THE Teddy Bear Sourcebook
FOR COLLECTORS AND ARTISTS

THE Teddy Bear Sourcebook

FOR COLLECTORS AND ARTISTS

ARGIE MANOLIS

BETTERWAY BOOKS

CINCINNATI, OHIO

Other fine Betterway Books are available from your local bookstore or direct from the publisher.

99 98 97 96 95   5 4 3 2 1

Library of Congress Cataloging-in-Publication Data

Manolis, Argie
    The teddy bear sourcebook for collectors and artists / by Argie Manolis.—1st ed.
        p.   cm.
    Includes indexes.
    ISBN 1-55870-386-1 (alk.paper)
    1. Teddy Bears—Information services—United States—Directories. I. Title.
NK8740.M36   1995
741.2—dc20   95-20963
                                                   CIP

Edited by Argie Manolis
Designed by Sandy Conopeotis Kent
Cover photo by Pamela Monfort Braun

Betterway Books are available at special discounts for sales promotions, premiums and fund-raising use. Special editions or book excerpts can also be created to specification. For details contact: Special Sales Manager, Betterway Books, 1507 Dana Avenue, Cincinnati, Ohio 45207.

Dedicated to arctophiles everywhere.

ACKNOWLEDGMENTS

So many people have helped make this book possible. From the moment Betterway Books decided to publish *The Teddy Bear Sourcebook*, we have had overwhelming support from the teddy bear community. It would be impossible to name everyone who called with suggestions and advice, took the time to talk to me at shows, and shared their encouragement. Thanks to all who helped!

Several people were especially helpful in the early stages of the project. Terrie Stong of Good Bears of the World introduced me to several key people in the teddy bear community and offered advice. Artists Debbie Kesling and Terri Effan spent several hours looking over the questionnaires used to gather information for the sourcebook and offered valuable suggestions.

A huge thank you to all the contributors: John Fey, Chester Freeman, Diane Gard, Linda Henry, Debbie Kesling, Neysa Phillippi and Ken Yenke, who wrote articles and provided photographs for the book and helped with the book's promotion, and Terri Effan, who acted as a consultant on the book. A special, heartfelt thanks to Chester Freeman, Debbie Kesling and Neysa Phillippi, who went beyond the call of duty as contributors. They were available as consultants whenever I had a question and they helped me gather resources. All three had enough faith in the project to promote the book before it had even been published!

Several people called or wrote with additional resources, and I am grateful to everyone who contributed. The following people sent a significant number of names and addresses: Hanna Gube of BearTique in Montreal, Canada; artist Karen Pringle of Ontario, Canada; Charles F. Woods of The Bear Castle in Nevada City, California, and Steve Schutt of Clarion, Iowa.

Finally, thanks to George Black, Bernice Makepeace, Janee McKinney, Lucy Rigg and Terrie Stong for taking the time to be interviewed for the book, and to Cynthia Powell, who sent two complimentary copies of her books.

Thanks again to everyone who contributed to this book by taking the time to fill out questionnaires, sending names and addresses of additional resources and calling or writing with encouraging words. It has been a pleasure to get to know each and every one of you, and your contributions are very much appreciated.

Argie G. Manolis

Argie Manolis
Editor
The Teddy Bear Sourcebook

ABOUT THE COVER

The photographs that appear on the cover of this book were chosen from hundreds of photographs by the book's designers to represent a variety of teddy bear artists' styles. The artists chosen sent bears on very short notice. Some even created bears just for the cover in less than a week!

Bears on the cover are by the following artists:

Front cover:

Top row, left to right: Vicky Lougher, Mary George, Jean Marie Mathers, Neysa Phillippi

Bottom row, left to right: Jean Marie Mathers, Neysa Phillippi, Neysa Phillippi

Miniature: Terrie Effan

Back cover:

Left, top to bottom: Doris Hoppe Riggs, Dee Hockenberry, Chester Freeman, Jean Marie Mathers

Right, top to bottom: Chester Freeman, Mary George, Dorothy DePaulo, Mary George

Miniature: Terrie Effan

CONTRIBUTORS

Terri Effan, who worked as a consultant on the book, helped with the initial research and the questionnaire development that played an instrumental role in the success of *The Teddy Bear Sourcebook*. She also provided several resources and was always available to provide advice and encouragement. Her miniature teddy bears appear on the cover of *The Teddy Bear Sourcebook*. Always hard-working and enthusiastic, Terri has been a big help in advertising, marketing and selling the book—even before its release!

John Fey, author of the introduction for collectors, is a long-time teddy bear collector and a partner in Fuzzy Bear Productions, which produces the annual Columbus Teddy Bear Fair and the Beary Merry Christmas Show in Columbus, Ohio. He is also the treasurer of Good Bears of the World. One of my first contacts in the wonderful world of teddy bears, John provided me with some much-needed advice at the 1994 Columbus Teddy Bear Fair, when *The Teddy Bear Sourcebook* was just a vague concept. He has also been a tremendous help with promotion and sales of the book. A true arctophile, John's enthusiasm and hard work have played a large part in the success of *The Teddy Bear Sourcebook*!

Chester Freeman, author of the introduction for artists, is an internationally acclaimed teddy bear artist from Geneva, New York and co-author of the children's book *Runaway Bear*. He has lectured widely on the therapeutic power of the teddy bear. A former minister, Chester has the caring demeanor of all true arctophiles. He was always available to provide an encouraging word while *The Teddy Bear Sourcebook* was being compiled. He helped gather resources, provided advice and sent his bears to my office for a long vacation while the book's designers planned the cover. His efforts to promote and sell the book have been phenomenal!

Diane Gard, author of the introduction to chapter three, is a well-known teddy bear artist and workshop instructor with a buoyant spirit. Diane, who lives near Denver, Colorado, has written several articles about teddy bears and has been featured in teddy bear publications throughout the world. Her inspiring article will help all readers find the creative child within!

Robin Gee, author of the interview that opens chapter six, is a freelance writer and former senior editor for *Writer's Digest Books*. She lives in Madison, Wisconsin. In her interview with Bernice Makepeace, chairperson of Winnie's Hometown Festival in Canada, she uncovers the long-forgotten, true story of Winnie-the-Pooh!

Linda Henry, author of the introduction to chapter two, is an award-winning teddy bear and doll artist from Canal Winchester, Ohio. Linda was quick to sign onto the project at the last minute despite a tight deadline schedule. A freelance commercial artist by trade, Linda's creativity is apparent in her article, which details how to find supplies in the most unusual places. Linda patiently provided advice throughout the process and has helped promote and sell *The Teddy Bear Sourcebook* in common and not-so-common places. Her article and enthusiasm have been a huge help!

Debbie Kesling, author of the article on miniature teddy bears and sidebars throughout the book, is an acclaimed miniature teddy bear artist who has been a true-blue believer in *The Teddy Bear Sourcebook* from the very beginning. Debbie's bears have been featured in publications around the world. She has produced a video on making miniature teddy bears and written articles on teddy bears and related topics. One of my first contacts, Debbie convinced us that *The Teddy Bear Sourcebook* was desperately needed and helped with the questionnaire development and initial research. Always generous and enthusiastic, Debbie provided advice, introduced me to key people in the industry and helped gather resources. She also provided several marketing and promotional ideas, and has been a big help in getting the word out about the book to arctophiles everywhere. Without Debbie's help, *The Teddy Bear Sourcebook* would have never have been published!

Neysa Phillippi, author of the introduction to chapter eight, is a well-known teddy bear artist and the organizer of Artists for Artists European tours. Her bears have appeared in publications throughout the world, including the cover of *The Teddy Bear Sourcebook*! Neysa was excited about the project from the very start, and has helped in more ways than I can count—providing advice, gathering resources, and marketing and selling the book in the U.S. and in Europe! Her efforts and hard work have been instrumental in the success of *The Teddy Bear Sourcebook*!

Meredith Wolf, author of the interview that opens chapter five, was an intern at Betterway Books during the summer of 1994. She graduated from Harvard in 1995 and now works at Abbeville Press. During her internship, she helped with the initial research and questionnaire development that made a huge difference in the success of *The Teddy Bear Sourcebook*. Her interview with Terrie Strong of Good Bears of the World will warm your heart!

Ken Yenke, author of the introduction to chapter four, is a true teddy bear expert. He has been researching the development and history of the teddy bear for more than ten years, and is an expert appraiser, lecturer and collector. I was introduced to Ken's vast knowledge of olde teddy bears when I met him at the 1994 Columbus Teddy Bear Fair. Since then, Ken has provided me some much-needed advice about collectible teddy bears and helped promote and sell the book. His expertise has been a great help!

Table of Contents

For Collectors

BY JOHN FEY

*A*n arctophile, derived from the Greek words for "bear" (arcto) and for "friend or lover of" (phile), is a person who loves bears. The term normally applies to a person who has an affection for the soft-sculpture art form that honors the bear portion of the animal kingdom. The teddy bear has served as a playmate and trusted companion for countless millions of children for the past ninety years and continues to bring joy to people of all ages. The teddy bear is so much more than just a child's toy. It is a universal symbol of love and comfort.

Teddy bear lovers come in all sizes, ages and nationalities, with varied preferences and motivations. Some need nothing more than one or two special companions in which to confide their secrets. Some still remember and cherish their childhood confidants, and yearn for that wisdom that only comes with tenure. Some choose to surround themselves with bears of all sizes, descriptions and ages, enjoying the acquiring as much as the acquisitions. Some see teddy bears as a shrewd monetary investment, while others are captured by the returning gaze of a furry face. Some collectors fancy the traditional appearance of the designs that first graced the teddy bears of the early 1900s. Other collectors choose the modern interpretations that present day bear makers use to expand the teddy bear's horizons. Whether the object of your adoration is just one or a thousand smiling fuzzy faces, you are truly an arctophile. You belong to a proud and noble society and are indeed in good company.

Aren't they all the same? When you proudly proclaim to a non-bear person that you are an arctophile, they say "huh?" If you tell them that your teddy bear collection numbers more than ten, they ask how you tell them apart, saying, "Aren't all teddy bears the same?" You then reply, "Of course not, silly! There are lots of different materials, fur finishes and construction techniques. Besides, they all have different names!"

The Birth of the Teddy Bear

There is only one original name, however. The term "teddy bear" began when Clifford K. Berryman's original cartoon, "Drawing the Line in Mississippi," first

Long-time bear collector John Fey will not admit to having a crowded house—but be sure to call in advance if you plan to visit so he and his wife Sharon can find a place for you to sit. John is treasurer of Good Bears of the World and a partner in Fuzzy Bear Productions, which produces the annual Columbus Teddy Bear Fair and the Beary Merry Christmas Show every year in Columbus, Ohio. John and Sharon are often spotted at teddy bear shows, pushing a baby buggy full of their bears. They live in Thornville, Ohio.

appeared in the *Washington Post* on November 16, 1902. The cartoon depicted President Theodore Roosevelt refusing to shoot a captured bear while on a hunting trip in Mississippi. The original cartoon disappeared. Berryman redrew the cartoon, making Teddy Roosevelt look more robust and making the bear look cuter and more appealing. This was the second and most publicized version of the famous cartoon.

Berryman's cartoon inspired Russian immigrants Morris and Rose Michtom to create a little jointed bear. According to legend, Morris Michtom wrote to President Roosevelt and asked permission to call the toy bear cub "Teddy Bear" in memory of the incident in Mississippi. The President supposedly answered the request in longhand, giving his permission but adding that

This miniature bear by Joan Laigh sits inside an antique pocket watch case advertising the Roosevelt-Fairbanks campaign in 1904.

he did not know if the name would help the stuffed animal business. Silly President! The Michtoms' toy bear business grew to become the Ideal Novelty and Toy Company. In 1903, the German Steiff Company also began marketing a stuffed and jointed bear. To this day, there is still speculation as to whether the Ideal or Steiff bear appeared first.

The Childhood Toy

In the early 1900s, Paul Piper, under the pen name Seymor Eaton, created a series of children's books, featuring two large bears, Teddy B and Teddy G. The books had beautifully illustrated color plates. Teddy B and Teddy G, known as the Roosevelt Bears, were the forebears of many famous storybook bears, destined to delight and inspire the imaginations of children. Any child knows and can list a host of storybook and cartoon bear characters.

Many of you had teddy bears when you were children, and you are fortunate if you still have your childhood teddies. My mother had two teddies that were her constant companions. The day I was born, she was late getting to the hospital because she washed the bears' clothes and had to wait for them to dry before leaving. I vaguely remember her bears, but they apparently did not survive my childhood. The only bear I remember having was a large unjointed panda with a metal nose. I fondly dubbed her Mrs. Bear. She did not survive my

childhood either, but I have since been able to find one that fits my memory of her.

A Token of Affection

Teddy bears always make the perfect gift. They just seem to say, "I love you," regardless of the occasion or the ages of the donors and recipients. My wife, Sharon, and I started our bear collection by giving each other bears for birthdays, anniversaries and other holidays. The bears were ideal symbols of our love.

The ultimate teddy token of affection has to be Happy Anniversary, a 1920s vintage Steiff bear that Paul Volpp bought for his wife Rosemary for their anniversary. Paul bought the bear for $86,350 in 1989, from an auction at Sotheby's in London. Happy Anniversary set the record for the most expensive teddy bear ever sold at public auction. She held that record until late 1994, when a 1904 Steiff bear named Teddy Lady was sold at Sotheby's for $171,500. Teddy Lady was bought by a Japanese soft toy manufacturer that intends to exhibit the bear as the centerpiece of a proposed teddy bear museum.

The late Colonel Robert Henderson, Teddy Lady's original owner and the founder of the British branch of Good Bears of the World, had a teddy bear with him at the Allied invasion of Normandy during World War II. Paul and Rosemary Volpp take Happy Anniversary with them all over the world. There are numerous stories of teddies that have made the faithful companions of adults. The late British actor, Peter Bull, always carried two little bears with him as traveling companions. He carried them in different pockets because the bears did not get along with each other.

The *Washington Post* quoted the late James Ownby, founder of Good Bears of the World, as saying, "There's a lot of hate, tension and fear in today's world that could be countered by the therapeutic effect of the teddy bear. There is something metaphysical about teddy bears that's hard to explain. But when you hold one in your arms, you can't help but smile."

A Legitimate Hobby

Collecting teddy bears is as legitimate as any other hobby. All respectable hobbies have certain similarities. They all have their pioneers. Teddy Roosevelt, Clifford Berryman, Morris and Rose Michtom, and Richard and Marguerite Steiff could all be considered teddy bear pioneers, as could many of the other early manufacturers. In more recent times we have to thank such arctophiles as Peter Bull, Pauline Cockrill, Dee Hockenberry, Ted Menten, Terry and Doris Michaud, Linda Mullins, Beverly Port, Helen Sieverling, Paul and Rosemary Volpp, and Carol-Lynn Rossel Waugh for protecting the teddy bear's heritage and passing it on to newcomers such as us.

All respectable hobbies have organizations, and teddy bear collecting is no exception. There are philanthropic organizations such as Good Bears of the World (GBW), the International League of Teddy Bear Clubs (ILTBC), and Teddy Bear Boosters of Northern California (TBBNC). There are organizations for bear makers such as the Teddy Bear Artist's Association (TBAA) and the Society of Miniature Artists Learning & Loving (SMALL). Last but certainly not least are the many groups for teddy bear collectors. Whether you have a fondness for a particular bear maker (e.g., Carol Black, Canterbury, Dean's, Muffy or Steiff) or collect all sorts of teddies, there is probably an organization for you to join. Check the Clubs chapter in this book. If there is not a teddy bear club in your area, perhaps you can find enough local teddy bear enthusiasts to start one.

Like other hobbyists, teddy bear collectors enjoy periodic gatherings where aficionados can share and expand their interests. Conventions and shows are great places to meet bear makers in person, find a concentrated multitude of teddies yearning for adoption, and rub elbows with other arctophiles. You can even meet famous bears. You can learn how to make a bear, dress a bear, repair a bear, wear a bear, decorate with a bear or collect a bear. Teddy bear conventions and shows are proliferating, and you can find them almost any time of year. Check the show chapter in this book for shows in your area, or plan your vacation around a show in a city you've always wanted to visit! Whether you are attending a Linda Mullins show in San Diego, a Pat Moore show in Seattle, the Teddy Bear Reunion in the Heartland show in Clarion, an ABC show in Schaumburg, a Toy Store show in Toledo, a Fuzzy Bear show in Columbus, a D.L. Harrison show in Timonium, a Disney show in Orlando, or any of the other fine shows, you will find bears, bear people and bears galore. Enjoy!

Finally, like other hobbies, teddy bear collectors have several periodicals and reference materials at their disposal. The leading teddy bear periodicals include *Teddy Bear & Friends* and *Teddy Bear Review* in the U.S. and *Huglets* and *Teddy Times* in the U.K. For bear makers, these magazines are teddy bear billboards, advertising

their bears to collectors worldwide. We collectors can use the magazines to preview the latest furry creations and update our wish lists.

Many bear collectors keep a library of reference books for consultation, general information or simple enjoyment. For reference materials, begin with this book. It includes a comprehensive section on teddy bear reference materials. Some of my favorites include *Button in Ear*, by Jurgen & Marianne Cieslik, *The Complete Book of Teddy Bears*, by Joan Green & Ted Menten, *The Teddy Bear Artist's Annual*, by Paul & Rosemary Volpp, Donna Harrison, & Dottie Ayers, *The Teddy Bear Book*, by Peter Bull, *The Teddy Bear Lovers' Catalog*, by Ted Menten, and *The Ultimate Teddy Bear Book*, by Pauline Cockrill.

Aren't They All the Same?

There are as many types of teddy bears as there are collectors! Teddies can be made from flat woven or knit fabric, upholstery fabric, ultrasuede, leather, animal pelts (new or recycled), acrylic fur, European plush, mohair (new or recycled), alpaca, wool blends, silk blends and even wood. The finishing variations include coloring, distressing, fur length, texture and custom trimming. Fur manufacturers apply some effects before fur reaches the bear makers. However, many bear makers now dye and distress the fur themselves. That, combined with the way bear makers cut the pattern pieces

Milo, by Bearly Friends, is just one of the many unusual bears in John's collection.

and trim the bear after construction, provides limitless opportunities for creative expression. Every artist and manufacturer listed in this book has his or her own special style.

There is more to a distinctive bear than the fur finish. Bear makers create their own unique patterns and choose from an assortment of different skeletal techniques and sizes, from minuscule to ceiling scrapers. They fill their bears with everything imaginable, from buckshot to barley. They sometimes give them voice boxes or music boxes—if the bears choose to speak. Finally, they individually stitch, carve or mold each face. When someone asks, "Aren't all teddies the same?" it just makes you want to growl! You calm down when you remember that once upon a time they all looked the same to you, too!

Bearafurnalia

Bearafurnalia is my term for bear-related accessories. Everybody needs stuff! Whether it is wearing apparel, items of adornment, household decorations, or something in which to carry a bear, you have to have it. My wife Sharon and I lost count of how many bear-related T-shirts and sweat shirts we have. At last count, I had thirty-five neckties with bears on them. We have a penchant for anything associated with bears.

Bearafurnalia can be found in the most unlikely places. For instance, Jack Nicklaus, known in the golfing world as the Golden Bear, promotes a line of golf shirts that display his emblem, an embroidered yellow bear. Arctophiles can find a multitude of appropriate amateur and professional organizations whose names and logos adorn hats, shirts, socks, suspenders, ties, etc. There are the Chicago Bears, Chicago Cubs, Boston Bruins, UCLA Bruins, Maine Black Bears and the Baylor Bears, just to name a few. Eagle Products, a graphics company in Kansas City, produces a line of shirts that advertise the imaginary beverage, Bear Whiz Beer. For the musically inclined arctophile, the Grateful Dead's colorful Dancing Bears logo can be found on a series of shirts.

Aside from such logos, shirts, sweaters, hats, visors, coats, neckties, trousers, suspenders, socks and shoes

---

Following Your Heart

When selecting bears to add to your collection, whether full-size or miniature, follow your heart. If you limit your purchases to teddies that you love, you will never be disappointed. Though teddy bears have the potential to go up in value, speculating in this "bullish" bear market can be risky. Basing your collection strictly on projected resale value is unwise. Don't overlook the fledgling artist when shopping for new additions to your bear family. Some of the finest work I have seen at recent bear shows has been the product of artists who have been working for only a year or so.

—Debbie Kesling

---

are all available with bear adornment. You can wear rings, bracelets, necklaces, earrings, watches and pins with bear adornment. You can buy teddy bear hubcaps. You can decorate your house from roof to basement with bears. You can display bear signs, posters, photographs, flags, draperies, wallpaper, throws, knickknacks and even bear furniture. Remember, anything worth doing is worth doing to excess!

Sharing the Love of Bears

While some people are content with a solitary relationship with their teddies, others would proclaim their proclivity to the world. I believe the most rewarding aspect of bear collecting is sharing your teddies with others. You can invite friends to your home to see your room(s) full of teddies or you can loan your teddies for displays in libraries and museums. You can introduce them during public talks to schools and social groups or photograph them for books and magazines. You can parade them around in a baby buggy (as Sharon and I do at bear shows), or just carry one under your arm or in your pocket. In each instance, you are sharing the joy of teddy bears with others. The essence of that joy is the magic that causes people to smile when they see or hold a teddy bear!

For Artists

BY CHESTER FREEMAN

*W*hat is it about teddy bears that attracts at least fifteen hundred people in the U.S. alone to make their own—and millions of people to collect them? For me, the teddy bear is not just a toy. It is an instrument of love. Its function is comfort. Its source of strength is in touch. Its power is mystical. Perhaps the reason that teddy bears are so universal in their appeal is that they allow us as adults to feel secure and hopeful while we confront our fears. When we hold onto our bears, they calm our anxieties.

I was an only child, and I vividly remember receiving my first teddy bear as a gift from my parents. Little did they realize that my teddy would become a playmate and friend. "Timmy" would fill the void I felt when I was alone. When I was being punished for doing something wrong, my teddy was always there to provide the comfort I needed. So, one could say my insights into teddy bear power stem from my childhood. After I grew up, my childhood bear remained at home with my parents and quietly waited for our eventual reunion.

The First Freeman Bears

Most people wonder how a former college chaplain ever became a teddy bear artist and author. It all occurred by happenstance. In the early 1980s while living in New England, I began to frequent antique shows. Occasionally I would notice an old teddy bear for sale. The bear would naturally cause me to reflect on my own childhood. As Christmas neared in 1982, a friend encouraged me to try to make a teddy, so I purchased a magazine with a how-to article on a jointed teddy bear and began to follow the directions. After I completed their pattern, I realized it looked more like a woodchuck than a teddy bear!

Thinking that I could do better, I designed my own pattern. During that Christmas season I hosted a faculty party, and several colleagues commented on the bear that I had made and wanted to know if I would make one for them. At first it was just a whimsical hobby—something fun to do in my spare time—and I said yes.

Chester Freeman, a former minister, is an internationally acclaimed teddy bear artist from Geneva, New York. He is also an expert on the therapeutic power of teddy bears. His bears have been featured in several books and publications, and he has written several articles about teddy bears. He is also the co-author of *Runaway Bear*, a children's book that brings his bears to life. He is holding the original fully jointed mohair bears that he created and designed for his first children's book.

Later that spring, word spread among the students that the chaplain was making teddies, so they invited me to participate in an artist festival. After this event, I was asked to participate in the first Amherst Teddy Bear Rally sponsored by the Chamber of Commerce. It was at that rally that businesses began to approach me about carrying my work.

More Than a Hobby

My hobby—which brought me a little extra income—began taking a different direction. Within the next three years my work appeared on the cover of the book *Teddy Bear Artists: The Romance of Making and Collecting Bears*, by Carol-Lynn Rossel Waugh (Hobby House Press, 1984). This exposure brought my work to the attention of a larger audience. Soon I was approached by a greeting card company that wanted to use my bears for their cards. That was very affirming.

As my small business grew, I needed to find suppliers. The local stores rarely had all the materials I needed, so I spent countless hours tracking down the necessary manufacturers. Today all you have to do is turn to the suppliers' chapter in this book to find multiple sources. Included are the sources for plush and mohair fabrics as well as all of the materials necessary to complete a finished bear with accessories. I wish *The Teddy Bear Sourcebook* had been available when I first started out, because it took me four years and a worldwide search to find all the materials that I needed to produce a quality bear.

My business began to grow as I worked at Amherst College and the University of Massachusetts. My personal ventures into the marketplace led me to believe that it was time to advertise. Fortunately for me, there was only one publication for teddy bear collectors at the time, so I placed a color ad in the magazine. It was very costly to have the photography, design and ad layout completed, but it ultimately paid off. I advertised in alternate issues to continue to build awareness.

A Source of Solace

During my stint as college chaplain I encountered a great deal of homesickness among the students. Invariably, the majority of the students I talked to had one item of security that connected them to home base. More often than not, this was their teddy bear. With so much focus on teddy bears in so many of the counseling sessions I conducted, I began to take them more seriously. Eventually I left the colleges to continue my education by doing a residency as an ecumenical hospital chaplain. In Hartford, Connecticut I began to seriously pursue the therapeutic value of the teddy bear. I found that using teddy bears in a hospital setting relieved anxiety and calmed adults as well as children.

During one of my pastoral visits I counseled an elderly lady in a hospital who had lost her will to live. Because of her depression and anxiety, she had begun to see the staff and others as threatening. As we talked, I could clearly see her tension reflected in her rigidity and in the way she clutched the bed sheets around her neck. Once we established a rapport, she began to open up. To my surprise, from under the covers she slowly revealed a teddy bear. After she had introduced me to her companion, we were able to talk on a heart-to-heart

level of trust and affection. The teddy bear was her one solace in the midst of this hospital environment.

Many people who are experiencing change or moving into the unknown reach out for something that brings them comfort. It is the teddy bear that frequently answers that need. Some psychiatrists are coming to recognize the therapeutic value of the teddy bear and are even recommending them as a form of therapy. The person most responsible for educating the academic community about this idea is Dr. Paul C. Horton of Meriden, Connecticut. In his book *Solace: The Missing Dimension in Psychiatry* (University of Chicago Press, 1981), he points out that solacing objects such as teddy bears and security blankets help us to recapture the great comfort we felt when we were young. Solacing objects are important for us during all stages of our lives.

Paramedics, police, fire departments and social service workers are beginning to use teddy bears as tools of the trade. The bears are given to children and adults who are alone and need support during a personal or medical crisis. In some hospitals, intensive care nurses find that teddy bears are helpful for patients who have just experienced open heart surgery. Because of the nature of the operation, many patients find it very difficult to cough, fearing they might break their stitches. Holding a teddy bear over the stitches helps relieve their anxiety, and they are able to cough without fear. Other hospitals use teddy bears to prepare children for surgical procedures. There are teddies that have incisions and wear casts and splints, eyeglasses and even prosthetic limbs. These special teddy bears lessen the fears of children. If you've ever had a doubt about the power of teddy bears, these examples illustrate ways in which making and giving a teddy bear can have a profound effect on those in need. This book is a great place to start your exploration of the teddy bear world because all of the resources are at your fingertips. You too can find satisfaction in sharing your handmade bears with others as I did.

My own research shows that teddy bears provide and promote hugging. Scientific research supports the theory that touch is necessary for the physical and emotional well-being of humans. Some individuals may have difficulty hugging another person, but they can hug a teddy bear. The act of hugging the teddy actually promotes wholeness for that individual. Teddy bears provide comfort in those withdrawn moments when we need to be alone. This is also true in the case of elderly persons who may be alone not by choice but as a result of circumstances beyond their control. The teddy bear has emotional energy that is transferred to us by a simple hug. The simple act of embracing a bear generates a feeling of security, trust, strength and even healing.

As I travel around the country lecturing on the therapeutic value of the teddy bear, new observations are constantly called to my attention. Over the past two years, hotels around the United States have reported seeing teddy bears in rooms occupied by traveling businesspeople. When asked about this phenomenon, both men and women confessed to carrying teddy bears in their briefcases. The stress from frequent traveling was lessened by having something from home that gave them a sense of security or "furbearance."

The Joys of Making Bears

One of the greatest joys of making teddy bears, which is shared by all the artists listed in this book, is the warmth that their creations evoke. Once people realize that I am a minister as well as a teddy bear artist, they are very willing to open up and seek counsel from me. I receive many letters from collectors, artists and enthusiasts sharing their concerns and reflections with me. The magic of the teddy bear is vividly illustrated in these letters. I would like to share a few of these with you.

"Our bear family is growing, and a friend recently told me I must take care not to substitute the bears for children or even a dog, which in his eyes, would be better company. I don't believe, however, that my bears are a substitute for anything—they can very well stand in their own right. I do see them, however, as symbols of a very happy childhood and a reminder of many fond memories and people I love. When I was very young, I would accompany my Grandmother to church every Sunday. She in her widow's black, me in my brand new red shoes, and teddy would be allowed to come to keep me out of mischief. When I tried to explain that teddy was the naughty one, she would say that there was room for improvement in both of us."

"Your bears are creating no little stir among our friends and acquaintances. Your bears have given us the most interesting opportunity to see, in some cases, even very close friends open up in new ways, becoming less restrained and admitting to lifelong
but secret teddy love. The most amazing thing is that it takes a bear, which after all is such a symbol of childhood, to break down the barriers of grownups."

Finding a Place in the Teddy Bear World

As I became more involved in studying the therapeutic value of teddy bears, I also became more adept at making them. As the demand for my bears grew, I had to make a crucial decision. Should I leave the comfort and security of a steady job and paycheck to become a teddy bear artist? Besides the financial implications, could my self-esteem handle it? There are about fifteen hundred teddy bear artisans in the United States today who design and handcraft bears as I do. Only ten of them are men. I definitely felt awkward and uncomfortable in the beginning. However, I found that it was really a matter of refocusing my vocation on making bears and watching the joy and healing powers they brought to their new owners.

I have now come to realize that my work is really an extension of my ministry. People who once were embarrassed that they used their teddy bears to comfort them in crisis times tell me that I've helped them to articulate their feelings. As I realized I had more of a national reputation, I also found that my work was recognized internationally. Artist-designed bears were gaining popularity around the world, and several commercial companies sought out artists to design bears. In 1987, I designed two bears for Merrythought Limited of England and soon began to seek out other international markets in Japan, Australia, New Zealand and Tasmania. Most of these contacts came through collector magazines and friends who traveled abroad.

At one point I thought that my business had grown enough to take on a few assistants. To meet the increase in demand for my product, I approached a sheltered workshop and began to involve workers with special needs in producing certain aspects of my work. After a struggle, the products began to approach my standards, but I felt the "look" that I had worked so long to achieve was suffering. I decided to cut back on the number of stores that I supplied and personally service all my accounts. Now I make each bear myself. This has allowed me to be selective about the stores that carry my line of bears and to control the look and quality of each bear. A single production artist can obviously only produce a small number of bears each year. My bears cannot be found in every store, but they are in select stores known

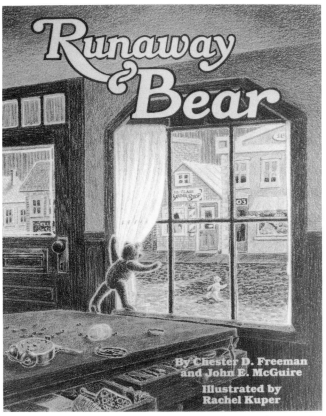

Runaway Bear, by Chester Freeman and John E. McGuire, is a heartwarming story about two teddy bears with very different personalities.

for high-quality collectibles. Today teddy bears are almost the third largest collectible in the world, so there is an ever expanding market for them. I have been making teddy bears for almost fourteen years.

Bears in Books

Whenever I get stressed out with the business of making teddies I turn to writing. As a freelance writer I have been able to write for a variety of magazines including *Teddy Bear Review* and *Teddy Bear and Friends*. Teddy bears became the inspiration for my first children's book, *Runaway Bear*, published by Pelican Publishing Company. This book was done in collaboration with two other artists: basketry craftsman John McGuire on

text, and illustrator Rachel Kuper. The story was composed spontaneously. Like many of the artists listed in this book, I always secretly fancied the idea of my stuffed animal becoming real. This was my opportunity to bring two of my bears to life.

Runaway Bear is a lavishly illustrated story that revolves around two bears made by a loving father as birthday gifts for his twin daughters. Once the bears are created, the adventure unfolds. One bear escapes and encounters animals in a mystical forest. While making himself feel big at the expense of their feelings, he fails to notice that he has ripped a stitch and is actually getting smaller by losing his stuffing. His fellow bear then seeks his return. The restoration of the arrogant bear and their last-minute return proves to be most entertaining. The central theme is one of kindness, caring, and a need for good friends. Bear collectors seem to enjoy my spin on why antique bears have shoe button eyes and wood shavings for stuffing. All the reviews have been very positive and the book has been adopted by several school systems and libraries around the country to be used as a teaching tool. The letters and reactions I encounter as a result of this book and its many messages have added a new dimension to my work.

A Special Bond

In recent months I have been traveling around the country presenting lectures, readings and programs for schools, libraries and other organizations. The thing that fascinates me is that the collectors of my work come to my book signings and embrace me as if they've known me forever. Never mind that it's the first time we've met—they own a bear I created and they feel that they're very close to me. This is the great reward about making teddy bears—you give a little of yourself to each person. Each artist listed in this book has a unique style, and, like me, has found fulfillment in making his or her own creations. An interest in teddy bears leads to the discovery of a whole new world. Teddy bears changed my life, and I think that they can make a difference in your life too!

1

Retail
Businesses

How to Use This Chapter

*T*eddy bear stores are where many collectors first find a yearning for their lovable bruins. Lured by an attractive store window or a catchy name, anyone who enters the store is fair game. This chapter is a comprehensive guide to these stores. The listings will tell you where the store is located, what merchandise it carries, when it is open and how you can pay for whatever you buy.

This chapter serves many purposes. If you are a new collector who has not yet found a favorite teddy bear store, you are sure to discover one here. New collectors may want to begin with the geographic index in the back of the book to locate stores in their area. Then, use the listings in this chapter to find out when the store is open as well as payment and layaway information.

Veteran collectors who are searching for a specific brand name bear or type of figurine, accessory or collectible should begin with the indexes in the back of the book. When you have located the item you want, check the listing to find out if mail order is available. Some of the businesses listed are mail order only, and the listing will say so. But even businesses that have store locations may sell through the mail if contacted by phone or fax.

If you want to purchase bears through the mail, call or write for a catalog if the listing says there is one available. Send a check or money order with your request if the listing gives a catalog cost. When you purchase an item through the mail, be prepared to pay an additional shipping cost. While mail order businesses may already include the shipping cost in the price, most stores that do occasional sales through the mail do not.

This chapter can also be used when planning a vacation. Whether you are driving cross-country or flying to a popular vacation spot, you are bound to feel at home in any nearby teddy bear store. The store may even carry bears and bear items that your home store does not! Again, use the geographical index to locate the store in or near your vacation spot.

Due to the publication time line, it is possible that stores listed may have added new items and cancelled others. Artist bears especially are bound to be in constant flux. Therefore, if you are driving far from home for a specific bear, it is wise to call first to make sure the bear is available and to verify the hours the store is open.

If you are a bear artist, you can use this chapter to locate shops that may be interested in carrying your bears. It is best to call for an appointment with the shop's owner or manager if you are in the area. If not, call to ask if they are looking for new bears, and then offer to send photos and other promotional materials.

All the information in these listings were provided by the owners or managers of the stores. In some cases, addresses are listed for major stores that never responded to our request for information. We have tried our best to verify these addresses. Again, remember that information is subject to change. Always call in advance if you are making a special trip.

All of these stores have wonderful collections that are bound to excite new and veteran collectors alike. These pages will tell you brand name bears, artist bears, miniature bears, accessories and collectibles that the store carries. Searching for that perfect bear and other bearafurnalia is part of the joy of collecting these lovable, fuzzy creatures. We hope the listings in this chapter will help!

Janee McKinney, Owner, Bears in the Wood

BY ARGIE MANOLIS

Janee McKinney, owner of Bears in the Wood, talks about the changes she's seen in the past twenty years—and why her store is still around.

When Janee McKinney moved to Palo Alto after leaving her job in advertising at *San Francisco Magazine*, she was determined to be the first woman salesperson for Porsche. Instead, she opened the country's first teddy bear store in Los Gatos, California.

It isn't quite as unlikely as it sounds. Janee had loved bears since she got her first one from her parents when she was eleven months old.

"Teddy was his name—real original—and he was always my number one toy," Janee says. "He was real to me. He was my little companion. Teddy was really a friend."

Her second bear, Georgie, was a gift from an aunt on her second birthday. Later, her mother made a few bears for her using patterns in a women's magazine, and she received a few bears as gifts from an old boyfriend as well.

When the Porsche job didn't pan out, she took a job at a store called The Wood Turn On. The store specialized in artist-made wood products, including handmade furniture, lamps and vases. She went to trade shows to

Janee and her husband, Howard, stand in front of their beloved store.

find products for the store—a perfect job for someone who had always loved to shop.

She also enjoyed decorating the store. That's where her small collection of seven teddy bears came in. She used them in the windows and throughout the store as props. She would set one on a wooden swing, for instance, or place a bear in a wooden toy airplane.

"Well, every day I sat there waiting for somebody to come in and buy all this wood stuff, and every day, it did not fail, somebody would bring one of my bears up to the counter and ask, 'How much is this?' " Janee recalls. "I would say, 'Well, he's not for sale, he's mine.' And I started to think, 'Boy, these could really sell.' "

She asked the store's owner if she could set up a section in the back of the store and sell teddy bears, and call it "Bears in the Wood."

"He laughed and said, 'That's really dumb.' " Janee says. "So I went home at night basically thinking, 'You know, that's really not stupid. I could do a store with teddy bears.' "

While working at *San Francisco Magazine*, she had pondered someday opening her own store. Many of her advertising accounts had been retail stores, and she

Janee McKinney receives her first teddy bear from parents Mildred and Harry Luttiken.

thought it would be wonderful to shop for merchandise for a store. When she thought of the Bears in the Wood idea, she couldn't let it go. She joined one of the woodworkers who had showed his furniture in The Wood Turn On, and they opened Bears in the Wood in Los Gatos. They were partners for about a year. He then left to pursue his own business.

Nevertheless, the name stuck. "It's always reminded me of Winnie-the-Pooh and the hundred acre wood," says Janee. "Also, it's fun to say. That has a lot to do with it." Bears in the Wood became the first store in the country to sell teddy bears only, opening in 1976.

"I remember meeting the vice president of Dakin at one of the first trade shows I went to looking for bear products," says Janee. "When I told him what I was doing, he said, 'You can't open a teddy bear store. That's ridiculous. You have to carry all sorts of other things. That will never work.' "

Little did he know that teddy bear collecting would become one of the most popular hobbies in the U.S., and that the store would survive for more than nineteen years.

Looking for Products

During those early years, Janee says, there really was no such thing as a teddy bear collector. "There had never been a limited edition bear or a numbered or signed bear, and there really weren't artist bears back then, either," Janee says. But English actor Peter Bull had just admitted to his love of teddy bears in his book, *The Teddy Bear Book.* Slowly, the world was learning about the wonder of antique teddy bears. Still, it took a while for modern bears to catch on as collectibles.

In the beginning, B.B. Bears (Basic Brown Bears) from Woods in Wood in San Francisco were the best selling bears in the store. Alresford bears from England were in second place. Often, Janee would see a bear she liked at a trade show, but she couldn't possibly buy it for the store because the minimum orders were so high.

"But back in those old days, I can remember the Gund rep at one of those trade shows persistently asking me to add their line to my store," Janee says. "And there was basically only one bear in their line that I was interested in, and that was Misty. I think back at that time, Gund had a five-hundred dollar minimum, and I couldn't order five-hundred dollars worth of Mistys. So we pleaded with Gund and Dakin and a lot of the other manufacturers to add more bears to their line. And as

you can see, that has happened, and they are a big part of the store today."

Other bear products were even more difficult to find at that time, Janee says. Card companies were especially difficult to buy from because they usually only had one or two cards in an entire line with teddy bears on them.

"Usually the cards were very juvenile," Janee says. "I would say, 'I need something with a teddy bear on it for adults.' Well, they kind of laughed at the beginning. I took a lot of heat because they thought teddy bears were just for kids."

Sometimes, she would give in and buy one-hundred dollars worth of one or two cards just to meet the company's minimum. "We all kind of laugh when we do inventory because we still have some cards from the old days when we had to order hundreds of dollars' worth of one or two cards," Janee says. "There are still some cards intermingled on the racks for around forty cents."

More Than a Trend

The hardest part of getting the store off the ground, Janee says, was convincing people that teddy bears were not just a trend. But she knew in her heart from the beginning that there would always be a need for teddy bears.

"There will always be the need for the magic that I think only a teddy bear can bring into people's lives," Janee says. "It seems like everybody needs the whimsy that a bear can release in this stress-related, serious world. And for some reason, it's OK if the bear initiates it."

Part of that magic has to do with childhood memories, Janee believes. "You remember your teddy bears. It seems like everybody had one," she says. "It was that bear that they were really able to confide in. My husband always says, 'We don't trust anyone who doesn't like bears.' I think it definitely takes a good person with a good personality to be able to relate to them."

Janee is proud to have been the first to sell bears made by some of the best names in bear artistry, including Cathy Bordi, Barbara Conley, Christine Jesser and Kathy Corley. Janee remembers Cathy Bordi arriving at the store with a basket full of bears and showing them to her. She thought it was wonderful, but never imagined that there would be more than fifteen hundred bear artists in the U.S. nearly twenty years later.

Janee credits the media support she received for helping her store in the beginning. When Bears in the Wood first opened, several newspapers and a TV newsmagazine did feature stories on the store. Word of mouth took care of the rest.

A Place for Fun

Loyal customers who have been coming to the store since Bears in the Wood opened in 1976 have kept business from waning when others followed Janee's lead. Now, hundreds of teddy bear stores later, customers still come to the store seeking a good time.

"People say they have fun in here," Janee says. "We try to greet everybody when they walk in the door, just as you'd welcome people to your house. We definitely make contact with them." Janee says all her employees love bears as much as she does. One of the reasons she decided not to franchise, she says, is because she couldn't stand the thought of her store losing that personal touch.

Janee says the staff encourages test hugging. "I tell the customers that you've got to pick up the bears. You've got to see how they feel. And they'll try it. And maybe that person hasn't hugged a bear in fifteen years. I like to experience the warmth they feel when they try it."

The store appeals to children as well. It includes a full-size log cabin with windows and window boxes, a bed and kitchen area. The cabin is modeled after the three bears' house from *Goldilocks and the Three Bears.*

Janee remembers a little girl who crouched down in the store and refused to leave. "She and her mother were arguing for the longest time, and I couldn't figure out what it was all about," Janee says. "Then I heard the mother say, 'Don't you understand? People don't live in bear stores!' "

Then there was a woman who came in the day of the space shuttle crash. "Remember that day? It was the most depressing day in the world," Janee says. "This lady came in and she said, 'I came here because I needed to feel good.' Maybe that's our secret, our uniqueness. We try to make everybody feel at home."

Surviving the Rough Times

Bears in the Wood has survived every hardship from difficult economic times to major earthquakes.

"Nineteen years ago when I opened it, I knew in my mind (of course, nineteen years younger then) that it

Muffy pays a visit to Bears in the Wood staff (from left to right): Robin Helfrich, Susie Greenberg, Angela Deniz, Howard McKinney, Bonnie Washington and Janee McKinney.

would work, because nothing had ever been done like it before," Janee says. "We've been through a lot of lows and highs. I mean, the economy definitely went way down for a few years there. But you just have to know how to buy for that. I've been fortunate not to get head over heels in inventory. It's a gamble. But we've been able to survive."

During the earthquake that was supposed to wipe Los Gatos off the map, the teddy bears fell on the floor and saved many of the breakable items in the store, Janee says. Los Gatos was also in danger during the fires in 1985, but they never got near the store.

"I think I've been lucky," Janee says. "because I've had a guardian bear all these years. A guardian bear with wings."

But there is more to the store's success than luck, and Janee is aware of that.

"I think the survival is due to our hard work and determination, and maybe a touch of stubbornness. We didn't want to throw the towel in when times got rough. Loyal customers have a lot to do with it. It's not easy being in business. There is a lot of competition out there, and you've just got to try your best every day. So far, it's worked."

Family Support

Support from her parents and her husband has been a big help, too. Her parents lent her the money to start the store.

"My dad passed away in 1978, and the store had been open since 1976," Janee says. "So he got to see the success. I know he's telling everybody up in heaven about Bears in the Wood and teddy bears. I put his favorite bear in his casket with him."

Janee's mother, now eighty-three, can still be found behind the counter of the store on Sundays. She loves working with people, and the loyal customers know her by name and love her dearly.

Janee's husband, Howard McKinney, is equally devoted to the store—but that took a little convincing.

"When I opened my business, there was a fly fishing store on the corner, and I remember the manager of that store walking in and saying, "What are you going to sell?' And I said, 'teddy bears.' And I could see him kind of roll his eyes. I knew he was thinking, 'Oh, she'll be here about three months.' "

That man ended up marrying Janee in 1982. Nineteen years after their first meeting, the fly fishing specialty store which he managed is long gone, but Bears in the Wood is still in the same location, and doing better than ever. And you'll often find Janee's husband behind the counter.

Lifelong Friendships

"We're real animal lovers, and that coincides with our love of teddy bears," Janee says. Janee's husband has a travel agency called Fishabout for fishing enthusiasts. He sends people all over the world on fishing trips. His business goes hand in hand with Bears in the Wood. Janee and her husband now host their own photographic safaris to Africa nearly every year.

"No one we met in Africa knew what a teddy bear was," says Janee. "We took some with us and gave them away. And this year, as a matter a fact, we got a Christmas card from a girl we met in Africa back in 1989, and it had a bear on it."

As a result of their safaris, they decided to open a section of the store called "On Safari." That section, the only part of the store with non-teddy bear items, includes native crafts, plush jungle animals, and other gifts representing Africa and the rain forests. A portion of the money raised from this section of the store goes to wildlife organizations.

This dedication to wildlife has also earned the McKinneys some lifelong friends. The codirector of the Cheetah Conservation Fund wrote in a thank-you letter, "I'm sure the teddy bears around the world would fully approve of helping the cheetah."

But perhaps the most amazing stories associated with Bears in the Wood are those about people who come to the store seeking friendship. For instance, there was the

couple who got out of a taxi and unloaded several pieces of luggage in front of the store. They walked in and told Janee, "We just flew into the San Francisco airport from Norway. We got a taxi and we told him we wanted to come to Bears in the Wood in Los Gatos. We read about your store in a book, and we wanted you to be our first stop in America."

"They've come back a couple times since then," Janee says. "We get a letter from them every year requesting calendars, and a bear of our choice to surprise them with, and some little odds and ends. And we send these things to them every year. They give me their Visa card number, and off it goes."

Janee says she never gets tired of owning a bear store. "Bear people are special," she says. "Getting back to that personality again: They are well-rounded, happy, interesting people."

Making Your Own Rules

One of the best things about owning your own business is that you get to make the rules. For Janee, there are very few, but they are stringent.

"We are such animal lovers that there's no way we will carry any bears made with real fur," she says. "There are a lot of people who say, 'Well, it's recycled. It's an old mink.' Well, I don't care. An animal still had to die to make that. So new or recycled, we have nothing made out of real fur. In this day and age, there's no excuse for that. Using real fur goes against the whole idea of a loving little teddy bear, and there are plenty of high-quality synthetic fabrics and mohairs out there to use."

Her only other rule is this: She will not buy artist bears from photographs. "I want hands on," she says. "A lot of times, a picture will make a bear look absolutely wonderful and he isn't. On the other hand, a picture can make him look awful and he's wonderful. It's so hard to tell in a picture."

Janee says the most enjoyable part of owning her own store is searching for merchandise. "When we go to a trade show, we don't just go to our regular vendors," she says. "We look through everything, because you never know when you'll find the perfect item hidden behind something else. We really work hard to try to find unique merchandise. Our bears come in all sizes, shapes and colors, and our customers come in all ages, origins and economics. We pride ourselves on having something for everyone."

Janee says her ability to choose items for the store

is based on instinct. "I've always been interested in shopping, or in being a consumer, so to speak. Maybe it's a sixth sense."

Or maybe not. She thinks for a moment, and says, "Every single thing you do is a steppingstone that leads to something else. Because I can fall back on just about everything I've ever done, jobwise, even from high school days."

Her interest in owning her own store was piqued through her clients while she was an advertising representative for *San Francisco Magazine*. Perhaps her shopping savvy comes partly from her experience working at a major department store during high school. And, she admits, that flower shop job she had in college taught her to make the most beautiful bows for the bears in her store.

"Somewhere along the way my husband and I took a small business class," she says. "And I realized that if I had thought about opening a bear store—if I hadn't just jumped in on it—maybe I wouldn't have done it.

So maybe it's good that I went with what I knew, with my own instincts."

A Statement of Affection

Janee was always sure that no one—regardless of age, sex or social status—could have too many teddy bears.

"I've always said that teddy bears are a statement of affection. You'd never give a teddy bear to someone you didn't like," she says. "Teddy bears to me are like friends. You can never have too many. When people ask me how many I have, I tell them I've never counted. I have absolutely no idea. That would be like sitting down and going through your phone book and counting your friends."

And that, she says, makes her sure that Bears in the Wood will be around as long as she is.

"I don't think the interest in bears will ever decrease," she says. "If the need for teddy bears ever went away, I honestly think that would be the end of the world."

Retail Listings

A BEAR IN SHEEP'S CLOTHING

Judith Shangold, owner
P.O. Box 770
Medford, MA 02155
Phone: 617-395-6491
Fax: 617-395-6491
Mail order only.
Catalog: free
Accepts: check, money order
Discounts: nonprofit organization, established businesses

MODERN BEARS:
U.S.A.: Boyds

ACCESSORIES:
Knitting and needlepoint patterns for clothing
Clothes: hats (for 10″ bears)
Miniature bear accessories: glasses
In business for 4 years

A LA CARTE ON THE AVENUE

Petrea Hamor, owner
P.O. Box 236
26540 Ave. of the Giants
Redcrest, CA 95569
Phone: 707-722-4517
    Phone orders accepted.
Hours: 10:30A.M.-4P.M.
Accepts: check, money order, Visa, MasterCard

MODERN BEARS:
U.S.A.: Gund
Artist bears: Laurie Clark, Margaret Lewis, Fay White
Miniature bears: Laurie Clark
In business for 2 years

A LITTLE HUG

Ed & Liz Oerding, owners
P.O. Box 317
Gleneden Beach, OR 97341
Phone: 503-764-2491
    Phone orders accepted.
Mail order only.
Accepts: check, money order, Visa, MasterCard, Discover
Discounts: frequent order

MODERN BEARS:
U.S.A.: Applause/Raikes, Wallace Berrie
Shows: OR, WA
In business for 8 years

A SWEET REMEMBRANCE

Paula Walton
172 Aspetuck Ridge Rd.
New Milford, CT 06776-5611
Phone: 203-355-5709
    Phone orders accepted.
Hours: by appointment
Catalog: $5, refundable with purchase.
Accepts: check, money order
Layaway: 25% down, 3 equal payments
Discounts: frequent customer
Old/special items: antique bears, bears manufactured between WWI and WWII, bears manufactured 1945-1970, antique bear collectibles, bunnies
Artist bears: Paula Walton
Miniature bears: Paula Walton

ACCESSORIES:
Clothes: custom order
Furniture: antique chairs, tables, cribs, etc.
Miniature clothes: custom made
Miniature furniture: antique toy chairs, cribs, etc.
More about these accessories: Antiques are one-of-a-kind. Selection varies. Not always available.
Bear collectibles: antique collectibles, paintings, prints, greeting cards, dummy boards
Shows: East Coast
In business for 9 years

ALL THINGS BRIGHT AND BEAUTIFUL

Box 43, Bridge St.
Waitsfield, VT 05673
Phone: 802-496-3997
    Phone orders accepted.
Hours: 7 days, 9A.M.-6P.M.
Accepts: check, Visa, MasterCard, Discover, American Express

MODERN BEARS:
Canada: Ganz Bros.
France: Nounours/Aux Nations/Ajena
Germany: Gebruder Hermann, Steiff
Italy: Trudi Giocattoli
U.K.: Canterbury, Deans, Lefray/Real Soft Toys, Little Folk, Merrythought, Paddington
U.S.A.: Boyds, California Stuffed Toys, Charlene Kinser Designs, Dakin, Gund, Lone Star, Madame Alexander Bears, The Manhattan Toy Co., Mary Meyer, Muffy, Vanderbear family, North American Bear Co. (other), Michaud Collection
Artist bears: Several, mostly New England artists. Selection constantly changing.
Figurines: Boyds Bearstone, Cast Art Industries, Cherished Teddies, Laura's Attic, Muffy, The Roosevelt Bears, United Design Corp.
In business for 23 years

AMERICAN TWIG

Steve & Deborah Potts, owners
1350½ Randall St.
Cortland, NY 13045
Second address:
160 Homer Ave.
Cortland, NY 13045
Phone: 607-753-1339
    Phone orders accepted.
Hours: by appointment
Catalog: $2, refundable with purchase.
Accepts: check, money order, Visa, MasterCard
Layaway: 50% down
Discounts: frequent customer, wholesale

ACCESSORIES:
Furniture: signed, original twig and wood chairs
Shows: Northeast
In business for 3 years

ANIMAL HAUS

7784 Montgomery Rd., Suite 9
Cincinnati, OH 45236

ANIMAL KINGDOM

Judy Moyer, owner
103 S. Allen St.
State College, PA
Phone: 814-237-2402 or 1-800-453-0014
  Phone orders accepted.
Fax: 814-237-3136
  Fax orders accepted.
Hours: M-W, F, 9:30A.M.-5:30P.M. TH, 9:30A.M.-8P.M. Sat, 9:30A.M.-5P.M. Sun, 11:30A.M.-4P.M. May-Jan. 1: open until 8P.M. F, Sat.
Catalog: $2, refundable with purchase.
Accepts: check, money order, Visa, MasterCard, Discover, American Express
Layaway: 10% down, 10% per month

MODERN BEARS:
Canada: Ganz Bros., Mighty Star
Germany: Steiff
Italy: Trudi Giocattoli
U.S.A.: Applause, Boyds, Russ Berrie, Dakin, Gund, The Manhattan Toy Co., Mary Meyer, Muffy, Vanderbear family

ACCESSORIES:
Glasses
Clothes: Boyds
Furniture: Boyds
Figurines: Boyds Bearstone
Bear collectibles: Paddington collectibles, Winnie-the-Pooh collectibles
In business for 5 years

ANYTHING GOES, INC.

Carmen Pedota, vice-president
P.O. Box 92
Anna Maria, FL 34216
Second address:
9801 Gulf Dr.
Anna Maria, FL
Phone: 813-778-4456 or 1-800-780-2327 for orders.
  Phone orders accepted.
Fax: 813-778-1906
  Fax orders accepted.
Hours: M-Sat, 10A.M.-5P.M.
Catalog available.
Accepts: check, money order, Visa, MasterCard, Discover, American Express
Discounts: bulk order, frequent customer
Old/special items: antique bears, bears manufactured between WWI and WWII, bears manufactured 1945-1970, antique bear collectibles

MODERN BEARS:
Canada: Ganz Bros.
Germany: Kathe Kruse Puppen, Schuco, Steiff
Italy: Lenci
U.K.: Canterbury, Merrythought, Paddington
U.S.A.: Applause/Raikes, Beaver Valley, Boyds, Cooperstown Bears, Gund, Madame Alexander Bears, Mary Meyer, Muffy, Vanderbear family, VIBs, North American Bear Co. (other), R. John Wright, Vermont
Artist bears: Goose Creek, McB, Ballard Baines, Bearons of La Jolla, Barbara's Originals, Bearly There
Miniature bears: Ballard Baines, Lisa Lloyd, Pat Carruka, Arlene Damisch, Roberta Rehm

ACCESSORIES:
Clothes: Muffy
Figurines: Boyds Bearstone, Muffy, The Roosevelt Bears, Steiff
Shows: FL
In business for 9 years

AVALON PRODUCTIONS

Linda Whelon, producer
P.O. Box 1973023
Portland, OR 97280-0730
Mail order only.
Accepts: check, money order

ACCESSORIES:
Adoption certificate. Includes all important information about the bear. Suitable for framing. Parchment/marble paper. Official seal from the Teddy Bear Empire.
In business for 2 years

B & J COLLECTIBLES

Jean Davis, owner
609 W. Broadway
Drumright, OK
Phone: 918-352-4067
  Phone orders accepted.
Hours: 10A.M.-5P.M.
Accepts: check, money order, Visa, MasterCard, Discover, American Express
Layaway: 33% down, 60 days
Discounts: bulk order
Old/special items: bunnies
MODERN BEARS:
U.S.A.: Applause/Raikes, Muffy, Vanderbear family, VIBs, North American Bear Co. (other)

Artist bears: Dolores Ribordy, Mary Ellen Brandt, Barbara Thomas, Bettina Groh, Susan White, Hazel Reeves
Miniature bears: Sharon Ballard, Janet Merchant

ACCESSORIES:
Clothes: NAB
Furniture: NAB, craft
Figurines: Cherished Teddies, Muffy, United Design Corp.
Bear collectibles: ornaments, postcards, stationery, tea sets, tins
Shows: OK
In business for 6 years

BABES 'N BEARS

Shanna Peterson, manager
5307-F FM 1960 West
Houston, TX 77069
Phone: 713-580-9229 or 1-800-460-9229 for orders
  Phone orders accepted.
Fax: 713-580-5384
Hours: M-Sat, 10A.M.-6P.M.
Catalog: $1, refundable with purchase.
Accepts: check, money order, Visa, MasterCard, Discover, American Express
Layaway available.
Discounts: certain products, specials
Old/special items: golliwogs, bunnies

MODERN BEARS:
Canada: Cuddly Toys, Ganz Bros.
Germany: Gebruder Hermann, Steiff
Italy: Trudi Giocattoli
U.K.: Canterbury, Little Folk, Merrythought, Paddington
U.S.A.: Applause/Raikes, Beaver Valley, Boyds, Russ Berrie, Cooperstown Bears, Dakin, Gund, Lone Star, Madame Alexander Bears, The Manhattan Toy Co., Mary Meyer, Muffy, Vanderbear family, VIBs, North American Bear Co. (other), R. John Wright, Michaud Collection
Artist bears: Joanne Mittchell, Joan Woessner, Michelle Brown, Bearly There, Ro Bears
Miniature bears: Carol Stewart, Mama's Babies, Akira, Gund

ACCESSORIES:
Jewelry
Clothes: Boyds, NAB Furniture available.
Miniature furniture available.
Figurines: Boyds Bearstone, Cast Art Industries, Cherished Teddies, Colour

Box Miniatures, Jan Hagara Collectibles, Laura's Attic, Lucy & Me, Muffy, The Roosevelt Bears, United Design Corp.

Bear collectibles: books about bears, books about collecting, jewelry, bear magazines, dollhouse miniatures, ornaments, Paddington collectibles, postcards, Smokey bear collectibles, stationery, tea sets, tins, Winnie-the-Pooh collectibles

Shows: TX

In business for 10 years

BARBIE'S BEARS

Barbie Hampton, owner
15172 Koyle Cemetery Rd.
Winslow, AR 72959
Phone: 501-634-5741
Phone orders accepted.
Mail order only.
Catalog: LSASE
Accepts: check, money order, Visa, MasterCard

MODERN BEARS:

Germany: Steiff
U.K.: Deans
U.S.A.: Boyds, Mary Meyer
Artist bears: Bearly There, Barbie's Bears

ACCESSORIES:

Clothes: sweaters, handmade outfits
Bear collectibles: books about collecting, boxes, bear magazines, stationery, tote bags, Winnie-the-Pooh collectibles

Shows: OK, MO, TX, AR

In business for 4 years

BEAR-A-DISE

Jyll Weissman, owner
359 Millburn Ave.
Millburn, NJ 07041
Phone: 201-376-2405 or 201-376-2406 or 1-800-376-BEAR for orders
Phone orders accepted.
Fax: 201-376-2405
Fax orders accepted.
Hours: M-Sat, 10A.M.-5:30P.M. Thanksgiving-Christmas, open 7 days.
Accepts: check, money order, Visa, MasterCard, American Express
Layaway: 33% down, 33% in 30 days, balance in 60 days

MODERN BEARS:

Germany: Steiff
U.K.: Canterbury, Deans, Bransgore
U.S.A.: Applause/Raikes, Boyds, Russ Berrie, Cooperstown Bears, Gund, Mary Meyer, Muffy, Vanderbear family, VIBs, North American Bear Co. (other)

Artist bears: Janet Reeves, Connie Roark, Sally Winey, Claire Herz, Marie Zimmerman, Sandy Dickl, Terry Hayes, Mary Timme, Jan Brouwer, Paula Egbert, Gloria Franks, Kathy Wallace, Sue Foskey, Marcia Sibol, Carolyn Lamothe, Debbie Stewart, Pat Lyons, Pat Murphy, Barbara Golden, Karen Meyer, Nancy Johnsen, Sandy Dineen, Chester Freeman, Martha DeRaimo, Jean Buchans, Donna Bobby, B&J Originals, Corbett Hollow, Lin Davies, Bear Brown, Brenda Dewey, Ann Cran-shaw, Jackie Morris, Linda Stafford, Carol Carini, Pat Hurley, Carol Martin, Vicky Lougher, Mati's Originals, Bev Wright, and more.

Miniature bears: Durae Allen, Linda Nelson, Maryann Gebhardt, Sherri Dodson, Janet Wilson, Brenda Dewey, Akira

ACCESSORIES:

Glasses
Clothes: Boyds, NAB, Tender Heart Treasures, hats
Furniture: twig chairs, pine beds, cradles, high chairs, J.P. Bartholomew wagons, swings
Figurines: Boyds Bearstone, NAB, Iris Arc crystal
Bear collectibles: books about bears, books about collecting, jewelry, bear magazines, dollhouse miniatures, ornaments, tea sets, tote bags, rubber stamps, calendars, framed photos

Shows: NJ, FL

In business for 2 years

BEAR-A-DISE LANDING

Jeanne Orlando, owner
1310 Boston Post Rd.
Guilford, CT 06437
Phone: 203-458-2378
Phone orders accepted.
Hours: T-Sat, 10A.M.-5P.M. Sun, 11A.M.-3P.M. Closed M.
Accepts: check, Visa, MasterCard

Layaway: 25% down, 30 days
Old/special items: bunnies

MODERN BEARS:

Canada: Ganz Bros.
Germany: Gebruder Hermann
Italy: Trudi Giocattoli
U.K.: Canterbury, Deans, Merrythought, Paddington
U.S.A.: Applause/Raikes, Boyds, Russ Berrie, Cooperstown Bears, Dakin, Gund, The Manhattan Toy Co., Muffy, Vanderbear family, VIBs, North American Bear Co. (other), Vermont

Artist bears: Anne Cranshaw, Donna Hodges, Joan Woessner, Chris Cassner, Serieta, Irene Heckel, Dee Hockenberry, Gloria Franks, Edda Seipel, Carol Kirby, Janet Reeves and more.

Miniature bears: Akira, Chris Cassner

ACCESSORIES:

Glasses, trunks, 8"-23"
Clothes available.
Furniture: wooden chairs, tables
Figurines: Boyds Bearstone, Muffy
Bear collectibles: books about bears, books about bearmaking, books about collecting, boxes, chinaware, postcards, stationery, tea sets, Winnie-the-Pooh collectibles

In business for 3 years

THE BEAR-EE PATCH

2461 San Diego Ave., 107
San Diego, CA 92110

THE BEAR EMPORIUM

Roseanna Camaioni, owner
955 Ashley Blvd.
New Bedford, MA 02745
Phone: 508-995-2221
Phone orders accepted.
Accepts: check, money order
Layaway: $50 minimum, 25% down, 30 days.
Discounts: bulk order, frequent customer, senior citizen, student
Old/special items: antique bears, bears manufactured between WWI and WWII, bears manufactured between 1945-1970, antique bear collectibles, bunnies

MODERN BEARS:

Canada: Cuddly Toys, Ganz Bros.
France: The French Bear Co.

Germany: Gebruder Hermann, Steiff
Italy: Trudi Giocattoli
U.K.: Big Softies, Canterbury, Little Folk, Merrythought, Paddington
U.S.A.: Applause/Raikes, Beaver Valley, Boyds, Russ Berrie, Dakin, Gund, Lone Star, The Manhattan Toy Co., Mary Meyer, Muffy, Vanderbear family, VIBs, North American Bear Co. (other), Michaud Collection, Avanti, Sun and Star, Hen and Holly, Bearly People, Bears & Co.
Artist bears: Linda Spiegel, Robert Raikes, Carol Black, Sue Foskey, Genie Buttica, Wendy Brent, Tilly, Granny Grady, Edith Winston, Karen M. Stanek, Christine Lamb and more.
Miniature bears: Mama's Babies, Bears & Co., Nanda's Bears and more.

ACCESSORIES:
Clothes: knitted
Furniture: handmade chairs
Figurines: Boyds Bearstone, Lucy & Me, Muffy, United Design Corp., brass figurines, crystal figurines, music boxes
Bear collectibles: books about bears, books about collecting, clothing for people, jewelry, bear magazines, ornaments, paintings, prints, stationery, tote bags, Winnie-the-Pooh collectibles, lamps, magnets
Shows: Northeast
In business for 9 years

BEAR ESSENTIALS

Harry Morgan, owner
3211 S. Vanwert Rd.
Villa Rica, GA 30180
Phone: 404-459-0672
      Phone orders accepted.
Accepts: check, money order
Layaway: 10% down, 3 months
Discounts: bulk order, frequent customer, club, nonprofit organization, senior citizens, students

MODERN BEARS:
Germany: Gebruder Hermann, Steiff
U.K.: Little Folk, Merrythought, Paddington
U.S.A.: Applause/Raikes, Russ Berrie, Cooperstown Bears, Gund, Mary Meyer, Muffy, Vanderbear family, VIBs, North American Bear Co. (other), Michaud Collection

ACCESSORIES:
Furniture: NAB
Miscellaneous: baskets, glasses, jewelry, shoes
In business for 10 years

THE BEAR FACTORY

Rhonda K. Dyer, owner
307 S. Main St.
St. Charles, MO 63301
Phone: 314-940-0047
      Phone orders accepted.
Hours: M-Sat, 10A.M.-5P.M. Sun, noon-5P.M.
Accepts: check, money order, Visa, MasterCard, Discover
Layaway: 10% down, 120 days
Old/special items: bunnies

MODERN BEARS:
Canada: Ganz Bros.
Germany: Gebruder Hermann, Steiff
U.K.: Canterbury, Deans, Merrythought, Paddington, English Teddy Bear
U.S.A.: Boyds, Russ Berrie, Dakin, Gund, Jona, Mary Meyer, VIBs, North American Bear Co. (other), Michaud Collection, Ty
Artist bears: Selection constantly changing. Please call for availability.
Miniature bears: Gund, Little Gem by Chu Ming Wu

ACCESSORIES:
Glasses
Clothes available.
Figurines: Lucy & Me
Bear collectibles: books about bears, books about bearmaking, books about collecting, jewelry, bear magazines, ornaments, postcards, prints, Smokey bear collectibles, tea sets
In business for 13 years

BEAR FRIENDS AND COMPANY, INC.

Cindy Trimper, president
806 S. 1st St.,
Inlet Village #18
Ocean City, MD 21842
Phone: 401-289-5651
      Phone orders accepted.
Hours: May-Sept. 15, 10A.M.-10P.M. Sept.-Oct., 10A.M.-6P.M. Nov.-Dec., 10A.M.-5P.M. Closed Jan.-Feb. 15. Open on weekends, Feb.-April.
Accepts: money order, Visa, MasterCard, Discover, American Express
Layaway: 90 days

MODERN BEARS:
Canada: Ganz Bros.
Germany: Hermann-Spielwaren, Steiff
U.K.: Canterbury, Deans, Little Folk, Merrythought, Paddington
U.S.A.: Applause/Raikes, Beaver Valley, Boyds, Russ Berrie, California Stuffed Toys, Cooperstown Bears, Dakin, Gund, Mary Meyer, Muffy, Vanderbear family, VIBs, North American Bear Co. (other), Vermont
Artist bears: Barbara Zimmerman, Stier Bears, Cathy Bordi, Sandra Shimel, Jerri Keller
Miniature bears: Akira, Jerri Keller

ACCESSORIES:
Glasses
Clothes: NAB, Boyds
Furniture: NAB
Figurines: Boyds Bearstone, Cherished Teddies, Lucy & Me, Muffy, Sarah's Attic, United Design Corp.
Bear collectibles: books about bears, books about collecting, clothing for people, jewelry, bear magazines, Paddington collectibles, postcards, prints, stationery, tea sets, tins, tote bags, Winnie-the-Pooh collectibles
In business for 11 years

BEAR HUGS

Suzanna DeNight, owner
7 Cooper Ave.
Marlton, NJ 08053
Phone: 609-596-2050 or 1-800-672-3277 for orders
      Phone orders accepted.
Fax: 609-983-0805
      Fax orders accepted.
Hours: M-TH, 10A.M.-5P.M. F, 10A.M.-8P.M. Sat, 10A.M.-4P.M. Sun, Nov. and Dec. only.
Accepts: check, money order, Visa, MasterCard, Discover, American Express
Layaway: 20% down, 2 months
Discounts: club, yearly anniversary

MODERN BEARS:
Germany: Steiff, Haida
U.K.: Canterbury, Little Folk, Merrythought, Paddington, English Teddy Bear Co.
U.S.A.: Applause/Raikes, Boyds, Cooperstown Bears, Gund, Mary Meyer, Muffy, Vanderbear family, VIBs, North American Bear Co. (other), Cherished Teddies

Artist bears: Sersha, Peggy Pearson, Elegant Creations, Carol Black, Bearly There, Kathy Sheppard, Sandra Dineen

Miniature bears: Sherri Dodson

ACCESSORIES:

Baskets, glasses

Clothes: sweaters, hats, assorted clothes

Furniture: desks, chairs, benches, beds, armoires, etc.

Figurines: Boyds Bearstone, Cherished Teddies, Colour Box Miniatures, Muffy

More about figurines: newsletter updates customers on other figurines available

Bear collectibles: books about bears, books about bearmaking, books about collecting, boxes, chinaware, clothing for people, jewelry, bear magazines, Paddington collectibles, paintings, postcards, pottery, prints, Smokey bear collectibles, stationery, tea sets, tins, tote bags, Winnie-the-Pooh collectibles

In business for 11 years

BEAR HUGS

Mary Nelson, manager

210 Sherman, #161

Coeur d' Alene, ID 83814

Phone: 208-664-2327

Phone orders accepted.

Hours: M-Sat, 9:30A.M.-9P.M. Sun, 11A.M.-6P.M.

Accepts: check, money order, Visa, MasterCard, Discover, American Express

Layaway available.

MODERN BEARS:

Canada: Ganz Bros.

Germany: Gebruder Hermann, Steiff

U.K.: Canterbury, Merrythought, Paddington

U.S.A.: Applause/Raikes, Boyds, Cooperstown Bears, Dakin, Gund, Lone Star, Muffy, Vanderbear family, VIBs, North American Bear Co. (other), Orzek, Mango, Michaud Collection

Artist bears: Several nationally known artists.

Miniature bears: Several nationally known artists.

ACCESSORIES:

Clothes: NAB, Boyds

Furniture: NAB

Figurines: Boyds Bearstone, Muffy, United Design Corp.

Bear collectibles: books about bears, books about bearmaking, books about collecting, boxes, jewelry, bear magazines, Paddington collectibles, paintings, Smokey bear collectibles, stationery, tea sets, Winnie-the-Pooh collectibles

In business for 5 years

BEAR HUGS—A BEAR EMPORIUM

Enid Carnahan, owner

7902 27th West

Tacoma, WA 98466

Second address:

409 Broadway

Seaside, OR 97138

Phone: 206-564-3700 or 503-738-3890

Phone orders accepted.

Hours: M-Sat, 10A.M.-5:30P.M. Open Sundays in December only.

Accepts: check, money order, Visa, MasterCard

Layaway: 33% down, monthly payments

Old/special items: antique bear collectibles

MODERN BEARS:

Canada: Ganz Bros., Mighty Star

Germany: Gebruder Hermann, Hermann-Spielwaren, Kathe Kruse Puppen, Steiff

New Zealand: Sheepskin Products

Switzerland: MCZ/Mutzali/Felpa

U.K.: Alresford, Big Softies, Canterbury, Little Folk, Merrythought, Paddington

U.S.A.: Applause/Raikes, Boyds, Russ Berrie, Charlene Kinser Designs, Dakin, Gund, Lone Star, The Manhattan Toy Co., Mary Meyer, Muffy, Vanderbear family, VIBs, North American Bear Co. (other), R. John Wright, Michaud Collection, Vermont

Artist bears: Joan Sonntag, Sue Chaffee, Rose Policky, Joan Gadano, Florence Gutemann, Linda Nelson, Carol Jones, Ann Inman, Linda Spiegel-Lohre, Judy Stutzman, Bev Miller, Linda Schaff, Janet Grant, Mar-Gare, Paula Egbert

Miniature bears: Akira, Sunday Flagg, Rose Policky, Marilyn Wade, Judy Scott, Marty Blackman

ACCESSORIES:

Glasses, jewelry, shoes

Clothes: Tender Heart, hand-knit clothing

Furniture: chairs, beds, armoires, tables, etc.

Miniatures: glasses

Miniature furniture available.

Figurines: Cherished Teddies, Lucy & Me, Muffy

Bear collectibles: antique collectibles, books about bears, books about bearmaking, books about collecting, chinaware, clothing for people, jewelry, bear magazines, ornaments, Paddington collectibles, postcards, prints, Smokey bear collectibles, stationery, tea sets, tins, tote bags, Winnie-the-Pooh collectibles

In business for 15 years

BEAR HUGS & BABY DOLLS

Cynthia Richards, owner

1184 Lexington Ave. (between 80th and 81st streets)

New York, NY 10028

Phone: 212-717-1514

Phone orders accepted.

Accepts: money order, Visa, MasterCard, American Express

Layaway: $200 minimum, 50% down

Discounts: collector club for arctophiles & Muffy collectors

Old/special items: antique bears, bears manufactured between WWI and WWII, bears manufactured 1945-1970 (all on consignment only, not always available), bunnies (Easter season only)

MODERN BEARS:

Canada: Ganz Bros.

Germany: Gebruder Hermann, Kathe Kruse Puppen, Steiff

Italy: Trudi Giocattoli

New Zealand: Bear With Us

U.K.: Canterbury, Merrythought, Paddington

U.S.A.: Applause/Raikes, Beaver Valley, Boyds, Charlene Kinser Designs, Cooperstown Bears, Dakin, Gund, Madame Alexander Bears, Muffy, Vanderbear family, VIBs, North American Bear Co. (other)

Artist bears: Several artists—including well-known, little-known and local.

Never buys from the same artist more than once a year.

Miniature bears: Gund, Little Gems, Half Nelsons

ACCESSORIES:

Glasses

Clothes: sweaters, custom made clothes, ever-changing selection designed by seamstress

Figurines: Muffy

Bear collectibles: books about bears, books about collecting, clothing for people, jewelry, postcards, stationery, tea sets, Winnie-the-Pooh collectibles

In business for 3 years

BEAR IN MIND, INC.

Fran Lewis, president

53 Bradford St. W.

Concord, MA 01742

Phone: 508-369-1167

Phone orders accepted.

Fax: 508-371-0762

Fax orders accepted.

Catalog: $1

Accepts: check, money order, Visa, MasterCard, Discover, American Express

Discounts: bulk order, nonprofit organization

Old/special items: bunnies

MODERN BEARS:

Canada: Cuddly Toys, Ganz Bros.

France: Nounours/Aux Nations/Ajena

Germany: Gebruder Hermann, Hermann-Spielwaren, Steiff

U.K.: Canterbury, Little Folk, Merrythought, Paddington

U.S.A.: Boyds, Charlene Kinser Designs, Cooperstown Bears, Dakin, Gund, Jona, Lone Star, Madame Alexander Bears, The Manhattan Toy Co., Mary Meyer, Muffy, Vanderbear family, VIBs, North American Bear Co. (other), R. John Wright, Michaud Collection, Vermont

ACCESSORIES:

Baskets, glasses

Clothes available.

Furniture available.

Miniature accessories: glasses

Miniature clothes available.

Miniature furniture available.

Figurines: Boyds Bearstone, Cherished Teddies, Laura's Attic, Lucy & Me, Muffy, The Roosevelt Bears, Sarah's Attic, United Design Corp.

Bear collectibles: books about bears, books about bearmaking, books about collecting, boxes, chinaware, clothing for people, jewelry, dollhouse miniatures, ornaments, Paddington collectibles, paintings, postcards, pottery, prints, Smokey bear collectibles, stationery, tea sets, tins, tote bags, Winnie-the-Pooh collectibles

In business for 18 years

BEAR NECESSITIES

Gwen Zimmerman and Chris Pisoni, owners

331 Main St.

Salinas, CA 93901

Phone: 408-758-4230

Phone orders accepted.

Accepts: check, money order, Visa, MasterCard, Discover

Layaway: 10% down, reasonable monthly payments

MODERN BEARS:

U.S.A.: Applause/Raikes, Boyds, Dakin, Gund, Mary Meyer, Muffy, Vanderbear, VIB, North American Bear Co. (other)

ACCESSORIES:

Glasses, jewelry

Clothes: sweaters

Figurines: Boyds Bearstone

In business for 6 years

THE BEAR PAWSE

Holly McLean-Aldis

502 S. Montezuma St.

Prescott, AZ 86303

Phone: 520-445-3800

Phone orders accepted.

Fax: 520-445-6763

Fax orders accepted.

Hours: M-Sat, 9:30 A.M.-5:30 P.M. Sun, 11 A.M.-3 P.M.

Catalog: $6 (video)

Accepts: check, money order, Visa, MasterCard, Discover, American Express

Discounts: frequent customer

Old/special items: antique bears, bears manufactured between WWI and WWII, bears manufactured 1945-1970, bunnies

MODERN BEARS:

Canada: Ganz Bros., Mighty Star

Germany: Grisly Spielwaren, Gebruder Hermann, Steiff, Haida

U.K.: Merrythought, Paddington

U.S.A.: Beaver Valley, Boyds, Russ Berrie, Cooperstown Bears, Dakin, Gund, Lone Star, The Manhattan Toy Co., Mary Meyer, Muffy, Vanderbear family, VIBs, North American Bear Co. (other), R. John Wright, Michaud Collection

Artist bears: Donna Hodges, Carol Martin, Diane Gard, Julie Jones, Ann Brown, CM Bears, Cuddly Jeans, Joan Woessner, Michauds, Kricket, Lorette Barrett, Gloria Franks, Ben Raffle, Lane Carpenter, Carol Ross

Miniature bears: Lisa Lloyd, Sherry Dodson, Linda Spiegel-Lohre, Carol Martin, Factoria Toy Works, Pat Carriker, Mama's Babies, Linda Schaff

ACCESSORIES:

Merrythought bear slippers (16"-18" bear), bear muff

Clothes: NAB, Boyds, Hermann

Figurines: Boyds Bearstone, Lucy & Me, Muffy, United Design Corp.

Bear collectibles: books about bears, books about bearmaking, books about collecting, bear magazines, ornaments, Paddington collectibles, Smokey bear collectibles, stationery, tea sets, tote bags, Winnie-the-Pooh collectibles, plaques, banks, teapots, salt & pepper sets

Shows: AZ

In business for 11 years

BEAR TRACKER, INT'L.

S. Silber, owner

265 S. Federal Hwy., Suite 315

Deefield Beach, FL 33441

Phone: 305-570-7940

Phone orders accepted.

Fax: 305-570-7940

Fax orders accepted 24 hours.

Hours: M-F, 10 A.M.-5 P.M.

Catalog: $3, refundable with purchase.

Accepts: check, money order, Visa, MasterCard, Discover, American Express

Layaway: 33% down, 90 days

Old/special items: bears manufactured 1945-1970, bunnies

MODERN BEARS:

Germany: Gebruder Hermann, Steiff

U.K.: Canterbury, Deans, Merrythought, Paddington

U.S.A.: Applause/Raikes, Beaver Valley, Boyds, Cooperstown Bears, Dakin, Gund, Lone Star, Madame Alexander

Bears, The Manhattan Toy Co., Muffy, Vanderbear family, VIBs, North American Bear Co. (other), R. John Wright, Michaud Collection, Vermont, Disney World annual teddy bear convention bears. Artists and manufacturers vary.

Artist bears: Several USA artists
Miniature bears: Steiff, Gund, Boyds

ACCESSORIES:
Baskets, glasses
Clothes: Boyds, NAB
Furniture: Boyds, artist
Figurines: Boyds Bearstone, Muffy
Bear collectibles: books about collecting, postcards, stationery, tea sets
Shows: FL
In business for 5 years

BEAR WITH US

Jennifer Anderson, owner
4690 N. Blackstone
Fresno, CA 93726
Phone: 209-222-8031
Phone orders accepted.
Hours: M-F, 10A.M.-5P.M. Sat, 10A.M.-3P.M.
Accepts: check, money order, Visa, MasterCard, Discover
Layaway available.
Discounts: club
Old/special items: bears manufactured 1945-1970, bunnies

MODERN BEARS:
Germany: Gebruder Hermann, Steiff
U.K.: Canterbury, Merrythought, Paddington
U.S.A.: Applause/Raikes, Boyds, Cooperstown Bears, Dakin, Gund, Lone Star, Mary Meyer, Muffy, Vanderbear family, VIBs, North American Bear Co. (other), Michaud Collection
Artist bears: Janet Reeves, Beth Kreische, Tea 'N Teddies, Denise Gluech, Chester Freeman, Pat Cathey, Teri Catia, Bearly There

ACCESSORIES:
Baskets
Clothes: NAB
Furniture: NAB
More about these accessories: large selection of Vanderbear clothing
Figurines: Boyds Bearstone, Cherished Teddies, Lucy & Me, Muffy
Bear collectibles: bear magazines, stationery, tea sets, tins

Shows: Fresno, CA
In business for 7 years

BEARAPHERNALIA

Chris & Fran Ruggles
4330 Barranca Pkwy, Suite 120
Irvine, CA 92714
Phone: 714-262-9444
Phone orders accepted.
Catalog: free
Accepts: check, money order, Visa, MasterCard
Layaway: 33% down, 33% in 30 days, balance in 60 days
Discounts: special sales on Muffy

MODERN BEARS:
Germany: Kathe Kruse Puppen, Schuco, Steiff
U.K.: Merrythought, Paddington
U.S.A.: Applause/Raikes, Beaver Valley, Boyds, Charlene Kinser Designs, Cooperstown Bears, Gund, Madame Alexander Bears, Muffy, Vanderbear family, VIBs, North American Bear Co. (other), R. John Wright, Michaud Collection, Vermont
Artist bears: Marcia Sibol, Martha Deraimo, Wendy Brent, Marie Zimmerman, Kathleen Wallace, Pam Holton, Terry John Woods, Rosalie Frishman, Barbara Ferrier

ACCESSORIES:
Baskets, glasses
Clothes available.
Furniture available.
Figurines: Boyds Bearstone, Cherished Teddies, Muffy
Bear collectibles: books about bears, books about bearmaking, books about collecting, jewelry, bear magazines, Paddington collectibles, postcards, Smokey bear collectibles, stationery, tea sets, tins, tote bags, Winnie-the-Pooh collectibles
In business for 5 years

GAIL R. BEARD

493 Bluff Dr.
Ozark, MO 65721
Phone: 417-581-5656 or 1-800-381-BEAR for orders
Phone orders: 9A.M.-9P.M.
Mail order only.
Bear collectibles: Gail makes teddy bear signs that say Teddy Bear Crossing,

Bear Hugs Ahead, and Teddy Bear Trail

BEARDEAUX BARN

8907 Warner Ave., Ste.166
Huntington Beach, CA 92647
Phone: 714-842-4460
Phone orders accepted.
Fax: 714-842-4460
Fax orders accepted.
Hours: M, 1P.M.-7P.M. W, F, 11A.M.-4P.M. First Sat. of month, 10A.M.-4P.M.
Catalog: $4
Accepts: check, money order, Visa, MasterCard
Layaway: 33% down, 33% in 30 days, balance in 60 days
Old/special items: antique accessories and collectibles

MODERN BEARS:
Germany: Steiff
U.S.A.: Boyds
Artist bears: Linda Johnson, Pam Holton, Debi Ortega, Linda Schaff, Maria Grimes, Marsha DeHaven, Bearly There and many more
Miniature bears: Many artists

ACCESSORIES:
Baskets, shoes
Clothes: antiques
Furniture: antiques and primitives
Figurines: Boyds Bearstone, Cherished Teddies, The Roosevelt Bears
Bear collectibles: antique collectibles, books about bearmaking, clothing for people, jewelry, bear magazines, dollhouse miniatures, stationery, tote bags
Shows: throughout USA
In business for 6 years

BEARING GIFTS

8600 Foundry St.
Savage, MD 20763
Phone: 301-498-6871
Phone orders accepted.
Hours: 7 days, 10A.M.-5:30P.M.
Accepts: check, money order, Visa, MasterCard
Layaway: 25% down, 30 days
Discounts: frequent customer
Old/special items: bunnies

MODERN BEARS:
Canada: Ganz Bros.
Germany: Grisly Spielwaren, Steiff
U.K.: Canterbury, Little Folk

U.S.A.: Applause/Raikes, Boyds, Russ Berrie, Cooperstown Bears, Dakin, Gund, Muffy, Vanderbear family, VIBs, North American Bear Co., Vermont, Bearly People, J.W. Wind
Artist bears: Bearly There, Durae Allen, Faye Touve, Mati's Originals
Miniature bears: Durae Allen, Tommy Smith, Kathy Rose

ACCESSORIES:
Stands
Clothes: sweaters
Furniture: chairs, swings, sleighs, carriages, high chairs, benches
Figurines: Boyds Bearstone, Cast Art Industries, Cherished Teddies, Muffy, United Design Corp. (Pennibears)
Bear collectibles: books about bears, books about bearmaking, books about collecting, chinaware, clothing for people, jewelry, bear magazines, ornaments, postcards, tea sets, tins
Shows: MD, PA

BEARLY AVAILABLE
Jean Myers, owner
31 Central Square New Rd., Rt. 9
Linwood, NJ 08221
Phone: 609-926-2272
Phone orders accepted.
Hours: M-Sat, 10A.M.-6P.M. Sun, by appointment.
Accepts: check, money order, Visa, MasterCard, Discover, American Express, MAC
Layaway: 33% down, monthly payments, 3 months
Discounts: club
Old/special items: golliwogs, bunnies

MODERN BEARS:
Germany: Steiff
U.K.: Canterbury, Deans, Merrythought, Paddington
U.S.A.: Applause/Raikes, Beaver Valley, Boyds, Charlene Kinser Designs, Dakin, Gund, Jona, Lone Star, Madame Alexander Bears, Mary Meyer, Muffy, Vanderbear family, VIBs, North American Bear Co. (other), R. John Wright, Vermont, All Stuffed Up, Ralph Lauren, Hen in the Holly, Bristol Bear Co., Bears & Co, Mango, Michaud Collection
Artist bears: Can't Bear to Part, Bear Brown, Nostalgic Bears, Mill Creek, Debbie Henderson, Santas With

Bears, and more—constantly changing.
Miniature bears: Akira, We Three Bears

ACCESSORIES:
Glasses, jewelry, artist-made houses for bears (all sizes), sets, backdrops
Clothes: sweaters, dresses, pants
Furniture: chairs, rocking horses, tables, benches
Figurines: Boyds Bearstone, Cherished Teddies, Colour Box Miniatures, Lucy & Me, Muffy, The Roosevelt Bears, United Design Corp.
Bear collectibles: books about bears, books about bearmaking, books about collecting, boxes, chinaware, clothing for people, jewelry, bear magazines, dollhouse miniatures, ornaments, Paddington collectibles, paintings, postcards, pottery, prints, stationery, tea sets, tins, tote bags, Winnie-the-Pooh collectibles
Shows: NY, NJ, MD
In business for 6 years

BEARS & BAUBLES
Georgia M. Carlson, owner
1603 Solano Ave.
Berkeley, CA 94707
Phone: 510-524-4794
Phone orders accepted.
Hours: T, W, Sat, 10A.M.-5:30P.M., TH, F, 10A.M.-7P.M.
Catalog: $5, refundable with purchase.
Accepts: check, money order, Visa, MasterCard, Discover, American Express
Layaway: 33% down, 90 days, no refunds
Discounts: occasional sales
Old/special items: antique bears, bears manufactured between WWI and WWII, bears manufactured 1945-1970, antique bear collectibles, bunnies

MODERN BEARS:
Canada: Ganz Bros.
Germany: Steiff (older), Haida
Italy: Trudi Giocattoli
New Zealand: Sheepskin Products
U.K.: Deans, Paddington
U.S.A.: Applause/Raikes, Boyds, Russ Berrie, Charlene Kinser Designs, Dakin, Lone Star, The Manhattan Toy Co., Mary Meyer, Muffy, Vanderbear family, VIBs, North American Bear Co. (other)
Artist bears: Norma Adwere, Janet

Hellerich, Sally Phillips, Florence Link, Gerry Williams, Sue Vouri, Patti Angel, Patricia Gye, C.J. Rankin, Wendy Brent
Miniature bears: Patti Angel, Leota Ordiway, Deborah CanHam, Akira

ACCESSORIES:
Glasses, hair ribbons, jewelry
Clothes: NAB, Boyds
Figurines: Muffy
Bear collectibles: books about bears, books about bearmaking, books about collecting, jewelry, bear magazines, Paddington collectibles, stationery
Shows: West Coast
In business for 9 years

BEARS & MORE
Linda Burner and Valerie Burner, owners
5849 W. Palmaire
Glendale, AZ 85301
Phone: 602-931-0339
Phone orders accepted.
Hours: M-Sat, 10A.M.-4P.M.
Accepts: check, money order, Visa, MasterCard
Layaway: 25% down, 25% per month
Discounts: after spending $200, get $20 off
Old/special items: antique bear collectibles, bunnies

MODERN BEARS:
Germany: Gebruder Hermann, Steiff
U.K.: Canterbury, Deans, Merrythought, Paddington
U.S.A.: Applause/Raikes, Boyds, Russ Berrie, Gund, The Manhattan Toy Co., Mary Meyer, Muffy, Vanderbear family, VIBs, North American Bear Co. (other)
Artist bears: Jeanne Green, Susan Corey, Ben Raffle, Melanie Hugby, Melanie Nathan, Barbara Koch, Valerie Burner, Ruth Milam, Country Orphan
Miniature bears: Shirley Howey, Jill Nelson

ACCESSORIES:
Baskets
Clothes: hand knit sweaters, hats
Bear collectibles: books about bears, books about collecting, ornaments, postcards, prints, tins, tote bags

BEARS BY THE BAY

302 Magnolia
Fairhope, AL 36532

BEARS BY THE SEA

K. Wilde, owner
680 Cypress St.
Pismo Beach, CA 93449
Phone: 805-773-1952
Phone orders accepted.
Fax: 805-773-5869
Fax orders accepted.
Hours: 7 days, 11A.M.-5P.M.
Accepts: check, money order, Visa, MasterCard, Discover, American Express
Discounts: club
Old/special items: antique bears, antique bear collectibles, bunnies

MODERN BEARS:
Canada: Cuddly Toys, Ganz Bros.
Germany: Steiff
U.K.: Merrythought
U.S.A.: Applause/Raikes, Boyds, Russ Berrie, Cooperstown Bears, Dakin, Gund, Madame Alexander Bears, The Manhattan Toy Co., Mary Meyer, Muffy, Vanderbear family, VIBs, North American Bear Co. (other), R. John Wright
Artist bears: Victoria Standard, Lisa Lloyd

ACCESSORIES:
Baskets, glasses, jewelry, shoes
Clothes: shirts, sweaters and more
Furniture: chairs
Figurines: Cherished Teddies, Lucy & Me, Muffy
Bear collectibles: books about bears, books about bearmaking, books about collecting, chinaware, clothing for people, jewelry, bear magazines, paintings, postcards, stationery, tea sets, tins, tote bags
In business for 4 years

THE BEAR'S DEN, INC.

Joyce M. Harper, owner
Cedar Hill Shopping Center
525 Cedar Hill Ave.
Wycokoff, NJ 07481
Phone: 201-444-9133 or 1-800-TEDDY BEAR for orders
Phone orders accepted.
Hours: M-W, F, Sat, 10A.M.-6P.M. TH, 10A.M.-8P.M.
Accepts: check, money order, Visa, Mas-

terCard, Discover, American Express
Layaway: 20% down, 30 days
Discounts: senior citizen
Old/special items: antique bears, bears manufactured between WWI and WWII, bears manufactured 1945-1970, bunnies

MODERN BEARS:
Canada: Ganz Bros., Mighty Star
Germany: Steiff
U.K.: Canterbury, Merrythought, Paddington
U.S.A.: Applause/Raikes, Boyds, Russ Berrie, Cooperstown Bears, Dakin, Gund, Lone Star, Madame Alexander Bears, The Manhattan Toy Co., Mary Meyer, Muffy, Vanderbear family, VIBs, North American Bear Co. (other), R. John Wright, Vermont
In business for 7 years

BEARS EVERYWHERE!

Pat Dietch, owner
703 Caroline St.
Fredericksburg, VA 22401
Phone: 703-371-8484 or 1-800-679-0040
Phone orders accepted.
Catalog: $2, refundable with purchase.
Accepts: check, money order, Visa, MasterCard, Discover, American Express
Layaway: 33% down, monthly payments, 30-120 days, depending on price
Discounts: buy 10 pieces, get one of equal value free, no time limit
Old/special items: bunnies

MODERN BEARS:
Germany: Gebruder Hermann, Steiff, Haida
U.K.: Canterbury, Deans, Merrythought, Paddington
U.S.A.: Beaver Valley, Boyds, Russ Berrie, Charlene Kinser Designs, Dakin, Gund, Jona, The Manhattan Toy Co., Mary Meyer, Muffy, Vanderbear family, VIBs, North American Bear Co.,Vermont, Smokey, Mati's Originals, All Stuffed Up, Play By Play (Coca-Cola), Bearland, Ty, Princess, Mango
Artist bears: Bearly There, Randie Bortnem, Irene Heckel, Gloria Franks, Joan Mescon, Gary Nett, Carol Black, Donna Hodges, Serieta Harrell, Mari Zimmerman, Wanda

Shope, Denise Killingsworth, Ruth Ann Maurer, Jackie Lescher, Christine Jesser, Heidi Steiner, Debra Stewart, Golden Harlequin, Janet Reeves, Susan Horn, Gilmur Rudley, Nancy Latham, Marsha Friesen, Terry Hayes, Cecelia Moupree, Vicky Lougher, Debi Reese, McB Bears, Sarah McClellen, Leanne Snyder, Wendy Brent, Pat Hurley, Maxine Hurst, Irene Weiser, Carol Carini, Lexington, Edda Seiple, Barbara Golden, Heidi Miller, Stuyvesant Bears, Wanda Cole, Grandpa Jingles and many more.
Miniature bears: Little Gem Bears, Pay Fye, Maxine Hurst, Lynn Musson, Leota Ordiway, Cathy Rose, Joyce Miller, Linda Nelson, Diane Sherman

ACCESSORIES:
Glasses, carriages, bicycles, pedal cars, planes
Clothes: NAB, sweaters
Furniture: NAB, tables, chairs, sofas, beds, etc.
Figurines: Boyds Bearstone, Cherished Teddies, Heart for Bears, Laura's Attic, Lucy & Me, Muffy, Chocolate Bear Essentials (Enesco), Pandannas (Enesco)
Bear collectibles: books about bears, books about bearmaking, books about collecting, chinaware, clothing for people, jewelry, bear magazines, Paddington collectibles, tea sets, Winnie-the-Pooh collectibles
In business for 6 years

BEARS GALORE DELIVERED TO YOUR DOOR

Rochelle Glass, partner
396 Academy Rd.
Winnipeg, Manitoba R3N 0B8, Canada
Phone: 204-488-2327
Phone orders accepted.
Fax: 204-942-1176
Fax orders accepted.
Hours: M-F, 9:30A.M.-5:30P.M. Sat, 10A.M.- 4P.M.
Accepts: money order, Visa, MasterCard
Layaway: 50% down, 3 months
Discounts: nonprofit organization, student
Old/special items: antique bear collectibles, bunnies

MODERN BEARS:

Canada: Ganz Bros., Mighty Star

Germany: Hermann-Spielwaren, Steiff

U.K.: Merrythought, Paddington

U.S.A.: Applause/Raikes, Boyds, Russ Berrie, Dakin, Muffy, Vanderbear family, VIBs, North American Bear Co. (other), Ty, Bearly People

Artist bears: J.R. Bears, It Bears Repeating, The Bearworks, Fred Bears, Heartspun

Miniature bears: Heartspun, Fred Bears, J.R. Bears

ACCESSORIES:

Baskets, glasses

Clothes: NAB

Furniture: rattan

Miniature bear accessories: baskets

Bear collectibles: ornaments, Paddington collectibles, postcards, stationery, tote bags

In business for 6 years

BEARS, HARES AND OTHER WARES

Bonnie H. Moose

500 W. 33rd St.

Baltimore, MD 21211-2745

Phone: 410-889-5061

Phone orders accepted.

Mail order only.

Bear collectibles: paintings, postcards, stationery, greeting cards, notepaper

More about collectibles: All of Bonnie's collectibles are custom artwork pieces based on watercolor wash on a pen and ink design

BEARS IN THE ATTIC

Ed & Kathy Carver, owners

227 Main St.

Reisterstown, MD 21136

Phone: 410-833-4900 or 1-800-BE-ATTIC for orders.

Phone orders accepted.

Fax: 410-833-4901

Fax orders accepted.

Hours: W-Sun, noon-5P.M.

Catalog: $3

Accepts: check, money order, Visa, MasterCard, Discover

Layaway: $60 minimum, 1 month to pay for every $100 spent

Discounts: occassional sales

Old/special items: bunnies

MODERN BEARS:

Canada: Ganz Bros., Mighty Star

Germany: Grisly Spielwaren, Gebruder Hermann, Steiff, sigikid, Haida, Miro Bears, Hermann Spielwaren

U.K.: Canterbury, Deans, Little Folk, Merrythought, Paddington, English Teddy Bear Company

U.S.A.: Beaver Valley, Boyds, Russ Berrie, Cooperstown Bears, Dakin, Gund, The Manhattan Toy Co., Mary Meyer, Muffy, North American Bear Co. (other), Michaud Collection, Westcliff, Liquid Blue, Ty, Princess Soft Toys, Woodland Enterprises, Orzek, Holly Designs, Hobby House Press

Artist bears: Susan Geary, Patsy Lane, Mary Jane Cheeks, Chris Cassner, Deanise Killingsworth, Robin Foley, Rick and Nancy Dannettel, Lana Rickabaugh, Suzan Golden, Michele Brown, Barbara Colgan, Joy McClenaghan, Cheryl Binder, Linda Ashcraft, Monty Sours, Terry Hayes, Ginny Rathall, Sally Winey, Joanne Johnson, Jutta Cyr, Diane Gard, Georgette Zlomke, Julie Wolff

Miniature bears: Jane Pogorzelski, Joy McClenaghan

ACCESSORIES:

Glasses, jewelry, signs, wagons

Clothes: sweaters

Furniture: handmade rocking chairs, chairs, buckboards, straight chairs, picnic tables

More about these accessories: Now offering special orders on accessories! Jewelry is sterling silver and 14K gold, hand designed by an artist. Many designs are available.

Figurines: Twigs

Bear collectibles: books about bears, books about collecting, bear magazines, tins

Shows: MD

In business for 4 years

BEARS IN THE WOOD

Janee McKinney, owner/president

59 N. Santa Cruz Ave.

Los Gatos, CA 95030

Phone: 408-354-6974

Phone orders accepted.

Hours: T-Sat, 10A.M.-5:30P.M. Sun, noon-5P.M. Closed M. Special holiday hours during Christmas season

Accepts: check, money order, Visa

Layaway: 50% down, 60 days, no refunds

Old/special items: antique bear collectibles

MODERN BEARS:

Canada: Ganz Bros.

Germany: Steiff

Italy: Trudi Giocattoli

U.K.: Deans

U.S.A.: Boyds, Russ Berrie, Charlene Kinser Designs, Cooperstown Bears, Dakin, Gund, The Manhattan Toy Co., Mary Meyer, Muffy, Vanderbear family, VIBs, North American Bear Co., R. John Wright

Other modern bears: Several other brands

Artist bears: Barbara Conley, Beverly Wright, Christine Jesser, Kathy Corley, Rosalind Chang, Darci Andrews, Maxine Hurst, Debbie Supnet, Karen Sawin and more

Miniature bears: Rosalind Chang, Kathryn Riley, Carolyn Willis, Victor Fortunato, Factoria Toy Works, Jimmy Wu and more

ACCESSORIES:

Glasses, jewelry, socks

Clothes available.

Furniture available.

Figurines: Lucy & Me, Muffy

Bear collectibles: books about bears, books about bearmaking, books about collecting, boxes, chinaware, clothing for people, jewelry, bear magazines, dollhouse miniatures, ornaments, paintings, postcards, pottery, prints, Smokey bear collectibles, stationery, tea sets, tins, tote bags, Winnie-the-Pooh collectibles, greeting cards

In business for 20 years

For more information, see the interview opening this chapter.

BEARS 'N MORE

Deb Schepker, owner

3004 Stony Point Rd.

Richmond, VA 23235

Phone: 804-323-3500

Phone orders accepted.

Hours: M-F, 10A.M.-6P.M. Sat, 10A.M.-5P.M. Extended holiday hours.

Accepts: check, Visa, MasterCard

Layaway: 20% down, 20% per month

Discounts: club, nonprofit organization

Old/special items: bunnies

MODERN BEARS:

Canada: Ganz Bros.

Germany: Grisly Spielwaren, Steiff

U.K.: Deans, Paddington

U.S.A.: Applause/Raikes, Boyds, Russ Berrie, Dakin, Gund, The Manhattan Toy Co., Mary Meyer, Muffy, Vanderbear family, VIBs, North American Bear Co. (other), J.J. Wind (Smokey Bear), The Michaud Collection

Artist bears: Linda Schaff, Julie Jones, Kimberly Hunt, Joy McClenaghan, Jerrie Keller, Linda Spiegel-Lohre, Claire Herz, Sue Foskey, Barbara Bessos, Gilmer Rudley, Joyce Beans, Debi Reese, Marilyn Jensen, Debby Blut, Maureen McElwain

Miniature bears: Kathy Rose, Barbara Garrett, Linda Schaff, Durae Allen, Gund

ACCESSORIES:

Glasses

Clothes: NAB, Tender Heart Treasures, handmade sweaters

Furniture: NAB

Figurines: Colour Box Miniatures, Muffy

Bear collectibles: books about bears, books about collecting, Smokey bear collectibles, tea sets, Winnie-the-Pooh collectibles

Shows: VA

In business for 9 years

BEARS 'N THINGS

D. Hockenberry and L. Oakley, owners

14191 Bacon Rd.

Albion, NY 14411

Second address:

space at Uncle Sam's Antiques,

9060 Main St.,

Clarence, NY 14031

Phone: 716-589-4066

Phone orders accepted.

Fax: 716-589-5190

Fax orders accepted.

Hours: 7 days, 11A.M.-5P.M.

Catalog: $10 for monthly list with photos. $17.50 foreign.

Accepts: check, money order, Visa, MasterCard

Layaway: minimum $500, 2 months

Discounts: dealer

Old/special items: antique bears, bears manufactured between WWI and WWII, bears manufactured 1945-1970, golliwogs, bunnies, antique bear collectibles

MODERN BEARS:

Germany: Steiff

U.S.A.: R. John Wright

Shows: NY, OH, MD, NJ

In business for 11 years

BEARS 'N WARES

Linda Farley, owner

312 Bridge St.

New Cumberland, PA 17070

Phone: 717-774-1261

Phone orders accepted.

Fax: 717-774-1766

Fax orders accepted.

Hours: Depends on season. Please call first.

Accepts: check, money order, Visa, MasterCard, Discover, American Express

Layaway available.

Old/special items: antique bear collectibles, golliwogs, bunnies

MODERN BEARS:

Germany: Gebruder Hermann, Kathe Kruse Puppen, Schuco, Steiff

U.K.: Canterbury, Little Folk, Merrythought, Paddington

U.S.A.: Applause/Raikes, Beaver Valley, Boyds, Charlene Kinser Designs, Cooperstown Bears, Dakin, Gund, Madame Alexander Bears, Muffy, Vanderbear family, VIBs, North American Bear Co. (other), R. John Wright, Michaud Collection, Vermont

Artist bears: Joan Woessner, Donna Hodges, Lane Carpenter, Octavia Chin, Marsha DeHaven, Charleen Kinser, Edda Seiple, Heidi Steinner and more

Miniature bears: Octavia Chin, Lisa Lloyd, Gund, Akira and more

ACCESSORIES:

Baskets, glasses

Clothes: NAB

Furniture: small chairs, etc.

Figurines: Boyds Bearstone, Cherished Teddies, Muffy, United Design Corp., Pennywhistle Lane (Enesco), Russian carved wooden bears

Bear collectibles: books about bears, books about collecting, boxes, jewelry, bear magazines, ornaments, paintings, postcards, stationery, tea sets, tins, Winnie-the-Pooh collectibles

In business for 11 years

THE BEARS OF BRUTON ST.

Debbie Wolf, owner

107 S. Bruton St.

Wilson, NC 27893

Phone: 919-243-1471 or 1-800-488-BEAR for non-local orders

Phone orders accepted.

Fax: 919-243-4792

Fax orders accepted.

Hours: T-Sat, 10A.M.-5P.M. Closed Sun and M.

Catalog: free

Accepts: check, money order, Visa, MasterCard, Discover, American Express

Layaway: 25% down, 90 days

Discounts: club

MODERN BEARS:

Germany: Gebruder Hermann, Steiff

U.K.: Canterbury, Merrythought, Paddington

U.S.A.: Applause/Raikes, Boyds, Dakin, Gund, Madame Alexander Bears, Muffy, Vanderbear family, VIBs, North American Bear Co. (other), Michaud Collection, Cherished Teddies

Artist bears: Gloria Franks, Monty & Joe Sours, Jodi Rankin, Janet Reeves, Marie Zimmerman, Edda Seiple, Barbara McConnell, Melodie Malcolm, Jenny Krantz, Nancy Green, Joan Woessner, Kathy Sheppard, Romerhaus, Tammie Lawrence, Steve Schutt, Linda Spiegel-Lohre

Miniature bears: Little Gems, Kathy Sheppard, Jenny Krantz

ACCESSORIES:

Glasses

Furniture available.

Figurines: Boyds Bearstone, Cherished Teddies, Muffy

Bear collectibles: books about bears, books about collecting, chinaware, jewelry, bear magazines, Paddington collectibles, postcards, stationery, tea sets, Winnie-the-Pooh collectibles

Shows: MD, VA, TN, FL, SC

In business for 7 years

BEARTIQUE
Hanna Gube, owner
3914 St. Denis
Montreal, Quebec H2W 2M2, Canada
Phone: 514-286-BEAR
Fax: 514-489-4526
Fax orders accepted.
Hours: W, Sat, Sun, 11 A.M.-6P.M. TH, F,
11 A.M.- 9P.M. Closed M,T.
Accepts: money order, Visa, MasterCard
Layaway: for tailor-made items, usually
40% down, 2 months; depends on
price

MODERN BEARS:
Canada: Ganz Bros.
U.K.: Canterbury, Deans, Merrythought,
Paddington
U.S.A.: Boyds, Russ Berrie, Coopers-
town Bears, Dakin, Gund, Mary
Meyer, North American Bear Co.,
Mango, Ty, Eden, Darling Exclusive
Imports
Artist bears: Apps-olutely Bears, Bear-
works, Bears by Lorna, Bears by
Eddie, Craiglatch Critters, Irmgard
Heidt, Woodland Creations, Bear
Magic, Rosemount Bear Co., Fred
Bears, P.M. Bears, Wee Treasures
Stenden House, Horne Canada, Bear
Links & Co., Linda Ferguson, McTar-
ish Teddys, Bearnettes' Collector
Originals, Rita Suasdell-Taylor,
Friendship Teddy Bear Factory, Can't
Bear to Part, Happy Tymes, Winey
Bears, Theodore & Co., Pat Fye Orig-
inals, Bearcraft, River Hills Bears,
Grin & Bear It, Nostalgic Bear Co.,
Carol Black Originals, Bearly There
Inc., Bearons of La Jolla, Just We
Bears
Miniature bears: Akira, Bears by Edie,
Joan Rankin, Standen House, Irmgard
Heidt

ACCESSORIES:
Clothes: sweaters, hats, overalls, dresses,
etc.
Furniture: stepbacks, closets, corner
cabinets, shelves, etc.
Figurines: Boyds Bearstone, Cherished
Teddies, United Design Corp.,
Dreamsickles, wooden carvings, Russ
Bear collectibles: books about bears,
books about collecting, jewelry, bear
magazines, ornaments, postcards,
prints, stationery, tins, Winnie-the-
Pooh collectibles, mugs, night lights,

musicals, baby shower items, soaps,
balloons, stickers, brass hooks, mobiles, letter openers, desk sets, honey
and marmalade, baby items, including
teethers, ice packs, musicals
In business for 1 year

BEARY BEST FRIENDS
Susan L. Paul
RD #8, Box 8643
East Stroudsburg, PA 18301
Second address:
Pocono Peddler's Village,
Tannersville, PA 18372
Phone: 717-620-2099
Phone orders accepted.
Hours: T-TH, Sun, 10A.M.-5P.M., F-Sat,
10A.M.-6P.M.
Accepts: check, money order, Visa, Mas-
terCard, Discover
Layaway available.
Old/special items: bunnies

MODERN BEARS:
U.S.A.: Boyds, Russ Berrie, Gund,
Muffy, Vanderbear family, VIBs,
North American Bear Co. (other)
Artist bears: Bankar Bears & Buddies,
Lin Wildlife Friends, Friends From
Frederick
Miniature bears: Gund

ACCESSORIES:
Glasses
Clothes: Boyds
Furniture: artist-made for shop
Figurines: Boyds Bearstone, Wedding
Bears by Showstoppers, Silver Deer
Bears
Bear collectibles: books about collect-
ing, bear magazines
In business for 1 year

BEARY SPECIAL FRIENDS
Elizabeth Kintz, owner
2981 W. 550 N.
Decatur, IN 46733
Second address:
152 S. Second St.,
Decatur, IN 46733
Phone: 219-547-4300
Phone orders accepted.
Hours: M-Sat, 10A.M.-5P.M. Sun, 1P.M.-
5P.M.
Accepts: check, money order, Visa, Mas-
terCard
Layaway: 20% down, 30 days
Discounts: bulk order, frequent cus-

tomer, club, nonprofit organization,
senior citizen, student
MODERN BEARS:
Germany: Haida
U.S.A.: Applause/Raikes, Boyds, Dakin,
Gund, Mary Meyer
Artist bears: Linda Spiegel-Lohre, The
Bear Lady, Jackie Morris, Jan Bonner,
Connie Roark, Paula Walton, Jackie
Strecher, Sally Winey, Kathy Kay,
Leeann Snyder, Memory Frost,
Sharon Agin, Edie Rase
Miniature bears: Lana Rickabaugh,
Sherri Dodson

ACCESSORIES:
Glasses, cars, wagons, airplanes
Clothes: hats, sweaters
Furniture: chairs, old stoves, washing
machines
Bear collectibles: books about collect-
ing, jewelry, bear magazines, tote
bags
Shows: IN
In business for 2 years

BENJAMIN BEAR
Sarah Rumsey, owner
1679 Barn Swallow Place
Marietta, GA 30062
Phone: 404-977-7592
Phone orders accepted.
Fax: 404-977-7592
Fax orders accepted.
Mail order only.
Catalog: LSASE
Accepts: check, money order, Visa, Mas-
terCard

MODERN BEARS:
Germany: Steiff
U.K.: Merrythought
U.S.A.: Beaver Valley, Boyds, Coopers-
town Bears, Lone Star, Muffy, Vand-
erbear family, VIBs, North American
Bear Co. (other), R. John Wright
Bear collectibles: books about bears,
jewelry, ornaments, postcards, statio-
nery, tea sets, Winnie-the-Pooh col-
lectibles
Shows: East Coast, Midwest, Southeast
In business for 8 years

BERRY PATCH
Terry Goetz, owner
P.O. Box 581
Lyons, CO 80540
Second address:

304½ Main
Lyons, CO
Phone: 303-823-9443
    Phone orders accepted.
Hours: 7 days, 11 A.M.-6 P.M.
Accepts: check, money order, Visa, MasterCard
Layaway: Flexible. Monthly payments required.
Discounts: Muffy club
Old/special items: bunnies

MODERN BEARS:
U.S.A.: Boyds, Gund, The Manhattan Toy Co., Mary Meyer, Muffy, Vanderbear family, North American Bear Co. (other)
Artist bears: Connie Roark, Ballard Baines, Susan Horn, Sher Masor, Terry Sevitz, Jeanette McPherson, Althea Leistikow, Janet Anderson, Carol Pearce, Deborah Didier, Kelly Dauterman
Miniature bears: Akira, Deborah Didier, local artists

ACCESSORIES:
Glasses, hair ribbons, jewelry
Clothes: sweaters
Miniature: hair ribbons
More about these accessories: Store has its own line of jewelry
Figurines: Boyds Bearstone, Muffy
Bear collectibles: books about bears, boxes, ornaments, postcards, tea sets, tins, Winnie-the-Pooh collectibles
Shows: CO
In business for 16 years

BOBBY BARE TRAP, INC.
Jeannie Bare, owner
2416 Music Valley Dr.
Nashville, TN 37214
Billing address:
P.O. Box 2852
Hendersonville, TN 37079
Phone: 615-872-8440 or 615-824-9372 (office)
    Phone orders accepted.
Fax: 615-822-0098
    Fax orders accepted.
Hours: Summer: 7 days, 8 A.M.-10 P.M. Winter: M-TH, 10 A.M.-7 P.M. F-Sat, 10 A.M.-8 P.M. Sun, 10 A.M.-6 P.M.
Catalog: free
Accepts: money order, Visa, MasterCard, Discover

MODERN BEARS:
Canada: Ganz Bros.
U.K.: Paddington
U.S.A.: Applause/Raikes, Boyds, Russ Berrie, Dakin, Gund, Lone Star, The Manhattan Toy Co., Mary Meyer, Muffy, Vanderbear family, VIBs, North American Bear Co. (other), Michaud Collection, Eden, Orzek, Princess
Artist bears: Joan Woessner, Carol Stewart, Ms. Noah, Linda Spiegel-Lohre, Sue Foskey
Miniature bears: Carol Stewart

ACCESSORIES:
Glasses, jewelry, rocking horses
Clothes: sweaters
Furniture: chairs, benches
Figurines: United Design Corp.
Bear collectibles: books about bears, books about collecting, clothing for people, jewelry, bear magazines, ornaments, Paddington collectibles, postcards, Winnie-the-Pooh collectibles
In business for 7 years

BROWN'S DOLL & BEAR BOUTIQUE
Meryl Brown, owner
420 N. Wilbur, #120
Walla Walla, WA 99362
Phone: 509-529-7552 or 1-800-532-3249 for orders
    Phone orders accepted.
Hours: M-F, 10 A.M.-7 P.M. Sat, 10 A.M.-6 P.M. Sun, noon-5 P.M.
Accepts: check, money order, Visa, MasterCard, American Express
Layaway: 20% down, 10% per month
Discounts: frequent customer
Old/special items: bunnies

MODERN BEARS:
Germany: Hermann-Spielwaren, Steiff
U.K.: Paddington
U.S.A.: Applause/Raikes, Boyds, Russ Berrie, Cooperstown Bears, Dakin, Gund, Lone Star, Mary Meyer, Muffy, Vanderbear family, VIBs
Artist bears: Bearly There, Dandilion Dreams, Joey Bears, Bev Dodd, Gretchen McKillip
Miniature bears: Little Gem Bears

ACCESSORIES:
Glasses, shoes, socks
Clothes: NAB, Tender Heart
Furniture: chairs, beds, etc.

Miniature: glasses, shoes, socks
Figurines: Boyds Bearstone, Cherished Teddies, Jan Hagara Collectibles, Lucy & Me, Muffy
Bear collectibles: books about bears, boxes, bear magazines, dollhouse miniatures, ornaments, Paddington collectibles, postcards, tea sets, tins, tote bags, Winnie-the-Pooh collectibles
In business for 6 years

BUTTONS BY JEFF
Jeff Ruhnke
4434 St. Louis Ave.
Chicago, IL 60632
Phone: 312-254-1086
Mail order only.
Accepts: check, money order
Discounts: club, Good Bears of the World
Bear collectibles: buttons, mirrors, magnets, cards and teddy bear ID cards made out of teddy bear photographs

CABBAGES & KINGS
Jeanette L. Keene, manager
6330 Lawrenceville Hwy.
Tucker, GA 30084
Phone: 404-934-0055
    Phone orders accepted.
Hours: M-F, 10 A.M.-6 P.M. Sat, 9:30 A.M.-5 P.M.
Accepts: check, money order, Visa, MasterCard, American Express
Layaway: 25% down, 90 days. More than $500: 6 months
Discounts: bulk order, frequent customer
Old/special items: bunnies

MODERN BEARS:
U.K.: Merrythought
U.S.A.: Beaver Valley, Gund, Douglas Cuddle, Ty, Creative Concepts, Tilly Collectibles, Ms. Noah
Artist bears: Wendy Brent, Nancy Bruns, Debora Ferguson, Donna Hodges, McB Bears, Jenny Krantz, Rosenbears
Miniature bears: Debora Ferguson, Mama's Babies
In business for 7 years

CAMERON AND SMITH, LTD.
Bob Smith, president
P.O. Box 637
Vero Beach, FL 32961

Phone: 407-778-7862 or 1-800-472-9862 for orders
Phone orders accepted.
Fax: 407-778-7862
Fax orders accepted.
Mail order only.
Catalog: $5, refundable with purchase.
Accepts: check, money order, Visa, MasterCard, Discover
Bear collectibles: boxes, Paddington collectibles, Winnie-the-Pooh collectibles
More about collectibles: Boxes are enamel or copper. Bears are handpainted on the boxes using an 18th-century technique.

CAROL'S DOLL HOUSE
Carol Nelson, owner
Oak Park Plaza
10761 University Ave. NE
Blaine, MN 55434
Phone: 612-755-7475
Phone orders accepted.
Hours: M, W, F, Sat, 10A.M.-5P.M. T, H, 10A.M.-9P.M.
Accepts: check, money order, Visa, MasterCard, Discover
Layaway: 25% down, $50 per month
Discounts: club
Old/special items: antique bears, bears manufactured between WWI and WWII, bears manufactured 1945-1970 (if available)

MODERN BEARS:
Germany: Gebruder Hermann, Hermann-Spielwaren, Steiff
U.S.A.: Applause/Raikes, Boyds, Dakin, Gund, Muffy, Vanderbear family, VIBs, Ty

ACCESSORIES:
Glasses
Clothes available.
Furniture available.
Figurines: Muffy
Bear collectibles: clothing for people, postcards
Shows: MN, IA, WI, IL
In business for 21 years

CAROL STEWART'S MINIATURE TEDDY BEARS, INC.
Carol Stewart, owner
903 NW Spruce Ridge
Stuart, FL 34994

Phone: 407-692-9067
Phone orders accepted.
Mail order only.
Catalog: $3, refundable with purchase
Accepts: check, money order, Visa, MasterCard
Artist bears: Carol Stewart
Miniature bears: Carol Stewart
Shows: Walt Disney World
In business for 12 years

CARROUSEL
Terry Michaud, owner
505 W. Broad St.
Chesaning, MI 48616
Phone: 517-845-7881
Phone orders accepted.
Fax: 517-845-6650
Fax orders accepted.
Hours: Depends on season—please call first
Accepts: check, money order, Visa, MasterCard, Discover, American Express
Layaway: 33% down, 33% in 60 days, balance in 90 days

MODERN BEARS:
U.S.A.: Michaud Collection
More about these bears: All original antique bears from the Michaud collection are on exhibit in the museum/showrooms.
Artist bears: Constantly changing selection. Artist bears from around the world.
Miniature bears: Several artists.

ACCESSORIES:
Clothes available.
Figurines: Michaud Collection (Sarah's Attic)
Bear collectibles: books about bears, books about bearmaking, books about collecting, jewelry, bear magazines, postcards, sweatshirts for adults
Shows: MD, OH, Walt Disney World
In business for 21 years

CASEY'S BEAR FACTORY
Rita Casey, owner
110 Village Landing
Fairport, NY 14450
Phone: 716-223-6280 or 716-425-3566
Phone orders accepted.
Catalog: video, $5; other, $2
Accepts: check, money order, Visa, MasterCard, Discover
Layaway: 10% down, 3 months

Old/special items: bunnies
MODERN BEARS:
Canada: Ganz Bros.
U.K.: Canterbury, Merrythought
U.S.A.: Applause/Raikes, Boyds, Russ Berrie, Gund, Ty
Artist bears: More than 90 artists
Miniature artist bears: 10 miniature bear artists

ACCESSORIES:
Glasses, jewelry
Clothes available.
Furniture available.
Miniature: baskets, glasses
Miniature furniture available.
Figurines: Boyds Bearstone
Bear collectibles: books about bears, books about bearmaking, books about collecting, clothing for people, jewelry, bear magazines, dollhouse miniatures, ornaments, paintings, postcards, prints, stationery, tea sets, tins, tote bags
In business for 4 years

CHANNEL ISLANDS GIFTS, FISHERMAN'S WHARF
Wendy Marsden, manager
2741 S. Victoria, Suite H
Oxnard, CA 93035
Phone: 805-985-2215
Phone orders accepted.
Hours: 7 days, 10A.M.-6P.M.
Accepts: check, money order, Visa, MasterCard, Discover, American Express
Layaway available.
Discounts: frequent customer, senior citizen, teacher's discount
Old/special items: bunnies

MODERN BEARS:
U.S.A.: Boyds, The Manhattan Toy Co., North American Bear Co.

ACCESSORIES:
Baskets, glasses
Clothes available.
Furniture available.
Figurines: Boyds Bearstone, Cairn Studio, Cast Art Industries
Bear collectibles: boxes, tea sets, tins, tote bags, Afghans, blankets
In business for 9 years

CHARMANT TEDDY BEARS

Donna McPherson and Armand
Thibodeau
RR #1 Napanee, Ontario K7R 3K6,
Canada
Phone: 613-354-6393
   Phone orders accepted.
Fax: 613-354-6393
   Fax orders accepted.
Hours: F, 6P.M.-9P.M., Sat, Sun, 11A.M.-
   6P.M., and by appointment
Accepts: check, money order, Visa
Layaway: 25% down, balance payment
   arranged
Artist bears: Charmant Teddy Bears,
   Northeast USA artist bears

ACCESSORIES:
Baskets
Clothes: handmade, vintage
Furniture: antique chairs, desks, etc.
Shows: NY, VT, MD, CT, MA, Ontario,
   England, Germany, Belgium, Holland

CHERI'S BEAR ESSENTIALS

3953 Broadway
Kansas City, MO 64111

CHERYL'S TOY BOX

Cheryl C. Lynch
P.O. Box 524
Oxford, NC 27656
Second address:
110 N. Mecklingberg Ave.
South Hill, VA
Phone: 919-693-8777
   Phone orders accepted.
Hours: M-Sat, 10A.M.-5P.M. Closed W,
   Sun.
Accepts: check, money order, Visa, Mas-
   terCard, American Express
Layaway: tailored to customer's needs
Discounts: club
Old/special items: bunnies

MODERN BEARS:
Germany: Steiff
U.K.: Paddington
U.S.A.: Applause/Raikes, Boyds, Gund,
   Muffy, Vanderbear family, VIBs,
   North American Bear Co. (other), R.
   John Wright
Artist bears: Gloria Franks, Brenda
   Dewey, Pat Fye, Pam Young, Anita
   Marlin, Sour bears
Miniature bears: Brenda Dewey, Pat
   Fye, Akira, Carol Stewart

ACCESSORIES:
Baskets
Furniture available.
Figurines: Cherished Teddies, Muffy
Bear collectibles: clothing for people,
   Paddington collectibles, Winnie-the-
   Pooh collectibles
Shows: MD, FL, IL, NJ, VA
In business for 14 years

CHRISTINA'S COLLECTIBLES

Teddy Bears & Dolls
Christina Steenmeijer, owner
66-134 Kam Hwy, #4
Haleiwa, HI 96712
Phone: 808-637-6429
   Phone orders accepted.
Fax: 808-595-0302
   Fax orders accepted.
Hours: 7 days, noon-5P.M.
Accepts: check, money order, Visa, Mas-
   terCard, Diner's Club and JCB
Layaway: 33% down, 2 months
Discounts: bulk order, frequent cus-
   tomer, club, nonprofit organization,
   senior citizen, student
Old/special items: bears manufactured
   between WWI and WWII, bears man-
   ufactured 1945-1970, antique bear
   collectibles, golliwogs, bunnies

MODERN BEARS:
Germany: Gebruder Hermann, Kathe
   Kruse Puppen, Steiff
Italy: Trudi Giocattoli
U.K.: Canterbury, Deans, Merrythought,
   Paddington
U.S.A.: Applause/Raikes, Boyds, Dakin,
   Gund, Madame Alexander Bears,
   Muffy, Vanderbear family, VIBs,
   North American Bear Co. (other)
Artist bears: Debi Reese, Jackie Palmer,
   Jackie Saraf, Maxine Hurst, Darlene
   Allen, Jackie Steenmeijer (U.K.),
   Gilmur Rudley
Miniature bears: Norine Oshiro, Lani
   Mall, Hawaii folk bears

ACCESSORIES:
Baskets, jewelry, shoes, socks
Clothes: Boyds, NAB
Furniture: Boyds, NAB, wicker chairs
Figurines: Boyds Bearstone, Cherished
   Teddies, Muffy
Bear collectibles: books about bears,
   books about bearmaking, books about
   collecting, chinaware, jewelry, bear
   magazines, paintings, postcards, pot-
tery, stationery, tea sets, Winnie-the-
Pooh collectibles

CHRISTMAS IN THE VILLAGE

Mary Navone & Bernadette Romeo
P.O. Box 173
66 Sheather St.
Hammondsport, NY 14840
Phone: 607-569-3100
   Phone orders accepted.
Accepts: check, money order, Visa, Mas-
   terCard, Discover
Layaway: 10% down, regular payments,
   90 days
Discounts: bulk order, frequent cus-
   tomer, club
Old/special items: bunnies

MODERN BEARS:
Canada: Ganz Bros.
U.S.A.: Boyds, Russ Berrie, Mary
   Meyer, Muffy
Artist bears: Bettina Groh
Miniature bears: Bettina Groh

ACCESSORIES:
Wagons
Clothes: sweaters
Furniture: chairs, etc.
Figurines: Boyds Bearstone, Dept. 56
In business for 17 years

CHRISTY'S

P.O. Box 509
Buckingham, PA 18912

CHUBBY'S CUBBY

Karen Nelson, owner
P.O. Box 215
204 Union St.
Occoquan, VA 22125
Phone: 703-491-1671
   Phone orders accepted.
Hours: 10A.M.-5P.M.
Accepts: check, Visa, MasterCard
Layaway: 20-25% down, flexible ar-
   rangements
Old/special items: bunnies

MODERN BEARS:
Canada: Ganz Bros.
U.S.A.: Jona, Madame Alexander Bears,
   Mary Meyer, Muffy, Vanderbear fam-
   ily, VIBs, North American Bear Co.
   (other), Lucy & Me, Bearly People,
   Princess Soft Toys, Cherished Teddy
   plush
Artist bears: Elizabeth Phillips
Miniature bears: Akira

ACCESSORIES:

Glasses, shoes, socks

Clothes: NAB, outfits for 10″-12″ bears

Furniture: NAB

Figurines: Heart for Bears, Lucy & Me, Muffy

More about figurines: Large selection of Lucy & Me

Bear collectibles: bear magazines, stationery, tea sets, tins

Shows: East Coast

In business for 4 years

CLASSIC DOLL & BEAR SHOPPE

Christy Simm, owner

73-386 El Paseo

Palm Desert, CA 92260

Phone: 619-773-0732 or 1-800-449-3655 for orders

Phone orders accepted.

Fax: 619-773-0723

Fax orders accepted.

Hours: M-Sat, 10A.M.-5P.M.

Catalog: free

Accepts: check, money order, Visa, MasterCard, Discover, American Express, Diner's Club

Layaway: 25% down, 4 months

Discounts: bulk order

Old/special items: bunnies

MODERN BEARS:

Canada: Ganz Bros.

Germany: Althans, Hermann-Spielwaren, H. Scharrer & Koch, Kathe Kruse Puppen, Steiff

Italy: Lenci

U.K.: Canterbury, Merrythought

U.S.A.: Applause/Raikes, Russ Berrie, Gund, Muffy, Vanderbear family, VIBs, North American Bear Co. (other)

Artist bears: Joanne Mitchell, Mike & Val Freeland, Wanda Shope, Jonnie St. Martin, Ruthann Mauer, Sue Newlin

Miniature bears: Steiff

ACCESSORIES:

Baskets

Clothes: NAB

Furniture: Victorian

Figurines: Jan Hagara Collectibles, Muffy

Bear collectibles: chinaware, bear magazines, ornaments, postcards, stationery, tea sets, tins, Winnie-the-Pooh collectibles

Shows: CA

In business for 6 years

CLAYTON'S GIFTS & TOYS, INC.

Bruce A. Roberts, president

5225 Main St.

Buffalo, NY 14221

Phone: 716-633-1995 or 716-633-1966

Phone orders accepted.

Hours: M, T, W, F, 10A.M.-6P.M. TH, 10A.M.- 9P.M. Sat, noon-5P.M.

Accepts: check, money order, Visa, MasterCard, American Express

Layaway: 10% restock fee

Discounts: bulk order, nonprofit organization

Old/special items: golliwogs (sometimes), bunnies

MODERN BEARS:

Canada: Ganz Bros.

Germany: Steiff

U.K.: Paddington, Nisbet

U.S.A.: Applause/Raikes, Charlene Kinser Designs, Dakin, Gund, Mary Meyer, Muffy, Vanderbear family, VIBs, North American Bear Co. (other), Vermont

Other modern bears: Zodiac, Peter Bull, signed

Bear collectibles: dollhouse miniatures, tea sets

In business for 76 years

COACH HOUSE COLLECTION

Susan Reeves, owner

43 E. Jefferson

Naperville, IL 60540

Phone: 708-355-9131

Phone orders accepted.

Hours: M-Sat, 9:30A.M.-5:30P.M. TH, 9:30A.M.-8P.M. Extended Christmas hours.

Accepts: Visa, MasterCard

Layaway: 20% down, 30 days or 50% down, 60 days

Discounts: club, nonprofit organization

Old/special items: bunnies

MODERN BEARS:

U.K.: Paddington

U.S.A.: Boyds, Dakin, Gund, Madame Alexander Bears, Muffy, Vanderbear family, VIBs, North American Bear Co. (other)

Artist bears: Linda Spiegel-Lohre, Donna Hodges, Golden Harlequins, Lynn West

ACCESSORIES:

glasses

Clothes: NAB

Figurines: Boyds Bearstone, Muffy

Bear collectibles: books about bears, jewelry, bear magazines, ornaments, postcards, prints, stationery, tins, Winnie-the-Pooh collectibles

In business for 11 years

COBBLESTONE ALLEY ANTIQUES

Dorothy Koehler, owner

657 N. Citrus Ave.

Crystal River, FL 34429

Phone: 904-795-0060

Phone orders accepted.

Hours: M-F, 10A.M.-5P.M. Sat, 10A.M.-4P.M.

Accepts: check, Visa, MasterCard, Discover, American Express

Layaway: 20% down, 30 days

Discounts: dealers and preferred customers

Old/special items: antique bears, bears manufactured between WWI and WWII, bears manufactured 1945-1970, antique bear collectibles, bunnies

MODERN BEARS:

Germany: Hermann-Spielwaren, Steiff

U.S.A.: Boyds

Artist bears: The Bear Fact, Beyer Bears, Jill Cisco, Edie Rase

Miniature bears: Jill Cisco

Figurines: Boyds Bearstone, United Design Corp.

ACCESSORIES:

Furniture: antique chairs, doll carriages, tables and more.

Bear collectibles: dollhouse miniatures, Smokey bear collectibles, tea sets

In business for 16 years

COLLECTABLE BEARS & GIFTS

Juanita & Mike Dowler, owners

1710 Briargate Blvd., #327

Colorado Springs, CO 80920

Phone: 719-535-8265

Phone orders accepted.

Fax: 719-578-1889

Fax orders accepted after 5:30

Hours: M-Sat, 10A.M.-9P.M. Sun, 11A.M.-6P.M.

Accepts: check, money order, Visa, MasterCard, Discover, American Express

Discounts: bulk order, frequent order

Layaway: $50 minimum. 10% down, payments every two weeks, 90 days or more with regular payments

MODERN BEARS:

Germany: Gebruder Hermann, Steiff

U.K.: Canterbury, Deans, Merrythought, Paddington, English Teddy Bear Co.

U.S.A.: Applause/Raikes, Beaver Valley, Russ Berrie, Cooperstown Bears, Dakin, Gund, The Manhattan Toy Co., Mary Meyer, Muffy, Vanderbear family, VIBs, North American Bear Co. (other), Vermont, Peek-a-Boos, Bearly People, Ty

Artist bears: Ro Bears, Annemade, Sarah Beara Bears, Bear Elegance, Bearly There, Redfield Bears, Kelly Dauterman, Corbitt Kids, Reg Bears, CM Bears and more

Miniature bears: Little Gems, We Three Bears, Carol Stewart, Debra Didier, Gund

Figurines: Cherished Teddies, Joybears, Laura's Attic, Lucy & Me, Michaud Collection, Muffy, The Roosevelt Bears, Sarah's Attic

Bear collectibles: books about bears, books about bearmaking, books about collecting, jewelry, bear magazines, postcards, Smokey bear collectibles, tea sets, Winnie-the-Pooh collectibles

In business for 2 years

COLLECTORS CHOICE

Karen Strickland
20118 Marilla St.
Chatsworth, CA 91311
Additional addresses:
Old Town Pomoma Mall Sp #148
Second St.
Pomona, CA
611 S. Palm Canyon
Sun Center, Ste. 16
Palm Springs, CA 92264
Phone: 818-886-6150, 818-885-0027
Phone orders accepted.
Fax: 818-885-0027
Fax orders accepted.
Hours: 10A.M.-5P.M.
Catalog: $20/year
Accepts: check, money order, Visa, MasterCard, Carte Blanche, Diner's Club
Layaway: 20% down, 60 days
Discounts: bulk order
Old/special items: antique bears, bears manufactured between WWI and

WWII, bears manufactured 1945-1970, golliwogs, antique bear collectibles, bunnies

MODERN BEARS:

Austria: Berg Spielwaren

Germany: Hans Clemens, Fechter, Gebruder Hermann, Hermann-Spielwaren, Schuco, Steiff

New Zealand: Sheepskin Products

U.K.: Chad Valley, Merrythought, Alpha Farnell, Deans

U.S.A.: Knickerbocker, Ideal, early American Character, Gund

Artist bears: Karen Strickland

Miniature bears: Karen Strickland

ACCESSORIES:

Baskets

Clothes: old

Furniture: old

Miniature clothes: old

Figurines: chalkware bear figurines, made from old chocolate candy molds

Bear collectibles: books about bears, books about bearmaking, books about collecting, Smokey bear collectibles, Winnie-the-Pooh collectibles

Shows: CA

In business for 7 years

COLLECTORS' DELIGHT

Karen Lee Lemon, owner
2104 Station Ct.
Elkhart, IN 46517
Phone: 219-293-1163 or 1-800-892-0443
Phone orders accepted.
Accepts: check, money order, Visa, MasterCard, Discover
Layaway: $100 minimum, 20% down, 3 equal monthly payments, 90 days
Discounts: club

MODERN BEARS:

Germany: Steiff

Italy: Trudi Giocattoli

U.K.: Canterbury, Merrythought, Paddington

U.S.A.: Raikes, Dakin, Gund, Mary Meyer, Muffy, Vanderbear family, VIBs, North American Bear Co. (other), Vermont

Artist bears: Janet Reeves, Gloria Franks

ACCESSORIES:

Clothes: NAB

Figurines: Boyds Bearstone, Cairn Studio, Cherished Teddies, Colour Box

Miniatures, Jan Hagara Collectibles, Michaud Collection, Muffy, The Roosevelt Bears, Sarah's attic

Bear collectibles: tea sets

In business for 9 years

COMFREY CORNER

Shalmir Pinney
565 Hebron Rd.
Heath, OH 43056
Second address:
Hibernation Bears Division DBA
Box 411
Granville, OH 43023
Fax: 614-366-9700
Fax orders accepted.
Hours: M-F, 10A.M.-7P.M. Sat, 10A.M.-4P.M.
Catalog: LSASE
Accepts: money order, Visa, MasterCard, Discover, certified check
Layaway: 20% down, 30-90 days, $5 restocking fee
Discounts: frequent order

MODERN BEARS:

Germany: Old World Christmas by Hermann

U.K.: Paddington

U.S.A.: Applause/Raikes, Russ Berrie, Gund, Madame Alexander Bears, Muffy, Vanderbear family, VIBs, North American Bear Co., Eden, Bonita

Artist bears: La Bearons, Mama's Babies

ACCESSORIES:

Baskets, shampoo, stands

Clothes: NAB

Furniture: NAB

Figurines: Kelly Bears, Muffy, Raikes, United Design Corp., Dept. 56, Schmid

Bear collectibles: books about bears, books about collecting, boxes, clothing for people, bear magazines, ornaments, Paddington collectibles, paintings, postcards, prints, tea sets, tins, tote bags, Winnie-the-Pooh collectibles, music boxes, gift bags

In business for 18 years

CONCEPTS, INC.

Jacqueline Bardner Smith
1342 SE 12th Terrace
Cape Coral, FL 33990
Mail order only.
Bear collectibles: postcards, calendars

More about collectibles: Postcards and calendars feature Blackberry Hollow bears that are created and photographed by Jacqueline Bardner Smith
In business for 26 years

CORNUCOPIA

Clifton Cane, owner
49 Commercial St.
Boothbay Harbor, ME 04538
Phone: 207-633-4838
Phone orders accepted.
Fax: 207-633-7504
Fax orders accepted.
Hours: 9A.M.-6P.M.
Accepts: Visa, MasterCard, Discover, American Express

MODERN BEARS:
U.S.A.: Boyds
Figurines: Boyds Bearstone
In business for 9 years

THE COUNTRY BEAR

Jay Hadly, owner
Rt. 73, Box 17
Skippack, PA 19474
Phone: 610-584-4055
Phone orders accepted.
Hours: 7 days, 10A.M.-4P.M.
Accepts: check, money order, Visa, MasterCard, Discover, American Express
Layaway: 30% down, 30 days
Old/special items: antique bears, bears manufactured 1945-1970, golliwogs, bunnies

MODERN BEARS:
Germany: Grisly Spielwaren, Gebruder Hermann, Schuco, Steiff
U.K.: Merrythought
U.S.A.: Boyds, Muffy
Artist bears: Janet Reeves, Bear Lady, Sue Foskey, Connie Roark, Sally Winey, Linda Sage, Louise Beniere, Jay Hadly, Linda Spiegel-Lohre, Carol Lamothe, Noel Hadly, Lonnie St. Martin
Miniature bears: Noel Hadly, Debbie Parks

ACCESSORIES:
Clothes: NAB
Bear collectibles: jewelry, Winnie-the-Pooh collectibles
Shows: MA, ME, CT, NY, MD, PA
In business for 14 years

COUNTRY CORNER

Margaret Barras, owner
1697 Main St.
Dunedin, FL 34698
Phone: 813-734-9563 or 1-800-771-3655 for orders
Phone orders accepted.
Hours: M-Sat, 10A.M.-5P.M.
Accepts: check, money order, Visa, MasterCard, Discover
Layaway: 33% down, 33% per month
Discounts: frequent order

MODERN BEARS:
Germany: Haida
U.K.: Canterbury
U.S.A.: Applause/Raikes, Boyds, Gund, Muffy, VIBs
Artist bears: Ann Carlo, Matty Originals, Mandalyne Bears
In business for 10 years

THE COUNTRY HOUSE

Norma and Mike Delano, owners
805 E. Main St.
Salisbury, MD 21801
Phone: 410-749-1959 or 1-800-331-3602 for orders
Phone orders accepted.
Fax: 410-548-3224
Fax orders accepted.
Catalog: $2, free with order
Accepts: check, money order, Visa, MasterCard, Discover, American Express
Layaway: 25% down, 3 months

MODERN BEARS:
Germany: Steiff
U.S.A.: Boyds, Muffy
Artist bears: varies

ACCESSORIES:
Baskets, glasses, jewelry
Clothes: NAB, Boyds
Furniture: NAB, wooden, wicker
Figurines: Boyds Bearstone, Cairn Studio, Cast Art Industries, Character Collectibles, Muffy, Cherished Teddies
Bear collectibles: jewelry, tea sets
In business for 12 years

THE COUNTRY NOOK

Gene Curtis, general manager
415 Main St.
P.O. Box 631
Presque Isle, ME 04769
Phone: 207-764-3211
Phone orders accepted.

Fax: 207-764-2387
Fax orders accepted.
Accepts: money order, Visa, MasterCard, Discover
Layaway available.

MODERN BEARS:
Germany: Steiff
U.K.: Canterbury
U.S.A.: Applause/Raikes, Boyds, Russ Berrie, Gund, Mary Meyer
Artist bears: cm Bears, Bearly There, Shirley Meyer, The Ohio River Bear Co., Chester Freeman, Jackie Strecker
Figurines: Boyds Bearstone, Michaud Collection, Sarah's Attic, United Design Corp.
Bear collectibles: books about collecting, paintings, stationery, tins
In business for 5 years

COUNTRY WARES OF FREDERICK

Nancy S. Hambright
8076 Geaslin Dr.
Middletown, MD 21701
Phone: 301-694-0990
Phone orders accepted.
Hours: M-Sat, 10A.M.-5P.M. Sun, noon-4P.M. From Thanksgiving until Christmas Eve: TH, F, Sat, 10A.M.-8P.M., Sun, noon- 6P.M.
Accepts: check, money order, Visa, MasterCard, Discover, American Express, most cards
Layaway: 50% down, 30 days, no fee
Discounts: frequent order, club

MODERN BEARS:
Canada: Cuddly Toys, Ganz Bros.
U.K.: Merrythought, Paddington
U.S.A.: Applause/Raikes, Boyds, Russ Berrie, Cooperstown Bears, Dakin, Gund, The Manhattan Toy Co., Mary Meyer, Muffy, Vanderbear family, VIBs, North American Bear Co. (other), The Michaud Collection
Artist bears: Bearly There, Sue Foskey, Chris Cassner
Miniature bears: Mama's Babies, Little Gems

ACCESSORIES:
Clothes: Boyds
Furniture: chairs
Figurines: Boyds Bearstone, Cherished Teddies, Muffy, United Design Corp.
Bear collectibles: books about bears, bear magazines, ornaments
In business for 7 years

CRESCENT BEAR & BATH BOUTIQUE

Michelle Kuelbs, owner
212 W. Main St.
Waunakee, WI 53597
Phone: 608-849-8339
Phone orders accepted.
Hours: M-W, 10A.M.-6P.M. TH, 10A.M.-
7:30P.M. F, 10A.M.-6P.M. Sat, 11A.M.-
5P.M. Nov. and Dec.: Sun, noon-4P.M.
Also by appointment
Accepts: check, money order, Visa, Mas-
terCard
Layaway: 33% down, 33% in 30 days,
balance in 60 days
Old/special items: bunnies

MODERN BEARS:
Germany: Steiff
U.S.A.: Applause/Raikes, Charlene
Kinser Designs, Gund, The Manhat-
tan Toy Co., Mary Meyer, Muffy,
North American Bear Co. (other), Ba-
sic Brown Bears, Folkmanis
Artist bears: Bearly There, Jeanette
McPherson, Barbara Troxel, Lenore
Dement, Louann Hendershot, Kathy
Biehlert, Leann Snyder, Joey
Morrison-Smith, Jacki Morris, Linda
Bayless, Jackie Strecker, Tammie
Lawrence, Naomi Laight, Jeanne
Greenbush, Kelli Kilby, Carol
Stewart, Ann Brown, Chester
Freeman, Chris Cassner, Linda Staff-
ord, Marsha Friesen, Mica Michelle
Friesen, Connie Roark, Ruth Ann
Mauer, Ballard Baines, Janet Reeves,
and more
Miniature bears: Kelli Kilby, Carol
Stewart, Gund

ACCESSORIES:
Baskets
Clothes: NAB, Basic Brown Bear
Furniture: wicker chairs
Bear collectibles: books about bears,
books about bearmaking, books about
collecting, boxes, clothing for people,
bear magazines, ornaments, Smokey
bear collectibles, stationery, tins, tote
bags, Winnie-the-Pooh collectibles,
Polar bears of Barbara Stone greeting
cards and calendars, other teddy bear
calendars, posters, Sierra Club bear
stationery and greeting cards
More about collectibles: Polar bear items
by Barbara Stone are featured on original works of art.

D 'N J BEARS & DOLLS

Lloyd & Sheila Cohen
18563 Main St.
Huntington Beach, CA 92848
Phone: 714-847-6266
Phone orders accepted.
Hours: M-TH, 10A.M.-5:30P.M. F, 10A.M.-
6P.M. Sat, 10A.M.-5P.M. Sun, noon-
4P.M.
Accepts: check, money order, Visa, Mas-
terCard, Discover, American Express,
traveler's checks
Layaway: 15% down, no refund. 15% re-
stocking fee if cancelled
Old/special items: bunnies
Discounts: club

MODERN BEARS:
Canada: Ganz Bros.
Germany: Hans Clemens, Gebruder Her-
mann, Steiff
Italy: Trudi Giocattoli
U.K.: Canterbury, Deans, Little Folk,
Merrythought, Paddington
U.S.A.: Applause/Raikes, Boyds, Russ
Berrie, California Stuffed Toys, Char-
lene Kinser Designs, Cooperstown
Bears, Dakin, Gund, Ideal, Lone Star,
The Manhattan Toy Co., Mary Meyer,
Muffy, Vanderbear family, VIBs,
North American Bear Co. (other), J.J.
Wind (military service bears), Ty,
Gorham Bears by Beverely Port (no
longer made)
Artist bears: Linda Johnson, Pam Hol-
ton, Pat Fye, Janet Reeves, Linda
Spiegel, Joan Woessner, Kathy Mul-
lins, Dee Hockenberry, Debi Ortega,
Tatum Egland, Chris Cassner, Deanna
Brittsan, Evelyn Penfield, Niki Kos-
tas, Penny Noble, Shirley Boynton,
Suzanne Rempfer, Suzanne Adler,
Pauline Weir, Pat Carriker, Sue Kruse,
Jimmy Woo, Connie Tagnoli, Sersha
Miniature bears: Pat Carriker, Jimmy
Wu, Pam Holton, Pauline Weir, Pat
Fye, Connie Tagnoli, Gund

ACCESSORIES:
Baskets, glasses, hair ribbons, shoes, vehicles, Radio Flyer wagons, small
cakes, mini food, tea sets, french ribbon, handmade items for holidays,
swings and other sundry items; Miniature baskets, glasses, shoes, vehicles,
Radio Flyer wagons
Clothes: manufactured, recycled,
custom-designed outfits and hats

Furniture: chairs, beds, etc.
Miniature clothes: handmade, custom
made outfits and hats
Miniature furniture: handmade
Figurines: Boyds Bearstone, Cherished
Teddies, Muffy, The Roosevelt Bears,
imports (without brand names)
Bear collectibles: books about bears,
books about bearmaking, books about
collecting, chinaware, bear magazines, ornaments, Paddington collectibles, postcards, Smokey bear collectibles, tea sets, Winnie-the-Pooh
collectibles
In business for 18 years

DAYDREAMS & TEA

Jennifer Canfield, owner
1265 S. Cleveland Massillon Rd.
Copley, OH 44321
Second address:
414 W. Main St.
Marblehead, OH 43440 (open April-No-
vember)
Phone: 216-666-1755, 216-666-2633 or
1-800-721-2633 for orders
Phone orders accepted.
Hours: 11A.M.-5P.M.
Accepts: check, money order, Visa, Mas-
terCard, Discover
Layaway: 33% down, 30 days
Discounts: frequent customer, club
Old/special itmes: golliwogs, bunnies,
antique bear collectibles

MODERN BEARS:
Germany: Gebruder Hermann, Her-
mann-Spielwaren, Steiff
U.S.A.: Applause/Raikes, Boyds, Gund,
Madame Alexander Bears, Muffy,
Vanderbear family, North American
Bear Co. (other)
Artist bears: Marta Weller, Joyce
Haughey, Michele Brown, Linda B.
Schaff, Kathy Moyer
Miniature bears: Akira

ACCESSORIES:
Baskets, glasses, hair ribbons, buggies,
sleighs, bear-size houses, barns, etc.
Clothes: NAB, Boyd
Furniture: NAB, Boyd, antique reproductions, child-size furniture
Figurines: Boyds Bearstone, Muffy
Bear collectibles: books about bears,
chinaware, clothing for people, dollhouse miniatures, stationery, tea sets,
tins, Winnie-the-Pooh collectibles

Shows: OH
In business for 4 years

DECIDEDLY DIFFERENT

Karen J. Sullivan, executive officer
590 N. Main St.
Vermilion, OH 44089
Phone: 216-967-4664
Phone orders accepted.
Hours: T-Sat, 10 A.M.-9 P.M. Sun, noon-5 P.M.
Accepts: check, money order, Visa, MasterCard
Layaway: 10% down, 2 months
Old/special items: bunnies

MODERN BEARS:
Canada: Ganz Bros.
Germany: Steiff, Paddington
U.S.A.: Beaver Valley, Boyds, Dakin, Gund, Mary Meyer, Muffy, Vanderbear family, VIBs, North American Bear Co. (other), Gina Softoys, Ty, Bearly People
Artist bears: Jackie Morris, Melodie Malcolm, Ann Inman, Debbie Reeves, Ballard Baines, O'Harabears, Ginny Rathell, Merry Mink, Michele Brown
Miniature bears: O'Harabears, Ballard Baines, Gund

ACCESSORIES:
Clothes: NAB (all)
Miniature accessories: glasses
Miniature clothes: Boyds
Figurines: Boyds Bearstone, Muffy, Thumbprint Teddies by Sunday Flagg
Bear collectibles: books about bears, books about collecting, bear magazines
In business for 4 years

THE DOLL ATTIC & CO.

Joan Pinney, owner
62 Brock St.
Kingston, Ontario K7L 1R9, Canada
Phone: 613-545-1085
Phone orders accepted.
Accepts: check, money order, Visa, MasterCard
Layaway: 20% down, 90 days
Discounts: frequent customer, nonprofit organization
Old/special items: golliwogs, bunnies

MODERN BEARS:
Canada: Ganz Bros., Binkley
Germany: Gebruder Hermann, Steiff

U.K.: Merrythought, Paddington
U.S.A.: Applause/Raikes, Boyds, Russ Berrie, Mary Meyer, Muffy, Ty, Oshkosh
Artist bears: Bears by Valerie, Cherie Friendship, Bears in Pairs
Figurines: Boyds Bearstone, Cherished Teddies
Bear collectibles: books about bears, stationery, tea sets, tins
Shows: Kingston, Ontario
In business for 24 years

THE DOLL & BEAR ORPHANAGE

Lucy Rouse, owner
2357 Main St.
Stratford, CT 06497
Phone: 203-386-9221
Phone orders accepted.
Hours: M-F, 10 A.M.-5 P.M. Sat, 10 A.M.-3:30 P.M.
Accepts: check, money order, Visa, MasterCard, Discover, American Express, Diner's Club
Layaway: 90 days, $2 service charge, refundable if paid 30 days before due date.

MODERN BEARS:
U.K.: Deans, Paddington
U.S.A.: Boyds, Cooperstown Bears, Gund, Muffy, Vanderbear family, VIBs, North American Bear Co. (other), Country Critters, Folkmanis
Artist bears: Linda Spiegel-Lohre, Carolyn Lamothe, Cindy Anschutz, Arnette, Shirley Hart, Bayless Creations

ACCESSORIES:
Shoes, socks
Clothes: NAB (all)
Figurines: Boyds Bearstone, Cherished Teddies, Muffy, United Design Corp.
Bear collectibles: books about bears, books about collecting, clothing for people (sweatshirts and T-shirts), jewelry, bear magazines, postcards, pottery, stationery, tea sets, Winnie-the-Pooh collectibles, Hamilton collector plates, pins
Shows: CT
In business for 5 years

THE DOLL & GIFT GALLERY

Christine C. Burnett, owner
P.O. Box 250, Rte. 284
Westtown, NY 10998

Phone: 914-726-3788
Phone orders accepted.
Hours: T-Sat, 11 A.M.-5 P.M. June-Dec. only: Sun, noon-4 P.M.
Accepts: check, money order, Visa, MasterCard, American Express
Layaway: 15% or more down, 1, 2 or 3 months depending on value of item. Deposits non-refundable.
Discounts: bulk order, frequent customer (occassionally)
Old/special items: bunnies

MODERN BEARS:
Germany: Gebruder Hermann, Steiff
U.K.: Merrythought, Paddington
U.S.A.: Applause/Raikes, Beaver Valley, Boyds, Gund, Mary Meyer, Muffy, Vanderbear family, VIBs, Michaud Collection, Vermont
Artist bears: Donna Hodges, Barbara McB Bears, Bearly There, Kathy Myers, and local artists
Miniature bears: Helen & Roger Morris, local artists

ACCESSORIES:
Baskets, glasses, hair ribbons, jewelry, shoes, socks
Clothes available.
Furniture available.
Miniature accessories: hair ribbons
Miniature clothes available.
Miniature furniture available.
Figurines: Boyds Bearstone, Muffy
Bear collectibles: books about bears, paintings, pottery, tea sets
Shows: NY
In business for 6 years

THE DOLL HOSPITAL & TOY SOLDIER SHOP

Stacey Parish, general manager
3947 W. 12 Mile Rd.
Berkley, MI 48072
Phone: 810-543-3115 or 1-800-551-PLAY
Phone orders accepted.
Fax: 810-543-0503
Fax orders accepted.
Hours: M-TH, Sat, 10 A.M.-5:30 P.M. F, 10 A.M.-8 P.M.
Accepts: check, money order, Visa, MasterCard
Layaway: 30% down, payments every 2 weeks, 60 days
Discounts: frequent orders

MODERN BEARS:

Germany: Gebruder Hermann, Kathe Kruse Puppen, Steiff

U.K.: Canterbury, Merrythought, Paddington

U.S.A.: Applause/Raikes, Boyds, Cooperstown Bears, Gund, Muffy, Vanderbear family, VIBs, North American Bear Co. (other), Vermont

Miniature bears: Gund

ACCESSORIES:

Clothes: NAB

Figurines: Muffy

Bear collectibles: books about collecting, dollhouse miniatures, tea sets

In business for 48 years

DOLL & MINI NOOK

Peg Szekely, owner

336 W. Broad St.

Quakertown, PA 18951

Phone: 215-536-4242 or 1-800-591-6886

Phone orders accepted.

Accepts: check, money order, Visa, MasterCard, Discover

Layaway: 25% down, monthly payments

Discounts: frequent orders

MODERN BEARS:

Germany: Steiff

U.S.A.: Dakin, Gund, Madame Alexander Bears, Mary Meyer, Friends from Frederick

Miniature bears: Gund

ACCESSORIES:

Glasses, jewelry, shoes, socks

Miniature accessories: baskets, glasses, shoes, socks

Figurines: Pennywhistle Lane (Enesco)

Bear collectibles: books about bears, books about collecting, jewelry, dollhouse miniatures, tea sets

Shows: PA, NJ

In business for 12 years

DOLLS, BEARS & FUNNY HARES

Daniel Epley & Joel Hoy, partners

6015 Johnson Dr.

Mission, KS 66202

Phone: 913-677-3055 or 1-800-480-3055

Phone orders accepted.

Fax: 913-677-3915

Fax orders accepted.

Hours: M-Sat, 10A.M.-6P.M.

Accepts: check, money order, Visa, Mas-

terCard, Discover, American Express

Layaway: up to $200: 10% down, 30 days. $200-$500: 25% down, 90 days. More than $500: 25% down, 120 days

Discounts: club

Old/special items: bunnies

MODERN BEARS:

Canada: Ganz Bros.

Germany: Steiff

U.S.A.: Boyds, Dakin, Gund, Mary Meyer, Muffy, Vanderbear family, VIBs, North American Bear Co. (other), R. John Wright, Ty

Artist bears: Gloria Franks, Martha DeRaimo, Jutta Cyr, Kathleen Wallace, Jackie Melerski-Saraf, Bettin Groh, Carol Modean, Chris Cassner, Dolores Groseck, Barbara Golden, Joel Hoy, Barbara Clark, Janet Reeves, Kim Hunt, Becky Coutras, Jennie Rettig, Linda Davis, Brenda Moorman, Sandi Russell, Claudia Weinstein, Janet Brouwer, Althea Leistikow, Eva Baldwin, Genie Buttitta, LouAnn Hendershot

Miniature bears: Susan McCay, Jo Ann Snyder, Jutta Cyr, Sandi Russell, Linda Davis

ACCESSORIES:

Jewelry, shoes, socks

Clothes: sweaters, NAB

Figurines: Boyds Bearstone, Muffy, Dept. 56

Bear collectibles: boxes, jewelry, bear magazines, ornaments, Winnie-the-Pooh collectibles

In business for 4 years

DOLLS & BEARS OF CHARLTON COURT

Adrienne Zisser, owner

1957 Union St.

San Francisco, CA 94123

Hours: Open M-Sat, hours vary

Accepts: check, money order, Visa, MasterCard, Diner's Club, JVB

Layaway: 90-120 days

Discounts: frequent customer, club, nonprofit organization, senior citizen, dealer

Old/special items: antique bears, bears manufactured between WWI and WWII, bears manufactured 1945-1970, golliwogs, bunnies, antique bear collectibles

MODERN BEARS:

Germany: Steiff

U.K.: Canterbury, Paddington

U.S.A.: Applause/Raikes, Charlene Kinser Designs, Gund, Madame Alexander Bears, Muffy, Vanderbear family, VIBs, North American Bear Co. (other)

Artist bears: Barbara Sixby, Kathleen Wallace, Linda Johnson, Tasi Watson, Karen Sheets, Sue Foskey, Barbara Wiltrout, Diane Martin, Carol Black, Maria Grimes, Suzanne Adler, Martha DeRaimo, Patricia Blair, Hillary Hulen, Sarah McClellan, Karen Garfinkle and many more.

Miniature bears: Debi Ortega, Heather VanNes, Heather Isaacs, Carol Stewart, Polly's Pals, Little Gems

ACCESSORIES:

Glasses, hair ribbons, jewelry

Clothes: old, handmade, NAB, hats, lace collars

Furniture: chairs, tables, trunks

Miniature clothes available.

Figurines: Muffy, artist bronze figurines

Bear collectibles: antique collectibles, chinaware, jewelry, ornaments, postcards, stationery, tea sets

In business for 13 years

DOLLS 'N BEARLAND

15001 N. Hayden, #104

Scottsdale, AZ 85260

Phone: 602-596-9947 or 1-800-359-9541 for orders

Phone orders accepted.

Fax: 602-596-9947

Fax orders accepted.

Hours: M-Sat, 9A.M.-5P.M.

Catalog: free with two loose stamps and envelope in USA; $3.50 foreign

Accepts: check, money order, Visa, MasterCard, Discover

Layaway: $2.50 fee, 25% down, 90 days for regularly priced items, 30 days for sale items. All sales final.

Discounts: collector savings club, package deals on some merchandise

MODERN BEARS:

Germany: Steiff

U.K.: Canterbury, Merrythought, Paddington

U.S.A.: Applause/Raikes, Boyds, Gund, Mary Meyer, Muffy, Vanderbear fam-

ily, VIBs, North American Bear Co. (other), Hen & the Holly
Artist bears: Bearly There, Bear Elegance
Miniature bears: Gund
In business for 14 years

DOLLSVILLE DOLLS & BEARSVILLE BEARS
461 N. Palm Canyon Dr.
Palm Springs, CA 92262
Phone: 619-325-2241 or 1-800-225-2327
Phone orders accepted.
Fax: 619-322-1691
Fax orders accepted.
Catalog: $2 (Bear-a-log and specials list); $1 old bear list
Accepts: check, money order, Visa, MasterCard, Discover, American Express
Layaway available.
Discounts: club, monthly specials
Old/special items: antique bears, bears manufactured between WWI and WWII, bears manufactured 1945-1970, golliwogs, bunnies

MODERN BEARS:
Germany: Gebruder Hermann, H. Scharrer & Koch, Steiff
U.K.: Canterbury, Chad Valley (old), Deans, Little Folk, Merrythought, Paddington
U.S.A.: Beaver Valley, Boyds, Charlene Kinser Designs, Cooperstown Bears, Gund, Lone Star, Muffy, Vanderbear family, VIBs, North American Bear Co. (other), The Michaud Collection, Vermont
In business for 16 years

DOWN BY THE STATION
Phyllis D. Phelps, secretary
150 W. Argonne
Kirkwood, MO 63122
Phone: 314-965-7833
Phone orders accepted.
Fax: 314-965-2601
Fax orders accepted.
Accepts: check, money order, Visa

MODERN BEARS:
U.S.A.: Boyds, Muffy, Vanderbear family, North American Bear Co. (other)

ACCESSORIES:
Clothes: NAB, Boyds
Furniture: chairs, etc., NAB
Figurines: Boyds Bearstone, Muffy
In business for 12 years

EAT YOUR SPINACH!
Kim & Garret Murphy, owners
475 El Camino Real, Suite 415
Millbrae, CA 94030
Phone: 415-697-5008
Phone orders accepted.
Fax: 415-697-5906
Fax orders accepted.
Mail order only.
Accepts: check, money order
Discounts: bulk order
Bear collectibles: teddy bear T-shirts and sweatshirts
Shows: Northern CA
In business for 2 years

ELENA'S DOLLHOUSES & MINIATURES
Helen Murray, owner
5565 Schueller Circle
Burlington, Ontario L7L 3T1, Canada
Phone: 905-333-3402
Phone orders accepted.
Hours: T-Sat, 10A.M.-4P.M., and by appointment
Catalog: SASE
Accepts: check, money order, Visa, MasterCard
Layaway: 25% down, 30 days
Discounts: senior citizen, wholesale
Miniature bears: Helen Murray
Bear collectibles: extensive selection of dollhouses and miniatures for bears
Shows: Ontario
In business for 4 years

ENCHANTED KINGDOM
Lisa Allen, manager & buyer
435 E. Illinois, Ste. 268
Chicago, IL 60611
Phone: 312-321-5464 or 1-800-758-9028 for orders
Phone orders accepted.
Fax: 312-321-5463
Fax orders accepted.
Hours: M-TH, 10A.M.-9P.M. F & Sat, 10A.M.-10P.M. Sun, 11A.M.-7P.M.
Accepts: check, Visa, MasterCard, Discover, American Express
Discounts: frequent customer
Layaway: $200 minimum, 25% per month
Old/special bears: bunnies

MODERN BEARS:
Germany: Steiff
U.K.: Paddington
U.S.A.: Applause/Raikes, Boyds, Russ

Berrie, Dakin, Gund, The Manhattan Toy Co., Mary Meyer, Muffy, Vanderbear family, VIBs, North American Bear Co. (other)
Artist bears: Maggie Anderson, Linda Spiegel-Lohre, JoAnne Adams, Middleton, Blessed Companion
Miniature bears: Maggie Anderson

ACCESSORIES:
Baskets, glasses
Clothes: NAB
Furniture: chairs, etc.
Figurines: Boyds Bearstone, Muffy
Bear collectibles: books about bears, books about bearmaking, books about collecting, bear magazines, Winnie-the-Pooh collectibles
In business for 5 years

ENCHANTMENTS
Mrs. Mary B. Strachan Blun, owner
311 Bull St.
Savannah, GA 31401
Phone: 912-231-9323 or 1-800-231-9345 for orders
Phone orders accepted.
Fax: 912-231-9345
Fax orders accepted.
Hours: M-Sat, 10A.M.-5:30P.M.
Accepts: check, money order, Visa, MasterCard, Discover, American Express
Layaway: terms vary

MODERN BEARS:
France: Jouet Berger
Germany: Hermann-Spielwaren, Steiff
U.K.: Canterbury, Merrythought
U.S.A.: Beaver Valley, Cooperstown Bears, Gund, The Manhattan Toy Co., Muffy, R. John Wright, Vermont
Artist bears: JoyceAnne Haughey, Jenny Krantz, Dee Hockenberry, Kathy Comish, Janet Reeves, Edda Seiple
Miniature bears: Jenny Krantz, Chu-Ming Wu, Steiff
Figurines: Goebel
Bear collectibles: books about bears, books about collecting, boxes, jewelry, bear magazines, prints, tea sets, tote bags, Winnie-the-Pooh collectibles
More about collectibles: boxes are Halcyon Days enamels
Shows: Southeast
In business for 3 years

ENCHANTWOOD
Roberta Berthold, owner
3415 Swinnerton Rd.
Hibbing, MN 55746
Phone: 218-263-7524
  Phone orders accepted.
Fax: 218-262-5689
  Fax orders accepted.
Hours: T-Sat, 10:30A.M.-5P.M. Nov.-
  Xmas, May-Sept., open Sun, noon-
  5P.M.
Catalog: free
Accepts: check, money order, Visa, Mas-
  terCard
Layaway available.
Discounts: frequent customer
Old/special items: bunnies

MODERN BEARS:
Germany: Gebruder Hermann, Steiff
U.S.A.: Boyds, Gund, Muffy, North
  American Bear Co. (other), Ty, Bun-
  nies By the Bay, Hen in the Holly
Artist bears: Tammy Lawrence, Muriel
  Townsend, Joan Woessner, Melodie
  Malcolm, Marie Zimmerman, Rosalie
  Frischman, Marti Steiger and more.
Miniature bears: Becky Wheeler, Fac-
  toria Toy Works, Kathy LaQuay,
  Carol Stewart, Jan Kahnke, Janie
  Comito, Kelley Kilby, Terrie Effan,
  Suzanne VB Rempfer, Randy Martin,
  Debbie Kesling, Debi Ortega, Little
  Gem Bears

ACCESSORIES:
Glasses
Clothes: NAB, Boyds, sweaters
Furniture: chairs, sofas, buggies, Victo-
  rian, wicker, wood
Miniature furniture available.
Figurines: Boyds Bearstone, Muffy, The
  Roosevelt Bears
Bear collectibles: books about bears,
  chinaware, jewelry, bear magazines,
  paintings, stationery, tea sets
Shows: MN, WI, IA, IL

FAIRYTALES, INC.
Jim & Rochelle Pokorn
3 South Park Ave.
Lombard, IL 60148
Second address:
49½ E. Washington
Hindsdale, IL 60521
Phone: 708-495-6909 or 1-800-495-
  6973 (out of state)
  Phone orders accepted.

Fax: 708-495-6553
  Fax orders accepted.
Hours: T-F, 11A.M.-6P.M. Sat, 11A.M.-
  5P.M.
Catalog available (in color).
Accepts: check, money order, Visa, Mas-
  terCard, Discover, American Express
Layaway: 3 equal payments in 3 months

MODERN BEARS:
Canada: Ganz Bros.
France: Nounours/Aux Nations/Ajena
Germany: Gebruder Hermann, Her-
  mann-Spielwaren, Steiff
Italy: Trudi Giocattoli
U.K.: Canterbury, Merrythought, Pad-
  dington
U.S.A.: Applause/Raikes, Beaver Valley,
  Boyds, Russ Berrie, Charlene Kinser
  Designs, Cooperstown Bears, Dakin,
  Gund, Gund Signature collection, Ma-
  dame Alexander, Mary Meyer, Muffy,
  Vanderbear family, VIBs, North
  American Bear Co. (other), R. John
  Wright, Michaud Collection, Ver-
  mont, Eden Toys. Also deals in sec-
  ondary market on Steiff, Muffy, The
  Vanderbears and VIBS.
Artist bears: Jeanne Greene, Pam
  Holton, Linda Schaff, Dorothy
  Marzolf, Joey Morrison Smith, Linda
  Johnson, Kimberly Hunt, Edda
  Seiple, Jutta Cyr, Bonnie Windell,
  Sandra Dickl, Anne Cranshaw, Car-
  olyn Lamothe, Sue & Randall Foskey,
  Karen Searl, Kathleen Wallace, Jo-
  anne Mitchell and more.
Miniature bears: Gund, Pam Holton,
  Linda Schaff, Dorothy Marzolf, Little
  Gem

ACCESSORIES:
Bear kits by Pam Holton, wagons
Clothes: Boyds, NAB
Furniture: chairs, benches
Miniature accessories: Wagons
Miniature clothes: Boyds, hand-knit
  sweaters
Miniature furniture: chairs, benches
Figurines: Boyds Bearstone, Muffy
Bear collectibles: books about bears,
  books about bearmaking, books about
  collecting, bear magazines, Padding-
  ton collectibles, stationery, tea sets,
  Bearstone bearwear pins, folkstones,
  Winnie-the-Pooh collectibles
Shows: Midwestern states
In business for 3 years

FANTASY BEARS
Jean Peterson
11070 Bellwood #2
Minocgua, WI 54548
Phone: 715-358-1969
  Phone orders accepted.
Mail order only.
Catalog: $1, refundable with purchase.
Accepts: check, money order
Discounts: bulk order, frequent cus-
  tomer, senior citizens
Old/special items: antique bear collect-
  ibles
Artist bears: Jean & Harry Peterson

ACCESSORIES:
Baskets, glasses, hair ribbons, jewelry,
  shoes, socks
Clothes available.
Miniature accessories: baskets
Miniature clothes available.
Miniature furniture available.
Bear collectibles: paintings, tea sets, tins
In business for 3 years

THE FANTASY DEN
Charlene Taylor, owner
25 Morehouse Ave.
Stratford, CT 06497
Phone: 203-377-2968
  Phone orders accepted.
Mail order only.
Catalog: $2.50, refundable with purchase
Accepts: check, money order
Layaway: varies with customer's needs
Discounts: bulk order, frequent cus-
  tomer, first order discount
Old/special items: golliwogs

MODERN BEARS:
Canada: Binkley
Germany: Grisly Spielwaren, Gebruder
  Hermann, Hermann-Spielwaren, sigi-
  kid, Miro, Clemens
U.K.: Alresford, Big Softies, Canterbury,
  Chad Valley, Deans, Little Folk, Mer-
  rythought, Paddington
U.S.A.: Dakin, Gund, The Manhattan
  Toy Co., Mary Meyer, Muffy, Vander-
  bear family, VIBs, North American
  Bear Co. (other), Eden Toys
Miniature bears: Gund, Clemens, Mer-
  rythought, Hermann

ACCESSORIES:
Clothes: NAB, knitted sweaters, T-shirts
  and shorts
Bear collectibles: books about bears,
  bear magazines, paintings, postcards,

prints, stationery, tea sets, all Vander-bear collectibles
Shows: NY, MA, CT
In business for 15 years

FOREST VIEW ENTERPRISES
Janet Curran, owner
P.O. Box 550
Yucaipa, CA 92399-0550
Phone: 909-797-7644
Fax: 909-797-7264
Fax orders accepted.
Mail order only.
Catalog: free
Accepts: check, money order

ACCESSORIES:
Jewelry
Bear collectibles: jewelry, appliqués, patches
More about collectibles: Jewelry includes enamelled and unenamelled pins and charms, made to customer's specifications. Embroidered appliqués and patches also made to customer's specifications.

FRAN LEWIS' BEAR IN MIND, INC.
Fran Lewis, president
53 Bradford St.
Concord, MA 01742
Phone: 508-369-1167
Phone orders accepted.
Fax: 508-371-0762
Fax orders accepted.
Hours: M-F, 10A.M.-5P.M. Sat, 10A.M.-4P.M.
Catalog: $1
Accepts: check, money order, Visa, MasterCard, Discover, American Express
Discounts: bulk order, occasional sales
Old/special items: bunnies

MODERN BEARS:
Canada: Ganz Bros.
Germany: Hermann-Spielwaren, Steiff
U.K.: Canterbury, Merrythought, Paddington
U.S.A.: Beaver Valley, Boyds, California Stuffed Toys, Charlene Kinser Designs, Cooperstown Bears, Dakin, Gund, Jona, The Manhattan Toy Co., Mary Meyer, Muffy, Vanderbear family, VIBs, North American Bear Co. (other), R. John Wright, Michaud Collection, Vermont
Other modern bears: several others
Artist bears: Several

Miniature bears: Akira, Wheeler, Gustafson, Schmid, and more

ACCESSORIES:
Baskets, glasses, hair ribbons, jewelry, shoes, socks
Clothes available.
Furniture available.
Miniature accessories: baskets, glasses, hair ribbons, jewelry, shoes, socks
Miniature clothes available.
Miniature furniture available.
Figurines: Boyds Bearstone, Cherished Teddies, Lucy & Me, Muffy, The Roosevelt Bears, United Design Corp.
Bear collectibles: books about bears, books about collecting, boxes, chinaware, clothing for people, jewelry, ornaments, Paddington collectibles, postcards, Smokey bear collectibles, stationery, tea sets, tins, tote bags, Winnie-the-Pooh collectibles
Shows: MA
In business for 18 years

FREDERICKTOWNE DOLL SHOPPE
Donna Gardner, president
116 East St.
Frederick, MD 21701
Phone: 301-698-1618 or 1-800-77-DOLLS for orders
Phone orders accepted.
Hours: T-F, 10A.M.-5P.M. Sat, 10A.M.-6P.M. Sun, noon-5P.M. Closed M.
Accepts: check, money order, Visa, MasterCard, Discover
Discounts: frequent order, club

MODERN BEARS:
Germany: Kathe Kruse, Steiff
Bear collectibles: books about bears, chinaware, clothing for people, bear magazines, dollhouse miniatures, postcards, stationery, tea sets
In business for 2 years

G & J COLLECTIBLES
Janice & George Parola
43 Oakfield Ave.
Freeport, NY 11520-1935
Phone: 516-868-8439
Phone orders accepted.
Fax: 516-379-1534
Fax orders accepted.
Mail order only.
Catalog: free
Accepts: check, money order
Old/special items: Steiff bears and ani-

mals manufactured 1945-1970, antique bear collectibles

MODERN BEARS:
Germany: Steiff
Miniature bears: Carries entire Steiff collection

GALLERY BEARS
Elaine F. Lamar, owner
809 SE Main St.
Roseburg, OR 97470
Phone: 503-673-6694
Phone orders accepted.
Fax: 503-673-0860
Hours: T-F, 10A.M.-5:30P.M. Sat, 10A.M.-5P.M.
Accepts: check, money order, Visa, MasterCard
Layaway: 90 days same as cash, no interest
Discounts: frequent customer
Old/special items: bunnies

MODERN BEARS:
U.K.: Canterbury, Paddington
U.S.A.: Applause/Raikes, Boyds, Dakin, Gund, Mary Meyer, Muffy, Vanderbear family, VIBs, North American Bear Co. (other)
Miniature bears: Gund, local artists

ACCESSORIES:
Patterns
Furniture: bent willow beds, rocking chairs, desks, NAB
Miniature accessories: baskets
Miniature furniture: wicker
Figurines: Boyds Bearstone, Muffy, local artists' fima clay figurines
Bear collectibles: books about bears, books about collecting, clothing for people, jewelry, ornaments, Paddington collectibles, paintings, postcards, pottery, prints, stationery, tea sets, tins, tote bags, Winnie-the-Pooh collectibles
In business for 10 years

GEPETTO'S COLLECTIBLES
Dale Williams and Dennis Smiley, owners
233 The Crossroads
Carmel, CA 93923
Phone: 408-625-6162
Phone orders accepted.
Hours: M-Sat, 10A.M.-6P.M. Sun, 11A.M.-5P.M.
Accepts: check, money order, Visa, Mas-

terCard, Discover, Diner's Club
Layaway: 33% down, 90 days
Discounts: bulk order
Old/special items: bunnies

MODERN BEARS:
France: Nounours/Aux Nations/Ajena
Germany: Althans, Gebruder Hermann, Hermann-Spielwaren, Steiff
Italy: Trudi Giocattoli
New Zealand: Sheepskin Products
U.K.: Alresford, Canterbury, Little Folk, Merrythought, Paddington
U.S.A.: Applause/Raikes, Beaver Valley, Charlene Kinser Designs, Gund, Madame Alexander Bears, The Manhattan Toy Co., Mary Meyer, Muffy, Vanderbear family, VIBs, North American Bear Co. (other), R. John Wright, The Michaud Collection
Artist bears: Cat Orlando, Jeanne Green, Barbara Whisnant, Barbara Sixby, Debi Ortega, Barbara McConnell, Von Haydershagt, Lynn Graham, Lane Carpenter, Donna Hodges, Gary Nett, Ann Inman Looms, Victoria Stanard, Judy Howard, Nancy Coker, Serietta Harrel
Miniature bears: Akira, Noreen Oshiro, Debi Ortega, Linda Nelson
Figurines: Cairn Studio, Cherished Teddies, Muffy, The Roosevelt Bears
Bear collectibles: books about bears, books about collecting, chinaware, jewelry, bear magazines, tea sets
In business for 13 years

GIGI'S DOLLS & SHERI'S TEDDY BEARS
6029 N. Northwest Hwy.
Chicago, IL 60631

GOLDEN RULE BEARS
Tom & Lorraine Young, owners
1103 Main St.
Sumner, WA 98390-1414
Phone: 206-863-0280 or 1-800-932-2327 for orders
Phone orders accepted.
Fax: 206-863-1780
Fax orders accepted.
E-mail: Bears4u@aol.com
E-mail orders accepted.
Hours: M-Sat, 10A.M.-5:30P.M. Sun, 11A.M.-4P.M. in Nov. and Dec.
Accepts: check, money order, Visa, MasterCard, Discover, American Express
Layaway: less than $100: 33% down, 30

days. More than $100: 33% down, 33% in 30 days, balance in 60 days. No fee.
Discounts: club
Old/special items: bunnies

MODERN BEARS:
Canada: Ganz Bros.
Germany: Gebruder Hermann, Steiff
U.K.: Canterbury, Merrythought, Paddington
U.S.A.: Applause/Raikes, Beaver Valley, Boyds, Russ Berrie, Cooperstown Bears, Dakin, Gund, Lone Star, Madame Alexander Bears, The Manhattan Toy Co., Mary Meyer, Muffy, Vanderbear family, VIBs, North American Bear Co. (other), R. John Wright, Michaud Collection, Vermont, Cuddle Toys, Eden, Mati's Originals, Orzek, Mango, Peek-a-Boo Bears, Folkmanis
Artist bears: Ann Inman-Looms, Ted Menten, Paula Egbert, Marguerite Good-Montesano, Judy Scott, Linda Schaff, Kim Hunt, Suzanne Rempfer, Alex Looms, Donna Hodges, Veronica Dooling, Tasi Watson, Pam Pontius, Sharon Queen, Bearly There, Ruthie O'Neill, Heidi Steiner, Pat Fye, Lori Murphy, Dave Scarpati, Jeanie Major and more
Miniature bears: Marti Blackman, Judy Scott, Suzanne Rempfer, Chu Ming-Wu, Linda Schaff, Akira

ACCESSORIES:
Glasses
Clothes: NAB, Boyds, Tender-Heart
Furniture: Boyds
Figurines: Boyds Bearstone, Cherished Teddies, Lucy & Me, Muffy, The Roosevelt Bears, United Design Corp., Danforth (pewter Winnie the Pooh), Charpente (porcelain Winnie the Pooh), Enesco Chocolate bears
Bear collectibles: books about bears, books about collecting, boxes, chinaware, clothing for people, jewelry, bear magazines, ornaments, Paddington collectibles, postcards, Smokey bear collectibles, stationery, tea sets, tins, Winnie-the-Pooh collectibles, rubber stamps, stickers
Shows: OR, WA
In business for 10 years

GOOD HEARTED BEARS
Gloria Meister
½ Pearl St.
Mystic, CT 06355
Phone: 203-536-2468
Phone orders accepted.
Accepts: money order, Visa, MasterCard

MODERN BEARS:
Germany: Steiff
U.K.: Paddington
U.S.A.: Applause/Raikes, Boyds, Charlene Kinser Designs, Cooperstown Bears, Dakin, Gund, Lone Star, Mary Meyer, Muffy, Vanderbear family, VIBs, North American Bear Co. (other)
Artist bears: Barbara Conley, Tracey Roe, Cathie Levy, Rosalie Frischmann, Dorothy DePaulo, Carol Pearce, Hillary Hulen, Carla Cubillas, Mary Holstad, Joan Woessner, Sue Newlin, Pat Murphy, Beth Lewis, Lori Baker, Deanna Brittsan, Ruth Ann Maurer, Barbara Whisnant, Linda Stafford, Althea Leistikow, Brenda Dewey, Jeanie Major, Ann Inman-Looms, Alex Looms, Heidi Steiner and more
Miniature bears: Durae Allen, Pat Carriker, Odette Conley, Arlene Damisch, Rose Policky, Julia Reardon, Heather VanNes, Stacy Pio, Suzanne Rempfer, Diane Pease, Pauline Weir and more

ACCESSORIES:
Glasses
Clothes available.
Furniture available.
Figurines: Cherished Teddies, Lucy & Me
Bear collectibles: books about bears, books about bearmaking, books about collecting, boxes, chinaware, clothing for people, jewelry, dollhouse miniatures, Paddington collectibles, postcards, stationery, tins, Winnie-the-Pooh collectibles
Shows: NY, MA, CT, FL, MD
In business for 14 years

GRANDMA'S BEARS WORKSHOP AND SHOWROOM
Ruth Clipperton Peters, owner
412 Hwy 43 E.
Harrison, AR 72601
Phone: 501-741-0273 or 1-800-297-

9230 for orders
Phone orders accepted.
Hours: M-TH, 10A.M.-4P.M. F, 10A.M.-
6P.M. Sat, Sun: call first.
Catalog: $3, refundable with purchase
Accepts: check, money order, Visa, Mas-
terCard
Layaway: 10% down, no monthly mini-
mum, no time limit
Discounts: frequent customer, GBW
member—5% discount
Artist bears: Ruth Clipperton Peters
Miniature bears: Ruth Clipperton Peters

ACCESSORIES:
Clothes: clothing made to fit Winston and
his cousins by Ruth Clipperton Peters
Bear collectibles: boxes, jewelry, ornaments
More about collectibles: boxes are
wooden, decorated with miniature
flocked bears, lace, flowers, miniature
toys, etc. Jewelry and ornaments have
a country look and are painted wood
bear shapes.
Shows: Central
In business for 6 years

GRIN & BEAR IT

Jan Vangeleren, owner
20 W. Chicago Ave.
Naperville, IL 60540
Phone: 708-357-4244
Phone orders accepted.
Fax: 708-357-0150
Fax orders accepted.
Hours: M-Sat, 10A.M.-5P.M.
Accepts: check, money order, Visa, Mas-
terCard, Discover, American Express
Old/special items: bunnies

MODERN BEARS:
France: Nounours/Aux Nations/Ajena
Germany: Gebruder Hermann, Her-
mann-Spielwaren, Steiff
U.K.: Canterbury, Deans, Merrythought,
Paddington
U.S.A.: Raikes (originals), Charlene
Kinser Designs, Cooperstown Bears,
Gund, Madame Alexander Bears,
Muffy, Vanderbear family, VIBs,
North American Bear Co., R. John
Wright, Michaud Collection
Artist bears: Goosecreek, Joanne Mitch-
ell, Ballard Baines, Donna Hodges,
Carol Black, Wendy Brent, Sonie
Monroe, Jill Kenny, Sherry Kozil,
Hillary Huben, Diane Gard, Karine

Masterson, Janet Reeves, Betsy
Reum, Jackie Lescher, Monty-Sue
Sours, Marge Knapp, Carol-Lynn
Rossel Waugh, Chester Freeman, Mi-
chaud Collection, Donna Bobby, Kim
Hunt, Dee Hockenberry, Randy Bort-
nem, Linda Henry, Barb Ferrier, Gary
Nett, Bearly Friends, Razzberries, Jer-
rie Keller and many more
Miniature bears: Clarice, Carol Stewart,
Durae Allen, Gund, Little Gems

ACCESSORIES:
Clothes: NAB
Figurines: Michaud Collection, Muffy
Bear collectibles: books about bears,
books about bearmaking, chinaware,
ornaments, paintings, tea sets, Win-
nie-the-Pooh collectibles
In business for 9 years

GROVES QUALITY COLLECTIBLES

Sue Groves
204 N. Main St.
Bluffton, OH 45817
Phone: 419-358-8559
Mail order address:
347 S. Jameson Ave.
Lima, OH 45805
Phone: 419-299-7177
Phone orders accepted.
Fax: 419-229-2737
Fax orders accepted.
Catalog: $2, refundable with purchase
Accepts: check, money order, Visa, Mas-
terCard, Discover
Layaway: 33% down, 60 days
Discounts: nonprofit organization, sales,
show specials
Old/special items: antique bears, bears
manufactured between WWI and
WWII, bears manufactured 1945-
1970, golliwogs, bunnies

MODERN BEARS:
Australia: Teddy & Friends
Canada: Ganz Bros.
France: The French Bear Co.
Germany: Althans, Fechter, Grisly
Spielwaren, Gebruder Hermann, Her-
mann-Spielwaren, Kathe Kruse Pup-
pen, Schuco, Steiff, sigikid
Italy: Lenci
Switzerland: MCZ/Mutzali/Felpa
U.K.: Alresford, Canterbury, Deans, Lit-
tle Folk, Merrythought, Paddington
U.S.A.: Applause/Raikes, Beaver Valley,
Boyds, Charlene Kinser Designs,

Cooperstown Bears, Dakin, Gund,
Lone Star, Mary Meyer, Muffy, Vand-
erbear family, VIBs, North American
Bear Co. (other), R. John Wright, Mi-
chaud Collection, Vermont, Ty, Bearly
People Other modern collectible
bears: Many additional brands
Artist bears: More than 300 artists
Miniature bears: Several artists

ACCESSORIES:
Baskets, glasses, hair ribbons, jewelry
Clothes available.
Furniture available.
Miniature Accessories: baskets, glasses
Miniature furniture available.
Figurines: Boyds Bearstone, Michaud
Collection, Muffy, Neuenschwander,
The Roosevelt Bears, Sarah's Attic,
Kris Kennedy, Gina Lee
Bear collectibles: books about bears,
books about bearmaking, books about
collecting, chinaware, clothing for
people, jewelry, bear magazines, doll-
house miniatures, ornaments, Pad-
dington collectibles, paintings, postcards, prints, Smokey bear
collectibles, stationery, tea sets, tins,
tote bags, Winnie-the-Pooh collectibles, silverware, napkin rings,
spoons, etc.
In business for 18 years

LINDA GRUNAU

3294 Woody Ln.
San Jose, CA 95132
Phone: 408-263-1026
Phone orders accepted.
Mail order available.
Bear collectibles: Embroidered logos
and designs for shirts, hats, bear
clothes, etc. Any logo or design can
be adapted.

HARPER GENERAL STORE

Barbara Lauver
RD 2, Box 512
Annville, PA 17003
Phone: 717-865-3456
Phone orders accepted.
Fax: 717-865-3813
Fax orders accepted.
Mail order only.
Catalog: $10/year
Accepts: check, money order, Visa, Mas-
terCard
Layaway: 25% down, 90 days

Old/special items: antique bears, bears manufactured between WWI and WWII, bears manufactured 1945-1970, antique bear collectibles

Miniature bears: Laurie Sasaki, Octavia Chin, Lisa Lloyd, Elaine Fujita Gamble, Sara Phillips

Shows: MD, NY, CA, TN, NJ, OH, Japan

In business for 22 years

HARVEY'S GIFTSHOP INC.
Penny Price, president
294 E. Main St.
Frostburg, MD 21532
Phone: 301-689-9266
   Phone orders accepted.
Fax: 301-689-3309
   Fax orders accepted.
Accepts: check, money order, Visa, MasterCard, Discover, American Express, direct billing
Layaway: $5 deposit, 12 weeks
Discounts: 20% off cash and carry
Old/special items: bunnies
Modern collectible bears: One-of-a-kind reproduction style old bears. Some are custom made in the shop.

ACCESSORIES:
Baskets, glasses
Furniture: wicker
Miniature furniture: wicker
Bear collectibles: reproductions of antique collectibles, books about bears, books about bearmaking, books about collecting, boxes, chinaware, jewelry, paintings, prints, tea sets, tins, bear paper dolls, greeting cards, stationery

In business for 65 years

HATFULL OF HUGGABLES
Ginny Fine, owner
11255 Woodruff Ave., #2
Downey, CA 90241
Phone: 310-803-5311
   Phone orders accepted.
Fax: 310-803-1034
   Fax orders accepted.
Hours: W-F, 11A.M.-4:30P.M. Sat, 10A.M.-3P.M.
Accepts: check, money order, Visa, MasterCard
Layaway: 33% down, 33% per month
Discounts: club

MODERN BEARS:
Germany: Gebruder Hermann, Kathe Kruse Puppen, Steiff

U.K.: Canterbury, Merrythought
U.S.A.: Applause/Raikes, Russ Berrie, Charlene Kinser Designs, Dakin, Gund, Muffy, Michaud Collection, Tide-Rider
Artist bears: 30 bear artists, change periodically. Shop exclusives and one-of-a-kind bears included.
Miniature bears: Several artists, change periodically

ACCESSORIES:
Furniture: chairs, nanny cradles, etc.
Miniature furniture: small chairs, trunks
Figurines: Muffy
Bear collectibles: books about bears, books about bearmaking, books about collecting, chinaware, bear magazines, ornaments, postcards, prints, stationery, tote bags, Winnie-the-Pooh collectibles

HELLO DOLLY SHOPPE, INC.
Nancy Netherton, owner
8445 International Dr., Suite 113
Orlando, FL 32819
Phone: 407-352-7344
   Phone orders accepted.
Hours: 7 days, 10A.M.-10P.M.
Accepts: check, money order, Visa, MasterCard, American Express
Layaway: 20% down, 30-60 days, larger purchases may have longer
Old/special items: bunnies

MODERN BEARS:
Canada: Ganz Bros.
Germany: Haida, Gebruder Hermann
U.K.: Canterbury
U.S.A.: Applause/Raikes, Dakin, Gund, Lone Star, Mary Meyer
Artist bears: Barbara Originals
Miniature bears: Miniatures made in Miami, FL

In business for 10 years

THE HEN NEST
Charlotte Doster, owner
5485 113th St. N.
Seminole, FL 34642
Phone: 813-398-1470 or 1-800-452-1273 for orders
   Phone orders accepted.
Fax: 813-398-1470
   Fax orders accepted.
Accepts: check, Visa, MasterCard, Discover, American Express
Layaway: 20% down, 60 days

Old/special items: antique bears, bears manufactured between WWI and WWII, bears manufactured 1945-1970, golliwogs, bunnies, antique bear collectibles

MODERN BEARS:
Germany: Gebruder Hermann, Steiff
U.K.: Canterbury, Deans, Merrythought, Paddington
U.S.A.: Boyds, Gund, Muffy, North American Bear Co. (other)
Artist bears: Joan Woessner, Donna Hodges, Janet Reeves, Lori Baker, Ann Carlo, Sheila Schuchert, Kathy Sheppard, Lori Ventimiglia, Pat Fye, Carolyn Jacobsen, Roberta Rehm, Kathleen Kelley, Althea Leistikow, Darlene Allen, Terry Hayes, Barbara McConnell, Joyce O'Sullivan, Steve Schutt, Doris Riggs
Miniature bears: Lori Ventimiglia, Kathleen Kelley, Roberta Rehm, Pat Fye, Terry Hayes
Bear collectibles: books about bears, books about bearmaking, books about collecting, boxes, chinaware, clothing for people, jewelry, bear magazines, dollhouse miniatures, ornaments, paintings, postcards, pottery, prints, Smokey bear collectibles, stationery, tea sets
Shows: FL

In business for 9 years

HICKORY DICKORY DOLLS & BEARS
Joan A. Tosko, owner
124 E. Aurora Rd.
Northfield, OH 44067
Phone: 468-2085 or 1-800-468-2085
   Phone orders accepted.
Hours: T-Sat, 10A.M.- 4:30P.M. Closed Sun and M.
Accepts: money order, Visa, MasterCard, Discover
Layaway: 25% down, 3 equal monthly payments
Discounts: frequent order

MODERN BEARS:
Germany: Steiff
U.K.: Merrythought, Paddington
U.S.A.: Boyds, Cooperstown Bears, Gund, Madame Alexander Bears, Muffy, Vanderbear family, R. John Wright
Artist bears: Jenny Krantz, Barbara Bessos

Miniature bears: R. John Wright, Jenny Krantz, Gund

In business for 6 years

THE HOME FOR WAYWARD BEARS

Marian & Selma Borken

P.O. Box 630031

Miami, FL 33163

Second address:

18407 W. Dixie Highway

Miami, FL 33160

Phone: 305-935-0730

Phone orders accepted. (Will hold for payment)

Fax: 305-985-8119

Fax orders accepted. (Will hold for payment)

Hours: TH, F, 2:30P.M.-5:30P.M. Sat, 11-5:30P.M. Also by appointment.

Catalog: $2

Accepts: check, money order, cashier check

Layaway: 50% down, 50% in 45 days

Old/special items: bears manufactured 1945-1970, golliwogs (handmade)

MODERN BEARS:

U.K.: Paddington

U.S.A.: Applause/Raikes, Russ Berrie, California Stuffed Toys, Dakin, Gund, Knickerbocker, VIBs, North American Bear Co. (other), bunnies

ACCESSORIES:

Baskets

Clothes: hand painted T-shirts

Bear collectibles: books about bears, clothing for people, Paddington collectibles, postcards, stationery, tote bags, Winnie-the-Pooh collectibles

More about collectibles: T-shirts are designed by Marian & Selma Borken and silk-screen printed. Tote bags and stationery also carry their original designs.

Shows: FL

In business for 3 years

HOUSE OF BEARS

Joan Fortmiller, owner

P.O. Box 384

Hudson, MA 01749

Phone: 508-562-4849 or 1-800-767-2327 for orders.

Phone orders accepted.

Mail order only.

Accepts: check, money order, Visa, MasterCard, Discover

MODERN BEARS:

U.S.A.: Applause/Raikes, Beaver Valley, Charlene Kinser Designs

ACCESSORIES:

Stands

Has extensive collection of new and retired Robert Raikes collectibles, including both manufactured and orginals

In business for 10 years

THE HOUSE OF THE CRAFTY MOUSE

Joanne DeBruin, owner

Miracle Mile Mini Mall

Rochester, MN 55901

Phone: 507-282-7711

Phone orders accepted.

Hours: M-F, 10A.M.-9P.M. Sat, 10A.M.-5P.M. Sun, 1P.M.-5P.M.

Accepts: check, Visa, MasterCard

Layaway: 7 days, no down payment. May call and extend time.

MODERN BEARS:

U.S.A.: Boyds, Mary Meyer

Artist bears: Teddies Are For Real

In business for 8 years

THE HUGGING BEAR INN & SHOPPE

Georgette Thomas, owner

RR #1, Box 32, Main St.

Chester, VT 05143

Phone: 802-875-2339 or 1-800-325-0519 for orders

Phone orders accepted.

Hours: 7 days, 9A.M.-6P.M.

Catalog: free

Accepts: check, money order, Visa, MasterCard, Discover, American Express, traveler's checks

Discounts: guests at inn receive 5-10% discount

Old/special items: bunnies

MODERN BEARS:

Canada: Ganz Bros.

Germany: Gebruder Hermann, Steiff

Italy: Trudi Giocattoli

U.K.: Canterbury, Little Folk, Merrythought, Paddington

U.S.A.: Applause/Raikes, Boyds, Russ Berrie, California Stuffed Toys, Charlene Kinser Designs, Dakin, Gund, Jona, Lone Star, The Manhattan Toy Co., Mary Meyer, Muffy, Vanderbear family, VIBs, North American Bear Co. (other), R. John Wright, The Michaud Collection, Ver-

mont, Special Effects, Eden, G.A.F., Ty, Bearly People, Douglas Cuddle Toys, Folkmanis, Charm

Artist bears: Bearly There, Donna Bjerke, Terry Skorstad, Terri Woods, Jill Kenny, Ann Cummings, Nancy Edmonds, Sarah McClellan, Cindy Bartosewcz, Carol Carini, Laurie Corbin, Jan Chapados, Francis Harper, Arnold Couture and more than 40 artists from around the world

Miniature bears: Deborah Didier, Diane Sherman, Akira, Lane Carpenter

ACCESSORIES:

Baskets, cradles, sleds, carriages

Clothes: NAB, sweaters, shirts, crocheted vests and hats

Furniture: chairs, benches, cradles, tables, chairs, etc.

Miniature accessories: Baskets

Miniature clothes: crocheted vests and hats

Figurines: Cherished Teddies, Colour Box Miniatures, Laura's Attic, Lucy & Me, Muffy, United Design Corp., Pennywhistles, Marydale pottery figurines, pewter figurines

Bear collectibles: books about bears, books about bearmaking, books about collecting, boxes, chinaware, clothing for people, jewelry, bear magazines, ornaments, Paddington collectibles, paintings, postcards, pottery, prints, stationery, tea sets, tins, tote bags, Winnie-the-Pooh collectibles, rubber stamps, magnets, keychains, musicals, music boxes

Shows: MA

In business for 13 years

HUNDRED ACRE WOOD

Carrie Davis, partner

2413 E. Harry

Wichita, KS 67211

Phone: 316-265-2727

Phone orders accepted.

Hours: M-Sat, 10A.M.-5:30P.M.

Accepts: check, money order, Visa, MasterCard

Layaway: 20% down, 60 days

Discounts: After $100 is spent, $10 off next purchase

Old/special items: bunnies

MODERN BEARS:

Germany: Steiff

U.K.: Paddington, The English Teddy Bear Co.

U.S.A.: Applause/Raikes, Boyds, Gund, Mary Meyer, VIBs, North American Bear Co. (other), Vermont

ACCESSORIES:

Baskets, glasses

Clothes: sweaters, Santa robes, occupational clothes

Furniture: willow, adirondack, pine

Miniature accessories: baskets

Figurines: Boyds Bearstone, Lucy & Me

Bear collectibles: books about bears, boxes, chinaware, clothing for people, jewelry, postcards, prints, stationery, tea sets, Winnie-the-Pooh collectibles

In business for 2 years

HYDE PARK ZOO

Jean B. Palermo, president

1624 W. Snow Circle

Tampa, FL 33606

Phone: 813-254-7736 or 1-800-826-1226 for orders

Phone orders accepted.

Fax: 813-228-0518

Fax orders accepted.

Accepts: check, money order, Visa, MasterCard, American Express

Layaway: 25% down, 30, 60 or 90 days

MODERN BEARS:

Canada: Ganz Bros.

Germany: Grisly Spielwaren, Gebruder Hermann, Steiff, sigikid

Italy: Trudi Giocattol

U.K.: Merrythought, Paddington

U.S.A.: Applause, Boyds, Russ Berrie, Dakin, Gund, The Manhattan Toy Co., Mary Meyer, Muffy, Vanderbear family, VIBs, North American Bear Co. (other)

Artist bears: Joanne Mitchell, Mary Jane Demko, Shirley Whitney, Serieta Harrell, Barbara Golden, Mati's Originals, French Bear Co., Donna Hodges, Sue Foskey

ACCESSORIES:

Glasses

Clothes: NAB

Furniture: chairs, benches

Figurines: Boyds Bearstone, Muffy

Shows: FL

In business for 8 years

I. CHILD

Richard Eldredge, owner

118 E. Tarpon Ave.

Tarpon Springs, FL 34689

Phone: 813-938-4730 or 1-800-556-4730 for orders

Phone orders accepted.

Hours: T-Sat, 10A.M.-5P.M. Additional hours seasonally.

Accepts: Visa, MasterCard, Discover

Layaway: 20% down, 30 days

Old/special items: bunnies

MODERN BEARS:

Canada: Ganz Bros.

Germany: Gebruder Hermann, Steiff

U.K.: Canterbury, Deans, Merrythought, Paddington

U.S.A.: Applause/Raikes, Boyds, Russ Berrie, Dakin, Gund, The Manhattan Toy Co., Muffy, North American Bear Co. (other), Michaud Collection, Vermont

Artist bears: Dee Hockenberry, Pat Fairbanks, Edie Rase, Mary Jane Demko, Jill Sisco, Yvonne Septfonds, Annemie Davis

Miniature bears: Jill Sisco, Little Gems

ACCESSORIES:

Glasses

Clothes: NAB, Boyds

Furniture: assorted

Figurines: Boyds Bearstone

Bear collectibles: books about bearmaking, books about collecting, bear magazines, postcards

In business for 2 years

INSPIRATIONS LIMITED

A. John Wiedefeld, owner

P.O. Box 9096

Cedar Pines Park, CA 92322

Phone: 909-338-6758 or 1-800-337-6758

Phone orders accepted.

Fax: 1-800-337-6758

Fax orders accepted.

Mail order only.

Catalog: $3 samples

Accepts: check, money order

Discounts: 50% wholesale discount

Bear collectibles: greeting cards, note cards and gift tags

Shows: CA

In business for 13 years

J & M WOODCRAFT

Jim & Maxine Richardson

2772 Mustang Ln.

Norco, CA 91760-2527

Phone: 909-371-6947

Phone orders accepted.

Mail order only.

Catalog: $1, refundable with purchase

Accepts: check, money order

Discounts: bulk order, frequent customer

ACCESSORIES:

Furniture: wooden tables & chairs, buckboards, high chairs, rockers, swings, bunk beds, playpens, wheelbarrows, chairs, special orders

Shows: CA

In business for 11 years

JOYCE'S DOLL SHOP

Al Harper & Debra Joyce Hines

4133 W. Main St.

Batavia, NY 14020

Phone: 716-344-2246 or 1-800-562-9065 for orders

Phone orders accepted.

Hours: M-Sat, 9:30A.M.-5P.M. Sun, noon-5P.M.

Catalog: free sales flyers

Accepts: check, money order, Visa, MasterCard, Discover, American Express

Layaway: 6 months

Discounts: bulk order, frequent customer, club

Old/special items: bunnies

MODERN BEARS:

Germany: Steiff

U.K.: Canterbury, Merrythought

U.S.A.: Applause/Raikes, Beaver Valley, Cooperstown Bears, Dakin, Gund, Madame Alexander Bears, Muffy, Vanderbear family, VIBs

Artist bears: Linda Spiegel-Lohre

Miniature bears: Gund, Steiff, Raikes

ACCESSORIES:

Clothes: NAB

Furniture: NAB

Figurines: Muffy

Bear collectibles: ornaments, tea sets

Shows: NY

In business for 14 years

JUSTIN TYMES CHRISTMAS COTTAGE

Peggy Gilmore, owner

13499 U.S. 41 S.E. #241

Ft. Myers, FL 33907

Phone: 813-489-0688

Phone orders accepted.

Hours: Sun, noon-5P.M., M, T, W, Sat, 10A.M.-6P.M., TH, F, 10A.M.-9P.M.

Accepts: check, money order, Visa, MasterCard

Layaway: 20% down, 90 days

Old/special items: bunnies

MODERN BEARS:

U.S.A.: Beaver Valley, Boyds, Gund, Lone Star, Madame Alexander Bears, Mary Meyer, Muffy, Vanderbear family

Artist bears: Terry Hayes, Jill Kenny, Jackie Melerski-Saraf, Margaret Ann Corbett, Marie Zimmerman, Joan Woessner, Barbara Ferrier, Joe & Monty Sours, Millie Gage, Edith Foks Ferrageau, Linda S. Stafford, Susan R. Smith, Carol Kirby, Ann Carlo, Veronica Dooling, Karen Sheets, Belle Hagerty, Sheila Schuchert, Carolyn Lamothe, Lonnie St. Martin

Figurines: Boyds Bearstone, Cast Art Industries, Character Collectibles, Cherished Teddies, Muffy, United Design Corp., Summerhill Crystal

Bear collectibles: stationery, tea sets

In business for 6 years

KEEPSAKE DOLLS & BEARS

Tom & Norma Huczek

P.O. Box 811

Abingdon, MD 21009-0811

Phone: 410-838-4954

Phone orders accepted.

Mail order only.

Hours: Call M-F, 9A.M.-5P.M. Leave message on weekends.

Catalog: free

Accepts: check, money order

Layaway: 25% down, 3 equal monthly payments, 90 days

Discounts: club

Old/special items: golliwogs (contemporary), bunnies

MODERN BEARS:

U.S.A.: Boyds, Gund, Muffy, Vanderbear family, VIBs, North American Bear Co. (other)

Artist bears: Jaisy Martin, Kimberly Hunt, Diane Martin, Dorothy DePaulo, Jan Brouwer, Mary George, Trudy Maderos/Marge Cochran, Mica Michele Friesen, Mary Wurster and more

Miniature bears: Durae Allen, Genesis Handsewn Miniatures by Tom, Carol Stewart, Deborah L. Drown, Stacy Pio, Deborah Jo Ferguson, Deborah Didier, Lana Rickabaugh, Tracy Main, Mary Fran Baldo and more

ACCESSORIES:

Clothes: sweaters

Bear collectibles: stationery, Winnie-the-Pooh collectibles

Shows: East Coast

In business for 6 years

KENDALLWOOD CRAFTS

Sandy

1092 Black Gap Rd.

Fayetteville, PA 17222

Phone: 717-352-9493

Phone orders accepted.

Mail order only.

Catalog: free

Accepts: check, money order

ACCESSORIES:

Jewelry

Clothes: hand-knitted sweaters

Bear collectibles: jewelry; Bear pins are handcrafted fabric pins with an attached teddy bear button. They can be worn by bears or humans.

In business for 2 years

LAUREL COTTAGE

Lori Woo, owner

1525 Aviation Blvd., #143

Redondo Beach, CA 90278-2800

Phone: 310-769-0590

Fax: 310-538-3453

Fax orders accepted from established customers only.

Mail order only.

Catalog: SASE with 75 cents postage

Accepts: check, money order

Layaway: $100 minimum, 25% down, 4 months

Bear collectibles: Winnie-the-Pooh collectibles

Shows: Disneyana

In business for 6 years

LIL' DAVID'S WOODBOX

David & Ingrid Lipscomb

Rt. 3, Box 205

Luray, VA 22835

Phone: 703-743-9336

Phone orders accepted.

Fax: 703-743-9336

Fax orders accepted.

Hours: by appointment

Accepts: check, money order, Visa, MasterCard, Discover

Layaway: 25% down, 3 equal payments, 3 months, no refunds—credit only

Discounts: frequent buyer

Old/special items: antique bears (bought and sold), golliwogs, bunnies, antique bear collectibles

MODERN BEARS:

Germany: Hans Clemens, Grisly Spielwaren, Gebruder Hermann, Hermann-Spielwaren, Steiff

Artist bears: Linda Beckman, Nancy Brown, Jody Battaglia, Doris Beck, Marsha Friesen, Renee Gladden, Shirley Howey, Kathleen Wallace, Judy Krantz, Donna McCurry, Barbara Troxel, Vicki Stephan, Joan Woessner, Catherine While, Terry Woods, Terri Hayes, Bears of the Abbey and more

Miniature bears: Carol Stewart, Patricia Carriker, Rose Policky, Jaimie Wu, Barbara Garrett

Bear collectibles: antique collectibles, books about bears, chinaware, jewelry, postcards, tea sets

Shows: MA, PA, NJ, MD, VA, FL, OH, MI, KY, MO, TX, OK, NY, CT, GA

In business for 11 years

LINDA'S LOV-LEZ HOUSE OF DOLLS, BEARS & MORE

Linda A. Kemp, owner

9103 Mentor Ave.

Mentor, OH 44060

Phone: 216-255-3655

Phone orders accepted.

Accepts: check, money order, Visa, MasterCard

Layaway: 33% down, 33% in 30 days, 33% in 60 days

Discounts: frequent customer, frequent sales

Old/special items: bears manufactured 1945-1970, bunnies

MODERN BEARS:

Canada: Ganz Bros.

Germany: Steiff

U.K.: Canterbury, Merrythought, Paddington

U.S.A.: Applause/Raikes, Boyds, Russ Berrie, Dakin, Gund, Madame Alexander Bears, Mary Meyer, Muffy, Vanderbear family, VIBs, Ty

Other modern manufactured bears: Kin, Takara

Artist bears: Denise Wade, Anita O'Hara, Diana Pinizotto, Bonnie O'Neill, Debbie Dennis and more

Miniature bears: Anita O'Hara, Diana Pinizotto, Debbie Dennis

ACCESSORIES:
Glasses, jewelry, swings, see-saws

Clothes: custom-made

Furniture: benches and more

Bear collectibles: books about bears, books about bearmaking, books about collecting, jewelry, postcards, stationery, tea sets

Shows: OH

In business for 5 years

LORINDA'S
Lorinda Emling, owner
6336 N. Oracle Rd., Suite 326-208
Tucson, AZ 85704
Phone: 602-628-3173
Phone orders accepted.
Mail order only.
Catalog: LSASE
Accepts: check, money order
Layaway: 25% down. Less than $100: 1 month. More than $100: 3 months
Old/special items: antique bears, bears manufactured between WWI and WWII, bears manufactured 1945-1970, bunnies

MODERN BEARS:
Germany: Steiff
Miniature bears: Steiff, occasionally old miniature bears. Specializes in Steiff animals, especially older animals.
Shows: AZ
In business for 7 years

MA MA BEARS
Norma Ganderson, owner
5268 Wethersfield Rd.
Jamesville, NY 13078
Additional addresses:
#1 Shoppingtown Mall
Dewitt, NY 13214;
Faneuil Hall Market
Boston, MA 02109
Phone: 315-446-GRRR, 617-557-GRRR or 1-800-446-BEAR for orders
Phone orders accepted.

Fax: 315-449-4007
Fax orders accepted.
Hours: M-Sat, 10A.M.-9P.M. Sun, noon-6P.M.
Accepts: check, money order, Visa, MasterCard, Discover, American Express
Layaway: 25% down, 60 days

MODERN BEARS:
Canada: Ganz Bros.
Germany: Hans Clemens, Grisly Spielwaren, Gebruder Hermann, Schuco, Steiff
Italy: Trudi Giocattoli
U.K.: Canterbury, Deans, Little Folk, Merrythought, Paddington
U.S.A.: Applause/Raikes, Boyds, Russ Berrie, California Stuffed Toys, Cooperstown Bears, Dakin, Gund, Jona, Lone Star, The Manhattan Toy Co., Mary Meyer, Muffy, Vanderbear family, VIBs, North American Bear Co. (other), R. John Wright, Michaud Collection, Vermont, J.J. Wind, Ty, Princess Soft Toys
Artist bears: Bearly There, Kathy Jordan, Chester Freeman
Miniature bears: Akira

ACCESSORIES:
Baskets, glasses
Clothes available.
Furniture available.
Miniature furniture available.
Figurines: Boyds Bearstone, Cherished Teddies, Lucy & Me, Muffy, The Roosevelt Bears
Bear collectibles: books about bears, books about bearmaking, books about collecting, chinaware, jewelry, bear magazines, dollhouse miniatures, ornaments, Paddington collectibles, postcards, stationery, tea sets, Winnie-the-Pooh collectibles
Shows: Northeast
In business for 11 years

MARILYN'S WORLD, INC.
Marilyn Kent, president
4630 Univeristy Dr.
Lauderhill, FL 33351
Phone: 305-742-7353
Phone orders accepted.
Fax: 305-742-6444
Fax orders accepted.
Hours: M-F, 10A.M.-5P.M. Sat, 11A.M.-4P.M.
Accepts: check, money order, Visa, Mas-

terCard, Discover, American Express
Layaway: 33% down, 120 days, no interest

MODERN BEARS:
U.K.: Canterbury, Merrythought
U.S.A.: Applause/Raikes, Cooperstown Bears, Dakin, Gund, Muffy, Vanderbear family, VIBs, Vermont
Artist bears: Linda Ashcraft, Debbie Altman, Durae Allen, Darci Andrews, Genie Buttita, Carol Black, Celia Baham, Wendy Brent, Mike & Val Freeland, Pat Fye, Sue & Margaret Corbett, Sue & Randall Foskey, Lenore DeMent, Deanna Brittsen, Dolores Groseck, Jo-An Gast, Donna Hodges, Terry Hayes, Holly Dyer, Suzanne Golden, Sereita Harrell, Debra Bedwel-Koonz, Susan B. Johnson, Heidi Miller, Rose Leshko, Mary Holstad, Wanda Shope, Robert Raikes, Yvonne Plakke, Gloria Rosenbaum, Joan Woessner, Barbara Whisnant, Karen Sawin, Julie Woolf, Susan Orr, John Paul Port, Mary Timme
Miniature bears: Jerri Booker, Renee Casey, Peggy Flemming, Jo-An Gast, Bev Landstra, Carol Stewart, Pauline Weir

ACCESSORIES:
Clothes: NAB
Figurines: Muffy
Bear collectibles: boxes, jewelry
More about collectibles: boxes are Crummels handpainted English enamel boxes. Jewelry is 14K and sterling silver bear jewelry.
Shows: FL
In business for 11 years

MARJ'S DOLL SANCTUARY
Marjory Timmerman, owner
5238 Plainfield Ave. NE
Grand Rapids, MI 49505
Phone: 616-361-0054
Phone orders accepted.
Fax: 616-361-0232
Fax orders accepted.
Hours: M-Sat 10A.M.-6P.M.
Catalog: $2, refundable with purchase
Accepts: check, money order, Visa, MasterCard, Discover
Layaway: 20% down, monthly payments

MODERN BEARS:
Canada: Ganz Bros.
Germany: Steiff, Hermann

U.K.: Canterbury, Merrythought, Paddington

U.S.A.: Applause/Raikes, Boyds, Russ Berrie, Cooperstown Bears, Dakin, Gund, Muffy, Vanderbear family, VIBs, North American Bear Co. (other), R. John Wright, Michaud Collection, Vermont

Artist bears: More than 55 artists

Miniature bears: Several artists

Figurines: Jan Hagara Collectibles, Kelly Bears, Michaud Collection, Muffy

Bear collectibles: books about bears, books about bearmaking, books about collecting, bear magazines, ornaments, postcards, stationery, tea sets, Winnie-the-Pooh collectibles

Shows: MI, MN, OH, WI, KY, IN, TN

In business for 8 years

MARLENE'S SPECIALTY SHOP

Marlene Violette, owner

Lewiston Mall, 20 East Ave.

Lewiston, ME 04240

Phone: 207-783-2031 or 207-483-4780
Phone orders accepted.

Hours: M-Sat, 9:30A.M.-9P.M. Sun, noon-5P.M.

Accepts: check, money order, Visa, MasterCard, Discover, American Express

Layaway: 20% down. Length of layaway depends on price

Discounts: club

Old/special items: bunnies

MODERN BEARS:

Germany: Steiff

U.K.: Canterbury, Merrythought

U.S.A.: Beaver Valley, Boyds, Russ Berrie, Cooperstown Bears, Gund, Madame Alexander Bears, Mary Meyer, Muffy, Vanderbear family, VIBs, North American Bear Co., R. John Wright, Tilly, Princess, Ty, Michaud Collection

Artist bears: Carol Black, Linda Spiegel-Lohre, Vermont Treadle, Grandpapa

Figurines: Boyds Bearstone, Jan Hagara, Muffy

Bear collectibles: paintings, tea sets, tote bags

In business for 12 years

MARTIN HOUSE DOLLS & TOYS

Linda Hartman, owner

46 Center St.

Thornhill, Ontario L4J 1E9, Canada

Phone: 905-881-0426
Phone orders accepted.

Fax: 905-886-6048
Fax orders accepted.

Hours: M-Sat, 10A.M.-5:30P.M. Sun, noon-5P.M.

Accepts: check, money order, Visa, MasterCard, American Express

Layaway: 20% down, 60 days or 25% down, 3 equal monthly payments

Discounts: bulk order, frequent customer, club

Old/special items: antique bears, bears manufactured between WWI and WWII, bears manufactured 1945-1970, golliwogs, antique bear collectibles, bunnies

MODERN BEARS:

Canada: Ganz Bros., Mighty Star

Germany: Kathe Kruse Puppen, Steiff

U.K.: Canterbury, Deans, Little Folk, Merrythought, Paddington

U.S.A.: Applause/Raikes, Beaver Valley, Boyds, Charlene Kinser Designs, Cooperstown Bears, Dakin, Gund, The Manhattan Toy Co., Mary Meyer, Muffy, Vanderbear family, VIBs, North American Bear Co. (other), Michaud Collection, Ty

Artist bears: McB Bears, Nostalgic Bear Co., Donna Hodges, Wendy Brent, Goose Creek, Joan Woessner, Bearly There, R. John Wright, Linda Harris, Sue McKay, Lesley Mallet, Jean Paccagnan and many more Canadian artists

Miniature bears: Phyllis Sirota, Frances Armstrong

ACCESSORIES:

Baskets, glasses, hair ribbons, swings, jewelry, shoes, socks

Clothes: complete outfits, handknit sweaters

Furniture: chairs, loveseats, NAB

Miniature accessories: baskets, umbrellas

Miniature clothes available.

Miniature furniture: chairs, loveseats, houses

Figurines: Boyds Bearstone, Cherished Teddies, Colour Box Miniatures, Jan Hagara Collectibles, Lucy & Me, Michaud Collection, Sarah's Attic

Bear collectibles: books about bears, books about bearmaking, bear magazines, dollhouse miniatures, orna-

ments, Paddington collectibles, paintings, postcards, pottery, prints, stationery, tea sets, tins, tote bags, Winnie-the-Pooh collectibles and more

Shows: Ontario

In business for 11 years

MARY D'S DOLLS & BEARS & SUCH

Mary Dee, proprietor

8409 W. Broadway

Minneapolis, MN 55445

Phone: 612-424-4375
Phone orders accepted.

Fax: 612-424-8643
Fax orders accepted.

Hours: M, F, Sat, 10A.M.-4P.M. T, W 10A.M.-6P.M. TH, 10A.M.-8P.M.

Catalog: $1

Accepts: money order, Visa, MasterCard, Discover

Layaway: 33% down, 33% in 30 days, balance in 60 days

Discounts: club

Old/special items: bunnies

MODERN BEARS:

Germany: Grisly Spielwaren Hermann-Spielwaren, Kathe Kruse Puppen, Steiff

Italy: Trudi Giocattoli

U.K.: Canterbury, Merrythought, Paddington

U.S.A.: Applause/Raikes, Boyds, Dakin, Gund, Madame Alexander Bears, Mary Meyer, Muffy, Vanderbear family, VIBs, North American Bear Co. (other), R. John Wright, Michaud Collection, Vermont

Artist bears: Donna Hodges, Bearons of La Jolla, Cranberry Mountain, Bearly There, Golden Harlequin, Gloria Franks, Bear Elegance, We're Bears, Von Hayderschott, Can't Bear To Part, Ribeary Bears, Blacklick Bears, Becky Wheeler

Miniature bears: Akira, Becky Wheeler, Pauline Weir, Dolores Ribordy

ACCESSORIES:

Baskets, glasses, shoes, socks, stands, cases

Clothes: professional clothes, holiday clothes, NAB

Furniture: tables & chairs, beds, park benches

Miniature accessories: glasses

Miniature furniture: tables & chairs, benches

Figurines: Boyds Bearstone, Cherished Teddies, Jan Hagara Collectibles, Muffy

Bear collectibles: books about bears, books about bearmaking, books about collecting, boxes, chinaware, jewelry, bear magazines, ornaments, Paddington collectibles, paintings, postcards, prints, stationery, tea sets, tins, tote bags, Winnie-the-Pooh collectibles

Shows: MN, WI, IL

In business for 15 years

BONITA L. WARRINGTON MCCONNELL

39619 Calle Cascada

Green Valley, CA 91350

Phone: 805-270-9016

Phone orders: 9A.M.-5P.M.

Mail order only.

Bear collectibles: handmade bear Christmas ornaments

Shows: CA

GRETCHEN MCKILLIP

45 W. Imperial Dr.

Walla Walla, WA 99362

Phone: 509-525-0395

Phone orders: 10A.M.-5P.M.

Mail order only.

Bear collectibles: pins with fabric sculpted bear heads with beading, vintage buttons, handmade bear purses, greeting cards from original drawings. All collectibles are made by Gretchen.

MINIATURE WORLD & GIFTS OF CAREFREE

Phyllis Risken, owner

99 Easy St., P.O. Box 5508

Carefree, AZ 85377

Phone: 602-488-2612

Phone orders accepted.

Accepts: check, money order, Visa, MasterCard, Discover, American Express

Layaway: 30-60 days

Discounts: certain items

MODERN BEARS:

Germany: Gebruder Hermann

U.S.A.: Applause/Raikes, Boyds, Dakin, Gund, Lone Star, Madame Alexander Bears, Muffy, Vanderbear family, VIBs, North American Bear Co. (other)

ACCESSORIES:

Baskets, glasses

Clothes available.

Furniture available.

Miniature accessories: baskets

Miniature clothes available.

Miniature furniture available.

Figurines: Boyds Bearstone, Muffy, United Design Corp.

Bear collectibles: books about bears, chinaware, jewelry, dollhouse miniatures, tea sets

Shows: AZ

In business for 21 years

MOM'S CEDAR CHEST

Wendy Starr Kirtland, owner

1831 Ximeno Ave.

Long Beach, CA 90815

Phone: 310-985-0089

Phone orders accepted.

Fax: 310-434-5558

Fax orders accepted.

Hours: M-Sat, 10A.M.-6P.M. Sun, noon-5P.M.

Accepts: check, money order, Visa, MasterCard, Discover

Layaway: $50 minimum, 20% down, 60 days

Discounts: frequent order discount on certain merchandise

Old/special items: bunnies

MODERN BEARS:

U.S.A.: Boyds, Gund, Muffy, Vanderbear family, Bunnies by the Bay

ACCESSORIES:

Glasses

Clothes: NAB, Boyds

Furniture: NAB, Boyds

Figurines: Boyds Bearstone, Cherished Teddies, Muffy

Bear collectibles: ornaments, stationery, tea sets, Winnie-the-Pooh collectibles

In business for 4 years

MOORE BEARS

John Moore, owner

P.O. Box 232, Route 896

Strasburg, PA 17579

Phone: 717-687-6954 or 717-687-7545

Phone orders accepted.

Hours: M-TH, 9A.M.-8P.M. F, Sat, 9A.M.-9P.M.

Catalog: $4, refundable with purchase

Accepts: check, money order, Visa, Mas-

terCard, Discover, American Express, MAC

Layaway: 10% down, 60 days, no refunds

Discounts: bulk order, in-store club

MODERN BEARS:

Canada: Ganz Bros.

Germany: Grisly Spielwaren, Gebruder Hermann, Steiff

U.K.: Canterbury, Deans, Little Folk, Merrythought, Paddington

U.S.A.: Applause/Raikes, Boyds, Russ Berrie, Dakin, Gund, Jona, The Manhattan Toy Co., Mary Meyer, Muffy, Vanderbear family, VIBs, North American Bear Co. (other), Vermont

Artist bears: cm Bears, Bailey Bears, Barbara's Originals, Bear Elegance, Bearly There, Bearons of La Jolla, Carol Black Originals, Busser Bears, Bears from Sandy's Heart, Cassner Bears, Crabapple Bears, Cranberry Mountain Bears, Chester Freeman, French Bear Co., Ginger Bears, Grumpie's Bears, Jaisy's Bear Hugs, Sheppard Seabears, Julie Jones, Joyful Bears, Just Wee Bears, MJ's Bears, Pat's Bears & Collectibles, Purely Neysa, Ribeary Bears, River Cottage Bears, River Hills Bears, Winey Bears, Teddies are for Real

Miniature bears: Akira, Bears by Debora, Little Critters, Carol Stewart Miniatures, Janet Wilson Bears and more

ACCESSORIES:

Kits, glasses, shoes, socks

Clothes: sweaters, play outfits, hats, scarves, collars, sweatsuits, sweatshirts, etc.

Furniture: upholstered and wooden chairs, rockers

Figurines: Boyds Bearstone, Cherished Teddies, Lucy & Me, Muffy

Bear collectibles: books about collecting, chinaware, clothing for people, bear magazines, Smokey bear collectibles, stationery, tea sets, Winnie-the-Pooh collectibles, greeting cards

In business for 10 years

MOSTLY BEARS

7355 Ralston Rd.

Arvada, CO 80002

MOUNTAIN CREATIONS

Shari Woodstein, owner
19055 E. 16th Pl.
Aurora, CO 80011
Phone: 303-343-7113
Phone orders accepted.
Mail order only.
Catalog: $2, refundable with purchase
Accepts: check, money order
Layaway: 25% down, 25% per month
Artist bears: Shari Woodstein
Miniature bears: Shari Woodstein

ACCESSORIES:
Swings, teeter totters
Clothes: sweaters, hats
Furniture: chairs
Miniature clothes: sweaters, hats
Shows: CO
In business for 3 years

MULBERRY STREET TOYS

Diane Green, manager
9310 Transit Rd.
East Amherst, NY 14051
Phone: 716-688-7112
Phone orders accepted.
Fax: 716-625-9559
Fax orders accepted.
Hours: M-Sat, 10A.M.-8P.M. Sun, noon-5P.M.
Catalog: free
Accepts: check, money order, Visa, MasterCard, Discover
Layaway: 20% down, 90 days, no refunds—store credit only
Discounts: special events, shoppers' card
Old/special items: bunnies

MODERN BEARS:
Germany: Steiff, Haida
Italy: Trudi Giocattoli
U.K.: Canterbury, Deans, Merrythought, Paddington
U.S.A.: Applause/Raikes, Boyds, Cooperstown Bears, Dakin, Gund, Mary Meyer, Muffy, Vanderbear family, VIBs, North American Bear Co. (other), Vermont, RJs-Polo, Bearly People
Artist bears: Linda Spiegel, Linda Hejna, Kathie Jordan, Coventry
Miniature bears: Debbie Ortega, Steiff, Akira (Deborah Canham), Adelle, Gund

ACCESSORIES:
Baskets, glasses, shoes, socks
Clothes: NAB, Boyds, regular doll clothes
Furniture: Boyds, doll furniture
Miniature accessories: baskets, glasses, shoes, socks, Radio Flyer wagons
Miniature clothes available.
Miniature furniture: doll furniture
Figurines: Muffy
Bear collectibles: books about bears, bear magazines, dollhouse miniatures, ornaments, Paddington collectibles, postcards, stationery, tea sets, tote bags, Winnie-the-Pooh collectibles
Shows: Western NY
In business for 11 years

NATURAL SETTINGS

Peter J. Carino, president
P.O. Box 104
Great River, NY 11739
Phone: 1-800-409-9603
Phone orders accepted.
Fax: 516-589-4093
Fax orders accepted.
Mail order only.
Catalog: free
Accepts: check, money order, Visa, MasterCard, Discover
Discounts: bulk order, frequent order (for distributors)
Bear collectibles: unique line of postcards, stationery and greeting cards
Offers a two-week free trial period to retail stores
Shows: Northeast
In business for 3 years

NEEDHAM HOUSE

Terry John Woods, Dale West
RR #1, Box 240, Eastham Rd.
Shrewsbury, VT 05738
Phone: 802-492-3715
Phone orders accepted.
Catalog: $4
Accepts: check, money order, Visa, MasterCard
Old/ special items: antique bear collectibles
Artist bears: Blackwoods Design

ACCESSORIES:
Clothes: antique
Furniture: antique, antique reproductions
Shows: New England states

In business for 7 years

NOBODY'S TEDDY

Lilly Roy, owner
2840 Biddle Ave.
Wyandotte, MI 48192
Phone: 313-246-3655 or 1-800-596-BEAR for orders
Phone orders accepted.
Fax: 313-285-2056
Fax orders accepted.
Hours: M-TH, 9:30A.M.-6P.M. F, 9:30A.M.-8P.M. in summer, and 9:30A.M.-6P.M. in winter. Sundays occasionally.
Accepts: check, money order, Visa, MasterCard, Discover, American Express
Layaway: special orders: 50% down
Other sales: 20% down, payments every 2 weeks
Discounts: store sales
Old/special items: bunnies

MODERN BEARS:
Germany: Gebruder Hermann, Kathe Kruse Puppen, Steiff
U.K.: Canterbury, Deans, Merrythought, Paddington
U.S.A.: Applause/Raikes, Boyds, Charlene Kinser Designs, Cooperstown Bears, Dakin, Gund, Mary Meyer, Muffy, VIBs, Michaud Collection, Vermont
Artist bears: Linda Spiegel-Lohre, Joann Mitchel
Miniature bears: Gund, Steiff

ACCESSORIES:
Glasses, leather suitcases
Clothes: robes, hats, sweaters, leather outfits, etc.
Furniture: beds, chairs
Figurines: Boyds Bearstone, Muffy
Bear collectibles: books about bears, books about collecting, boxes, bear magazines, ornaments, Paddington collectibles, postcards, stationery, Winnie-the-Pooh collectibles, Coca-Cola bears, straws, key chains, teddy tum tum
In business for 3 years

NOW & THEN ANTIQUES & GIFTS

Anne Doorley, owner
292 Main St.
Nyack, NY 10960
Second address:
20 Powderhorn Rd.

Ardsley, NY 10502

Phone: 914-693-1557 or 914-353-1797
  Phone orders accepted.

Hours: W-Sun, 11A.M.-5P.M.

Accepts: check, money order, Visa, MasterCard

Layaway: 33% down, 33% in 30 days, balance in 60 days

Old/special items: antique bears, bears manufactured between WWI and WWII, bears manufactured 1945-1970, antique bear collectibles

MODERN BEARS:

U.S.A.: Applause/Raikes, Boyds, Charlene Kinser Designs, Cooperstown Bears, Gund, Ideal, Mary Meyer, Muffy, Vanderbear family, VIBs, North American Bear Co. (other), R. John Wright

Artist bears: varies

Miniature bears: varies

ACCESSORIES:

Baskets, glasses

Clothes available.

Furniture available.

Miniature accessories: glasses, hair ribbons

Miniature furniture available.

Bear collectibles: books about bears, postcards, Winnie-the-Pooh collectibles

Shows: NJ, NY

In business for 21 years

OLD-TIMERS ANTIQUES

Elizabeth Neitz, owner
3717-B South Dixie Hwy.
West Palm Beach, FL 33405

Phone: 407-832-5141
  Phone orders accepted.

Fax: 407-832-5141
  Fax orders accepted.

Hours: M-Sat, 10A.M.-5P.M. 24-hour fax and answering machine

Catalog: $10/year

Accepts: check, money order, Visa, MasterCard, American Express

Layaway available.

Discounts: monthly sales on selected items

Old/special items: antique bears, bears manufactured between WWI and WWII, bears manufactured 1945-1970 (all Steiff), antique bear collectibles

MODERN BEARS:

Germany: Steiff

Miniature bears: Steiff

ACCESSORIES:

Baskets

Clothes: collars, sweaters

Bear collectibles: books about Steiff bears, books about collecting, Steiff jewelry, postcards, tea sets, tote bags, watches, signs

Shows: FL, NY, OH, Midwest

In business for 8 years

OUT OF THE WOODS

Steve Orique & Alan Clark
3516 Lydia Lane
Modesto, CA 95357

THE OWL'S NEST

Beth Riedl, owner
P.O. Box 6599
Carmel, CA 93921

Phone: 408-624-5509
  Phone orders accepted.

Hours: Summer: M-Sat, 10:30A.M.-5P.M. Winter: varies

Accepts: check, money order, Visa, MasterCard, American Express

Layaway: 33% down, 3 months

Old/special items: golliwogs, bunnies

Artist bears: Cindy Martin, Pam Young, Barbara Ferrier, Mary George, Carol Pearce, Pat Murphy, Sandy Fleming, Terri Hayes, Kathy Corley, Connie Hindmarsh, Kathy Wallace, Lori Murphy and more

Miniature bears: Diane Turbarg, Pam Holton, Kelli Kilby, Heather Isaacs, Roger Morris, Vic Fortunato, Pat Carriker, Sarah Misserian, Linda Nelson, Brenda Dewey and more

Miniature furniture: Rough Rider, Teddy Roosevelt chairs by Pamm Bacon

Shows: IL, NY, CT, MA, NY, MD, VA, FL

In business for 14 years

THE PAPER PLACE & DOLL PLACE

Tami Tammen, manager
212 S. River Ave.
Holland, MI 49423

Phone: 616-392-7776
  Phone orders accepted.

Second address:
118 Washington St.

Grand Haven, MI 49417

Fax: 616-392-2499
  Fax orders accepted.

Hours: Holland: M, TH, F, 9A.M.-9P.M. T, W, Sat, 9A.M.-6P.M. Grand Haven: M-TH, Sat, 9A.M.-6P.M. F, 9A.M.-9P.M. Call for seasonal hours.

Catalog: $3, refundable with purchase

Accepts: check, money order, Visa, MasterCard, Discover

Layaway: 20% down, $3 layaway fee. 60 days—12 months depending on purchase price.

Old/special items: bunnies

MODERN BEARS:

Canada: Ganz Bros.

Germany: Grisly Spielwaren, Gebruder Hermann, Steiff, Miro

U.K.: Canterbury, Merrythought, Paddington

U.S.A.: Applause/Raikes, Boyds, Dakin, Gund, Mary Meyer, Muffy, Vanderbear family, VIBs, North American Bear Co. (other), Middleton, Orzek Bears

More about these bears: Retired Dakin only. Muffy Gingerbear, Snowflake and other retired NAB pieces.

Artist bears: Sue Foskey, Donna Hodges, Renee Gladden, Joyce Haughey, McBee Bears, Harlequin Bears, Old Tyme Teddy Bears, KC & The Bears, Jane Kidder, Jenny Krantz, Just Wee Bears, Luvables & Huggables, Maryanna, Wiseman, Beverly Port for Gorham, Quite a Bear Company

Miniature bears: German, Gund, handmade Chu-Ming Wu

ACCESSORIES:

Clothes: Vanderbear clothes, sweaters, Santa coats

Figurines: Muffy, Pooh bear by Michel & Co.

Bear collectibles: books about bears, books about collecting, bear magazines, ornaments, Paddington collectibles, postcards, stationery, tea sets, tote bags, Winnie-the-Pooh collectibles, paper dolls, rubber stamps

In business for 12 years

PAT'S KOUNTRY KITCHEN & KOLLECTIBLES

Patricia Brink, owner
70 Mill Rock Rd.
Old Saybrook, CT 06475

Phone: 203-395-3349
Phone orders accepted.
Fax: 203-388-6669
Fax orders accepted.
Hours: 10A.M.-7P.M.
Accepts: check, Visa, MasterCard

MODERN BEARS:
U.S.A.: Boyds, Russ Berrie, The Manhattan Toy Co.
Artist bears: Odette Conley, Nancy Conley, Bev White, Diane Sherman Turbarg
Miniature bears: Odete Conley, Nancy Conley, Diane Sherman Turbarg

ACCESSORIES:
Glasses
Clothes: Boyds
Furniture: chairs
Miniature furniture: rocking chair horse or rooster
Figurines: Boyds Bearstone
Bear collectibles: books about bears, ornaments, postcards, prints, stationery, tea sets
In business for 2 years

PAW PRINTS
Kristina Shankel
351 South Frost
Saginaw, MI 48603-6029
Phone: 517-793-5256
Phone orders accepted.
Mail order only.
Bear collectibles: postcards, prints
More about collectibles: Postcards and prints are all based on photographs by Kristina Shankel

PEARLBEAR TOGS—PEARLBEAR DESIGNS
Pearl Frank, president
157 Countryside Dr.
Summit, NJ 07901
Phone: 908-665-0381
Phone orders accepted.
Mail order only.
Catalog: $3, refundable with purchase.
Accepts: check, money order, Visa, MasterCard, American Express
Layaway available on bears
Artist bears: Pearlbear Designs

ACCESSORIES:
Purses
Clothes: Pearlbear Togs—clothing for any size bear, hats. Custom orders also available.
Miniature accessories: purses

Miniature clothes: Pearlbear Togs, custom orders, hats
Shows: NJ
In business for 9 years

PEWTER CLASSICS DOLLS & BEARS
Linda Dryer, owner
3584 Bromley SE
Grand Rapids, MI 49512
Phone: 616-942-8822 or 1-800-833-3655 for orders
Phone orders accepted.
Fax: 616-942-5848
Fax orders accepted.
Catalog: free
Accepts: check, money order, Visa, MasterCard, Discover
Layaway: 20% down, monthly payments, 90 days
Discounts: club

MODERN BEARS:
Germany: Steiff
U.S.A.: Boyds, Gund, Madame Alexander Bears, Mary Meyer, Muffy, Vanderbear family, VIBs, North American Bear Co. (other), Michaud Collection, Bearly People
Artist bears: McB Bears, Bearons of La Jolla, Carol Black, Carol Darling, Linda Spiegel, Penny Noble, Linda Nelson, LuAnn Linton, Kay Elmore, Barbie's Bears, Gloria Rosenbaum, Sue Foskey, Michelle Debevic, Cathy Wilder
Miniature bears: Linda Nelson, LuAnn Linton, Jessie Wilder

ACCESSORIES:
Jewelry
Miniature accessories: baskets
Figurines: Boyds Bearstone, Cairn Studio, Cast Art Industries, Cherished Teddies, Jan Hagara Collectibles, Laura's Attic, Michaud Collection, Muffy, Sarah's Attic, United Design Corp.
Bear collectibles: books about bears, chinaware, clothing for people, jewelry, bear magazines, tea sets, tins
Shows: MI, OH, IL
In business for 11 years

PICKWICK PURVEYORS
Jacklyn Gualtieri, owner
8 Spring Ridge Dr.
Berkeley Hts, NJ 07922
Phone: 908-508-1711

Fax: 908-665-9333
Fax orders accepted.
Mail order only.
Catalog: $3, refundable with purchase
Accepts: check, money order, Visa, MasterCard

MODERN BEARS:
Germany: Haida
U.S.A.: Boyds
Artist bears: Jacklyn M. Gualtieri and more
Bear collectibles: books about bears, jewelry, bear magazines, stationery, tea sets
Shows: Northeast
In business for 6 years

THE PIED PIPER
Robyn Hussey, manager
350 S. Main St.
Plymouth, MI 48170
Phone: 313-459-3410 or 1-800-336-3410
Phone orders accepted.
Hours: M-TH, 10A.M.-5:30P.M. F, 10A.M.-8P.M. Sat, 10A.M.-5:30P.M. Sun, noon-5P.M.
Accepts: check, money order, Visa, MasterCard, Discover, American Express
Layaway: 20% down. payments every 2 months
Discounts: artist bear club: buy 5 at full retail price and 6th is free

MODERN BEARS:
Germany: Steiff
U.K.: Canterbury, Merrythought, Paddington
U.S.A.: Applause/Raikes, Boyds, Dakin, Gund, Madame Alexander Bears, Muffy, North American Bear Co. (other)
Artist bears: Annemade, The Bear Lady, Bearaphanalia, Martha DeRaimo, FoxFire, Golden Harlequin, Goose Creek, Hug A Bear, Grandpapa Jingles, Just Wee Bears, Lori Murphy, Pawquette, Ro Bears, Steiner Bears, Stuf'd Stuff, Von Hayderschatt

ACCESSORIES:
Baskets, glasses, jewelry
Furniture: white wicker, Boyds twig
Bear collectibles: books about bears, books about collecting, tea sets

R & M TRADING CO.
Linda Miller
614 Carriage Dr.
Batavia, IL 60510
Phone: 708-879-8154 or 1-800-688-8890
  Phone orders accepted.
Mail order only.
Catalog: available
Accepts: check, money order, Visa, MasterCard
Miniature bears: China imports, Akira
Bear collectibles: jewelry, tins, tote bags, English porcelain bear mugs, Teddy Bear Picnic puzzle
More about collectibles: Mug designs include: old bears, teddies and toys, Christmas bears, playtime bears, vintage bears and cars. They are sold in sets of three and come in 8 oz. and 10 oz.
In business for 2 years

JOAN RANKIN
155 Hochelaga St. W.
Moose Jaw, Saskatchewan S6H 2C2
Canada
Phone: 306-692-3341
  Phone orders: 8 A.M.-8 P.M.
Mail order only.
Bear collectibles: handmade teddy bear notecards featuring photographs of Joan's bears.
Shows: Alberta; Toronto, Ontario

THE RARE BEAR COLLECTOR
Juliet Savage and Lynn Van Name, partners
21 Mill Hill Rd., P.O. Box 612
Woodstock, NY 12498
Phone: 914-679-4201 (shop) or 914-679-5769 (mail order)
  Phone orders accepted.
Fax: 914-679-5769
  Fax orders accepted.
Hours: 11 A.M.-5 P.M. Extended hours during summer and holiday season
Catalog: $2
Accepts: check, money order, Visa, MasterCard
Layaway: 25% down, 25% per month
Discounts: frequent customer, club
Old/special items: antique bears, bears manufactured between WWI and WWII, bears manufactured 1945-1970, golliwogs, bunnies, antique bear collectibles

MODERN BEARS:
Germany: Grisly Spielwaren, Gebruder Hermann, Hermann-Spielwaren, Schuco, Steiff
U.K.: Wendy Boston, Canterbury, Chad Valley, Deans, Lefray/Real Soft Toys, Merrythought, Paddington
U.S.A.: Applause/Raikes, Beaver Valley, Boyds, Charlene Kinser Designs, Cooperstown Bears, Dakin, Gund, Ideal, Knickerbocker, Muffy, Vanderbear family, VIBs, North American Bear Co. (other), R. John Wright, Michaud Collection
Artist bears: Linda Noreika, Tammy Lawrence, Debbie Curtis, Heidi Steiner, Lori Ann Baker, Sally Winey, Sharon Dressman, Carol Martin, Carol Cavallaro, Kerry Ann Trueman, Debra Bedwell Koontz, Stier Bears
Miniature bears: Factoria Works, Mama, Kathy Rose

ACCESSORIES:
Glasses, musical instruments (8"-12" bears)
Clothes: sweaters, jackets, robes, NAB
Furniture: chairs, benches, NAB
Figurines: Boyds Bearstone, Muffy, The Roosevelt Bears, Mini Maria (hand-painted, pewter, jointed figurines made in England)
Bear collectibles: books about bears, books about bearmaking, books about collecting, chinaware, clothing for people, jewelry, bear magazines, prints, stationery, tea sets, tote bags
Shows: Northeast
In business for 6 years

THE ROCKING HORSE GALLERY
803 Caroline St.
Fredericksburg, VA 22401
Phone: 703-371-1894
  Phone orders accepted.
Hours: M-Sat, 11 A.M.-5 P.M. Sun, 1 P.M.-5 P.M.
Catalog: $5, refundable with purchase
Accepts: check, money order, Visa, MasterCard, Discover, American Express
Layaway: 33% down, 33% in 30 days, balance in 60 days
Old/special items: bunnies

MODERN BEARS:
Germany: Grisly Spielwaren, Steiff
U.K.: Canterbury, Merrythought, Paddington

U.S.A.: Beaver Valley, Boyds, Russ Berrie, Charlene Kinser Designs, Gund, Madame Alexander Bears, Muffy, Vanderbear family, VIBs, North American Bear Co. (other), Michaud Collection, Vermont
Artist bears: Large selection. Selection constantly changes.
Miniature bears: Carol Stewart

ACCESSORIES:
Rocking horses for 20"-36" bears
Clothes available.
Furniture: chairs, benches
Miniature furniture: chairs, benches
More about these accessories: custom-made accessories available
Figurines: Boyds Bearstone, Muffy
Bear collectibles: books about bears, books about collecting, jewelry, bear magazines, Paddington collectibles, paintings, prints, Smokey bear collectibles, stationery, Winnie-the-Pooh collectibles
Shows: Eastern USA
In business for 15 years

RUTH'S FLOWERS & GIFTS
Susan Minor, owner
108 S. Crittenden
Marshfield, MO 65706
Phone: 417-468-3110
  Phone orders accepted.
Fax: 417-468-7480
  Fax orders accepted.
Hours: M-F, 8:30 A.M.-5 P.M. Sat, 9 A.M.-2 P.M.
Accepts: check, money order, Visa, MasterCard, Discover, American Express
Layaway: 20% down, 30 days
Old/special items: bunnies

MODERN BEARS:
U.S.A.: Boyds, Russ Berrie & Co.
Artist bears: bears and bunnies custom made with silk and dried flowers

ACCESSORIES:
Clothes: Boyds
Furniture: chairs, benches
Figurines: Boyds Bearstone
Bear collectibles: jewelry, tea sets, calendars
In business for 7 years

THE SANDPIPER
George E. Geib, owner
500 Cypress, #51
Pismo Beach, CA 93449

Phone: 805-773-0122 or 1-800-451-0810
Phone orders accepted.
Hours: 7 days, 10:30A.M.-5:30P.M.
Accepts: money order, Visa, MasterCard, Discover, American Express
Layaway: 33% down, 3 monthly payments

MODERN BEARS:
Germany: Steiff
U.S.A.: Boyds, Russ Berrie, Gund
Artist bears: Nona's Bears, Toni La Ciero, Joan Woessner, Leota Ordiway
Miniature bears: Akira, Solo Bears

ACCESSORIES:
Baskets, glasses
Clothes: Boyds
Figurines: Boyds Bearstone, United Design Corp., Dept. 56, Russ Berrie, Teddy Town, Teddy Babies, Teddy Bear Family
Bear collectibles: chinaware, jewelry, ornaments, paintings, pottery, prints, tea sets, greeting cards
More about collectibles: Pottery is Mill Creek Blue Mountain pottery. Nancy Phelp's watercolors and Donna Jacobsen's compressed charcoal on white birch are available.
Shows: CA
In business for 9 years

SARA'S BEARS & GIFTS
Sally A. Wells, owner
173 S. Yonge St.
Ormond Beach, FL 32174
Phone: 904-673-7272 or 1-800-988-4073
Phone orders accepted.
Catalog: free
Accepts: check, money order, Visa, MasterCard, Discover, American Express
Layaway: 25% down, 3 payments in 3 months
Discounts: frequent shopper's card ($20 discount after $200 spent)

MODERN BEARS:
Germany: Hermann-Spielwaren, Steiff
Italy: Trudi Giocattoli
U.K.: Canterbury, Merrythought, Paddington
U.S.A.: Applause/Raikes, Beaver Valley, Boyds, Russ Berrie, Cooperstown Bears, Dakin, Gund, Lone Star, Madame Alexander Bears, Mary Meyer, Muffy, Vanderbear family, VIBs,

North American Bear Co. (other), Michaud Collection
Artist bears: Edda Seiple, Joyce Haughey, Barbara Bessos, Jenny Krantz, Stephanie Daniels, Janet Reeves, Dee Hockenberry, Michaud
Miniature bears: Sherry Dodson

ACCESSORIES:
Baskets, glasses, hair ribbons, jewelry, shoes, socks
Clothes: custom-made
Furniture: wicker, wood
Miniature accessories: baskets
Miniature furniture available.
Figurines: Boyds Bearstone, Cherished Teddies, Michaud Collection, Muffy, Sarah's Attic
Bear collectibles: books about bears, books about bearmaking, books about collecting, boxes, chinaware, clothing for people, jewelry, bear magazines, Paddington collectibles, postcards, pottery, stationery, tea sets, tins, tote bags, Winnie-the-Pooh collectibles
Shows: FL
In business for 4 years

SASSY CATS & FRIENDS
Martha Thompson, owner
5 Hendersonville Rd.
Asheville, NC 28803
Phone: 704-274-1701
Phone orders accepted.
Accepts: check, money order, Visa, MasterCard, Discover, American Express
Layaway: 20% down, payments every 2 weeks
Discounts: bulk order, frequent customer, club
Old/special items: bunnies

MODERN BEARS:
Germany: Gebruder Hermann
U.K.: Canterbury, Deans, Merrythought
U.S.A.: Boyds, Gund, Michaud Collection
Artist bears: Donna Hodges, Robin Rive (New Zealand)

ACCESSORIES:
Baskets, glasses
Furniture available.
Figurines: Boyds Bearstone, Cherished Teddies, Colour Box Miniatures, Laura's Attic, Michaud Collection, Sarah's Attic, United Design Corp, Pennywhistle Lane

More about these figurines: Large selections of each
Bear collectibles: books about bears, books about collecting, boxes, jewelry, postcards, pottery, prints, Smokey bear collectibles, stationery, tea sets, tins, tote bags
In business for 10 years

THE SILLY OLD BEAR SHOP
Daniel Wilson, owner
80 Queen St., #1
Niagara on the Lake, Ontario L0S 1J0, Canada
Phone: 905-468-5411
Phone orders accepted.
Fax: 905-468-5411
Fax orders accepted.
Hours: Apr. 1-Dec. 31: 7 days, 10A.M.-5P.M. Jan. 1-Mar. 31: weekends only, 11A.M.-4P.M. Summer: 10A.M.-8P.M.
Catalog: free
Accepts: money order, Visa, MasterCard, American Express
Discounts: bulk order, frequent order, CAA and AAA members

MODERN BEARS:
U.S.A.: Gund
Artist bears: Rita Bond, Margaret Walpole, Louise Apps, Karen Pringle (The "B" Group)
Bear collectibles: books, gift cards, postcards, stationery, tins, Winnie-the-Pooh collectibles, including: dinnerware, wrapping paper, ceramics, gift bags, videos, rubber stamps, and several additional Poo items. Baby registry and gift certificates available.
In business for 2 years

SLADES DOLLS AND BEARS
Janie Slade, manager/buyer
328 S. Phillips Ave.
Sioux Falls, SD 57102
Phone: 605-332-5012
Phone orders accepted.
Hours: T-Sat, 10A.M.-5:30P.M. Sun, 11A.M.-2P.M. Mondays and evenings by appointment
Accepts: check, money order, Visa, MasterCard, Discover
Layaway: 33% down, 33% in 30 days, balance in 60 days. Extended time for items of $100 or more
Discounts: frequent customer
Old/special items: bunnies

MODERN BEARS:

Germany: Gebruder Hermann

U.K.: Merrythought

U.S.A.: Applause/Raikes, Boyds, Cooperstown Bears, Dakin, Gund, Mary Meyer, Muffy, Vanderbear family, VIBs, North American Bear Co. (other), Ty, Bearly People

Artist bears: Dee Hockenberry, Carol Modean, Muriel Townsend, Cindy Bartosewcz, Susan K. Orr, Julie K. Wolff, Steve Schutt

Miniature bears: Linda's Little Corner of the World

ACCESSORIES:

Glasses, jewelry

Clothes: sweaters

Furniture: chairs

Figurines: Boyds Bearstone, Cherished Teddies, Pennywhistle Lane (Enesco)

Bear collectibles: books about bears, books about collecting, chinaware, clothing for people, jewelry, ornaments, postcards, prints, stationery, tea sets, tote bags, Winnie-the-Pooh collectibles, paper dolls, plates

Shows: Midwest

In business for 1 year

SLEEPY HOLLOW

Cynthia Kline, owner

59 S. Green St.

East Stroudsburg, PA 18301

Phone: 717-421-8700 or 717-424-7711

Phone orders accepted.

Hours: Sat, Sun, 9A.M.-5P.M. Holidays (Memorial Day, July 4, etc.) 9A.M.-5P.M.

Accepts: check, money order, Visa, MasterCard

Layaway: downpayment is flexible, minimum 20%. Monthly payments.

Discounts: bulk order, frequent customer

Old/special items: bunnies

MODERN BEARS:

Germany: Steiff

U.K.: Merrythought

U.S.A.: Beaver Valley, Boyds, Gund, Lone Star, Muffy, Vanderbear family, VIBs, North American Bear Co. (other)

Artist bears: Donna Hodges, Linda Spiegel-Lohre, Barbar McConnell, Susan Redstreake-Geary, Lin's Wildlife Friends

ACCESSORIES:

Glasses, jewelry

Clothes: Boyds, dresses

Furniture: Boyds, handmade oak chairs, beds, high chairs, cradles

Figurines: Boyds Bearstone, Muffy, The Roosevelt Bears

Bear collectibles: jewelry, bear magazines, ornaments, stationery, tea sets, Winnie-the-Pooh collectibles

In business for 3 years

SOMETHING UNIQUE

Carla J. Gilstrap, partner

114 E. Main

Jenks, OK 74037

Phone: 918-299-3322 or 1-800-382-3277 for orders

Phone orders accepted.

Fax: 918-455-0495

Fax orders accepted.

Hours: M-Sat, 10:30A.M.-5P.M. Sun, 1P.M.-5P.M.

Accepts: check, money order, Visa, MasterCard, Discover

Layaway: 25% down, 60 days

Discounts: frequent customer, club

MODERN BEARS:

U.K.: Deans

U.S.A.: Applause/Raikes, Boyds, Mary Meyer, Vermont

Artist bears: Monica Murray, Bear Brown Collectibles, Dorothy Word, Charlene Terry

ACCESSORIES:

Baskets, glasses, shoes, socks, books for bears

Clothes available.

Furniture available.

Figurines: Boyds Bearstone

Bear collectibles: tea sets, tote bags, miniature glassware, depression patterns

Shows: OK

In business for 4 years

STRICTLY BEARS

Julie Atherton

4 Public Square

Medina, OH 44256

Phone: 216-722-1225

Phone orders accepted.

Accepts: check, money order, Visa, MasterCard, Discover

Layaway: 33% down, 33% in 30 days, balance in 60 days

Discounts: special order

MODERN BEARS:

Canada: Ganz Bros.

Germany: Steiff, Hermann

U.K.: Deans, Merrythought, Paddington, Canterbury

U.S.A.: Applause, Beaver Valley, Boyds, Cooperstown Bears, Dakin, Gund, Madame Alexander Bears, Mary Meyer, Michaud Collection, Muffy, Vanderbear family, North American Bear Co. (other), Vermont, Ty, Russ, Bearly People, Mango, The Manhattan Toy Co., Charlene Kinser Designs

Artist bears: Traci Alexander, Lori Baker, Bearfoot Bears, Bear Facts, The Bear Lady, Bears In The Woods, Blackwoods Designs, Jan Bonner, Randie Bortnem, Carol Cavallaro, Cassner Bears, Cranberry Mountain, Ann Cranshaw, Marsha DeHaven, Down Beary Lane, Deanna Duvall, Holly Dyer, Gloria Franks, French Bear Co., Sue Foskey, Diane Gard, Jean Gardano, H.M. Bears, Shirley Hart, Terry Hayes, Debbie Hines, Donna Hodges, Jenny's Teddies, Diane Johnson, Julie Jones, Just Wee Bears, Barb Koch, Jenny Krantz, Lillibet, Sydney Marshall, Martha's Bears, McB Bears, Terry McVicker, Joanne Mitchell, Jackie Morris, Kathy Moyer, Ted Menten, Murphy Bears, Kathy Nearing, Half Nelson, Purely Neysa, Sally Pohling, Ohio River, Old Time Teddies, Joyce O'Sullivan, Sandy Perrine, Janet Reeves, Rosenbear Designs, Judy Fossilli, Edda Seiple, Mitzi Sindelar, Linda Spiegel-Lohre, Terumi Bears, Lin Van Houten, Joan Woessner, Zoar Bears and more

Miniature bears: Lisa Lloyd, Carol Stewart

Figurines: Sarah's Attic

In business for 10 years

THE STRONG MUSEUM GIFT SHOP

Beverly Kosky, manager

1 Manhattan Square

Rochester, NY 14618

Phone: 716-263-2700 X 208

Phone orders accepted.

Fax: 716-263-2493

Fax orders accepted.

Hours: M-Sat, 10A.M.-5P.M. Sun, 1P.M.-5P.M.

Accepts: check, Visa, MasterCard, Discover

Discounts: museum membership discount

MODERN BEARS:

Germany: Steiff

U.S.A.: Applause/Raikes, Boyds, Russ Berrie, Gund, The Manhattan Toy Co., Muffy, North American Bear Co. (other)

ACCESSORIES:

Clothes: Boyds, NAB

Furniture: wicker chairs, benches

Figurines: Boyds Bearstone

Bear collectibles: books about bears, books about collecting, chinaware, jewelry, dollhouse miniatures, ornaments, postcards, stationery, tea sets, tins, tote bags

In business for 12 years

STUF'D & STUFF

Cay Eckland, owner

10001 Westheimer, #1450A

Houston, TX 77042

Phone: 713-266-4352

Phone orders accepted.

Hours: M-Sat, 10A.M.-6P.M.

Catalog: $1, refundable with purchase.

Accepts: check, money order, Visa, MasterCard, Discover, American Express

Layaway: 25% down, 25% each month

Old/special items: golliwogs, bunnies

MODERN BEARS:

Canada: Ganz Bros.

Germany: Gebruder Hermann, Hermann-Spielwaren, Steiff

Italy: Trudi Giocattoli

U.K.: Canterbury, Deans, Little Folk, Merrythought, Paddington

U.S.A.: Applause/Raikes, Boyds, Russ Berrie, Charlene Kinser Designs, Dakin, Gund, The Manhattan Toy Co., Mary Meyer, Muffy, Vanderbear family, VIBs, North American Bear Co. (other), Mati's Originals, Michaud Collection

Artist bears: Bearly There, Joanne Mitchell, Michele Brown, Lorna-Dee Johnson, Carol Pearce, Carol Loucks, Jeanette McPherson, Carol Carini, Sonie Monroe, Susie Sims, Sara McClelland, Joyce Ann Haughey, Elaine Adams, Terry John Woods

Miniature bears: Foxfire, Chu Ming Wu, Betty Suarez, Betty Sutton, Gund, Akira

ACCESSORIES:

Glasses, ice cream sets

Clothes: NAB, Tender Heart, handmade sweaters

Furniture: NAB, various chairs, ice cream sets

Miniature accessories: cars, golf carts

Figurines: Cherished Teddies, Michaud Collection, Muffy, Sarah's Attic, United Design Corp.

Bear collectibles: books about bears, books about bearmaking, books about collecting, jewelry, bear magazines, ornaments, Paddington collectibles, postcards, stationery, tea sets, tote bags, Winnie-the-Pooh collectibles

Shows: Houston, TX

In business for 14 years

THE STUYVESANT BEAR

Tamara L. Demarest, owner

P.O. Box 72

Stuyvesant, NY 12173

Second address:

Rt. 9

Sunnyside Business Center

Stuyvesant, NY 12173

Phone: 518-758-2838 or 1-800-492-2327 for orders

Phone orders accepted.

Fax: 518-758-2838

Fax orders accepted.

Hours: W-Sat, 10A.M.-4P.M. Sun, 11A.M.-3P.M. Changes are possible. Please call first.

Catalog: $3, refundable with purchase

Accepts: check, money order, Visa, MasterCard

Discounts: bulk order

Artist bears: Stuyvesant Bears, more to come

ACCESSORIES:

Furniture: one-of-a-kind bear beds

Shows: MA, CT

In business for 6 years

SUE'S BEAR HAUS

Susan E. Markel, VP & Sec.

1950 Carlisle Rd.

York, PA 17404

Phone: 717-767-5300 or 1-800-569-5174

Phone orders accepted.

Hours: M, T, TH, F, 10A.M.-6P.M. W, 10A.M.-8P.M. Sat, 10A.M.-2P.M.

Accepts: check, money order, Visa, MasterCard, Discover

Layaway: $40-$199: 20% down, 30 days. $200-$399, 30% down, 60 days. More than $400, 30% down, payments every two weeks, 90 days.

Discounts: bulk order, frequent customer

Old/special items: bunnies

MODERN BEARS:

Germany: Steiff

U.K.: Canterbury

U.S.A.: Boyds, Gund, Mary Meyer, Muffy, Vanderbear family, VIBs, North American Bear Co. (other), Mango

Artist bears: Edda Seiple, Chris Cassner, Sandra Shimel, Judy Bohnert, Barbara's Originals, Sandra Dickl, Gail Clifford, Sally Winey

ACCESSORIES:

Boyds pins

Clothes: sweaters, NAB

Furniture: small chairs, benches

Figurines: Boyds Bearstone, Cherished Teddies, Laura's Attic, Lucy & Me, Muffy

Bear collectibles: books about bears, books about collecting, jewelry, bear magazines, ornaments, postcards, prints, stationery, tea sets, gift baskets with bears inside for all different occasions (birthday, new baby, etc.) and rooms (bath, kitchen) of your home.

Shows: PA, MD

In business for 3 years

SWAN'S NEST

Rosemary Swan, owner

RR1, Box 21

E. Lebanon, ME 04027-9708

Phone: 207-457-1845

Phone orders accepted.

Mail order only.

Catalog: $5 w/ photos, refundable with purchase. Free w/o photos.

Accepts: check, money order, Visa, MasterCard

Layaway: 40% down, 30% for each of next two months. Flexible.

Discounts: Credit for free bear for every 10 bears bought

Old/special items: bunnies

Artist bears: Artist bears from England, Scotland, Wales, Australia and New Zealand. List varies, but includes the following: Wales: Bocs Teganau,

Amanda Heugh; England: Bo Bears, Bedford Bears, Waifs & Strays, Ancestral Collector Bears, Barbara Ann, Only Natural, Zena Arts, Appletree Bears, Thread Bears, Madrigal Designs, Bedford Bears, Bo Bears, Naomi Laight, Companion Bears, Michaela Parnell-Mica Bears; Scotland: Changelings, Dormouse Designs; Australia: Andee's Bears, Athans Steffen's Bears, Karla Mahanna, Lorraine Keen.

Miniature bears: Catherine White, Michaela Parnell-Mica (England)

Bear collectibles: clothing for people, jewelry, bear magazines, postcards, stationery, tote bags

Shows: Northeast

In business for 4 years

SWEATER YOUR BEAR

Bobbie Halligan, owner
109 Andover Rd.
Greenville, SC 29615
Phone: 803-244-8066
Mail order only.
Catalog: $2, refundable with purchase
Accepts: check, money order
Discounts: bulk order

ACCESSORIES:

Clothes: hand-knit sweaters (5″-17″ bears)

Shows: NC

In business for 4 years

SYMONS SPECIALTIES

Sheila and Richard Symons
P.O. Box 60978
Fairbanks, AK 99706
Phone: 907-474-2161 or 1-800-478-7628 for orders (AK only)
Phone orders accepted.
Mail order only.
Catalog: free price list
Accepts: check, money order, Visa, MasterCard
Bear collectibles: Teddy bear glycerine soap. Soaps come in several colors. Come in either a two-pack or on a 450%″ square card with a color coordinated polka dot border and three balloons inscribed with "It's a Girl!" "It's a Boy!" or "I Love Baths!" It appears as though the teddy bear is holding the balloons on the cards. The cards also have a bow at the top.

In business for 5 years

THE TALKING TEDDY

Steve & Susan Swickard, owners
P.O. Box 1380
Estes Park, CO 80517
Second address:
521 Lone Pine Dr.
(on Hwy. 34 East)
Estes Park, CO 80517
Phone: 970-586-6483 or 1-800-TED-BEAR for orders only
Phone orders accepted.
Fax: 970-586-2728
Fax orders accepted.
Hours: M-Sat, 10A.M.-5P.M. Sun, 1P.M.-5P.M. Mid-June to Labor Day: M-Sat, 9A.M.-9P.M. Sun, noon-9P.M.
Catalog: $2.50
Accepts: check, money order, Visa, MasterCard, Discover, traveler's checks (in person)
Layaway: 50% down, 60 days, no substitutions
Discounts: club
Old/special items: bears manufactured between WWI and WWII, antique bear collectibles, golliwogs

MODERN BEARS:

Canada: Ganz Bros., Mighty Star
Germany: Gebruder Hermann, Kathe Kruse Puppen, Steiff, sigikid
Italy: Trudi Giocattoli
U.K.: Merrythought, Paddington, The English Teddy Bear Company
U.S.A.: Raikes, Boyds, Charlene Kinser Designs, Cooperstown Bears, Dakin, Gund, Lone Star, Madame Alexander Bears, The Manhattan Toy Co., Mary Meyer, Muffy, Vanderbear family, VIBs, North American Bear Co. (other), R. John Wright, Michaud Collection, Ty, Mango, Peek-a-Boo, Michal/Charpente, Smokey Bear, Eden Toys, Rupert, Fiesta, Gina
Artist bears: Bearly There, Tammie Lawrence, Sher Masor, Kay Elmore, Ruth Gallagher, Donna Hodges, Marsha DeHaven, Sarah McClelland, Steve, Lin and John Van Houten, Nan Wright, Terry Woods, Carol & Henry Martin, Karen Sheets, Terry Klink, Iris Voorhis, Carol Black, Mad Hatted Bears, Jenny Rettig, Grandpa-pa Jingles, Pat Murphy, Carol Martin
Miniature bears: Lisa Lloyd, Pat

Carriker, Carol Stewart, Anita Oliver, Rose Policky, Sherri Dodson, Factoria Toy Works, Akira

ACCESSORIES:

Glasses, shoes, socks, buggies, trikes, rocking horses

Clothes: sweaters, outfits (large selection)

Furniture: chairs, beds

Miniature furniture: chairs, beds, tables

Figurines: Boyds Bearstone, Cherished Teddies, Colour Box Miniatures, Lucy & Me, Michaud Collection, Muffy, Ravenwood, The Roosevelt Bears, United Design Corp., Penni Bears, Paddington, Celeb Teds

Bear collectibles: books about bears, books about bearmaking, books about collecting, boxes, chinaware, clothing for people, jewelry, bear magazines, ornaments, Paddington collectibles, paintings, postcards, pottery, prints, Smokey bear collectibles, stationery, tea sets, tins, tote bags, Winnie-the-Pooh collectibles, food items, stickers, rubber stamps, greeting cards, posters, calendars, honey products, original artwork

In business for 11 years

TED E. BEAR SHOPPE

Gail C. Jochen, president
E. Jane Ruprecht, vice-president
2120 Tamiami Trail N.
Naples, FL 33940
Phone: 813-261-2225 or 1-800-814-BEAR
Phone orders accepted.
Hours: June-Oct.: M-Sat, 10A.M.-6P.M. Oct.-May: M-Sat, 10A.M.-9P.M., Sun, noon-5P.M.
Catalog: free newsletter
Accepts: check, money order, Visa, MasterCard, Discover, American Express
Layaway: 20% down, 60 days
Old/special items: bunnies

MODERN BEARS:

Canada: Ganz Bros.
Germany: Gebruder Hermann, Steiff
Italy: Trudi Giocattoli
U.K.: Canterbury, Deans, Merrythought, Paddington
U.S.A.: Applause/Raikes, Beaver Valley, Boyds, Russ Berrie, Cooperstown Bears, Dakin, Gund, Muffy, Vanderbear family, VIBs, North American

Bear Co. (other), R. John Wright, Michaud Collection

Artist bears: Gloria Franks, Joanne Mitchell, Jenny Kranz, Edda Sieple, Jay Hadley III, Barbara Golden, Wendy Brent, Joyce Haughey, O'Hara Bears, Mati's Originals, Winey Bears, Capricious Creatures, Ballard Baines

Miniature bears: Sherri Dodson, Ballard Baines, O'Hara Bears

ACCESSORIES:

Baskets, glasses, wagons, boxes

Furniture: wooden benches, twig chairs

Figurines: Cherished Teddies, Colour Box Miniatures, Joybears, Laura's Attic, Lucy & Me, Michaud Collection, Muffy, United Design Corp.

More about figurines: large selection

Bear collectibles: books about bears, books about bearmaking, books about collecting, bear magazines, Smokey bear collectibles, stationery, tea sets, tins, Winnie-the-Pooh collectibles, windsocks, Cuddlekins

More about collectibles: large selection of ornaments: Enesco, Boyds, Applause, Muffy and more

In business for 3 years

TED E. HUGS

450 Amwell Rd.

Belle Mead, NJ 08502

TEDDY BAR CIRCA 1900

Steve and Sybille Howard

3458 S. Service Rd.

Oakville, Ontario L6J 4Z3, Canada

Second address:

Circle M Antique Market

Hwy. 5 Dundas

Flamborough, Hamilton, Ontario

Phone: 905-827-4096 or 905-689-6492

Phone orders accepted.

Hours: Sun, 8A.M.-5P.M. During the week by appointment only.

Accepts: check, money order

Layaway: 20% down, 30 days or individual terms depending on customers' needs

Discounts: bulk order, frequent customer, dealer

Old/special items: antique bears, bears manufactured between WWI and WWII, bears manufactured 1945-1970, golliwogs, bunnies, antique bear collectibles

MODERN BEARS:

Germany: Gebruder Hermann, Steiff

U.K.: Merrythought, Gabrielle Designs, Paddington

Artist bears: Linda Harris, Debi Hill

ACCESSORIES:

Glasses, jewelry

Figurines: Russian bear figurines

Bear collectibles: antique collectibles, books about collecting, bear magazines, postcards, tea sets, Winnie-the-Pooh collectibles

More about collectibles: Large selection of antique bear items, including black forest memorabilia and baby plates

Shows: Southern Ontario

In business for 3 years

TEDDY BEAR CROSSING

Karen Theisman, owner

34 S. Sierra Madre St.

Colorado Springs, CO 80903

Phone: 719-473-2327

Phone orders accepted.

Hours: M-F, 9A.M.-6P.M. Sat, 9A.M.-4P.M. Closed Sun.

Accepts: check, money order, Visa, MasterCard, Discover, American Express

Layaway: 25% down, 90 days

Old/special items: bunnies

MODERN BEARS:

Germany: Steiff

Italy: Trudi Giocattoli

U.K.: Paddington

U.S.A.: Applause/Raikes, Boyds, Russ Berrie, Dakin, Gund, Lone Star, The Manhattan Toy Co., Mary Meyer, Muffy, Vanderbear family, VIBs, North American Bear Co. (other)

Artist bears: Kelly Dauterman, Mary Kaye Lee, Dorothy DePaulo, Arlene Anderson, Sher Masor, Remi Kramer, Kathleen Wallace, Ruth Ann Mauer, Sarah Neuscheler and more

Miniature bears: Diane Cart, Mary Kaye Lee, Pat Carriker, Akira

ACCESSORIES:

Glasses

Clothes: T-shirts, sweaters

Furniture: wicker, wood, twig chairs

Figurines: Cherished Teddies, Colour Box Miniatures, Lucy & Me, Muffy, The Roosevelt Bears, United Design Corp.

Bear collectibles: books about bears, books about bearmaking, books about

collecting, boxes, clothing for people, bear magazines, ornaments, Paddington collectibles, postcards, stationery, tea sets, tins, tote bags, Winnie-the-Pooh collectibles

In business for 6 years

THE TEDDY BEAR DEN

Pam Ecott, owner

1775 E. Tropicana Ave.. #15

Las Vegas, NV 89119

Phone: 702-736-2696

Phone orders accepted.

Hours: M-Sat, 10A.M.-5P.M.

Accepts: check, money order, Visa, MasterCard

Layaway: $50 minimum, 33% down, 60 days, 2 bear maximum

MODERN BEARS:

U.K.: Paddington

U.S.A.: Applause/Raikes, Boyds, Russ Berrie, Dakin, Gund, Lone Star, Mary Meyer, Muffy, Vanderbear family, VIBs, North American Bear Co. (other)

Artist bears: Randie Bortnem, Wanda Shope, Marie Zimmermann, Gloria Franks, Ann Inman-Looms, Heidi Miller, Karen Sheets, Barbara Brown, Carol Black, Barbara Golden, Kathleen Wallace, Ruth Ann Mauer, Chris Cassner, Sandy Shimel, Barbara Sixby, Lenore Dement, Diane Martin, Linda Stafford, Mica Michele Friesen, Sandra Dineen, Lori Nerdahl, Marie Warling and more

Miniature bears: Jane Pogorzelski, Factoria Toyworks, Deborah Didier, Stacy Pio

ACCESSORIES:

Clothes: sweaters

Furniture: chairs, wagons

Figurines: Boyds Bearstone, Cherished Teddies, Heart for Bears, Muffy, United Design Corp.

Bear collectibles: bear magazines, ornaments, postcards, stationery, tins

In business for 7 years

TEDDY BEAR DEPOT

Mike Pipkin, owner

2228 Valley View Mall

Dallas, TX 75240

Phone: 214-934-2327

Phone orders accepted.

Fax: 817-488-0260
Fax orders accepted.
Hours: M-Sat, 10A.M.-9P.M. Sun, noon-5P.M.
Accepts: check, money order, Visa, MasterCard, Discover, American Express
Layaway: 25% down, 3 equal payments, no fees
Old/special items: bunnies

MODERN BEARS:
Germany: Steiff
Italy: Trudi Giocattoli
U.K.: Paddington
U.S.A.: Applause/Raikes, Boyds, Russ Berrie, Cooperstown Bears, Dakin, Gund, Lone Star, Muffy, Vanderbear family, VIBs, North American Bear Co. (other), R. John Wright
More about these bears: Current and retired Muffy and family
Artist bears: Bear Brown Collectibles
Miniature bears: Akira

ACCESSORIES:
Clothes: NAB
Furniture: NAB
Figurines: Cherished Teddy, Muffy
Bear collectibles: books about bears, books about collecting, clothing for people, jewelry, tea sets, Winnie-the-Pooh collectibles

THE TEDDY BEAR GARDEN
Nola Hart and Ruth Fraser
366 Eglinton Ave.
Toronto, Ontario M5N 1A2, Canada
Phone: 416-322-3277
Phone orders accepted.
Fax: 416-322-5527
Fax orders accepted.
Hours: M, 10A.M.-5P.M. T, W, F, Sat, 10A.M.-5:30P.M. TH, 10A.M.-7P.M. Summer: same, except TH, 10A.M.-5:30P.M. Oct.-Dec.: additional hours on Sun, noon-4P.M.
Calalog: free newsletter
Accepts: check, money order, Visa, MasterCard, American Express
Discounts: club
Old/special items: antique bears, bears manufactured between WWI and WWII, bunnies

MODERN BEARS:
Canada: Ganz Bros.
Germany: Steiff
U.K.: Canterbury, Merrythought, Paddington

U.S.A.: Boyds, Russ Berrie, Dakin, Gund, Lone Star, The Manhattan Toy Co., Mary Meyer, Muffy, Vanderbear family, North American Bear Co. (other), Ty
Artist bears: Bear Magic Canada, Linda Ferguson, Hana Franklin, Bridgett Furhoff, Joyce Jones, Terrie Kroeker, Joan Links, Rhonda Castel, Doreen Schmitt, Sharon Tomlinson, Renata Weitzenbauer, Carol Cowan, Ruth Fraser, Nola Hart and more
Miniature bears: Ruth Fraser, Marlene Scott, Renate Weitzembauer, Colleen McLaughlin, Joan Roberts, K. Clarke

ACCESSORIES:
Clothes: handmade outfits, sweaters
Figurines: Boyds Bearstone, Colour Box Miniatures
Bear collectibles: books about bears, books about bearmaking, books about collecting, jewelry, bear magazines, postcards, tea sets, tote bags, Winnie-the-Pooh collectibles
In business for 5 years

TEDDY BEAR JUNCTION
Linda Higby and Roxanna Parker, owners
300 Broadway
Chico, CA 95928
Phone: 916-894-5500
Phone orders accepted.
Hours: M-F, 10A.M.-6P.M. Sat, 10A.M.-6P.M. Sun, noon-4P.M.
Catalog: free newsletter
Accepts: check, money order, Visa, MasterCard, Discover
Layaway: Up to $100: 25% down. More than $100: 20% down. Payments every 30 days. Length of layaway depends on amount of purchase.
Old/special items: bunnies

MODERN BEARS:
Canada: Ganz Bros.
Germany: Hermann-Spielwaren, Steiff
U.K.: Canterbury, Merrythought, Paddington
U.S.A.: Applause/Raikes, Beaver Valley, Boyds, Russ Berrie, Charlene Kinser Designs, Dakin, Gund, Mary Meyer, Muffy, Vanderbear family, VIBs, North American Bear Co. (other), Vermont, Michaud Collection
Artist bears: Creations by Marti, Ann Brown, Teddies for Real by Jesser,

Whiteley Woods, Teddy Bear Farm
Miniature bears: Little Gem Bears

ACCESSORIES:
Jewelry, grocery carts, petite steamer trunks, mini metal cars and planes (that Muffy can drive)
Clothes: sweaters
Figurines: Cherished Teddies, The Roosevelt Bears
Bear collectibles: books about bears, books about collecting, jewelry, bear magazines, ornaments, stationery, tins, Winnie-the-Pooh collectibles, Oscar and Bertie wall plaques, (some musical) puzzles, key and coat hangers, wall magnets
Shows: CA
In business for 9 years

THE TEDDY BEAR MUSEUM OF NAPLES GIFT SHOP
Deanne Kee, office manager
2511 Pine Ridge Rd.
Naples, FL 33942
Phone: 813-598-2711 or 1-800-681-2327
Phone orders accepted.
Fax: 813-598-9239
Fax orders accepted.
Catalog: free first edition
Accepts: check, money order, Visa, MasterCard
Layaway: 20% down, 3 months

MODERN BEARS:
Canada: Ganz Bros.
Germany: Grisly Spielwaren, Heike Gump, Gebruder Hermann, Schuco, Steiff
U.K.: Canterbury, Merrythought, Paddington
U.S.A.: Applause/Raikes, Russ Berrie, Dakin, Gund, Lone Star, The Manhattan Toy Co., Mary Meyer, Muffy, Vanderbear family, VIBs, North American Bear Co. (other), Mango, All Stuffed Up, Eden, Michaud Collection
Artist bears: Joyce Haughey, Bonnie Moose, Rita Casey, John Sawyer, Barbara Golden, Jean Burhans, Jill Kenny, Robin Platt, Beth Kammerer, Jeanine Frost, Dee Hockenberry, Beverly White, Cheri Fuller, Connie Johnson, Karla Singer, Kathy Nearing, Nic Nichols, Jenny Krantz, Fred Slater, Elizabeth Becket, Ed and

Helen Duggan, Edda Seiple, Kathleen Wallace, Anne-Marie VanGelder, Linda Ferguson, Geri Chilcutt, Sally Winey, Jennifer Round, Heike Gump, Georgine Palka, Patricia Merrick, Linda Novack, Cheri Fuller, Connie Johnson

Miniature bears: Bonnie Moose, Roberta Rehm, Carol Stewart

ACCESSORIES:

Clothes: NAB

Bear collectibles: books about bears, books about bearmaking, books about collecting, boxes, clothing for people, jewelry, bear magazines, dollhouse miniatures, ornaments, postcards, prints, Smokey bear collectibles, stationery, tea sets, tote bags, Winnie-the-Pooh collectibles

In business for 5 years

THE TEDDY BEAR ROOM

John Nixon, owner
169 Wortley Rd.
London, Ontario N6C 3P6 Canada
Phone: 519-432-4041
  Phone orders accepted.
Fax: 519-432-3031
Hours: M-Sat, 10A.M.-5P.M.
Catalog: free
Accepts: money order, Visa

MODERN BEARS:

Germany: Hermann-Spielwaren, Schuco, Steiff
U.K.: Canterbury, Merrythought
U.S.A.: Gund
Bear collectibles: books about bears, books about collecting, chinaware, jewelry, bear magazines, postcards
In business for 5 years

TEDDY BEAR SPECIALTIES

Carol-Anne Fisher, owner
138 Mill St.
Georgetown, Ontario L7G 2C1, Canada
Phone: 905-873-8522
  Phone orders accepted.
Hours: Closed W, 10A.M.-5P.M. TH, F, 10A.M.-7P.M. Sat, 10A.M.-5P.M., Sun, noon-5P.M.
Catalog: free newsletter
Accepts: check, money order, Visa, MasterCard, American Express
Layaway: negotiable. Usually 25% down, 60 days
Discounts: frequent order

MODERN BEARS:

Canada: Mighty Star
Germany: Gebruder Hermann, Steiff
U.K.: Canterbury, Merrythought, Paddington
U.S.A.: Applause/Raikes, Boyds, Cooperstown Bears, Gund, Mary Meyer, Muffy, Vanderbear family, VIBs, North American Bear Co. (other)
Artist bears: Donna Lee Wilson, Sue McKay, Trudy Yelland, Cherie Friendship, Linda Hejna and more Selection constantly changing
Miniature bears: Trudy Yelland

ACCESSORIES:

Clothes: NAB, hand-knit sweaters
Figurines: Boyds Bearstone, Colour Box Miniatures, Jan Hagara Collectibles, Muffy
Bear collectibles: books about bears, books about bearmaking, books about collecting, clothing for people, jewelry, bear magazines, paintings, postcards, prints, stationery, tote bags, Winnie-the-Pooh collectibles, afghans, ornaments
More about collectibles: clothing and jewelry is Canadian-made
Shows: Ontario
In business for 4 years

TEDDY BEAR STATION

Andelyn Cooper
13464 Cleveland Ave. N.W.
Uniontown, OH 44685
Phone: 216-699-1779
  Phone orders accepted.
Hours: M-Sat, 11A.M.-5P.M.
Catalog: $3, refundable with purchase
Accepts: check, money order, Visa, MasterCard, Discover
Layaway: 20% down, 60 days, no fees. Payments due biweekly.
Old/special items: bunnies

MODERN BEARS:

Canada: Ganz Bros.
Germany: Gebruder Hermann, Steiff
U.K.: Canterbury, Deans, Merrythought, Paddington
U.S.A.: Applause/Raikes, Beaver Valley, Boyds, Russ Berrie, Cooperstown Bears, Dakin, Gund, Mary Meyer, Muffy, Vanderbear family, VIBs, North American Bear Co. (other), Michaud Collection, Vermont, Cherished

Teddies plush, Lucy & Me, Bearly People, Mango, Spoontiques
Artist bears: Sersha, Just Wee Bears, Purely Neysa, Crabapple, Bearons of La Jolla, Carol Earle, Kathy's Bears, Cranberry Mountain, Pumpkin Patch, Golden Harlequin, Judy Bears, Bearly Angels, Busser Bears, Pendletons, China Cupboard, Sue Newlin, Hotchkin Bears, From the Heart, Ruth Elliott, Tea-Berry Hollow, cm Bears, Bonner Bears, Treasured Bears, Chester Freeman, Treasured Teddies, McB Bears
Miniature bears: Akira, Pendletons, Gund, Beary Little Bears

ACCESSORIES:

Baskets, glasses, hair ribbons, jewelry, shoes
Clothes: sweaters, outfits
Furniture: wood, wicker
Miniature accessories: glasses, jewelry
Miniature furniture: wood, wicker
Figurines: Cherished Teddies, Lucy & Me, Muffy
Bear collectibles: books about bears, books about bearmaking, books about collecting, boxes, chinaware, clothing for people, jewelry, bear magazines, dollhouse miniatures, ornaments, Paddington collectibles, postcards, prints, stationery, tea sets, tins, tote bags, Winnie-the-Pooh collectibles
Shows: Eastern states surrounding OH
In business for 7 years

TEDDY BEAR'S PICNIC TOY SHOP

Selene Higgins, owner
#205-2250 Oak Bay Ave.
Victoria, BC V8R 1G5, Canada
Phone: 604-598-5558
  Phone orders accepted.
Fax: 604-598-5558
  Fax orders accepted.
Hours: M-F, 10A.M.-5:30P.M. Sat, 10A.M.-6P.M. Sun, 11-4P.M., summer only.
Catalog: $3, refundable with purchase.
Accepts: money order, Visa, MasterCard, American Express
Layaway: 20% down, no service charge
Discounts: bulk order, frequent customer, nonprofit organization

MODERN BEARS:

Canada: Ganz Bros., Mighty Star, Binkley, Standen house
Germany: Steiff

Italy: Trudi Giocattoli

U.K.: Canterbury, Merrythought, Deans

U.S.A.: Applause/Raikes, Boyds, Dakin, Gund, Mary Meyer, Muffy, Vanderbear family, VIBs, North American Bear Co., Ty, Country Critters

Artist bears: Patricia Gye, June Slack, Joan Rankin, Bow Bears, Cath Wood, Bears and Bedtime, Bransgore Bears, Beech Bears

Miniature bears: Biddesden Bears, June Slack, Lorna Hopkins, Little Gem Bears

ACCESSORIES:

Furniture: antique-type high chairs, beds, prams

Figurines: Boyds Bearstone, Colour Box Miniatures, Jan Hagara Collectibles, Muffy, Upcott Bears (Devon, U.K.)

Bear collectibles: books about bears, books about collecting, clothing for people, ornaments, postcards, prints, stationery, tea sets, tins, Winnie-the-Pooh collectibles, magnets, pins, greeting cards, puzzles

More about collectibles: Some pins and magnets and one line of photo cards are made in Canada

In business for 7 years

TEDDY BEARS TO GO

Vivian R. Lambrecht, president
897 W. Park Ave.
Ocean, NJ 07712
Phone: 908-493-4455 or 1-800-284-2327
  Phone orders accepted.
Fax: 908-493-8050
  Fax orders accepted.
Hours: M-F, 9 A.M.-6 P.M. Sat, 10 A.M.-3 P.M.
Accepts: check, money order, Visa, MasterCard, Discover, American Express
Layaway: 20% down, monthly payments
Discounts: bulk order, frequent customer, senior citizen

MODERN BEARS:

Canada: Mighty Star
Germany: Gebruder Hermann, Steiff
Italy: Trudi Giocattoli
U.K.: Canterbury, Merrythought, Paddington
U.S.A.: Applause/Raikes, Boyds, Russ Berrie, California Stuffed Toys, Cooperstown Bears, Dakin, Gund, Lone Star, Madame Alexander Bears, The Manhattan Toy Co., Mary Meyer,

Muffy, Vanderbear family, VIBs, North American Bear Co. (other)

Artist bears: Bearly There, Nostalgic Bear Co.

Miniature bears: Akira

ACCESSORIES:

Glasses, hair ribbons, jewelry, shoes, socks

Clothes available.

Furniture: wicker chairs

Bear collectibles: jewelry, bear magazines, Paddington collectibles, Smokey bear collectibles, Winnie-the-Pooh collectibles

In business for 9 years

TEDDY BEARS TO GO

Harriet Valdez, owner
1900 Route 70, Suite 210
Lakewood, NJ 08701
Phone: 908-477-2400 or 1-800-348-2327 for orders
  Phone orders accepted.
Fax: 908-477-7166
  Fax orders accepted.
Hours: M, T, TH, 9 A.M.-6 P.M. W, F, 9 A.M.-8 P.M. Sat, 9 A.M.-5 P.M. Sun, 10 A.M.-4 P.M.
Accepts: money order, Visa, MasterCard, Discover, American Express, MAC (in person)
Layaway: 25% down, 90 days
Discounts: frequent customer, free shipping for orders of more than $100, local coupons

MODERN BEARS:

Canada: Ganz Bros.
Germany: Gebruder Hermann, Steiff
Italy: Trudi Giocattoli
U.K.: Canterbury, Deans, Merrythought, Paddington
U.S.A.: Applause/Raikes, Boyds, Russ Berrie, Cooperstown Bears, Dakin, Gund, Madame Alexander Bears, The Manhattan Toy Co., Mary Meyer, Muffy, Vanderbear family, VIBs, North American Bear Co. (other), Vermont, Bearly People

Artist bears: Kathleen Wallace, Lynn Gatto, Sandy Dineen, Vilma Ervin, Mary Kolar, Zoolatana, Donna Hodges, Bunnies by the Bay, Terry-bears and more

Miniature bears: Akira, Steiff

ACCESSORIES:

Baskets, glasses, hair ribbons, shoes, socks

Clothes available.

Furniture available.

Figurines: Boyds Bearstone, Folkstones, Cherished Teddies, Laura's Attic, Lucy & Me, Muffy, United Design Corp.

Bear collectibles: books about bears, books about bearmaking, books about collecting, chinaware, bear magazines, Paddington collectibles, paintings, postcards, stationery, tea sets, Winnie-the-Pooh collectibles

In business for 6 years

TEDDY BEARS & US

Bobbi Bohrman, proprietor
340 S. Liberty St.
Orwigsburg, PA 17961
Phone: 717-366-1366
Hours: T-F, 10 A.M.-5 P.M. Sat, 10 A.M.-4 P.M.
Accepts: check, Visa, MasterCard
Discounts: frequent customer, senior citizen, coupons in local newspaper
Old/special items: bunnies

MODERN BEARS:

Germany: Gebruder Hermann, Steiff
Italy: Trudi Giocattoli
U.S.A.: Boyds, Russ Berrie, Dakin, Mary Meyer, Muffy, Vanderbear family, VIBs, North American Bear Co. (other)

Artist bears: Frances Harper, Janet Reeves, Carolyn Lamothe, Marcia Sibol, Millie Gage, Linda Schaff, Susan Redstreake Geary, Anne Cranshaw, Kathleen Wallace, Vicki Stephan, Grandma Lynn, Ruth Ann Mauer, Lori Murphy

Figurines: Boyds Bearstone, Cherished Teddies, Lucy & Me, Muffy, Paddington (Enesco)

Bear collectibles: books about bears, bear magazines, ornaments, Paddington collectibles, tea sets, tins, Winnie-the-Pooh collectibles

In business for 3 years

TEDDY TOGS

Elizabeth S. Mabry, owner
P.O. Box 9563
Bend, OR 97708

Phone: 503-382-7959
Phone orders accepted.
Mail order only.
Catalog: $2 and SASE
Accepts: check, money order
Clothes: original clothes for bears

TEDDY TOWN USA
23 Whitebridge Rd.
Nashville, TN 37205

TEDDY TRIBUNE WAREHOUSE
Barbara Wolters, owner
254 W. Sidney
St. Paul, MN 55107
Phone: 612-291-7571
Phone orders accepted.
Catalog: video mail order catalog $6
Accepts: check, money order
Layaway: 30% down, 90 days
Old/special items: antique bears, bears
manufactured between WWI and
WWII, bears manufactured 1945-
1970, antique bear collectibles, golli-
wogs, bunnies

MODERN BEARS:
Stock varies—always a large selection
More about these bears: Will also sell
artist's bears on consignment. See list-
ing in chapter eight for details
Artist bears: varies
Miniature bears: varies

ACCESSORIES:
Baskets, glasses, hair ribbons, jewelry,
shoes, socks
Clothes: handmade, commercial
Furniture: handmade, commercial
More about these accessories: stock
varies
Figurines: stock varies
Bear collectibles: books about bears,
books about bearmaking, books about
collecting, boxes, chinaware, clothing
for people, jewelry, bear magazines,
dollhouse miniatures, ornaments,
Paddington collectibles, paintings,
postcards, pottery, prints, Smokey
bear collectibles, stationery, tea sets,
tins, tote bags, Winnie-the-Pooh collectibles, stock varies—always a wide
selection
Shows: Teddy Tribune Event, St. Paul,
MN
In business for 2 years

TEDDY'S
1961 Route 33
Hamilton Square, NJ 08690

TEDDY'S CORNER
Kathy Fleming, manager
526 Pine St.
Glenwood Springs, CO 81601
Phone: 303-945-2087
Phone orders accepted.
Fax: 303-945-7030
Fax orders accepted.
Hours: 7 days, 9A.M.-5:30P.M.
Accepts: check, money order, Visa, Mas-
terCard, Discover, American Express
Layaway: 33% down, 33% in 30 days,
balance in 60 days
Old/special items: bunnies

MODERN BEARS:
U.K.: Paddington
U.S.A.: Applause/Raikes, Boyds, Russ
Berrie, Gund, Lone Star, Madame Al-
exander Bears, Mary Meyer, Muffy,
Vanderbear family

ACCESSORIES:
Baskets
Clothes: NAB
Furniture available.
Figurines: Boyds Bearstone, Jan Hagara
Collectibles, Michaud Collection,
Muffy, Sarah's Attic, United Design
Corp.
Bear collectibles: books about bears,
books about collecting, jewelry, post-
cards, Smokey bear collectibles, sta-
tionery, tea sets, tins, tote bags, Win-
nie-the-Pooh collectibles
In business for 6 years

TERRY BEARS
Terry Boryk, owner
12 E. Main St.
Oyster Bay, NY 11771
Phone: 516-922-6972
Phone orders accepted.
Fax: 516-922-6972
Fax orders accepted.
Hours: M-Sat, 10A.M.-5P.M.
Accepts: check, money order, Visa, Mas-
terCard, American Express
Layaway: 20% down, 60 days
Discounts: frequent customer, club

MODERN BEARS:
Germany: Gebruder Hermann, Steiff
U.K.: Merrythought
U.S.A.: Applause/Raikes, Beaver Valley,

Boyds, Mary Meyer, Muffy, Vander-
bear family, VIBs, North American
Bear Co. (other), Vermont, Bearly
People
Artist bears: Joan Woessner, Donna
Hodges, Barbara Golden, Jill Kenny,
Teresa Bonenfant, Cat Orlando
Miniature bears: Steiff, Norma Thomas,
Donna Hodges, Joan Roberts

ACCESSORIES:
Jewelry
Clothes: NAB, clothes for Donna Hod-
ges's "Michelle"
Furniture: NAB
Figurines: Boyds Bearstone, Lucy &
Me, Muffy, United Design Corp.
Bear collectibles: jewelry
In business for 6 years

THEODORE ROOSEVELT INAUGURAL HISTORICAL SITE
Janice Tomaka, special events
coordinator
641 Delaware Ave.
Buffalo, NY 14202
Phone: 716-884-0095
Phone orders accepted.
Fax: 716-884-0330
Fax orders accepted.
Accepts: check, money order, Visa, Mas-
terCard
Discounts: volunteers or members

MODERN BEARS:
U.S.A.: Russ Berrie, Dakin, Gund, Mary
Meyer, Muffy, Vanderbear family,
North American Bear Co. (other),
Vermont
Artist Bears: Genie Buttitta (commemo-
rative Teddy Roosevelt bear); Trudy
Yelland (Teddy Roosevelt bear)
Bear collectibles: books (Ho Phi Le col-
lection), jewelry, dollhouse minia-
tures, postcards, tote bags
In business for 24 years

THEODORE ROOSEVELT MEDORA FOUNDATION
Sandy Tjaden, manager, retail merchan-
dising
918 E. Divide Ave.
Bismarck, ND 58501
Second address:
Box 198
Medora, MD 58645
Phone: 701-623-4444
Phone orders accepted.

Fax: 701-223-3347
Fax orders accepted.
Hours: Winter, 8:30A.M.-5P.M. Summer, 8:30A.M.-8:30P.M.
Accepts: check, money order, Visa, MasterCard, American Express

MODERN BEARS:
U.S.A.: Applause/Raikes, Boyds, Russ Berrie, Dakin, Mary Meyer, Muffy, Vanderbear family, Ty
Figurines: Boyds Bearstone, Cast Art Industries, Lucy & Me, Sarah's Attic, United Design Corp.
Bear collectibles: books about bears, jewelry, tea sets, tins, tote bags

M. MICHELE THORP
36910 Edgehill Rd.
Springfield, OR 97478
Mail order only.
Phone: 503-747-4812
Phone orders: 8A.M.-9P.M.
Bear collectibles: T-shirts, paintings, prints, stationery, tea sets, paper dolls
Shows: OR, WA, CA, CO, AZ, New England

TILLIE'S
Tillie A. Stover, owner
918 Coronado Blvd.
Universal City, TX 78148
Phone: 210-658-1444
Phone orders accepted.
Hours: M-Sat, 10A.M.-5:30P.M.
Accepts: check, money order, Visa, MasterCard, Discover, American Express
Layaway: 6 months, no refunds. Longer for purchases of more than $1,000
Old/special items: bunnies

MODERN BEARS:
Germany: Kathe Kruse Puppen, Steiff, Paddington
U.S.A.: Applause/Raikes, Beaver Valley, Boyds, Charlene Kinser Designs, Dakin, Gund, Lone Star, Muffy, Vanderbear family
Artist bears: Beaver Valley, Bear Brown, Wendy Brent, Jo Ann Mitchell, McB Bears, Mamma's Babies
Miniature bears: Mama's Babies, Akira Trading Co., Steiff

ACCESSORIES:
Glasses
Clothes: Boyds
Furniture: Boyds
Figurines: Boyds Bearstone, Cast Art

Industries, Cherished Teddies, Jan Hagara Collectibles, Michaud Collection, Ravenwood, The Roosevelt Bears, Sarah's Attic, United Design Corp.
Bear collectibles: books about bears, chinaware, jewelry, ornaments, Paddington collectibles, postcards, tea sets
In business for 19 years

TOUCH MY HEART DOLLS, BEARS AND GENTLE FRIENDS
Norma Carroll, owner
P.O. Box 36342
Cincinnati, OH 45236
Phone: 513-791-5270
Phone orders accepted.
Mail order only.
Catalog: SASE
Accepts: check, money order, Visa, MasterCard
Layaway: less than $600: 3 months, 4 equal payments. Up to 1 year on expensive pieces. Will work with the customer on special pieces, circumstances
Old/special items: antique bears, bears manufactured between WWI and WWII, bears manufactured 1945-1970, golliwogs, bunnies, antique bear collectibles

MODERN BEARS:
Artist bears: Janet Reeves, R.J. Wright, Regina Brock, Heidi Steiner
Miniature bears: antiques only
Bear collectibles: books about collecting
Shows: MD, IL, OH, IN, MI, NY, KS, MO, NJ, PA
In business for 5 years

THE TOY SHOPPE
Barrie & Danny Shapiro, owners
11632 Busy St.
Richmond, VA 23236
Phone: 804-379-7995 or 1-800-447-7995
Phone orders accepted.
Fax: 804-379-2780
Fax orders accepted.
Hours: M-Sat, 9:30A.M.-5P.M.
Catalog: free
Accepts: check, money order, Visa, MasterCard, Discover
Layaway: 25% down, 1 year to pay. Can also take equal monthly payments

from credit card or post-dated checks
Discounts: vary
Old/special items: golliwogs, bunnies

MODERN BEARS:
France: The French Bear Co.
Germany: Schuco, Steiff, Haida
U.S.A.: Beaver Valley, Charlene Kinser Designs, Gund, North American Bear Co., R. John Wright
Artist bears: Bearly There, Barbara Golden, Tru's Bears, T-Bone Bears, Purely Neysa, Linda Schaff, Martha DeRaimo, Goose Creek, Capricious Creatures and more
Miniature bears: Stacy Pio and more

THE TOY STORE
Beth Savino, owner
Franklin Park Mall
Toledo, OH 43623

TOYS & TREASURES
Linda Horsey, owner
3076 17th St.
Sarasota, FL 34234
Phone: 813-954-2327
Phone orders accepted.
Hours: M-Sat, 10A.M.-5P.M. Extended holiday hours
Catalog: $1
Accepts: check, money order, Visa, MasterCard, Discover
Layaway: 20% down, 90 days. Length can be extended for large purchases.
Discounts: club
Old/special items: golliwogs, bunnies

MODERN BEARS:
Canada: Ganz Bros.
Germany: Hans Clemens, Gebruder Hermann, Schuco, Steiff
U.K.: Canterbury, Deans, Little Folk, Merrythought, Paddington
U.S.A.: Applause/Raikes, Boyds, Dakin, Gund, Muffy, Vanderbear family, VIBs, North American Bear Co. (other), Michaud Collection
Artist bears: Constantly changing
Miniature bears: Constantly changing. Akira Trading, Sherry Dodson, Leota Ordiway, Gund, Linda Stafford, Linda Speigel, Celia Baham

ACCESSORIES:
Baskets, carts, wagons, etc.
Clothes: NAB, Boyds
Furniture: chairs, etc.
Miniature accessories: baskets

Miniature furniture: chairs, benches, dollhouse minis (1 inch scale)

Figurines: Boyds Bearstone, Jan Hagara collectibles, Muffy

Bear collectibles: books about bears, books about bearmaking, books about collecting, chinaware, clothing for people, jewelry, bear magazines, dollhouse miniatures, ornaments, Paddington collectibles, paintings, postcards, prints, stationery, tea sets, Winnie-the-Pooh collectibles

Shows: FL

In business for 3 years

TREASURED TEDDIES

7 Hayes Ct.
Wilmington, DE 19808

TRULY UNIQUE GIFT SHOP

Joanne and Gary Fratrich, owners
RR #3, Box 7327, Rt. 4 East
Rutland, VT 05701

Phone: 802-773-7742
Phone orders accepted.

Fax: 802-773-7378
Fax orders accepted.

Accepts: check, money order, Visa, MasterCard, Discover, American Express

Old/special items: bunnies

MODERN BEARS:

U.S.A.: Boyds

Artist bears: JK Bears, Treadle Bears, Bears of Corbett Hollow

ACCESSORIES:

Clothes: Boyds

Figurines: Boyds Bearstone

In business for 11 years

TUTTI ANIMAL (TOYS INTERNATIONAL)

Constance R. Hoepner, v.p.
3333 Bear St.
Costa Mesa, CA 92626

Phone: 714-549-8771 or 714-545-2505
Phone orders accepted.

Hours: M-F, 10A.M.-9P.M. Sat, 10A.M.-7P.M. Sun, 11A.M.-6:30P.M.

Accepts: check, money order, Visa, MasterCard

Discounts: nonprofit organizations

MODERN BEARS:

France: Nounours/Aux Nations/Ajena

Germany: Gebruder Hermann, Kathe Kruse Puppen, Schuco, Steiff

Italy: Trudi Giocattoli

U.K.: Canterbury, Merrythought, Paddington

U.S.A.: Applause/Raikes, Charlene Kinser Designs, Cooperstown Bears, Dakin, Gund, Madame Alexander Bears, The Manhattan Toy Co., Muffy, Vanderbear family, VIBs, North American Bear Co. (other),Cascade Toy, Douglas Cuddle Toys, Best Ever, Kathy Kreations, Folkmanis

Artist bears: Linda Nelson, Pam Holton, Linda Spiegel-Lohre

Miniature bears: Pam Holton

ACCESSORIES:

Clothes: NAB

Furniture: NAB

Bear collectibles: tea sets

In business for 9 years

2 BEARS TEDDY BEARS

Pauline Renpenning, owner
1904-20 Ave. N.W.
Calgary, Alberta T2M 1H5, Canada

Phone: 403-282-4770
Phone orders accepted.

Fax: 403-282-4770
Fax orders accepted.

Hours: M-Sat, 10A.M.-6P.M. Sun, noon-5P.M.

Accepts: check, money order, Visa, MasterCard, American Express

Layaway: 33% down, 33% in 1 month, balance in 2 months

Old/special items: bunnies

MODERN BEARS:

Canada: Mighty Star, Paddington

U.K.: Paddington

U.S.A.: Applause/Raikes, Boyds, Russ Berrie, Gund, Mary Meyer, Muffy, Vanderbear family

Artist bears: Heidi Ott (U.K.), Barbara Troxel, Mary Kaye Lee, Linda Spiegel-Lohre, Jodi Rankin, Joyce Reichard, Nancy Bruns, Lorna Dee Johnson, Jeanne Green, Carol and Henry Martin, Doris King, Anne Cranshaw, Jeanette Demanovich, Jackie Lescher, Judy Rossilli, Christine Lamb, Karen Loewen, Ted Menten, Nancy Rygg, Sue & Randall Foskey, Victoria Stanard, Pat Cathey, Carol Cavallaro, Paulette Tucker, Lou Ann Hendershot, Sherri Dodson, Beverly Martin Wright, Jutta Cyr, Lorna Hopkin, Vivian Fritze, Heather Smith, Joan Rankin, John Renpen-

ning, Jo Ann Klassen, Sharon Tomlinson, Trudy Teneycke, Joan Stevenson

Miniature bears: Maggie Anderson, Pat Williams, Deborah Didier, Julia Deimert, Edie Barlishen, May-Britt Mykietiak, Janet Desjardine, Barb Butcher, Trudy Labbe

ACCESSORIES:

Furniture: handcrafted loveseats, chairs, etc.

Figurines: Boyds Bearstone

Bear collectibles: books about bears, books about bearmaking, books about collecting, clothing for people, jewelry, bear magazines, postcards, stationery

In business for 5 years

UNIQUE PRODUCTS

Joan P. Schwartz, president
6510 Newman Circle East
Lakeland, FL 33811

Phone: 813-644-6899
Fax: 813-644-6899
Mail order only.

Catalog: SASE

Accepts: check, money order

ACCESSORIES:

Furniture: handcrafted wood furniture, including chairs, desks, benches and beds

Miniature furniture: handcrafted wood furniture, including swings and benches

In business for 3 years

VILLAGE BEARS & COLLECTIBLES

Don & Ann Gehlbach
5128 Ocean Blvd
Sarasota, FL 34242

Phone: 813-346-2667
Phone orders accepted.

Fax: 813-349-5806
Fax orders accepted.

Hours: T-Sat, 11A.M.-5P.M.

Photos available.

Accepts: money order, Visa, MasterCard, American Express

Layaway: 33% down, 33% in 1 month, balance in 2 months, no refunds

Discounts: Collectors' Club

Old/special items: bears manufactured between WWI and WWII, bears manufactured 1945-1970, golliwogs, antique accessories

MODERN BEARS:

Germany: Gebruder Hermann, Steiff, Haida, Bing, Grizly

U.K.: Big Softies, Canterbury, Deans, Merrythought, Paddington, Rupert, Lakeland, Gabrielle, Nisbet

U.S.A.: Beaver Valley, Boyds, Eden, Cooperstown Bears, Dakin, Gund, Mary Meyer, Muffy (new and retired), Vanderbear family (new and retired), North American Bear Co., R. John Wright

Artist bears: Australian: J. Laing. British: Atlantic Bears, Bo Bears, Bocs Teganau, Bodriggy, Amanda Heugh, Charnwood, Martha Gregory, Mother Hubbard, Naomi Laight, Teddystyle Sunny Bears, Yvonne Plakke. American: Barbara Troxel, Bearly There, McB, Blackwoods, Blacklick, Donna Hodges, Mary Holstad, Linda Beckman, Log Cabin, Pam Holton, Leota Ordiway, River Hills, Shoestrings, Heidi Steiner, Tammie Lawrence, Pat Murphy, Beverly Martin Wright, Stier Bears

Miniature bears: British: Anita Oliver, Pawsonality, Kathryn Riley, Shoebutton, Wood-u-like, Bodriggy American: Chu Ming Wu, Bears By Bert, Deborah Drown, Linda Beckman, Paulette Svec

ACCESSORIES:

Glasses, jewelry, cars, toys, quilts, luggage, wagons

Clothes: sweaters, vests, hats, ties, knickers, collars, robes, pajamas

Furniture: tables, chairs, beds, armoires

Miniature furniture: wooden

Figurines: Cherished Teddies, Michaud Collection, Muffy, The Roosevelt Bears, Pennywhistle Lane (Enesco), Dept. 56, Winnie the Pooh

Bear collectibles: books about bears, books about collecting, chinaware, clothing for people, jewelry, bear magazines, dollhouse miniatures, ornaments, Paddington collectibles, postcards, stationery, tea sets, tins, greeting cards, Winnie-the-Pooh collectibles

In business for 3 years

VILLAGE SQUARE OF FOUNTAIN

Sue Tangen, owner
#99 Main St., P.O. Box 110
Fountain, MN 55935
Phone: 507-268-4406
Phone orders accepted.
Accepts: check, Visa, MasterCard, Discover

MODERN BEARS:

U.S.A.: Boyds

Artist bears: local artists

ACCESSORIES:

Glasses, shoes, socks
Clothes available.
Furniture available.
Miniature clothes available.
Miniature furniture available.

Figurines: Boyds Bearstone

Bear collectibles: books about bears, stationery

In business for 3 years

VIRGINIA'S 5TH AVENUE DOLLS & BEARS

531 5th Ave. South
Naples, FL 33940

WHITE BEAR ANTIQUES & TEDDY BEARS LTD.

Jo Jones, owner
1301 E. 15th St.
Tulsa, OK 74120
Phone: 918-592-1914 or 1-800-676-8195 for orders
Phone orders accepted.
Hours: M-Sat, 10 A.M.-5 P.M. Sun, 1 P.M.-5 P.M.
Accepts: check, money order, Visa, MasterCard, Discover
Layaway: 25% down, 3 equal payments, 90 days
Discounts: club
Old/special items: antique bears, bears manufactured between WWI and WWII, bears manufactured 1945-1970, golliwogs, bunnies, antique bear collectibles

MODERN BEARS:

Germany: Grisly Spielwaren, Gebruder Hermann, Steiff

U.K.: Canterbury, Merrythought, Paddington

U.S.A.: Applause/Raikes, Beaver Valley, Boyds, Russ Berrie, Cooperstown Bears, Dakin, Gund, Lone Star, Madame Alexander Bears, The Manhattan Toy Co., Mary Meyer, Muffy,

Vanderbear family, VIBs, North American Bear Co. (other), Michaud Collection

Artist bears: Ro Bears, Glass Dragon, Stier Bears, Bear Brown, Short Mt. Trading Co., Stearny's Bears, Classic Traditions by M. Murray

Miniature bears: Diane Cart, Akira Trading Co., Jane Merchant, Linda Moore

ACCESSORIES:

Glasses, shoes, socks

Furniture: chairs, beds

Figurines: Boyds Bearstone, Cherished Teddies, Joybears, Michaud Collection, Muffy, The Roosevelt Bears, United Design Corp.

Bear collectibles: books about bears, books about collecting, boxes, chinaware, jewelry, bear magazines, ornaments, Paddington collectibles, postcards, prints, Smokey bear collectibles, stationery, tea sets, tote bags, Winnie-the-Pooh collectibles

Shows: MO, OK

In business for 5 years

WILLIAMS

William Bowen
5150 Yonge St., Concourse Level
North York, Ontario M2N 6L8, Canada
Phone: 416-590-0335
Phone orders accepted.
Accepts: money order, Visa, MasterCard
Layaway: 50% down, 30 days, costs of delivery
Old/special items: bunnies

MODERN BEARS:

U.S.A.: Gund, Attic Toys, Ty

In business for 8 years

WONDERLAND

Linda Gruskin, owner
6812 Stirling Rd.
Hollywood, FL 33024
Phone: 305-967-8222
Phone orders accepted.
Hours: M-F, 11 A.M.-6 P.M. Sat, 10 A.M.-4 P.M.
Accepts: check, money order, Visa, MasterCard, Discover, American Express
Old/special items: antique bears, bears manufactured between WWI and WWII, bears manufactured 1945-1970, golliwogs, bunnies, antique bear collectibles

MODERN BEARS:

Germany: Grisly Spielwaren, Gebruder Hermann, Hermann-Spielwaren, Schuco, Steiff

U.K.: Canterbury, Chad Valley, Merrythought, Paddington

U.S.A.: Applause/Raikes, Beaver Valley, Russ Berrie, California Stuffed Toys, Cooperstown Bears, Dakin, Gund, Muffy, Vanderbear family, VIBs, North American Bear Co. (other), R. John Wright, Michaud Collection

Artist bears: Joanne Mitchell, Gloria Franks, Michelle Brown, Dee Hockenberry, Marcia Sibol, Joyce Houghey, Janet Reeves, Pat Murphy, Kathy Moyer, Kathy Wilder, Denise Wade, Judy Howard, Etta Seiple, Barbara Bessos, Michauds, Jeanette McPherson, Linda Farrell, Debbie Reese, Karine Masterson, Marsha Frieson, Mica Michele, Terri Klink, Chester Freeman, Linda Spiegel-Lohre, Melodie Malcolm, Kathy Nearing, Diane Gard, Barbara McConnell, Gary Neth, Lenore Dement, Laura Orzek

Miniature bears: Kathy LaQuay, Sherry Dodson, Debra Drown

ACCESSORIES:

Carriages

Clothes: sweaters

Furniture: beds, lounge chairs, high chairs, cribs, chairs, sofas

Miniature accessories: carriages

Miniature furniture: beds, lounge chairs, high chairs, cribs, chairs, sofas

Figurines: Cherished Teddies

Bear collectibles: books about bears, books about collecting, chinaware, bear magazines, dollhouse miniatures, ornaments, Paddington collectibles, tea sets, tote bags, Winnie-the-Pooh collectibles

Shows: FL

In business for 5 years

WRITE IMPRESSIONS
Cheryle Challe
143 James St. South
Hamilton, Ontario L8P 3A1
Canada
Phone: 905-522-8241
Hours: M-F, 10A.M.-5:30P.M., Sat, 10A.M.-5P.M.
Accepts: check, money order, Visa, MasterCard
Layaway available.

MODERN BEARS:

U.K.: Paddington
U.S.A.: Gund, Mary Meyer
Artist bears: local artists
Figurines: Boyds Bearstone

THE WRITE SHOP
Connie Young, owner
96 Nashaway Rd.
Bolton, MA 01740
Additional addresses:
476 Main St.
Bolton, MA;
554 Main St.
Harwich Port, MA
(open summers only)
Phone: 508-779-5292
Phone orders accepted.
Hours: T-Sat, 10A.M.-5P.M. Summer: T-Sun, 10A.M.-9P.M.
Catalog: free
Accepts: check, Visa, MasterCard
Layaway: full payment, ten-day hold
Artist bears: Miss Addie's Attic

YE OLDE TEDDY BEAR SHOPPE
624 Main St.
Irwin, PA 15642

YESTERDAY'S LORE
Donald Stephenson, president
P.O. Box 1055, 26 Honeysuckle Lane
Nashville, IN 47448
Phone: 812-988-1123
Phone orders accepted.

Hours: 10A.M.-5P.M.
Accepts: check, money order, Visa, MasterCard
Layaway available.
Old/special items: bunnies

MODERN BEARS:

Canada: Ganz Bros.
U.S.A.: Boyds
Artist bears: Stuf'd Stuff

ACCESSORIES:

Glasses
Clothes: sweaters, hats
Figurines: Boyds Bearstone
Bear collectibles: jewelry, ornaments, tea sets

ZEPHYR IMPRESSIONS
Vince Claerhout, owner
405-5 St. S.
Lethbridge, Alberta T1J 2B6, Canada
Phone: 403-320-8876
Phone orders accepted.
Hours: M, T, W, F, Sat, 10A.M.-5:30P.M. TH, 10A.M.-9P.M.
Accepts: check, money order, Visa, MasterCard, American Express
Discounts: bulk order, frequent customer

MODERN BEARS:

Canada: Bears & Bedtime
Germany: Steiff
U.K.: Merrythought
Scotland: Hantel
More about these bears: Sells all limited edition pieces by Steiff and Merrythought
Miniature bears: Edie Barlishen, Hantel
Bear collectibles: boxes
More about collectibles: Enamel boxes produced by Crummles of England with the bear motif, including a music box with the teddy bear picnic

In business for 8 years

2

Suppliers

How to Use This Chapter

*A*ll bear artists share a common struggle: finding quality supplies at reasonable prices. When artists are just beginning their businesses, they often find it especially difficult to locate suppliers. But the search is never over. Even experienced bear artists are constantly looking for new supplies and better deals.

In this chapter, we have listed contact information for several suppliers to make the search easier. We have tried to be as all-inclusive as possible, and therefore have made no judgements about the quality or pricing of the items sold. Each artist will have to make those decisions for herself. Linda Henry's article gives wonderful advice for requesting samples and maximizing your buying.

Many of these suppliers are mail order only. Those with store locations include location addresses and store hours. All listings include payment possibilities, discounts available, delivery information and specific items sold. Areas where the company may sell their products at shows are also listed for some suppliers. Some supplier listings include addresses only. In these cases, the companies either did not respond to our request for information, or we learned about them too late to request detailed information. In either case, we have verified their addresses so that artists can contact them about items sold.

While most of the suppliers listed are businesses with their own offices, several are businesses run out of a home—particularly those suppliers that sell patterns and kits only. As always, be courteous when contacting these suppliers by phone, and take time zone differences into account.

Finding and purchasing supplies does not have to be frustrating. These listings, along with Linda Henry's excellent article, make it easy. Linda has wonderful advice for purchasing supplies, as well as ideas for locating supplies in unlikely places. Good luck in your search!

The Search for Supplies Made Easy

BY LINDA HENRY

*H*ow fortunate is today's teddy bear artist to have so many resources at her fingertips! In the early 1970s, when artist-made bears were just making their way into the market, quality bearmaking supplies were hard to find. It was not until about 1983 that suppliers such as Edinburgh Imports began offering mohair and alpaca to eager artists. At that time, Edinburgh Imports had a one-page price list offering only about six fabrics. Today, they offer more than sixteen pages of furs, patterns and bear-making supplies.

As the availability of materials and instruction in the art of bear making has dramatically increased, so too has the number of teddy bear makers. In the early days, there were less than five hundred artists worldwide. Today's figures are closer to twenty-five hundred to thirty-five hundred! The artist archives at the Teddy Bear Museum in Naples, Florida, includes more than fifteen hundred artists in the U.S. alone.

When I started making bears in 1987, resource books such as this one did not exist. Early artists had to rely on networking with other artists who were willing to share information on the resources they had found. Today supplies may be easily purchased through the large number of suppliers that you will find in this chapter.

Armed with this listing of resources, you are ready to begin your exciting adventure into the world of teddy bear-making. As you peruse the listings, you may find that several different companies offer what you are looking for. Begin by contacting those companies and asking for their price lists and sample cards. This way, you may compare their quality and pricing before placing an order.

Using Patterns and Kits

Several suppliers in this book offer patterns and kits. Ron Block of Edinburgh Imports and the Teddy Bear Artists' Association recommends that the beginning bear maker start by ordering a kit and a book such as *How to Make and Sell Quality Teddy Bears*, by Doris and Terry Michaud. Books such as this one will cover the art of designing your own pattern, helpful shortcuts and various marketing opportunities for selling your

Linda Henry, a freelance commercial artist, began her bear-making career in 1987 when she and her husband, Mike, began designing their own original teddy bears. She has won several national competitions and has been nominated for the TOBY award. Her bears have been featured in several books and publications, and she has written feature articles for several magazines as well. She has designed bears for several manufacturers, including L.L. Knickerbocker and Silent Sentiments. She lives in Canal Winchester, Ohio.

bears. Other books that may be helpful are listed in chapter 8. There are also videotapes available on the art of bearmaking, and several workshops offered across the country. They, too, are listed in chapter 8.

On a helpful note, Edinburgh Imports offers a toll-free number (1-800-EDINBRG in the USA and Canada) as a "hotline" for anyone with questions on how to solve specific bear-making problems. Ron says that they have walked many a bear artist through the art of turning a "classic crown joint" over the years!

While many bear artists started out using kits or books of patterns, professional artists design their own patterns. By developing your own unique pattern and style, you will truly be able to call yourself a teddy bear artist. When developing your pattern, you may find it helpful to cut your first original bear out of an old blanket to get the "feel" for the bear without investing in costly materials during the early trial and error stages.

Placing Your Order

Now that you are ready to place your order, you may want to consider buying a small amount of fur, a few eyes, and other supplies, to see how they work on your bears before buying in bulk. Don't forget to consider any specials that the supplier might be offering. Specials offer you the opportunity to try out their newest and highest quality fabrics at lower prices.

You will need to know how long the supplier's delivery time is. Most vendors will offer several options, including next day air if you are desperate to meet a deadline. You also need to know how backlogged the supplier is to figure out how long it will take your order to be processed.

It's also important to note that all of the German fur manufacturers take three weeks off in August for their "holiday"! Alas, many an artist has fallen victim to this delay in the past. They have found the perfect fur for their fall and Christmas shows, only to learn that the supplier was out of stock. Edinburgh Imports suggests that you place your fur order during the period from April to June to be shipped by August 1. This way, the distributor can make sure he has the fur that you need in stock prior to the German "holiday" downtime.

Most companies offer several payment options, including check, charge and C.O.D. Make sure you are aware of the additional charges for C.O.D. service. Because you are buying wholesale, be prepared to give the supplier your vendor's license (resale) number for their records.

It may be wise to inquire about their return policies as well. Sometimes a two-inch sample does not have the same impact as two yards of the same fabric. Some distributors may also have a restocking charge for returned merchandise.

Purchasing Fur: Potential Problems

When buying any fur, especially natural furs such as mohair or alpaca, you should be aware that dye lots may differ slightly with each new bolt that your supplier receives. I questioned Ron Block about this, and he told me that mohair manufacturers in Europe receive their raw materials from several different "fur communities." While manufacturers try to maintain consistency,

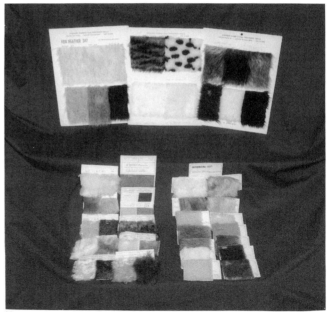

Here are some examples of fabric sample cards which can be ordered from suppliers. The top sample is from Monterey Mills; the bottom left, from Edinburgh Imports, and the bottom right is from Intercal Trading Co.

goats or llamas of different communities have been raised on different diets and in different climates, resulting in inconsistency in the texture and oil contents of the fur. This in turn affects the manner in which the dye is absorbed.

While these color differences are slight, they may be a nuisance if you have only enough fur to finish half a bear and are hoping to order more to complete it. Try to avoid this by ordering enough fur to finish your projects. Distressed and wavy furs will likewise differ in the amount of swirl from bolt to bolt. This is caused by differences in the moisture content of the fur during processing.

If you are planning a larger limited edition and you want to be assured that it will all come from the same bolt, Edinburgh Imports offers artists the opportunity to put a hold on the total amount they will need and to buy portions over time. For example, you are able to put fifteen yards on hold, and purchase the fur in five-yard increments over a three-month period. Check with other suppliers for similar programs.

Making the Most of a "Bear Budget"

If the cost of mohair is not within your budget, or you're looking for a way to introduce a lower price range into your line, consider purchasing domestic plush. There are several American manufacturers who offer excellent quality fabrics at a fraction of the cost of mohair.

If you are planning to convert an existing pattern from mohair to plush, you should be aware that the backings are very different. Mohair has a tightly woven backing that will conform more closely to your pattern. Plush, on the other hand, will stretch considerably, depending on such factors as the tightness of the weave, the amount of sizing on the backing, and the density and firmness of the stuffing used.

You may find it helpful to stabilize the backing before cutting by applying your own sizing. Make a mixture of white all-purpose glue and water. Try a four-to-one ratio at first (four parts water to one part glue), although you may want to adjust it depending on the stiffness desired. Apply with a brush and let it dry thoroughly before cutting. There are also iron-on backings that may be purchased at most fabric stores.

As the teddy bear market continues to become more competitive, retail pricing could be an important key to your success. The lower cost of domestic plush may give beginners an edge by allowing them to offer lower priced bears. It will also give them the opportunity to experiment with new or unusual pattern ideas and fabric treatments.

Broadening Your Creative Horizons

With a little extra creative effort on your part, inexpensive plush fabrics can be transformed into some really exciting, unique bears! To achieve that "worn," antique look, try boiling some acrylic fur in a large pot for an hour or so. Dry it in a hot dryer. Avoid brushing the fur to maintain that distressed look.

Although acrylic fabrics have a natural tendency to resist dyes, you can enhance the color of an acrylic bear by using watered down acrylic paints. Brushing the bear after it has completely dried will soften the color and remove the stiffness from the fur.

Mohair and alpaca, on the other hand, will readily accept commercial and natural dyes because they are natural fibers. I know several artists who buy only white fur, giving them the opportunity to create a limitless number of colors. When hand-dyeing, use only the highest quality permanent dyes. Craft and art supply stores usually have a good selection of colors on hand.

If you decide to custom mix your own colors, I recommend that you keep a notebook of the formulas with exact measurements so you can duplicate those lovely colors again. An added note: Wet fabric will always appear darker than when it is dry. Always test your color on a small piece of the fabric to be dyed and allow it

Bearnardo, a 17" mohair bear by Linda Henry, has a porcelain face—just one of the many creative options that bear artists can adopt.

to dry thoroughly to make sure that it's really the color you want. Using a hair dryer can speed up this testing process.

A number of artists combine their fur creations with other media. I am also a porcelain doll artist and have incorporated original porcelain faces into several of my bears. Other artists have been extremely successful using wood, wool felt, polymer clay or resin faces to create teddy bears that are uniquely their own.

Advantages to Co-op Buying

When I started making bears, I had very little capital. Fortunately, two other teddy bear artists in my area, Jackie Morris and Sher Masor, offered to let me join them in a co-op buy of mohair. This was to their advantage also since a larger order meant that they qualified for a larger quantity discount. Jackie also shared her sources for high-quality domestic plush at reasonable prices. I immediately called Monterey and ordered their price list and sample pack. I noticed that they offered several different grades of fiberfill stuffing in bulk. I found another friend, Jodi Rankin, who wanted to go together with me to make the minimum purchase. We were delighted with the quality of this stuffing, bought at the lowest price we had come across. This spirit of sharing is one of the finest qualities of the teddy bear artists' community.

Alternate Suppliers

When searching for supplies, remember never to limit yourself. There are hundreds of places to search for specific supplies, and many supplies can be found at shows and stores that have nothing to do with teddy bears. While there are too many of these less conventional suppliers to list in this book, the following ideas should provide a starting point for your search.

Doll supply shops offer a wide variety of items that may be used for teddy bears also. Most will carry plastic pellets, armature, costume patterns and accessories such as shoes, hats, glasses and parasols. If you lean toward the "vintage" look, antique shops offer a nostalgic array of accessories and props. Upholstery shops are a wonderful place to look for some of the tools of the trade such as needles, upholstery thread and fabric for miniature bears and paw pads. Craft supply stores usually carry a wide variety of fabric dyes, paints, doll stands and other supplies and accessories. Art supply stores will also offer paints and dyes, and many carry the new plastic clays that can be baked in your home oven to create noses, snouts, claws and even whole bears!

While shopping at your local fabric store, inquire as to whether or not they have special order books. Often they will contain samples of more unusual fabrics, such as upholstery velvets and Ultrasuede, with relatively low minimum purchases. There are several fabric and sewing machine shops in my area that periodically have fabric swaps. This is a good way to utilize those smaller scraps of mohair that you can't find a use for but just hate to throw away. Seamstresses, quilters and weavers occasionally like to add textures to their creations, and they may have some wonderful pieces of fabric they would be willing to trade with you. If there are no fabric swaps in your area, why not talk to your local shop about organizing one?

Leather supply stores not only carry various grades of leather and suedes, but dyes and accessories, too. I use their softer glove leathers for paw pads and noses. Accessories for Western or Native American bears can be found in these stores, too. For convenience, I use

Tandy Leather's catalog. It's more than 130 pages long and costs $2.50. Write to them at Tandy Leather Company, Advertising Dept., P.O. Box 791, Fort Worth, TX 76101.

There are numerous types of specialty stores you can use as a resource in developing your own "style." Christmas, Victorian, Western and Native American shops can offer ideas and accessories to personalize your bears. Don't overlook outlet and toy stores for doll clothing and accessories. My Cory bear is designed to wear baby clothes, so I'm always looking for darling baby shoes or headbands at department stores or baby shops. Don't overlook the pet departments for grooming tools or maybe a nice bear collar. Taking time to browse in these shops is fun and stimulating. You may find supplies and accessories that you never considered using before. At the very least, you will come away with a head full of new ideas for unique bear creations!

Shopping at Home

Finally, don't forget about catalogs. Doll catalogs, sewing notions catalogs and art supply catalogs have dyes, paints, plastic clays and other supplies that can be used in bearmaking. Clock catalogs often have music boxes that can be used in bears. One of my favorite catalogs is from Clotilde, which offers hundreds of sewing notions at a 20 percent discount. Write to: Clotilde Inc., 2 Sew Smart Way B8031, Stevens Point, WI 54481-8031, or call 1-800-772-2891. If you're interested in seeing what catalogs have to offer, I suggest you start by ordering a catalog directory such as Shop At Home Craft Collection, 2080 S. Holly St., P.O. Box 221050, Denver, CO 80222-9050. They offer dozens of catalogs for you to pick from with brief descriptions of each one.

Another way to shop without leaving home is through one of the numerous television shopping networks. While they do not offer a constant source for any particular supply, you may be able to find an accessory or craft supply at a reasonable price that can be delivered right to your door. I have purchased lovely wooden doll stands this way, and was very pleased with the quality and price. Occasionally they will offer craft supplies and demonstrate their uses. Not only do you not have to leave home, but you can be productive while shopping if you watch with a lap full of "bears in progress."

Finally, don't forget to check the most obvious, and often the most overlooked, places-in your own home. There are probably items in your attic, basement or garage that can be used to make bears. I have used moss, rocks and bark from my own backyard to create delightful habitats for my bears. When I travel, I try to collect unusual items that I can't find at home. I have boxes of feathers, pine cones, sea shells, sand, coral, driftwood and even bones just waiting to add that special touch to just the right bear.

Shows and Sales

Make sure you take advantage of teddy bear and doll shows where suppliers display their wares and are available to answer any questions you may have. Many shows and conventions offer seminars focusing on locating resources and how to work with new materials. See chapter 6 for some of these shows. Antique shows and sales offer the same resources that can be found in antique shops, sometimes at lower prices. Finally, dog shows are the perfect place to find high-quality dog grooming tools, and these are excellent for grooming teddy bears!

No matter where you live in the country, there are sales going on every day. Check your local paper for auctions, estate sales, flea markets and garage sales. I usually look for boxes of fabrics and trims or craft sewing supplies. You never know when you may come away with a box full of treasures! I have even been known to go through people's trash (much to the embarrassment of my twelve-year-old daughter, Jessica). On a recent walk I salvaged some perfectly good plastic shelving. And every artist knows you can never have too much shelving! I have even heard stories of people pulling vintage teddy bears from garbage cans, thus rescuing them from a gruesome fate at the city dump. Truly one man's trash is another man's treasure!

"800" Directories

What should you do if you come across a wonderful fabric or trim at a shop that has only a limited stock? Many times you will find the manufacturer's name printed somewhere on the bolt. There is now a directory of "800" numbers available by dialing 1-800-555-1212. If a manufacturer has a toll-free number, the operator will be able to supply it. Many large companies have minimum orders that may require more than you are willing to invest. Ask for their price lists and sample cards. Again, you may find that there are other artists that are willing to co-op to help you meet your minimum.

Sources of Inspiration

Your local library probably has several books on teddy bear patterns and on period costume designing. Browse through the children's section to rejuvenate your memories of classic fairy tales and nursery rhymes. Even the well-established artist may benefit by finding a new "source of inspiration." Ideas can be found every day in the most ordinary places!

While discussing this topic with my family, my daughter suggested McDonald's as a resource. While my husband thought that was humorous, I was immediately reminded of the "Fast-Food" teddy bear article by Carol-Lynn Rossel Waugh and the delightful "Ronald McDonald and the Hamburgler" bears created by Beverly White for a Ronald McDonald House auction. You never know when you may be called upon to create something out of the ordinary!

Bearmaking—a Lifetime of Adventure

Whether you are now ready to make your first bear, or you've been making bears for thirty years, we hope that the ideas and sources presented here will broaden the scope of your creative endeavors. Finding wonderful new resources and experimenting with creative ideas can be half the fun. Best of all, every day will bring you closer to a world of teddy bear loving friends!

Suppliers

A. ROOSEVELT BEAR CO.
Alexia Roosevelt
1016 Nandina Way
Sunnyvale, CA 94086
Phone: 408-739-4659
   Phone orders accepted.
Fax: 408-738-6614
   Fax orders accepted.
Mail order only.
Catalog: $3 in USA; $5 foreign (Full-color catalog of 34 jointed bears and bunnies)
Allow 3-6 days for delivery
Accepts: check, money order, Visa, MasterCard
Discounts: bulk order, preferred customer, wholesale
Shows: MD, FL, IL, CA

SUPPLIES FOR REGULAR BEARS:
Eyes: glass, pre-looped, safety eyes, shank
Mohair: curly, distressed, feathered, regular, string, tipped, wavy
Joints: disks and washers, hardboard, tap bolts
Patterns: bear kits, bear patterns (6"-17" bears), clothing patterns (included with bear patterns)
Paws: facile suede, Ultrasuede
Stuffing: Dacron/fiberfill, pellets
Tools: brushes, cotter keys
Other: Persian wool

SUPPLIES FOR MINIATURE BEARS:
Eyes: glass, pre-looped
Fur: mohair, Ultrasuede
Joints: disks and washers, hardboard, lock nuts
Paws: facile suede, Ultrasuede
Stuffing: Dacron/fiberfill, pellets
Tools: brushes
In business for 4 years.

ANIMAL CRACKERS PATTERN CO.
5824 Isleta SW
Albuquerque, NM 87105
Phone: 505-873-2806 or 1-800-274-2327
   Phone orders accepted.
Store location at above address.

Hours: M-F, 9A.M.-5P.M. Please call, hours change periodically.
Catalog: $2, refundable with purchase.
Allow 1 week for delivery.
Accepts: check, money order, Visa, MasterCard, COD
Discounts: bulk order

SUPPLIES FOR REGULAR BEARS:
Eyes: glass, pre-looped, safety, shoe button
Furs (non-mohair): acrylic plush, alpaca plush, rayon, upholstery velvet
Mohair: curly, distressed, feathered, regular, string, tipped, wavy
Joints: loc-line armature systems, cotter pins, disks and washers, hardboard, lock nuts, plastic doll joints, pop rivets, tap bolts
Patterns: bear kits, bear patterns, clothing patterns
Paws: Ultrasuede, wool
Stuffing: pellets
Tools: brushes, loc-line pliers, needles, pop rivet settlers, stuffing tools
Other supplies for regular bears: growlers, jewelry findings, music boxes, ribbons, nylon thread, nut drivers, scissors, awl, pearl cotton thread

SUPPLIES FOR MINIATURE BEARS:
Eyes: bead, glass, pre-looped, on wires
Fur: mohair, upholstery velvet, Ultrasuede
Joints: cotter pins, disks and washers, hardboard
Paws: Ultrasuede
Stuffing: pellets, lead shot
Other supplies for miniature bears: ribbons, jewelry findings

ACCESSORIES FOR REGULAR BEARS:
Glasses, hair ribbons, jewelry, stands, birch bark canoes, hats, parasols, violins, brass horns, baseball bats, rolling pins, tin and wooden buckets
Clothes for regular bears: ready-made patterns or kits, sweaters

ACCESSORIES FOR MINIATURE BEARS:
Hair ribbons, jewelry, stands
In business for 13 years

BARBIE'S BEARS
Barbie Hampton, owner
15172 Koyle Cemetary Rd.
Winslow, AR 72959
Phone: 501-634-5741
   Phone orders accepted.
Mail order only.
Accepts: check, money order, Visa, MasterCard
Patterns, Fur and other supplies available.

BASICALLY BEARS
Mary Ellen Brandt
825 7th St. SE
Oelwein, IA 50662
Phone: 319-283-3748
   Phone orders accepted.
Mail order only.
Catalog: SASE
Allow 1-2 weeks for delivery.
Accepts: check, money order, Visa, MasterCard
Shows: IL, MO, KS

SUPPLIES FOR REGULAR BEARS:
Eyes: shoe button
Joints: lock nuts, tap bolts, metal disks and washers

ACCESSORIES FOR REGULAR BEARS:
Antique glasses, sunglasses, children's shoes, infants' shoes and Cabbage Patch Kid shoes.
In business for 11 years

BEAR CLAWSET
Suzanne B. Irvin, Marcia L. Campbell
27 Palermo Wk.
Long Beach, CA 90803
Phone: 310-434-8077
Mail order only.
Catalog: $2 US, $3.50 Canada
Allow 5-10 days for delivery.
Accepts: check, money order
Shows: CA

SUPPLIES FOR REGULAR BEARS:
Eyes: glass, pre-looped, wire, safety, shank
Furs (non-mohair): cotton, imported German synthetic

Mohair: curly, distressed, feathered, regular, string, tipped, wavy, kinky curly

Joints: cotter pins, disks and washers, hardboard, lock nuts, plastic doll joints, pop rivets

Patterns: bear kits, bear patterns, sweater patterns, costume patterns

Paws: felt (100% imported wool), pig suede

Stuffing: pellets

Tools: brushes, hemostats, needles, tweezers

Other supplies for regular bears: embroidery thread, growlers, jewelry findings, no-no and yes-no mechanisms, squeakers, pattern boards

SUPPLIES FOR MINIATURE BEARS:

Eyes: glass, on wires

Fur: mohair, upholstery velvet

Joints: cotter pins, disks and washers, hardboard

Patterns: miniature bear kits, miniature bear patterns

Paws: felt

Stuffing: pellets

Tools: hemostats, stuffing sticks

ACCESSORIES FOR REGULAR BEARS:
Glasses, stands

ACCESSORIES FOR MINIATURE BEARS:
Stands
In business for 14 years

BEAR HUGS
Mary Nelson
210 Sherman, #161
Coeur d'Alene, ID 83814
Phone: 208-664-2327
Phone orders accepted.
Store location: same
Hours: M-Sat, 9:30A.M.-9P.M.
Sun, 11A.M.-6P.M.
Accepts: check, money order, Visa, MasterCard, Discover, American Express

SUPPLIES FOR REGULAR BEARS:

Eyes: glass, pre-looped, wire, shoe button

Furs (non-mohair): imported German synthetic

Mohair: curly, distressed, feathered, regular, string, tipped, wavy

Joints: cotter pins, disks and washers

Patterns: bear patterns

Paws: felt

Stuffing: Dacron, fiberfill, pellets

Tools: brushes

Other supplies for regular bears: embroidery thread, growlers

SUPPLIES FOR MINIATURE BEARS:

Eyes: glass, pre-looped, on wires

Fur: mohair, upholstery velvet

Joints: cotter pins, disks and washers

Patterns: miniature bear patterns

Paws: felt

Stuffing: Dacron, fiberfill, pellets

Tools: brushes

ACCESSORIES FOR REGULAR BEARS:
Stands

Clothes for regular bears: hand-knit sweaters

Furniture for regular bears: Muffy
In business for 5 years.

A BEAR IN SHEEP'S CLOTHING
Judith Shangold
P.O. Box 770
Medford, MA 02155
Phone: 617-395-6491
Fax: 617-395-6491
Mail order only.
Catalog: free
Allow 1 week for delivery.
Accepts: check, money order
Discounts: nonprofit organization, established businesses

SUPPLIES FOR REGULAR BEARS:

Patterns: clothing patterns, including knitting patterns for 10″ animals, and needlepoint/cross-stitch charts for vests

ACCESSORIES FOR MINIATURE BEARS:
Glasses

Clothes for miniature bears: straw hats
In business for 4 years

BEAR STREET
Dale Junker
415 W. Foothill Blvd.
Claremont, CA 91711

BEAR TRACKER, INC.
Gary Silber
201 SE 15th Terrace
Deerfield Beach, FL 33441

BEAR-A-DISE
Jyll Weissman, owner
359 Millburn Ave.
Millburn, NJ
Phone: 201-376-2405, 201-376-2406
or 1-800-376-BEAR for orders

Fax: 201-376-2405
Accepts: check, money order, Visa, MasterCard, American Express, layaway

BEARDEAUX BARN
8907 Warner Ave., Ste. 166
Huntington Beach, CA 92647
Phone: 714-842-4460
Phone orders accepted.
Fax: 714-842-4460
Fax orders accepted
Accepts: check, money order, Visa, MasterCard
Large selection of supplies

BEARS & BAUBLES
Georgia Carlson
1603 Solano Ave.
Berkeley, CA 94707
Phone: 510-524-4794
Phone orders accepted.
Hours: T, W, Sat, 10A.M.-5:30P.M.
TH, F, 10A.M.-7P.M.
Catalog: $3, refundable with purchase.
Allow 3-5 weeks for delivery.
Accepts: check, money order, Visa, MasterCard, Discover, American Express
Discounts: occasional sales
Shows: CA

SUPPLIES FOR REGULAR BEARS:

Eyes: glass, pre-looped, wire, safety, shoe button

Furs (non-mohair): acrylic plush, alpaca plush, distressed plush, dralon, dual plush, rayon

Mohair: curly, distressed, feathered, regular, string, tipped, wavy

Joints: cotter pins, disks and washers, hardboard, lock nuts, plastic doll joints

Patterns: bear kits, bear patterns, clothing patterns (limited selection)

Paws: facile suede, felt, leather cloth, Ultrasuede, velvet

Stuffing: Dacron, fiberfill, pellets

Tools: brushes, needles

Other supplies for regular bears: growlers, music boxes, ribbons

SUPPLIES FOR MINIATURE BEARS:

Eyes: glass, pre-looped, wire

Fur: mohair, upholstery velvet, Ultrasuede

Joints: cotter pins, disks and washers, lock nuts

Patterns: miniature bear kits, miniature

bear patterns, miniature clothing patterns (limited selection)
Paws: facile suede, felt, Ultrasuede, ultra leather
Stuffing: Dacron, fiberfill, pellets
Tools: brushes, needles
Other supplies for miniature bears: ribbons

ACCESSORIES FOR REGULAR BEARS:
Glasses, hair ribbons, jewelry, stands
Clothes for regular bears: hats, sweaters in limited quantities
Furniture for regular bears: limited items

ACCESSORIES FOR MINIATURE BEARS:
Hair ribbons, stands
In business for 8 years

BEARS & BEDTIME MFG INC.
4803-52 Ave.
Stony Plain, AB T72-1C4
Phone: 403-963-6300 or 1-800-461-BEAR
Phone orders accepted.
Fax: 403-963-2134
Fax orders accepted.
Store location
Catalog: free

SUPPLIES FOR REGULAR BEARS:
Eyes: glass, safety
Furs (non-mohair): German, Canadian and American synthetics
Mohair: German
Bear patterns: assorted

SARA BERNSTEIN'S DESIGNS
Sara Bernstein
10 Sami Ct.
Englishtown, NJ 07726
Mail order only.
Catalog: $1 + SASE
Allow 1-2 weeks for delivery.
Accepts: check, money order
Discounts: bulk order
Shows: NJ

SUPPLIES FOR REGULAR BEARS:
Patterns: bear patterns
In business for 11 years

BIDDESDEN BEARS
Laurie & Mark Spurdle
720 Parkside Rd.
West Vancouver, British Columbia
V7S 1P3, Canada
Mail order only.

Catalog: $2, refundable with purchase.
Allow 2 weeks for delivery.
Accepts: check, money order
Shows: Alberta

SUPPLIES FOR MINIATURE BEARS:
Patterns: miniature bear kits
In business for 3 years

BOLEK'S CRAFT SUPPLIES
330 N. Tuscarawas Ave., P.O. Box 465
Dover, OH 44622-0465

BORG TEXTILE CORP.
P.O. Box 697, 105 Maple St.
Rossville, GA 30741

BY DIANE
1126 Ivon Ave., BR
Endicott, NY 13760

CARROUSEL
505 W. Broad St.
Chesaning, MI 48616
Phone: 517-845-7881
Phone orders accepted.
Fax: 517-845-6650
Fax orders accepted.
Store location at above address.
Hours: Hours vary, call first.
Allow 10 days for delivery.
Accepts: check, money order, Visa, MasterCard, Discover, American Express
Shows: Baltimore, MD

SUPPLIES FOR REGULAR BEARS:
Eyes: glass, wire
Furs (non-mohair): acrylic plush, alpaca plush, modacrylic plush
Mohair: curly, distressed, feathered, regular, string, tipped, wavy mohair blends, end pieces, closeouts
Joints: disks and washers, pop rivets
Patterns: bear kits, bear patterns

SUPPLIES FOR MINIATURE BEARS:
Patterns: miniature bear patterns

ACCESSORIES FOR REGULAR BEARS:
Glasses, shoes, socks
Clothes for regular bears: knitted and sewn
In business for 21 years

CARVER'S EYE CO.
Irene Ruppel
P.O. Box 16692
Portland, OR 97216

CASEY'S BEAR FACTORY
Rita Casey
110 Village Landing
Fairport, NY 14450
Phone: 716-223-6280
Phone orders accepted.
Store location at above address.
Hours: T-Sat, 10A.M.-5P.M.
H, 10A.M.-9P.M.
Catalog: $2
Allow 2 weeks for delivery.
Accepts: check, money order, Visa, MasterCard, Discover
Discounts: bulk order
Shows: IL, MA, NJ, NY

SUPPLIES FOR REGULAR BEARS:
Eyes: glass, pre-looped, safety, shank, shoe button
Furs (non-mohair): acrylic plush, alpaca plush, artificial silk plush, cashmere, distressed plush, dual plush, modacrylic plush, rayon, silk blends
Mohair: curly, distressed, feathered, regular, string, tipped, wavy
Joints: loc-line armature systems, disks and washers, hardboard, lock nuts, plastic doll joints, pop rivets, swivel tilt neck joints, tap bolts, flexline
Patterns: bear kits, bear patterns, clothing patterns
Paws: facile suede, Ultrasuede
Stuffing: Dacron, fiberfill, pellets
Tools: brushes, cotter keys, hemostats, loc-line pliers, needles, tweezers
Other supplies for regular bears: embroidery thread, growlers, music boxes, no-no and yes-no mechanisms, ribbons, voice boxes

SUPPLIES FOR MINIATURE BEARS:
Eyes: bead, glass, pre-looped
Fur: mohair, upholstery velvet, Ultrasuede
Joints: cotter pins, disks and washers, hardboard, lock nuts
Patterns: miniature bear kits, miniature bear patterns, miniature clothing patterns
Paws: facile suede, felt, Ultrasuede
Stuffing: Dacron, fiberfill, pellets
Tools: brushes, hemostats, minifasturn pliers, needles, sidecutters, tweezers
Other supplies for miniature bears: ribbons, jewelry findings

ACCESSORIES FOR REGULAR BEARS:
Baskets, glasses, hair ribbons, jewelry, shoes, socks, stands

Clothes for regular bears available.
Furniture for regular bears: chairs

ACCESSORIES FOR MINIATURE BEARS:
Baskets, glasses, hair ribbons, jewelry, shoes, socks, stands
Furniture for miniature bears: chairs
In business for 4 years

CHARMANT TEDDY BEARS

Donna McPherson and Armand Thibodeau
RR #1
Napanee, Ontario K7R 3K6, Canada
Phone: 613-354-6393
Fax: 613-354-6393
Accepts: check, money order, Visa, MasterCard

SUPPLIES FOR REGULAR BEARS:
Fur: acrylic fabrics

CLASSIC TRADITIONS

Monica Murray
P.O. Box 728
Jenks, OK 74037
Phone: 918-299-5416
  Phone orders accepted.
Mail order only.
Accepts: check, money order, Visa, MasterCard
Shows: OK, MO, CA

SUPPLIES FOR REGULAR BEARS:
Eyes: glass, pre-looped, wire
Furs (non-mohair): rayon
Mohair: curly, distressed, feathered, regular, string, tipped, wavy
Joints: cotter pins, disks and washers, hardboard
Patterns: bear patterns
Paws: felt, Ultrasuede
Stuffing: pellets
Tools: brushes, cotter keys, hemostats, needles
Other supplies for regular bears: growlers

SUPPLIES FOR MINIATURE BEARS:
Eyes: bead, glass, pre-looped, wire
Fur: mohair, upholstery velvet, Ultrasuede
Joints: cotter pins, disks and washers, hardboard
Patterns: miniature bear patterns
Paws: felt, Ultrasuede
Stuffing: pellets
Tools: brushes, hemostats, minifasturn pliers, needles

In business for 8 years

CONCEPTS, ETC.

Jacqueline B. Smith
1342 SE 12th Ter.
Cape Coral, FL 33990
Mail order only.
Allow 2 weeks for delivery.
Accepts: check

SUPPLIES FOR MINIATURE BEARS:
Patterns: miniature bear kits, miniature bear patterns, miniature clothing patterns
Tools: needles, tweezers, scissors
In business for 6 months

COUNTRY STUFFINS

Elaine K. Maines
8307 Sunburst Dr.
Cincinnati, OH 45241
Phone: 513-777-0276
  Phone orders accepted.
Mail order only.
Allow 9 weeks for delivery.
Accepts: check, money order
Discounts: bulk order

SUPPLIES FOR REGULAR BEARS:
Furs (non-mohair): tan-, white- and gray-piled acrylic plush
Patterns: bear kit includes all pieces and instructions for 25″ tan bear. No stuffing included.
In business for 7 years

CR'S CRAFTS

P.O. Box 8-5S
Leland, IA 50453
Phone: 515-567-3652
  Phone orders accepted.
Fax: 515-567-3071
  Fax orders accepted.
Store location: 109 5th Ave. West, Leland, IA
Hours: 8:30 A.M.-3:30 P.M.
Catalog: $2
Allow 4-6 weeks for delivery.
Accepts: check, money order, Visa, MasterCard, Discover

SUPPLIES FOR REGULAR BEARS:
Eyes: glass, pre-looped, wire, safety, shank
Furs (non-mohair): acrylic plush, crushed viscose, distressed string cotton, curly, fun fur
Mohair: distressed, feathered, dense, regular, string, kinky curly, ultra sparse
Joints: loc-line armature systems, body wire frames, cotter pins, metal disks and washers, hardboard, lock nuts, plastic doll joints, armature systems (skele-bend)
Patterns: bear kits, bear patterns, clothing patterns (more than twenty clothing patterns for 9″-28″ bears: sports, military outfits, dresses, overalls and more)
Paws: facile suede, felt, leather cloth, Ultrasuede, velour, suede cloth, 100% wool felt, wool blend felt
Stuffing: fiberfill, pellets
Tools: brushes, hemostats, loc-line pliers, needles, 8″ and 12″ stuffing tools
Other supplies for regular bears: embroidery thread, growlers, jewelry findings, music boxes, ribbons, voice boxes, pearl cotton, safety noses, leather-look noses, flocked noses, heart-shaped noses, extra strong thread, musical bank slots

SUPPLIES FOR MINIATURE BEARS:
Eyes: bead, glass, pre-looped, wire, small safety and shank eyes
Fur: mohair, Ultrasuede, extra short pile fur, velour
Joints: cotter pins, disks and washers, hardboard, lock nuts
Patterns: miniature bear kits, miniature bear patterns, miniature clothing patterns
Paws: felt, Ultrasuede, velour, suede cloth, 100% wool felt, wool blend felt
Stuffing: dacron, fiberfill, pellets
Tools: brushes, hemostats, needles, 8″ stuffing tools
Other supplies for miniature bears: ribbons, jewelry findings, safety noses, pearl cotton, extra strong thread

ACCESSORIES FOR REGULAR BEARS:
Baskets, glasses, hair ribbons, jewelry, shoes, socks, stands, trikes, wagons, swings, tractor, roller blades, skateboard, teeter-totter, sled, wood skis, tea sets, purses, wire trikes, ice skates, pacifiers, rattles, umbrellas
Clothes for regular bears: For 12″-17″ bears, many styles, including sweaters and professional outfits; hats, many styles, including football helmets
Furniture for regular bears: rocking chairs, wicker chairs, beach chairs

ACCESSORIES FOR MINIATURE BEARS:
Baskets, glasses, hair ribbons, jewelry, shoes, socks, stands, carriages, rocking horses, trikes
Clothes for miniature bears: hats (many styles)
Furniture for miniature bears: school desks, rocking chairs, wicker chairs, beach and director's chairs, benches
In business for 12 years

DELANEY'S BEAR HOUSE
JoAnne Delaney
7316 E. McKinley
Scottsdale, AZ 85257
Phone: 602-947-6077
Phone orders accepted.
Mail order only.
Catalog: free
Allow 4-5 days for delivery.
Accepts: check, money order
Discounts: bulk order

SUPPLIES FOR REGULAR BEARS:
Joints: cotter pins, disks and washers, hardboard, lock nuts, pop rivets
In business for 11 years

DISCO JOINTS AND TEDDIES
Shirley Voelker
305 Bedford Rd.
Kitchener, Ontario N2G 3A7, Canada
Phone: 519-576-1472
Phone orders accepted.
Mail order only.
Catalog: SASE, allow 1-3 weeks for delivery.
Accepts: check, money order, Visa
Shows: Ontario, Canada

SUPPLIES FOR REGULAR BEARS:
Eyes: glass, pre-looped, safety, shoe button
Furs (non-mohair): acrylic plush
Mohair: curly, distressed, feathered, regular, string, tipped, wavy
Joints: cotter pins, disks and washers, hardboard, lock nuts, plastic doll joints, pop rivets, swivel tilt neck joints, tap bolts, flex limb
Patterns: bear kits, bear patterns
Paws: facile suede, felt, Ultrasuede
Stuffing: Dacron, fiberfill, excelsior, pellets
Tools: brushes, needles
Other supplies for regular bears: growlers, music boxes, pearl cotton, nylon thread

SUPPLIES FOR MINIATURE BEARS:
Patterns: miniature bear kits

ACCESSORIES FOR REGULAR BEARS:
Glasses, stands
In business for 11 years

DOLLSPART
The Teddy Works
8000 Cooper Ave., Bldg. 28
Glendale, NY 11385
Phone: 1-800-336-3655 or 718-326-4971

DONNA BEARS
Donna
5204 Godfrey Rd.
Godfrey, IL 62035
Phone: 618-466-0080 or 1-800-848-5514
Phone orders accepted.
Store location: same
Hours: M-Sat, 10A.M.-5P.M.
Allow 1 week for delivery.
Accepts: check, money order, Visa, MasterCard, Discover, American Express
Discounts: preferred customer
Shows: IL, NY

SUPPLIES FOR REGULAR BEARS:
Eyes: glass, pre-looped, wire, shoe button
Mohair: curly, distressed, feathered, regular, string, tipped, wavy
Joints: loc-line armature systems, cotter pins, disks and washers, hardboard, lock nuts, tap bolts
Patterns: bear kits, bear patterns, clothing patterns
Paws: facile suede, felt, leather cloth, Ultrasuede, velvet
Stuffing: Dacron, fiberfill, pellets
Tools: brushes, cotter keys, hemostats, loc-line pliers, needles, tweezers
Other supplies for regular bears: embroidery thread, growlers, music boxes, ribbons

SUPPLIES FOR MINIATURE BEARS:
Eyes: glass, pre-looped, wires
Fur: mohair, Ultrasuede
Joints: cotter pins, disks and washers, hardboard
Patterns: miniature bear kits, miniature bear patterns
Paws: facile suede, felt, Ultrasuede
Stuffing: Dacron, fiberfill, pellets
Other supplies for miniature bears: ribbons

ACCESSORIES FOR REGULAR BEARS:
Glasses, hair ribbons, jewelry, shoes, socks, stands
Clothes for regular bears available.

ACCESSORIES FOR MINIATURE BEARS:
Baskets, hair ribbons
Furniture for miniature bears available.
In business for 3 years.

EDINBURGH IMPORTS, INC.
Elke Block
P.O. Box 722
Woodland Hills, CA 91365
Phone: 818-591-3800 or 1-800-334-6274 outside CA, including Canada
Phone orders accepted.
Fax: 818-591-3806
Fax orders accepted.
Store location: 23961 Craftsman Rd., Ste. E, Calabasas, CA 91302
Hours: 8:30A.M.-4:30P.M. with appointment
Catalog: free
Allow 1 day for delivery.
Accepts: check, money order, Visa, MasterCard, Discover, credit
Discounts: bulk order. monthly discounted specials.
Shows: more than 100 shows yearly

SUPPLIES FOR REGULAR BEARS:
Eyes: glass, pre-looped, wire, safety, shoe button, paperweight
Furs (non-mohair): acrylic plush, alpaca plush, artificial silk plush, distressed plush, dual plush, modacrylic plush, rayon, silk blends (mohair/silk, alpaca/silk), wool (curly & swirly), cotton string, rayon distressed, curly and matted multi-color synthetics, alpaca w/ guard
Mohair: curly, distressed, feathered, regular, string, tipped, wavy, mixtures, sparse, different colored backing, country (natural backing), extra dense, color blends
Joints: loc-line armature systems, cotter pins, disks and washers, hardboard, lock nuts, pop rivets, swivel tilt neck joints, tap bolts
Patterns: bear kits, bear patterns
Paws: felt
Stuffing: pellets
Tools: brushes, cotter keys, loc-line pliers, needles, stuffing sticks
Other supplies for regular bears: growlers, no-no and yes-no mechanisms

SUPPLIES FOR MINIATURE BEARS:
Eyes: glass, wire
Fur: upholstery velvet, synthetic
Joints: cotter pins, disks and washers, hardboard
Patterns: miniature bear kits, miniature bear patterns
Paws: felt
Stuffing: pellets
Tools: brushes, minifasturn pliers, needles

ACCESSORIES FOR REGULAR BEARS:
Stands

ACCESSORIES FOR MINIATURE BEARS:
Stands
In business for 10 years

EMILY FARMER
P.O. Box 2911
Sanford, NC 27330

ENTERPRISE ART
2860 Roosevelt Blvd.
Clearwater, FL 34620

PEGGY J. FLEMING
P.O. Box 12114
Des Moines, IA 50312
Phone: 515-277-8060
Phone orders: 9A.M.-9P.M.
Patterns: bear kits (from Peggy's original designs)

GOLDEN FUN KITS
Berene Epp
10697-FWP
Golden, CO 80401-0600
Mail order only.
Catalog: $1
Allow 1-2 weeks for delivery.
Accepts: check, money order
Discounts: bulk order
Shows: CO

SUPPLIES FOR REGULAR BEARS:
Eyes: pre-looped, safety, life-lyk eyebacks
Furs (non-mohair): acrylic plush, a variety of animal furs
Joints: cotter pins, disks and washers, hardboard, plastic doll joints, flexlimb
Patterns: bear kits, bear patterns, clothing patterns
Paws: vinyl koala paws
Stuffing: pellets
Tools: brushes, stuffing tools, basting pins

Other supplies for regular bears: growlers, music boxes, voice boxes, electronic growlers, squeakers, noses (plastic and flocked)
In business for 15 years

GOOSEBERRY HILL
Dennis Pace
1881 Old Lincoln Hwy.
Coalville, UT 84017
Phone: 801-336-2116 or 801-336-2780
Phone orders accepted.
Store location at above address.
Hours: 8A.M.-5P.M.
Catalog: free
Allow 10 days for delivery.
Accepts: check, money order, Visa, MasterCard
Discounts: bulk order
Shows: wholesale only, TX

SUPPLIES FOR REGULAR BEARS:
Eyes: safety, shank
Mohair: curly, distressed, feathered, regular, string, tipped, wavy
Joints: cotter pins, disks and washers, hardboard, pop rivets
Patterns: bear kits, bear patterns, clothing patterns
Paws: felt
Other supplies for regular bears: embroidery thread, nylon, ribbons

SUPPLIES FOR MINIATURE BEARS:
Fur: mohair
Joints: cotter pins, disks and washers
Patterns: miniature bear kits, miniature bear patterns
Other supplies for miniature bears: ribbons

ACCESSORIES FOR REGULAR BEARS:
Hair ribbons
In business for 16 years

THE GREAT CANADIAN PATTERN CO.
Candy Milliard
424 West 28th St.
North Vancouver, British Columbia V7N 2S3
Canada
Mail order only.
Catalog: $3, allow 2 days for delivery.

SUPPLIES FOR REGULAR BEARS:
Patterns: bear patterns, bear kits (more than 3 dozen patterns and kits for patterns ranging from 7"-24")

HEART PRODUCTIONS
Gretchen McKillip or Catie Walker
45 W. Imperial Dr.
Walla Walla, WA 99362
Phone: 509-525-0395 or 509-529-8868
Fax: 509-522-0747
Mail order only.

SUPPLIES FOR REGULAR BEARS:
Patterns: bear kits, bear patterns, clothing patterns

SUPPLIES FOR MINIATURE BEARS:
Patterns: miniature bear kits, miniature bear patterns, miniature clothing patterns

HEMER HOUSE DESIGNS
Jane Perala
Site G, C-43, RR 2
Nanaimo, British Columbia V9R 5K2, Canada
Phone: 604-722-3134
Phone orders accepted.
Mail order only.
Catalog: $3, refundable with purchase.
Allow 4-6 weeks for delivery.
Accepts: check, money order, Visa, MasterCard
Discounts: bulk order
Shows: Alberta, British Columbia

SUPPLIES FOR REGULAR BEARS:
Patterns: bear kits, bear patterns

SUPPLIES FOR MINIATURE BEARS:
Patterns: miniature bear kits, miniature bear patterns

HERB BEARIES
Lisa Rupp
P.O. Box 627
Westfield, IN 46074
Phone: 317-844-9162 or 1-800-634-2543
Phone orders accepted.
Mail order only.
Catalog: $1
Allow 3-4 days for delivery.
Accepts: check, money order, Visa, MasterCard
Discounts: free pattern with order of $30
Shows: IN

SUPPLIES FOR REGULAR BEARS:
Joints: hardboard, lock nuts
Patterns: bear kits, bear patterns

ACCESSORIES FOR REGULAR BEARS:
Gift tags, owner certificates, pillows, flowerpots

Clothes for regular bears: hats, aprons
Furniture for regular bears: twig furniture
In business for 2 years

PAM HOLTON DESIGNS

Pam Holton
P.O. Box 5022/423
Lake Forest, CA 92630
Phone: 714-951-8074
Phone orders accepted.
Mail order only.
Catalog: $1
Allow 5-10 days for delivery.
Accepts: check, money order, Visa, MasterCard
Discounts: $3 coupon with order
Shows: IL, CA

SUPPLIES FOR REGULAR BEARS:
Patterns: bear kits and patterns for more than 26 bears, sizes 4″-10″, clothing patterns
In business for 12 years

INTERCAL TRADING GROUP

1760 Monrovia, Suite A-17
Costa Mesa, CA 92627
Phone: 714-645-9396
Phone orders accepted.
Fax: 716-645-5471
Fax orders accepted.
Store location at above address.
Hours: by appointment
Catalog: 2 stamps; $2 foreign
Allow 1 day for delivery.
Accepts: check, money order, Visa, MasterCard
Shows: various

SUPPLIES FOR REGULAR BEARS:
Eyes: glass, pre-looped, shoe button
Furs (non-mohair): acrylic plush, alpaca plush, rayon, string cotton
Mohair: curly, distressed, feathered, regular, string, tipped, wavy. Only U.S. source for English mohair, including distressed, vintage finish, feather finish, kinky curly
Joints: cotter pins, disks and washers, hardboard, lock nuts
Paws: felt
Tools: brushes
Other supplies for regular bears: embroidery thread, growlers

SUPPLIES FOR MINIATURE BEARS:
Eyes: glass, wire
Fur: mohair

Joints: cotter pins, disks and washers, hardboard
Paws: felt
In business for 11 years

J & J CREATIVE SUPPLIES, INC.

510 Vista Park Dr., Bldg. #5
Pittsburgh, PA 15205

J.D. BABB, INC.

Diane Babb
1126 Ivon Ave.
Endicott, NY 13760-1431
Phone: 607-754-0391
Phone orders accepted.
Fax: 607-754-0391
Fax orders accepted.
Mail order only.
Catalog: $2
Allow 7-14 days for delivery.
Accepts: check, money order, Visa, MasterCard
Discounts: bulk order
Shows: IA, MA, MD

SUPPLIES FOR REGULAR BEARS:
Eyes: glass, wire, safety
Furs (non-mohair): acrylic plush, modacrylic plush
Mohair: curly, distressed, feathered, regular, string, tipped, wavy
Joints: loc-line armature systems, cotter pins, disks and washers, hardboard, lock nuts, plastic doll joints, pop rivets, tap bolts, skele-bend armature systems
Patterns: bear kits, bear patterns, clothing patterns (more than 50 for small, medium, large and preemie bears)
Paws: facile suede
Stuffing: pellets
Tools: brushes, hemostats, loc-line pliers, needles
Other supplies for regular bears: growlers

SUPPLIES FOR MINIATURE BEARS:
Eyes: glass on wire, plastic safety
Fur: mohair, upholstery velvet
Joints: cotter pins, disks and washers, hardboard, washers
Patterns: miniature bear kits, miniature bear patterns
Paws: facile suede, Ultrasuede
Stuffing: pellets
Tools: brushes, hemostats

ACCESSORIES FOR REGULAR BEARS:
Glasses, stands
In business for 21 years

ANITA KELSEY

12345 Lake City Way NE #198
Seattle, WA 98125
Phone: 206-365-8753
Patterns: bear patterns from Anita's original designs. Anita is also a dealer for Edinburgh Imports.

GRETCHEN MCKILLIP

45 W. Imperial Dr.
Walla Walla, WA 99362
Phone: 509-525-0395
Phone orders: 10A.M.-5P.M.
Mail order only
Patterns: bear patterns, bear kits designed by Gretchen

KATHY MCMICHAEL

647 Pleasant
Walla Walla, WA 99362
Phone: 509-529-2295
Phone orders accepted.
Mail order only.
Allow up to 4 weeks for delivery.
Accepts: check, money order, Visa, MasterCard, Discover
Shows: OR

SUPPLIES FOR REGULAR BEARS:
Eyes: glass, pre-looped, safety
Furs (non-mohair): acrylic plush, German synthetic
Mohair: curly, distressed, feathered, regular, string, tipped, wavy
Joints: disks and washers, hardboard, lock nuts
Patterns: bear kits, bear patterns
Paws: Ultrasuede
Stuffing: Dacron, fiberfill, pellets
Tools: brushes
Other supplies for regular bears: music boxes, pearl cotton, wired ribbon

ACCESSORIES FOR REGULAR BEARS:
Glasses, hair ribbons, stands
Clothes for regular bears: velvet hats
In business for 11 years

MONTEREY, INC.

1725 E. Delavan Dr.
Janesville, WI 53545

MY VERY OWN BEAR
Vivian Fritze
#1406 12141 Jasper Ave.
Edmonton, Alberta T5N 3X8, Canada
Phone: 403-482-6800
    Phone orders accepted.
Fax: 403-482-6811
    Fax orders accepted.
Mail order only.
Catalog: $5, refundable with purchase.
Allow 4 weeks for delivery.
Accepts: check, money order
Shows: Western Canada

SUPPLIES FOR MINIATURE BEARS:
Patterns: miniature bear kits
In business for 4 years

NEVER A DULL NEEDLE
3101 Silina, Suite 101
Virginia Beach, VA 23452

NEWARK DRESSMAKER SUPPLY
6473 Ruch Rd.
Lehigh Valley, PA 18002-0730

PANDA-MONIUM
R.R. 3, Box 206
Elwood, IN 46036

PICKWICK PURVEYORS
Jacklyn Gualtieri
8 Spring Ridge Dr.
Berkeley Heights, NJ 07922
Phone: 908-508-1711
    Phone orders accepted.
Fax: 908-665-9333
    Fax orders accepted.
Mail order only.
Catalog: $3, refundable with purchase.
Allow 2-6 weeks for delivery.
Accepts: check, money order, Visa, MasterCard
Discounts: bulk order
Shows: NJ, RI, MA

SUPPLIES FOR REGULAR BEARS:
Patterns: bear kits, bear patterns
In business for 6 years

PIECEMAKERS, INC.
1720 Adams Ave.
Costa Mesa, CA 92626
Phone: 714-641-3112
    Phone orders accepted.
Fax: 714-641-2883
    Fax orders accepted.
Store location: same

Hours: M-F, 10A.M.-9P.M. Sat, Sun, 10A.M.-5:30P.M.
Allow 1-2 weeks for delivery.
Accepts: check, money order, Visa, MasterCard, Discover
Shows: GA, TX, CA

SUPPLIES FOR REGULAR BEARS:
Eyes: glass, pre-looped, safety, shank
Furs (non-mohair): acrylic plush, alpaca plush, silk blends (silk/alpaca)
Mohair: curly, distressed, feathered, regular, string, tipped, wavy
Joints: disks and washers, hardboard, lock nuts, plastic doll joints
Patterns: bear kits, bear patterns
Paws: felt, wool
Stuffing: fiberfill, pellets
Tools: brushes, hemostats, needles, tweezers
Other supplies for regular bears: embroidery thread, jewelry findings, music boxes

SUPPLIES FOR MINIATURE BEARS:
Eyes: bead, glass, pre-looped
Fur: mohair
Joints: disks and washers, lock nuts, joint kits
Patterns: miniature bear kits, miniature bear patterns
Paws: felt
Stuffing: fiberfill, pellets
Tools: hemostats, needles, tweezers
Other supplies for miniature bears: ribbons, jewelry findings

ACCESSORIES FOR REGULAR BEARS:
Glasses, hair ribbons, jewelry, stands

ACCESSORIES FOR MINIATURE BEARS:
Glasses, hair ribbons
In business for 18 years

QUILTERS' QUARTERS
Connie Archambault
595 Mt. Pleasant Rd.
Toronto, Ontario M4S 2M5, Canada
Phone: 416-487-1047
    Phone orders accepted.
Store location: same
Hours: M-F, 10A.M.-6P.M.
Sat, 10A.M.-5:30P.M.
Accepts: check, money order, Visa, MasterCard

SUPPLIES FOR REGULAR BEARS:
Eyes: glass, pre-looped, wire, safety
Furs (non-mohair): acrylic plush

Mohair: curly, distressed, feathered, regular, string, tipped, wavy
Joints: cotter pins, disks and washers, hardboard
Patterns: bear kits, bear patterns
Paws: felt, Ultrasuede, ultra leather
Stuffing: Dacron, fiberfill, pellets
Tools: brushes, cotter keys, hemostats, needles
Other supplies for regular bears: embroidery thread, growlers, jewelry findings, ribbons

SUPPLIES FOR MINIATURE BEARS:
Eyes: bead, glass, wire
Fur: mohair, Ultrasuede
Joints: cotter pins, disks and washers, hardboard
Patterns: miniature bear kits, miniature bear patterns
Paws: felt, Ultrasuede
Stuffing: Dacron, fiberfill, pellets
Tools: brushes, hemostats, needles
Other supplies for miniature bears: ribbons, jewelry findings

ACCESSORIES FOR REGULAR BEARS:
Wagons, trikes, bear shelves (''Bear'' is carved into the wood)
In business for 6 years

SHIRLEY ANN GIFTS
Shirley Lentsch
1139 Autumn St.
Roseville, MN 55113
Mail order only.
Catalog: $2
Accepts: check, money order
Discounts: free pattern with $50 order

SUPPLIES FOR REGULAR BEARS:
Patterns: bear patterns (large selection), clothing patterns
In business for 7 years

BARBARA IRWIN SHYNKARYK
6811 Cairns Ct.
Richmond, British Columbia V7C 5E6, Canada
Phone: 604-275-9096
    Phone orders: anytime
Patterns: bear patterns designed by Barbara

SOUTH P.A.W. BEARS
Patricia Chambers
P.O. Box 121172
Fort Worth, TX 76121
Mail order only.

Catalog: $1, refundable with purchase.
Allow 2-4 weeks for delivery.
Accepts: check, money order, Master-
Card
Shows: KS, OK, TX

SUPPLIES FOR REGULAR BEARS:
Eyes: glass, wire
Furs (non-mohair): acrylic plush, vin-
tage fabrics
Mohair: regular
Joints: disks and washers, tap bolts
Patterns: bear patterns, clothing patterns
Paws: felt, vintage fabrics
Stuffing: Dacron, fiberfill
Tools: brushes, hemostats, needles
Other supplies for regular bears: em-
broidery thread, jewelry findings, rib-
bons

SUPPLIES FOR MINIATURE BEARS:
Eyes: glass
Other supplies for miniature bears: rib-
bons, vintage findings, polymer clay

ACCESSORIES FOR REGULAR BEARS:
Baskets decorated with polymer clay
bears

ACCESSORIES FOR MINIATURE BEARS:
Display cabinets
In business for 6 years

SPARE BEAR PARTS
Linda Mead
P.O. Box 56-W
Interlochen, MI 49643
Phone: 616-275-6993
Phone orders accepted.
Fax: 616-275-6230
Fax orders accepted.
Mail order only.
Catalog: $1.25
Shipped next day.
Accepts: check, money order, Visa, Mas-
terCard, Discover, COD
Discounts: bulk order
Shows: Midwest; FL

SUPPLIES FOR REGULAR BEARS:
Eyes: glass, pre-looped, wire, safety,
shoe button
Furs (non-mohair): acrylic plush, distressed plush, modacrylic plush, silk
blends
Mohair: distressed, regular, wavy
Joints: body wire frames, cotter pins,
disks and washers, hardboard, lock
nuts, pop rivets, tap bolts
Patterns: bear kits, bear patterns

Paws: facile suede, felt
Stuffing: Dacron, fiberfill, excelsior, pellets, wood wool
Tools: needles, brushes, stuffing tools
Other supplies for regular bears: growlers, music boxes, pearl cotton, sew in
labels, wide-waisted stands, hand aid
support gloves, videos on bearmaking, learning kit series kits

ACCESSORIES FOR REGULAR BEARS:
Glasses
In business for 6 years

STANDARD DOLL CO.
23-83 31st St.
Long Island City, NY 11105
Phone: 718-721-7787

STANISLAUS IMPORTS
Jonnie Weingarten
41 14th Ave.
San Francisco, CA 94103
Phone: 415-431-7122 or 1-800-848-
1986
Phone orders accepted.
Fax: 415-431-4365
Fax orders accepted.
Hours: M-F, 9 A.M.-2 P.M.
Catalog: $5 and tax number, allow 3
weeks for delivery.
Accepts: check, money order, Visa, busi-
ness check
Discounts: bulk order
Shows: Toy Fair, Germany; Various
hobby shows; HIA show; ACCI show

SUPPLIES FOR REGULAR BEARS:
Eyes: pre-looped, wire, safety, sew-on
eyes
Joints: loc-line armature systems, plastic
doll joints
Tools: hemostats, loc-line pliers, tweezers
Other supplies for regular bears: growlers, jewelry findings, music boxes,
ribbons

SUPPLIES FOR MINIATURE BEARS:
Glass, on wires

ACCESSORIES FOR REGULAR BEARS:
Baskets, glasses, jewelry, shoes, socks,
stands
Furniture for regular bears available.

A SWEET REMEMBRANCE
Paula Walton
172 Aspetuck Ridge Rd.
New Milford, CT 06776-5611

Phone: 203-355-5709
Phone orders accepted.
Mail order only.
Catalog: $5, refundable with purchase.
Allow 2 weeks or less for delivery.
Accepts: check, money order, layaway
Discounts: buy 5, get 6th at half price
Shows: East Coast

SUPPLIES FOR REGULAR BEARS:
Joints: disks and washers, lock nuts
Patterns: bear patterns
Tools: needles

ACCESSORIES FOR REGULAR BEARS:
Clothes for regular bears: custom-made
clothing (by special order)
In business for 11 years

TAYLOR'S CUTAWAYS & STUFF
Jim Taylor
2802 E. Washington St.
Urbana, IL 61801-4699
Mail order only.
Catalog: $1
Allow 5-10 days for delivery.
Accepts: check, money order, Visa, Mas-
terCard

SUPPLIES FOR REGULAR BEARS:
Eyes: safety
Furs (non-mohair): fur by the pound,
long pile
Joints: plastic doll joints
Patterns: bear kits, bear patterns

TEDDYS BY TRACY
Tracy Main
32 Pikehall Pl.
Baltimore, MD 21236
Phone: 410-529-2418
Phone orders accepted.
Fax: 410-529-2418
Fax orders accepted.
Mail order only.
Catalog: $5, refundable with purchase.
Allow 2 weeks for delivery.
Accepts: check, money order, Visa, Mas-
terCard
Discounts: bulk order
Shows: MD, IL

SUPPLIES FOR MINIATURE BEARS:
Eyes: onyx, seed beads, Austrian Flat-
back crystals
Fur: Ultrasuede, more than 40 colors of
upholstery velvet
Joints: disks and washers, cotter pins in
¼" and ½", hardboard

Patterns: miniature bear kits, miniature bear patterns

Paws: facile suede, Ultrasuede, more than 100 colors available

Tools: hemostats (3 sizes), needles, quilter's needles

Other supplies for miniature bears: silk ribbon in 18 colors, organdy ribbon, Bunka, doll buttons, four sizes of display domes

More about these supplies for miniature bears: Sample ring of Ultrasuede available for $15. Sample card of silk ribbon available for $12. Sample of spark organdy ribbon available for $7.50.

ACCESSORIES FOR MINIATURE BEARS:

Furniture for miniature bears: miniature furniture sold at shows

In business for 5 years

THE TEDDY TAILOR

Jeanne M. Klein
P.O. Box 234
Sutherlin, OR 97479
Phone: 503-459-9517
  Phone orders accepted.
Mail order only.
Catalog: $3 in USA; $5 foreign
Allow 10 days for delivery.
Accepts: check, money order, Visa, MasterCard
Discounts: bulk order
Shows: OR

SUPPLIES FOR REGULAR BEARS:

Patterns: bear kits, bear patterns
In business for 9 years

TEDDY TOGS

Elizabeth S. Mabry
P.O. Box 9563
Bend, OR 97708
Phone: 503-382-7959
  Phone orders accepted.
Mail order only.

Catalog: $2 + SASE
Accepts: check, money order
Shows: Pacific Northwest

SUPPLIES FOR REGULAR BEARS:

Patterns: knitted clothing patterns

ACCESSORIES FOR REGULAR BEARS:

Clothes for regular bears: knitted clothing
In business for 9 years

2 BEARS TEDDY BEARS

Ted, Pauline & John Renpenning
1904-20 Avenue N.W.
Calgary, Alberta T2M 1H5, Canada
Phone: 403-282-4770
  Phone orders accepted.
Fax: 403-282-9234
  Fax orders accepted.
Store location: same
Hours: M-Sat, 10A.M.-6P.M. Sun, noon-5P.M.
Catalog: $5, refundable with purchase.
Allow 1-2 weeks for delivery.
Accepts: check, money order, Visa, MasterCard, American Express
Discounts: bulk order on mohair only
Shows: Manitoba, Saskatchewan, Alberta, British Columbia

SUPPLIES FOR REGULAR BEARS:

Eyes: glass, pre-looped, wire, safety, shoe button

Furs (non-mohair): acrylic plush, alpaca plush, cashmere, rayon

Mohair: curly, distressed, feathered, regular, string, tipped, wavy

Joints: disks and washers, hardboard, lock nuts

Patterns: bear kits, bear patterns

Paws: felt (Merino wool), Ultrasuede

Stuffing: pellets, steel shot

Tools: brushes, needles, stuffing sticks

Other supplies for regular bears: embroidery thread, yes-no mechanisms, voice boxes, pearl cotton

SUPPLIES FOR MINIATURE BEARS:

Eyes: bead, glass, pre-looped, on wires, onyx

Fur: mohair, upholstery velvet, Ultrasuede

Joints: cotter pins, disks and washers, hardboard, lock nuts

Patterns: miniature bear kits, miniature bear patterns

Paws: Ultrasuede

Stuffing: pellets, steel shot

Tools: brushes, needles

ACCESSORIES FOR REGULAR BEARS:

Stands
Furniture for regular bears available.
In business for 5 years

TYDD'S TEDDIES

50 West 4th St.
Hamilton, Ontario L9C 3M4, Canada

PAMELA WOOLEY

5021 Stringtown Rd.
Evansville, IN 47711
Phone: 812-464-2521
  Phone orders accepted.
Fax: 812-464-2521
  Fax orders accepted.
Mail order only.
Catalog: SASE
Allow 3-4 days for delivery.
Accepts: check, money order, Visa, MasterCard
Shows: IL, CA

SUPPLIES FOR REGULAR BEARS:

Eyes: shoe button (antique)

ACCESSORIES FOR REGULAR BEARS:

Clothes for regular bears: circa 1915 white starched collars with button studs
In business for 9 years

YLI CORPORATION

45 West 300 North
Provo, UT 84601

3
Artists

How to Use This Chapter

*T*here are thousands of artists in the USA and Canada, and there is no way we could have gathered information from all of them for this book. However, there is a large selection of artist listings on the pages that follow that will give collectors a good starting point for locating bears that meet their fancy. Our only requirement for inclusion in the sourcebook was that the artists had to make and sell their own designs. Some well-known artists chose not to be included due to the large volume of orders and phone calls they receive, and we honored their request. We only included those artists who returned a questionnaire before the deadline.

Listed are full- and part-time artists; artists that sell their bears in retail stores, at shows, or out of their homes; artists with years of experience and several honors and publications to their credit and artists who are just entering the teddy bear community. We have made absolutely no judgements about the quality of workmanship, and have attempted to be as all-inclusive as possible. We aim to provide information about well-known artists and to give new artists exposure.

All information in these listings was provided by the artists. We have tried to provide information that is as up-to-date as possible, but keep in mind that artists' work is constantly changing, and the listing may not be 100 percent correct. The contact and catalog information was provided so that collectors would be able to contact the artist about his/her creations and learn of any changes in style and design. Artists also provided the photographs used. They are meant to serve as examples of the artist's work, and may not be available at the time of publication. In fact, many are one-of-a-kinds. All photographs were printed in black-and-white in order to keep the book affordable. When provided, the photos were included directly above the artist's name.

Many artists listed have fax machines in their homes or elsewhere that they can use to receive orders and other information. Before faxing a request for information or an order, check to see if the phone and fax numbers are the same. If they are, it is probably best to call the artist first and let him or her know you will be sending a fax. Make sure to mark all faxes with your name, address, phone and fax number, as well as the name, address, phone and fax number of the recipient. Some fax numbers listed are shared by more than one person or business, so complete information is important.

Whether you are contacting an artist by phone or fax, be mindful of the recipient's location and take time zone differences into account. Although some listings state that the artist accept calls at anytime, it is usually best not to phone or fax late at night or very early in the morning. Fax machines and ringing phones can be very disruptive, especially for those artists who have families and work out of their homes. Most artists have listed the hours that they will take calls. Please pay careful attention to this information, and if you are having a hard time reaching an artist, leave a message!

As a matter of courtesy, never stop by an artist's home or studio unannounced unless the listing specifically states that walk-in customers are welcome. Many artists welcome home appointments and have listed how much advance notice they will need to prepare for such a visit.

If you are making a special trip to a specific store in order to purchase an artist's bear, be sure to call the store first. Stores are often changing the artist bears they carry, and you don't want to make a pointless trip.

The artists listed in this chapter offer a wide variety of creative designs and use all kinds of materials. The chapter includes everything from miniature bears to big bears, traditional bears to trendy bears and bare bears to fully dressed bears. There are artists who will make heirloom bears out of recycled fur, and artists who stick solely to synthetics or mohair. If you are looking for miniature bears, the miniature bear index at the back of the book will make your search simpler. No matter what you are looking for in this chapter, you are sure to find an artist who has created the bear of your dreams!

Outside the Lines: A Perspective on Creativity

BY DIANE GARD

*M*y eyes were bright and eager with anticipation, glowing with the reflection of the pretty pink candles. I had already made my special wish, so I quickly inhaled, and with all the force of my four-year-old energy, I blew out the tiny flames. Later, I whispered my wish to my mom. In my child's wisdom, I knew that this was how it was done. It had always worked before. The next morning, as I rubbed the sleep out of my eyes, I saw, at the foot of my bed, that my wish had appeared . . . a brand new box of sixty-four Crayola crayons! (My sister always wished for a pony—she is still waiting.)

Inside the magic green and gold box was a kaleidoscope of colors, each with its pristine paper wrapping and perfectly shaped tip. When I brought out the coloring books, I was a little sad, knowing that these crayons would never again be new. But I loved to draw and found immense joy in seeing the colors magically transform themselves on paper.

Going Outside the Lines

When I was little, I was careful to stay inside the lines. I expertly filled in the larger areas with perfect parallel strokes. Everything was the right shade or hue. The trees were burnt sienna with forest green leaves. The sky was sky blue, of course, and the sun, yellow gold. I printed my name carefully on each page. My parents praised my "perfect" drawings. "Isn't she talented to be able to stay inside the lines!" they said. Many of my drawings were displayed on the refrigerator gallery for all to admire. I enjoyed the attention and praise. With my tiny ego sated, I filled more pages in the coloring books, all neat and precise.

The years when I was between the ages of six and nine were blissful. I was a big sister and I was in school. I knew the rules and followed most of them. Being perfect still got good praise. But another concept was beginning to emerge, a simple view on creativity that eventually became an inspiration and ultimately a lifelong philosophy. I observed that some rules didn't make sense and that breaking them didn't make the sky fall. Being

Diane Gard has been making bears since 1982. She was born in Denver, Colorado and still lives at the foot of the colorful Rocky Mountains. She began sewing and creating her own designs when she was 12 years old, and received formal training at Colorado State University in Ft. Collins. Diane has worked in various creative fields while raising two young children. Her bears have been featured in several publications, and she has written widely on the subject of teddy bears. She regularly presents workshops on bearmaking.

perfect was an adult concept, I realized, and finding delight from within was often as rewarding as applause.

I celebrated this new passion by drawing purple trees, red skies and green cats. Sometimes I went outside the lines! My strokes were bolder and impulsive and I made up imaginary animals and abstract shapes. I was using my imagination to its limit and I was having great fun! Art was free from rules, and creating became an obsession. It seems ironic to me now that it took thirty years to recapture my long-dormant appetite for creativity in the world of teddy bear artistry.

A Child's Imagination

Since 1982, I have designed and made teddy bears, those whimsical, quizzical-eyed bears with a heart. My bears are sometimes traditional, often unconventional, likely to be frivolous, and-now that I am getting older myself—a little eccentric. Is there such a big difference between eccentricity and childishness? I still love the exemption from rules and the challenge of imagination. I enjoy watching children and learning from them the freedom to fantasize, as I did with two classes of talented grade schoolers.

In 1993, I received two packages in the mail. Each contained stories, drawings and letters from two second-grade classes, one in Virginia and one in Arizona. Their teachers, both teddy bear lovers, had conceived inventive assignments for their students. In one class, they each wrote a story about Marisa Bearenson, one of my long-legged fashion bears. Each student sent me a story in a hand-drawn eight-page book. The stories

are spontaneous and bright, funny and sometimes poignant. The kids have described Marisa going to the mall and shopping. She has bought a cat and taken it to the movie, made a Halloween costume out of discarded clothes and had her hat stolen. She has disguised herself as a toy in a department store so she could be adopted, and she's had a manicure. Each page of the books is illustrated in such a way as to tell a story in itself. Marisa, the heroine, seemingly has no boundaries, just as the books are free in their form.

The second class sent me crayon drawings accompanied by letters, each describing a bear they had invented. They noted the bear's features, size, clothing and marketability. The children had designed their bears carefully and with great attention to detail. Nothing was too far out for them. David's bear holds a water gun, and when

The Business of Bear Artistry: What Every Artist and Collector Should Know

For many artists, bearmaking is a hobby, with the majority of the rewards coming in the form of camaraderie with customers and other artists as opposed to income. An amazing number of bear makers come from high-tech/high-stress backgrounds. Terrie Effan, for example, used to be a nuclear engineer! I was an engineer at I.B.M. before I started making bears. The teddy bear world is, for the most part, a very "warm and fuzzy" place-much friendlier than most large business environments.

Unfortunately, good feelings don't pay the bills! In many cases, these artists depend upon their teddy bear income to make ends meet. They must price their bears accordingly, allowing them to earn a wage that justifies their giving up corporate positions. Keep in mind, however, that less expensive bears are not necessarily inferior, nor are higher priced bears undeniably superior.

As demand for an artist's work increases, that artist has several options. He or she may simply maintain a waiting list, notifying customers as bears become available. A deposit may or may not be required. This method works quite well for artists who create limited editions, as well as those who do not mind the pressure of having customers waiting for particular pieces. Keep in mind that not all artists have a catalog or price list. Quite a few bear artists make one-of-a-kind bears and do not take orders. Before contacting artists regarding their

bears, please check their listing in this book to see what their policies are.

Another way for artists to handle increased demand is to adjust the price range of their bears accordingly. An artist, working unassisted, can only make so many bears each year. Artists with particularly low production but high product demand can command much higher prices for the few bears produced than if they made hundreds of bears each year.

As orders pile up, some bearmakers recruit helpers to ease the load. These assistants may be family members, friends, or even pieceworkers in the Orient. Artists may have assistants simply trace patterns and cut pieces for them, or they may have entire bears produced by these helpers. Although there is nothing wrong with mass-produced or manufactured bears, not all artists getting help with their bears make it clear that they do so. A wise collector will ask artists if they do all the work themselves, or if they have assistance. Artist bears are generally considered to be made completely by the artist. It has been argued that even the Great Masters of the art world have as students prepare their canvases for them, but with artist bears, every stitch is part of the artistic process. Honesty is always the best policy, and any compromise jeopardizes the integrity and future of the hobby.

—Debbie Kesling

you squeeze its stomach, water will come out of the gun. Rachael's bear has a waterproof belly that turns into a rainbow when it gets wet. Emily designed a Rock and Roll bear named Taz, who "breaks all the rules." Some bears are eight feet tall and will cost $2.99. Another has Silly Putty hands for climbing walls. There is even one who is the President and invites you to dinner! I was charmed and totally humbled by the rich imaginations of the children. These seven- and eight-year-olds hold the magic of life in their hearts with unaffected vision and ingenuity, untouched yet by adult discipline. I now take special pleasure in sharing these letters, stories and slides of their drawings in presentations at shows.

The Child in Each of Us

It became apparent to me through this experience that pure creative genius is that of a child's. My research showed that I was not alone in this theory. Pablo Picasso, on speaking of the true genius of children, said, "When I was their age I could draw like Raphael, but it has taken me a lifetime to learn to draw like (children)." Picasso cultivated certain childlike personality features. In his artwork he searched for the simplest underlying shapes and strove to capture all the details of a visual experience on paper—all characteristics of the art of children.

Young children have the freedom of time to let their imaginations roam, to ask questions about the marvels that inspire awe, and then to pursue these questions and master their skills. They think nothing of doing something over and over until they get it right. As adults, we believe we are fettered by time. We are used to mastering a task quickly and when we can't, we get discouraged and often give up. Others are challenged to solve the problem.

One of our greatest "problem solvers," and perennial children, was Albert Einstein. Einstein was aware of the parallels between his thought patterns and those associated with children. He once asked, "How did I come up with the theory of relativity? The reason, I think, is that a normal adult never stops to think about the problems of space and time. These are the things which (one) thought of as a child. But my intellectual development was retarded, as a result of which I began to wonder about space and time only when I had already grown up." Einstein is also quoted as saying, "Imagination is more important than knowledge." He prided himself on the preservation of certain childlike aspects, such as curiosity and defiance of convention. Like other

creators, he placed the mind and spirit of the young child on a pedestal. Only in the past century have artists in all fields shown an interest in the symbolic works of young children, and like Einstein and Picasso, an abiding curiosity about children's minds.

We are now into the second decade of the resurgence of teddy bear collecting, and as I look around at the thousands of wonderful teddy bear faces, I see creations inspired by the perfect imagination drawn from the genius of childhood innocence. It hasn't taken us a lifetime like Picasso or Einstein. Perhaps teddy bear artists are closer to that "inner place" because the teddy bear itself is the classic symbol of childhood. Like children, these artists are serious in their work, and yet aren't afraid to be delightfully silly. But it is not easy to make the transition from adult discipline to childish freedom.

Letting Go of the Rules

Although I still continue to create my unique teddy bears, I now teach teddy bear-making classes several times a year. I begin the classes by guiding each student through the difficult process of designing their own original pattern. I believe that by adulthood we have been taught to view everything on a proportional scale. For instance, on an architect's rendering, you can see that the trees and the shrubs and the people are all in a certain scale to match the size of the building. If the people were too tall or the trees too short, it would look wrong to us. In teddy bear-making, we don't have to follow those rules anymore, but it is difficult to unlearn a concept so ingrained.

As my students are drafting the patterns for their new bears, they might ask questions like: "Is this leg too long?" or "Is this tummy too fat?" or "Will this nose look right?" My answer is always, "I don't know, what do you think?" There is no answer because there are no rules in art. If there were, we would have no Picassos or Mozarts or Warhols. Most important, I believe bear-making is a genuine art form, where one searches his or her heart to discover that purity of vision drawn from the child within, and to create a remarkable teddy bear with the unique personality that comes from the spirit of the artist. I am dismayed when I see a bear that looks like the bear of another artist. I have a vision of a huge blank canvas just waiting to be filled with the brushstrokes of an inventive mind. Each artist possesses the gift of wonder that will become the heart of the bear.

In my classes, I encourage the students to be spontaneous rather than worrying about following written in-

What You Should Know About Mass-Manufacturing Your Designs

If you are a well-established artist with more customers than you can handle, you have probably considered the possibility of mass-manufacturing your bears. Though some manufacturers actively seek out talented artists to add to their design teams, many rely on the talents of in-house designers. On the other hand, a motivated artist can approach a company, asking for the opportunity to design for them. If you feel you are ready to offer design services to a manufacturer, you will probably need to send them a portfolio of your work. This would include photos of your bears, articles featuring your bears that have appeared in books and periodicals, and any other items that would give the company a "feel" for your style.

When a company is looking at a particular design for mass-production, they are asking themselves the following questions: Will this bear be appealing and marketable? Will we be able to manufacture it for a reasonable price? Are the necessary supplies for this design readily available? If the manufacturer expresses interest, make certain you have a contract, and that you understand the terms of the agreement. You will probably be given deadlines, and you will be expected to meet those deadlines, so be realistic in your expectations.

The prospect of seeing your designs mass-manufactured may be very appealing, but there is a downside, as well. Typically, the payment you receive for your design is not very large. You may receive royalties based upon the number of bears sold from your designs, at the rate of a few cents per bear. The prototype bear you give the manufacturer will probably not be returned to you. There could be negative repercussions from other artists, as mass-production is sometimes considered to be "selling out."

On the positive side, if you have more customers than you can handle, mass-manufacturing your designs may be the appropriate path for you. This also may be true if the price of your original pieces is out of the range of the majority of collectors, or if you have good designs that you are simply tired of making. In the end, only you can make the choice that is right for you!

—*Debbie Kesling*

---

structions. I hope they come away with a truer understanding of the process of creating. They start with a vision. Putting that vision onto a one-dimensional piece of paper is sometimes frustrating. But as I watch the students struggle with the process, I see untapped creativity begin to break through. The looks on their faces slowly change from bewildered concentration to confident smiles as the realization of long-hidden talent emerges. Their eyes grow bright with surprise as they see their vision taking shape. I stare in wonderment as they see the furry mohair, and I share their excitement at the discovery of this new form of self-expression. The atmosphere is palpable with enthusiasm.

Life-Long Friendships

I am not surprised, though, as I see the students hugging and exchanging addresses at the end of the class. They enthusiastically keep in touch with me and with each other. It brings back memories from my first years of making bears and the forging of new friendships that I still cherish today. The world of bear artistry has been from its beginning a sharing and friendly community. It still amazes me that although all of us are in competition with each other at shows, we still remain loyal friends and cheer each other's successes. In elementary school, our report cards had a section where the teacher noted our abilities to share and to "work and play well with others." I think we all deserve a check mark in the box marked "excellent!"

All of these aspects of being a teddy bear artist are parts of the creative process. A characteristic of creativity is its most remarkable joining of the child and the adult. If the genius of childhood is the key to the imagination, then as adults, we need to practice seeing things from the perspective of a child. Get down there and look up at the world, visualize time and space. Practice being a little silly. Does it really matter any more what the neighbors think? And buy a box of sixty-four Crayola crayons . . . hold them in your hands, smell the wax, find the bright purple one and color outside the lines. You might just create a masterpiece! 🐾

Artists

GLORIA GAY ADAMS
The Bearfoot Bear
1594 Gangl Dr.
Stow, OH 44224
Phone: 216-688-8475
Phone orders: M-F, 6A.M.-9P.M. Sat,
9A.M.-5P.M.
Price range: $50-$150
Size range: 12"-17"
The Bearfoot Bears have two teddy bears
hand stenciled on each footpad. They
have big eyes and are made from im-
ported mohair. Gloria has a line of
dressed bears with wigs and eyelashes
and a line of "Dreambearies," made
from mohair and muslin, that look like
they are sleeping.
Shows: Midwest, mostly OH
Stores: Groves Quality Collectibles,
Bluffton, OH
Mail order: 4-6 weeks
Accepts: check, money order, C.O.D.
Has been making bears for 9 years
Publications: Teddy Bear Artists' Annual

JANIECE ROBERTA ADAMS
P.O. Box 633
Paradise, CA 95967
Phone: 916-872-3593 or 1-800-8-
BEARS-9 for orders through store
Phone orders: 8A.M.-9P.M.
Price range: $35-$450
Size range: 12"-6'
Shows: CA
Stores: Country Touch, Paradise, CA
Catalog/Photos: $1, refundable with pur-
chase
Mail order: 2-4 weeks
Accepts: check, money order, Visa, Mas-
terCard, Discover, American Express
Has been making bears for 5 years
Awards: Teddy Bear Convention, Ne-
vada City
Publications: newspapers

CAROL ADRIAN
Adrian Bears
2206 30th St., White Township
Beaver Falls, PA 15010

Phone: 412-847-0324
Phone orders: anytime
Price range: less than $35-$200
Adrian Bears are reproductions of old
bears. They are made from distressed
German mohair and have glass eyes.
All are jointed with wood joints.
Noses are shaved and bears are dis-
tressed to simulate wear.
Home Appointments: a few days
Shows: PA, OH, MI
Catalog/Photos: $2, refundable with pur-
chase
Mail order: 4-6 weeks
Accepts: check, money order
Has been making bears for 11 years

NORMA ADWERE-BOAMAH
Pewter Bears
1310 Portland Ave.
Albany, CA 94706
Phone: 510-524-8053
Price range: $100-S300
Size range: 2"-24"
Pewter bears are one-of-a-kind bears by
Norma. Each bear has a pewter bear
button on its heart.
Home Appointments: 2-3 days
Shows: CA
Stores: Bears & Baubles, Berkeley, CA
Accepts: check, Visa, MasterCard, Dis-
cover, American Express
Has been making bears for 6 years
Awards: TBBNC, 1st, 1992; 2nd, 1994;
Marin Needlearts Show, 1st, 1991;
1st, 1992; Best of Class, 2nd, 1993;
1st, 4th, 1994

DARLENE ADAMS ALLEN
Raspbeary Bears of Bearen Forest
881 Rich Dr.
Oviedo, FL 32765
Phone: 407-359-0891
Phone orders: 10A.M.-6P.M.
Price range: $50-$350
Size range: 4½"-20"
Raspbeary Bears of Bearen Forest have
center seam heads, rounded tummies,
long arms, short legs and a silver nail

stud in the right ear. Darlene signs
both feet of each bear.
Shows: FL, IL, WA
Stores: The Hen Nest, Seminole, FL;
Victoria's Collectibles, Winter
Springs, FL; A Country Treasure,
Kaileua, HI; MBR Bears & Dolls,
Staten Island, NY; As You Like It,
Glen Rose, TX; Spoiled Rotten, Mill
Creek, WA
Catalog/Photos: $2, refundable with pur-
chase
Mail order: 1 week
Accepts: check, money order
Has been making bears for 10 years
Publications: Teddy Bear Artists' An-
nual; Contemporary Artists Price
Guide

JANET ANN ANDERSON
Janet Ann Anderson and Bears
32705 St. Moritz Dr.
Evergreen, CO 80439
Phone: 303-670-0343
Phone orders: 9A.M.-6P.M.
Price range: $100-$300
Size range: 4", 6", 9", 16"
Janet's bears are made of quality mohair
and glass or antique shoe button eyes.
They are fully jointed. She uses a
unique separate snout construction,
and her paw design is her trademark.
Her bears are dressed in very detailed
clothing, featuring cross-stitching,
embroidery and smocking on their
outfits, plus hand-knitted sweaters
and crocheted and quilted accessories.
Each bear is designed and created entirely by Janet.

Waiting list: 6 weeks
Home Appointments: 2 weeks
Shows: Midwest, occasionally in East
Stores: Mostly Bears, Arvada, CO; Colorado Doll Faire, Ft. Collins, CO; Marj's Doll Sanctuary, Grand Rapids, MI; Mary D's Dolls & Bears & Such, Minneapolis, MN; Christy's, Buckingham, PA; Bear Tracks, Pittsburgh, PA
Catalog/Photos: 45 cents per photo, refundable with purchase
Mail order: 2 weeks
Accepts: check, money order, Visa, MasterCard
Has been making bears for 11 years
Publications: TB&F

KARA L. ANDERSON
Love's Labours
428 Highland Terr.
Phone: 609-589-5818
Phone orders: 10A.M.-4P.M.
Price range: $35-$150
Size range: 2"-3"
Love's Labours include Tummy Teddies, 3" teddies with 1" miniature "rooms" in their tummies (i.e. 1:144 scale nursery as the tummy of a bear in pink or blue pajamas; a 1:144 scale Christmas living room as the tummy of a Santa bear, etc.) Sew 'n Sews are 2" and 3" teddies with a sewing theme, such as pincushions and dress forms. Kara makes several other bears, and most have miniature accessories and/or are part of a miniature vignette. Some include a music box.
Waiting list: 3-6 months
Home Appointments: 1 week
Shows: everywhere
Catalog/Photos: $3, refundable with purchase
Mail order: 2 weeks-6 months
Accepts: check, money order
Has been making bears for 13 years
Publications: TB&F

> ONLY BUY A BEAR IF YOU LIKE IT, AND DON'T PUT IT IN A CLOSET, BUT DISPLAY IT PROMINENTLY FOR FREQUENT HUGS. AND DON'T BE EMBARRASSED TO TALK TO YOUR BEAR.
> — *Pauline Renpenning, owner, 2 Bears Teddy Bears, Alberta, Canada*

JUDITH ANDERSON EPPOLITO
Ashenberry Collectibles
7383 Liffey Ln.
Liverpool, NY 13088-4607
Phone: 315-451-1573
Phone orders: 7 days, 8A.M.-9P.M.
Price range: $50-$300
Size range: 3"-21"
Ashenberry Collectibles are unique, long-snouted bears made of 100% mohair. They have glass or shoe button eyes and are stuffed with pellets and/or fiberfill. Some are self-standing. Judith's line also includes teddy bear friends such as rabbits, cats and dogs.
Shows: MA, NY, MD, CT
Catalog/Photos: $2
Mail order: 4 weeks
Accepts: check, money order, Visa, MasterCard
Has been making bears for 4 years

LOUISE APPS
Apps-olutely Bears
58 Duncan Dr.
St. Catharines, Ontario L2N 3P4, Canada
Phone: 905-935-8411
Phone orders: 9A.M.-9P.M.
Price range: less than $35-$200
Size range: up to 18"
Apps-olutely Bears are individually designed bears with character and personality. They are all handstitched with Ultrasuede pads. Their looks vary with the use of different materials, including mohair, real fur or German plush. Accessories range from ribbons and collars to Louise's own self-designed and hand-knitted apparel. Handcrafted props are also used.
Waiting list: 1 month
Home Appointments: flexible
Shows: Southern Ontario
Stores: Silly Old Bear Shop, Niagara-on-

the-Lake, Ontario; Beartique, Montreal, Quebec; Historical Museum, Niagara-on-the-Lake, Ontario
Accepts: check, money order
Has been making bears for 5 years
Publications: Toy Box Magazine; Victorian Harvester

SHELLEY ARMSTRONG-PLAUNT
Rabbit Creek Bears
9 Oak St.
Whitehorse, Yukon Y1A 4A9, Canada
Phone: 403-633-4419
Phone orders: 10A.M.-10P.M.
Fax: 403-668-4349
Price range: $100-more than $450
Size range: 4"-18"
Rabbit Creek Bears are artist designed, costumed bears depicting some aspect of life "north of 60 degrees," including Inuit and Native costumes, various Santa bears, gold panners, trappers, Royal Canadian Mounted Police and fishermen. Shelley uses synthetic furs and some mohair and other natural furs. Polar bears are a specialty, but other colors are available. All are costumed with much attention to detail and authenticity.
Shows: Calgary, Alberta; Toronto, Ontario
Stores: Bauff Springs Gallery, Canmore, Alberta; Frontierland, Whitehorse, Yukon; Yukon Native Products, Whitehorse, Yukon
Catalog/Photos: $2.50, refundable with purchase
Mail order: 4-6 weeks
Accepts: check, money order
Has been making bears for 10 years
Awards: White Hat Teddy Contest, 1st, Best Overall, 1993; 1st, 1994
Publications: TB&F; TBR; Victorian Harvester; calendar by Yukon Women's Directorate

LINDA ASHCRAFT
Expressions by Ashcraft
5510 Hauser Lk. Rd.
Post Falls, ID 83854
Phone: 208-773-9800
Phone orders: anytime
Price range: $100-more than $450
Size range: 3"-28"
Expressions by Ashcraft have wool felt faces and are sculptured and airbrushed. Linda is one of the only bear

artists who uses airbrushing, so her bears are quite unique.

Waiting list: very short

Home Appointments: 1 day

Shows: Midwest, East, South, Northwest, West

Stores: Marilyn's World, Lauderhill, FL; The Rocking Horse Gallery, Fredericksburg, VA; The Honey Bee Bear Shoppe, East Bridgewater, MA; Out of the Woods, Modesto, CA; My Friends & Me, Leesburg, VA; Anything Goes, Anna Maria, FL

Catalog/Photos: $10, refundable with purchase

Mail order available.

Accepts: check, money order, Visa, MasterCard

Has been making bears for 12 years

Publications: TB&F, TBR, Linda Mullins's books

DIANE M. BABB

by Diane

1126 Ivon Ave.

Endicott, NY 13760-1431

Phone: 607-754-0391

Phone orders: 9 A.M.-9 P.M.

Fax: 607-754-0391

Fax orders accepted.

Price range: $35-more than $450

Size range: 6"-20"

Diane's bears range from whimsical to realistic, with antique reproductions somewhere in the middle.

Waiting list: 2-6 weeks

Home Appointments: 2 weeks

Shows: East, Midwest, South

Catalog/Photos: $2

Mail order available.

Accepts: check, money order, Visa, MasterCard

Has been making bears for 21 years

Publications: Bialosky Teddy Bear Catalog I & II; Contemporary Teddy Bear Price Guide

CELIA BAHAM

Celia's Teddies

1562 San Joaquin Ave.

San Jose, CA 95118

Phone: 408-266-8129

Phone orders: 7 A.M.-9 P.M.

Fax: 408-978-2888

Fax orders accepted.

Price range: $50-$450

Size range: 3½"-28"

Celia's Teddies are slim bears with long necks. They wear hand-knit sweaters and are young looking. Celia makes Roosevelt bears that stand on all fours, with sculpted faces and large eyes. They have pellet-filled bent legs. She also makes one-of-a-kinds with handstitched noses, glass eyes, jointed faces and necks and loc-line arms and legs. She also makes embroidered clown-faced bears.

Waiting list: no more than 6 weeks

Home Appointments: 1 week

Shows: CA, FL, MD, IL, Canada

Stores: Bears In The Woods, Los Gatos, CA; Toys & Treasures, Sarasota, FL; Paisley Bear, Ft. Lauderdale, FL; The Teddy Bear Museum of Naples, Naples, FL; Monique Kooman, Rotterdam, Netherlands; Teddy Bears of Witney, Oxfordshire, UK; Arundel Teddy Bears, West Sussex, UK

Catalog/Photos: $5, refundable with purchase

Mail order: 6 weeks for orders; 2 weeks for bears in stock

Accepts: check, money order, Visa, MasterCard

Has been making bears for 24 years

Awards: Golden Teddy nominee, twice; TBBNC, Best of Show, twice; ABC, 1st; many 1st, 2nd, 3rd at local and national shows

Publications: TBR; TB&F; Tribute To Teddy Bear Artists; Bearland; Official Price Guide to Antique and Modern Teddy Bears; Teddy Bear Lover's Companion; Complete Book of Teddy Bears; many calendars by Ron Kimball

MARILYN DIANE BALKE

Balke Bears

P.O. Box 1248

Yreka, CA 96097

Phone: 916-598-2700

Phone orders: 8 A.M.-9 P.M.

Price range: $35-$300

Size range: 2"-23"

Balke bears have great personalities. Marilyn often hears people say, "What great faces!"

Shows: Northern CA

Catalog/Photos: $2, refundable with purchase

Mail order: 3 weeks

Accepts: check, money order

Has been making bears for 11 years

Publications: TBR

EDIE BARLISHEN

Bears by Edie

42 Greer Crescent

St. Albert, Alberta T8N 1T8, Canada

Phone: 403-459-5786

Phone orders: 8 A.M.-10 P.M.

Price range: less than $35-$300

Size range: 1"-40"

Edie Bears are all original designs handmade completely by Edie. Tiny velour bears come in eighteen styles and sizes. Her limited edition miniature bears come in mohair, rayon and upholstery velvet. They are fully jointed and carry the tiny velour bears. Her limited edition regular bears are fully jointed and dressed, accessorized or bare. They are stuffed with Poly-Fil or pellets. Her giant bears (34"-39") are tall, one-of-a-kind accessorized bears. Finally, her "Play it Again" bears are made from recycled vintage fabrics and are one-of-a-kind.

Shows: Alberta, Manitoba

Stores: Treasures & Toys, Edmonton, Alberta; 2 Bears Teddy Bears, Calgary, Alberta; Ferrar Miniature Works, Calgary, Alberta; BearTique, Montreal, Quebec; Zephyr Impressions, Lethbridge, Alberta

Catalog/Photos: $3

Mail order: 1 month

Accepts: check, money order

Has been making bears for 8 years

Awards: The Bear Fair, Calgary 1993, 1st & 2nd; Klondike Days Exhibition, Edmonton, 2nd place and merit, 1993; 1st, 3rd, 1994.

Publications: TBR, TB&F, Victorian Harvester, Great Teddy Bear Connection Video

ELAINE BARNUM

Bears by Barnum
10128 S. 2460 E.
Sandy, UT 84092
Phone: 801-943-2930
Phone orders: 7 days, 8A.M.-10P.M.
Price range: $150-$200
Size range: 12"-19"

Bears by Barnum are fully jointed, mohair bears with German glass eyes. Their paws are pigskin suede. Elaine firmly stuffs each bear with Poly-Fil. She completes each bear alone, from its design development to its final grooming and dressing. The bears' clothes are also custom designed by Elaine. She carefully names each bear to match its personality. Most are one-of-a-kind.

Home Appointments: 1-2 hours
Shows: UT, CO
Catalog/Photos: $2.50, refundable with purchase
Mail order: 4-6 weeks
Accepts: check, money order
Has been making bears for 5 years
Awards: TBBNC, 2nd, 3rd, 1993

CINDY BARTOSEWCZ

Hilltop Bears
RR# 1, P.O. Box 18, North Hill Rd.
Readsboro, VT 05350
Phone: 802-423-7004
Phone orders: 7 days, 8A.M.-9P.M.
Price range: $50-$250
Size range: 7"-20"

Hilltop Bears are designed and made by Cindy. They are fully jointed and made from mohair, alpaca and occasionally synthetic. They have expressive personalities accomplished by needle sculpting, meticulous trimming and embroidery.

Waiting list: 2 weeks
Home Appointments: 2 days
Shows: Northeast, mostly VT and MA

Stores: Hugging Bear Inn & Shoppe, Chester, VT; Slades Dolls & Bears, Sioux Falls, SD; Casey's Bear Factory, Fairport, NY; Crescent Bears, Waunakee, WI; Groves Quality Collectibles, Lima, OH
Catalog/Photos: $2, refundable with purchase
Mail order: 1-2 weeks
Accepts: check, money order, Visa, MasterCard
Has been making bears for 7 years
Publications: TBR, TB&F

LYNDA BAYLESS

Bayless Creations
Bear Lover's Treasure Chest
10 Edward Ave.
Syosset, NY 11791
Phone: 516-921-5622
    Phone orders accepted.
Fax: 1-800-554-7642
    Fax orders accepted.
Price range: $50-$200
Waiting List: 4-8 weeks
Stores: Bear Lover's Treasure Chest, Syosset, NY; Beary Nice Gifts (wholesale only), 1-800-554-7642
Catalog/Photos: $1, refundable with purchase
Mail order: 4-8 weeks
Accepts: check, money order
Has been making bears for 11 years

GAIL R. BEARD

Merrywoods Bears
493 Bluff Dr.
Ozark, MO 65721
Phone: 1-800-381-BEAR
Phone orders: 9A.M.-9P.M., or leave message
Price range: less than $35-$100
Size range: 1½"-10"

Merrywoods Bears include Ozark Bob or Bobette, car companions that come with a cup holder for the door, a scarf and a straw hat. Gail also makes teddy head ornaments and pins that are 1½" in height. They are made of short mohair with felt knit hats. Buddy Bear is a 5½" bear made of upholstery fabric with felt paw pads. Phantom of the Opbeara is a 5" gold Ultrasuede with long mohair fur. Finally, Valentino is a 4" red bear with silver metallic dots with a stuffed heart on his foot.

Home Appointments: 1 week
Shows: Midwest
Catalog/Photos: $4
Mail order: 1-4 weeks
Accepts: check, money order, Visa, MasterCard
Has been making bears for 7 years

SHEILA ANNE BERGNER

Toys in the Attic
4964 Paxton Rd.
Oak Lawn, IL 60453
Phone: 708-425-3702
Phone orders: anytime
Price range: $50-$350
Size range: 6"-22"

Toys in the Attic bears are made of mohair. They are fully jointed with Ultrasuede paw pads, embroidered noses and glass eyes. Some are dressed and some wear just a ribbon. Sheila spends a great deal of time on the dressed bears' outfits. She loves to use unusual fabrics and special laces and trims. Many have special props, such as sleds, which she designs herself.

Waiting list: 3 weeks
Home Appointments available.
Shows: Midwest
Catalog/Photos: $10, refundable with purchase
Mail order: 3-4 weeks
Accepts: check, money order
Has been making bears for 4 years

SARA BERNSTEIN

Sara Bernstein's Dolls and Teddys
10 Sami Ct.
Englishtown, NJ 07726
Phone: 908-536-4101
Phone orders: 10A.M.-9P.M.
Price range: $35-$200
Size range: 4"-10"

Sara Bernstein makes and designs all her bears. They are made of 100% mohair, with glass eyes and wool felt. They are fully jointed and have a nostalgic feel, with long snouts and large humps. Sara also makes Pandas, clowns and bellhop bears.

Shows: NJ, PA
Catalog/Photos: $3.50 for bear catalog; $1.50 for pattern catalog
Mail order: 3 weeks
Accepts: check, money order
Has been making bears for 11 years

ELAINE BILLIARD

Billiard Bears
8055 Windfall Way
Colorado Springs, CO 80908
Phone: 719-495-0366
Phone orders: 9A.M.-9P.M.
Price range: $100-$250
Size range: 2½"-20"

Billiard Bears include fully jointed miniature bears made of upholstery fur and Ultrasuede paws. Elaine's 11"-18" bears are made of mohair, alpaca or wool and have Ultrasuede or wool felt paws, shoe button or glass eyes, and are stuffed with Poly-Fil or pellets. Griz, a 20" mohair bear, has clay claws, an open mouth and a growler. He has glass eyes, black Ultrasuede paws and looks like a real bear.

Shows: Midwest
Catalog/Photos: $3, refundable with purchase
Mail order: 4 weeks

Accepts: check, money order
Has been making bears for 12 years

KATHY BINDERT

Bear Mountain
307 N. Front St.
Wilmington, NC 28401
Phone: 910-762-3575
Phone orders: 10A.M.-5:30P.M.
Fax: 910-762-3575
  Fax orders accepted.
Price range: $100-more than $450
Size range: 11"-19"

Bear Mountain bears are made from recycled fur coats. Kathy enjoys making family heirlooms.

Shows: East Coast
Catalog/Photos: $2, refundable with purchase
Mail order: 1-2 months
Accepts: check, money order, Visa, MasterCard, Discover
Has been making bears for 4 years
Awards: Best in Show, Best Newcomer

RITA BOND

Rita B's Bears
400 Vine St., Apt 405
St. Catharines, Ontario L2M 3S3, Canada
Phone: 905-646-3831
Phone orders: 9A.M.-5P.M.
Price range: less than $35-$200
Size range: 3"-18"

Rita B's Bears are mainly mohair, with some acrylic. Most are not dressed, but some come with accessories. All are handsewn and finished by Rita. Her distressed, aged bears are excelsior stuffed and have glass or shoe button eyes. Others are stuffed with pellets or Poly-Fil. All are fully jointed, and some come with their life stories on paper.

Home Appointments: 1 week
Shows: Ontario; OH
Stores: Silly Old Bear, Niagara-on-the-

Lake, Ontario; Teddy Bear Mansion, Jordan, Ontario; Enchanted Forest, Hamilton, Ontario; Historical Museum, Niagara-on-the-Lake, Ontario
Accepts: check, money order
Has been making bears for 8 years
Publications: Toy Box Magazine, Victorian Harvester, Hayes Dana Contact

JAN BONNER

Bonner Bears & Friends
318 Caren Ave.
Worthington, OH 43085
Phone: 614-436-1571
Phone orders: 9A.M.-5P.M.
Price range: $50-$300
Size range: 5"-42"

Bonner Bears are based on the traditions and occurrences of Jan's family. She enjoys putting a bit of childlike whimsy in each bear. Although several are plain mohair, many feature needlework, quilting, smocking, French hand sewing, stencil and counted cross-stitch. Costumes are designed to incorporate these skills.

Home Appointments: 1 week
Shows: Midwest
Stores: Groves Quality Collectibles, Lima, OH; Strictly Bears, Medina, OH; Village Bears & More, Shrieve, OH; A Show of Hands, Cincinnati, OH
Catalog/Photos: $2, refundable with purchase
Mail order: 8-10 weeks
Accepts: check, money order
Has been making bears for 19 years
Awards: Best Craft, Chris Kindlmart, Canton Art Institute; Honorable Mention, Westerville Music & Arts Festival; Ohio State Fair, Best of Show; Featured on White House Christmas tree, 1993
Publications: TBR; Contemporary Teddy Bear Price Guide; Teddy Bear Artists' Annual; 1993 Bialoski & Friends calendar

JERRI BOOKER
From the Heart Creations
P.O. Box 254
Kootenai, ID 83840
Phone: 208-263-5583
Phone orders: 8A.M.-8P.M.
Price range: $50-$450
Size range: 3"-36"
From the Heart Creations include jointed, mohair miniature bears. Jerri also makes jointed 15"-30" bears with metal paws and noses. They are made of German synthetic, with glass eyes and floss noses. The metal paws are all handcut, hammered and polished.
Home Appointments: 1 day
Shows: WA, OR, ID, CA
Stores: Whats Hot, Sandpoint, ID; Bear Hugs, Tacoma, WA; Marilyn's World, Lauderhill, FL; Country Gifts, Stevenson, WA; Dolls & Friends, Bellevue, WA; The Old Miller Place, Aurora, OR
Catalog/Photos: $1-$2, refundable with purchase
Mail order: 1-4 weeks
Accepts: check, money order, Visa, MasterCard, American Express
Has been making bears for 12 years
Awards: Seattle Mardi Paws show, 2nd; TBBNC, 3rd

SHIRLEY BOYINGTON
Bearington Bears
3419 Charlemagne
Long Beach, CA 90808
Phone: 310-425-5288
Phone orders: 9A.M.-5P.M.
Price range: $150-more than $450
Size range: 6"-36"
Bearington Bears have the quality and facial expressions of Steiff bears. Shirley uses mohair, hand blown eyes, merino wool paws and growlers. Some wear antique clothes.
Home Appointments: 3 days

Shows: CA
Stores: The Bear-ee Patch, San Diego; The Bear Necessities, Solvang, CA; Marilyn's World, Lauderhill, FL; Hatful of Huggables, Downey, CA; D & J Bears & Dolls, Huntington Beach, CA
Has been making bears for 11 years
Awards: ILTBC, 1st, Best of Show
Publications: TB&F; Helen Seiverling Price Guide; Tribute To Teddy Bear Artists

GINGER T. BRAME
The Piece Parade
7405 Lake Tree Dr.
Raleigh, NC 27615
Phone: 919-870-1881
Phone orders: anytime
Price range: $50-$250
Size range: 5"-17"
The Piece Parade bears are all designed and created by Ginger. She pays attention to every detail, from the shape of the foot to the curve of the ear. Each bear is fully jointed and made of the finest quality materials, including imported mohair and handblown glass eyes. All noses are handstitched. Paw and foot pads are Ultrasuede. They are stuffed with polyester fiberfill or pellets, and each bear wears a tiny jingle bell and has a sewn in label. Many are one-of-a-kind, and a few are made in very limited editions.
Waiting list: 12 weeks
Home Appointments: varies
Shows: Southeast, Mid-Atlantic, Northeast, Midwest
Stores: Pam Hebbs, London, UK; Dolls in the Attic, Victoria, Australia
Catalog/Photos: $2
Mail order: at least 12 weeks
Accepts: check, money order, Visa, MasterCard, American Express, layaway
Has been making bears for 11 years

Awards: TOBY nominee, 1994; several show awards.
Publications: The Teddy Bear Encyclopedia; The Ultimate Teddy Bear Book; Contemporary Teddy Bear Price Guide; The Art of Making Teddy Bears; TBR, TB&F, Country Almanac; Tribute to Teddy Bear Artists

MARY ELLEN BRANDT
Basically Bears
825 7th St. SE
Oelwein, IA 50662
Phone: 319-283-3748
Phone orders: 8A.M.-8P.M.
Price range: $50-$400
Size range: 6"-24"
Basically Bears are made from recycled real fur such as mink, raccoon, muskrat, seal, fox, stone marten and even skunk. Mary Ellen preserves family heirlooms by making a fur collar into a bear or a family fur coat into several bears, cats or bunnies. Her bears are all lined, stuffed with fiberfill or pellets. She has a large supply of antique shoe button eyes and uses glass eyes on larger bears. She uses mohair and plush fabric only rarely.
Waiting list: 2-6 weeks
Home Appointments: 2-3 days
Shows: Midwest; OK; Schaumburg, IL; IA; Kansas City, MO
Stores: Bears & Hares Collectibles, Tulsa, OK; Teddy Bears To Go, Lakewood, NJ; Prairie Clothing, Amana, IA
Catalog/Photos: SASE, refundable with purchase
Mail order: 2-6 weeks
Accepts: check, money order, Visa, MasterCard
Has been making bears for 11 years
Publications: Complete Book of Teddy Bears; TB&F (ads)

PAMELA BRANTLEY-WOOLEY

5021 Stringtown Rd.
Evansville, IN 47711
Phone: 1-800-359-3305
Phone orders: 9A.M.-9P.M.
Fax: 812-464-2521
Fax orders accepted.
Price range: $200-more than $450
Size range: 4"-34"
Pamela's bears are described as having soulful and expressive faces. They tend to pout, and seem to empathize with our daily aches and pains.
Shows: Schaumburg, IL; Orange, CA; Boston, MA
Catalog/Photos: $7.50
Mail order: 4-6 months
Accepts: check, money order, Visa, MasterCard
Has been making bears for 11 years
Awards: Golden Teddy, 1989, 1990, 1992; TOBY nominee, 1991, 1993
Publications: Complete Book of Teddy Bears; Teddy Bear Artists' Annual; Teddy Bear Artists Price Guide; Random House Guide to Teddy Bears; TBR, cover, 1991

ACACIA BRISBOIS

Acacia's Teddies
11698 Graton Rd.
Sebastopol, CA 95472
Phone: 707-829-1358
Phone orders: 9A.M.-9P.M.
Price range: less than $35-$150
Size range: 5"-16"
Acacia's Teddies are original designs. She uses old fur and wool coats to create bears. She recycles old furs and wool coats and gives them a new life as one-of-a-kind teddy bears. The real fur bears have leather paws from old coats. She also makes mohair bears in a range of sizes. Seasonal specials and special orders are always welcome.
Home Appointments: 1 day
Shows: CA
Stores: Meyers, East Brunswick, NJ
Catalog/Photos: $5, refundable with purchase
Mail order: 1 week
Accepts: check, money order
Has been making bears for 3 years

DEANNA BRITTSAN

Bears by Deanna Brittsan
1155 Uppingham Dr.
Thousand Oaks, CA 91360
Phone: 805-492-1040
Phone orders: 10A.M.-10P.M.
Price range: $50-$350
Size range: 5"-24"
Deanna's bears are known for their aged look. Her Santa Bear is popular. Some of her bears are dressed to look old, and some are made out of old-looking fabric. She dyes their fur herself.
Waiting list: 3-6 months
Home Appointments: 1 month
Shows: San Diego, CA; Clarion, IA
Stores: Rose Cottage, Thousand Oaks, CA; Bear Tracks, Pittsburgh, PA; Good Hearted Bears, Mystic, CT; Animal Haus, Ltd., Cincinnati, OH; Hatfull of Huggables, Downey, CA
Catalog/Photos: $5, refundable with purchase
Mail order: 2-3 weeks
Accepts: check, money order, Visa, MasterCard, Discover
Has been making bears for 14 years
Awards: Sacramento Fair, 1st, 1987; Golden Teddy Award, 1989, 1993; ILTBC awards; TOBY nominee, 1992
Publications: TBR; TB&F; A Berry Merry Christmas; Contemporary Teddy Bear Price Guide; Teddy Bear Artists' Annual; Complete Book of Teddy Bears

JEANETTE BRONSON

Bronson Bear Works
Route 1, P.O. Box 32-Z
Globe, AZ 85501
Phone: 602-425-9253
Phone orders: 9A.M.-5P.M.
Price range: $35-$200
Size range: 8"-21"
Bronson Bear Works bears are handcrafted from Jeanette's original patterns using German mohair and alpaca fabrics as well as some German synthetics. They have glass eyes, embroidered noses and Ultrasuede feet, and are stuffed with Poly-fil and/or pellets. Many have growlers. They are decorated with silk or French wire-edged ribbons or lace, and have a fancy button in the center of their bows. Their left feet are hand signed

and dated. All are fully jointed. Some are limited editions.
Home Appointments: 1 week
Shows: AZ
Catalog/Photos: $1
Mail order: 4 weeks
Accepts: check, money order
Has been making bears for 11 years
Awards: Tucson Annual Doll Show Competition, 1st
Publications: TBR

ANN A. BROWN

Ann's Little Brown Bears
P.O. Box 1475
Corrales, NM 87048
Phone: 505-898-4817
Phone orders: 8A.M.-6P.M.
Price range: $35-$250
Waiting list: 2-3 months
Home Appointments: 1 day
Shows: IL, MO, OK
Stores: The Bear Pawse, Jack Henry Bears, Teddy Bear Junction
Catalog/Photos: $2, refundable with purchase
Mail order: 6-8 weeks
Accepts: check, money order
Has been making bears for 3 years
Awards: Golden Teddy Award, 1994
Publications: Teddy Bear Times, 1993

BARBARA BROWN

Barbara's Bears
3855 Startouch Dr.
Pasadena, CA 91107
Phone: 818-351-5006
Phone orders: 8A.M.-8P.M.
Price range: $50-$250
Size range: 5"-30"
Barbara's bears have sweet faces with shiny black eyes and lush, plush fur. They are usually dressed as childlike bears
Shows: CA, CO, FL, IA
Stores: Mostly Bears, Arvada, CO;

Teddy Bear Den, Las Vegas, NV; The Rocking Horse Gallery, Fredericksburg, VA; Bearly Available, Linwood, NJ; Terry Bears, Oyster Bay, NY; Animal Haus, Ltd., Cincinnati, OH

Catalog/Photos: $3, refundable with purchase

Mail order available. Time varies.

Accepts: check, money order

Has been making bears for 11 years

Awards: Several 1st, 2nd, 3rd place ribbons; invited to be featured artist at Disneyland

Publications: Tribute to Teddy Bear Artists; Teddy Bear Artists' Annual; Contemporary Teddy Bear Price Guide; TBR; TB&F; many bear club magazines

NANCY L. BROWN
Nac-B Bears
5441 Windermere
Grand Blanc, MI 48439
Phone: 810-694-5421
Phone orders: 8 A.M.-9 P.M.
Price range: $35-$250
Size range: 6"-21"

Nac-B Bears are fully jointed mohair bears with an old-fashioned look or a cute expression. Nancy dresses them in themes ranging from country to Victorian.

Home Appointments: 1 day
Shows: MI
Catalog/Photos: $2, refundable with purchase
Mail order: 1-3 weeks
Accepts: check, money order, Visa, MasterCard
Has been making bears for 6 years

BARBARA BUTCHER
Heartspun Teddy Bears
502-6801-59 Ave.
Red Deer, Alberta T4P 1B3, Canada
Phone: 403-342-6686
Phone orders: evenings
Price range: $35-$100
Size range: 1½"-8"

Heartspun Teddy Bears are made from uphostery velvet (minis), mohair (straight and distressed) and alpaca. Barbara handstitches all miniature bears. They are fully jointed, and most have onyx bead eyes. All have Ultrasuede paw pads. The larger bears all have glass eyes, are fully jointed and

have either wool felt or Ultrasuede paw pads. Most of the bears Barbara makes are undressed.

Shows: Alberta
Stores: 2 Bears Teddy Bears, Calgary, Alberta; Bear Essentials, Victoria, British Columbia; Bears Galore, Winnipeg, Manitoba
Catalog/Photos: $1
Mail order: 4-6 weeks
Accepts: check, money order
Has been making bears for 6 years
Publications: TB&F

GENIE BUTTITTA
Genie B's Bears
942 Brighton Rd.
Tonawanda, NY 14150
Phone: 716-834-5369
Phone orders: 9 A.M.-9 P.M.
Price range: $50 and up
Size range: 2¼"-23"

Genie B's Bears are miniature to large bears with highlighted eyes. Genie has been told her bears have character in their faces.

Home Appointments: 1 week
Shows: East, Midwest
Stores: Hugging Bear Inn & Shoppe, Chester, VT; Basically Bears, Hampton, NH; Franklin Toy & Collectible, Sarasota, FL; My Friends & Me, Leesburg, VA
Catalog/Photos available
Mail order: 8-10 weeks

CAROL JEAN CARINI
Carini's Critters
257 Main St., P.O. Box 62
West Rutland, VT 05777
Phone: 802-438-5051
Phone orders: 8 A.M.-9 P.M.
Price range: $50-$350
Size range: 6¾"-30"

Carini's Critters are old-fashioned looking mohair or alpaca bears with 100%

wool felt paws. Carol uses either handblown glass or antique shoe button eyes. Her bears are stuffed with either Poly-Fil and pellets or excelsior. They have long limbs, humped backs and large feet.

Waiting list: up to 6 weeks
Home Appointments: 1-2 days
Shows: Northeast, mostly New England
Catalog/Photos: $5
Mail order: 3-4 weeks
Accepts: check, money order, Visa, MasterCard
Design manufactured by Mary Meyer Corp.
Has been making bears for 9 years
Publications: TBR, cover and article; TB&F

ANN M. CARLO
Original Designs by Ann M. Carlo
1427 Treetop Dr.
Palm Harbor, FL 34683
Phone: 813-785-4394
Phone orders: 8 A.M.-8 P.M.
Price range: $35-$300
Size range: 2½"-22"

Ann's bears are fully jointed, and most have bent arms and legs. She handstitches the noses and makes them slightly upturned. The bears have glass or shoe button eyes and are stuffed with pellets or Poly-fil. Some have silk embroidery on the paw pads.

Home Appointments: 1 week
Shows: FL, CT, RI, IL, VA
Stores: Betty's Victorian Cottage, Seaview, WA; Doll Tapestry, Lantana, FL
Catalog/Photos: free
Mail order: 4-6 weeks
Accepts: check, money order
Has been making bears for 5 years
Publications: TB&F

LAURA CARUSO
The Country Bear
10465 Big Hand Rd.
Columbus Twp., MI 48063
Phone: 810-727-1737
Phone orders: 9A.M.-8P.M.
Price range: $125-$450
Waiting list: 12-16 weeks
Size range: 2½"-26"
The Country Bear bears are designed and created in the antique style. Laura makes each bear entirely by herself. Most are one-of-a-kind. They are made to look very old and are slightly slumped with a well-loved look. She uses excelsior pellets and fiberfill to give each bear the feel she wants. She also ages her mohair using a special process. Many bears are dressed in antique clothing.
Shows: MI
Stores: A Matter of Taste, Romeo, MI; Groves Quality Collectibles, Lima, OH; Teddy Bear Station, Germany
Catalog/Photos: $5
Mail order: 3 weeks
Accepts: check, money order, Visa, MasterCard
Has been making bears for 14 years
Awards: TOBY nominee, 1992
Publications: TBR, TB&F

RITA CASEY
Casey Creations
17 Lodge Pole Rd.
Pittsford, NY 14534
Phone: 716-425-3566
Phone orders: anytime
Price range: $35-$300
Waiting list: 4-6 weeks, special orders
Home Appointments available.
Shows: MA, IL, NY
Stores: Casey's Bear Factory, Fairport, NY; Bearly Available, Linwood, NJ; Bear-A-Dise, Millburn, NJ
Catalog/Photos: $2 catalog; $5 video
Mail order: 6 weeks
Accepts: check, money order, Visa, MasterCard, Discover
Has been making bears for 9 years

DIANA RENEE CASEY
Renee's Bears & Other Things
11245 183rd St., Suite 170
Cerritos, CA 90703
Phone: 310-860-8647
Phone orders: 10A.M.-8P.M.

Price range: $50-$150
Size range: 2½"-11"
Renee's Bears include miniatures that average 3". She dresses most of them in hats, dresses, etc. Some are fairies, bees, engineers, ballerinas and on and on. Renee puts a highlight dot on their eyes and nose. This final step brings her teddies to life. She handmakes all clothing and completes all the work. She also makes larger bears, but they are very limited.
Shows: West Coast
Stores: Marilyn's World, Lauderhill, FL; The Owl's Nest, Carmel, CA; The Bear Necessities, Solvang, CA; Kids In The Neighborhood, Garden Grove, CA; Turn of the Century, Arroyo Grande, CA; Growlies-Friends of the Fur, Scotland
Catalog/Photos: 50 cents for photos, $1 for catalog, refundable with purchase
Mail order: varies
Accepts: check, Visa, MasterCard
Has been making bears for 5 years
Awards: Linda's Doll And Bear Show, 2 2nds, 3rd
Publications: Antique Collector magazine, Orange County Metropolitan magazine

CHRISTINE CASSNER
Cassner Bears
P.O. Box 416
Arendtsville, PA 17303
Phone: 717-677-6925
Phone orders: 24 hours
Price range: $35-more than $450
Size range: 5"-32"
Cassner Bears are designed and made entirely by Christine. She makes child-safe bears and collector quality bears. Each edition is limited depending on the availability of the fur and/or accessory. She uses American synthetic,

German synthetic, mohair, alpaca and assorted blended furs.
Stores: Bear-A-Dise Landing, Guilford, CT; Country Wares of Frederick, Frederick, MD; Codori's Bavarian Gift Shop, Gettysburg, PA; Piroska's Gift Shop, Mansfield, OH; Bears By The Bay, Fairhope, AL; Crescent Bear & Bath, Waunakee, WI; D 'N J Bears & Dolls, Huntington Beach, CA; Dolls, Bears & Funny Hares, Mission, KS; Sue's Bear Haus, York, PA; The Teddy Bear Den, Las Vegas
Mail orders available.
Accepts: check, money order
Has been making bears for 7 years

PAT A. CATHEY
T-BRRRs
3227 W. Enoch Rd.
Deer Park, WA 99006
Phone: 509-276-5227
Phone orders: 7 days, 8A.M.-9P.M.
Price range: $35-$250
Size range: 7"-21"
Pat's bears all have rather large heads for their body size. They have "pug" turned up noses. Pat designs and does all the work on each bear.
Home Appointments: 1 week
Shows: West Coast
Catalog/Photos: $4, refundable with purchase
Mail order: 3 weeks
Accepts: check, money order, COD
Has been making bears for 7 years
Awards: Grand Champion Bears; Reserve Champion Bears
Publications: TBR; TB&F

CHERLYNN ROSE CATHRO
Stuff 'N Such
P.O. Box 30, Site 5, RR 12
Calgary, Alberta T3E 6W3
Canada
Phone: 403-686-1631
Phone orders: 8A.M.-7P.M.
Price range: $50-$250
Size range: 6"-13"
Stuff 'N Such are an endearing collection of primarily mohair bears with onyx eyes and suede paw pads. Cherlynn uniquely details each bear. These whimsical bears are lovingly named to reflect their distinct personalities. No two are the same. They are made to be wonderful expressions of love.

Stores: Crabapple Cottage, Calgary, Alberta
Accepts: money order
Has been making bears for 2 years

BETTY CHEZEN
730 N. 73rd E. Ave.
Tulsa, OK 74115
Phone: 918-835-1439
    Phone orders: 9A.M.-5P.M.
Price range: $35-$100
Size range: 10″ and up
Betty's bears are made of mohair, fabric or fur.
Home Appointments available.
Shows: KS, OK
Accepts: check, money order
Has been making bears for 11 years

CYNTHIA L. CHRISTMAN
CYNDI
8777 Herrnhutter Strass
Kempton, PA 19529
Phone: 610-756-6301
Phone orders: 10A.M.-7P.M.
Price range: $35-$150
Size range: 6″-30″
CYNDI bears are one-of-a-kind, unique bears made of various materials, including mohair, acrylic plush, alpaca plush, rayon and cotton furs. Cyndi also makes child-safe bears using safety eyes. Collector bears have glass eyes. She likes to set up a theme display for her bears at shows.
Shows: Northeast, Middle Eastern states
Accepts: check, money order, Visa, MasterCard
Has been making bears for 6 years

MARILYN RUTH CHURCH
Bears in Pairs
61 Hettersley Dr.
Ajax, Ontario L1T 1V4, Canada
Phone: 905-427-8318
Phone orders: all day
Price range: less than $35-$250
Size range: 6″-8″
Bears in Pairs are dressed very fashionably, with silks, velvets and fancy fabrics, but Marilyn also uses all other fabrics. She makes bears in two colors. Her bears in pairs include Mr. and Mrs. Santa Claus and Romeo and Juliet.
Home Appointments: 2-3 days
Shows: Ontario, Quebec

Stores: Pickering Crafters Marketplace, Pickering, Ontario; Crafters Marketplace, Mississauga, Ontario; The Doll Attic, Kingston, Ontario
Catalog/Photos: $5, refundable with purchase
Mail order: 4-5 weeks
Accepts: check, money order
Has been making bears for 3 years

LAURE CLARK
Briar Rose Sentiments
1951 Peninsula Dr.
Arcata, CA 95521
Phone: 707-442-2084
Phone orders: 7 days, 8A.M.-8P.M.
Fax: 707-443-2579
    Fax orders accepted.
Price range: $100-more than $450
Size range: 3½″-36″
Briar Rose Sentiments bears are made of top-quality materials to last a lifetime or longer. Laure's favorite materials are mohair and other natural fur fabrics, German glass eyes, Ultrasuede for paws, Poly-Fil stuffing and pearl cotton for noses. Most are fully jointed. Her characters tend to favor prominent snouts and somewhat long limbs. Almost any bear can be made to stand by itself, and some include wire in arms for posing. Her bears wear minimal clothing.
Home Appointments: 7 days
Shows: CA, OR
Stores: Heuer's Florist, Eureka, CA; A La Carte On The Avenue, Redcrest, CA; The Dolls & Bears of Charlton Court, San Francisco; Baa-Baa Sheepskins, Eureka, CA
Catalog/Photos: $5, refundable with purchase
Mail order: up to 12 weeks
Accepts: check, money order, Visa, MasterCard, layaway
Has been making bears for 4 years

Awards: several show awards since 1993
Publications: Folkart Treasures Magazine, 1993

BARBARA J. CLARK
Mississippi Honey Bears
Rt. 1, P.O. Box 30
Lake, MS 39092
Phone: 601-775-3339
Phone orders: 9A.M.-9P.M.
Price range: $90 and up
Size range: 11″-32″
Mississippi Honey Bears are usually made of mohair and have shoe button eyes. Barbara likes big feet, long arms and humps on her bears. She often hand dyes the mohair, and enjoys working with colors such as plum, pink and red. Her bears usually wear only a neck ribbon or a vest.
Shows: TX, OK, GA, KY
Stores: Bear Lace Cottage, Fletcher, NC; Dolls, Bears & Funny Hares, Mission, KS; White Bear Antiques, Tulsa, OK; Pied Piper, Plymouth, MI; Bears By The Bay, Fairhope, AL; Rock-A-Bye Lady, Madison, IN
Catalog/Photos available.
Mail order available.
Accepts: check, money order, Visa, MasterCard
Has been making bears for 6 years

SHIRLEY M. CLARK
Cornucopia Art & Craft
P.O. Box 3056
Sherwood Park, Alberta T8A 2A6, Canada
Phone: 403-922-3664
Phone orders: 9A.M.-8P.M.
Price range: $50-$250
Size range: 6″-24″
Cornucopia Art & Craft bears are fully costumed in clothing based on historical designs. All bears and costumes are designed and handcrafted by

Shirley. She uses natural fibers such as mohair, alpaca and wool, as well as German synthetics. Her bears are often created for special scenes, such as "Tea Party" or "Beartown Saloon."

Waiting list: 4-6 weeks

Home Appointments: 1-2 days

Shows: Western Canada

Stores: Treasures & Toys, Edmonton, Alberta

Catalog/Photos: $5, refundable with purchase

Mail order: 4-6 weeks

Accepts: money order, Visa

Has been making bears for 9 years

Awards: Klondike Days Exposition, Best Overall Doll & Toy; Bear Fair, 1993, 1st; 1994, 1st; Best Booth Award

Publications: TBR, Victorian Harvester, Teddy Bear Connection Video, Alberta Craft Council Magazine, local newspapers

DONNA BEANLAND CLAUSTRE
Donna Claustre Originals
1202 La Brad Ln.
Tampa, FL 33613
Phone: 813-961-7158
Phone orders: 9A.M.-5P.M.
Price range: $75-$350
Size range: 6″-18″

Donna Claustre Originals are made of German mohair, glass eyes and Ultrasuede paws. They are stuffed with pellets and have tinted faces and many unusual body and facial concepts. Donna has more than 25 designs. One example is an 8″ or 10″ bear with a suede, center seam face, handpainted eye features and glass eyes, a turned-up nose, bent arms, fat lower body, large feet dressed as caricatures, and some clothing as part of the body.

Shows: CT, RI, MA, FL, IA, CA, Germany

Stores: J & L Collectibles, Tampa, FL; stores in Germany

Catalog/Photos available.

Mail order: 4-6 weeks

Accepts: check, money order, Visa, MasterCard

Has been making bears for 13 years

Awards: Florida State Fair, Best of Show; Christmas Show, Ft. Lauderdale; Best of Show; June Show, Ft. Lauderdale; blue ribbon; Blue Northern Teddy Boosters

Publications: TB&F, Teddy Bear Artists' Annual; Bears for All Seasons; Contemporary Teddy Bear Price Guide; Puppen & Spielzeug; Teddy Bear Encyclopedia; radio and TV talk shows

SHARON R. CLEMENT
Clement Collectibles
8001 E. 88th Pl.
Kansas City, MO 64138
Phone: 816-765-1004
Phone orders: 7P.M.-10P.M.
Price range: less than $35-$100
Size range: 1″-3½″

Clement Collectibles are fully thread jointed miniatures. Some have glass eyes and suede paw pads. Sharon gives them all cute faces and smiles.

Home Appointments: 1 day

Shows: Midwest

Stores: Cheri's Bear Essentials, Kansas City, MO; K.C. Toy & Miniature Museum, Kansas City, MO; Mini Temptations, Overland Park, KS

Catalog/Photos: $1, refundable with purchase

Mail order: 4-6 weeks

Accepts: check, money order

Has been making bears for 11 years

Awards: ATBAG, 1989

Publications: National Doll & Teddy Bear Collector; TB&F; Nutshell News; Teddy Tribune

GAIL M. CLIFFORD
Made on the Meadow
201 Meadow Ln.
Vestal, NY 13850
Phone: 607-754-8578
Phone orders: 9A.M.- 9P.M.
Price range: $100-$350
Size range: 10″-24″

Made on the Meadow bears are one-of-a-kind teddy bears in vintage clothing and accessories. Gail makes mohair bears only.

Home Appointments: 1 day

Shows: East, Midwest, West

Stores: The Rocking Horse Gallery, Fredericksburg, VA; Bears By The Bay, Fairhope, AL; The Bear Pawse, Prescott, AZ; The Cinnamon Bear, Hilton Head, SC; Sue's Bear Haus, York, PA; The Hugging Bear Inn & Shoppe, Chester, VT; Our Front Porch, Pittsford, NY

Catalog/Photos: $2.50, refundable with purchase

Mail order: 4-5 weeks

Accepts: check, money order, Visa, MasterCard, layaway

Has been making bears for 4 years

Publications: Rocking Horses; TBR, 1993; TB&F, 1994

PAULINE M. CONRAD
Bingen Bears
2356 S. 4th St.
Allentown, PA 18103
Phone: 610-797-1852
Phone orders: anytime
Fax: 610-797-6478
Fax orders accepted.
Price range: $35-$300
Size range: 1¼″-17″

Bingen Bears are handsewn with glass eyes. Each bear looks right at you, as if to say, "Pick me up, please." Pauline specializes in special orders for such things as sports, hobbies and dance recitals. If you give her a photograph, she can make a bear to look like it. Most are one-of-a-kind, and she prefers her smaller bears.

Waiting list: 6 months
Home Appointments: a few days
Catalog/Photos: Price of photos depends on request
Accepts: check, money order
Has been making bears for 7 years

MARGARETANN CORBETT
The Bears of Corbett Hollow
5729 Lawsons Hill Ct.
Alexandria, VA 22310
Phone: 703-960-5112
Phone orders: 9A.M.-9P.M.
Price range: $150-$350
Size range: 15"-28"
The Bears of Corbett Hollow are all original designs and completely handcrafted by MargaretAnn. They are made of the finest imported mohair and have glass eyes and leather paw pads. They are filled with Poly-fil and/or pellets. Distinguishing features include their large, low ears and their distinctive large, handsewn noses. The bears are generally dressed in actual children's clothes. Most also wear socks and shoes.
Shows: VA, FL, MD, PA, CT, NY, NJ, MA, RI, IL, AZ
Stores: The Rocking Horse Gallery, Fredericksburg, VA; Justin Tymes Christmas Cottage, Ft. Myers, FL; Treasured Teddies, Wilmington, DE; Truly Unique Gift Shoppe, Rutland, VT
Catalog/Photos: $5, refundable with purchase
Mail order: 6-8 weeks
Accepts: check, money order, Visa, MasterCard
Has been making bears for 9 years
Awards: Several local and regional Best of Show awards

REBECCA W. COUTRAS
Joint Venture
5013 Ashley Dr.
Nashville, TN 37211
Phone: 615-833-7961
Phone orders: 7A.M.-9A.M.; 5P.M.-10P.M.
Price range: $100-$350
Size range: 10"-26"
Joint Venture bears are made of mohair, often curly or vintage finish mohair. Becky uses imported, black glass eyes, Ultrasuede for pads and mostly Poly-Fil stuffing. She uses a bolt/locknut and disc for joints. Most of her bears are one-of-a-kind. The nose varies from bear to bear, depending on what fits the bear's character. She is constantly changing patterns. Most of her bears are doing something. She likes to capture the actions, expressions and character of children. She uses vintage and recycled clothing and handmakes many accessories.
Waiting list: 3-4 weeks
Home Appointments: 1 week
Shows: IL, FL, MO, VA, TN
Stores: The Rocking Horse Gallery, Fredericksburg, VA; Dolls, Bears & Funny Hares, Mission, KS
Catalog/Photos: $2 for photos
Mail order: 3-4 weeks
Accepts: check, money order
Has been making bears for 4 years

> I BELIEVE THAT BEAR ENTHUSIASTS SHOULD STRIVE FOR DIVERSIFIED COLLECTIONS, INCLUDING THE MOST COMMON BEARS SUCH AS MUFFY, STEIFF AND GUND, AS WELL AS A MIX OF FIGURINES AND ACCESSORIES. A NICE MIX KEEPS ANY COLLECTION INTERESTING.
> — *Linda Farley, owner, Bears 'n Wares, New Cumberland, PA*

ANITA LOUISE CRANE
The Bearlace Cottage
P.O. Box 702, 311 Main St.
Park City, UT 84060
Phone: 801-649-8804
Phone orders: 8A.M.-8P.M.
Price range: $100-more than $450
Shows: San Diego
Catalog/Photos: $5-$7
Mail order: 4-8 weeks
Accepts: check, money order, Visa, MasterCard, American Express
Has been making bears for 13 years
Awards: Linda Mullins' show, Best of Show, Best Victorian Bear, 1994
Publications: TB&F; Dolls, Bears & Collectibles (Australia); Victoria Magazine; Tribute to Teddy Bear Artists; Many Country Homes & Gardens crafts books; Hallmark cards; and her own book, Teddy Bear Magic

ANNE ELIZABETH CRANSHAW
E. Willoughby Bear Company
2 Star Rd.
Cape Elizabeth, ME 04107
Phone: 207-767-4183
Phone orders: 9A.M.-5P.M.
Fax: 207-767-4183
Fax orders accepted.
Price range: $50-$450
Waiting list: 2 months
Home Appointments available.
Shows: Northeast, Midwest, South, West, Northwest

Stores: All Things Bright & Beautiful, Waitsfield, VT; Bear Hugs & Baby Dolls, New York, NY; Animal Haus, Cincinnati, OH; Bear-a-dise, Millburn, NJ; Bear-A-Dise Landing, Guilford, CT; Childhood Fantasies, Lagrangeville, NY; Betty's Victorian Cottage, WA; Groves Quality Collectibles, Lima, OH; Hatfull of Huggables, Downey, CA; Teddy Bear Treasures, Albany, NY; Mama Bears, Fayetteville, NY; Teddy Bears And Us, Schuykill Haven, PA; Marlene's of Lewiston, Lewiston, ME; Verna Mae Collectibles, Greenwood, NE; Owl Shop, Inc., Worcester, MA; Westport Antiques, Portland, ME; Paisley Bear, Ft. Lauderdale, FL; J. Nelson Collection, Portland, ME; Persnickety Peddler, Aroma, CA; Arundel Teddy Bears, West Sussex, England; Porter Emporium, Porter, ME; Bears of Witney, Oxfordshire, UK; Lichfield Collectable Bears, Lichfield, Staffs, UK; Strictly Bears, Medina, OH; The Teddy Bear Shoppe, Northampton, UK; Kiss Me, Switzerland; 2 Bear Teddy Bears, Calgary, Alberta

Catalog/Photos: $3, refundable with purchase

Mail order: 1-2 months

Accepts: check, money order, Visa, MasterCard

Has been making bears for 12 years

Awards: Golden Teddy nominee, 1993; ATBAG Conference, 1st, 2nd, 3rd, 1988; 1st, 1987; Teddy Bear Faire, Del Mar, CA, 1st, 2nd, 3rd, 1988; Magic of Teddy Bears, Baltimore, 3rd, 1988; Somebear Over the Rainbow, Chicago, Two 3rds, 1988; 3rd, Brenda Dewey's

Publications: The Complete Book of Teddy Bears; Teddy Bear Artist's Annual; The Teddy Bear Lover's Companion; Tribute to Teddy Bear Artists

JUTTA R. CYR

Bearaphanalia Bears™
343 Manora Rd. NE
Calgary, Alberta T2A 4R7, Canada
Phone: 403-248-9231
Phone orders: 9A.M.-5P.M.
Fax: 403-248-9399
  Fax orders accepted.
Price range: $150-more than $450

Size range: 4½"-24"

Bearaphanalia Bears include Gator, the flagship of Jutta's company, a bear with long, exaggerated arms and legs who is very poseable.

Waiting list: 6 months

Home Appointments: 2 days

Shows: Schaumburg, IL, Walt Disney World

Stores: Walt Disney World and Epcot Center, Orlando, FL; Dolls, Bears & Funny Hares, Mission, KS; Bear Essentials, Victoria, British Columbia; Candy Bear Shoppe, Cochrane, Alberta; Pied Piper, Plymouth, MI; Esther Kaufmann's Teddy Corner, Zwillikon, Switzerland; Anything Goes, Inc., Anna Maria, FL; FairyTales, Inc., Lombard, IL; Bears Galore, Winnipeg, Manitoba; Meine Kleine Teddy, Welt, Ulzburg, Germany; Abington's Animals, Calgary, Alberta

Catalog/Photos: $10, refundable with purchase

Mail order: 6-8 months

Accepts: check, money order

Has been making bears for 8 years

Publications: TBR, cover and feature; Victorian Harvester; Insight on Collectibles; Toy Box Magazine; TB&F; Edmonton Journal Newspaper; Calgary Herald Newspaper; numerous TV appearances, including CTV national news.

JEANETTE ANNE-MARIE DANCEY
Dreamweaver Bears
P.O. Box 3686
Smithers, British Columbia V0J 2N0, Canada
Phone: 604-847-3110
Phone orders: 9A.M.-9P.M.
Fax: 604-847-9707
  Fax orders accepted.
Price range: $50-$450
Size range: 6"-28"

Dreamweaver Bears are 100% handcrafted and designed by the artist. Jeanette gives them real personalities and uses the highest quality German synthetics, mohair, glass eyes and German growlers. Many are one-of-a-kind, and some are limited editions of 25 or less. Many come with handcrafted wooden accessories, including skis, snowboards, planes and presentation stands.

Shows: Vancouver, British Columbia; Alberta

Catalog/Photos: $5, refundable with purchase

Mail order: 6 weeks

Accepts: money order

Has been making bears for 7 years

Awards: Canada-wide Bear Fair, 1st and 2nd, 1993; Calgary Bear Fair, 2nd, 1994

Publications: TB&F; TBR; many newspapers; Calgary television interviews, 1990, 1994

DOROTHY FERN DARDEN

The Teddy Bear Farm
6441 Moss Ln.
Paradise, CA 95969
Phone: 916-877-7543
Phone orders: 9A.M.-5P.M.
Price range: $35-more than $450
Size range: 12"-6'

The Teddy Bear Farm bears are different than other flat-faced, big-eared bears. They are instant heirlooms. Dorothy has been designing and making bears since 1969, and she holds 23 copyrights. Seamstresses help her in production, but she only hires the best! She has a sign in her window that says, "If we are home, we are open." Teddy bears are her life.

Home Appointments: 1 week

Shows: CA

Stores: Teddy Bear Junction, Chico, CA; Country Touch, Paradise, CA; Orgen Teddies, Eugene, OR

Catalog/Photos: $3

Mail order: 2-4 weeks

Accepts: money order, American Express

Has been making bears for 27 years

Awards: several blue ribbons

Publications: TBR, several newspaper articles, several times on TV

MARY DAUB

Mary's Secret Garden
410 East Ayre St.
Newport, DE 19804
Phone: 302-994-1124
Phone orders: 9A.M.-6P.M.
Fax: 302-994-9473
Fax orders accepted.
Price range: $350-$400
Size range: 18"-72"

Mary's Secret Garden bears are made of synthetics, mohair and alpaca. They are realistic and do not look like teddy bears, although they are just as cuddly. They feature details such as sculpted noses, leather pads, eyeliner and open mouths with soft sculpted lips. Finger and toe pads are defined individually. Realistic eyes are set into a "socket," creating lifelike expressions. The eyes are authentic glass taxidermy eyes. She uses real human hair eyelashes. Soft rubber curved claws adorn each toe. All bears are fully positionable so that they can stand, sit up, cross their legs, hold a bottle or cling to their owners.

Shows: International Toy Fair, New York
Stores: G.S.A. Management, Inc., Franklin, IN; Suzanne's, Phoenix; Sweetness & Light, Yardley, PA; Cabbage Rose Ltd., Vienna, VA; Empress Doll Boutique, Laurel, DE, The Apple Basket, Rochester Hills, MI; Victorian Doll Shop, Northville, MI; Kits & Kaboodle, Indianapolis; The Toy Shoppe, Richmond, VA; Petite Mon Ami, Wiscassett, ME; Martin House Dolls & Toys, Ontario; Treasured Teddies, Bear, DE; Porter Emporium, Inc., Porter, ME; Zip's Toys To Go, Ardmore, PA
Photos available.
Mail order available.
Accepts: check, money order, Visa, MasterCard
Has been making bears for 2 years
Publications: TB&F (ads)

DEANNA DAULT

Bearly Trainable
15849 Gooseberry Way
Apple Valley, MN 55124
Phone: 612-431-0741
Phone orders: anytime
Price range: $35-more than $450
Size range: 9"-24"

Bearly Trainable bears are mostly made of mohair. They are filled with pellets or Poly-Fil. Most wear ribbons. The muzzles are all shaved. Deanna gives them all potbellies, and some have humps.

Shows: Midwest
Stores: Collectible Showcase, Bloomington, MN
Mail orders available.
Accepts: check, money order
Has been making bears for 4 years
Publications: TB&F, TBR

KELLY DAUTERMAN

Acorn Hollow
2227 Split Rock Dr.
Colorado Springs, CO 80919
Phone: 719-260-0663
Phone orders: 10A.M.-10P.M.
Price range: $100-$250
Size range: 12"-24"

Acorn Hollow bears are made of the best materials and have glass or shoe button eyes. They are fully jointed and very traditional, with long arms and a hump. Kelly sometimes creates whimsical bears. She designs her bears and does all the work herself. Most are one-of-a-kind.

Waiting list: 1-6 months
Home Appointments: 2 weeks
Shows: Across USA
Stores: several worldwide
Catalog/Photos: $10, refundable with purchase
Mail order: varies; never more than 6 months
Accepts: check, money order
Has been making bears for 12 years
Awards: several contests
Publications: Teddy Bear Times, newspaper

LINDA AND GARETH DAVIES

Lin Wildlife Friends
611 Red Oak Ln.
Tannersville, PA 18372
Phone: 717-629-5629
Phone orders: 9A.M.-6P.M.
Price range: $50-$250
Size range: 6"-30"

Lin Wildlife Friends are original designs modeled after traditional German-style bears. Linda and Gareth use only mohair or other wools and antique shoe button or glass eyes. They make most of the bears' accessories, including jewelry, leather collars and hand-knit sweaters. Some bears include a vintage item, such as an antique quilt blanket. Others feature jewelry accents.

Waiting list: 2-6 weeks
Home Appointments: call
Shows: Northeast
Stores: Teddy's Treasures, Kutztown, PA; The Salt Box Country Store, Canton, OH; Beary Best Friends, Tannersville, PA; White Fox Antiques, Clarion, IA; 1764 House, Stewartsville, NJ; Treasured Teddies, Wilmington, DE; General Stark's Store, Derry, NH
Catalog/Photos: $5, refundable with purchase
Mail order: 2-6 weeks
Accepts: check, money order
Has been making bears for 9 years

EVELYN MARRERO-DAVILA

Eve's Bears & Treasures
333 Morrowfield Ave.
Elmira, NY 14904
Phone: 607-734-6342
Phone orders: M-Sat, 9A.M.-9P.M.
Price range: $35-$250
Size range: 9"-18"

Eve's Bears & Treasures are mainly custom-order bears made of recycled materials such as mink coats, quilts and clothing. She also sells bears made of other, more traditional materials such as mohair, acrylics, etc. Her one-of-a-kind Beary Patch Collection includes very popular bears made of vintage fabrics or unusual recycled materials, such as tweeds and cashmere.

Home Appointments: 1 week
Stores: Clorinda's Country Cottage, Elmira, NY; Touch of Country, Elm-

ira, NY; Auntie Emm's, Elmira, NY; Country & Thyme Market, Chenango Bridge, NY
Catalog/Photos available.
Mail order: 2-4 weeks
Has been making bears for 11 years
Publications: newspaper articles

E. R. JOAN DAY
Daysie Bears
927 Cantabrian Dr. SW
Calgary, Alberta T2W 1M2, Canada
Phone: 403-281-8326
Phone orders: 9A.M.-8P.M.
Price range: less than $35-$200
Size range: 8″-24″
Daysie Bears are crafted with love from imported mohair and acrylic pile. Joan uses leather for paw pads and sometimes leather noses. Her bears tend to look very traditional and will withstand the test of time. She thinks of them as "forever" bears. They are born in a variety of colors and textures.
Catalog/Photos: $2
Home Appointments: 2 days
Shows: Western Canada
Accepts: check, money order
Has been making bears for 10 years
Awards: local bear fair, 3rd

JULIA DEIMERT
Bear Essentials by Julia
157 Coventry Pl. N.E.
Calgary, Alberta T3K 4A6, Canada
Phone: 403-226-0627
Price range: less than $35-$150
Size range: 2″-12″
Bear Essentials by Julia are fully jointed. Most are dressed in researched, historically accurate costumes. Costumes are made of antique materials with many handmade features, such as a thread crocheted dress on an angel bear, a hand-knit sweater on a small boy bear and thread crocheted collars. Julia also makes jester bears with limbs that snap on and off, and bear heads in roses to form everlasting bouquets. She also makes one-of-a-kind bear pins which are quite popular.
Shows: Calgary, Alberta
Stores: 2 Bears Teddy Bears, Calgary, Alberta; Quilted Bear, Calgary, Alberta

Catalog/Photos: $3
Mail order: 8-10 weeks
Accepts: check, money order
Has been making bears for 4 years
Awards: Calgary Exhibition & Stampede, 2nd

TAMARA L. DEMAREST
The Stuyvesant Bear
P.O. Box 72
Stuyvesant, NY 12173
Phone: 1-800-492-BEAR
Phone orders: 10A.M.-4P.M. or leave message
Fax: 518-758-2838
Fax orders accepted.
Email: *P-PRUR68A
Price range: $35-$250
Size range: 10″-24″
The Stuyvesant Bears are 100% mohair, jointed teddies with handblown glass eyes and German felt paw pads. All are handmade by Tamara. Each comes with a certificate of authenticity, and all are signed and include the logo paw print on each left paw. All bears come with the story of the Stuyvesant Bear and how he came to be.
Shows: MA, CT
Stores: Tree House Toys, Ltd, Portsmouth, NH; Silly Old Bear, Seattle; Bears Everywhere, Fredericksburg, VA; Fister's, S. Weymouth, MA
Catalog/Photos: $3, refundable with purchase
Mail order: 7-10 days
Accepts: check, money order, Visa, MasterCard
Has been making bears for 6 years
Publications: TB&F

IF A BEAR TALKS TO YOU,
YOU MUST ADOPT IT ON THE SPOT.
— *Pauline Renpenning, owner, 2 Bears Teddy Bears, Alberta, Canada*

DOROTHY DEPAULO
DePaulo's
185 S. Garrison
Lakewood, CO 80226
Phone: 303-232-1353
Phone orders: 9A.M.-9P.M.
Price range: $100-$450
Size range: 6″-24″
Dorothy's bears are made of imported mohair with glass eyes. Most have leather noses. A great deal of special attention is given to create an individual expression for each face. Most of her bears are limited editions of about 25
Waiting list: 6-8 weeks
Home Appointments: 1 day
Shows: Rocky Mountains and East Coast
Stores: Mostly Bears, Arvada, CO; Good Hearted Bears, Mystic, CT; Keepsake Dolls & Bears, Abingdon, MD; Teddy Bear Crossing, Colorado Springs, CO
Catalog/Photos: $2, refundable with purchase
Mail order: 6-8 weeks
Accepts: check, money order
Has been making bears for 5 years
Awards: Longmont Doll & Bear Show, 1st, 1992; Hotel Colorado-Glenwood Springs, 1st, 1994; 3rd, 1993
Publications: TB&F
One of Dorothy's bears was chosen to appear on the cover of this book.

TO SHOW A CHILD WHAT HAS ONCE
DELIGHTED YOU,
TO FIND A CHILD'S DELIGHT
ADDED TO YOUR OWN,
SO THAT THERE IS NOW A
DOUBLE DELIGHT SEEN IN
THE GLOW OF TRUST AND AFFECTION—
THIS IS HAPPINESS!
— *motto poem, Daydreams & Tea, Copley, Ohio*

BETTIE DEPUE
My Favorite Things
615 Belmont Rd.
Grand Forks, ND 58201
Phone: 701-775-9846
Phone orders: 9 A.M.-8 P.M.
Price range: $100-$250
Size range: 12″-20″

My Favorite Things bears are made of mohair or alpaca. They have glass or antique shoe button eyes. Bettie soft sculpts their faces, and each has his own unique personality.

Shows: Midwest
Stores: Bears & Hares Collectibles, Tulsa, OK; Lindsey's Doll Cottage, Nashville; TeddyTown USA, Nashville; Cheri's Bear Essentials, Kansas City, MO
Accepts: check, money order
Waiting list: 4-6 weeks
Has been making bears for 11 years

MARTHA DERAIMO
Martha's Bears
635 Hickory, Suite 142
West Bend, WI 53095
Phone: 414-338-6954
Phone orders: 10 A.M.-4 P.M.
Price range: $100-$350
Size range: 4″-40″

Martha's Bears are usually dressed, and each has antique accessories. Martha loves detail, and her characters often come with complete accessories. For instance, she has a cowbear with chaps, gun, holster, boots and hat; an actress with a trunk of make-up, theater gills, and jewelry, and a teacher with old books, a bell, a watch and a chalkboard.

Shows: CA, IL, FL, NJ
Stores: The Rocking Horse Gallery, Fredericksburg, VA; Bears By The Bay, Fairhope, AL; Bearly & More, E. Amherst, NY; Dime A Dance, Cedarburg, WI; Teddy Bears of Witney, Oxfordshire, UK; Strictly Bears, Medina, OH; Dolls, Bears & Funny Hares, Mission, KS; Bearaphanalia, Irvine, CA
Catalog/Photos: $3 (photos), refundable with purchase
Mail order: 3-6 weeks
Accepts: check, money order, Visa, MasterCard
Has been making bears for 11 years
Awards: Schaumburg, 1st, 2nd, 1992; Two 1sts, 1994; Golden Teddy nominee, 1994
Publications: TBR, cover & article, 1992; 4th Teddy Bear Price Guide; Collectors' History of Teddy Bears, Past & Present II; Tribute to Teddy Bear Artists

JANET DESJARDINE
Tiny Teddies
Ste. 206-580 13th St. NW
Portage La Prairie, Manitoba R1N 3R2, Canada
Phone: 204-857-9202
Phone orders: day or evening
Price range: $35-$50
Size range: 1½″-3″

Tiny Teddies come in a variety of designs, including a Panda. Janet handstitches all bears, and they are usually made of lightweight upholstery velvet with Ultrasuede paw pads. They have glass bead eyes and stitched noses. Most are fully jointed.

Home Appointments: 1 day
Shows: Manitoba
Stores: 2 Bears Teddy Bears, Calgary, Alberta; Teddy's Treasures, Edmonton, Alberta; Craft Cupboard, Winnepeg, Manitoba
Catalog/Photos: $2, refundable with purchase
Mail order: 2-4 weeks
Accepts: check, money order
Has been making bears for 3 years
Publications: TB&F, The Victorian Harvester

BRENDA DEWEY
Cosmic Nites
8015 Brimfield St.
Clinton, NY 13323
Phone: 315-853-6077
Phone orders: 9 A.M.-5 P.M.
Price range: $50-more than $450
Size range: 2½″-9″

Cosmic Nites bears are best known for the unique colors Brenda uses. Almost every bear is hand-dyed. She also does a lot of sculpting and detailing in her work. Most of her bears are on the fantasy side of life, modeled after wizards, jesters, trolls and dragons. Some have two-jointed heads.

Shows: FL, CA, IL, NJ, Canada, England
Stores: Bear Tracks, Pittsburgh; Out of the Woods, Modesto, CA; Good Hearted Bears, Mystic, NJ; The Rocking Horse Gallery, Fredericksburg, VA; Sue Pearson, UK; J & L Collectibles, Tampa
Accepts: check
Has been making bears for 17 years
Awards: Golden Teddy, 1991; Collectors Choice, 1988; Best of Show, 1992
Publications: TBR, Complete Book of Teddy Bears, Tribute to the Teddy Bear Artist

SANDRA DICKL

Sankar Bears & Buddies
110 Wayne St.
Stroudsburg, PA 18360
Phone: 717-424-2131
Phone orders: 8A.M.-9P.M.
Price range: $50-$350
Size range: 4½"-28"

Sankar Bears & Buddies bears are designed and handmade entirely by Sandra. Styles vary from the slim traditional look to the very plump with a look of innocence. Her bears are known for their piercing eyes. They are fully jointed, and many have bendable arms. Nifty is unique in that she has the traditional 5-way joints, plus jointed knees. Sandra's bears are stuffed with Poly-Fil, plastic pellets and steel pellets. She uses imported mohair and synthetics. She prefers bare bears, but dresses some in antique dresses and accessories.

Waiting list: 6-10 weeks
Home Appointments: 1 hour-1 week
Shows: Northeast and Southeast
Stores: Beary Best Friends, Tannersville, PA; Bear-a-Dise, Millburn, NJ; Fairy-Tales, Lombard, IL; Arundel Teddy Bears, West Sussex, UK; Kaufmann's Teddy Bear Corner, Zwillikon, Switzerland; Treasured Teddies, Wilmington, DE; Moore Bears, Strasburg, PA; Ted E. Hugs, Belle Mead, NJ; Bears By The Bay, Fairhope, AL
Catalog/Photos: $4
Mail order: 6-10 weeks (sometimes less)
Accepts: check, money order, Visa, MasterCard
Has been making bears for 11 years
Awards: several show awards
Publications: Contemporary Teddy Bear Price Guide

SANDRA ANN DINEEN

Sandy's Bearly Bruins
11 Huntington Ct.
Toms River, NJ 08753
Phone: 908-255-6924
Phone orders: 9A.M.-10P.M.
Price range: $100-$300
Size range: 13"-23"

Sandy's Bearly Bruins are made with German or English mohair, German glass eyes, noses embroidered with German cotton floss, and wool felt paws. The bears are fully jointed using hardboard discs, nuts and bolts. Some bears are dressed in vintage clothing to give them an antique look. Others wear handmade clothing or hand-knit sweaters, scarves and bows.

Waiting list: 2-4 weeks
Home Appointments: 1 week
Shows: MA, NJ, MD, RI, CN, IL, PA
Stores: Teddy Bears To Go, Lakewood, NJ; Rocky & His Friends, Medford, NJ; Bear-A-Dise, Millburn, NJ; The Teddy Bear Den, Las Vegas; Cumbrian Quilt Works, Cumbria, UK; Fantastic Balloons & Bears, Charlottesville, VA
Catalog/Photos: $5, refundable with purchase
Mail order: 2 weeks
Accepts: check, money order, Visa, MasterCard
Has been making bears for 5 years
Awards: Timonium, 5th, 1993; 3rd, 1994

DIANA DOBROWSKI

Diana's Teddy Bear Shop
HC 71 Box 7320
Wibaux, MT 59353
Phone: 406-795-2354
Phone orders: anytime
Price range: $50-$100
Size range: 2"-35"

Diana's bears come in all sizes, shapes and colors. They are stitched with the same amount of love from their sculptured faces to their padded feet. Some wear scarves and hats that Diana crochets. She also makes little wool pants, jackets or dresses for some of her bears. Many become family heirlooms made from recycled fur coats.

Waiting list: 4-6 weeks
Home Appointments: 1 day
Shows: SD, WY, ND, MT
Stores: Bear Paw Gallery, Sidney, MT
Catalog/Photos: free
Mail order: 4 weeks
Accepts: check
Has been making bears for 11 years
Awards: Local fair, Grand Champion Best of Show
Publications: Golden West Electric Co-op Magazine

VERONICA DOOLING

Bearly Legal Bears
3818 S. 66th St., Unit D
Tacoma, WA 98409
Phone: 206-473-7307
Phone orders: M-Sat, 8A.M.-5P.M.
Fax: 206-471-1323
Fax orders accepted.
Price range: $80-$500
Size range: 6½"-30"

Bearly Legal Bears are 100% mohair bears with glass or shoe button eyes and are polyester-, pellet-, and/or cotton-filled. Some have armature in their arms and/or legs. Paw pads are wool felt or Ultrasuede. Each bear is designed and created exclusively by Veronica. They have handstitched noses. Most are not dressed. All are limited editions.

Waiting list: 12 weeks
Shows: Across USA
Photos: sample color photos, $2
Mail order: 12 weeks
Accepts: check, money order, Visa, MasterCard, layaway
Has been making bears for 3 years
Awards: NW Club Ted, Best Artist Bear, 1994
Publications: TBR (ads)

LINDA LOUISE DORR

aDORRable bears
1735 NW 101st St.
Clive, IA 50325
Phone: 515-223-1764
Phone orders: 8 A.M.-10 P.M.
Price range: $95-$400
Size range: 8"-31"

aDORRable Bears are made in the style of old Steiff bears. Linda gives them deep-set eyes, a distinctive bridge of snout, long arms and a hump on the back. Some are dressed. Linda prefers nautical clothing, which she designs, or vintage children's clothing. Linda does all the work on every bear.

Waiting list: 2-4 weeks
Home Appointments: 1 week
Shows: Midwest
Catalog/Photos: $2, refundable with purchase
Mail order: 2-4 weeks
Accepts: check, money order
Has been making bears for 9 years
Awards: Golden Teddy

ROYALE DOWNES

Bearables by Royale
31 Gladeview Crescent SW
Calgary, Alberta T3E 4X7, Canada
Phone: 403-242-8437
Phone orders: normal business hours
Price range: less than $35-$100
Size range: less than 1"-8"

Bearables by Royale include miniature figurines made from a polymer sculpting compound. They are less than 1" tall and are individually handcrafted to reflect cherished moments in life. Royale also creates bears made of German synthetic fur and English and German mohair. These bare teddies have personality and appeal. They are 4"-8" tall, fully jointed, and have glass eyes and Ultrasuede paws. They are

stuffed with polyester and steel pellets.
Home Appointments: short notice
Shows: Calgary, Alberta
Stores: Old & Crafty, Cochrane, Alberta
Has been making bears for 6 years
Publications: TB&F

SHARON DRESSMAN

The Bear Basket
Rt. 4, P.O. Box 338
Morgantown, WV 26505
Phone: 304-599-3070
Phone orders: 9 A.M.-9 P.M.
Size range: Most 2"-4", some up to 12"

The Bear Basket teddy bears are miniatures, but they do have some bigger brothers. All are handsewn, original designs. They are made of clipped mohair, upholstery fabric or a suede-look velour, and are stuffed with fiberfill or plastic pellets or both. Sharon's bears come in a wide range of colors and are both traditional and nontraditional. She has Pandas as well.

Shows: OH, MI, PA, MD
Stores: Groves Quality Collectibles, Lima, OH; Muriel's Doll House, Plymouth, MI; Bear Tracks, Upper St. Clair, PA; Teddy Bears of Witney, Witney, Oxfordshire, UK; Good Hearted Bears, Mystic, CT; Country Arts & Antiques, Cincinnati, OH
Catalog/Photos: free
Mail order: 4-6 weeks
Accepts: check, money order
Has been making bears for 6 years

BEGINNING BEARMAKERS: ALWAYS KEEP YOUR FIRST BEAR AND SOME OF THE BEARS ALONG THE WAY SO YOU CAN SEE HOW FAR YOUR SKILLS HAVE COME AND WHERE YOU NEED TO GO NEXT. STRIVE ALWAYS FOR PERFECTION.
— *Cindy Michalski, artist, Westminster, CO*

DEBORAH L. DROWN

Born Again Bears
P.O. Box 167
Grant, FL 32949
Phone: 407-725-5270
Phone orders: 9 A.M.-9 P.M.
Price range: $50-$150
Size range: 1¾"-3½"

Born Again Bears are just one of a selection of miniature animals Deborah creates. They are very detailed.

Home Appointments: 1-2 days
Shows: East Coast
Stores: Village Bears, Sarasota, FL; 1764 House, Stewartsville, NJ; Bears & Dolls, Anchorage, AK; Bears By The Bay, Fairhope, AL; Cheri's Bear Essentials, Kansas City, MO; Dolls & Other Bear Necessities, San Clemente, CA; JeJo's, Pocatello, ID; Out of the Woods, Modesto, CA; Town & Country, Wilmington, DE; Keepsake Dolls and Bears, Abingdon, MD
Catalog/Photos: $1
Mail order: 3-4 weeks
Accepts: check, money order, Visa, MasterCard
Has been making bears for 5 years

DEANNA DUVALL

My Bears & Whimsy
1405 Birch St.
Forest Grove, OR 97116
Phone: 503-359-9264
Phone orders: 8 A.M.-4 P.M.

Price range: $100-$350
Size range: 9″-23″
My Bears & Whimsey are very traditional, with humped backs, long arms, and faces that are stern yet sweet. Deanna uses mohair, glass or shoe button eyes, and pearl cotton for noses, mouths and claws. The mohair is custom dyed when working on a special project. She dresses the bears in either vintage clothing or originally designed costumes.
Home Appointments: 1 week
Stores: The Owl's Nest, Carmel, CA; Groves Quality Collectibles, Lima, OH
Catalog/Photos: $2
Mail order: up to 6 weeks
Accepts: check, money order
Has been making bears for 18 years
Awards: Teddy and Me, 1st, 1982
Publications: Teddy Bear Artists; Teddy Bear Artists' Annual; Teddy Bear Price Guide, TBR

PENNY DYER

Bears By Penny
#206-2776 Pine St.
Vancouver, British Columbia, Canada
Phone: 604-731-6260
Phone orders: 6P.M.-9P.M.
Price range: $50-$100
Size range: 8″-15″
Bears By Penny are mainly mohair, fully jointed bears with glass eyes and Ultrasuede paw pads. Her bears are often accessorized with hats, collars or ties that she has designed and made. She also has been experimenting with dyeing fur.
Shows: British Columbia; Alberta
Catalog/Photos: $1, refundable with purchase
Mail order: up to 4 weeks
Accepts: check, money order
Has been making bears for 3 years
Publications: Teddies Own Journal

HOLLY DYER

Hollybearys
203 S. Water St.
Mt. Blanchard, OH 45867
Phone: 419-694-5301
Phone orders: 9A.M.-11P.M.
Price range: $50-$200
Size range: 3″-20″
Hollybearys are fully jointed. They all

have some type of hump and perky expressions and smiles. Holly stuffs them with polyester, plastic pellets, steel shot and excelsior. Her bears are happy and make people smile. Most are nontraditional and slightly unusual.
Home Appointments: 3 days
Shows: Midwest; Toronto, Ontario
Stores: Groves Quality Collectibles, Bluffton, OH; Marilyn's World, Lauderhill, FL; Dolls & Other Bear Necessities, San Clemente, CA; Love's A Bear Necessity, Metamora, IN; The Teddy Bear Garden, Ltd., Toronto, Ontario
Catalog/Photos available.
Mail order: 6-8 weeks
Accepts: check, money order
Has been making bears for 11 years

NANCY EDMUNDS

Wood-N-Bear
P.O. Box 274, Church St. Ext.
Wallingford, VT 05773
Phone: 802-446-2814
Phone orders: 9A.M.-9P.M.
Price range: $50-$150
Size range: 6″-20″
Wood-N-Bear bears have longer noses and bigger bellies than most bears. Nancy likes it when she can make the faces say, "I need a hug." She doesn't antique or dress her bears, although a ribbon is a must.
Home Appointments: 1 day
Shows: East Coast
Stores: All Things Bright & Beautiful, Waitsfield, VT; Hugging Bear Inn & Shoppe, Chester, VT; Magic Sleigh, Manchester, VT; Truly Unique, Rutland, VT
Catalog/Photos: free flyer, $5 photos, refundable with purchase
Mail order: 4-6 weeks
Accepts: check, money order, Visa, MasterCard
Has been making bears for 6 years
Publications: TB&F

TERRI EFFAN

Terri's Baskets and Bears
1280 S. Raisinville Rd.
Monroe, MI 48161
Phone: 313-242-5601
Phone orders: 7 days, 9:30A.M.-9:30P.M.
Price range: $50-$150

Size range: 1⅝″-14″
Terri's Bears are usually miniature dressed and undressed bears. She works with a variety of fabrics and colors and rarely makes the same bear twice. She also makes teddy bear purses from 250%″ to 14″ (an evening bag teddy). All her miniatures are made from upholstery fabric and Ultrasuede with glass or black onyx bead eyes. Full size bears are made of German mohair with glass eyes. Each bear is made entirely by Terri, usually one at a time from start to finish. Her son has the right to keep all bears he likes for his own collection.
Home Appointments: 1 week
Shows: KS, MO, OH, MI, IL, Toronto, Ontario
Stores: Judy's Teddies & Treasures, Olympia, WA; The Toy Store, Toledo, OH
Catalog/Photos: $2, refundable with purchase
Mail order: 4-6 weeks
Accepts: check, money order
Has been making bears for 4 years
Terri acted as a consultant for this book. Three of her bears were chosen to appear on the cover.

JACQUELINE ENGLAND

Woodland Creations
2633 Kinnerton Cres.
Mississauga, Ontario L5K 2B1
Canada
Phone: 905-822-9197
Phone orders: 9A.M.-9P.M.
Price range: $50-more than $450
Size range: 15″-21″
Woodland Creations are made of mohair or alpaca, have glass eyes, pop-rivet joints and leather or Ultrasuede paws. Jacqueline's Musical Carousel has four dressed teddies riding white mohair bruin bears. They have glass eyes

and are fully jointed. The carousel base is solid oak, approximately 17" in diameter, with brass poles and fittings. The bears ride around the carousel in time to the music.

Home Appointments available.

Shows: Ontario

Stores: Visual Arts Center, Mississauga, Ontario; Crafter's Marketplace, Mississauga, Ontario

Catalog/Photos: $2, refundable with purchase

Mail order: 2-3 weeks

Accepts: money order, Visa

Has been making bears for 3 years

Publications: TBR (ad)

BEVERLY JEAN ERICKSEN

46-065 Konohiki St. 3631
Kaneohe, HI 96744
Phone: 808-235-6634
Price range: $35-$150
Home appointments available.
Shows: HI

JENNIFER ELIZABETH FAIR

Pennyfarthing Originals
10 Teesdale Pl. #1504
Scarborough, Ontario M1L 1K9, Canada
Phone: 416-691-3656
Phone orders: 7:30P.M.-10P.M.,
or leave message
Price range: less than $35-$200
Size range: 8"-14"

Pennyfarthing Originals come in a variety of fabrics, including mohair, brightly colored acrylics, cotton string, alpaca, denim, velvet and Christmas quilted fabric. Some are non-jointed and cuddly, like children's bears, and others have a more "grown-up" appeal. Jennifer is also experimenting with growlers and musical devices.

Shows: Southern Ontario

Catalog/Photos: free

Mail order: 2 weeks

Accepts: check, money order, Visa

Has been making bears for 2 years

PAT R. FAIRBANKS

PRFect Pals
P.O. Box 20553
St. Petersburg, FL 33702
Phone: 813-526-6301
Phone orders: 7A.M.-9P.M.
Price range: $50-$250
Size range: 3"-30"

PRFect Pals bears are made of a variety of vintage materials as well as new imported furs and mohair. Pat also makes custom bears from real fur or other old coats and a variety of one-of-a-kind bears. Most have large noses and large, imported glass eyes. She has bears with five- and six-piece heads.

Waiting list: 2-4 weeks

Home Appointments: 2-3 hours

Shows: FL, Midwest

Stores: I. Child, Tarpon Springs, FL

Photos: SASE

Mail order: 2 weeks

Accepts: check, money order

Has been making bears for 6 years

Publications: Bear Tracks

LINDA LEE FARRELL

Hearthfire Bears
8250 NW 68th Ter.
Tamarac, FL 33321
Phone: 305-722-6697
Phone orders: anytime
Price range: $95-$300
Size range: 6"-20"

Heartfire Bears come in both plush and

mohair. Linda also makes bears from recycled fur coats and some special request bears. Most of her bears are dressed. All are designed and created by Linda and are fully jointed. Some have music boxes or growlers.

Waiting list 6 weeks

Home Appointments: 1 week

Stores: Wonderland, Inc., Hollywood, FL; Margaritaville, New Orleans, LA

Mail order: 4-6 weeks

Accepts: money order, bank check

Has been making bears for 5 years

Publications: TBR

BARBARA J. FICKERT

Second Childhood
406 Tennyson Dr.
Oakville, Ontario L6L 3Z1, Canada
Phone: 905-827-6744
Phone orders: anytime
Price range: $35-$125
Size range: 1½"-4"

Second Childhood bears have black onyx bead eyes and a friendly "take me home" appeal. The smallest bears are made of Ultrasuede in typical teddy bear colors, including honey, beige, cinnamon and chocolate. All are jointed and wear silk ribbon bows. Larger bears are crafted from a variety of smooth or distressed plush fabrics. Most wear a ribbon or collar. Some wear hats, scarves, vests and jewelry.

Home Appointments: 2-3 days

Shows: Ontario

Catalog/Photos: $2, refund with purchase

Mail order available.

Accepts: money order, Visa

Has been making bears for 4 years

DORYCE KATHLEEN FINCH

Finch's Musical Bears
340 State St. SE
Grand Rapids, MI 49503

Phone: 616-454-6466
Phone orders: 10A.M.-10P.M.
Price range: less than $35-$200
Size range: 6″-24″
Finch's Musical Bears are stuffed with fiberfill, jointed and musical. Doryce makes them "not too grouchy looking."
Home Appointments: 2 days
Shows: MI, IN, OH, IL, WI
Catalog/Photos: $3, refundable with purchase
Mail order: 3 months
Accepts: check, money order
Has been making bears for 15 years

PEGGY J. FLEMING
P.O. Box 12114
Des Moines, IA 50312
Phone: 515-277-8060
Phone orders: 9A.M.-9P.M.
Price range: $50-$150
Size range: 1″-6″
Peggy's minature stuffed and jointed bears are usually made of upholstery velvet. She sometimes works in mohair or alpaca blends. Most are not dressed because she doesn't like to cover their bodies, which are important to their designs. Prominent noses are a common feature on all her bears. They have been described as funny looking, and often make people laugh. Each has Peggy's initials embroidered on the left hip.
Waiting list: depends on order
Home Appointments: 2 weeks
Shows: Midwest
Stores: Donna Bears, Godfrey, IL; Cheri's Bear Essentials, Kansas City, MO; Marilyn's World, Lauderhill, FL; Groves Quality Collectibles, Lima, OH; Treasured Teddies, Wilmington, DE; Donna's Country Collection, West Des Moines, IA
Catalog/Photos: $3

Mail order: 6-8 weeks
Accepts: check, money order, Visa, MasterCard
Has been making bears for 5 years
Awards: ribbon, Iowa State Fair
Publications: TB&F

SUE FOWLER
The Jane Street Bear Company
2823 Jane St.
Port Moody, British Columbia V3H 2K7, Canada
Phone: 604-469-9123
Price range: less than $35-$50
Size range: 2″-12″
The Jane Street Bear Company bears are all original designs. They are mainly done in mohair, but some are made of acrylic furs. Sue's bears are often dressed in a hand-knit sweater or a full costume. All are fully jointed. The larger bears have glass eyes. The miniatures have bead eyes. Sue enjoys creating special bears and has made a number of bears in outfits requested by customers.
Home Appointments: 1 week
Shows: Western Canada
Catalog/Photos: $3, refundable with purchase
Mail order: 1 week
Accepts: check, money order, postal C.O.D. service
Has been making bears for 4 years
Awards: The Bear Fair, 2nd, 1994

GLORIA FRANKS
by Goose Creek
Rt. 1, P.O. Box 221B
Walker, WV 26180
Phone: 304-628-3174
Phone orders: anytime
Fax: 304-628-3174
Fax orders accepted.
Price range: $250-$450
Size range: 18″-30″
by Goose Creek bears are large bears that are usually dressed. Gloria uses flex limb in the arms. They wear dresses ranging in style from Victorian to country. Her Teddy Toddlers are 30″ and wear regular toddler clothes. They stand on their own and have lockline in their arms and legs.
Waiting list: 6-8 weeks
Shows: several shows—locations vary
Catalog/Photos: stamped envelope

Mail order: 6-8 weeks
Accepts: check, money order, Visa, MasterCard
Has been making bears for 11 years
Awards: several show awards

RUTH E. FRASER
Bears Abundant
156 Shaughnessy Blvd.
Willowdale, Ontario M2J 1J8, Canada
Phone: 416-493-2944
Fax: 416-322-5527
Price range: $50-$300
Size range: 1⁵⁄₁₆″-15″
Bears Abundant bears include miniatures designed for a ¹⁄₁₂th scale to look proportionate in a dollhouse. Ruth has designed some one-of-a-kind series, including her Gem bears. These are based on the color and texture of each gem chosen, with a piece of the gem added to each bear. Her one-of-a-kind series includes bears from 3½″-15″.
Shows: Toronto, Ontario; Tokyo, Japan
Stores: The Teddy Bear Garden, Toronto, Ontario
Photos: free
Accepts: money order, Visa
Design manufactured by Ty, Inc.
Has been making bears for 20 years

> BE YOURSELF—YOU WILL BE HAPPY YOU DID!
> — *Ann Horne, artist, North York, Ontario*

CHESTER DANIEL FREEMAN, JR.
Chester Freeman Bears
398 S. Main St.
Geneva, NY 14456-2614
Phone: 315-781-1251
Phone orders: 9A.M.-4P.M.
Fax: 315-781-0643
Fax orders accepted.
Price range: $100-$400
Size range: 10″-16″
Chester's designs have become recognized for their classic proportions and ensuring quality. Each bear's uniqueness results from the combination of the finest fabrics in silk, mohair and alpaca, meticulous sculpting of the bear's body parts, and the hand-embroidered features. Chester's limited production ensures buyers that personal attention has been given to each order, and no compromise in quality

is ever made. His bears are well known to collectors and retail establishments, and they appear in numerous price guides that chart their annual increase in value.

Waiting list: 3-4 months
Home Appointments: 1-2 days
Shows: Midwest, West Coast, Northeast
Stores: Linger Awhile, Titusville, FL; Cheri's Bear Essentials, Kansas City, MO; Cape Fear Christmas House, Wilmington, NC; Childhood Fantasies, La Grangeville, NY; Bears 'N Hares, Tulsa, OK; Grin & Bear It, Naperville, IL
Catalog/Photos: free with SASE
Mail order: 6 weeks
Accepts: check, money order
Has been making bears for 14 years
Awards: Legislative Resolution for artistic achievement for teddy bear artistry and the publication of Run Away Bear issued by the senate of New York state; selection of bears to the Children's Museum of Indianapolis
Publications: Teddy Bear Artists: The Romance Books of Making and Collecting Bears; The Official Price Guide to Antiques and Collectibles; The Official ID and Price Guide to American Country Collectibles; The Official Price Guide to Antique and Modern Teddy Bears; Contemporary Teddy Bear Price Guide, TBR, TB&F, Teddy Bear Times, Colonial Homes, Early American Life, Country Living, Country Almanac
See the artists' introduction to this book written by Chester. Two of Chester's bears were chosen to appear on the cover of this book.

PENNY CRANE FRENCH
back mountain bears
RR 1, P.O. Box 159
Trout Run, PA 17771

Phone: 717-634-2741
Phone orders: 9 A.M.-9 P.M.
Price range: $50-$200
Size range: 9"-22"
back mountain bears are made from a wide variety of fabrics, including acrylic, alpaca, mohair and European plush. Penny makes character bears and soft, huggable styles. All her bears have large, happy smiles, meant to evoke smiles from all who see them.
Waiting list: 4-6 weeks
Shows: East Coast, Mid-Atlantic
Catalog/Photos: SASE
Mail order: 1 week-10 days
Accepts: check, money order, Visa, MasterCard
Has been making bears for 24 years
Awards: Several ribbons in area contests, including 1sts; state and chapter juried member of the PA Guild of Craftsmen
Publications: TBR; TB&F; newspapers

CHERIE FRIENDSHIP
Friendship Teddy Bears
21 Ridgevale Dr.
Markham, Ontario L6B 1A8, Canada
Phone: 905-294-5658
Phone orders: 9 A.M.-7 P.M.
Price range: $100-$250
Size range: 9"-22"
Friendship Teddy Bears are fully jointed, mohair bears made from Cherie's original designs. They have glass or antique shoe button eyes. Some have growlers. Bears are usually bare and tend to be traditional. Some are aged to look antique.
Home appointments available.
Shows: Toronto, Ontario
Stores: Grandma's Treasures, Unionville, Ontario; Teddy Bear Garden, Ontario; Crafter's Marketplace, Mississauga, Ontario

Catalog/Photos: $5, refundable with purchase
Mail order: 30 days
Accepts: check, money order, MasterCard
Has been making bears for 4 years
Publications: Victorian Harvester

VIVIAN FRITZE
Fritze Bears
#1406 12141 Jasper Ave.
Edmonton, Alberta T5N 3X8
Canada
Phone: 403-482-6800
Phone orders: 9 A.M.-8 P.M.
Fax: 403-482-6811
Fax orders accepted.
Price range: $50-$400
Size range: 2"-30"
Fritze Bears are all original designs by Vivian. She uses the best materials, including mohair, alpaca, antique wool, German synthetics, glass eyes and Ultrasuede and leather. She stuffs her bears with fiberfill, plastic and steel pellets. She makes both limited and open editions, and personalities are guaranteed.
Waiting list: 2-3 months
Home Appointments: 1 day
Shows: Western and Eastern Canada
Stores: Treasures & Toys, Edmonton, Alberta; 2 Bears Teddy Bears, Calgary, Alberta; Martin House Dolls & Toys, Thornhill, Ontario; Beartique, Montreal, Quebec
Catalog/Photos: $5, refundable with purchase
Mail order: 8-12 weeks
Accepts: check, money order
Has been making bears for 4 years
Publications: The Victorian Harvester

JEAN GADANO & MITZI FRY
Tabby's Bear
P.O. Box 18145
San Jose, CA 95158
Phone: 408-998-5680
Phone orders: anytime
Fax: 408-723-7056
Fax orders accepted.
Price range: $50-more than $450
Size range: 9"-22"
Tabby's Bears are made of mohair, imported plush or old wool coats. Jean and Mitzi have used polyester fiber filling or plastic pellets inside the bears. Undressed bears are adorned with ribbons or lace collars, bow ties, hats and eyeglasses. Dressed bears are adorned with the finest fabrics available as well as vintage fabrics. They use antique baby shoes, eyeglasses and jewelry to accessorize. They make a unique bear with a mohair head and a body made from an old wool coat, adorned with antique buttons on the body. All bears have glass eyes and an Ultrasuede covered nose.
Home Appointments: 1 day
Shows: West Coast, Southwest, Midwest, East Coast
Catalog/Photos: $1, refundable with purchase
Mail order: 4-6 weeks
Accepts: check, money order, Visa, MasterCard
Have been making bears for 11 years
Awards: TBBNC, Gold Medals, 1989, 1990; Blue Ribbon, 1990; ATBAG, Blue Ribbon, 1987; 2 Blue Ribbons, 1988; Portland Paws Lincoln City Convention, Blue Ribbon, 1992
Publications: Teddy Bear Artist Annual, Contemporary Teddy Bear Price Guide, Teddybaren

DIANE GARD
A Bear With A Heart
1005 West Oak St.
Fort Collins, CO 80521
Phone: 303-484-8191
Phone orders accepted.
Fax: 303-484-0090
Fax orders accepted.
Price range: $150-more than $450
Size range: 12"-36"
Bears With A Heart are whimsical, quizzical-eyed bears with a style all their own. Diane creates her unique character bears with a less traditional look while remaining true to the most endearing qualities of the essential teddy bear. From the impish "Weisenheimer," with his squirting flower to the long-legged sophistication of the fashion model bear, "Marisa Bearenson," all of Diane's original designs are characterized by a trademark red glass heart on each bear's chest.
Shows: across USA, Walt Disney World, Europe
Brochure/Photos: $3, refundable with purchase
Mail order: 2-4 months
Accepts: check, money order, Visa, MasterCard, American Express
Has been making bears for 13 years
Awards: Golden Teddy; TBBNC, Best of Show; numerous ribbons and awards at competitions, shows and conventions; bear on display at the Museum of American History of the Smithsonian Institute in Washington, D.C.
Publications: ToyBox, cover and article; TBR, 2 covers and articles; Teddy Bear Times, cover and article, TB&F, articles; Hugglets; BeerBericht,; Teddy Bear Artists' Annual, cover; Teddy's Bearzaar; Teddy Bear Lover's Companion; The Joy of Teddy Bears; The Complete Book of Teddy Bears; Teddy Bears Past & Present; Tribute to Teddy Bear Artists; The Teddy Bear Encyclopedia; Contemporary Teddy Bear Price Guide; Teddy Bears; newspapers
See the article opening this chapter written by Diane.

JO-AN GAST
Jo-G Collectibles
19647 U Ave.
Steamboat Rock, IA 50672
Phone: 515-858-5769
Phone orders: 7 A.M.-9 P.M.
Price range: $50-$350
Size range: 2"-38"
Jo-G Collectibles are entirely handcrated by Jo-an. She also makes and designs all patterns and clothing. Her miniature bears are handstitched. The medium to large bears have Jo-G exclusive muscle arms. All have humpbacks and potbellies. She uses mohair except for the 2" bear, which is made of upholstery fabric. Her bears are stuffed with Poly-Fil or a combination of pellets and Poly-Fil.
Home Appointments: 1 day
Shows: IA, IL, MO, MN, KS
Stores: Marilyn's World, Lauderhill, FL; Casey's Bear Factory, Fairport, NY; Animal Haus Ltd., Cincinnati, OH
Catalog/Photos: $4, refundable with purchase
Mail order: 2-3 weeks
Accepts: check, layaway
Has been making bears for 7 years
Awards: TOBY nominee, 1991
Publications: TBR; TB&F

NANCY LYNN GATTO
Limerick Bear
59 Jones Rd
Wallingford, CT 06492

Phone: 203-265-0757
Phone orders: 10 A.M.-10 P.M.
Price range: $50-$400
Size range: 6½"-24"

Limerick Bears are loosely jointed and softly stuffed. Nancy prefers the antique look in bears, and she trims and stains their noses to give them a loved look. They are stuffed with many different materials.

Waiting list: 1 month
Home Appointments: 1 day
Shows: CT, VT, MA, IL, PA, MD, FL, NY, NJ
Stores: Teddy Bears To Go, Lakewood, NJ; The Paisley Bear, Ft. Lauderdale, FL
Catalog/Photos: $2, refundable with purchase
Mail order: 4-6 weeks
Accepts: check, money order, Visa, MasterCard

Has been making bears for 11 years

Publications: Teddy Bear Artists' Annual; Contemporary Teddy Bear Price Guide; TB&F; TBR

SUSAN REDSTREAKE GEARY
New Mexico Bear Paws
2 Trueman Ct.
Baltimore, MD 21244
Phone: 410-298-8459
Phone orders: anytime
Price range: $100-more than $450
Size range: 6"-36"

New Mexico Bear Paws bears have furry faces and are made of mohair. They come with antique props such as boxes and cans, hat boxes, clothing and accessories. Susan creates many theme bears and sets with pets. She also makes bears modeled after historical people. All bears come with a sterling silver bear charm in their left ear.

Waiting list: 1-2 months

Home Appointments: 1 day to 1 week
Shows: MD, PA, VA
Stores: The Rocking Horse Gallery, Fredericksburg, VA
Photos: $3, refundable with purchase
Mail order: 1-2 months
Accepts: check, money order

Has been making bears for 7 years

Awards: TOBY, 1993; National Teddy Roosevelt Bear Contest, 1993, Golden Teddy nominee.
Publications: TBR, pattern designs and articles

MARY GEORGE
Mary George Bears
46713 Camelia Dr.
Canton, MI 48187
Phone: 313-453-6814
Phone orders: anytime, preferably 8 A.M.-8 P.M.
Price range: $85-more than $450
Size range: 8"-30"

Mary George Bears are reminiscent of antique bears. Mary's designs incorporate features found in bears made in the early 1900s, including long arms, big feet, triangular-shaped heads, boot button eyes and humps in back. She uses a variety of mohair styles and colors, but all materials are consistent with those used to make antique bears.

Waiting list: 3-4 months
Shows: Midwest
Stores: Owl's Nest, Carmel, CA; My Friends & Me, Leesburg, VA
Catalog/Photos: $1 for postage
Mail order: 3-4 months
Accepts: check, money order

Has been making bears for 8 years

Awards: Two Best of Show awards; TOBY nominee, 1994

Three of Mary's bears were chosen to appear on the cover of this book.

LINDA GIESECKE
Bearly Mine
279 Carlton Ave.
Piscalaway, NJ 08854
Phone: 908-968-8939
Phone orders: 9 A.M.-8 P.M.
Price range: $35-$250
Size range: 7"-22"

Bearly Mine bears are made of imported mohair or recycled coats. They are handmade by Linda.

Waiting list: 4-6 weeks
Shows: Northeast
Stores: Ted E. Hugs, Belle Mead, NJ; Gerri's Doll Den, Babylon, NY; Shanah's Gifts, Smithtown, NY; Coomer's, Plano, TX; The Magpies Nest, Canterbury, Kent, UK; Casey's Bear Factory, Fairport, NY
Catalog/Photos: $2, refundable with purchase
Mail order: 6 weeks
Accepts: check, money order

Has been making bears for 6 years

WENDY GITT
Gwendy Bears
1101 Sheaffer Rd.
Elizabethtown, PA 17022
Phone: 717-367-4396
Phone orders: 9 A.M.-9 P.M.
Price range: $50-$200
Size range: 16"-20"

Gwendy Bears tend to be children. They have a slender build with long limbs and black glass eyes and are made of mohair or synthetic furs. Wendy sometimes sculptures the upper eye area. They have stitched noses. Boys have shoulders and girls have noticeable hips and cute little potbellies. Arms are often bendable. They have a very innocent, intent look, and are a little serious. Wendy loves to give them old-fashioned names.

Accepts: check, money order

Has been making bears for 2 years

CYNTHIA GLICKMAN
Willow Creek Bears & Bunnies
2531 Bowker Ct.
Carmichael, CA 95608
Phone: 916-482-3239
Phone orders: 9 A.M.-5 P.M.
Price range: $50-$450
Size range: 2"-48"

Willow Creek Bears feature cross-stitch

on their paws and clothing. They are all original designs, and almost all are one-of-a-kinds. Cynthia uses the finest mohair, alpaca, silk blend fur, glass eyes and leather or Ultrasuede for paws. Her bears are jointed with wooden discs and stuffed with Poly-Fil and pellets for a "huggy" feel. Many are trimmed in antique laces and flowers and wear baby clothing. All noses are hand-embroidered.

Waiting list: 2 months
Home Appointments: 2-3 days
Shows: CA, OR, WA, AZ, IL, FL
Stores: Huckleberry Junction, Naperville, IL
Accepts: check, money order, Visa, MasterCard
Has been making bears for 5 years
Awards: California State Fair, 2 1sts, 2nd, 3rd, Best of Show, 1993; 1st, 3rd, 1994; TBBNC, 2nd

BARBARA GOLDEN
Can't Bear To Part
3932 Digby Ct., #10
Richmond, VA 23233
Phone: 804-747-3779
Phone orders: 9A.M.-9P.M.
Price range: $200-$450
Size range: 9"-26"

Can't Bear to Part bears are known for their personality and body language. Their facial features are very sculptured. Barbara gives some bears tiny teeth and freckles. Smaller bears sit on handmade couches.
Has been making bears for 5 years
Awards: TOBY nominee, 1994
Publications: TB&F; TBR; Teddy Bear Times

CHERYL GORDON
20 Laurel Ln.
Wolcott, CT 06716
Phone: 203-879-5835
Phone orders: leave message on machine
Price range: less than $35-$150
Size range: 6"-24"

Cheryl's designs are all original, based on antique bears. There are about 25 new designs each year. Most are one-of-a-kind. She limits her production to about two hundred bears per year. All are produced by Cheryl with no outside help.

Waiting list: 6 months
Home Appointments: 2 weeks
Shows: MA, CT
Accepts: check, money order
Has been making bears for 15 years
Awards: Baltimore Zoo Bear Show

SHONDRA-TANIA GRANT-FAIN
Bitterman's Courtyard Collection
3237 Dellwood Rd. W.
Waynesville, NC 28786
Phone: 704-926-3577
Phone orders: anytime
Price range: $50-$300
Size range: 1"-3½"

Bitterman's Courtyard Collection are all unique designs and unusual ideas. Shondra uses the best materials she can find, including genuine Ultrasuede. No matter how small the bear, she uses traditional jointing. All her bears are either limited editions or one-of-a-kind. They come with a beautiful walnut stand with an engraved plate bearing the "Bitterman's Courtyard Collection" name, the name of the bear and the official edition number.

Waiting list: 2 months
Home Appointments: call
Shows: Southeast
Stores: Hyacinths for the Soul, Asheville, NC; Miniature Cottage, Inc., Nashville; Gepetto's, Cherokee, NC; Nana's Dolls & Collectibles, Grove City, OH; Putnam's Landing, Dallas
Photos: $3 (one photo free)
Mail order: 8-12 weeks
Accepts: money order
Has been making bears for 7 years

NADINE GRAVATT
Ravenwood Designs
Ravenwood Farm
57 Red Valley Rd.
Cream Ridge, NJ 08514

Phone: 609-758-3068
Phone orders: 8A.M.-8P.M.
Price range: $100-more than $450
Size range: 12"-28"

Ravenwood Designs are one-of-a-kind or very small editions. Nadine's bears are made with all kinds of antique accessories that she buys at antique shows or flea markets. She tries to make bears that have their own looks and personalities. She makes her own patterns and does all the clothes herself.

Waiting list: 2 months
Home Appointments: 1 week
Accepts: check, money order
Has been making bears for 5 years
Awards: TOBY Nominee, 1994; many 1st place ribbons at bear shows
Publications: TB&F, cover, June 1993. Beer Bericht cover Summer 1993 "Amsterdam"

JEANNE E. GREEN
Buttonbush
7445 W. Cactus Rd.
Ste. 211-126
Peoria, AZ 85381
Phone: 602-412-1110
Phone orders: 10A.M.-5P.M.
Price range: $100-$450
Size range: 5"-25"

Buttonbush bears have a center seam face and double, handstitched noses. They have unique profiles and concerned souls. Jeanne uses extra long imported furs for each of her original designs. They come in limited editions of less than ten or one-of-a-kinds.

Home Appointments: 1-2 days
Shows: IL, AZ, CA, CO
Stores: Bears & More, Glendale, AZ; Gepetto's, Carmel, CA; Animal Haus Ltd., Cincinnati, OH; The Bear Pawse, Prescott, AZ; Hugging Bear Inn & Shop, Chester, VT; Treasured

Dolls & Specialties, La Conner, WA
Catalog/Photos: $2
Mail order: 1 week
Accepts: check, money order, layaway
Has been making bears for 10 years
Awards: ATBAG, 1st
Publications: TB&F; Contemporary
Teddy Bear Price Guide; Teddy Bear
Times; TBR

BETTINA F. GROH

The Glass Dragon
420 Sunview Cir.
Blue Springs, MO 64014
Phone: 816-228-6402
Phone orders: 9A.M.-9P.M.
Price range: $35-$300
Size range: 3"-36"

The Glass Dragon teddy bears are handmade by Bettina from design to completion. She has decided not to add
outside help to assure her clients of
the highest quality possible. Each bear
is signed and numbered, and the designs are changed frequently. Limited
editions may be as few as ten. Bettina
also makes bears from recycled items
of sentimental value to her customers.
She is sensitive to the issue of using
animal fur and will only use recycled
fur.
Waiting list: 60-90 days
Home Appointments: 1 day
Shows: NY, TX, OK, KS, MO
Stores: Dolls, Bears & Funny Hares,
Mission, KS; White Bear Antiques,
Tulsa, OK; Christmas In The Village,
Hammondsport, NY
Catalog/Photos: free
Mail order: varies
Accepts: check, money order, Visa, Mas-
terCard
Has been making bears for 6 years
Awards: Collectors' Jubilee, Tulsa, OK,
Best Bear Artist, 1994

DOLORES GROSECK

The Bears of Southampton
443 Militia Hill Rd.
Southampton, PA 18966
Phone: 215-355-0879
Phone orders: anytime
Price range: $150-more than $450
Size range: 12"-22"

The Bears of Southampton are often
made using mixed media, especially
clay and sculpture. Dolores tries to in-
tegrate unrelated objects into a design
project. The bears' bodies are somewhat traditional. Dolores is known for
her dressed bears, which she still prefers, but lately her bears have become
bare, making her more sensitive to
subtle aspects such as the tilt of the
head and the paw pads.
Shows: West, Midwest, East
Stores: Marilyn's World, Lauderhill, FL;
Christy's, Buckingham, PA; Groves
Quality Collectibles, Lima, OH; Bear
Tracks, Pittsburgh; Honey Bee Bear
Shoppe, East Bridgewater, MA;
Dolls, Bears & Funny Hares, Mission,
KS; Owl of the Woods, Modesto, CA;
Owl's Nest, Carmel, CA
Catalog/Photos: $5, refundable with pur-
chase
Mail order: 6 months
Accepts: check
Has been making bears for 11 years
Awards: Golden Teddy Award
Publications: TBR; Offical Guide to An-
tique and Modern Teddy Bears; Offi-
cial Guide to Antiques and Collect-
ibles; Complete Book of Teddy Bears

LINDA GRUNAU

Lindan
3294 Woody Ln.
San Jose, CA 95132
Phone: 405-263-1026
Phone orders: anytime
Fax: 408-263-1026
Fax orders accepted.
Price range: $50-$150
Size range: 12"-15"

Lindan Bears are usually mohair, with
Ultrasuede paw pads and glass or shoe
button eyes. They are stuffed with
Poly-Fil or pellets. Kristopher with a
K is mohair, and comes with lederho-
sen, an alpine horn, and a Tyroleon
hat. He also comes with a tape of Alpine horn music.

Shows: CA, WA, IL, MI
Photos available.
Mail order available.
Accepts: check
Has been making bears for 15 years
Publications: TBR

SUZI GRUNIN

Suzi's Bears
One Michael Dr.
South Easton, MA 02375
Phone: 508-238-3980
Phone orders: 10A.M.-7P.M.
Price range: $85-$220
Size range: 13"-29"

Suzi's Bears are jointed. They are classic
teddy bears with long arms. They are
made of mohair, alpaca or top-quality
synthetics. They have very expressive
faces, and each one has its own distinct personality.
Home Appointments: 1-2 days
Shows: MA, CT, RI
Mail order: 4 weeks
Accepts: check, money order, Visa, MasterCard
Has been making bears for 7 years

JACKLYN GUALTIERI

Pickwick Purveyors
8 Spring Ridge Dr.
Berkeley Heights, NJ 07922
Phone: 908-508-1711
Phone orders: 9A.M.-5P.M.
Fax: 908-665-9333
Fax orders accepted.
Price range: $35-$350
Size range: 2½"-24"

Jacklyn designs and makes her line of
"Most Best Bears" from start to finish. They are made of luxury fur fabrics, and many are one-of-a-kind, with
the largest edition at 12. Bears often
wear costumes. When possible, the
costumes are constructed from vintage fabrics, ribbons and trims.

Home Appointments: 1 day
Shows: NJ, MA, CT, RI, PA, MD, NY
Catalog/Photos: $3, refundable with purchase
Mail order: 1 week
Accepts: check, money order, Visa, MasterCard
Publications: TB&F, TBR
Has been making bears for 4 years

APRIL WHITCOMB GUSTAFSON
149 Main St.
Boylston, MA
Phone: 508-869-6329
Phone orders: Mon-Thurs, evenings;
Fri & Sat, days
Price range: $100-$1,000
Size range: 3″ and under
April's bears are fully jointed bears sculpted from a low-fire clay, then covered with velvets, leathers, suede and silk for clothing. Some have open mouths with tongues and teeth. Some have head-tail movement, metal jaws and realistic paw pads. Most are limited editions of fifty or less. They come in their own handmade quilted hat boxes, which April's mother makes.
Waiting list: 3-4 weeks
Home Appointments: 1 week
Shows: MA
Catalog/Photos: free
Mail order: 4-6 weeks
Accepts: check, money order
Design manufactured by Schmid, Inc.
Has been making bears for 16 years
Awards: 2 Golden Teddy Awards; 1 TOBY; ATBAG award
Publications: TB&F; TBR; Tribute to Teddy Bear Artists; Teddy Bear Catalog; Teddy Bear Artists: The Romance of Making and Collecting Teddy Bears; Teddy Bear Lovers Catalog; A Hug of Bears; Guide to American Miniaturists; The Miniatures Catalog;

Sky Magazine; Teddy Bear Times; Nutshell News; Official Price Guide to Antique and Modern Teddy Bears

PATRICIA NOEL GYE
Wayfarer Bears
10539 McDonald Park Rd.
Sidney, British Columbia V8L 3J2, Canada
Phone: 604-656-9571
Fax: 604-656-5233
    Fax orders accepted.
Price range: $100-more than $450
Size range: 5″-36″
Wayfarer Bears are traditional, fully jointed mohair bears. Patricia uses handblown glass eyes and Ultrasuede paws. They are big bears with wonderful faces.
Home Appointments: 2 hours-2 days
Shows: West Coast of North America, Nevada City, CA, Napa, CA, Lincoln City, OR, Seattle, WA, Victoria and Richmond, British Columbia, Calgary, Alberta
Stores: Teddy Bears Picnic, Victoria, British Columbia, Theodore's Bear Emporium, London, UK
Catalog/Photos: $3, refundable with purchase
Mail order: up to 2 months
Accepts: check, money order
Has been making bears for 12 years
Awards: Several 1st place show awards
Publications: TB&F; TBR; The Victorian Harvester

BELLE HAGERTY
B J's Bears
627 E. Franklin
Macomb, IL 61455
Phone: 309-833-5883
Phone orders: anytime
Price range: $50-$250
Size range: 5″-30″
BJ's Bears are all original designs. They

are made of mohair or alpaca from Germany and England. Belle uses handblown glass enameled eyes and suede or Ultrasuede paws. She makes limited editions from three to one hundred, and some one-of-a-kind bears. Most of her designs are inspired by family members or people she meets.
Home Appointments: 5 days
Shows: Midwest, Southeast
Stores: Teddy Bears of Witney, Oxfordshire, UK; Essentially Dolls & Bears, Kalamazoo, MI; Donna Bears, Bethalto, IL; Something Special, Pigeon Falls, TN; The Bear-ee Patch, San Diego; Jan Dolls & Bears, Godfrey, IL
Catalog/Photos: free
Mail order: 2-4 weeks
Accepts: check, money order, layaway
Has been making bears for 9 years
Publications: TBR

SUSAN KATHLEEN HALBERT
PocketBears
7151 Speedway Blvd., Suite 310
Tucson, AZ 35710-1317
Phone: 602-750-1506
Phone orders: 7 days, 9 A.M.-5 P.M.
Price range: $50-$150
Size range: ¾″-3″
PocketBears are all designed and handmade by Susan. They are all fully jointed, made of upholstery plush and stuffed with fiberfill. She occasionally creates dressed or character bears, but her heart belongs to good, basic bare bears.
Stores: Toys 'N Tiques, Tucson, AZ; Doll Cottage, Tucson, AZ; Old Pueblo Miniatures, Tucson, AZ
Catalog/Photos: $1.50
Mail order: 7-10 days
Accepts: check, money order
Has been making bears for 5 years

BARBIE HAMPTON

Barbie's Bears
15172 Koyle Cemetery Rd.
Winslow, AK 72959
Phone: 501-634-5741
Phone orders: 8A.M.-8P.M.
Price range: $50-$100
Size range: 10"-24"

Barbie's Bears are fully jointed and made of synthetics and mohair. They have antique shoe button eyes and are stuffed with Poly-Fil and pellets. Most are one-of-a-kinds, and Barbie dresses them in vintage clothing and accessories.

Home Appointments: 1 day
Shows: South
Stores: J & L Collectibles, Tampa, FL; Bears & Hares Collectibles, Tulsa, OK; Groves Quality Collectibles, Lima, OH; Pewter Classics Dolls & Bears, Grand Rapids, MI
Catalog/Photos: $1
Mail order: 4-6 weeks
Accepts: check, money order, Visa, MasterCard
Has been making bears for 4 years
Awards: blue ribbons at local craft fairs

BETTY J. HANSEN

Hansen Bears
10622 Bryant St., Sp. #30
Yucaipa, CA 92399
Phone: 909-797-4975
Phone orders: 9A.M.-4P.M.
Price range: $35-$200
Size range: 9"-16"

Hansen Bears are original patterns by Betty. She uses German mohair, glass eyes and Ultrasuede or leather for paw pads. All noses are handstitched. Discs and cotter pins are used, and discs are handmade. Bears sometimes come with handmade benches and wooden toys. Betty makes an unusual button bear with fur body, head and

hands, and strung buttons for arms and legs. Button bears are fully dressed and are made with about 50 buttons.

Home Appointments: 1 week
Shows: CA, AZ, OR, NJ, IA
Catalog/Photos: $2, refundable with purchase
Mail order: 3 weeks
Accepts: check, money order
Has been making bears for 16 years
Publications: TBR; TB&F; Country Home Magazine

KATHLYN MARIE HARDIN

Bear Tales
1408 N. Geronimo Dr.
Independence, MO 64058
Phone: 816-796-0712
Phone orders: 8A.M.-8P.M.
Price range: $100-$200
Size range: 8"-22"

Bear Tales bears are made of mohair or German synthetics. Kathlyn stuffs them with pellets and fiberfill. She uses antique shoe buttons for the eyes. They are all jointed and have leather or Ultrasuede paw pads. She also makes bears out of old fur coats by order.

Home Appointments: 1 week
Shows: MS, OK, KS, CO
Catalog/Photos: $2, refundable with purchase
Mail order: 2-4 weeks
Accepts: check, money order
Has been making bears for 3 years
Awards: Greater Kansas City Doll & Bear Show, 1st

TEDDIES ARE TRULY THE KEEPERS OF OUR HEARTS—
OUR DEEPEST SECRETS AND OUR WILDEST DREAMS!
— *Nancy Moorehead, artist, Archer City, TX*

FRANCES HARPER

. . . apple of my eye. . .
233 Main Ave.
S. Hampton, NH 03827
Phone: 603-394-7927
Phone orders: 9A.M.-9P.M.
Price range: $65-$385

. . . apple of my eye . . . bears are made to look like old-time, traditional bears. They are excelsior-filled. Frances uses 100% mohair, black button eyes and sometimes, growlers.

Waiting list: 4-6 weeks
Home Appointments: 2-3 days
Shows: MA, CT, NJ, MD, PA, OH, Germany
Stores: Christy's, Buckingham, PA; Teddy Bears of Witney, Oxfordshire, UK; Basically Bears at Garrison Knoll, Stratham, NH
Catalog/Photos: $3
Mail order: 4-6 weeks
Accepts: check, money order, Visa, MasterCard
Has been making bears for 9 years

LINDA HARRIS

Beariations
54 Berkinshaw Cres.
Don Mills, Ontario M3B 2T2, Canada
Phone: 416-445-9417
Phone orders accepted.
Price range: $100-more than $450
Beariations bears are one-of-a-kind. Linda creates a new pattern for each one and hand sews it using only the finest materials. She chooses accessories with great care, and often incorporates antique fabrics and accessories.

Shows: Toronto
Accepts: check, Visa
Design manufactured by Ty, Inc.
Has been making bears for 6 years
Awards: TOBY, 1991; several additional awards

NOLA HART
Bears from the Hart
90 Berkinshaw Cres.
Don Mills, Ontario, Canada
Phone: 416-444-4038
Fax: 416-322-5527
Price range: $50-$250
Size range: 6″-15″
Bears from the Hart are mostly one-of-a-kind, long-limbed bears. They are made out of a variety of textured mohairs. Nola is interested in antiquing her designs using tea and coffee stains, and wearing the fur down to give her bears that "bear with history" look. She does some limited editions of 20 or fewer.
Shows: Toronto, Ontario; Tokyo, Japan
Stores: The Teddy Bear Garden, Toronto, Ontario
Catalog/Photos: free
Mail order: 6 weeks
Accepts: check, money order, Visa, MasterCard, American Express
Design manufactured by Ty, Inc.
Has been making bears for 6 years

RUTH E. HARVEY
Harvey & Harvey Bears
106-206 W. Shawneetown Rd.
Thompsonville, IL 62890
Phone: 618-627-2229
Phone orders: anytime
Price range: $50-$300
Size range: 10″-25″
Harvey & Harvey Bears each have their own personalities. Ruth often uses a pattern with a center head seam. This bear is jointed and is called T-Bruin. She also makes a non-jointed bear called Alex. Both patterns are constantly changing.
Waiting list: 3-4 weeks
Home Appointments: 2-3 days
Shows: IL
Stores: Little Treasures Dolls & Bears,

West Frankfort, IL; Arts & Crafts Marketplace, Whittington, IL
Catalog/Photos: free
Mail order: next day
Accepts: check, money order
Has been making bears for 7 years
Awards: DuQuoin, Illinois State Fair, 1st
Publications: TB&F

BETTY JANE HAYENGA
Goodnews Bears
P.O. Box 802
Combes, TX 78535
Phone: 210-425-5604
Phone orders: anytime
Price range: $150-$300
Size range: 12″
Goodnews Bears are created to be as authentic to Betty's Scottish heritage as possible. They are all original designs made from distressed British mohair and dressed in the tartan of the customer's choice. Each bear is 5 times jointed and painstakingly detailed with a personality all its own. She spends long hours making kilts, shirts, tams and sporrans, knitting hose and sweaters, and tuning the bagpipes.
Shows: TX, AZ, AR, MI, IL, IN, PA, MS
Catalog/Photos: price list and description free
Mail order available.
Accepts: check, money order, Visa, MasterCard
Has been making bears for 14 years
Awards: Teddy Bear Jubilee, Best of Show, 1991; other Best of Show awards
Publications: articles in 1980s

IRENE HECKEL
Grin & Bear It
P.O. Box 186, 28 Alder Dr.
Mystic Beach, NY 11951
Phone: 516-281-9393

Phone orders: 9 A.M.-9 P.M.
Price range: $150-$400
Size range: 9″-22″
Grin & Bear It bears are all original designs with emphasis on faces and jointing. For instance, Irene may joint the head in various ways to gain the greatest range of movement. Most bears are stuffed with Poly-Fil and pellets for more weight and a "real bear" feel. All have a pewter logo pin in their left ear.
Shows: East Coast
Stores: Bears Everywhere, Fredericksburg, VA; Bear-A-Dise Landing, Guilford, CT; BearTique, Montreal, Quebec; Knight's Collectibles, Saugatuck, MI; Tomorrow's Treasures, Robbinsville, NJ; Empress Doll Boutique, Laurel, DE
Catalog/Photos: free
Mail order: 1 week
Accepts: check, Visa, MasterCard
Has been making bears for 10 years
Publications: TBR

LINDA A. HEJNA
Crabapple Bears
24 Balbach Drive
Checktowaga, NY 14225
Phone: 716-631-5236
Phone orders: 8 A.M.-10 P.M.
Price range: $50-$150
Size range: 6″-16″
Crabapple Bears are completely designed and made by Linda. They are jointed and are made of materials imported from Germany. Linda uses glass or shoe button eyes, and also makes all accessories and clothing.
Home Appointments: 1 or 2 days
Shows: Eastern States
Stores: Mulberry Street Toys, East Amherst, NY; Teddy Bear Station, Uniontown, OH; Buffalo Candle & Craft Outlet, Buffalo, NY; Country Corners,

Dunedin, FL; Teddy Bear Museum of Naples, Naples, FL; Moore Bears, Strasburg, PA
Catalog/Photos: $4, refundable with purchase
Mail order: 2-3 weeks
Accepts: check, money order
Has been making bears for 8 years

LOU ANN HENDERSHOT
The Von Haydershcatt Collection
1420 W. New York Ave.
Oshkosh, WI 54901
Phone: 414-231-6235
Phone orders: 9 A.M.-9 P.M.
Price range: $100-$400
Size range: 6"-20"

The Von Hayderschatt Collection bears have long arms and legs and plump bodies. Lou Ann makes bears with long, narrow snouts and also short, thick snouts. Eyes are well sunk, and close set to medium set, depending on the "age" of the bear. Noses are double-embroidered on all bears over 8", forming a three-dimensional nose. Most noses are triangular, although she does some "nostril" noses. Her bears always have claws, and identification labels are on the bear's left leg.
Waiting list: 3 months
Home Appointments: 1 month
Shows: IL, WI
Stores: Gepetto's, Carmel, CA; International House, Orland Park, IL; Teddy Bears of Witney, Oxfordshire, UK; Dolls, Bears & Funny Hares, Mission, KS; Pied Piper, Plymouth, MI; Bear Necessities, Saginaw, MI
Catalog/Photos: $2
Mail order: 3-4 months
Accepts: check, money order, layaway
Has been making bears for 7 years
Awards: ABC shows, three 2nds
Publications: A Victorian Country Christmas Magazine

BILLIE MARIE HENDERSON
Billee's Beasties
9312 Santayana Dr.
Fairfax, VA 22031
Phone: 703-273-7162
Phone orders: anytime
Price range: $95-$425
Size range: 2½"-33"

Billee's Beasties come in miniature sizes, some dressed. She also makes a 25"-33" classic bear with a swivel tilt neck, and 9" dressed bears.
Waiting list: 6 weeks-3 months
Home Appointments: 1 week
Catalog/Photos available.
Mail order: 6 weeks-3 months
Accepts: check, money order
Has been making bears for 11 years
Awards: Golden Teddy
Publications: Tribute to Teddy Bear Artists; Teddy Bear Artists Annual; Complete Book of Teddy Bears; Guide to Antique and Modern Teddy Bears; Price Guide to Teddy Bears

PATTI MARIE HENDRIKS
P.M. Bears
RR #1
Brucefield, Ontario N0M 1J0, Canada
Phone: 519-522-0454
Phone orders: 9 A.M.-9 P.M.
Price range: $50-$200
Size range: 6"-22"

P.M. bears come in about 12 different designs that are constantly changing. Patti uses both plush and mohair. Some bears are dressed as characters, and some wear only ribbons and collars. Most styles are distressed or antiqued. She likes to use antique accessories such as jewelry, lace and real furs. Patti is told her bears all have a look to their noses that is identical to her own.
Shows: Ontario
Stores: Natalie Anne's Room, Bayfield,

Ontario; Originals, Stratford, Ontario; BearTique, Montreal, Quebec
Photos: $3.50, refundable with purchase
Accepts: check, Visa
Has been making bears for 6 years
Awards: Hug-In award, 2nd
Publications: Ontario Townsman, Teddy Bear Tribune

LINDA REBECCA HENRY
Bearloom Bears
230 Kramer St.
Canal Winchester, OH 43110
Phone: 614-837-5383
Phone orders: 9 A.M.-7 P.M.
Fax: 614-837-8011
Fax orders accepted.
Price range: $75-$600
Size range: 7"-26"

Bearloom Bears are handmade by Linda. She uses mohair, alpaca, and European and domestic plush. All her bears have glass eyes and are fully jointed. Some bears have original porcelain faces sculpted by Linda.
Shows: Midwest, South
Stores: The Toy Store, Toledo, OH; Groves Quality Collectibles, Lima, OH; Playhouse, Chillicothe, OH; Bruno Bar, Germany; Grin & Bear It, Naperville, IL; Bears Everywhere, Fredericksburg, VA
Waiting list: 2 months
Mail order: 2 months
Accepts: check, money order, Visa, MasterCard
Design manufactured by Silent Sentiments; L.L. Knickerbocker Co.
Has been making bears for 11 years
Awards: Schaumburg, 3 awards; Baltimore, 2 awards; Columbus Teddy Bear Fair, 3 awards; nominated for TOBY
Publications: Teddy Bear Artists' Annual; Contemporary Teddy Bear Price

Guide; TB&F; Tribute To Teddy Bear Artists

See the article opening chapter 2 written by Linda.

JUDITH ANN HICKMOTT
Homespun Country Bears
6005 Barkwood Ln.
Sylvania, OH 43560
Phone: 419-885-1526
Phone orders: 8 A.M.-10 P.M.
Price range: $35-$150
Size range: 8"-16"
Homespun Country Bears are made from real fur, such as mink, raccoon and lamb. Judith makes 8"-11" fat bears. Her plush bears are made to order. She likes to make family heirloom bears out of customers' fur coats.
Waiting list: 1 month
Home Appointments: 1 day
Shows: MI, OH
Accepts: check, money order
Has been making bears for 11 years
Awards: GBW, 1st; Paste Tence, 2nd
Publications: Bear Tracks

LOUISE AND GLENN HIGGINS
Higgins' Bears
RR #2 Box 157
Spencer, IN 47460
Phone: 812-829-4284
Phone orders: 8 A.M.-6 P.M.
Price range: $35-$200
Size range: 6"-30"

Higgins' Bears are designed by Glenn and Louise, and they take great care to keep their quality high. The bears are made of both mohair and synthetic furs. There are open editions, limited editions and one-of-a-kind bears. Glenn and Louise each have talents that mesh well when creating a bear.
Home Appointments: 1 week
Shows: IN, OH, KY, WI, MI, IL, FL, GA, OK, PA, KS
Stores: Temptations, Indianapolis; The Teddy Bear Den, Las Vegas; Beary Special Friends, Decatur, IN; Heirloom Dolls & Treasures, Naperville, IL; International House, Naperville, IL; The Collectors, Culver, IN
Catalog/Photos: $7, refundable with purchase
Mail order: 1 month
Accepts: check, money order, Visa, MasterCard
Has been making bears for 6 years

DEBI HILL
Wannabee Bears
150 Durham St. W
Lindsay, Ontario K9V 2R5, Canada
Phone: 705-324-5069
Phone orders: 6 P.M.-11 P.M.
Fax: 705-328-3572
Fax orders accepted.
Price range: $100-$350
Size range: 6"-30"
Wannabee Bears are original heirloom teddies created with a little nostalgia. Antiqued mohair and vintage accessories suggest bears of a bygone era. Debi's artistry includes medieval jesters, gollis, whimsical fairie bears with unique button on wings, tattered teddies and many one-of-a-kind bears.
Waiting list: 6 weeks
Shows: several in USA and Canada
Catalog/Photos: $5, refundable with purchase

Mail order: 6-8 weeks
Accepts: check, money order
Has been making bears for 5 years
Publications: Victorian Harvester, cover

DEE HOCKENBERRY
Bears N Things
14191 Bacon Rd.
Albion, NY 14411
Phone: 716-589-4066
Phone orders: 9 A.M.-5 P.M.
Fax: 716-589-5190
Fax orders accepted.
Price range: $200-$350
Size range: 11"-15"
Dee's bears are traditional mohair bears. They are all jointed. Many are limited editions or one-of-a-kinds. Many are dressed.
Waiting list: 1 month
Stores: Teddy Bear Museum, Naples, FL; I. Child, Tarpon Springs, FL; Village Bears & Collectibles, Sarasota, FL; Belle's, Charlotte, NC; Enchantments, Savannah, GA, Bear-A-Dise Landing, Guilford, CT
Photos available.
Mail order: 4 weeks
Accepts: check, money order, Visa, MasterCard
Has been making bears for 15 years
Publications: Complete Book of Teddy Bears; The Ultimate Teddy Bear Book; Teddy Bear Artists' Annual; Teddy Bears; Teddy Bear Lover's Postcard Book; Santa Dolls; Contemporary Teddy Bear Price Guide; Tribute To Teddy Bear Artists; TB&F
One of Dee's bears was chosen to appear on the cover of this book.

BETH DIANE HOGAN
Some Bears & Other Beasts
5629 N. Bonfair Ave.
Lakewood, CA 90712
Phone: 310-633-3474

Price range: $35-$200
Waiting list: 5 months
Home Appointments: 1 week
Shows: CA, IL, WA
Accepts: check
Has been making bears for 13 years
Awards: Golden Teddy
Publications: Teddy Men

JOAN MARIE HOLLENBACH
Just Joanie's
P.O. Box 411
Orwigsburg, PA 17961
Phone: 717-366-3649
Phone orders: 8 A.M.-8 P.M.
Price range: $35-$100
Size range: 2½"
Just Joanie's bears are handmade by
   Joan. Their arms and legs move. Her
   newer bears are 12" tall, made of En-
   glish mohair with glass eyes and
   leather paw pads. They are called
   "Just Joanie's Little Bear Babies."
Home Appointments: 1 week
Catalog/Photos: $1, refundable with pur-
   chase
Mail order: 2 weeks
Accepts: money order
Has been making bears for 11 years
Publications: TB&F

PATRICIA HOLSTINE
H.C.&E., Inc.
HCR 30, Box 185
Lincoln, MT 59639
Phone: 406-362-4583
Phone orders: 8 A.M.-8 P.M.
Price range: less than $35-more than
   $450
Size range: 15"-20"
H.C.&E., Inc. bears all have jointed
   heads. Several have leather eyelids
   and leather noses. Patricia makes
   faces that are untraditional. Each bear
   is guaranteed, or the money is re-
   funded.

Waiting list: 3 weeks
Home Appointments: 2 days
Shows: West, Midwest
Catalog/Photos: $3, refundable with pur-
   chase
Mail order: 30 days
Accepts: check, money order, Visa, Mas-
   terCard
Has been making bears for 20 years
Awards: Kerby, 2nd; Beary Precious
   Bears, 3rd
Publications: TBR (ads)

PAM HOLTON
Pam Holton Designs
P.O. Box 5022-423
Lake Forest, CA 92630
Phone: 714-951-8074
Phone orders: 9 A.M.-4:30 P.M.
Price range: $100-$200
Size range: 4½"-10"
Pam's smaller bears are handstitched, and
   her larger bears are machine stitched,
   except for the handstitched head and
   paws. Most of her bears are weighted.
   Many are mohair, with the exception
   of some alpaca bears.
Shows: Schaumburg, IL; San Diego
Stores: D&J Bears, Huntington Beach,
   CA; Bearaphernalia, Irvine, CA;
   Beardeaux Barn, Huntington Beach,
   CA; HuckleBeary Junction, IL
Catalog/Photos available.
Mail order available.
Accepts: check, money order, Visa, Mas-
   terCard
Has been making bears for 15 years
Publications: Tribute to Teddy Bear Art-
   ists

CINDY L. HOM
CH Bears
P.O. Box 157
Red Oak, IA 51566
Phone: 712-623-9166

Phone orders: M-F, before 8 A.M. or after
   5 P.M. Weekends, anytime.
Price range: $35-$150
Size range: 1⅝"-6½"
CH bears are made of mohair and uphol-
   stery velvet. Cindy occassionally hand
   dyes the fabric. Her bears have a
   young, contemporary look. She makes
   one bear to fit inside a lipstick tube.
   She also makes a bear purse and a bear
   muff.
Home Appointments: 2 days
Shows: Midwest
Stores: Donna's Dolls & Country Col-
   lectibles, West Des Moines, IA
Catalog/Photos: $2, refundable with pur-
   chase
Mail order: 1-2 weeks
Accepts: check, money order
Has been making bears for 9 years

LORNA HOPKIN
Bears by Lorna
1104 Southglen Dr. SW
Calgary, Alberta T2W 0X1, Canada
Phone: 403-253-1471
Phone orders: 9 A.M.-5 P.M.
Price range: $100-$200
Size range: 3½"-15"
Bears by Lorna are fully jointed bears
   made of mohair, alpaca or rayon.
   Some have hand-knit sweaters, vests,
   scarves or hats.
Waiting list: 6 weeks
Shows: Calgary, Alberta
Stores: Bear Essentials, Victoria, British
   Columbia; Two Bears Teddy Bears,
   Calgary, Alberta; Teddy Bears of Wit-
   ney, Witney, Oxfordshire, UK; Deb-
   bie's Safari, Fremont, CA; Doll
   House, Halifax, Nova Scotia
Photos: $5, refundable with purchase
Mail order: 4-6 weeks
Accepts: money order, Visa
Has been making bears for 6 years
Awards: Bear Fair, 2nd
Publications: TBR, Victorian Harvester,
   Today's Maturity

SUSAN L. HORN
Susan Horn Bears
1963 McKinley
Ypsilanti, MI 48197
Phone: 313-481-1611
Phone orders: 9A.M.-10P.M.
Address and phone number will change
late 1995.
Price range: $195-$400
Size range: 4¾"-28"
Susan dresses most of her bears. She uses
vintage items and special dying to
achieve an "olde" effect. Her bears
are often dressed in sweaters that can
serve as jackets or dresses based on
the articles Susan gives them.
Waiting list: 3 months
Shows: MI, OH, IN, IL, GA, KY
Stores: Groves Quality Collectibles,
Bluffton, OH; Bears Everywhere,
Fredericksburg, VA; Arundel Teddy
Bears, Arundel, West Sussex, UK;
Berry Patch, Lyons, CO
Photos: $4, refundable with purchase
Mail order: 3 months
Accepts: check, money order, Visa, Mas-
terCard
Has been making bears for 4 years
Publications: TBR, TB&F

ANN HORNE
bears by Ann Horne
27 Quincy Cres.
North York, Ontario M2J 1C5, Canada
Phone: 416-494-8728

Phone orders: 9A.M.-9P.M., or leave mes-
sage
Fax: 416-494-8728
Fax orders accepted.
Price range: $50-$200
Ann Horne's bears are one-of-a-kind,
nostalgic bears reminiscent of a "by-
gone age." They are made with new
fabrics and dressed in vintage clothes
and accessories. Old fabrics are used
for styles that are reminscent of Ger-
man bears. They have big feet, long,
hugging arms and whimsical expres-
sions.
Home Appointments: 1 day
Shows: Eastern and Southern Ontario;
NY
Photos available.
Mail order: 6-8 weeks
Accepts: check, money order
Has been making bears for 19 years

DAWN ELIZABETH HOUSTON
Honey Bears
Route 1, Box 84
Maryville, MO 64468
Phone: 816-582-8608
Phone orders: 9A.M.-9P.M.
Price range: $50-$200
Size range: 7"-26"
Honey Bears are handstuffed, hump-
backed bears. Some are dressed. All
have glass eyes and lambsuede paw
pads. They are often described as
sweet looking because of their large
eyes and perfectly trimmed muzzles.
Dawn occasionally uses pellets, but
mainly uses a special kind of stuffing
and a lot of muscle to achieve a very
firm bear.
Home Appointments: 1 day
Shows: Midwest
Catalog/Photos: free
Mail order: 4-6 weeks
Accepts: check, money order, Visa, MasterCard
Has been making bears for 4 years
Awards: Missouri State Fair blue ribbons; Nodaway County (MO) blue
ribbons; Teddy Bear Jubilee Champion Fund-raiser Bear, 1st runner up,
1992
Publications: TBR, 1993

SHIRLEY E. HOWEY
Shirley Howey Bears
2064 E. Birchwood
Mesa, AZ 85204
Phone: 602-833-7307
Phone orders: 9A.M.-9P.M.
Price range: $50-$100
Size range: 2"-6"
Shirley's bears are completely handsewn
from fabrics ranging from woolens
and calicos to upholstery velveteens
and mohair. Some are accessorized
with tiny quilts and toys. All are iden-
tified with a charm replica of Shirley's
logo with her signature on it. Most are
one-of-a-kind.
Home Appointments: 1 day
Shows: Southwest
Stores: Bears & More, Glendale, AZ;
The Armoire Collection, Scottsdale,
AZ; Carrousel, Chesaning, MI; Parlor
Bears, Lincoln City, OR; Animal
Haus Ltd., Cincinnati, OH
Accepts: check, money order
Has been making bears for 10 years
Publications: TBR, Teddy Bear Artists'
Annual, Contemporary Teddy Bear
Price Guide, Joy of Teddy Bears, The
Teddy Bear Lover's Companion,
Teddy Tales Bear Repeating, Too

JOEL HOY
Joel's Bears
5126 Russell
Mission, KS 66202
Phone: 913-831-2258
Phone orders: 10A.M.-6P.M.
Fax: 913-677-3915
Fax orders accepted.
Price range: $50-$200
Size range: 10"-20"
Joel's bears are made of mohair, alpaca
or European synthetics. Dressed bears
are available in several sizes. All bears
and their clothing are designed and
made by Joel.
Waiting list: 4-6 weeks
Stores: Dolls, Bears & Funny Hares,
Mission, KS
Photos: $2, refundable with purchase
Mail order available.
Accepts: check, money order, Visa, Mas-
terCard, Discover, American Express
Has been making bears for 4 years

THOMAS P. HUCZEK
Genesis Bears
P.O. Box 811
Abingdon, MD 21009-0811
Phone: 410-838-4954
Phone orders: M-Sat, 8A.M.-6P.M.
Price range: less than $35-$150
Size range: 2″-5″
Genesis Bears are contemporary minia-
   ture bears designed and handsewn by
   Tom. They are made with upholstery
   fabric with fabric, felt or leather paw
   pads. Several bears released in 1995
   are made of mohair. They have center
   seam heads and stitched claws. They
   are fully jointed and filled with poly-
   ester fiberfill. Some are weighted with
   copper shot. They are decorated but
   not dressed. All are limited editions of
   25 or less.
Shows: VA, MD, NJ, PA, DE
Catalog/Photos available.
Mail order: 2 weeks
Accepts: check, money order
Has been making bears for 4 years

PATRICIA A. HURLEY
Pat's Bears & Collectibles
2465 Townfield Lane
Virginia Beach, VA 23454-6539
Phone: 804-721-2475
Phone orders: 9A.M.-7P.M.
Price range: $50-$450
Size range: 7″-28″
Pat's Bears are made from American
   acrylic furs, English mohairs and vin-
   tage quilts, but her specialty is real fur.
   All bears are jointed with Masonite
   hardboard discs, screws and lock nuts.
   The most expensive bears have Ger-
   man glass eyes, and the acrylics gen-
   erally have plastic eyes. Her bears are
   registered with the state of Pennsylva-
   nia.
Shows: Mid-Atlantic region
Stores: The Rocking Horse Gallery,
   Fredericksburg, VA; Moore's Bears,
   Strasburg, PA; Bears Everywhere,
   Fredericksburg, VA; Old Town Gifts,
   Petersburg, VA; Bear Hugs, Marlton,
   NJ, Chubby's Cubby, Occaquan, VA
Catalog/Photos: free
Mail order: 4 weeks
Accepts: check, money order, Visa, Mas-
   terCard
Has been making bears for 16 years

DONNA LOU INSCO
Donna Insco Bears
HRC 63, Box 149
Richwoods, MO 63071
Phone: 314-678-2759
Phone orders: F, Sat, Sun, 9A.M.-6P.M.
Price range: $75-$250
Size range: 9″-24″
Donna's bears are old-fashioned looking,
   with long arms, big feet and glass or
   shoe button eyes. Most are made of
   mohair, but she also makes synthetic
   bears. Some are dressed in old- fash-
   ioned outfits. All are fully jointed and
   stuffed with Poly-Fil or pellets and
   Poly-Fil. Her bears have sweet faces
   with wistful smiles.
Shows: Midwest
Catalog/Photos: $3, refundable with pur-
   chase
Mail order: 4-8 weeks
Accepts: check, money order
Has been making bears for 7 years

JOAN T. JACOBSEN
Heart 'n Sole
9 Maple Ave.
Stockholm, NJ 07460
Phone: 201-697-1590
Phone orders: 9A.M.-8P.M.
Price range: $50-$100
Size range: ⅞″-3½″
Heart 'n Sole bears are entirely handsewn
   miniatures made from upholstery fur.
   Each bear is fully jointed and has glass
   eyes and Ultrasuede paws and pads.
   Some are dressed, and some wear silk
   bows. Joan tries to incorporate a
   theme or an accessory with each bear.
Shows: NJ, NY, PA, CT, RI
Catalog/Photos: $3, refundable with pur-
   chase
Mail order: 4-6 weeks
Accepts: check, money order
Has been making bears for 3 years
Awards: Sussex County Fair, 1st, 1994

VIRGINIA J. JASMER
Jazzbears
1974 Lomond Ave.
Springfield, OR 97477
Phone: 503-746-2175
Phone orders: 8A.M.-8P.M.
Price range: $100-$300
Size range: 8″-24″
Jazzbears are made of imported furs and
   imported glass eyes. They are fully
   jointed and have meticulously stitched
   noses in a variety of colors with a
   sweet look. Virginia adorns her bears
   with beautiful ribbons, antique laces
   or artist-created clothing.
Waiting list: 1 month
Home Appointments: 1 day
Shows: Northwest, West Coast, all Pat
   Moore shows
Stores: Old Miller Place, Aurora, OR;
   Bear Hugs, Tacoma, WA; Bear Hugs,
   Seaside, OR; Verna Mae Collectibles,
   Greenwood, NE; Mrs. Smith's Col-
   lectibles, Twin Falls, ID
Photos: free
Mail order: 1 month
Accepts: check, money order, Visa, Mas-
   terCard
Has been making bears for 10 years
Publications: Complete Book of Teddy
   Bears

JOANN JOHNSON
Joey Bear
P.O. Box 697
Denmark, WI 54208
Phone: 414-863-6334

Phone orders: answering machine
Price range: $150-$350
Size range: 9"-26"
Joey Bears are made individually, usually of mohair or alpaca, although JoAnn likes to experiment with different materials. They are stuffed with Poly-Fil and beads to give them adequate heft and feel. German glass eyes or antique shoe buttons are used to give their faces a warm and profound expression. The paws are either German felt, Ultrasuede or suede. Each bear wears a signature Joey Bear label in his back, and his right foot is signed by JoAnn.
Waiting list: 4-8 weeks
Shows: Midwest
Stores: Newport House, Ellison Bay, WI; Oscars, Appleton, WI
Catalog/Photos: free
Mail order: 2-4 weeks
Accepts: check, money order
Has been making bears for 4 years

DENISE M. JOHNSON
Ginny Rae Bear Family
2119 Sage Dr.
Ft. Collins, CO 80524
Phone: 303-484-4690
Phone orders: anytime
Email: JJohnson@aphis.Ag.GOV
Price range: $50-$200
Size range: 7"-30"
Ginnie Rae Bear Family bears are made of vintage fur coats (dated 1800s-1960s). Examples are sheared beaver, Persian lamb, mink and beaver. Because of this, there is a limitation to how many bears can be made out of each piece. Each bear is a one of one edition unless the customer asks otherwise. Denise uses more than 20 different patterns. Some stand, some have eyelids, some have pellet tummies. She also does mohair and special orders using customer's fur and chosen design.
Home Appointments: 1 day
Shows: CO, AR
Stores: Mountain Zoo, Estes Park, CO; Victorian Attic, Estes Park, CO; Teddy's Corner, Glenwood Springs, CO; L.J. Design, Mesa, AZ; Geneva Waterfront, Lake Geneva, WI; Annie's Country Store, Loveland, CO
Catalog/Photos: $3 photos, $5 video, refundable with purchase

Mail order: 1 week
Accepts: check, money order, Visa, MasterCard, layaway
Has been making bears for 8 years

VIVIAN F. JOSEPHS
978 Kern St.
Richmond, CA 94805
Phone: 510-237-2234
Phone orders: 10A.M.-6P.M.
Price range: $100-$150
Size range: 18"
Vivian's bears are fully jointed and all have growlers. They are soft and cuddly and come in different colors and different clothing patterns. Her bears are her own design.
Home appointments available.
Photos available.
Mail order: 4-6 weeks
Accepts: money order
Has been making bears for 7 years
Publications: TBR

SUSAN & BRIAN JUDGE
Willow Bear Cottage
R.R. #1
Red Deer, Alberta T4N 5E1, Canada
Phone: 403-346-8209
Phone orders: 7A.M.-11P.M.
Fax: 403-346-8209
Fax orders accepted.
Price range: $50-$300
Size range: 7"-27"
Willow Bear Cottage bears are made of top-quality mohair or German synthetic plush. German glass eyes are always used. Noses are hand-embroidered using German floss. Paws and pads vary between Ultrasuede and merino wool. Joint sets are always hardboard discs, bolts, washers and locknuts. Susan uses either plastic or steel pellets, Poly-stuffing or combinations of both.
Waiting list: 1-3 weeks
Shows: Western and Eastern Canada
Accepts: check, money order, Visa
Has been making bears for 4 years
Awards: The Bear Fair, 2nd

> LOVE WHAT YOU DO AND DO IT WITH LOVE AND THE RESULTS WILL BE LOVED!
> — *David Murray, artist, Cape Coral, FL*

DIANA ROWE JULET
Di's Vintage Bear Collection
3754 Kipling
Berkley, MI 48072
Price range: $50-$300
Size range: 8"-22"
Di's Vintage Bear Collection bears are made of mohair. They are fully jointed and have antique shoe button eyes. They are dressed in vintage clothing or accessories.
Shows: Midwest, FL
Stores: A Matter of Taste, Romeo, MI; Doll Hospital & Toy Soldier Shop, Berkley, MI; The Hugging Bear Inn & Shoppe, Chester, VT
Catalog/Photos: $2.50, refundable with purchase
Mail order: 4-6 weeks
Accepts: check, money order, Visa, MasterCard
Has been making bears for 4 years
Publications: TBR; local newspaper; The Sparkling Star

> DOCUMENT YOUR COLLECTION WITH A VIDEO CAMERA, AND INCLUDE THE RECEIPT IN THE PICTURE FOR INSURANCE CLAIMS.
> — *Jan Bonner, artist, Worthington, OH*

LINDA KAI
Kahiau Teddy Bears
47-394-2 Hui Iwa St.
Kaneohe, HI 96744
Phone: 808-239-7679
Phone orders: noon-5P.M.
Price range: $100-$150
Size range: 6"-18"
Kahiau Teddy Bears are handsewn by Linda.
Accepts: check, money order
Has been making bears for 10 years

BETH KAMMERER
The French Bear Co.
105 W. 19th Ave.
Hutchinson, KS 67502
Phone: 316-665-8344
Phone orders: anytime
Fax: 316-665-8344
Fax orders accepted.
Price range: $100-$400
Size range: 6"-26"
The French Bear Co. bears come in a
wide range of unique designs, from
realistic to whimsical to traditional.
Beth designs and handcrafts each
bear. Most are limited editions. They
are exquisitely detailed and of the fin-
est materials. She also makes Bear-
dolls—a combination of bears and
dolls.
Waiting list: 4-8 weeks
Home Appointments: a few days
Shows: Midwest, Southwest, East
Stores: The Toy Shoppe, Richmond, VA;
Moore Bears, Strasburg, PA; Teddy
Bear Museum, Naples, FL; Stictly
Bears, Medina, OH; Barenhohle, Ger-
many; Groves Quality Collectibles,
Lima, OH; Wonderland, Inc., Holly-
wood, FL; Village Bears & Collect-
ibles, Sarasota, FL; The Hen Nest,
Seminole, FL; Hyde Park Zoo,
Tampa, FL; Simply Lovely Gift
Shoppe, Fords, NJ; Teddys, Hamilton
Square, NJ; Teddy Bears To Go, Lake-
wood, NJ; Joyce's Doll Shop, Batavia,
NY; TeddyTown USA, Nashville, TN;
Marj's Doll Sanctuary, Grand Rapids,
MI; Mostly Bears, Arvada, CO
Catalog/Photos: varies, refundable with
purchase
Mail order: 4-8 weeks
Accepts: check, money order, Visa, Mas-
terCard
Has been making bears for 6 years
Awards: Kansas City show awards

LORI JEAN KARLUK
849 Goodman St.
Scranton, PA 18512
Phone: 717-383-0716
Fax: 717-383-0716
Price range: $50-$200
Size range: 8"-20"
Lori's bears are made of fine synthetics
or mohair. Some are also crocheted.
They are fully jointed and stuffed with
polyester fiberfill or excelsior. They
have glass eyes and Ultrasuede paw
pads. Lori is also a professional cro-
chet craft designer, and most of her
bears' clothes are hand crocheted. All
bear and clothing designs are original.
Catalog/Photos: large SASE
Mail order: 4-6 weeks
Has been making bears for 7 years
Publications: Bear-E-Tale Bears, Patterns by Lori Jean Karluk; Crochet
Patterns by Herrschners, cover story

JERRIE KELLER
Jerrie's Thread Bears
8236 Fernwood Dr.
Norfolk, VA 23518
Phone: 804-588-6222
Phone orders: anytime
Price range: $150-$200
Size range: 10"-22"
Jerrie's Thread Bears are sometimes
dressed. She is best known for her
bear called "Cowboy." He rides a
wooden rocking horse and is dressed
in a handmade Ultrasuede cowboy
suit. He has a mustache. He is a real
attention getter, and the story about
how Roy Rogers has one in his mu-
seum in Victorville, CA always makes
a sale—usually to men! She also has
a bear that Roy Rogers autographed
for her.
Waiting list: 2-4 weeks
Home Appointments: 1 day
Shows: East, Northeast
Stores: Bears 'N More, Richmond, VA;
Bear Friends & Company, Ocean City,
MD; Teddy's, Hamilton Square, NJ;
Fantastic Balloons & Bears, Char-
lottesville, VA; Bears By The Bay,
Fairhope, AL; Doll Cottage, Fallsten,
MD
Catalog/Photos: $2
Mail order: 2 weeks
Accepts: check, money order, Visa, Mas-
terCard

Has been making bears for 9 years
Publications: TBR; TB&F

ANITA KELSEY
The Fuzzy Bear Co.
12345 Lake City Way NE, #198
Seattle, WA 98125
Phone: 206-365-8753
Phone orders: anytime
Price range: $35-$350
Size range: 10"-23"
The Fuzzy Bear Co. bears are fully
jointed and made from German mohair, synthetic fabrics and real fur
from recycled fur coats. Anita's original designs include leather noses and
leather paw pads with styrene insoles
so the bears can stand alone on flat
feet. Growlers or music boxes are
available. Clothing is minimal. Baby
bears wear bonnets and diapers; boy
bears wear collars and ties; and girl
bears wear lace collars with ribbons.
Anita has a baby bear that rotates as
music plays.
Waiting list: 6 weeks to 3 months
Home Appointments: anytime
Shows: WA, OR
Stores: Bearadise, Seattle; Choice 88,
Bellevue, WA; Country Christmas,
Sea-Tac, WA
Mail order available.
Accepts: check, money order, Visa, Mas-
terCard
Has been making bears for 13 years
Awards: Best of Northwest, 1st

JILL S. KENNY
J.K. Bears
161 Middle Road
Milton, VT 05468
Phone: 802-893-4073
Phone orders: 8 A.M.-9 P.M.
Price range: $100-$250
Size range: 11"-22"
J.K. Bears are designed and made by Jill.

They are made of mohair and have Ultrasuede paws, glass or antique shoe button eyes and hand embroidered noses. They are stuffed with pellets and Poly-Fil. Many are hand dyed in a wide range of traditional and nontraditional colors.

Waiting list: 3-4 weeks

Home appointments available.

Shows: East Coast, Midwest

Stores: Terry Bears, Oyster Bay, NY; Truly Unique, Rutland, VT; Grin & Bear It, Naperville, IL; Justin Tymes, Ft. Myers, FL; Bobby's Land of Animals, Long Grove, IL; Exclusively Vermont, Stowe, VT; Hugging Bear Inn & Shoppe, Chester, VT; Exclusively Vermont, Stowe, VT; Mountain Valley Bears, Wausau, WI

Photos: $4

Mail order: 2-4 weeks

Accepts: check, money order, Visa, MasterCard

Has been making bears for 13 years

MYRNA JEAN KERNS

MJ's Bears
890 Maurine Dr.
Columbus, OH 43228-3118
Phone: 614-274-1924
Phone orders: 8A.M.-8P.M.
Price range: less than $35-$250
Size range: 2½"-20"

MJ's bears are fully jointed and made of German mohair or upholstery fabric. Paws are wool felt or Ultrasuede, as well as the pads, when applicable. Myrna uses glass or old shoe buttons for eyes, and sometimes plastic. Her bears are stuffed with Polyester fiber or plastic pellets. She makes many one-of-a-kind bears. All are designed and made from start to finish with no outside help.

Home Appointments: one week

Shows: OH, PA

Stores: Moore Bears, Strasburg, PA; Broken Arrow Accents, Pataskala, OH

Catalog/Photos: $7 catalog; $3 photos, refundable with purchase

Mail order: 3-4 weeks

Accepts: check, money order

Has been making bears for 7 years

DEBBIE KESLING

Bears by Debbie Kesling
8429 Lambert Dr.
Lambertville, MI 48144
Phone: 313-856-7197
Phone orders: 10:30A.M.-midnight
Email: dkesling@Norden1.com
Fax: 313-856-7197
Price range: $150-$300
Size range: ⅝"-2¾"

Debbie tries to capture a big bear look in miniature. These tiny teddies are made of upholstery fabric and Ultrasuede, and are traditionally jointed. Each bear is one-of-a-kind. She may create more than one of a particular design, but never duplicates bears exactly.

Shows: Midwest, East Coast

Mail order: Sells what is on hand

Accepts: check, money order, Visa, MasterCard

Design manufactured by Akira Trading Co.

Has been making bears for 12 years

Awards: Golden Teddy Award, 1991

Publications: TBR, cover, feature and other articles; Teddy Bear Artists' Annual; Antique and Modern Teddy Bears; TB&F See the article opening the miniature bear index and the sidebars in this chapter and in the introduction for collectors by Debbie.

KELLI ANN KILBY

Kelli's Kollectibles
P.O. Box 2824
Rancho Cucamonga, CA 91729
Phone: 909-980-3887

Phone orders: 9A.M.-midnight
Fax: 909-941-4607
Fax orders accepted.
Price range: $65-$250
Size range: 1½"-4½"

Kelli's Kollectibles are colorful, fantasy bears. They are fully jointed and hand sewn. Kelli enjoys using shiny fabrics and glittery accents. She also makes miniature bear pins, earrings and jewelry, and enjoys making other animals to go along with her bears.

Waiting list: 1-2 months

Shows: West Coast, Midwest, Europe, East Coast, Northern CA

Stores: Enchantwood, Hibbing, MN; The Owl's Nest, Carmel, CA

Photos: $5, refundable with purchase

Mail order: 1-2 months

Accepts: check, money order

Has been making bears for 17 years

Awards: TOBY nominee, 1992, 1993, 1994; Golden Teddy nominee, 1993, 1994

Publications: Salute to American Teddy Bear Artists; TB&F; TBR; Teddy Bear Times; Bear Bericht

JAN KINKADE

J.K. Bears
3712 16th St. Rd.
Greeley, CO 80634
Phone: 303-330-5410
Phone orders: anytime
Fax: 303-352-1402
Fax orders accepted.
Price range: $50-$450
Size range: 6"-36"

J.K. Bears are usually made of mohair, and most are one-of-a-kind. Jan also makes some limited editions.

Waiting list: varies

Home Appointments: 1 week

Stores: Mostly Bears, Arvada, CO; JR Collectibles, Tampa, FL; The Zoo, Estes Park, CO

Accepts: check, money order, Visa, MasterCard

Has been making bears for 5 years

Awards: Longmont, CO bear show, blue ribbon

CHARLOTTE KIRSCHNER

Lovable Huggables
22722 Stagg St.
West Hills, CA 91304
Phone: 818-347-6151

Phone orders: 8 A.M.-8 P.M.
Price range: $50-$150
Size range: 19"
Lovable Huggables say "Love Me." They are designed and handmade by Charlotte.
Shows: West
Accepts: check, money order
Has been making bears for 4 years

JEANNE M. KLEIN
The Teddy Tailor
P.O. Box 234
Sutherlin, OR 97479
Phone: 503-459-9517
Phone orders: 8 A.M.-6 P.M.
Price range: $35-$300
Size range: 4"-36"
The Teddy Tailor bears are distinctively styled by Jeanne and feature excellent quality workmanship. They come in a variety of sizes, designs and materials.
Waiting list: 3-6 months
Home Appointments: 1 week
Shows: Pacific Northwest
Stores: Shingle Towne Antiques, Dillard, OR; Gallery Bears, Roseburg, OR; Angels In The Attic, Roseburg, OR; Daisy Kingdom, Portland, OR
Accepts: check, money order, Visa, MasterCard
Has been making bears for 10 years
Awards: Roseburg Doll & Bear Show, Best of Show; Bears Ahoy Convention, 1st
Publications: TBR, National Doll and Teddy Bear Collector, Joint Adventures, National Examiner

TERRI KLINK
Yesterday's Memories
5034 N. 76 St.
Milwaukee, WI 53218
Phone: 414-462-6267
Phone orders: anytime
Price range: $50-more than $450

Size range: 3¼"-48"
Yesterday's Memories bears are traditional. Terri also makes a separate collection of reproductions of early 1900s bears that are made to look very old. Some even have "moth holes" in their pads. Her bears are excelsior-stuffed with antique shoe button eyes.
Waiting list: varies
Shows: From coast to coast
Mail order: 6-8 weeks
Accepts: check, money order, Visa, MasterCard
Has been making bears for 7 years
Awards: Bright Star, Indianapolis, Best of Show, 1991; San Jose, CA, 1st, 1993; Schaumburg, IL, 1st, 1994

> LOVE AND A SENSE OF HISTORY ARE VITAL TO BEAR COLLECTING.
> — *Carol Adrian, artist, Beaver Falls, PA*

MARY J. KOLAR
Pochung Mountain Bears
29 Lauren Ln.
Sussex, NJ 07461
Phone: 201-875-8301
Phone orders: anytime
Price range: $50-$250
Size range: 11"-23"
Pochung Mountain Bears are all original designs by Mary. They are made of German and English mohair. They have glass or shoe button eyes, floss noses and moth proof felt pads.
Shows: NJ, NY, PA, MA
Stores: Teddy Bears To Go, Lakewood, NJ; Doll & Gift Gallery, Westown, NY
Catalog/Photos: $3, refundable with purchase
Mail order: 2 weeks
Accepts: check, money order, Visa, MasterCard, Discover, American Express
Has been making bears for 3 years

> "BEAR HUNTS ARE LOTS OF FUN, BUT DON'T GET TOO CAUGHT UP IN THE THRILL OF THE CHASE FOR THE POPULAR BEAR. YOU MIGHT OVERLOOK THE PERFECTLY WONDERFUL BEAR ON THE SHELF BEHIND YOU THAT COULD BRING YOU GREAT PLEASURE ON A DAY-TO-DAY BASIS."
> — *Jennifer Anderson, owner, Bear With Us, Fresno, CA*

CATHY KOVACS
Cooey's Bears
13 Casswallen Cres.
52505 Rge. Rd. 214
Ardrossan, Alberta T0B 0E0, Canada
Price range: $35-$150
Size range: 5"-20"
Cooey's Bears are usually made of various types of mohair. Cathy sometimes uses German plush. The bears' features are exaggerated, including long noses, big paws and big feet. Cathy has a variety of different designs and looks.
Home Appointments: few days
Shows: Edmonton, Calgary
Stores: Treasures & Toys, Edmonton, Alberta
Catalog/Photos available.
Mail order: 2-3 weeks
Accepts: check, money order
Has been making bears for 7 years

SHERRY KOZIL
Guys & Dolls by Sherry Kozil
15 Rolling Hills Dr.
Barrington Hills, IL 60010
Phone: 708-426-1147
Phone orders: 10 A.M.-8 P.M.
Fax: 708-426-1148
Fax orders accepted.
Price range: $150-$350
Size range: 11"-24"
Guys & Dolls bears are fully jointed and made of mohair. Sherry's bears are modern, and she likes to do fashion bears. Her favorite bear is about 20", with a thinner body. Her fashion female bears have sweet faces and look cuddly. Sherry is partial to white bears with blue eyes and pink noses.
Waiting list: 3-4 weeks
Shows: Midwest
Stores: Grin & Bear It, Naperville, IL
Catalog/Photos: $3, refundable with purchase

Mail order available.
Accepts: check, money order
Has been making bears for 2 years

IVA JEAN KRISTEK
Kristek Bears
19311 Johnson Rd.
South Bend, IN 46614
Phone: 219-299-0730
Phone orders: 8 A.M.-10 P.M.
Price range: $50-$350
Size range: 2"-24"
Kristek bears are made of mohair or alpaca, have glass eyes and are fully jointed. Iva Jean designs and makes all bears and clothing herself. Most of her bears are dressed in quality materials, with outfits made especially for each bear. She often uses wool and leather in her clothing, and many of her boy bears wear leather hats, a popular detail. Her miniatures are dressed in great detail. She double-stitches her bears for extra durability.
Home Appointments: 2 days
Shows: Midwest, FL, MA
Stores: Ken & Elaine's Dolls, Centerville, OH; B & J Fine Dolls, Shipshewana, IN; The Teddy Bear Shop, Marietta, OH
Catalog/Photos: free
Mail order: 4 weeks
Accepts: check, money order, Visa, MasterCard
Has been making bears for 3 years

DWYLINE A. KRUGER
Dwyline's Kruger Bears
39 Jib Ct.
Pleasant Hill, CA 94523
Phone: 510-798-8297
Phone orders: M-F, 8 A.M.-10 P.M. weekends, 9 A.M.-6 P.M.
Price range: $25-$250
Size range: 3"-30"
Dwyline's Kruger Bears include several

different styles. She has "Fanny-Pack" purse bears made of German mohair or plush. She makes "Cyrano," of German-tipped mohair or plush with a red satin, ruffled collar and an imported black-and-silver ribbon bow. Her "Jester Bears" are center seam head bears on sticks with big collars and pointed hats. She also makes miniature bears that are completely handstitched, and several one-of-a-kind bears. All bears are double stitched.
Home Appointments: 1-2 weeks
Shows: CA, Boston, MA area
Catalog/Photos: $2, refundable with purchase
Mail order: varies
Accepts: check, money order
Has been making bears for 4 years
Awards: TBBNC, honorable mention
Publications: bear magazines (ads)

KAREN LYNN KUNST
Kunstwerks
P.O. Box 4155
Shrewsbury, MA 01545
Phone: 508-756-5453
Phone orders: 8 A.M.-5 P.M.
Price range: $50-$100
Size range: ½"-1¾"
Kunstwerks are original designs and miniaturized replicas. They are completely handsewn and stuffed by Karen. They are fully five jointed with disc and/or thread joints. Karen uses upholstery fabric, Ultrasuede and mohair. Larger sizes (2"-6") can be special ordered.
Waiting list: one month
Home Appointments: 1 day
Shows: Northeast
Catalog/Photos: $3, refundable with purchase
Mail order available.
Accepts: check, money order

Has been making bears for 4 years

LYNDA KUNZ
Lynda's Teddies
P.O. Box 308
Shokan, NY 12481-0308
Phone: 914-657-2102
Phone orders: M-F, 5 P.M.-9 P.M. and weekends
Price range: $50-$150
Size range: 1½"-2½"
Lynda's Teddies are miniatures with wonderful expressions. They are fully jointed and fit nicely into 1" scale doll-houses.
Shows: Northeast, Mid-Atlantic, Midwest, Northwest
Catalog/Photos: $2
Waiting list: 1-6 months
Mail order: 4 weeks, or notice will be sent
Accepts: check, money order, international postal money order
Has been making bears for 15 years
Awards: Linda Mullins show, 2nd, 1994; Teddy Tribune Original Teddy Bear Contest, 2nd, 1992; 2nd, 1993; Bristol Great Teddy Bear Jamboree, 1st and 2nd, 1992; Artisan, Toy Bears, 1993
Publications: Tribute to Teddy Bear Artists; TBR, 1992, 1994; The Sparkling Star, 1993, 1994; 1994 Designer Teddy Bear Calendar; Doll Life, 1993, cover and article; Nutshell News, 1993; The Teddy Tribune, 1993; Bear Tracks, 1992; Dolls in Miniature, 1992; TBR, 1992; Tiny Teddies, Dolls, Toys & Teddy Bears, 1992

> "BEARS ARE CUTEST WHEN THEY'RE DOING "HUMAN THINGS." USE THEM IN YOUR HOLIDAY DECORATING."
> — *Elizabeth Kintz, owner, Beary Special Friends, Decatur, IN*

KATHY LACQUAY
Bearskins
845 LaSalle Pl.
St. Cloud, MN 56301
Phone: 612-654-9352
Phone orders: 7 A.M.-8 P.M.
Price range: $50-$200
Size range: ⅝"-3"
Bearskins are unique miniature bears made of natural deerskin. They are completely designed and handstitched on the outside by Kathy. They are fully jointed and have embroidered noses, mouths and claws. Their Czechoslovakian glass bead eyes catch your attention with their many expressions. Most Bearskins are costumed, most notably the Native American bears, which are elaborately decorated with beadwork and feathers. All bears are signed, dated and numbered limited editions.
Home Appointments: 2-3 days
Shows: Midwest
Stores: Cheri's Bear Essentials, Kansas City, MO; Enchantwood, Hibbing, MN; Groves Quality Collectibles, Lima, OH; Teddytown USA, Nashville, TN; Wonderland, Inc., Hollywood, FL
Catalog/Photos: free with SASE
Mail order: 14 working days
Accepts: check, money order
Has been making bears for 3 years
Awards: local awards

> TAKE A LOOK INTO MY LIQUID GLASS EYES
> DON'T YOU WANT TO TAKE ME HOME?
> DON'T YOU KNOW I'LL BE FOREVER YOURS?
> — *Gloria Adams*

DEBORAH L. M. LANE
Bear With Me by Debbie Lane
7 Pleasant Rd.
High Bridge, NJ 08827
Phone: 908-638-4973

Phone orders: anytime
Fax: 908-638-4973
  Fax orders accepted.
Price range: less than $35-more than $450
Size range: 1½"-42"
Bear With Me bears are designed and made completely by Deborah. She makes one-of-a-kind and limited edition pieces, including character bears and miniature to large bears made of acrylic, mohair, alpaca, old fur coats, plaid flannels and wools. Special orders are welcome.
Waiting list: 4-6 weeks
Home Appointments: 1 week
Stores: Crispins of Andover, MA; Basically Bears, Stratham, NH; Janie Babes & Bears, Farmington, ME
Catalog/Photos: free
Mail order: 4-6 weeks
Accepts: check, money order, Visa, MasterCard, layaway
Has been making bears for 5 years
Publications: Lewiston Sun Journal

ROXANNE LANKFORD
Bitty Bears
4595 Anderson Rd.
Stone Mountain, GA 30083
Phone: 404-298-0717
Phone orders: 9 A.M.-9 P.M.
Fax: 404-298-0717
  Fax orders accepted.
Price range: $35-$100
Size range: 1"-7"
Bitty Bears have adorable faces. Roxanne looks for unusual furs and uses mohairs, German synthetics, and vintage fabrics from coats. The bears 6" and up have disc joints; smaller bears are thread jointed. Paws are usually Ultrasuede, and eyes are black glass or onyx. Many are filled with buckshot and feel good when held in a palm.
Shows: South

Stores: Gepetto's, Carmel, CA; Justin Tymes, Ft. Myers, FL; Marilyn's World, Lauderhill, FL; Daisy Farm, Miami, FL
Catalog/Photos: $2, refundable with purchase
Mail order: 2 weeks
Accepts: check, money order, Visa, MasterCard, Discover, American Express
Has been making bears for 4 years
Awards: OK show, 2nd

TERRI LARSON
Plum St.
1134 Plum St.
Lincoln, NE 68502
Phone: 402-474-4855
Phone orders: anytime
Price range: less than $35-$300
Size range: 5"-34"
Plum Street bears have a classic look and are available in a variety of sizes. Terri uses German mohair and glass eyes. She does many bears dressed in antique children's clothes and shoes. Undressed bears come with a choice of either a button collar or a ribbon.
Waiting list: 6-8 weeks
Home Appointments: 1 day
Shows: IA, CO, MO, KS, WI, IL, OK, NE
Stores: Christmas Lane, Lincoln, NE; Mostly Bears, Arvada, CO; The Berry Patch, Lyons, CO
Catalog/Photos: $3, refundable with purchase
Mail order: 2-3 weeks
Accepts: check, money order, Visa, MasterCard, layaway
Has been making bears for 5 years

> BUY BEARS BECAUSE YOU LOVE THEM. BUY STOCK
> IF YOU ARE LOOKING FOR AN INVESTMENT RETURN.
> — *Sarah Rumsey, owner, Benjamin Bear,*
> *Marietta, GA*

TAMMIE J. LAWRENCE
Tammies' Teddys'
717 Dakota St.
Holton, KS 66436
Phone: 913-364-4256
Phone orders: 10A.M.-9P.M.
Fax: 913-364-4256
Fax orders accepted.
Price range: $58-more than $450
Size range: 4"-40"
Tammies' Teddys' are antique replicas
from the pre-1930 era. They are cre-
ated from distressed mohair and worn
to look old and antique. They have
German glass or antique shoe button
eyes, and their paw pads often have
holes to expose excelsior stuffing.
Bears are stuffed with a combination
of Polyester filling, pellets and excel-
sior, depending on the look Tammie
wants. Many are dressed in antique
clothing and adorned with antique
jewelry, vintage flowers and old toys.
Catalog/Photos: $2
Mail order: 2-4 weeks
Accepts: check, money order and layaway available
Has been making bears for 14 years
Publications: TBR, cover, 1991; The Official Guide to Antique and Modern
Teddy Bears; The Teddy Bear Lovers
Companion; Collectors Guide to Miniature Teddy Bears, greeting cards and
stickers from Susan's Card Company;
TB&F

DO NOT USE CHEAP METHODS OR MATERIALS THAT
MAY COMPROMISE THE INTEGRITY OF YOUR BEARS.
TAKE THE CARE AND TIME REQUIRED FOR EACH BEAR
TO BE SPECIAL AND WORTHY OF CARRYING YOUR
NAME. IF YOU CRAFT EACH BEAR AS IF IT WERE
YOUR FIRST, THERE WILL BE NO
DISAPPOINTMENTS OR REGRETS.
— *Cherlynn Cathro, artist, Calgary, Alberta*

ALTHEA LEISTIKOW
Bears by Althea
1025 SW Taylor
Topeka, KS 66612-1714
Phone: 913-232-9649
Phone orders: 10A.M.-10P.M.
Price range: $35-more than $450
Size range: 3½"-32"
Bears by Althea have a classic look and
sweet faces. Althea's costumes have
been praised. She uses unusual and an-
tique, vintage materials in creating her
bears and costuming. A clean looking
line in design is important to her, as
well as the sweet spirit of the bear.
Home Appointments: 1 week
Shows: North, South, East, West, Mid-
west
Stores: Dolls, Bears & Funny Hares,
Mission, KS; The Hen's Nest, Semi-
nole, FL; The Bear's Corner, Tyler,
TX; The Paisley Bear, Ft. Lauderdale,
FL; Bear Tracks, Pittsburgh; White
Bear Antiques and Teddy Bears, Tulsa
Photos available.
Mail orders available.
Accepts: check
Has been making bears for 12 years
Awards: Golden Teddy; local awards be-
ginning 1984.
Publications: The Teddy Bear Lover's
Companion; Complete Book of Teddy
Bears; Tribute to Teddy Bear Artists;
Teddy Bear Artists' Annual; Official
Price Guide to Antique and Modern
Teddy Bears; Contemporary Teddy
Bear Price Guide; TB&F; TBR;
Teddy Bear Times

JACQUELYN LESCHER
Jenny's Teddies
903 Woodward Ave.
Rothschild, WI
Phone: 715-355-4495
Phone orders: 9A.M.-8P.M.
Price range: $100-$250

Shows: WI, IL, IA
Stores: Finch's Nest, Waukesha, WI; An-
imal Haus Ltd., Cincinnati, OH
Waiting list: 4-5 months
Mail order available.
Accepts: check, money order, Visa, Mas-
terCard
Has been making bears for 9 years

TIGER LILY
Tiger Lily Enterprises
P.O. Box 373
Hopatcong, NJ 07843-0373
Price range: $150-$300
Size range: 1½"-24"
Tiger Lily Enterprises bears are entirely
artist-made, and production is very
limited. Tiger creates her own de-
signs, and all materials used are the
very best.
Waiting list: about 6 weeks
Home appointments available.
Catalog/Photos: $2.50
Mail order: varies; average 6 weeks
Accepts: check, money order
Has been making bears for 6 years

DIANA LIND
Wee Treasures
573 Concord End Rd.
P.O. Box 242
Hillsboro, NH 03244
Phone: 603-464-5895
Phone orders: 10A.M.-9P.M.
Price range: less than $35-$250
Size range: 8"-27"
Wee Treasures are traditional, 5-way
jointed bears made in a wide variety
of mohairs. Diana uses feathered and
distressed furs, mostly in natural col-
ors, but also enjoys using pink, red,
lavender and blue fur for variety. She
has a 12½" bear that comes in his own
wooden box, and a one-of-a-kind
stamp collector bear with joints in his
elbows so he can use tweezers and a
magnifying glass as he works on his
stamp album. Diana also does mother
and baby sets and plush pellet bears.
Shows: Northeast
Stores: Parkside Gallery, Hillsboro, NH;
Sharon Arts Center, Sharon, NH;
Meredith-Laconia Arts & Crafts,
Meredith, NH; Wolfeboro League of
New Hampshire Craftsmen, Wolfeboro, NH; League of New Hampshire
Craftsmen, North Conway, NH; Craft-

ings, Manchester, NH; Concord Arts & Crafts, Concord, NH; League of NH Craftsmen, Hanover, NH; Sandwich Home Industries, Center Sandwich, NH
Accepts: check, money order
Has been making bears for 16 years

LISA H. LLOYD
Bears of Lloyd
1110 Opal Dr.
Prescott, AZ 86303
Phone: 520-778-1489
Phone orders: M-F, 8A.M.-5P.M.
Fax: 520-778-1489
Fax orders accepted.
Price range: $100-$300
Size range: 1"-3"

Bears of Lloyd are made with careful attention to quality, symmetry, consistency and detail. Lisa makes sure the placement of eyes, nose, mouth and ears are exactly within 1/64" to achieve the intended look and expression. Her bears are handsewn and designed entirely by her. They are made of upholstery fur and handstitched with no visible stitches. They are fully jointed, firmly stuffed and have glass bead eyes and embroidered features. Most stand unaided, and each comes with a dated, signed and numbered heart sequin.
Waiting list: 3-6 months
Home Appointments: 1 month
Shows: Chicago; CA; FL
Stores: The Bear Pawse, Prescott, AZ; The Talking Teddy, Estes Park, CO; Doll Emporium, Smyridge, South Africa; Theodore's Bear Emporium, London, UK
Catalog/Photos: $3
Mail order: 3-6 months
Accepts: check, money order, Visa, MasterCard
Has been making bears for 8 years

Awards: Golden Teddy Awards, 1991, 1993; TOBY nominee, 1990, 1991, 1992, 1993; Golden Teddy Nominee, 1994
Publications: TB&F, feature article, 1991; TBR, 1993; Collector's Guide to Miniature Teddy Bears

RITA LOEB
Tiny Teddy Company
2995 Van Buren Blvd., A13-145
Riverside, CA 92503
Phone: 909-780-9410
Phone orders: 10A.M.-9P.M.
Fax: 909-780-5141
Fax orders accepted.
Price range: $50-$150
Size range: 1½"-4"

Tiny Teddy Company bears are easy to spot. They are tiny bears with round tummys. Each has an individual personality, and most have names by the time they are completed. Most of Rita's little bears have tails and are filled with lead shot to sit nicely.
Shows: West Coast
Catalog/Photos: $5, refundable with purchase
Mail order: 1-2 weeks
Accepts: check, money order
Has been making bears for 5 years
Awards: ILTBC, 1st; 1995 Golden Teddy nominee
Publications: TB&F, 1994, 1995

> THERE IS NO SUCH THING AS AN UNLOVED TEDDY BEAR. EVEN IF HE DID NOT QUITE MEET THE ARTIST'S EXPECTATIONS, HE WILL HAVE APPEAL TO SOMEONE, SOMEWHERE. A TEDDY SPEAKS TO EACH OF US INDIVIDUALLY WHILE AT THE SAME TIME SPREADING UNIVERSAL LOVE.
> — *Janet Desjardine, artist, Portage La Prairie, Manitoba*

VICKY JOANNE LOUGHER
Elegant Creations
513 Woodglen Dr.
Chesapeake, VA 23320
Phone: 1-800-TED-DY09
Phone orders: before 10P.M.
Price range: $50-more than $450
Size range: 4"-30"

Elegant Creations have very elaborate and detailed costumes. Vicky uses many vintage fur pieces, feathers and jewelry to adorn her bears. She is noted for using fur pieces to adorn her elegant ladies. Most of her elegant ladies have an elongated body and tend to be on the thin side. Most bears also wear hats, which Vicky makes.
Waiting list: 4-8 weeks
Home Appointments: 1 day
Shows: VA, OH, NY, CT, MA, RI, NJ, MD, FL, TX, IN, KY, GA, PA, MI
Catalog/Photos: $4, refundable with purchase
Mail order: 4-8 weeks
Accepts: check, money order, Visa, MasterCard
Has been making bears for 3 years
Awards: several 1st and 2nd place ribbons, Timmonium. One of Vicky's bears was chosen to appear on the cover of this book.

PAT LYONS
Free Spirit Bears
120 N. Leroux, #101
Flagstaff, AZ 86001

Phone: 602-779-0602
Phone orders: daytime hours
Fax: 602-779-0602
  Fax orders accepted.
Price range: $150-$200
Size range: 8″-20″
Free Spirit Bears are Native American
  bears made of authentic accessories
  such as buckskin, bows and arrows
  and shields. Pat gives each bear a
  name that ties into its clothing and/or
  accessories. The bears are made com-
  pletely by Pat.
Waiting list: 2 weeks-2 months
Home Appointments: accept walk-ins
Shows: FL, IL, MD
Stores: Honey Bee Bear Shoppe, East
  Bridgewater, MA; Bearly Ours, Flag-
  staff, AZ; Animal Haus, Ltd., Cincin-
  nati, OH; Teddy Bears of Witney,
  Oxfordshire, UK; Bear-A-Dise, Millb-
  urn, NJ; Anything Goes, Anna Maria,
  FL
Catalog/Photos: $3
Mail order: 2-4 weeks
Accepts: check, money order, Visa, Mas-
  terCard, Discover
Has been making bears for 5 years
Awards: TOBY nominee, 1993
Publications: TBR, Cover & Story,
  1993; 1994 calender by Silver Vi-
  sions; Tribute to Teddy Bear Artists

EDWARD J. MACKERT

Quite A Bear Company
4010 Hancock Cir.
Atlanta, GA 30340-4242
Phone: 404-270-1026
Phone orders available.
Fax: 404-270-1154
  Fax orders accepted.
Price range: $40-$220
Size range: 12″-17″
Quite A Bear Company is a partnership
  of three bear artists who make bears
  out of real mink or fur. Bears are
  stuffed with Poly-Fil and have jointed
  heads, arms and legs. Each is made
  individually from a 20-piece pattern.
  They have pig skin pads and are artist
  signed and dated. The company will
  also make special order bears out of
  heirloom furs.
Catalog/Photos: $2, refundable with pur-
  chase
Accepts: check, money order, Visa, Mas-

terCard, Discover, American Express,
COD
Has been making bears for 4 years

KARROL J. MACKERT

Quite A Bear Company
4010 Hancock Cir.
Atlanta, GA 30340-4242
Phone: 404-270-1026
  Phone orders accepted.
Fax: 404-270-1154
  Fax orders accepted.
Price range: $40-$220
Size range: 12″-17″
Quite A Bear Company is a partnership of
  three artists who make bears out of real
  mink or fur. Bears are stuffed with Poly-
  Fil, and their heads, arms and legs are
  jointed. Each bear is made individually
  from a 20-piece pattern and has pig skin
  pads. They are artist signed and dated.
  The company also makes special order
  bears out of heirloom furs.
Catalog/Photos: $2, refundable with pur-
  chase
Stores: Swan Coach House, Atlanta, GA;
  shops across the country and in Japan
  and Germany
Accepts: check, money order, Visa, MasterCard, Discover, American Express,
  COD
Has been making bears for 4 years
Publications: CNN's Real News for Kids

JOSEPHINE LOIS MADIGAN

Aunt Lois' Dolls & Teddies
Madigan's Miniatures
1 Illicks Mill Rd.
Bethlehem, PA 18017-3746
Phone: 610-691-3887
Phone orders: 9A.M.-2P.M.
Price range: $35-$200
Size range: 6″-9″
Aunt Lois' Teddies are completely hand-
  sewn by Josephine. Some are dressed
  as professionals, such as doctors and
  nurses, or hobbyists, such as golfers
  and gardeners. Others wear large bows.
Home Appointments: 1 week
Catalog/Photos: available.
Mail order: 1 week
Accepts: check, money order
Has been making bears for 30 years
Awards: Teddy Bears Picnic, Peddler's
  Village, PA, 1st

TRACY MAIN

Teddys By Tracy
32 Pikehall Pl.
Baltimore, MD 21736
Phone: 410-524-2418
Phone orders: 10A.M.-8P.M.
Fax: 410-529-2418
  Fax orders accepted.
Price range: $35-$100
Size range: 1″-3″
Teddys by Tracy have an antique look. She
  likes to dress some of the bears. They
  are fully jointed, even the 1″ bear.
Shows: MD, FL, CA, IL, NJ
Stores: Bear Tracks, Pittsburgh; Pam
  Hebbs, Whetstone, UK
Catalog/Photos: available.
Mail order: 2-4 weeks
Accepts: check, money order, Visa, Mas-
  terCard
Has been making bears for 5 years

JEANIE MAJOR

Huckleberry Woods
3277 Long Lake Rd. SE
Port Orchard, WA 98366
Phone: 206-871-3180
Phone orders: 9A.M.-9P.M.
Price range: $100-$150
Size range: 8″-16″
Huckleberry Woods bears are all mohair,
  fully jointed, and stuffed with a com-
  bination of polyester fiberfill and
  plastic pellets. Jeanie uses imported
  glass or shoe button eyes. Some bears
  are dressed. She enjoys using two
  tones, such as black mohair with pur-
  ple for her blackberry bear, yellow
  with white for her banana cream bear,
  and two-tone Pandas.
Home Appointments: 1 day
Shows: West Coast
Stores: Basically Bears, Hampton, NH;
  Bears By The Bay, Fairhope, AL;
  Good Hearted Bears, Mystic, CT; The
  Paisley Bear, Ft. Lauderdale, FL; Bear
  Tracks, Pittsburgh; The Honey House,
  Shoreview, MN
Catalog/Photos: $1, refundable with pur-
  chase
Mail order: 1 week if in stock
Accepts: check, money order
Has been making bears for 14 years
Awards: Puyallup Fair, 1st, 1994; Club
  Ted, 1st, 1994; Rocky Mountain
  Teddy Show, 1st, 1994; ATBAG
  Conference, 1st, 1988; NW Club

Teddy Artist, 1st, 1993; and more
Publications: Complete Book of Teddy Bears, TBR, 1989 and 1991; TB&F, 1991

MELODIE MARIE MALCOLM
Fancy Stuffins
73698 CSAH 15
Dassel, MN 55325
Phone: 612-275-3794
Phone orders: 9 A.M.-8 P.M.
Price range: $50-$400
Size range: 4"-32"
Fancy Stuffins are bent knee, pellet-filled baby bears or traditional straight leg and long-armed bears. Melodie often dresses them in vintage clothing. They are made of sparse kinky or vintage finish mohair. She also designs and makes country look and storybook fashions. Her bears look very lovable and great care is taken to trim each face just right for individual expressions.
Waiting list: varies
Home Appointments: a few days
Shows: Midwest
Stores: A Matter of Taste, Romeo, MI; Decidedly Different, Vermilion, OH; Marj's Doll Sanctuary, Grand Rapids, MI; Wonderland, Hollywood, FL; Groves Quality Collectibles, Lima, OH; Enchantwood, Hibbing, MN; The Doll Buggy, Excelsior, MN; Esther Kaufmann's Teddy Corner, Switzerland; Der TeddyBar, Germany; Mostly Bears, Arvada, CO; Teddies Treasures, Albany, NY; Bears of Bruton Street, Wilson, NC; Gepetto's, Carmel, CA
Catalog/Photos: $4
Mail order: 60 days
Accepts: check, money order, Visa, MasterCard
Has been making bears for 13 years

Awards: Teddy Tribune Events, 1st, 1990; 1st, 1991; 1st, 1992
Publications: Contemporary Teddy Bear Price Guide; TBR; TB&F

PATTI K. MALEY
PM Teddies
906 Broadview Blvd.
Glen Burnie, MD 21061
Phone: 410-787-1455
Phone orders: 10 A.M.-8 P.M.
Price range: $50-$150
Size range: 7"-12"
PM Teddies are mostly one-of-a-kind. Patti gives them all smiles.
Shows: Mid-Atlantic, Northeast
Stores: Victoria's Collectibles, Winter Springs, FL
Catalog/Photos: free
Mail order: 4-6 weeks
Accepts: check, money order
Has been making bears for 3 years

Publications: TB&F, 1994

LORRAINE MALL
Lani's Dolls and Bears
3790 Anuhea St.
Honolulu, HI 96816
Phone: 808-735-9008
Phone orders: 8 A.M.-5 P.M.
Price range: $35-$100
Size range: 1½"-3"
Lani's Bears are handsewn and fully jointed. They are made of upholstery fabric with Ultrasuede paw pads, bead eyes and hand-embroidered noses. All pieces are turned and then stuffed. Many of Lorraine's bears are part of a series, such as the "Hat series" (various fancy hats), "Uniform series" (uniforms with fancy braids) or the Hawaiian series (easily identifiable Hawaiian costumes or accessories).
Home Appointments: at least one day
Shows: Hawaii
Stores: Teddy Bears & Dolls, Haleiwa, HI
Accepts: check, money order
Has been making bears for 4 years

> ROSES ARE NICE,
> CANDY IS, TOO,
> BUT NEITHER SAY "I LOVE YOU"
> LIKE TEDDY BEARS DO!
> — *Nancy Edmunds, artist, Wallingford, VT*

LESLEY KATHRYN MALLETT
FredBears
154 Cambridge Ct.
Richmond Hill, Ontario L4C 6E7
Canada
Phone: 905-731-3257
Phone orders: 10 A.M.-5 P.M.
Price range: $50-$300
Size range: 1"-31"
FredBears are mostly one-of-a-kind and are made of luxury fabrics, including mohair, alpaca and cashmere. Lesley likes long-legged bears, and most come with accessories such as bells, keys or vests that will not crush the fur. She makes some limited editions for stores. Each bear is a part of her, and she loves to introduce others to the world of bears.
Shows: Canada
Stores: Martin House, Thornhill, Ontario; Teddy Bear Garden, Toronto, Ontario, Teddy Bear Specialties, Georgetown, Ontario
Catalog/Photos: free photos, $5 catalog, refundable with purchase
Mail order: 3 weeks
Accepts: check
Has been making bears for 18 years

SUSAN K. MANSFIELD JONES
Toys Stuffed & Handmade by Susan
23 Sabrina Dr.
Etobicoke, Ontario M9R 2J4
Canada
Phone: 416-242-6446
Phone orders: 9 A.M.-5 P.M.
Price range: less than $35-$150
Size range: 3"-36"
Susan's bears are made out of many different furs, including Borg/Polyester English furs and domestic American furs along with alpaca, silk, velvet, wool and mohair. She tries to be versatile with her materials. She stuffs her bears with pellets or Polyester. All

bears are designed by Susan. She uses both safety eyes and glass eyes, and sometimes music boxes and growlers. She enjoys using leather a great deal as well.

Waiting list: 1 month
Home Appointments: 1 week
Accepts: check
Shows: East and Middle Canada
Has been making bears for 34 years
Awards: Canadian convention, 3rd, 1989; 2nd, 1991; honorable mention, 1993

> New bear artists should find a skill they especially enjoy and do well and incorporate that skill into their bear making.
> — Diane Pease, artist, Exton, PA

JUDY MANTLO

J. Mantlo Bears
7204 Carriage Rd. NE
Albuquerque, NM 87109
Phone: 505-884-7966
Phone orders: anytime
Price range: $100-$150 (wholesale)
Size range: 3"-12"

Judy's bears have many handmade accessories. For instance, the 4" pirate has a peg leg, an eyepatch, a parrot on his shoulder, a handmade sword, a leather belt, and a pirate chest complete with map and coins.

Waiting list: 2-3 months
Home Appointments available.
Shows: IDEX in Dallas; NY Toy Fair
Stores: Chickadee & Holly, Grand Haven, MI; Suzanne's, Phoenix, AZ; The Doll Collection, Dallas, TX; Collectors Alley, Friendswood, TX; Dear Little Dollies, Bellmore, NY; Turner Doll Shop, Bloomington, IN
Catalog/Photos: $2, refundable with purchase
Mail order: 2-3 months
Accepts: check, money order, COD
Has been making bears for 17 years
Awards: Golden Teddy nominee, 1993

> Small legs and arms can be neatly turned with an unsharpened lead pencil with an eraser.
> — Diana Dobrowski, artist, Wibaux, MT

CAROL MARTIN

cm Bears
515 N. 4th St.
Arkansas City, KS 67005
Phone: 316-442-1132
Phone orders: anytime
Price range: $50-more than $450
Size range: 8"-36"

cm Bears are made of mohair and are fully jointed. They have stitched noses and paws, and sometimes leather pads. The head is a 4-piece center seam head with glass eyes. Carol designs and makes all her bears. They come with a brass name plate. They are stuffed with Poly-Fil and have a bag of steel weight in the belly. Many patterns are limited.

Home Appointments: same day
Shows: TX, OK, KS, MO, PA, OH, MI, VT, MD, ME, MA, CO
Stores: The Talking Teddy, Estes Park, CO; Cheri's Bear Essentials, Kansas City, MO; Moore Bears, Strasburg, PA; White Bear Antiques, Tulsa, OK; 2 Bears Teddy Bears, Calgary, Alberta; The Bear Corner, Tyler, TX; The Rare Bear, Woodstock, NY; The Honey Bee Bear Shoppe, East Bridgewater, MA; The Doll Cradle, Merriam, KS; The Rocking Horse Gallery, Fredericksburg, VA; Bear-a-dise, Millburn, NJ; Porter Emporium, Porter, ME; The Mountain Zoo, Estes Park, CO; Hatful of Huggables, Downey, CA; Larkspur Lane, New Hope, PA; TESO, Presque Isle, ME; The Rosebud Toy Co's Emporium, East Arlington, VT; Groves Quality Collectibles, Lima, OH
Catalog/Photos: $6 VHS video brochure, refundable with purchase
Mail order: 10 days or less
Accepts: check, money order, Visa, MasterCard
Has been making bears for 11 years

Awards: TX, MO, PA shows, 1st, 2nd, 3rd place ribbons; Bill Boyd Teddy Bear Jubilee, chairman's choice award, 1993, 1994

CAROLYN MARTIN

Laveen Bear Country
P.O. Box 349
Laveen, AZ 85339
Phone: 602-237-4928
Phone orders: 7 A.M.-9 P.M.
Price range: $50-$350
Size range: 5"-28"

Laveen Bear Country bears are all original designs. Carolyn makes leather faces, giving them a shaved look with a unique touch. She also creates many open-mouth designs with teeth. No two faces are the same. Three of her bears have tears on their faces.

Stores: The Bear Pawse, Prescott, AZ; Dolls Plus, Mesa, AZ
Catalog/Photos: $1, refundable with purchase
Waiting list: 4-6 weeks
Mail order: 4-6 weeks
Accepts: check, money order
Has been making bears for 11 years
Awards: State Fair-2nd.
Publications: TBR, 1994; Teddy Bear Artists' Annual; Contemporary Teddy Bear Price Guide

> Share your knowledge of techniques, sources for supplies, and love of bears with everyone. The investment will reap wonderful friends and more new creations for everyone!
> — Pat R. Fairbanks, artist, St. Petersburg, FL

DIANE L. MARTIN
Blue Moon Bears
5665 Azalea Cir.
Pollock Pines, CA 95726
Phone: 916-644-7939
Phone orders: 10A.M.-8P.M.
Price range: $50-more than $450
Size range: 7″-50″

Blue Moon Bears are designed and made solely by Diane. They are all made of mohair, fully jointed, and handstuffed or pellet-filled with glass or old shoe button eyes. They all have an "old timey" look with smiling faces, and are all dressed or accessorized with vintage clothes and materials.
Waiting list: 4 months
Home Appointments: 1 month
Shows: West Coast
Stores: Hatfull of Huggables, Downey, CA; Suzanne's, Phoenix; Dolls & Bears of Charlton Court, San Francisco; Dolls in the Attic, Victoria, Australia; Verna Mae's Collectibles, Greenwood, NE; Out of the Woods, Modesto, CA
Catalog/Photos: $3, refundable with purchase
Mail order: 4 months
Accepts: check, money order
Has been making bears for 9 years
Awards: show and bear club awards
Publications: TBR; TB&F; Country Home

RANDALL DAVID MARTIN SR.
Lil' Brother's Bears
P.O. Box 8154
Toledo, OH 43605
Phone: 419-697-0371
Phone orders: 10A.M.-5P.M.
Price range: $50-$250
Size range: 1½″-3″

Lil' Brother's Bears are one-of-a-kind teddy bears featuring high-quality workmanship, invisible seams, and traditional (not string) jointing. While most of Randall's bears are traditional, he occasionally makes character bears. His bears are constructed of the highest quality materials and are handsewn with the greatest attention to detail. They are all charming and unique, and their faces are meant to say, "Please take me into your heart and home."
Waiting list: 2-3 weeks
Shows: Midwest
Stores: Groves Quality Collectibles, Lima, OH.
Mail order available.
Accepts: check, money order
Has been making bears for 2 years
Publications: TBR; TB&F

DOROTHY L. MARZOLF
Dottie Bears of Silver Farms
4539 Silver Valley Lane
Traverse City, MI 49684
Phone: 616-947-7128
Phone orders: 10A.M.-5P.M.
Price range: $50-$300
Size range: 5″-24″

Dottie Bears of Silver Farms are made of mohair, have glass eyes, and are fully jointed. Dorothy believes that it's important for the bear to look right at you. Dorothy's smaller bears (5″) are filled with Poly-Fil and steel shot so that they can sit and stand well.
Waiting list: 2-6 months
Home Appointments: 1 day
Shows: South, East, Midwest
Stores: Teddy Bears of Witney, Oxfordshire, UK; Children's World, Traverse City, MI; The Doll Cottage, Naperville, IL; Toys That Teach, Midland, MI; Coach House Collections, Naperville, IL
Catalog/Photos: $5
Mail order: immediately

Accepts: check, money order, Visa, MasterCard
Has been making bears for 8 years
Publications: TB&F; TBR; Traverse City Record Eagle; Country Lines Magazine

SHER MASOR
The Wicker Buggy
469 Crandall Dr.
Worthington, OH 43085
Phone: 614-848-5231
Price range: $50-$300
Size range: 1¼″-24″

The Wicker Buggy bears come in an unlimited variety of styles and looks. Sher specializes in miniature bears and Halloween designs. Small eyes and a "serious whimsy" are two of her trademarks. She often incorporates old or antique fabrics and accessories. She also enjoys experimenting with designs that are a radical departure from traditional teddy bear shapes. One such line is her folk art bears. She enjoys mixing unusual combinations of colors, fabrics, accessories and body proportions.
Home Appointments: depends on stock
Shows: OH
Stores: The Berry Patch, Lyons, CO; The Talking Teddy, Estes Park, CO; Teddy Bear Crossing, Colorado Springs, CO; Bare Essentials, Jackson Hole, WY
Mail order available.
Accepts: check, money order
Has been making bears for 19 years
Awards: Columbus Teddy Bear Fair, 2nd, 1991
Publications: Nutshell News, show scene, 1991; Country Living, 1986; Teddy Bear Artists' Annual; Contemporary Teddy Bear Price Guide; Rocky Mountain Miniature Magazine, 1984

JEAN MARIE MATHERS
Camelot Bears
95 Jamie St.
Islip Terrace, NY 11752
Phone: 516-277-1552
Phone orders: 8A.M.-8P.M.
Price range: $35-$250
Size range: 8"-24"
Camelot Bears are completely handmade one at a time from start to finish. They are made of imported mohair, German acrylic or luxurious domestic acrylic. The bears have handstitched noses, hand-trimmed faces, German blown glass eyes and old-fashioned fiber board joints. Camelot Bears are all limited editions, unique and true collectibles.
Shows: MA, CT
Stores: Nook & Cranny Collectibles, Islip, NY; Oakdale Country Elegance, Oakdale, NY; Hugging Bear Inn & Shoppe, Chester, VT; Carolyn's Card & Gift, Lake Ronko Koma, NY; Cinnamon Bear, Hilton Head Island, NC
Catalog/Photos: $3, refundable with purchase
Mail order: 1 week
Accepts: check, money order, Visa, MasterCard
Has been making bears for 2 years
Three of Jean's bears were chosen to appear on the cover of this book.

> WORK TOGETHER WITH OTHER ARTISTS, BOTH OLD AND NEW, IN SUPPORT OF THIS TRULY WONDERFUL ART FORM. ALSO, REMEMBER THAT NO ONE BEAR, OR METHOD, IS PERFECT OR BETTER THAN ANY OTHER.
> — *Vivian Fritze, artist, Edmonton, Alberta*

RUTHANN MAURER
RuthAnn's Old Time Teds
P.O. Box 1213
La Quinta, CA 92253
Phone: 619-564-3373
Phone orders: 7 days, 8A.M.-8P.M.
Price range: $50-$350
Size range: 5"-26"
RuthAnn's Old Time Teds are made of mohair and are fully jointed. They have glass eyes and wool felt paw pads. RuthAnn is often told that they have sweet expressions.
Waiting list: 6 months
Home Appointments: 1 day
Shows: Southern CA
Stores: Bears Everywhere, Fredericksburg, VA; Teddy Bear Den, Las Vegas; Teddybaren und Plusch, Germany; The Bear Necessities, Solvang, CA; Virginia's 5th Ave. Dolls & Bears, Naples, FL
Catalog/Photos: $5
Mail order: 6-8 weeks
Accepts: check, money order, Visa, MasterCard, 90-day layaway
Has been making bears for 9 years
Awards: Golden Teddy Award
Publications: TB&F, local newspaper

KAREN MAZARIN-STANEK
Bearables
53-1 Myano Ln.
Stamford, CT 06902
Phone: 203-323-9290
Phone orders: 9A.M.-6P.M.
Price range: $50-$300
Size range: 5"-20"
Bearables are all Karen's own patterns. She uses imported mohair, alpaca and glass eyes. She mills the wooden joints herself. All bears are fully jointed and contain growlers.
Waiting list: 4 weeks
Home Appointments: 2 weeks

Shows: CT, MA, MD, NJ, RI, NY, OH, NH, PA
Catalog/Photos: free
Mail order: 4-6 weeks
Accepts: check, money order, Visa, MasterCard
Has been making bears for 9 years

BONITA L. WARRINGTON MCCONNELL
Bonita
39619 Calle Cascada
Green Valley, CA 91350
Phone: 805-270-9016
Phone orders: 9A.M.-5P.M.
Price range: $100-$200
Size range: 4"-18"
Bonita's bears are fully jointed bears made of mohair, alpaca or wool. They have leather paws and glass or antique shoe button eyes. Bonita makes country theme character bears. Some wear jeans. She also makes unclothed bears and miniature bears.
Waiting list: 1 month
Shows: CA
Mail order: 1 month
Accepts: check, money order
Has been making bears for 11 years
Awards: TOBY, blue ribbons, 2nds, 3rds from various bear shows
Publications: Teddy Bears Past & Present II

CAROL MCINTYRE
The Treasure Box
P.O. Box 141
Montrose, British Columbia, Canada
Phone: 604-367-6262
Phone orders: after 1P.M.
Price range: $50-$150
Size range: 14"-20"
The Treasure Box bears are made of quality synthetics or mohair in a range of colors. Carol uses glass eyes and leather or suede leather for paws. Some are simply dressed with bow

ties and vests for boys or lace collars for girls. Some have only ribbon bows. Each bear is named and has a ribbon tag with the name and year sewn onto the back. They are all made with love.

Home Appointments: 1 day
Stores: The Cellar Fibre Studio, Rossland, British Columbia; The Green Porch, Saskatoon, Saskatchewan
Accepts: check, money order
Has been making bears for 3 years

SUSAN AND MARK MCKAY

Bears of the Abbey
1103 Queens Ave.
Oakville, Ontario L6H 4E9, Canada
Phone: 905-844-BEAR
Phone orders: 7 days, 8:30A.M.-8P.M.
Price range: $150-$450
Size range: 6"-18"

Bears of the Abbey are made of the finest materials, including extra dense mohairs and alpacas, leathers and genuine suede. Garments are made of wool with silks and satins. Susan and Mark will often find pieces of antique lace or lace collars to use for accenting as well as antique doll and baby dresses. Many of their bears have noses accented a darker color, and many have eyebrows for added expression. Some are colored with fabric paints.

Waiting list: 6 months
Shows: Canada-East, Midwest
Catalog/Photos: $3, refundable with purchase
Mail order: 3-6 months
Accepts: check, money order, Visa, MasterCard
Has been making bears for 5 years
Awards: 2 TOBY nominations, 1993
Publications: TB&F; TBR

MAUREEN AND FARLEY MCKENZIE

Far-Maur Bears
7403-82 St. Edmonton, Alberta T6C 2X2 Canada
Phone: 403-465-0112
Phone orders: 9A.M.-6P.M.
Price range: $35-$200
Size range: 6"-21"

Far-Maur Bears are fully jointed and have glass eyes. They are traditional bears with center gussets, humps and sway backs. Maureen and Farley use

new plush, vintage fabric and real fur recycled from old coats.

Home Appointments: 2 days
Shows: Alberta
Stores: Treasures & Toys, Edmonton, Alberta
Accepts: check, money order
Has been making bears for 3 years

GRETCHEN MCKILLIP

Hometown Bears
45 W. Imperial Dr.
Walla Walla, WA 99362
Phone: 509-525-0395
Phone orders: 10A.M.-5P.M.
Fax: 509-522-0747
Fax orders accepted.
Price range: less than $35-$300
Size range: 2"-more than 24"

Hometown Bears are small editions and one-of-a-kinds. Gretchen does all the work, from the first stitch to the last. She is constantly changing designs. She strives to keep her faces interesting and touching. Her bizarre bears take the most work, and she often keeps them because they have become part of the family . . . although they sometimes sneak out and go home with a new mom or dad.

Waiting list: 2-4 weeks
Home Appointments: varies
Shows: West
Stores: Brown's Doll & Bear Boutique, Walla Walla, WA; The Hawthorne Gallery, Dayton, WA
Photos available.
Mail order: varies
Accepts: check, money order
Has been making bears for 8 years
Awards: Bearwitched mini show, 1st, 2nd; Victorian Harvester best bear Christmas contest, 1994; local fairs
Publications: TB&F; TBR; Victorian Harvester

KATHLEEN ROSE MCMICHAEL

Kathleen Rose Bears
647 Pleasant
Walla Walla, WA 99362
Phone: 509-529-2295
Phone orders: anytime
Price range: $50-$450
Home Appointments: varies
Shows: Northwest
Has been making bears for 16 years
Awards: local fairs, bear shows, Doll Castle Museum
Publications: Northwest Doll & Teddy Bear Collector

FLORA MEDIATE

Flora's Teddys
190 Malcolm Dr.
Pasadena, CA 91105
Phone: 818-796-1220
Phone orders: anytime
Price range: less than $35-$200
Size range: 7"-18"

Flora's Teddys are made from a variety of different furs. She makes different types of bears, and makes a new bear every year especially for the summer convention in Orange.

Home Appointments: 1 week
Shows: Southern CA
Catalog/Photos: $1.50
Accepts: check, money order
Has been making bears for 16 years
Awards: California State Fair Golden Bear Award; several blue ribbons
Publications: TB&F; The Complete Book of Teddy Bears; Teddy Bear Artists' Annual; Teddy Bear Price Catalog; Contemporary Teddy Bear Price Guide

GINNIE MERIGOLD

Meri Bears
P.O. Box 45
Green Lake, WI 54941
Phone: 414-294-3725

Phone orders: 8A.M.- 8P.M.
Price range: $50-$250
Size range: 5″-24″

Meri Bears are made of mohair and occasionally alpaca. They are fully jointed with handblown glass eyes and either suede or wool paw pads. Ginnie does some limited editions, but most are one-of-a-kind. She makes one-of-a-kind Santas, jesters and clowns with elaborate embroidery and beading.

Home Appointments: 1 day
Shows: FL, Midwest
Stores: International House, Orland Park, IL; International House, Naperville, IL; Teddy Bears, Witney, Oxfordshire, UK
Catalog/Photos: $4, refundable with purchase
Mail order: 2 weeks
Accepts: check, money order, Visa, MasterCard
Has been making bears for 6 years
Awards: Schaumburg Convention, 1st, 1993, 1994

JOAN D. MESCON
To Be Treasured
22011 Malden St.
West Hills, CA 91304
Phone: 818-883-5025
Phone orders: 9A.M.-9P.M.
Fax: 818-883-6691
Fax orders accepted.
Email: AOL-TEDDYBRR
Price range: $85-$400
Size range: 6″-22″

To Be Treasured bears are made of mohair and other materials of the finest quality. All are handsewn and one-of-a-kind. Each bear has its own personality, and is either dressed or left undressed to fit the personality. All come with a signed certificate of authenticity and a photograph of the bear.

Home Appointments: 3 days

Shows: Western region
Stores: Animal Haus Ltd., Cincinnati, OH; Bears Everywhere, Fredericksburg, VA; Virginia's 5th Avenue Dolls & Bears, Naples, FL; The Bear Necessities, Solvang, CA; The Owl's Nest, Carmel, CA
Catalog/Photos: $.50 per photo, refundable with purchase
Mail order: 1 week
Accepts: check, money order, COD
Has been making bears for 9 years
Awards: ILTBC conference and show, 1st, 1992, 1993; 2nd, 1992; The 4 Dolls and Teddy Bear Show, 1st, 1993, 1994; 2nd 1994

DEBRA METLER
Debbie's Grizzlies
4274 Claire
West Bloomfield, MI 48323
Phone: 818-855-1874
Phone orders: 9A.M.-5P.M.
Price range: less than $35-$200
Size range: 8″-36″

Debbie's Grizzlies are all handmade original designs. They are fully jointed and made with mohair, string cotton, or unusual fabrics. They are stuffed with Polyester, pellets or excelsior and have antique shoe button, glass or safety eyes. Each bear is one-of-a-kind. Most are dressed in handmade clothes, including sweaters, hats, coats and vests. Some are bare.

Shows: MI, OH, IN, MA, IL
Catalog/Photos: $2.50, refundable with purchase
Mail order: 3-4 weeks
Accepts: check, money order
Has been making bears for 4 years

CINDY MICHALSKI
Cindy Michalski Originals
P.O. Box 623
Westminster, CO 80030

Phone: 303-426-4802
Phone orders: 8A.M.-8P.M.
Price range: $50-$100
Size range: 2″-4″

Cindy Michalski Originals are miniature bears sewn entirely by hand. She makes both plain and dressed bears in many different styles, including clowns, jesters, ballerinas and Santas. She uses upholstery velvet and some mohair for the bodies and Ultrasuede for the paw pads. Her bears are fully jointed and the seams are turned for a cleaner look. She spends a lot of time on the faces.

Home Appointments: 1 week
Shows: CO
Catalog/Photos: $2, refundable with purchase
Mail order: 3-4 weeks
Accepts: check, money order
Has been making bears for 5 years
Awards: ribbons at local shows
Publications: TB&F, 1994

RICHARD MICHELSON
RicPaul Enterprises, Inc.
P.O. Box 407, 7 Austin Rd.
Tully, NY 13159-0407
Phone: 315-696-5676
Phone orders: 7A.M.-6P.M.
Fax: 315-696-5676
Fax orders accepted.
Price range: less than $35-$100
Size range: 20″

RicPaul Enterprises, Inc. includes bears based on characters from Richard's books. For instance, the Christmas book has a 20″ bear and two 10″ elves. The Valentine book has a 15″ bear, a 10″ angel and a 10″ April Fools doll. As books are released, they are packaged with a bear (20″ or shorter) and manufactured by Commonwealth Toy Co. All sets are numbered and autographed and limited editions certified to be one-of-a-kind. The first one was sold on QVC network.

Waiting list: 6-8 weeks
Home Appointments: 4-6 weeks
Stores: throughout the world
Catalog/Photos: $2, refundable with purchase
Mail order: 6-8 weeks
Accepts: check, money order
Design manufactured by Commonwealth Toy Co.

Has been designing bears for 10 years

SHIRLEY M. MILLER
Boo-Teek Bears
304 S. 34th St.
Allentown, PA 18104
Phone: 610-437-9812
Phone orders: M-F, 6-10P.M. Sat-Sun,
   8A.M.-10P.M.
Fax: 610-481-8702
   Fax orders accepted.
Price range: $50-$200
Size range: 9″-18″
Boo-Teek bears are designed by Shirley.
   Instead of a traditional "country"
   look, she aims for a city look in her
   bears. She uses mohair fabrics, glass
   eyes and nut/bolt joints. She uses ei-
   ther Ultrasuede or kidskin gloves for
   paw pads.
Home Appointments: 1 week
Stores: Teddies Treasures, Kutztown, PA
Catalog/Photos: $2/photo, refundable
   with purchase
Mail order: 4-5 weeks
Accepts: check, money order
Has been making bears for 3 years
Publications: TB&F

CANDY MILLIARD
Bramble Bears
424 West 28th Street
North Vancouver, British Columbia
V7N 2J3, Canada
Phone: 604-988-1985
Fax: 604-988-0147
Price range: $100-$350
Size range: 9″-24″
Bramble Bears come in old-fashioned
   styles with a variety of detailing.
   Candy's bears have slightly larger
   ears, and eyes that are set close to-
   gether.
Waiting list: one month
Home Appointments: several days
Shows: Western Canada

Catalog/Photos: $2, refundable with pur-
   chase
Mail order: 6 weeks
Accepts: check, money order
Has been making bears for 3 years

SARAH DENISE MISSERIAN
Bearahs by Sarah
39975 Cedar Blvd., #330
Newark, CA 94560
Phone: 510-659-8981
Phone orders: anytime after noon
Price range: $50-$150
Size range: 1¼″-3½″
Bearahs by Sarah are sand filled and fully
   jointed. The sand adds a unique feel
   and weight to the bear. Sarah's bears
   are all made of upholstery velvet and
   mohair. They have Ultrasuede paw
   pads, and some have Ultrasuede muz-
   zles.
Shows: MA, CA
Stores: The Owl's Nest, Carmel, CA;
   Teddies Plus, Albany, NY
Waiting list: 8-10 weeks
Catalog/Photos: $6.50
Mail order: 2 weeks
Accepts: check
Has been making bears for 5 years
Awards: TBBNC, 1st, 1992; 1st, 1993; 2
   honorable mentions, 1994
Publications: TB&F, 1994

SONIE MONROE
Sonie Bears
3318 Darvamy Dr.
Dallas, TX 75220
Phone: 214-357-8795
Phone orders: 8A.M.-8P.M.
Fax: 214-357-0221
   Fax orders accepted.
Price range: $50-$300
Size range: 8″-28″
Waiting list: 6-12 weeks
Home Appointments: varies
Shows: MA, MO, OK, TX, AZ

Stores: Bear Corners, Tyler, TX; Doll
   Collection, Dallas, TX; Stuffin Stuff,
   Houston, TX; Grin & Bear It, Naper-
   ville, IL; Betty's Victorian Cottage,
   Seaview, WA; Bears & Hares, Tulsa,
   OK
Catalog/Photos: $3
Mail order: 1 month
Accepts: check, money order, Visa, Mas-
   terCard, layaway
Has been making bears for 8 years

NANCY JOANNE MOOREHEAD
The Teddy Bear Gang
P.O. Box 25, 610 S. Oak
Archer City, TX 76351-0025
Phone: 817-574-2247
Phone orders: 8A.M.-10P.M.
Price range: $50-$200
Size range: 2½″-34″
The Teddy Bear Gang Bears are designed
   and made completely by Nancy. All
   bears feature glass eyes and top-
   quality materials and accessories. All
   are fully jointed. Nancy uses every-
   thing from old quilts to mohair for her
   designs. Most are one-of-a-kind, and
   some miniatures are limited editions.
   Ultrasuede to tapestry to felt are used
   for paw and foot pads. Noses are
   handstitched and filled with Poly-Fil
   and/or pellets. Each teddy is stuffed
   with an unlimited amount of hugs so
   you can always get one back.
Waiting list: 6 weeks or longer
Home Appointments: 1 day
Shows: TX, OK
Accepts: check, money order
Has been making bears for 5 years
Awards: 2nd, Kansas City Jubilee; 1st,
   Teddy Bear Affair
Publications: local newspaper

BONNIE H. MOOSE
Bears, Hares & Other Wares
500 W. 33rd St.
Baltimore, MD 21211-2745
Phone: 410-889-5061
Phone orders: 8 A.M.-9 P.M.
Price range: $35-$250
Size range: 1"-18"
Bears, Hares and Other Wares bears are made of upholstery fabrics (for minis) and mohair, synthetic string, alpaca and acrylics (for larger bears). Some bears have growlers, music buttons or music boxes. Bonnie makes many designs with open mouths. Many may be paired with other animals, including kittens, dogs and rabbits.
Shows: MD, OH
Stores: Rocking Horse Gallery, Fredericksburg, VA; Teddy Bear Museum Shop, Naples, FL
Waiting list: 2 months
Catalog/Photos: free
Mail order: 4-6 weeks
Accepts: check, money order
Has been making bears for 4 years
Awards: Golden Teddy nominee, 1993; TOBY nominee, 1993; Maryland State Fair blue ribbons, 1992, 1993, 1994.
Publications: TB&F, 1993, 1994

JACKIE J. MORRIS
Blacklick Bears
6977 Tomahawk Trail
Reynoldsburg, OH 43068
Phone: 614-866-5429
Phone orders: 8 A.M.-9 P.M.
Fax: 614-866-5429
Fax orders accepted.
Price range: $100-$300
Size range: 6"-19"

Blacklick bears come in a variety of shapes and sizes and are all original patterns. Jackie enjoys experimenting with design and fabrics, but her bears have a couple consistent features. Their eyes are always relatively close together. Their muzzles are always clipped to show their facial expressions, and their noses are always simple triangles, slightly raised from the muzzle. If they are dressed, their clothes are always simple and unpretentious.
Shows: throughout US, Europe
Stores: Groves Quality Collectibles, Bluffton, OH; Honey Bee Bear Shoppe, East Bridgewater, MA; Pluschland, Switzerland; brunobaer, Germany; Strictly Bears, Medina, OH
Waiting list: 2 months
Catalog/Photos: $3
Mail order: 8 weeks
Accepts: check, money order, Visa, MasterCard
Has been making bears for 9 years
Awards: Golden Teddy Award, 1991; several show awards
Publications: TBR; Country Home Magazine; Teddy Bear Artists' Annual; Contemporary Teddy Bear Price Guide

SUZANNE IRENE MORRIS
Short Stuff
15 Westview Dr.
Hoquiam, WA 98550
Phone: 206-533-4555
Phone orders: 9 A.M.-7 P.M.
Fax: 206-533-1753
Fax orders accepted.
Price range: $50-$150
Size range: 10"-24"
Short Stuff bears are one-of-a-kind soft sculptured bears made of heavy wool blend or thermal loggers outdoor socks. Some are made of argyle or red

heel socks. They have Ultrasuede noses and plastic or glass eyes, some with eyelashes. Paw pads are Ultrasuede or suede, and pads on hands are circular, zigzag sewn pads. They have armatures in their arms and legs. Suzanne dresses her bears in fine-quality infant clothes, shoes and socks, or decorates them with silk flowers and matching baskets. She makes each bear from start to finish with no outside help.
Shows: Pacific Northwest
Stores: Lil' Iodines, Ocean Shores, WA; Suzy's Collectibles, St. Helena, CA
Catalog/Photos: photos must be returned
Mail order: depends on time of year
Accepts: check, money order, Visa, MasterCard
Has been making bears for 11 years
Publications: TBR, 1994

DEBORAH LYNN MOUNT
3851 Wallwerth
Toledo, OH 43612
Phone: 419-476-7579
Phone orders: anytime
Price range: $50-$100
Size range: 21"
Deborah's bears are made of domestic plush to keep prices down and U.S. pride up. She makes large bears modeled after big, old bears. Her bears have expressions of empathy. Her Oklahoma roots come through in her bears' attire and names like "Roy" and "Hoyt." Her baby bears wear smocked bonnets.
Home Appointments: ½ hour
Shows: Midwest
Stores: The Toy Store, Toledo, OH; The Teddy Bear Depot, Toledo, OH; Cottage Antiques, Toledo, OH; Hickory Dickory Dolls & Bears, Northfield, OH
Catalog/Photos: available.
Mail order available.
Has been making bears for 3 years

KATHLEEN A. MOYER
Kathy's Bears
4528 Whyem Dr.
Akron, OH 44319
Phone: 216-644-0849
Phone orders: 9 A.M.-8 P.M.
Price range: $100-$250
Size range: 8"-24"
Kathy's Bears are made of the finest German and English mohair and have German glass eyes and Ultrasuede paw pads. They are stuffed with pellets and/or Poly-Fil and have traditional hardboard joints. Noses are made of pearl cotton and are stitched 2-4 times for a raised look. Many are dressed. All bears and their clothing are made solely by Kathy. Some have loc-line armature in the arms. Kathy also makes distressed bears using finished American seal fur with all of the above features.
Waiting list: 8-12 weeks
Home Appointments: 1-2 weeks
Shows: OH
Stores: Wonderland, Inc., Hollywood, FL; Strictly Bears, Medina, OH; Groves Quality Collectibles, Lima, OH; Teddy Bear Station, Uniontown, OH; Daydreams & Tea, Cuyahoga Falls, OH; Raggedy Teds, Massillon, OH; Babes & Bears, Houston, TX
Catalog/Photos: $2, refundable with purchase
Mail order: 2 weeks
Awards: Hower House Teddy Bear Parade, 1994, three 1sts; two 2nds; two 3rds.
Publications: TBR, TB&F

LORI A. MURPHY
Teddy Bears by Lori Murphy
6604 Kaestner Ct.
Citrus Heights, CA 95621
Phone: 916-726-1557
Phone orders: all hours

Price range: $50-$250
Size range: 7"-20"
Lori's bears are traditional, jointed mohair bears with sweet faces. Many are dressed in vintage clothes and accessories, including hats and lace collars. They are made and designed entirely by Lori.
Waiting list: 1 month
Home Appointments: varies
Shows: Northern CA, OR, WA
Stores: Owl's Nest, Carmel, CA; Golden Rule Bears, Sumner, WA; Pied Piper, Plymouth, MI; Antique Affairs, Renton, WA; Past & Presents, Vacaville, CA
Catalog/Photos: $2, refundable with purchase
Mail order: 1 month
Accepts: check, money order
Has been making bears for 8 years
Awards: California State Fair, blue ribbons
Publications: TBR; TB&F

PATRICIA MURPHY
Murphy Bears
6900 Jennings Rd.
Ann Arbor, MI 48105
Phone: 313-761-6288
Phone orders: 9 A.M.-5 P.M.
Fax: 313-761-8717
Price range: $100-more than $450
Size range: 12"-28"
Murphy Bears are hand-dyed traditional designs by Pat. Many are one-of-a-kind. Some have antique clothing and accessories. Some have wonderful, hand-designed and hand-knit sweaters by Jean Trombley.
Waiting list: 8-12 weeks
Home Appointments: 1 week
Shows: Midwest, East Coast, Europe
Stores: Bear Tracks, Pittsburgh; Animal Haus Ltd., Cincinnati, OH; Kits and Kaboodle, Indianapolis, IN; Wonderland, Inc., Hollywood, FL; Verna Mae

Collectibles, Greenwood, NE; Bears Out of the Woods, Modesto, CA; Good Hearted Bears, Mystic, CT; Hidden Treasures, Erie, PA; Bear-a-Dise, Millburn, NJ; Damals, Germany; Magpies Nest, UK; Strictly Bears, Medina, OH; Bear Hugs, Coeur D'Alene, ID; Teddy Bears Picknick, Netherlands; Berengoed, Netherlands; Sobries Collector Shop, Belgium
Catalog/Photos: $2, refundable with purchase
Mail order: 2 weeks
Accepts: check, money order
Has been making bears for 11 years
Publications: Contemporary Teddy Bear Price Guide; Bearland

DAVID WILLIAM MURRAY
Intellagents, Inc.
1227 SE 9th Ter.
Cape Coral, FL 33909
Phone: 813-772-5957
Phone orders: 24 hours
Fax: 813-574-1008
Fax orders accepted.
Price range: $250-$300
Size range: 12"-16"
David's bears, The Hibearnators, are unique bears true to the slogan, "Our teddies bear a second look!" At first glance, they look like any other bear, but reach into hidden pouches to reveal a totally new bear. They have hidden second faces, paws and body parts. You actually get two bears in one! They are handstitched and crafted with high-quality goods. Each bear is hand-decorated, signed and numbered and comes with a collectible trading card.
Home Appointments: as needed
Shows: New York, NY
Catalog/Photos: free
Mail order: 30 days
Accepts: money order, Visa, MasterCard
Has been making bears for 13 years
Publications: TBR, TB&F

HELEN LENA MURRAY
Elena's Dollhouses & Miniatures
5565 Schueller Cir.
Burlington, Ontario L7L 3T1, Canada
Phone: 905-333-3402
Phone orders: T-Sat, 10 A.M.-4 P.M.
Price range: less than $35-$100

Size range: 1⅞"-3"

Helen's bears are handmade one at a time using upholstery velvets or mohairs with authentic leathers and suedes for paws and pads. They are jointed, Polyester stuffed and have hand-embroidered faces with glass beads or buttons for eyes. All dressings are 100% natural fabrics. Designs are Helen's own, and new designs are always being born.

Waiting list: 2 weeks-3 months

Home Appointments: 1 month

Shows: Great Lakes, Ontario

Stores: Wee Two, Oakville, Ontario; Pied Piper Miniatures, Buffalo, NY; Mini-World, Australia

Catalog/Photos: LSASE

Mail order: 4-6 weeks

Accepts: check, money order, Visa, MasterCard

Has been making bears for 4 years

Awards: MET show, 1994

Publications: Miniature Collector, 1994 & Mountie Bear

MONICA MURRAY
Classic Traditions
P.O. Box 728
Jenks, OK 74037
Phone: 918-299-5416
Phone orders: 9A.M.-6P.M.
Price range: $35-more than $450
Size range: 1"-3 feet

Classic Traditions bears are old looking bears with magical faces. Monica uses vintage clothes and accessories.

Shows: throughout USA, and one international trip per year

Stores: White Bear Antiques, Tulsa, OK; Something Unique, Jenks, OK

Catalog/Photos: free

Mail order: ASAP

Accepts: check, money order, Visa, MasterCard, layaway

Has been making bears for 9 years

Publications: TB&F, cover; newspapers

MAY-BRITT MYKIETIAK
BIM Bears
888 Alder Ave
Sherwood Park, Alberta T8A 1V5, Canada
Phone: 403-467-1023
Phone orders: 8A.M.-9P.M.
Price range: $50-$100
Size range: 1"-6"

BIM Bears are handstitched to ensure that the details stay true to the original design. May-Britt usually uses the best quality mohair and cashmere. Occasionally she will be inspired by synthetic. Her bears have real joints and usually have steel pellets among the Polyester filling. This makes them heavy and somewhat posable.

Waiting list: 6-8 weeks

Shows: Edmonton, Alberta; Calgary, Alberta

Stores: Treasures & Toys, Edmonton, Alberta, 2 Bears Teddy Bears, Calgary, Alberta

Has been making bears for 3 years

Awards: Safeway Klondike, 2nd

SUSAN WEBER NAGLE
Susies Sewn Originals
15 Laird St.
West Lawn, PA 19609
Phone: 610-678-0627
Phone orders: anytime
Price range: $50-$100
Size range: 6"-20"

Susie's Sewn Originals are mink teddy bears from customers' old fur coats. Susan also sells bears made from vintage mohair. Her teddy bears wear hand-knit sweaters.

Waiting list: 1 month

Home Appointments: 1 week

Shows: MD, PA, VA

Catalog/Photos: $3.50, refundable with purchase

Mail order: 1 month

Accepts: check, money order, Visa, MasterCard

Has been making bears for 10 years

KATHY NEARING
My Kind of Bear
38 Montague St.
Binghamton, NY 13901
Phone: 607-648-6122
Phone orders: 8A.M.-8P.M.
Price range: $50-$300
Size range: 9"-24"

My Kind of Bear bears are made of top-quality mohair with glass eyes. Kathy embroiders the noses. The bears are fully jointed. Some have flex limb. Some are dressed.

Home appointments available.

Shows: Northeast

Stores: Bears By The Bay, Fairhope, AL; The Teddy Bear Museum of Naples, Naples, FL; Delightful Dolls & Toys, Johnson City, NY

Catalog/Photos: available.

Mail order available.

Accepts: check, money order, Visa, MasterCard

Has been making bears for 8 years

LORI A. NERDAHL
Forever Friends
2119-E. 32nd Ct.
Davenport, IA 52807
Phone: 319-355-0723
Phone orders: before 9P.M.
Price range: $50-more than $450
Size range: 4"-36"

Forever Friends bears are made of top-quality fabrics, mainly mohair, and are fully jointed. They have suede paws and glass eyes. Most are filled with a mixture of polyester and pellets. Lori gives many of her bears bent legs, sweet baby faces and baby clothing. Some of her bears are two-faced and can cry or sleep. They are trimmed in laces, ribbons and roses in pastel color themes.

Waiting list: 2-3 months

Home appointments available.

Shows: IL, IA, CA, FL, MD

Stores: Hatfull of Huggables, Downey, CA; Bobby's Land of Animals, Long Grove, IL; International House, Naperville, IL; The Teddy Bear Den, Las Vegas; The Rocking Horse Gallery, Fredericksburg, VA

Catalog/Photos: $6, refundable with purchase

Mail order: 2 months

Accepts: check, money order, Visa, MasterCard

Has been making bears for 10 years

Awards: ABC Unlimited Productions, 1st, 2nd, 3rd

Publications: TBR, Country Home Magazine

SARAH NEUSCHELER

Sarah Beara Bears

2840 S. Wabash Cir.

Denver, CO 80231

Phone: 303-755-2030

Phone orders: M-F, 8A.M.-5P.M.

Price range: $50-$200

Size range: 8"-20"

Sarah Beara Bears are fully jointed and made from quality imported mohair with glass eyes. Most are filled with a combination pellet/Poly-Fil filling to give them a posable look. Sarah gives them an innocent, lovable face guaranteed to melt anyone's heart. Some bears lean more toward the juvenile bear look.

Home Appointments: 1 day

Stores: Teddy Bear Crossing, Colorado Springs, CO; Colorado Doll Faire, Ft. Collins, CO; Collectable Bears &

Gifts, Colorado Springs, CO; Finch's Nest, Waukesha, WI; Heart 2 Heart Inc., Davidson, NC

Catalog/Photos: $3, refundable with purchase

Mail order: 6-8 weeks

Accepts: check, money order

Has been making bears for 6 years

LANA NORLIN

Reliving Memories

1701 S. Center St.

Marshalltown, IA 50158

Phone: 515-752-4943

Phone orders: evenings or weekends

Price range: $50-$100

Size range: 15"

Reliving Memories bears are real fur bears from old fur coats. Lana also makes a variety of mohair bears. All are her own patterns. They all have their own personalities and are jointed in the head, arms and legs.

Waiting list: 8 weeks

Home Appointments: 1 month

Shows: IA

Mail order: 8 weeks

Accepts: check, money order

Has been making bears for 10 years

ANITA O'HARA

O'Harabears by Anita O'Hara

228 Prospect St.

Wellington, OH 44090

Phone: 216-647-3993

Phone orders: 9A.M.-4P.M.

Price range: $50-$100

Size range: 1¼"-6"

Made of upholstery velvet or mohair, O'Harabears by Anita O'Hara are fully jointed and stuffed with Polyester fiberfill. Some have a mix of Poly-Fil and copper shot for extra weight. Anita uses glass eyes on larger bears and glass bead or onyx bead eyes on tiny ones. She likes to use a variety of colors and fabrics to make unique creations.

Home Appointments: 1 week

Shows: Midwest

Stores: Ted E. Bear Shoppe, Naples, FL; Linda's Lov-Lez Bears, Mentor, OH

Catalog/Photos: list-free, photos $5, refundable with purchase

Mail order: 2 weeks

Accepts: check, money order

Has been making bears for 6 years

ELIZABETH ANNE OKINAKA

Clasic Collectables of Hawaii

P.O. Box 912

Volcano, HI 96785

Phone: 808-968-8126

Phone orders: anytime

Price range: $50-$350

Size range: 3"-36"

Classic Collectables of Hawaii are completely handsewn by Elizabeth. She uses the best fur and mohair with hand-dyed felt for paws. She also makes ceramic snouts and ceramic faces. All bears are special examples of the love she wishes to share with other bear lovers.

Waiting list: 3 weeks

Home Appointments: 2 weeks

Shows: HI, CA

Stores: Christina's Collectibles, Haleiwa, HI; Rainbow's End Store, Mountain View, HI

Catalog/Photos: $3, refundable with purchase

Mail order: 3-6 weeks

Accepts: money order, Visa

Has been making bears for 8 years

RUTHIE O'NEILL

1220 S. 74th St.

Tacoma, WA 98408

Phone: 206-474-0404

Phone orders accepted.

Price range: $50-$200

Size range: 8"-17"

Ruthie's bears are very flexible and fully jointed.

Waiting list: 1 month
Home Appointments: 1 week
Shows: WA, OR
Accepts: check
Has been making bears for 11 years
Awards: several 1st place ribbons
Publications: TB&F, TBR

LEOTA ORDIWAY
Solo Bears
4104 Tretorn Ave.
Bakersfield, CA 93313
Phone: 805-835-8508
Phone orders: anytime
Price range: $50-$150
Size range: 2½"-8"

Solo Bears are designed in the older, more traditional fashion. Leota has made reproductions of old teddy bears and then scaled them down to small sizes. Her 2½" teddies are made from handclipped mohair. She uses glass eyes that have pupils. For her 6" Victorian ladies, she uses vintage fabric, including hats. One 6" bear she makes wears a dress made from vintage hankies.

Home Appointments: varies
Shows: CA, OR, Midwest, Northeast, Southeast
Stores: Bear Necessities, Solvang, CA; Teddy Bears of Witney, Oxfordshire, UK; Briscoes Doll & Bear, Sutter Creek, CA; Bear Street, Claremont, CA; Casey's Bear Factory, Fairport, NY; JP Gallery of Gifts, Cocoa Village, FL
Photos available.
Mail order: 6-8 weeks
Accepts: check, money order, Visa, MasterCard
Has been making bears for 8 years
Awards: ATBAG, Best of Show, 1989; Teddy Tribune, 2nd, 1990; Teddy

Bear Jubilee, 1st, 1991; 2nd, 1993; Schaumburg, 1st

NORINE MIYUKI OSHIRO
Norine O-Bears of Hawaii
919 12th Ave.
Honolulu, HI 96816
Phone: 808-735-1539
Phone orders: 7 days, 9 A.M.-8 P.M.
Price range: less than $35-$200
Size range: ⅝"-3"

Norine O-Bears of Hawaii are miniature bears with their own warm personalities. They are fully jointed, turned and made with glass bead eyes, onyx, Ultrasuede, upholstery fabric and German mohair. Her miniatures are all sewn by hand and take more than 8 hours to make. She is always designing new bears.

Waiting list: 3-7 months
Home Appointments: 2-3 days
Shows: HI
Stores: Christina's Collectables, Haleiwa, HI; Gepetto's, Carmel, CA
Catalog/Photos: free
Mail order available.
Accepts: check
Has been making bears for 5 years

DEBORAH ANN PALERMO
Oak Forest Originals
10940 NW 15th St.
Pembroke Pines, FL 33026
Phone: 305-436-6006

Phone orders: 5 P.M.-9 P.M.
Price range: $35-$350
Size range: 6"-24"

Oak Forest Originals are created from start to finish by Deborah. She works excusively in mohair and Ultrasuede. Her bears have glass or shoe button eyes and may be stuffed with Poly-Fil or pellets. Claws are embroidered upon request.

Shows: FL
Stores: Daisy Farm, Inc., Miami, FL
Photos: free
Mail order: 6 weeks
Accepts: check, money order
Has been making bears for 4 years
Awards: TOBY nominee, 1994; Among the Flowers Bear Competition, Best in Show, 1994

GEORGENE LYNNE PALKA
George's Jungle
5516 Hill Ct.
Nashville, TN 37220
Phone: 615-832-9073
Phone orders: 7 A.M.-7 P.M.
Fax: 615-832-9073
Fax orders accepted.
Price range: $50-$200
Size range: 4"-25"

Georgene's bears are usually one-of-a-kind or very limited editions, with a few open editions. Most are undressed. Georgene strives to make unique bears that are more of an art form than a toy.

Home Appointments: 1 day
Shows: Central, South, North, East, Europe
Stores: TeddyTown USA, Nashville, TN; Babes 'n Bears, Houston, TX; Teddy Bear Museum, Naples, FL; Slades Dolls & Bears, Sioux Falls, SD
Catalog/Photos: $5, refundable with purchase, and LSASE
Mail order: 6 weeks-6 months

Accepts: check, money order, Visa, MasterCard, COD
Has been making bears for 7 years

DIANE C. PEASE
Piece by Pease Teddy Bears
328 Huffman Dr.
Exton, PA 19341
Phone: 610-363-9391
Phone orders: 9A.M.-9P.M.
Price range: $59-$140
Size range: 1″-3¼″
Piece by Pease Teddy Bears are all completely handstitched by Diane. Almost all her undressed bears have the unique feature of a tail. Because of difficulties with costuming, her dressed bears do not have a tail. She adds details to her bears using various embroidery, smocking and knitting skills on a tiny scale.
Waiting list: 2 months or more
Home Appointments: 3-4 days
Shows: East Coast
Stores: Good Hearted Bears, Mystic, CT
Catalog/Photos: free with request
Accepts: check, money order
Has been making bears for 4 years
Publications: TB&F, TBR
Awards: Best of Show, Annual Teddy Bear Fest in Strasburg, PA, 1992; 2nd, Timonium, 1992 and more

E. KAY PECK
Kde Signed It!
18617 Jiretz Rd.
Odessa, FL 33556
Phone: 813-920-6350
Phone orders: 9A.M.-6P.M.
Price range: $50-$400
Size range: 3″-45″
Kde Signed It! Bears come in a wide range of styles, from an old style to funky, fun bears. Kay makes one-of-a-kind and special order bears.
Waiting list: 3-5 months

Home Appointments: 1 week
Has been making bears for 13 years
Awards: Craft show in South FL

JANE PERALA
Hemer House Designs
Site G, C-43, R.R.2
Nanaimo, British Columbia V9R 5K2, Canada
Phone: 604-722-3134
Phone orders: 10A.M.-5P.M.
Price range: $100-$200
Size range: 10″-20″
Hemer House Designs are fully jointed, mohair bears with Ultrasuede paws and glass or shoe button eyes. They have embroidered noses. Some are dressed. Jane makes a variety of styles and uses a variety of mohair finishes.
Shows: British Columbia, Alberta
Stores: The Quilted Duck, Nanaimo, British Columbia
Catalog/Photos: $5, refundable with purchase
Mail order: 4-6 weeks
Accepts: money order, Visa, MasterCard
Has been making bears for 3 years
Awards: The Bear Fair, Calgary, Alberta, 2nd, 1994
Publications: The Victorian Harvester

JEAN PETERSON
Fantasy Bears
11070 Bellwood #2
Minocqua, WI 54548
Phone: 715-358-1969
Phone orders: 8A.M.-6P.M.
Price range: $35-$150
Size range: 5″-24″
Fantasy Bears come in several different styles. Jean makes all types of sportsmen bears and special holiday bears, such as a Mama Bear for Mother's Day. Mama bear is red, wears a pearl necklace and earrings, a real fur martin stole and a big floppy flowered hat. She carries a bouquet of a dozen red roses and an original 2″ × 2″ Mama's Day card.
Waiting list: 3 weeks
Home Appointments: 3 days
Catalog/Photos: $2, refundable with purchase
Mail order: 2 weeks
Accepts: check, money order, Visa, MasterCard
Has been making bears for 3 years

NEYSA PHILLIPPI
Purely Neysa
45 Gorman Ave.
Indiana, PA 15701-2244
Phone: 412-349-1225
Phone orders: 7 days, 9A.M.-9P.M.
Fax: 412-349-3903
Fax orders accepted.
Price range: $50-$400
Size range: 9″-42″
Purely Neysa bears are character bears that have been described as "not your normal bear"—whatever "normal" is! They are made of German and English mohair and string cotton as well. Neysa's plush line has been discontinued, but some are still available for purchase. Her plush bears are dressed, and her mohair bears are bare.
Home Appointments: same day
Shows: PA, OH, MD, FL, MO, IL, Europe, England
Stores: Teddy Bear Station, Uniontown, OH; The Toy Shoppe, Richmond, VA; Teddy Bear Junction at Norge Station, Williamsburg, VA; Bears Everywhere, Fredericksburg, VA; Groves Quality Collectables, Lima, OH; Worsley's Dolls & Bears, Butler, PA; Moore Bears, Strasburg, PA; Strictly Bears, Medina, OH; Candy Bear Shoppe Ltd. Cochrane, Alberta; Barenhohle, Germany; Bruno Baer, Germany; Bimbo Exclusief, The Netherlands; De JoJo, The Netherlands; Heike Gumpp, Germany; Lace Symphony, Belgium; Das Barle, Germany
Catalog/Photos: $6, refundable with purchase of more than $100
Mail order: will send when payment clears
Accepts: check, money order, Visa, MasterCard
Has been making bears for 12 years
Awards: several show ribbons

Publications: Contemporary Teddy Bear
  Price Guide; Puppen & Spielzeug
  Magazine; BeerBericht Magazine
  (Holland), 1994; Bright Star's News-
  letter; newspapers; local TV
See the article opening Chapter 8 by
  Neysa. Three of Neysa's bears were
  chosen to appear on the cover of the
  book.

JANET PINCKNEY
Maui Bears
10317 169th Ave. SE
Renton, WA 98059
Phone: 206-226-4775
Phone orders: noon-4P.M.
Price range: $50-$100
Size range: 1"-3½"
Maui Bears are jointed and have black
  onyx eyes, Ultrasuede pads, humped
  backs and sweet little faces. Janet's
  mohair bears range in size from 2½"-
  3½", and are made of sparse or dense
  mohair fabric. The upholstery fabric
  bears range in size from 1"-3". She has
  been making miniature bears for 10
  years and is always trying new things
  and exploring and collecting new ma-
  terials.
Stores: Secret Garden, Bellevue, WA
Waiting list: 4-6 weeks
Photos: $1
Mail order: 4-6 weeks
Accepts: check, money order, COD
Has been making bears for 11 years
Publications: TB&F, 1995

> BEAR ARTISTS, DON'T BE AFRAID TO TRY ALMOST
> ANYTHING. THERE ARE NO RULES FOR ARTISTRY,
> AND HALF THE FUN IS CREATING
> TOTALLY NEW DESIGNS!
> — *Susan & Mark McKay, artists,*
> *Oakville, Ontario*

STACY M. PIO
Mrs. Bear E. Pio's
1964 N. Hollywood Rd.
Nekoosa, WI 54457
Phone: 715-886-4014
Phone orders: noon-4P.M.
Price range: $50-$100
Size range: 2¾"-4½"
Mrs. Bear E. Pio's bears are five-jointed
  and made of mohair or upholstery fab-
  ric. They have German glass or onyx
  eyes and Kopok stuffing. Stacy hand
  stitches all her bears, and each comes
  with a signed and numbered hang tag.
Stores: The Toy Shoppe, Richmond, VA;
  Good Hearted Bears, Mystic, CT; The
  Teddy Bear Den, Las Vegas; Ted E.
  Bear Shoppe, Naples, FL
Waiting list: 8-12 weeks
Catalog/Photos: $2
Mail order: 6-8 weeks
Accepts: check, money order
Has been making bears for 2 years

JANE POGORZELSKI
Honey Bear Creations
RR 1, Box 8E
New Berlin, IL 62670
Phone: 217-488-7930
Phone orders: 7A.M.-7P.M.
Price range: less than $35-$200
Size range: 1¼"-8"
Honey Bear Creations include small
  bears made of upholstery fabric, Ul-
  trasuede or felt that are fully jointed.
  Jane's bears are bare except for a col-
  lar, bib or vest. All are original de-
  signs. They are totally handsewn and
  can be fiberfill, plastic pellet or steel
  shot filled.
Waiting list: 2 months
Home Appointments: 2 days or more
Shows: Midwest
Catalog/Photos: $2, refundable with pur-
  chase
Mail order: 2-3 months

Accepts: check, money order, Visa, MasterCard
Has been making bears for 11 years

PAM PONTIOUS
Pamda Bears
P.O. Box 5896
Bellingham, WA 98227
Phone: 206-647-2218
Phone orders: anytime
Price range: $100-$400
Size range: 2¼"-24"
Pamda Bears are always smiling. Pam
  likes to work with mohair and German
  synthetics. Most of her bears prefer
  subtle costuming, and they absolutely
  refuse to wear shoes! They say a bear
  is meant to have "bare" feet.
Waiting list: 4 months
Home Appointments: 1 week
Shows: Pacific Northwest, New England,
  Clarion, IA
Stores: Basically Bears, Hampton, NH;
  Golden Rule Bears, Sumner, WA; Par-
  lor Bears, Lincoln City, OR; Books
  'N' Bears, Florence, OR; The Wood-
  shed, Dillard, OR
Catalog/Photos: $5, refundable with pur-
  chase
Mail order: 4 months
Accepts: check, money order, Visa, Mas-
  terCard
Has been making bears for 8 years
Awards: Seattle, 1st; Chicago, 2nd

STEPHANIE PORCIELLO
Miss Addie's Attic
1 Corbett Lane
Winslow, ME 04901
Phone: 207-873-1713
Phone orders: 9A.M.- 9P.M.
Price range: $200-$400
Size range: 24"-34"
Miss Addie's Attic has three collections
  of bears to offer. The Weaver Creek
  Folks are limited edition, originally

designed bears of a rustic nature. All fabrics are tea-dyed to capture the look of times past. The Heirloom Collection bears are also original designs and Victorian in dress. The Christmas past collection consists of Santa-Paws, an old world Santa, and other characters of old.

Waiting list: 3-4 weeks
Home Appointments: 1 day
Shows: ME, MA
Stores: Golden Sails, Ogunquit, ME; Living Arts of Kennebunk, Kennebunk, ME; The Write Shop, Harwich Port, MA
Catalog/Photos: available.
Mail order: 3-4 weeks
Accepts: check, money order, Visa, MasterCard
Has been making bears for 4 years
Publications: The Waterville Morning Sentinel; TBR

CYNTHIA POWELL
P.O. Box 940061
Maitland, FL 32794-0061
Phone: 407-365-2327
Phone orders: 9A.M.-5P.M.
Price range: $150-$200
Size range: ⅜"-3"
Cynthia's bears are handsewn miniatures in very limited numbers. Many of her designs are inspired by large and small antique teddies. She makes fancy-colored bears or tiny teds with hidden surprises.
Catalog/Photos: $3
Mail order: varies
Accepts: check, money order, layaway
Has been making bears for 9 years
Awards: TOBY; Golden Teddy; Timonium, 1st; Schaumburg, 1st
Publications: A Collector's Guide to Miniature Teddy Bears; Teddy Bear Artists' Annual; The Official Price Guide to Teddy Bears; The Complete

Book of Teddy Bears; Tribute to Teddy Bear Artists

KAREN I. PRINGLE
Craiglatch Critters
11 Rodger St.
St. Catharines, Ontario L2N 3J5, Canada
Phone: 905-937-1411
Phone orders: 9A.M.-8:30P.M.
Price range: $50-$250
Size range: 2"-14"
All Craiglatch Critters are Karen's own original designs. Straw-Bear-y Fairy is a 3" gossamer winged bear. Sky Grey is a 13" mink colored silk rayon, fully jointed bear with a downcast head and flowers clasped behind his back. Sniffles is a 14" fully jointed distressed old gold mohair bear with a runny nose and eyes. The Ring-Bear-er is a 12" white, fluffy jointed bear with a white satin dicky sewn in and a bow tie—a perfect gift for your ringbearer after the wedding.
Waiting list: 4-6 weeks
Home Appointments: 1-2 weeks
Shows: Ontario; NY; OH
Stores: The Silly Old Bear Shop, Niagara-on-the-Lake, Ontario; The Owl & The Pussycat, Niagara-on-the-Lake, Ontario
Mail order: 4-6 weeks
Accepts: check, money order, 50% deposit on all orders
Has been making bears for 8 years
Publications: Toy Box Magazine; newspapers; Lincoln County Board of Education magazine

JOAN RANKIN
JR Bears
155 Hochelaga Street W.
Moose Jaw, Saskatchewan S6H 2C2, Canada
Phone: 306-692-3341
Phone orders: 8A.M.-8P.M.

Price range: $100-$300
Size range: 6"-20"
JR Bears are almost exclusively made of natural fiber plushes, including mohair, alpaca, mohair/silk, mohair/alpaca and occasionally rayon. They all have German glass eyes, leather pads and embroidered noses and are fully jointed. Most are firmly stuffed with polyester, but some are stuffed with pellets and Poly-Fil for a softer effect. Most are one-of-a-kinds, with a few small limited editions and one open edition. She likes to dress her bears in accessories such as caps, scarves, vests or collars. Some are fully dressed. All wear a JR Bears logo pin.
Waiting list: 1 month
Home Appointments: 1 day
Shows: Alberta, Ontario
Stores: Teddy Bears' Picnic, Victoria, British Columbia; Bears Galore, Winnepeg, Manitoba; Treasures & Toys, Edmonton, Alberta; Woodruffs, Winchester, UK
Catalog/Photos: available.
Mail order available.
Accepts: check, money order
Has been making bears for 8 years
Publications: TBR; Victorian Harvester, 1992, 1993; Toybox, 1993; The Teddy Bear Encyclopedia

EDITH E. RASE
Beary Collectibles
4601 Grayview Ct., C201
Tampa, FL 33609-1932
Phone: 813-286-7032
Phone orders: until 7P.M.
Price range: $50-$300
Size range: 4"-35"
Beary Collectibles bears are usually completely handstitched. Edie prefers the old look of traditional, early bears. Ninety percent of her bears are one-of-a-kind. They are not perfect, but,

like humans, they talk. Edie enjoys seeing children's eyes light up when they hug a bear.

Shows: South, Northeast, Central states

Stores: J & L Collectibles, Tampa, FL; Collectable Alley Antiques, Crystal River, FL; Antiques In Design, N. Belleais Bluffs, FL; Victorian Rabbit, St. Petersburg, FL; 12th St. Antiques, Palm Harbor, FL; Picket Fence, Winter Haven, FL

Waiting list: 30-45 days

Catalog/Photos: $3 (photos); $5 (catalog), refundable with purchase

Mail order: 4 weeks

Accepts: check, money order

Has been making bears for 5 years

Awards: State Fairs, several 1sts and 2nds

Publications: TB&F, 1994

DORIS A. REECE

Doris Reece Bears

556 Shorecliff Dr.

Rochester, NY 14612

Phone: 716-621-5773

Phone orders: 9A.M.-7P.M.

Price range: $50-$200

Size range: 7″-26″

Doris's bears are made of mohair and are fully jointed. All have a tiny ribbon in the left ear and are described as having sweet faces.

Home Appointments: 2 weeks

Shows: NY, MA, CT, PA

Catalog/Photos: $3

Mail order: 3 weeks

Accepts: check, money order

Has been making bears for 17 years

Publications: TBR, 1994

JANET REEVES

Hug-A-Bear

640 E. Wheeler Rd.

Midland, MI 48640

Phone: 517-631-3625

Phone orders: 9A.M.-8P.M.

Fax: 517-631-3625

Fax orders accepted.

Price range: $100-$400

Size range: 8″-24″

Hug-a-bear bears are antique style with long arms and legs. Janet uses either mohair or alpaca with Ultrasuede or wool paw pads. Her bears have humps on their backs and glass or antique shoe button eyes. Some are dressed. A few have inner soles and are free standing.

Waiting list: 8-16 weeks

Home Appointments: 3-4 days

Shows: Midwest, East, South and West

Stores: Bears & Hares Collectibles, Tulsa, OK; Bear-a-Dise, Millburn, NJ; Dolls, Bears & Funny Hares, Mission, KS; Ye Olde Teddy Bear Shoppe, Irwin, PA; Ted E. Bear Shoppe, Naples, FL; Animal Haus Ltd., Cincinnati, OH

Catalog/Photos: $4

Mail order: 6-12 weeks

Accepts: check, money order, Visa, MasterCard, layaway

Has been making bears for 11 years

Awards: Golden Teddy Award, 1989; several show awards

Publications: TB&F; TBR; Teddy Bear Artist Annual; Teddy Bear-Annalee's & Steiff Animals; Teddy Bear and Friends Price Guide; Official Price Guide to Antique and Modern Teddy Bears; TV, newspapers in Germany; Teddybaren (German book)

ROBERTA A. REHM

Bears by Bert

8577 Lantana Dr.

Seminole, FL 34647

Phone: 813-398-7346

Phone orders: after 5P.M.

Price range: $50-$200

Size range: 2″-4″, 9″-16″

Bears by Bert are mostly miniature bears. They are usually undressed. Roberta likes to work with a variety of fabrics, and some are hand-dyed. She also makes mohair and German plush bears from 9″ to 16″. They are also undressed.

Shows: FL

Stores: The Hen Nest, Seminole, FL; Village Bears and Collectables, Sarasota, FL; J & L Collectibles, Tampa, FL

Mail order available.

Accepts: check, money order

Has been making bears for 6 years

SUZANNE V.B. REMPFER

Suzy Bears

1296 Notting Hill Drive

San Jose, CA 95131-3611

Phone: 408-441-6329

Phone orders: 10A.M.-8P.M.

Price range: $50-$200

Size range: 1¼″-3″

Suzy Bears are completely handsewn and designed by Suzy. She uses upholstery fabric and some mohair at 3″. Her bears are fully jointed and have glass or onyx eyes, Ultrasuede pads and embroidered noses and claws. They come in limited editions and one-of-a-kinds.

Shows: West Coast

Stores: Golden Rule Bears, WA

Waiting list: 8-12 weeks

Catalog/Photos: $3, refundable with purchase

Mail order: 8-12 weeks

Accepts: check, money order, Visa, MasterCard

Has been making bears for 7 years

Awards: Lincoln City, 1st, 1994; 1st, 1993; 2nd, 1992; TBBNC, 1st, 1993; 1st, 2nd, 3rd, 1994

JOHN RENPENNING

Johnny Bears

1904 20th Ave. NW

Calgary, Alberta T2M 1H5, Canada

Phone: 403-282-4770

Phone orders: M-Sat, 10A.M.-6P.M. Sun, noon-5P.M.

Fax: 403-282-9234

Fax orders accepted.

Price range: $200-$400

Size range: 12″-19″

Johnny Bears are very hard stuffed character bears. They have a bronze head on the upper part of the left arm.

Stores: 2 Bears Teddy Bears, Calgary, Alberta

Catalog/Photos: free

Mail order: 2 weeks

Accepts: check, money order, Visa, MasterCard, American Express

Has been making bears for 3 years

Awards: Calgary Stampede, 2nd, 1993; 3rd, 1994

Publications: TB&F, 1994

BETSY L. REUM
Bears-in-the-Gruff
1303 Moores River Dr.
Lansing, MI 48910-1250
Phone: 517-482-9511
Phone orders: 9 A.M.-5 P.M.
Price range: $50-$400
Size range: 5"-22"
Bears-in-the-Gruff bears feature quality workmanship and great faces. Betsy spends a great deal of time working on the noses. They are embroidered with shaped nostrils. Creative costuming and character development make Betsy's bears truly unique.
Waiting list: 6-8 weeks
Home Appointments: 1 week
Shows: Midwest; Baltimore; Seattle; San Diego; Philadelphia; UK
Catalog/Photos: photos must be returned
Mail order: 6-8 weeks
Accepts: check, money order
Has been making bears for 10 years
Publications: TBR; Complete Book of Teddy Bear Artists; Teddy Bear Artists Annual; Teddy Bears; Tribute to Teddy Bear Artists

DOLORES RIBORDY
The Bears Cottage
1129 W. 22nd St.
Casper, WY 82604
Phone: 307-266-3857
Phone orders: all week, days and evenings
Price range: $50-$200
Size range: 3½"-16"
Ribearys, Dolores's bears, are made mostly from mohair and have glass eyes and embroidered noses. They are fully jointed and stuffed with fiberfill or pellets. Each bear comes with a certificate and a short story about the bear. Dolores uses suede or Ultrasuede on all bears, and the corners of their mouths are tilted up and are for-

ever happy. She does some dressed bears, but most are bare. Occasionally she will paint around their eyes, muzzles or noses. They are completely made by Dolores.
Waiting list: 6 months-1 year
Home Appointments: 2 days
Stores: Marj's Doll Sanctuary, Grand Rapids, MI; Mostly Bears, Arvada, CO; Nicolaysen Art Museum Gift Shop, Casper, WY; Dear Prudence, Tokyo, Japan; Moore Bears, Strasburg, PA; The Teddy Bear Den, Las Vegas; Groves Quality Collectibles, Bluffton, OH; Past & Present Antiques, Mission, KS; Why Knot Inn, Algonac, MI; Mary D's Dolls & Bears & Such, Minneapolis; Bearing Gifts, Anaheim, CA; Meadowlark Gallery, Douglas, WY; B & J Collectibles, Drumright, OK
Catalog/Photos: color photos, $4, catalog, $1, refundable with purchase
Mail order: 3 months or more
Accepts: check, money order, Visa, MasterCard, layaway
Has been making bears for 6 years
Awards: National Artist of the Year, 2nd, 3rd, 1989; Teddy Tribune Convention, 1st, 1990, two 3rds, 1989; two 2nds, 1991
Publications: Teddy Tribune, article, 1991; Moore Bears Collectible Catalog, 1993; local newspapers, 1988-1989; TBR, 1993

EDITH MARIE RICHMOND
6044 Dixon
Toledo, OH 43613
Phone: 419-475-7267
Phone orders: 6 A.M.-11 P.M.
Price range: less than $35-$150
Size range: 2"-16"
Edith's bears come in a variety of materials, but all are jointed and have glass eyes and Ultrasuede pads. Some have hand-knitted sweaters or clothes sewn

by Edith, but most wear only ribbons or other neckwear. Edith loves to try new fabrics that others might find strange.
Home Appointments: 2-3 days
Stores: Teddy Bear Depot, Toledo, OH
Photos: $.50 or 3/$1.00
Mail order: 1-2 weeks
Accepts: check, money order
Has been making bears for 11 years
Awards: Teddy Bear Fair, 2nd place, 1991; County fair, Reading, PA, 3 blue ribbons, 1992

LANA RICKABAUGH
Warm Fuzzies
218 N. Main
Maryville, MO 64468
Phone: 816-582-2609
Phone orders: M-F, 10 A.M.-5 P.M. Sat, 10 A.M.-4 P.M.
Price range: $35-$150
Size range: 1¾"-4"
Warm Fuzzies are Lana's own original patterns. Many are small limited editions or one-of-a-kinds. She believes in reasonable prices. She wants her bears to look at you with a soulful expression that says "Love Me."
Shows: Midwest
Stores: The Teddy Bear Den, Las Vegas; Bears In The Attic, Reistertown, MD; Beary Special Friends, Decatur, IN; Keepsake Dolls & Bears, Abingdon, MD
Waiting list: 1 month
Photos: $3, refundable with purchase
Mail order: 2-4 weeks
Accepts: check, money order
Has been making bears for 3 years

DORIS HOPPE RIGGS
Beguiling Bears
1989 Byram Dr.
Clearwater, FL 34615
Phone: 813-446-8094

Phone orders: noon-9P.M.
Price range: $300-$350
Size range: 8"-26"
Beguiling Bears are made of mohair, German plush and sometimes fun fur. Her bears will almost always be wearing a hat. If not, they will have a large 1930s style bow.
Shows: CT, PA, FL
Stores: J&L Collectibles, Tampa, FL; The Hen Nest, Seminole, FL; Casey's Bear Factory, Fairport, NY
Photos available.
Accepts: check
Has been making bears for 6 years
Publications: TB&F, 1994
One of Doris's bears was chosen to appear on the cover of this book.

CELIA M. ROBERTS
CMR Huggables LTD.
201 Arnett Dr.
P.O. Box 248
Pitsburg, OH 45358
Phone: 513-692-6122
Phone orders: 9A.M.-9P.M.
Fax: 513-692-6122
 Fax orders accepted.
Price range: $35-$200
Size range: 7½"-25"
CMR Huggables Ltd. bears are fully jointed. All have round ultra-leather noses that are padded and handsewn and Ultrasuede paws. Celia makes mohair and plush bears. A special bear she makes is a bald grandfather.
Home Appointments: 1 week
Shows: FL, GA, KY, MD, MI, OH, PA, IN, WI
Stores: Our Collection, Centerville, OH; Country Originals, Englewood, OH; Crispin's Bears, Andover, MA; Gooseberry Farm, West Carollton, OH; Hobbs House of Dolls, Marietta, GA; Ken & Elaine's Dolls, Centerville, OH; Roy R Eve Land, Peachtree City, GA
Catalog/Photos: free brochure
Mail order: 4 weeks
Accepts: check, money order, Visa, MasterCard
Has been making bears for 4 years
Publications: TB&F, TBR

WENDY LYNN ROBINSON
Bears by Wendy Robinson
14286 Felty Pl.
Dale City, VA 22193
Phone: 703-680-5027
Phone orders: 11A.M.-9P.M.
Price range: $100-$250
Size range: 12"-27"
Wendy's bears have a "cute" look with a perfectly embroidered nose and mouth, even eyes, and just the right size ears. Her bears are also well stuffed, and most people are surprised by the weight when they lift one.
Stores: The Rocking Horse Gallery, Fredericksburg, VA
Catalog/Photos: $3, refundable with purchase
Mail order: 3-6 weeks
Accepts: check, money order
Has been making bears for 2 years

EVA MAY ROETTGER
Bearly Eva's Den
32 Forest Ave.
Southbridge, MA 01550-2416
Phone: 508-764-2665
Phone orders: 9A.M.-9P.M.
Price range: $35-$300
Size range: 2"-36"
Bearly Eva's Den bears are completely designed and handmade by Eva. Most of her bears are made of mohair, but she also uses plush or vintage fabrics.

They are completely jointed, and some are one-of-a-kind.
Shows: ME, MA, CT
Stores: League of American Crafters, Sturbridge, MA; Porter Emporium, Porter, ME
Waiting list: 1 month
Catalog/Photos: $2, refundable with purchase
Mail order: 4 weeks
Accepts: check, money order, Visa, MasterCard
Has been making bears for 11 years
Awards: Woodstock fair, blue ribbons
Publications: TB&F; TBR; Inside Worcester

SAYURI SAKI ROMERHAUS
Romerhaus Bears
951 S. Alvord Blvd.
Evansville, IN 47714
Phone: 812-473-7277
Phone orders: anytime
Price range: $150-more than $450
Size range: 1"-14"
Romerhaus Bears have gained international recognition for Saki's unique designs and whimsical approach. Saki creates each bear entirely with no outside help. The Romerhaus bears live in the ninteenth century in a rural community designed by Saki and her husband, Richard. They are designed to wear nineteenth century "genteel country" clothing which Saki makes from real nineteenth century fabrics and laces. Saki concentrates on her miniature designs, and there are always new characters in the community. Saki's Sayuri GartenBaer Collection includes miniature bears with delicate wings.
Waiting list: 4-6 weeks
Home Appointments: 2 days
Catalog/Photos: $10 USA; $12.50 foreign
Mail order: 2-3 weeks

Accepts: check, money order, Visa, MasterCard

Awards: ABC Schaumburg convention, 1st; Del Mar, CA show, Best of Show; 3rd Award Miniatures, Baltimore; Golden Teddy Award, 1991

Publications: 1986 Bialosky & Friends Teddy Bear Calendar; The Complete Book of Teddy Bears; Teddy Bear Artists Annual; TB&F; TBR; Toy-Box; German, Dutch and Japanese periodicals; calendar and greeting cards by Silvervisions; A Tribute to Teddy Bear Artists

KIMBERLY RUFF
Bears 'N Blossoms
2927 Fairview Ln.
American Falls, ID 83211
Phone: 208-226-2634
Phone orders: 8 A.M.-9 P.M.
Price range: $100-$400
Size range: 8½"-26"

Bears 'N Blossoms bears are made of German mohair and have glass eyes and wool felt paws. They are fully jointed and pellet and fiberfilled. They have adorable, sweet baby faces. Kimberly usually decorates them with vintage laces, French and silk ribbons and beautiful one-of-a-kind hats.

Waiting list: 2-6 months
Home Appointments: 1 day
Shows: ID, UT, CA
Stores: International House, Orland Park, IL; The Rocking Horse Gallery, Fredericksburg, VA; The Bear-ee Patch, San Diego; Bears Everywhere
Catalog/Photos: $6, refundable with purchase.
Mail order available.
Accepts: check, money order, Visa, MasterCard
Has been making bears for 5 years

SANDRA M. RUSSELL
SMR Bears
12000 W. 99th Terrace
Lenexa, KS 66215
Phone: 913-888-2177
Phone orders: anytime
Price range: less than $35-$100
Size range: 3"-28"

SMR Bears are usually under 6". These miniature and small bears are all handstitched. Sandi's larger bears are made of recycled fur coats, and many

of them are also handstitched. Some newer bears are made out of mohair. All are made from her own designs and patterns. They are string and disc jointed, center seam and gusset designs. She uses Poly-Fil, pellets and steel shot for stuffing. Her faces are what draw people to her bears. Each bear is one-of-a-kind with its own personality.

Waiting list: 4-6 weeks
Home Appointments: 1 week
Shows: KS, OK, MO
Stores: Dolls, Bears & Funny Hares, Mission, KS
Catalog/Photos: none
Mail order: 4-6 weeks
Accepts: check, money order
Has been making bears for 3 years

NANCY RYGG
Nancy Rygg Originals
8217-8th Ave. N.
Seattle, WA 98115
Phone: 206-522-4145
Phone orders: M-F, after 6 P.M.; Sat-Sun, all day
Price range: $100-$250
Size range: 12"-24"

Nancy Rygg Originals are fully jointed and made of mohair and alpaca. Most are pellet stuffed, because her customers like how they feel, and are more posable that way. She often uses heirloom dresses, bibs, fabrics and laces, so many of her bears are one-of-a-kind pieces.

Waiting list: 1-2 months
Home Appointments: 1 week
Shows: Seattle
Stores: Bear Hugs, Coeur d'Alene, ID; Vicki's Gifts & Collectibles, Woodland Hills, CA; 2 Bears Teddy Bears, Calgary, Alberta; Undeniable Treasures, Renton, WA; Teddy Bear Den, Las Vegas; MBR Bears, Staten Island,

NY Catalog/Photos available.
Mail order: approximately 1 month
Accepts: check, money order
Has been making bears for 7 years
Awards: Golden Teddy Awards, 1990, 1991; invitation to 1st Disneyland Bear Show

BONNIE SAUERWINE
Bonnie Bears
206 N. Robinson Ave.
Pen Argyl, PA 18072
Phone: 610-863-5207
Phone orders: 8 A.M.-8 P.M.
Price range: $50-$250
Size range: 6"-30"

Bonnie Bears are lovingly created and made of the highest quality fabrics. Most are made of mohair or alpaca, are fully jointed and have glass or antique shoe button eyes. They come in one-of-a-kind or very limited editions. All bears are made entirely by Bonnie.

Waiting list: 6-8 weeks
Home Appointments: 1 week
Shows: Timmonium, MD
Catalog/Photos: $1 per photo
Mail order: 8 weeks
Accepts: check, money order, Visa, MasterCard
Has been making bears for 6 years

M. REGINA SAUNDERS
Quite A Bear Company
4010 Hancock Cir.
Atlanta, GA 30340-4242
Phone: 404-270-1026
Phone orders accepted.
Fax: 404-270-1154
Fax orders accepted.
Price range: $40-$220
Size range: 12"-17"

Quite A Bear Company is a partnership among three bear artists who make bears out of real mink or fur. The bears are stuffed with Poly-Fil and have jointed heads, arms and legs. A twenty piece pattern is used to make each bear, and each is individually made. All have pig skin pads and are artist-signed and dated. The company also makes special-order bears from heirloom furs.

Catalog/Photos: $2, refundable with purchase

Stores: Swan Coach House, Atlanta, GA; stores across the country and in Japan and Germany

Accepts: check, money order, Visa, MasterCard, Discover, American Express, COD

Has been making bears for 4 years

Publications: CNN's Real News for Kids

KAREN R. SAWIN

Wondersmith
130 Fig Tree Lane, #2a
Martinez, CA 94553-6503
Phone: 510-370-8198
Phone orders: anytime
Fax: 510-370-8198
Fax orders accepted.
Price range: $50-more than $450
Size range: 1¾" and up
Wondersmith bears come in all shapes and sizes. Karen's pellet-filled bears with "sleepy" eyes are very popular. She has a Santa series of one-of-a-kind 18" bears, complete with clothing and Christmas accessories. Her Mardi Gras and Mardi Gras junior bears are 19" and 12" bears with inset Ultrasuede faces, each completed with a one-of-a-kind, handpainted free design. All her bears and other creatures are created with a touch of whimsy.

Waiting list: 4-5 weeks

Home Appointments: 1 week

Shows: Northwest, Midwest

Stores: Marilyn's World, Lauderhill, FL; Bears & Baubles, Berkeley, CA; Bears In The Wood, Los Gatos, CA; Teddy Bears of Witney, Oxfordshire, UK; Parlor Bears, Lincoln City, OR; Bear Street, Claremont, CA

Photos: free

Mail order: 4-5 weeks

Accepts: check, money order

Has been making bears for 15 years

Awards: TBBNC, 1st, 1994

Publications: TBR, 1993, 1995; TB&F, 1993, 1994

PEGGY LYNN SCALE

P. Bear & Company
2264 N. 62nd St.
Wauwatosa, WI 53213
Phone: 414-258-5331
Phone orders: M, W, F evenings
Price range: $50-$200
Size range: 9"-18"
P. Bear and Company bears are original designs. As soon as Peggy positions the eyes, her bears seem to come to life, and she cannot stop until they are finished. She uses a small room in the attic of her old house as a factory. She feels that the reward of a customer's smile is the best part of making bears.

Waiting list: 4-6 weeks

Home Appointments: 2 weeks

Shows: IL, WI

Accepts: check, money order

Has been making bears for 5 years

Publications: TBR

JOANNE M. SCHALK

Bears and Bearwear by Jo
7312 Davis St.
Morton Grove, IL 60053-1703
Phone: 708-470-1956
Phone orders: 9A.M.-10P.M.
Price range: $35-$200
Size range: 7"-24"
Bears by Jo are fully jointed mohair and synthetic bears with glass or safety eyes. They are fiber-filled and/or pellet stuffed. Some have clothes and/or accessories. Special feature bears include tan line cubs—bears in swim suits with lighter fur under them, complete with beach accessories. Tie-dye Teds are hippie bears with white or dyed fur and tie dyed paws and T-shirts. Mardi Gras bears are purple mohair bears with purple, gold and green trimmed vests and masks, carrying and wearing beads and doubloons. Flora-Victorias are various colored mohair bears with matching floral print paws and ruffle collar. Joanne also makes bear clothes.

Home Appointments: 1 week

Shows: IL, MN, WI, MI, IA, MS, KS

Stores: Teddy Tribune Warehouse, St. Paul, MN; The Parking Lot, Inc., Evanston, IL

Catalog/Photos: SASE

Mail order: varies

Accepts: check, money order

Has been making bears for 12 years

Awards: Teddy Tribune awards

Publications: Teddy Tribune Magazine; TBR

CHERYL SCHMIDT

It Bears Repeating
11343-123 S.
Edmonton, Alberta T5M 0G1, Canada
Phone: 403-452-0065
Phone orders: 9A.M.-4P.M.
Price range: $50-$300
Size range: 6"-20"
It Bears Repeating bears are one-of-a-kind, nontraditional bears. Cheryl will use any materials that say "bear" to her! She uses a lot of soft sculpture techniques, and her bears have long, thin legs. They look like fuzzy people. They are fully jointed with glass eyes. She sometimes accessorizes them, but rarely costumes them.

Waiting list: 8 weeks

Home Appointments: varies

Shows: East and West Canada; Northwest US

Accepts: check, money order

Has been making bears for 4 years

Awards: Bear Fair, 1st, 1993; 1st, Best of Show, 1994; Klondike Day Arts and Crafts, 1st, 1994

ERIKA SCHROEDER

Mutti Bears
HCO-1, Box 167
Hudson, NY 12534
Phone: 518-828-6390
Phone orders: anytime
Price range: $50-$250
Size range: 7"-22"
Mutti Bears are made entirely of recycled real fur garments. Erica uses leather or suede for paw pads, leather noses and glass eyes. All are fully jointed.

Waiting list: 6-8 weeks

Home appointments available.

Shows: Northeast

Catalog/Photos: free

Mail order: immediate. Special orders take 2-3 months.

Accepts: check, money order

Has been making bears for 7 years

SHEILA DARLENE SCHUCHERT

S.S. Sugar Bears
P.O. Box 2179
Brandon, FL 33510

Phone: 813-681-6662
Phone orders: 10 A.M.-6 P.M.
Price range: $50-$300
Size range: 8"-11", 16"-21"

S.S. Sugar Bears are made of imported mohair and are fully jointed. They have glass eyes, Ultrasuede pads and are stuffed with Poly-Fil and pellets or pellets only. One unique feature of Sheila's 16" and 21" bears are their knobby knees. All of her bears have tails. She makes both dressed and undressed bears, and most are limited editions.

Shows: FL, VA, IL, KS, GA, PA, MI, MD
Stores: The Hen Nest, Seminole, FL; Village Bears & Collectibles, Sarasota, FL; My Friends & Me, Leesburg, VA; The Rocking Horse Gallery, Fredericksburg, VA; Justin Tyme's, Ft. Myers, FL; Fantastic Balloons & Bears, Charlottesville, VA
Accepts: check
Has been making bears for 3 years
Awards: People's Choice, 1st
Publications: TB&F, TBR

WILMA IRENE SCHUMACHER

Willy Bears
38 Flagstaff Close
Red Deer, Alberta T4N 6V1, Canada
Phone: 403-343-6438
Phone orders: 9 A.M.-9 P.M.
Fax: 403-885-5120
Fax orders accepted.
Price range: $35-$250
Size range: 3½"-36"

Willy Bears are made of German and English mohair and synthetics, with Ultrasuede or leather paw pads. They are fully jointed and stuffed with Poly-Fil or pellets. Some have steel shot pellets. Wilma gives each bear its own character and personality. They have shoe button glass eyes and hand-embroidered noses and mouths. She has specially designed bears for some customers.

Shows: Calgary, Edmonton, Red Deer
Stores: Hug-a-Bear Express, Edmonton, Alberta; Hug-a-Bear Express, Red Deer, Alberta
Mail order: 2-3 weeks
Accepts: money order
Has been making bears for 6 years

STEVE SCHUTT

Bear-"S"-Ence
201 First Ave. NW
Clarion, IA 50525
Price range: $150-more than $450
Size range: 3"-40"

Bear-"S"-Ence bears are original designs by Steve. They are constructed with fine materials, some of antique or vintage origin. Each bear is marked on the back of the head with a brass rivet with his logo. Bears feature horizontal, thin embroidered noses— Steve's trademark.

Shows: FL, CA, IA
Stores: My Friends & Me, Leesburg, VA; Honey Bee Bear Shoppe, East Bridgewater, MA; J & L Collectibles, Tampa, FL; White Fox, Clarion, IA
Waiting list: 6 months or more
Accepts: check, Visa, MasterCard
Design manufactured by Bearly There
Has been making bears for 15 years
Awards: ATBAG Artist Choice, Golden Teddy and Toby nominations, Numerous Blue ribbons at regional shows across the USA and abroad
Publications: Better Homes and Gardens Special Interest Publication, Country Living, Country Home, TBR, TB&F, Teddy Bear Times, Linda Mullins books, Gerry Giley books, Ted Menten books, Hoyle cards and calendars; HH Press books

KAREN SEARL

Karen's Treasures
86 W. Main St.
Georgetown, MA 01833
Phone: 508-352-6664
Phone orders: 9 A.M.-8 P.M.
Price range: $50-$400
Size range: 5"-29"

Karen's Treasures are designed and crafted by Karen. They are made of German or English mohair, alpaca or synthetics. They are fully jointed with Ultrasuede paws and are signed and dated. Some are limited editions. They are filled with pellets, Dacron or excelsior. Most are chubby, with sweet smiles.

Home Appointments: 2 weeks
Shows: Eastern states
Stores: FairyTales, Lombard, IL; Basically Bears, Stratham, NH; All Things

Bright & Beautiful, Waitsfield, VT; Country Bear, Carmel, ME
Catalog/Photos: free
Mail order: 1 month
Accepts: check, money order, Visa, MasterCard
Has been making bears for 9 years
Publications: TBR; newspapers

WILLIAM C. SESSIONS

Jingle Bell Bears
3605 Columbine Dr.
Modesto, CA 95356
Phone: 209-529-0513
Phone orders: 8 A.M.-10 P.M.
Price range: $50-$250
Size range: 10"-28"

Jingle Bell Bears are made of the finest quality imported German and/or English mohair and/or plush synthetic. They have German glass blown eyes and suede leather paw pads, and are stuffed with Poly-Fil and/or pellets. Their arms, legs and head are jointed. All designs are originals by William. They have handsewn faces and claws. Each bear wears a jingle bell, and the left rear foot is signed "J.B. Bear."

Waiting list: 2-3 months
Home appointments available
Shows: CA, OR, WA
Stores: Past & Present, Vacaville, CA; Twiggs, Carmel, CA; The Bear Necessities, Solvang, CA; Hugging Bear Inn & Shoppe, Chester, VT
Photos: at cost, refundable with purchase
Mail order: 60-90 days
Accepts: check, money order
Has been making bears for 6 years
Awards: TBBNC, 3rd, 1994

MYRNA & BERT SEVA

A Bear to Remember
P.O. Box 823
Murray Hill Station
New York, NY 10016
Phone: 212-779-2257
Phone orders: M-Sat, 9 A.M.-5 P.M.
Price range: $50-$400
Size range: 2"-30"

A Bear To Remember bears are mostly one-of-a-kind or very limited, numbered editions. Myrna and Bert are also open to requests for commissioned work. All their bears are personally designed and made. They come in both mohair and plush, dressed and undressed.

Shows: NY, MA, ND, PA, CT
Mail order: 3-4 weeks
Accepts: check, money order
Has been making bears for 4 years
Publications: TBR

KRISTINA SHANKEL

Paw Prints
851 S. Frost
Saginaw, MI 48603-6029
Phone: 517-793-5256
Price range: less than $35-$100
Size range: 4"-18"

Paw Prints bears come in a variety of shapes and colors, but there are some common features. All are fully jointed, polyester stuffed and have cheerful expressions. Unique features include the open mouth creations. The mouth can be pushed up to create a closed mouth look if desired. Many of Kristina's creations have padded wires in their limbs, tails, ears and/or wings for endless posing possibilities.

Shows: MI
Catalog/Photos: photos $1; complete color brochure, $3, refundable with purchase
Mail order: 2-4 weeks
Accepts: check, money order
Has been making bears for 10 years

DENIS R. SHAW

Denis's Den
P.O. Drawer A
LaHonda, CA 94020
Phone: 415-747-0549
Phone orders: anytime
Price range: $50-more than $450
Size range: 7"-18", 36"-84"

Denis's Den bears are real-looking bears on all fours, jointed and unjointed. They have unique face joints (behind the ears) called "Quizzy Face joints."

Some have double-jointed necks. Denis also makes more traditional bears. He has more than 230 designs. His Bedi-Terres bears are multi-colored bears from another planet with wings.

Home Appointments: 1 day
Shows: CA, FL, IL, OR, CO
Stores: The Honey Bee Bear Shoppe, East Bridgewater, MA; Gregg Alexander's Gifts, Kennebunkport, ME; Campbell's Collectibles, Crown Point, IN
Catalog/Photos: $3, refundable with purchase
Mail order: 3 months
Accepts: check, money order
Has been making bears for 10 years
Awards: California State Fair, 1st, 1987; 1st, 1988; Brenda Dewey's Show, Best in Show, 1992; TBBNC, Best in Show, 1993; 2nd, 1994
Publications: The Complete Book of Teddy Bears; Bearland; Tribute to Teddy Bear Artists; Teddy Bear Artist Annual; Teddy Bears (Grey); Contemporary Teddy Bear Price Guide; Beer Bericht; TBR; TB&F; Teddy Bear Times; Bear Tracks; Antiques & Collections

LINDA SHEPARD

Huggables by Lindy
7833 Valley Flores Dr.
West Hills, CA 91304
Phone: 818-704-0981
Phone orders: 9A.M.-9P.M.
Price range: $50-$350
Size range: 10"-32"

Huggables by Lindy are fully jointed mohair or alpaca bears. They are designed by Linda.

Home Appointments: 1 week
Shows: CA, Midwest
Stores: Theodore's Shoppe, Malibu, CA
Mail order: wait depends on stock
Accepts: check, money order, Visa, MasterCard
Has been making bears for 4 years

> THERE ARE NO SHORTCUTS FOR QUALITY BEARS. FROM DESIGN TO LAYOUT TO CUTTING, TIME AND PATIENCE ARE ESSENTIAL IN THE BEGINNING.
> — *John Renpenning, artist, Calgary, Alberta*

KATHLEEN M. SHEPPARD

Sheppard Seabear Sanctuary
3005 Bluff Blvd.
Holiday, FL 34691
Phone: 813-934-6349
Phone orders: M-F, after 4P.M., weekends
Price range: $50-more than $450
Size range: 3"-26"

Sheppard Seabear Sanctuary bears are traditional style mohair bears. All are jointed and have a noisemaker (squeaker, growler or music box). All feature a cross-stitched logo on their foot pad, and many have cross-stitching on their paw pads. Kathleen releases a special edition with a music box every Christmas.

Waiting list: 4-6 weeks
Home appointments available.
Shows: PA, NJ, FL
Stores: Moore Bears, Strasburg, PA; Teddy's, Hamilton Square, NJ; Bear Hugs, Marlton, NJ; Bears of Bruton Street, Wilson, NC; J & L Collectibles, Tampa, FL; The Hen Nest, Seminole, FL
Catalog/Photos: free
Mail order: 4-6 weeks
Accepts: check, money order
Has been making bears for 6 years
Awards: J & L Collectibles contest, 1st, 1991; 1st, 1992
Publications: TB&F

DIANE SHERMAN-TURBARG

Bear in the Woods
399 W. Pond Meadow Rd.
Westbrook, CT 06498
Phone: 203-399-6493
Phone orders: M-Sat, anytime
Price range: $300-$350
Size range: 1½"-26"

Bears in the Woods bears are made of new and old vintage fabrics. Diane makes her bears look like old, loved teddies, and enjoys reproducing old bears she has seen in articles.

Waiting list: 30 days
Home Appointments: 2 weeks
Shows: East Coast, West Coast, Chicago
Stores: Good Hearted Bear, Mystic, CT; Pat's Kountry Kollectibles, Old Saybrook, CT; Bearly & More Toys, East Amherst, NY; Hugging Bear Inn and Shoppe, Chester, VT; Owl's Nest, Carmel, CA; Christy's, Buckingham, PA
Catalog/Photos: $1 per photo
Mail order: 30 days
Accepts: check, money order, Visa, MasterCard
Has been making bears for 16 years
Awards: Several show awards.
Publications: TBR, TB&F, The Artist Annual

NITA JEAN SHIELDS

Born Again Bears
1650 Emmaus Rd. NW
Palm Bay, FL 32907
Phone: 407-951-2207
Phone orders: anytime
Price range: $100-$150
Size range: 9"-20"
Born Again bears are handcrafted to the customer's specifications from recycled furs that they supply. They are fully jointed with hardboard disks and rivets, fully lined, and filled with polyester. They have embroidered noses, Ultrasuede paws, glass eyes and either a crocheted collar or a wired French ribbon bow.
Waiting list: 4-6 weeks
Home Appointments: 1 week
Shows: Northeast, Southeast
Catalog/Photos: free
Mail order: 4-6 weeks
Accepts: check, money order, Visa, MasterCard
Has been making bears for 14 years
Awards: Several 1st place show awards.
Publications: TBR, TB&F (ads)

KAREN SHIREY

Muffin Entrprises Inc.
429 S. 18th St.
Camp Hill, PA 17011
Phone: 800-338-9041
Phone orders: 8 A.M.-5 P.M.
Fax: 717-761-7883
Fax orders accepted.

Price range: less than $35
Size range: 17"
Karen's patented bears, Sir Koff-A-Lot and Kiddie Kub, are designed to serve as post-op pillows for patients doing respiratory therapy following surgery. Their firm, flat, seamless backs serve as splints for incisions made in open heart, theracic or abdominal surgery. They also are a source of comfort for patients who are feeling frightened and vulnerable after surgery.
Shows: continental USA, Europe
Catalog/Photos: free
Mail order: 1 week
Accepts: check, money order, Visa, MasterCard
Design manufactured by Bantam Collections
Has been making bears for 11 years
Publications: TB&F; TBR; Bear Tracks

BARBARA IRWIN SHYNKARYK

B. Irwin Bears
6811 Cairns Ct.
Richmond, British Columbia V7C 5L6, Canada
Phone: 604-275-9096
Phone orders: anytime
Price range: $50-$350
Size range: 6"-32"
B. Irwin Bears are primarily made from German mohair, but Barbara also uses imported synthetics. They are completely jointed with glass eyes, except for bears made for children, which have safety eyes and joints. Her bears resemble the older traditional style. She often dresses them in vintage clothes or clothes made with antique lace embellishments.
Waiting list: 2 months
Home Appointments: 1 day
Shows: Western Canada
Catalog/Photos: $5, refundable with purchase
Mail order: 2 months
Accepts: check, money order
Has been making bears for 13 years
Publications: Victorian Harvester

MARCIA SIBOL

Bar Harbor Bears
P.O. Box 498
Bear, DE 19701
Phone: 302-368-0012
Phone orders: 10 A.M.-8 P.M.

Fax: 302-368-0012
Fax orders accepted.
Price range: $150-more than $450
Size range: 6½"-63"
Bar Harbor Bears are handcrafted, fully jointed mohair bears. Marcia does all the work herself. Some are costumed in vintage clothing and some wear original clothing made by Marcia.
Waiting list: 3-6 months
Shows: CA, MD, NJ
Catalog/Photos: $5
Mail order: 3-6 months
Accepts: check, Visa, MasterCard
Has been making bears for 12 years
Awards: Golden Teddy, 1sts at various bear shows
Publications: Bearland; Teddy Bear Lover's Companion; Teddy Bears; Artist's Annual; Complete Book of Teddy Bears

DONNA RUTH SIMPSON

Cedar Hollow Creations
13716 2nd Ave.
Tacoma, WA 98444
Phone: 206-536-BEAR
Phone orders: 8 A.M.-9 P.M.
Price range: $35-$200
Size range: 4"-24"
Cedar Hollow Creations come to life through the special creative talents and imagination of Donna. Only the best imported furs are used, as well as Ultrasuede, felted wool, brocades or other fine fabrics. All bears 4" and smaller are completely handstitched. The larger bears have some machine stitching. Most are limited editions of 5; others are one-of-a-kind.
Home Appointments: 1 week
Shows: West Coast
Catalog/Photos: $2.50, refundable with purchase, unless photo is not returned.
Accepts: check, money order
Has been making bears for 3 years

> As a bear artist, I believe that if you believe in your work, other people will, too. Don't just make the "in" thing. If you believe in magic, you can create it.
> — *Kelly Dauterman, artist, Colorado Springs, CO*

BARBARA SIXBY
Zucker Bears
3965 Duke Ct.
Livermore, CA 94550
Phone: 510-373-0720
Phone orders: 8 A.M.-6 P.M.
Fax: 510-373-0720
Fax orders accepted.
Price range: $80-more than $450
Size range: 3"-30"
Zucker Bears are known for their large noses, close set eyes and impish grins. Barbara has a wide variety of sizes and styles. She makes traditional, caricature and old-time teddys. Her Old Time Teddies resemble antique bears that have had years of loving. She also produces a line of yes/no bears, that say no when their tails are moved from side to side and yes when their tails are moved up and down.
Home appointments available.
Shows: across USA
Stores: Niles Antiques, Fremont, CA, and many more. Write or call for complete list.
Catalog/Photos: $3 and LSASE
Mail order: 4-6 weeks
Accepts: check, money order, Visa, MasterCard
Has been making bears for 13 years
Publications: Tribute to Teddy Bear Artists; TBR; TB&F; Official Price Guide to Antique and Modern Teddy Bears; Teddy Bear Lovers Catalog; Teddy Bear Lover's Companion

SHERIDAN SKINNER
Sher Bears, Inc.
19630 Blue Clover Ln.
Monument, CO 80132
Phone: 719-481-4260
Phone orders: 8 A.M.-9 P.M.
Fax: 719-632-7266
Fax orders accepted.
Price range: $50-more than $450

Size range: 8"-24"
Sher Bears are one-of-a-kind mohair bears that come in many different styles. Some are very zany characters who definitely have an attitude. Sheridan also makes Teddy Bearskin rugs and mohair and Ultrasuede bear purses.
Home Appointments: 1 day
Shows: CO, West, Northwest
Catalog/Photos: $5, refundable with purchase
Mail order: 1-6 weeks
Accepts: check, Visa, MasterCard
Has been making bears for 5 years
Awards: ILTBC, chairman's choice award, 1994

FREDERICK M. SLAYTER
3020 N. Federal Hwy., Suite 10
Ft. Lauderdale, FL 33306
Phone: 305-563-5353
Phone orders: 8:30 A.M.-2 P.M.
Price range: $250-more than $450
Size range: 10"-24"
The Paisley Bears include signature bears, made from 175- to 300-year-old hand-woven paisley. Frederick also makes character bears out of mohair. They are usually one-of-a-kind. His character sculptures are mohair with wire armature. They are fully costumed. He also has some regular mohair bears.
Shows: FL, CA, WA, TX, IL
Waiting list: 2 weeks
Catalog/Photos: free
Accepts: check
Has been making bears for 15 years
Awards: regional, national and international awards
Publications: Tribute to Teddy Bear Artists; Complete Book of Teddy Bear Artists

JONAN SNEERINGER
Remnant Bears & Furry Friends
1812 Mesa Ave.
Eureka, CA 95503-6828
Phone: 707-444-3590
Phone orders: 9 A.M.-8 P.M.
Price range: $50-more than $450
Size range: 7"-28"
Remnant Bears are quality-made whimsical bears. Jonan uses mohair, alpaca or pendleton wool. Each bear is original, demonstrating the love Jonan has for the craft.
Home Appointments: 1 day
Shows: CA, TX, IL
Stores: Creative Touch, Ferndale, CA; Old Town Crafters, Eureka, CA
Catalog/Photos: $4
Mail order: 1 month to 150% months
Accepts: check, money order, Visa, MasterCard
Has been making bears for 11 years
Awards: Humboldt Co. Fair, 1st, 4th; Quota Club Doll Show, 1st; 4-Dolls Show, 2nd

LEEANN M. SNYDER
Busser Bears
320 S. Fourth St.
Upper Sandusky, OH 43351-1406
Phone: 419-294-4823
Phone orders: anytime
Fax: 419-294-3588
Fax orders accepted.
Price range: $50-more than $500

Size range: 11"-30"

Busser Bears are very whimsical and off the wall. They are what you would call real characters. All eyes are set farther back than usual. They have longer snouts than most bears and meticulously sewn noses. They are very smooth, and many people can't believe they are handsewn. The bears truly express Leann's unique sense of humor and her belief that there's not enough laughter in the world.

Home Appointments: 1-2 weeks

Shows: OH, MI, IN, IL, KY, PA, MA, FL, GA

Stores: Moore Bears, Strasburg, PA; Groves Quality Collectibles, Lima, OH; Toy Shoppe, Midlothian, VA; Teddy Bear Station, Uniontown, OH; Bears Everywhere, Fredericksburg, VA; Bears 'N More, Richmond, VA

Catalog/Photos: $5, refundable with purchase

Mail order: 2-3 weeks

Accepts: check, money order, Visa, MasterCard

Has been making bears for 3 years

MONTY & JOE SOURS

The Bear Lady
Route 1, Box 40
Golden City, MO 64748
Phone: 417-537-8340
Phone orders: anytime
Fax: 417-537-8340
Fax orders accepted.
Price range: $100-more than $450
Size range: 7¼"-25"

The Bear Lady bears are a distinct line of high-quality artist bears made of mohair plush. Most are free standing, with Monty & Joe's unique cast pewter weights in the feet. Monty & Joe's designs have the features of real bears while retaining the warmth of a teddy. They have created their own handspun

and handwoven mohair plush fabric. Each bear is created as an individual art piece and no two are entirely identical. Their bears are featured in numerous museums around the world.

Waiting list: up to 6 weeks

Home Appointments: 1 day

Shows: Major shows nationwide

Stores: Teddy Bears of Witney, Oxfordshire, UK; The Country Bear, Skipjack, PA; The Rocking Horse Gallery, Fredericksburg, VA; Bears of Bruton Street, Wilson, NC; Carrousel by Michaud, Chesaning, MI; The Bear Corner, Tyler, TX; Martin House Dolls & Toys, Thornhill, Ontario; Munchener Puppenstuben Zinnfiguren, Germany; Marj's Doll Sanctuary, Grand Rapids, MI; The Honey Bee Bear Shoppe, E. Bridgewater, MA; Bears In The Attic, Reistertown, MD; Justin Tymes, Ft. Myers, FL; Good Hearted Bears, Mystic, CT; Bears By The Bay, Fairhope, AL; The Toy Store, Toledo, OH; Ted E. Bear Shoppe, Naples, FL; Ken & Elaine's Dolls, Centerville, OH; Beary Special Friends, Decatur, IN; The Bears Cottage, Corpus Christi, TX; Cheryl's Toy Box, Oxford, NC

Catalog/Photos: $4, refundable with purchase

Mail order: 2 weeks

Accepts: check, money order, Visa, MasterCard

Has been making bears for 15 years

Awards: Golden Teddy Award, 1992

Publications: TBR; TB&F, articles and cover; Contemporary Teddy Bear Price Guide; Best of TB&F; Midwest Motorist; several newspaper articles

JAN ELAINE SPARKS

Rocky Bottom Creations
141 Rocky Bottom Rd.
Sunset, SC 29685-9729
Phone: 803-878-9773
Phone orders: 7 A.M.-7 P.M.
Fax: 803-878-9773
Fax orders accepted.
Price range: $35-$270
Size range: 9"-24"

Jan's Heart 'n' Sole bears are created in the style and feeling of bears from the first forty years of the century. They have an internal suede heart with a quote inside it, and they have recycled suede pads and soles (hence Heart and

Sole). They are fully jointed, and many of the materials used are recycled. Jan's bears are made from various materials, including mohair, wool, faux fur, upholstery fabric, tapestry, blankets, real fur, old coats and clothing and quilts.

Waiting list: 6-8 weeks

Home Appointments: 1 day

Shows: SC, NC, GA, VA, TN, MA

Catalog/Photos: $1, refundable with purchase

Mail order: 2-8 weeks

Accepts: check, Visa, MasterCard

Has been making bears for 4 years

Awards: Central Summer Festival, Best of Show; Historic Pendleton Festival, 1st; Williamston Spring Water Festival, Best of Division; Georgia Apple Festival, Best of Show

Publications: newspapers; The Sparkling Star

LINDA S. STAFFORD

Log Cabin Bears
12116 Redwood Hwy.
Wilderville, OR 97543
Phone: 503-474-0639
Phone orders: 9 A.M.-5 P.M.
Price range: $50-$300
Size range: 6"-24"

Log Cabin Bears are all original, copyrighted designs and are made of the finest materials, including mohair (regular, extra dense, two-toned, distressed and vintage), Marino, alpaca and rayon (one bear only). All are fully jointed and have imported glass or antique shoe button eyes. Noses, mouths and claws are embroidered using the finest German pearl cotton yarn. Snouts are carefully handtrimmed. Linda makes all bears entirely herself. They may have wool scarves, cotton bandannas or ties, fancy ribbons, little pinecones, tiny starched collars. All accessories are chosen carefully for the bear.

Shows: West Coast

Stores: Bear-a-Dise, Millburn, NJ; Toys & Treasures, Sarasota, FL; Village Bears & Collectibles, Sarasota, FL; Crescent Bear & Bath Boutique, Waunakee, WI; Teddy Bear Den, Las Vegas; Bears In The Attic, Reisterstown, MD

Waiting list: 4-6 weeks

Catalog/Photos: $3.50

Mail order: 1-3 weeks

Accepts: check, money order, international money order

Has been making bears for 11 years

Awards: Golden Teddy Award, 1988

Publications: Teddy Bear Artists' Annual, A Beary Merry Christmas, TBR (ads)

CONNIE STARK

Honey Bug Bears
18798 National Pike
Frostburg, MD 21532

Phone: 301-689-3722

Phone orders: anytime

Fax: 301-689-3722

Fax orders accepted.

Price range: $35-$150

Size range: 4"-20"

Honey Bug Bears are limited edition mohair bears with glass eyes and Ultrasuede paw pads. Connie designs and makes all the bears herself.

Waiting list: 3 weeks

Home Appointments: 1 week

Shows: MD, PA

Catalog/Photos: $2, refundable with purchase

Mail order: 3 weeks

Accepts: check, money order, Visa, MasterCard

Has been making bears for 11 years

VICKI STEPHAN

Raspbearies
418 Howard St.
Northboro, MA 01532

Phone: 508-393-7864

Phone orders: 8A.M.-9P.M.

Price range: $35-$400

Size range: 5"-25"

Raspbearies are usually contemporary in style. Vicki uses unique accessories. Her Raspbeary Preserves are bears in canning jars, and Mainley Bear sports

a rack of moose antlers, for instance. Her large and medium bears have lockline armature. Many designs can stand on all fours or sit in a doggy style pose. Some have armature in their necks for more flexible posing.

Waiting list: 2-10 weeks

Home Appointments: 1 day

Shows: New England

Stores: Christy's, Buckingham, PA; Casey's Bear Factory, Fairport, NY; Lil' David's Woodbox, Luray, VA

Catalog/Photos: $2, refundable with purchase

Mail order available.

Accepts: check, money order

Has been making bears for 11 years

CAROL STEWART

Carol Stewart's Miniature Teddy Bears, Inc.
903 NW Spruce Ridge
Stuart, FL 34994

Phone: 407-692-9067

Shows: Walt Disney World Teddy Bear Convention

Catalog/Photos: $3, refundable with purchase

Accepts: check, money order, Visa, MasterCard

Has been making bears for 12 years

DEBORAH L. STEWART

Stewart Studios
P.O. Box 555
Acton, MA 01720

Phone: 508-263-6799

Phone orders: 8A.M.-7P.M.

Price range: $50-$200

Size range: 7"-18"

Stewart Studios bears are made of domestic plush, German plush or mohair. Most are stuffed with pellets and/or Poly-Fil. Deborah gives them all either eyelids or eyebrows.

Shows: MA, NY, NJ, PA, CT, MD

Stores: Bear-In-Mind, Concord, MA; Bears Everywhere, Fredericksburg, VA; Shanah's, Smithtown, NY; Bear-A-Dise, Millburn, NJ; Gallery of Dolls, Northport, NY

Catalog/Photos: $5, refundable with purchase

Mail order: 4-6 weeks

Accepts: check, money order, Visa, MasterCard, COD

Has been making bears for 8 years

Publications: The Arctophile; TBR; Yankee Magazine

JACKIE STRECKER

Arbor Bears
5603 Frankenmuth Rd.
Vassar, MI 48768

Phone: 517-823-3155

Phone orders: anytime

Price range: $50-$200

Size range: 8"-15"

Arbor bears are fully jointed and made from various mohairs. All are original designs and all work is done by Jackie. Some bears have wire in their arms and legs for posing. Some have outfits made from material Jackie weaves herself.

Home Appointments: 1 week

Shows: Midwest, East

Stores: All Things Bright & Beautiful, Waitsfield, VT; Rosebud Toy Co. Shops, East Arlington, VT; Bear Leigh of Bearskin Neck, Rockport, MA; Nobody's Teddy, Wyandotte, MI; Bear Necessities, Saginaw, MI; The Village Peddlery, Oakland, ME

Catalog/Photos: $2, refundable with purchase

Mail order: 2 weeks

Accepts: check, money order

Has been making bears for 9 years

Publications: TB&F

STACEY NOELLE STUCKY

Tattered Ear Bear
123 Pasto Rico
Rancho
Santa Margarita, CA 92688

Phone: 714-589-9886

Phone orders: 9A.M.-9P.M.

Price range: $100-$150

Size range: 2½"-9"

Tattered Ear Bears are reminiscent of teddy bears popular in Germany in the early 1900s. Stacy's miniature bears are antique replicas made of mohair rather than the usual upholstery fabric. She tries to create expressive faces for all her bears. Most have curved arms, longer legs and cone-shaped snouts. They are fully jointed internally, even the 2½" size.

Waiting list: 3 months
Home Appointments: 1-2 weeks
Shows: CA, IL, MD
Stores: D 'N J Bears & Dolls, Huntington Beach, CA; Teddy Bears of Witney, Oxfordshire, UK; Growlies of Gloucester, Johnstone, Scotland; Out of the Woods, Modesto, CA
Catalog/Photos: $2, refundable with purchase
Mail order: 1 week
Accepts: check, money order, Visa Design manufactured by Gund
Has been making bears for 6 years
Awards: West Coast Crystal Teddy Bear Artist Award, 2nd; TBBNC, 2nd
Publications: TB&F, TBR, A Tribute to Teddy Bear Artists

DOROTHY GALEN STUHR
Heart Hugs
P.O. Box 1526
Alpine, CA 91903-1526
Phone: 619-445-1690
Phone orders: 7 days, 7A.M.-9P.M.
Price range: $50-$150
Size range: 3½"-36"
Heart Hugs Bears are made of the best materials available with careful attention to detail. Every bear is made completely by Dorothy from the design concept to the final stitch. Her goal is to create a teddy bear that speaks to a person's heart through the simplicity and empathy on its face. She also makes bears from felt she has made herself using raw wool and centuries-old methods. These bears are entirely

handstitched and fully jointed. Each bear is one-of-a-kind.
Stores: Beary Patch, San Diego
Waiting list: 4-8 weeks
Catalog/Photos: $2, refundable with purchase
Mail order: 4-8 weeks
Accepts: check, money order
Has been making bears for 5 years
Awards: Del Mar Fair, 1st, 2nd, special award, 1992; 2nd, 1994; Linda Mullins's West Coast Crystal Teddy Competition, 3rd, 1994
Publications: TBR, 1994; Alpine Sun Newspaper, 1994

BETTY SUE SUAREZ
Bears, Bears And Bears
524 N. 42nd W. Ave.
Tulsa, OK 74127
Price range: $50-$300
Size range: 2½"-24"
Bears, Bears And Bears are usually long-armed, humpbacked bears that look somewhat like bears of the 1930s. Betty likes to pair golliwogs with the larger bears. Most are bare, but some are dressed in 1930s-like rompers. Her miniatures are also mostly bare, but a few jesters and fairies are included every year.
Home Appointments: 1-2 weeks
Shows: Midwest and South
Stores: Cheri's Bear Essentials, Kansas City, MO; Stuff 'N Stuffed, Houston, TX; Bear Street; White Bear Antiques and Teddies, Tulsa
Mail order available.
Accepts: check, money order
Has been making bears for 17 years
Awards: Several 1st, 2nd and 3rd place awards at shows

LESLIE ANNE TAYLOR
Sleepy Hollow Bears
112 E. Jefferson Ave.
Danville, KY 40422
Phone: 606-236-1728
Phone orders: 9A.M.-6P.M.
Price range: $50-$300
Size range: 10"-36"
Sleepy Hollow Bears are fully jointed and made of mohair or plush and glass eyes. Her bears have embroidered noses. All are dressed in handmade clothing and custom designed handmade sweaters.

Waiting list: 2-3 weeks
Home Appointments: 2 days
Shows: Midwest, South Central, North Central
Catalog/Photos: $5, refundable with purchase
Mail order: 3-4 weeks
Accepts: check, Visa, MasterCard
Has been making bears for 6 years
Publications: TB&F

DARLENE TAYLOR
Originals by Darlene
20201 Rd. #236
Strathmore, CA 93267-9661
Phone: 209-568-1091
Phone orders: 10A.M.-6P.M.
Fax: 209-568-1291
Price range: $50-$450
Size range: 9"-36"
Originals by Darlene have great personalities and are dressed in original costumes or in the buff. Darlene's bears, both antique reproductions and original creations, are numbered and come with a certificate of ownership fit for framing.
Waiting list: 2-3 weeks
Home Appointments: 2 days
Shows: Pacific Coast, inland
Photos: $3, refundable with purchase
Mail order: 2-3 weeks
Accepts: check, money order
Has been making bears for 16 years
Awards: Tulore County Fair, twenty 1sts-2nds; California State Fair, five 1sts, Best of Class
Publications: children's newspaper, Tokyo, Japan; U.K. Teddy Bear Guide; TB&F

MARY L. THIELE
Mary T's Teddy Bears & Bunnies
496 N. McCarrons Blvd.
Roseville, MN 55113
Phone: 612-489-6491

Phone orders: 9 A.M.-5 P.M.
Price range: $35-$250
Size range: 6"-30"
Mary T's Teddy Bears are all fully jointed. They are made of mohair, old fur coats, old quilts and synthetics. Most of Mary's bears are one-of-a-kind or limited editions of up to 10.
Shows: Midwest
Stores: Keeping Room, White Bear Lake, MN; Honey House, Shoreview, MN; Country School House, Maple Plain, MN; Reindeer House, Minneapolis
Photos: $1
Mail order: 3-4 weeks
Accepts: check, money order
Has been making bears for 11 years
Publications: Teddy Bear Tribune; local newspaper

NORMA ELIZABETH THOMAS
Norma's Teddies
4886 Luther St.
Riverside, CA 92504
Phone: 909-683-3765
Phone orders: daytime
Price range: $35-$100
Size range: 1¾"-5"
Norma's Teddies come in many different styles. She makes holiday bears for Christmas, Halloween, Thanksgiving and St. Patrick's Day. She also makes a Bo Peep and a 3½" jester, among others, as well as some just plain bears. Some of her 5" bears are mohair. Her smaller bears are made of upholstery fur.
Waiting list: 2 weeks
Home Appointments: 1 week
Shows: West, mostly Southern CA
Stores: Terry's Teddy Bears, Oyster Bay, NY
Catalog/Photos: free photos
Mail order: 2-3 weeks
Accepts: check

Has been making bears for 4 years
Awards: ribbons at club meetings
Publications: TB&F, 1994

M. MICHELE THORP
Mossy Log Studio
36910 Edgehill Rd.
Springfield, OR 97478
Phone: 503-747-4812
Phone orders: 8 A.M.-9 P.M.
Price range: $50-more than $450
Size range: 3½"-30"
Mossy Log Studio bears have hand-painted paw pads, Ultrasuede or trimmed fur, set in muzzles, and traditional humps. Michele also gives them tails. They are all original patterns based on photographs of real bears.
Shows: OR, CA, WA, New England, CO, AZ, NY, IL
Stores: Bears & Dolls, Anchorage, AK; Parlor Bears, Lincoln City, OR
Waiting list: 3 months
Catalog/Photos: $6
Mail order available.
Accepts: check, money order
Has been making bears for 10 years
Publications: TB&F, cover and article, 1992; TBR, 1992, 1993

> TEDDY BEARS ARE OUR AMBASSADORS OF
> WHIMSY TO THE WORLD!
> — *Penny Crane French, artist, Trout Run, PA*

MARY A. TIMME
Timbears
2870 N. Range Ave.
Colby, KS 67701
Phone: 913-462-2782
Phone orders: anytime
Price range: $50-$350
Size range: 6"-24"
Timbears are all intelligent looking instead of dopey, victimized or too-sad-for-words. Mary makes everything except for a couple of hats. She is working toward one-of-a-kind bears. She has made a unique Rodeo Cowboy Series of bears.
Home Appointments: 1 hour-1 day
Shows: TX, FL, CA, CO, IL
Stores: Bear-A-Dise, Millburn, NJ; Marilyn's World, Lauderhill, FL; Antique Furnishings, Las Vegas; Busy B's Antiques, Corpus Christi, TX; MBR Bears, Staten Island, NY

Catalog/Photos: $6
Mail order: 6 weeks
Accepts: check, money order, Visa, MasterCard
Has been making bears for 5 years
Awards: Best of Show
Publications: TBR

SHARON M. TOMLINSON
The BearWorks
312-125 Bamburgh Cir.
Scarborough, Ontario M1W 3G4
Canada
Phone: 416-495-1516
Phone orders: anytime
Fax: 416-495-1217
Fax orders accepted.
Price range: $50-$300
The BearWorks bears are handcrafted, designed and created wholly by Sharon. She uses only the best materials, including mohair, alpaca, antique shoe button eyes, Ultrasuede, Merino wool felt. Every bear sports a "BearWorks" logo pin and either an imported ribbon or an antique fabric bow. Sharon sometimes dresses her bears, especially if she can find an antique outfit.
Home Appointments: 3 days
Shows: North Central U.S., Canada
Stores: Dollina, Toronto, Ontario; Teddy Bear Gardens, Toronto, Ontario; Teddy Bears Galore, Winnipeg, Manitoba; Williams Gifts, Toronto, Ontario; Martin House Dolls & Bears, Thornhill, Ontario; All Things Bright And Beautiful, Waitsfield, VT; BearTique, Montreal West, Quebec; 2 Bears Teddy Bears, Calgary, Alberta
Catalog/Photos: $4 U.S.; $5 Canada, refundable with purchase
Mail order: 6 weeks
Accepts: money order, Visa, MasterCard, certified personal check
Publications: Victorian Harvester; Toybox Magazine
Has been making bears for 5 years

> TEDDY BEARS MAKE YOUR INNER CHILD FEEL LOVED
> AND COMFORTED AND REALLY HELP HEAL THE
> WOUNDS OF THE PAST.
> — *Melodie Malcolm, artist, Nassel, MN*

MURIEL TOWNSEND
Cranberry Mountain Bears
5900 325th Ave. NW
Princeton, MN 55371
Phone: 612-389-2753
Phone orders: anytime
Price range: $100-$250
Size range: 6"-36"
Cranberry Mountain Bears are teddy
   bears for the adult collector. Muriel
   uses vintage clothes and fabrics. She
   makes many one-of-a-kind bears.
Home Appointments: at least 2 days
Shows: Midwest, East coast
Stores: Mary D's Dolls & Bears, Brook-
   lyn Park, MN; Cheri's Bear Essen-
   tials, Kansas City, MO; Mostly Bears,
   Arvada, CO; Bobby's Land of Ani-
   mals, Long Grove, IL; Bittersweet
   Collection, Wenham, MA; Moore
   Bears, Strasburg, PA
Catalog/Photos: SASE
Mail order: 4-6 weeks
Accepts: check, money order, Visa, Mas-
   terCard
Has been making bears for 11 years
Awards: Teddy Tribune convention, 1st,
   People's Choice Award; Teddy Bear
   Jubilee, 1st, 1990; Timonium, Best of
   Show, 1993; ABC Productions, 1st,
   1993
Publications: Ted Menten's book; The
   Teddy Tribune

> PLEASE DO NOT GET UP ONE DAY AND SAY,
> "I'M GOING TO START A BEAR BUSINESS."
> DON'T GO INTO IT ONLY FOR THE MONEY.
> YOU'VE GOT TO LOVE THEM FIRST—
> DON'T USE THEM.
> — *Shondra-Tania Grant-Fain, artist,*
> *Waynesville, NC*

BARBARA A. TROXEL
Bear Den Hollow
Route 1, Box 48
Muscoda, WI 53573
Phone: 608-739-3410
Phone orders: anytime
Price range: $50-$400
Size range: 4½"-27"
Bear Den Hollow bears are made of Ger-
   man mohair, alpaca and wool with
   fine glass or old shoe button eyes.
   Barbara specializes in bears under 6".
   She also has a golliwog edition each
   year, with sizes ranging from 6" to 12".
Shows: MO, IL, MI, MN, OH
Stores: Animal Haus, Ltd., Cincinnati,
   OH; Bear Corner, Tyler, TX; Bear
   Hugs, Coeur D'Alene, ID; Bobby's
   Land of Animals, Long Grove, IL;
   Cheri's Bear Essentials, Kansas City,
   MO; Lil' David's Woodbox, Luray,
   VA
Catalog/Photos: $3, refundable with pur-
   chase
Mail order: 3-4 weeks
Accepts: check, money order, Visa, Mas-
   terCard
Has been making bears for 11 years

LAURA H. TURNER
Windsor Cottage Crafts
P.O. Box 252
New Windsor, MD 21176
Phone: 410-875-2850
Phone orders: day and evening

Price range: $50-$200
Size range: 4"-16"
Windsor Cottage Crafts bears are original
   designs based on older bears, com-
   bined with antique accessories. Laura
   has been a bear artist for 15 years and
   an antique dealer for more than 20,
   and the two vocations have blended
   very well.
Waiting list: 2 months
Home Appointments: 1 week
Shows: East
Photos available.
Mail order: 2 months
Accepts: check, money order, Visa, Mas-
   terCard
Has been making bears for 15 years
Awards: Two Best of Show awards
Publications: Teddy Bear Artists; Teddy
   Bear magazines; Teddy Bear price
   guides; Santa Price Guide

SUZAN J. VEJTASA
Golden Harlequin Bears
9950 Donner St.
P.O. Box 711831
Santee, CA 92071
Phone: 619-449-5482
Phone orders: 9 A.M.-5 P.M.
Fax: 619-449-4722
   Fax orders accepted.
Price range: $100-more than $450
Size range: 10"-31"
Golden Harlequin Bears have unique
   faces, combed into place to give them
   an original look. They are made of
   fine-quality materials. Suzan uses
   unique fabrics and laces in costuming.
   She is also known for her artistry of
   noses and over faces, and gives her
   bears personalities of love.
Waiting list: 6-8 weeks
Stores: Bear With Us, Lichfield Staffs,
   UK; Ribbon House Dolls & Bears,
   Leicestershire, UK; Doll Folly, Man-
   hatten, KS; Geppetto's, Carmel, CA;
   Coach House Collectibles, Naper-
   ville, IL; Teddy Bear Station, Union-
   town, OH
Catalog/Photos: available.
Mail order: 6-8 weeks
Accepts: check, money order
Has been making bears for 6 years
Awards: TOBY nominee; Del Mar Faire

SONJA VIOLETTE
Miss Addie's Attic
1 Corbett Lane
Winslow, ME 04901
Phone: 207-873-1713
Phone orders: 9 A.M.-9 P.M.
Price range: $200-$400
Size range: 24"-34"
Miss Addie's Attic has three collections of bears to offer. The Weaver Creek Folks are limited edition, originally designed bears of a rustic nature. All fabrics are tea-dyed to capture the look of times past. The Heirloom Collection is also of original design and Victorian in dress. The Christmas past collection consists of Santa-Paws, an old world Santa, and other characters of old.
Waiting list: 3-4 weeks
Home Appointments: 1 day
Shows: ME, MA
Stores: Golden Sails, Ogunquit, ME; Living Arts of Kennebunk, Kennebunk, ME; The Write Shop, Harwich Port, MA
Photos available.
Mail order: 3-4 weeks
Accepts: check, money order, Visa, MasterCard
Has been making bears for 4 years
Publications: The Waterville Morning Sentinel; TBR

LISA A. VOLLRATH
Fuzzybottom Bears
85 Pershing Cir.
Denison, TX 75020
Phone: 903-786-3160
Phone orders: 7 days, 9 A.M.-9 P.M.
Price range: $150-more than $450
Size range: 6"-24"
Fuzzybottom Bears are made of English and German mohair. They have Ultrasuede paw pads, glass eyes and are fully jointed. Lisa makes some bears with wire armatures. They are elaborately costumed and very detailed.
Shows: TX, OK
Catalog/Photos: $3, refundable with purchase
Mail order: 2 weeks if in stock
Waiting list: 4 weeks
Accepts: check, money order
Has been making bears for 3 years
Awards: Teddy Bear Collectors of Norman, Best of Show, 1993

Publications: TB&F

DENISE M. WADE
Dirty Knees & Friends
7440 Lauren J. Dr.
Mentor, OH 44060
Phone: 216-255-1906
Phone orders: 8 A.M.-8 P.M.
Fax: 216-431-1738
Fax orders accepted.
Price range: $50-$250
Size range: 11"-22"
Dirty Knees & Friends are completely made by Denise. Each bear has a green suede shamrock on the right thigh. The shamrock and the name dirty knees are registered trademarks.
Stores: Wonderland, Inc., Hollywood, FL; Linda's Lov-Lez, Mentor, OH; Rhay's Treasures, Willoughby, OH
Catalog/Photos: $3
Mail order: 4 weeks
Accepts: check, money order, Visa, MasterCard
Has been making bears for 16 years
Awards: blue ribbons at county fair

CATIE WALKER
Rosebud & Co.
309 W. Alder
Walla Walla, WA 99362
Phone: 509-529-8868
Phone orders: 9 A.M.-9 P.M.
Price range: $35-$100
Size range: 3" and under
Rosebud & Co. bears are all designed by Catie. They are handsewn and jointed with embroidered noses and glass bead eyes. Catie uses upholstery velvets and Ultrasuede. She also makes teddy bear pins, decorated with silk ribbon, charms and beading. She incorporates beading on most of her bears as well.
Home Appointments: 2 days
Shows: OR, WA
Catalog/Photos: free
Mail order: 4-6 weeks
Accepts: check, money order
Has been making bears for 9 years
Awards: local awards
Publications: Word Book of Bears; TB&F

DO IT FOR LOVE, NOT FOR MONEY!
— *Ruth E. Fraser, artist, Willowdale, Ontario*

KATHLEEN WALLACE
Stier Bears
2540 Pottstown Pike
Spring City, PA 19475
Phone: 610-469-3155
Phone orders: 9 A.M.-11 P.M.
Price range: $100-more than $450
Size range: 7"-40"
Stier Bears are usually vintage style, fully jointed mohair bears with glass or shoe button eyes. They have growlers and are stuffed with Poly-Fil or pellets. Kathleen is known for her large bears, but also makes many smaller bears. She uses many types of mohair, including curly, sparse and straight. She also uses many colors, from golds to traditional bear colors. Most have bell or lace collars.
Waiting list: 6-8 weeks
Home Appointments: 1 day
Shows: MA, NY, CT, MD, CA, NJ, FL, KS, MI, IL, AZ
Stores: Akkermar Baren-Goed, Holland; Christy's, Buckingham, PA; Groves Quality Collectibles, Lima, OH; Teddy Bear Den, Las Vegas; Teddy Bears of Witney, Oxfordshire, U.K.; The Teddy Bear Museum, Naples, FL
Catalog/Photos: $3, refundable with purchase
Mail order: 6-8 weeks
Accepts: check, money order, Visa, MasterCard
Has been making bears for 14 years
Awards: Many 1sts and 2nds at shows; TOBY nominee
Publications: Complete Book of Teddy Bears; Artists Annual; TB&F; Tribute to Teddy Bear Artists; Early American Life magazine; Toy Box magazine

BETTY J. WALSH
B2 bears
896 Pauline Ave.
Columbus, OH 43224

Phone: 614-268-8161
Phone orders: 9 A.M.-7 P.M.
Fax: 614-268-8161
Fax orders accepted.
Price range: $50-$100
Size range: 2"-25"
B2 Bears are completely handsewn by Betty. She has recently started using antique fabrics on her bears. Her favorites are her Santa bears, because each is one-of-a-kind. She uses antique or vintage accessories with each bear.
Home Appointments: 1 week
Shows: MD, OH, TN, MI, KY, GA
Stores: Betty's Uptown, Columbus, OH; Tortoise Shell, Columbus, OH; Teddy Bears of Witney, Oxfordshire, UK; Magpie's Nest, Canterbury, U.K.; Teddy Bears Picknick, Holland
Catalog/Photos: $2, refundable with purchase
Mail order: 2 weeks
Accepts: check, money order
Has been making bears for 4 years

PAULA DIANE WALTON
A Sweet Remembrance
172 Aspetuck Ridge Rd.
New Milford, CT 06776-5611
Phone: 203-355-5709
Phone orders: anytime
Price range: $35-$350
Size range: 5"-32"
A Sweet Remembrance bears are generally very serious, antique style bears with a strong tendency toward romanticism. Paula works mainly in mohair, but at times she uses vintage real fur from old coats (never new fur). She embellishes her bears with antique lace, vintage clothing and hats, antique glasses, etc. Even her bare bears are graced with pure silk ribbons. When she makes bear clothing, she often uses pintucking and lace inser-

tion. Her bears are fully jointed and have glass or antique shoe button eyes and embroidered noses and features.
Home Appointments: same day (call first)
Shows: East Coast
Stores: Rhonda Sanders, Gettysburg, PA; Basically Bears, Hampton, NH; The Bear Nostalgia, Hughson, CA; Crafty Mouse, Rochester, MN
Catalog: $5, refundable with purchase
Mail order: 1-2 weeks
Accepts: check, money order, layaway
Has been making bears for 9 years
Publications: Better Homes & Gardens Holiday Crafts, 1994; Cross Stitch & Country Crafts, 1994; 1993; Better Homes & Gardens Holiday Cooking, 1993

ULLA-MARIA WARLING
Swedie Bear
2359 Medina Ave.
Simi Valley, CA 93063
Phone: 805-584-BEAR
Phone orders: 9 A.M.-9 P.M.
Price range: $50-$200
Size range: 10"-30"
Swedie Bears are fully jointed bears with a unique muzzle design. They have stuffed fabric noses (not just stitched) and deep life-like eyes—some with eyelashes. Ulla-Maria strives to make them look very cuddly.
Waiting list: 4 weeks
Home Appointments: 2 days
Shows: CA, NV, AZ
Stores: Teddy Bear Den, Las Vegas; Marilyn's World, Ft. Lauderdale, FL
Catalog/Photos: $2, refundable with purchase
Mail order: 2 weeks
Accepts: check, money order, Visa, MasterCard, Discover, American Express, layaway, installments
Has been making bears for 11 years
Awards: Several local bear club contest awards; Linda Mullins's show, theme booth award; several awards for theme bear displays
Publications: Holiday Newspaper Publications; Club Publications

CAROL-LYNN ROSSEL WAUGH
5 Morrill St.
Winthrop, ME 04364-1220
Phone: 207-377-6769

Phone orders: 5 P.M.-7 P.M. Do not call during day!
Fax: 207-377-6769
Price range: $100-more than $450
Size range: 2"-25"
Carol-Lynn's bears have intelligent expressions featuring embroidered eyebrows, large noses and big smiles. Her bears are recognizable across a room full of bears because they look like they are ready to speak to the viewer. Mostly undressed, they all have the same saucy personalities.
Waiting list: 6 months to 1 year
Home Appointments: 6 weeks
Shows: New England
Photos: $5, refundable if returned.
Mail order: 1 month
Accepts: check, money order
Design manufactured by: Russ Berrie & Co; Annette
Has been making bears for 20 years
Publications: Teddy Bear Artists: The Romance of Making & Collecting Teddy Bears; Teddy Bear Artists' Annual; Contemporary Teddy Bear Price Guide; The Teddy Bear Companion; Tribute to Teddy Bear Artists; Official Price Guide for Antique and Modern Teddy Bears; TBR; TB&F; Teddy Bear Encyclopedia; Collector's Guide to Miniature Teddy Bears; Official Guide to Antiques & Collectibles; Who's Who Of American Women

DIETER WEIHERT
Bear Branch
3523 Tree Lane
Kingwood, TX 77339
Phone: 713-358-3736
Phone orders: 9 A.M.-9 P.M.
Price range: $100-$200
Size range: 15"-20"
Bear Branch bears are designed and handmade by Dieter. All bears are made of German mohair and Merino

wool. They are double stitched, fully jointed, firmly stuffed and have glass eyes. Some bears are made to stand alone. Some have growlers.

Waiting list: 4 weeks

Home Appointments: 1 day

Shows: TX

Stores: Stuf'd 'N Stuff, Houston, TX; Sterling Events, Kingwood, TX; The Three Bears, Houston, TX

Catalog/Photos: $5, refundable with purchase

Mail order: 1 week

Accepts: check, money order

Has been making bears for 4 years

Publications: TBR; TB&F

MELISSA WEISS

Bears by Melissa

P.O. Box 47

Elkwater, Alberta T0J 1C0, Canada

Phone: 403-893-2172

Phone orders: 9 A.M.-9 P.M.

Price range: less than $35-$200

Size range: 9"-36"

Bears by Melissa are made of synthetics and mohair. Designs include: traditional, fully jointed bears; bean bag bears stuffed with beans or plastic pellets; clown bears; and pajama bag bears. Melissa handmakes and double stitches each bear. Most are childsafe, but they have been collected by adults as well.

Shows: Southern Alberta

Stores: Damon Lane's, Medicine Hat, Alberta

Accepts: check, money order

Has been making bears for 7 years

Awards: The Bear Fair, honorable mention, 2nd, 1994

CHRISTINA WEMMITT-PAUK

Bear Works

281 Green Briar Rd.

Beech Mtn., NC 28604

Phone: 704-387-4755

Phone orders: 9 A.M.-6 P.M.

Fax: 704-387-2637

Fax orders accepted.

Price range: $100-more than $450

Waiting list: depends on piece

Home appointments available.

Shows: OH, CA

Stores: The Rocking Horse Gallery, Fredericksburg, VA; The Honey Bee Bear Shoppe, East Bridgewater, MA; Anything Goes, Inc., Anna Maria, FL;

The Hen's Nest, Seminole, FL; Sherry's Teddy Bears, Inc., Chicago

Has been making bears for 8 years

Awards: Golden Teddy Nominee; Best of Show, Ft. Lauerdale FL; Pinehurst NC; Fayettville NC; Strong Museum; ABC, 1st, 2 years

Publications: TBR, TB&F, Teddy Bear Artist Price Guide, newspapers

LINDA M. WENTZEL

The Bearest of Them All

252 Garretson Lane

Mansfield, TX 76063

Phone: 817-478-7790

Phone orders: 7 P.M.-9 P.M.

Price range: $35-$250

Size range: 9"-23"

Home Appointments: 1 week

Shows: TX, OK, IN

Stores: Friends In The Attic, Mansfield, TX

Mail order available.

Accepts: check, Visa

Has been making bears for 4 years

Publications: Mansfield News Mirror

SHARON A. WEST

Western Heritage

Rt. 6, Box 620

Shawnee, OK 74801

Phone: 405-275-5542

Phone orders: 8 A.M.-10 P.M.

Price range: less than $35-$300

Size range: 1¼"-27"

Western Heritage bears are antique in style and made of mohair, except for two very small designs that Sharon makes out of upholstery fabric.

Home appointments available.

Shows: OK, AR, TX, KS

Mail order available.

Accepts: check, money order

Has been making bears for 5 years

Awards: Teddy Bear Collectors of Norman, 1st, 2nd, 3rd

MARJORIE E. WEST

Beary Happy Bears

628 S.A. Road

Arvada, WY 82831

Phone: 307-736-2237

Phone orders: 7 A.M.-9 P.M.

Price range: $50-$200

Size range: 16"-21"

Beary Happy Bears are fully jointed mohair bears. Some have closed mouths, but most have open mouths with soft-sculptured teeth, which are patented. Marjorie's bears have either shoe button eyes or glass eyes. Some are dressed.

Catalog/Photos: free

Mail order: 2 weeks

Accepts: check, money order

Has been making bears for 2 years

Awards: Billings, MT Doll & Bear Show, 3 blue ribbons; Newcastle, WY Doll Show, 2 committee's choice ribbons

BECKY ANN WHEELER

Becky's Bears

20-104 Ave. NW

Coon Rapids, MN 55448

Phone: 612-757-9548

Phone orders: 9 A.M.-9 P.M.

Price range: $50-$150

Size range: 1"-4"

Becky's Bears are made of vintage velvets that are no longer being produced. They are entirely handsewn and fully jointed, usually with discs.

She uses blown German glass or onyx eyes. All her bears have either hand-made collars or vintage trims.

Shows: East, Midwest

Stores: Mary D's Dolls & Bears & Such, Brooklyn Park, MN; Kmitsch Girls, Stillwater, MN; Market Square Antiques, Chandler, AZ, Arundel Teddy Bears, Sussex, UK; Bears & Friends of Brighton, Sussex, UK

Catalog/Photos: free

Mail order: 8 weeks

Accepts: check, money order

Has been making bears for 5 years

Awards: Golden Teddy Award, 1994; Toby Award, 1994

Publications: TB&F, TBR, Teddy Bear Times

SHIRLEY WHITNEY

The Bears of Whitney Woods

16026 Surrey Dr.

Hudson, FL 34667

Phone: 813-863-5591

Phone orders: 9A.M.-9P.M.

Price range: $100-$300

Size range: 8"-23"

The Bears of Whitney Woods are all named after foods. Shirley enjoys using different textures of fabric. Most bears have fuzzy faces.

Waiting list: 3 weeks

Home Appointments: 1 week

Shows: South, FL, Midwest

Stores: MBR Bears & Dolls, Staten Island, NY; Bear-A-Dise Landing, Guilford, CT; Hyde Park Zoo, Tampa, FL

Catalog/Photos: free

Mail order: 5 working days

Accepts: check, money order, Visa, MasterCard

Has been making bears for 6 years

LISA DEVORE WILDMAN

The Stuffed Menagerie

P.O. Box 2236

Santa Cruz, CA 95062

Phone: 408-427-2199

Phone orders: 10A.M.-5P.M.

Price range: $35-$400

Size range: 4"-23"

The Stuffed Menagerie bears are fully jointed bears made of mohairs, alpaca, wool, mohair blends, cotton and synthetics. Lisa also makes bears out of old fur coats of any fur except rabbit fur. She uses glass, leather, shoe button or safety eyes. Paw pads are made of upholstery fabric, wool felt or Ultrasuede. Her bears are stuffed with Poly-Fil or pellets. Most are one-of-a-kind. Lisa is always looking for new furs and trying new things.

Waiting list: 4-6 weeks

Home Appointments: 1 week

Shows: Across US

Accepts: check, money order, Visa, MasterCard, American Express, layaway

Has been making bears for 17 years

JANET A.C. WILSON

Handmade Treasures

22 Sally Ann Ct.

Stewartstown, PA 17363

Phone: 717-993-3041

Phone orders: 9A.M.-5P.M.

Price range: $100-$200

Size range: 1⅞"-3"

Handmade Treasures bears are hand-stitched and fully wire and disk jointed. Most are made of upholstery fabric with black onyx or glass bead eyes. Faces are embroidered and paw pads are Ultrasuede. Janet dresses most of her bears, but the clothes are not glued on. Many of their props are also made by Janet.

Waiting list: 9-12 months

Shows: MD, MA, IL, FL

Stores: Bear Tracks, Pittsburgh; J & L Collectibles, Tampa, FL; Paisley Bear, Ft. Lauderdale, FL; Theodore's Bear Emporium, London, UK

Catalog/Photos: $2, refundable with purchase

Mail order: 9-12 months

Accepts: check, money order

Has been making bears for 5 years

Awards: Golden Teddy Award, 1993; Two TOBY nominations, 1993; Two Golden Teddy nominations, 1994

Publications: TBR; TB&F

DONNA LEE WILSON

325 James St. S., Apt. 411

Hamilton, Ontario L8P 3B7, Canada

Phone: 905-525-2259

Phone orders: 10A.M.-8P.M.

Price range: $50-$300

Size range: 6"-40"

Donna's bears are usually made of mohair and are always fully jointed. They express a variety of emotions, including happy, whimsical, wistful, contemplative—but never sad or angry. Donna makes bears ranging from completely bare to fully dressed. She develops the bear's character while making the bear, and names the bear after it is finished.

Home Appointments: 1 day

Shows: Ontario; Calgary, Alberta; Buffalo, NY; OH

Stores: Teddy Bear Specialties, Georgetown, Ontario; Write Impressions, Hamilton, Ontario

Photos: free if returned, $1.50 per photo if not

Mail order: 2-3 weeks

Accepts: check, money order

Has been making bears for 11 years

SALLY A. WINEY
Winey Bears
900 Market St.
Lemoyne, PA 17043
Phone: 717-774-7447
Phone orders: 8A.M.-8P.M.
Fax: 717-737-0231
  Fax orders accepted.
Price range: $50-$400
Size range: 4"-30"
Winey Bears are designed and handmade
  by Sally. Most are made of mohair and
  alpaca, but occasionally she will use
  synthetics. She makes limited edi-
  tions, especially for stores. The best
  known Winey Bears are "Rainbow
  Bears," along with their offshoots,
  "Lollipops" and "Neopolitans." All
  of these bears are made of dyed white
  mohair. Most are one-of-a-kind due to
  the hand-dying process.
Shows: across USA
Stores: Winey Bears, Lemoyne, PA;
  Bears By The Bay, Fairhope, AL;
  Bear-a-Dise, Millburn, NJ; Moore
  Bears, Strasburg, PA; Teddy Bears To
  Go, Lakewood, NJ
Catalog/Photos: $3.50, refundable with
  purchase
Mail order: 4-6 weeks
Accepts: check, money order, Visa, Mas-
  terCard
Design manufactured by Ty, Inc.
Has been making bears for 13 years
Awards: several show awards from
  around the country
Publications: Tribute to Teddy Bear Art-
  ists; TBR; TB&F

MICHAEL JOHNSTON WOESSNER
Bear Elegance Exclusives/
Realistic Design Bears
P.O. Box 300920
Escondido, CA 92030
Phone: 619-746-5132
Phone orders: 9A.M.-5P.M.
Fax: 619-737-9838
  Fax orders accepted.
Price range: more than $450
Size range: 23"-64"
Waiting list: 1-3 months
Home Appointments: 2 days
Shows: San Diego
Catalog/Photos: available
Mail order: available
Accepts: check, money order, Visa, Mas-
  terCard
Has been making bears for 4 years
Awards: Two TOBY awards, 1993. One
  TOBY, 1994

JOAN MARIE WOESSNER
Bear Elegance Exclusives
1150 Fern St.
Escondido, CA 92027
Phone: 619-746-5132
Phone orders: 9A.M.-5P.M.
Fax: 619-737-9838
  Fax orders accepted.
Price range: $84-$500
Size range: 11½"
Bear Elegance Exclusives are made
  mostly with German mohair and glass
  eyes, and Ultrasuede or felt paws and
  feet. A noticeable feature of Joan's
  bears is the mink used for eyelashes.
Shows: Linda Mullins's shows, Disney
  World Teddy Bear & Doll Convention
  ILTBC Convention, CA
Stores: Animal Haus, Ltd., Cincinnati,
  OH; Bobby Bear Trap Inc., Nashville,
  TN; Bear Tracks, Pittsburgh; Bears
  By The Bay, Fairhope, AL; Bear Tree,
  Anaheim, CA; Bears & Wares, New
  Cumberland, PA

Photos available.
Mail order: 2-3 weeks
Accepts: check, money order, Visa, Mas-
  terCard
Has been making bears for 11 years
Awards: 2 TOBY awards, 1991; ILTBC
  convention, Best of show, 1991, 1992
Publications: Complete Book of Teddy
  Bears; Teddy Bear Artists' Annual;
  Teddy's Past & Present, 1 & 2; TB&F;
  Teddy Bear Magazines, Holland &
  Germany

CATHERINE WOOD
Wee Treasures
1421 Lynwood
Port Coquitlam, British Columbia
V3B 6G9, Canada
Phone: 604-944-2643
Phone orders: 8A.M.-6P.M.
Fax: 604-469-3031
  Fax orders accepted.
Price range: $35-$300
Waiting list: 3-4 weeks
Home Appointments: 5-10 days
Shows: Pacific Northwest
Stores: Teddy Bear Picnic, Victoria, Brit-
  ish Columbia; Bear Essentials, Victo-
  ria, British Columbia; Beartique,
  Montreal, Quebec; Sidney Antiques,
  Sidney, British Columbia; Billies
  Country, Surrey, British Columbia;
  Red Balloon Toy Shop, Duncan, Brit-
  ish Columbia
Catalog Photos: available
Mail order: available
Accepts: check, Visa
Has been making bears for 6 years
Awards: 1st, 2nd, Strawberry Social
  Convention; prizes at club events
Publications: Victoria Harvester; Teddy
  Bear Times

TERRY JOHN WOODS
Blackwoods Design
Rt. 1, Box 840
Eastham Rd.
Shrewsbury, VT 05738
Phone: 802-492-3715
Phone orders: anytime
Price range: $100-$400
Size range: 10"-27"
Blackwoods Design bears are old look-
  ing, traditional bears with center seam
  heads. Terry uses a special dyeing pro-
  cess to age the bears. No two are alike.
  Special orders are available.

Waiting list: 2-4 months
Home Appointments: 1 week
Shows: MA, CT
Catalog/Photos: $3
Mail order: 2-4 months
Accepts: check, money order, Visa, MasterCard
Has been making bears for 7 years
Publications: TBR; TB&F

SHARI WOODSTEIN
Mountain Creations
19055 E. 16th Pl.
Aurora, CO 80011
Phone: 303-343-7113
Phone orders: M-F, 5:30P.M.-9P.M.; Sat,
8A.M.- 6P.M.
Price range: less than $35-$150
Size range: 3"-26"
Mountain Creations bears have individually sculpted faces. Shari's bears are made with recycled fur, synthetic fur, or burlap, velvets and miscellaneous materials.
Home Appointments: 1 day
Shows: CO, NE
Catalog/Photos: $2, refundable with purchase
Mail order: 3-4 weeks
Accepts: check, money order
Has been making bears for 2 years
Awards: Several 1st and 2nd place show awards

PAT A. WOODWORTH
Bears By Paw
464 Boughton Hill Rd.
Honeoye Falls, NY 14472
Phone: 716-624-4507
Phone orders: anytime
Price range: $50-$300
Size range: 8"-24"
Bears by Paw are fully jointed and are made from mohairs, alpacas and imported plushes. Pat also makes bears from recycled fur coats. Most of her

bears have glass eyes and Ultrasuede paw pads, and all have a birthmark (an embroidered paw print) on the left foot. She also makes memory bears from coats, blankets, gloves (for paw pads), bathrobes, or any other fabric out of which the customer would like to have a lasting remembrance.
Home Appointments: 1 day
Shows: East; Midwest
Stores: Casey's Bear Factory, Fairport, NY
Catalog/Photos: $5, refundable with purchase
Mail order: 4-6 weeks
Accepts: check, money order, Visa, MasterCard, Discover
Has been making bears for 6 years

PATRICIA WOOLLEY
Teddy Traveler
708-8th St.
Manhattan Beach, CA 90266
Phone: 310-374-8055
Phone orders: anytime
Fax: 310-374-3132
Fax orders accepted.
Price range: less than $35-$200
Patricia makes bear paintings, 12" × 14" and 16" × 20". Her work is done in watercolor or acrylic paint. She has three series of bear paintings, including Provencal village bears, antique bears and fine art bears. These are sold as prints, but she also sells originals.
Home appointments available.
Shows: CA, IA
Catalog/Photos: available
Mail order: 2-3 weeks
Accepts: check, money order
Has been making bears for 16 years
Awards: ATBAG, 1st, 1985; Old Hometown Fair, 1986; many art shows in CA and France
Publications: Teddy Bear Artists

JACQUELINE M. WRIGHT
Animal Crackers Pattern Co.
5824 Isleta SW
Albuquerque, NM 87105
Phone: 505-873-2806
Phone orders: 9A.M.-5P.M.
Fax: 505-243-1106
Fax orders accepted.
Price range: less than $35-$400
Size range: 5"-22"
Animal Crackers Pattern Co. bears are mohair bears with hand embroidered noses and glass eyes. Many contain music boxes or growlers and are dressed. All bears and clothing are original designs by Jacqueline.
Waiting list: 1-2 months
Home Appointments: 2-5 days
Catalog/Photos: $2, refundable with purchase
Mail order: 1-2 weeks
Accepts: check, money order, Visa, MasterCard, COD- $4.50 charge
Has been making bears for 13 years
Awards: Toby, 1994; Norman Teddy Bear Affair, best of show
Publications: TB&F

TRUDY YELLAND
Tru's Bearables
132 Tisdale St. N
Hamilton, Ontario L8L 5M6, Canada
Phone: 905-528-0702
Phone orders: anytime
Price range: $50-$250
Size range: 2½"-22"
Tru's Bearables miniature bears are made of mohair and upholstery fabric. Trudy enjoys making vintage style bears. Her two faced baby bears are all jointed. She uses the best fabric and produces all the bears herself.
Home Appointments: 1-2 weeks
Shows: NY, OH, Boxborough, MA
Mail order: 5 weeks
Accepts: check
Has been making bears for 6 years
Awards: bear on display at the Theodore Roosevelt Inaugural National Historic Site
Publications: local newspaper; TBR, 1990

TERI ZANETTI
Heart For Bears
2311-6 Sycamore Glen Dr.
Sparks, NV 89434

Phone: 702-355-7117
Phone orders: 8A.M.-6P.M.
Price range: less than $35
Size range: under 2″
Waiting list: 2 weeks
Heart for Bears bear figurines are designed and hand sculpted by Teri from start to finish. They are made of German polymer clay, and all details are made with the clay or etched on. Teri is sure to give each bear a different look, rather than simply changing what the bear is wearing or holding. All figurines come with a personalized hangtag, and most are limited editions.
Stores: Baa Baa Black Sheep, Sparks, NV; Jan's Hallmark, Reno, NV; Bears Everywhere, Fredericksburg, VA; Cheri's Bear Essentials, Kansas City, MO; Simply Lovely Gift Shoppe, Fords, NJ; Country Crossing Gift Shoppe, Chester, MD; The Teddy Bear Den, Las Vegas; Gregg Alexander's Gifts, Kennebunkport, ME; The Wright Place, Sierra City, CA
Catalog/Photos: photos $1
Mail order: 4 weeks
Accepts: check, money order
Has been making bears for 6 years
Publications: TB&F; TBR

DEBBIE ZIBRIK
Dear Bears
4797 Quebec St.
Vancouver, British Columbia V5V 3M2, Canada

Phone: 604-872-5954
Phone orders: anytime
Fax: 604-872-2508
Fax orders accepted.
Price range: $35-$250
Size range: 10″-24″
Dear Bears are fully jointed, traditional real fur bears featuring embroidered noses, glass eyes and Ultrasuede/leather paws. Each is numbered and signed by the bear artist. Each wears a brass medallion inscribed with the poem "I was once a coat."
Shows: Pacific Northwest; Alberta
Stores: Willows 'N Wishes, Port Alberni, British Columbia; East of Java, Port McNeil, British Columbia; West Coast Wonders Gift Shoppe, West Vancouver, British Columbia; Heritage Gifts & Crafts, Inc.; Kelowna, British Columbia; Teddy Bears Picnic, Victoria, British Columbia; Peasantries, Vancouver, British Columbia; Snowberries, Whistler, British Columbia; Blue Coyote Gallery, Vancouver, British Columbia; Mandeville Gardens, Burnaby, British Columbia
Accepts: check, money order, Visa
Has been making bears for 3 years
Awards: Calgary Bear Fair, 3rd
Publications: Bear Fair Tymes, Victorian Harvester

MARIE ZIMMERMANN
Paw Quette Bears
251 Van Bee Dr.
Williams Bay, WI 53191

QUALITY KEEPS YOUR TENDER TEDDY BEAR AND SOULFUL FRIEND AROUND FOR MORE THAN ONE LIFETIME.
— *Jeanne E. Green, artist, Peoria, AZ*

Phone: 414-245-1724
Phone orders: 8A.M.-10P.M.
Price range: $50-$450
Size range: 9″-32″
Paw Quette Bears have a whimsical, "canine" look, perhaps due to the fact that Marie has worked as a research specialist at the Wisconsin Veterinary School. A second "antique" look was added in 1992, and Marie enjoys making them both.
Waiting list: 4-6 months
Home Appointments: 2-5 days
Shows: Midwest, East Coast, South
Stores: Bear-A-Dise, Millburn, NJ; Animal Haus, Ltd., Cincinnati, OH; Dolls In The Attic, Victoria, Australia; Teddy Bear Den, Las Vegas; Bears of Bruton St., Wilson, NC; Gepetto's Collectables, Carmel, CA; Bearaphernalia, Irvine, CA; The Bear Necessities, Solvang, CA
Catalog/Photos: $5, refundable with purchase
Mail order: varies
Accepts: check, money order, Visa, MasterCard
Has been making bears for 7 years
Awards: show awards
Publications: Michaud's Contemporary Teddy Bear Price Guide, 1990

4
Manufacturers

How to Use This Chapter

*N*o sourcebook would be complete without manufacturers' listings. These manufacturers are just some of the many that make and sell teddy bears and teddy bear items. We have attempted to include as many as possible. If a particular manufacturer did not respond, we tried our best to verify the address and list the address alone. Otherwise, we have included as much information as possible, including basic contact information, sales information, USA and Canadian distributors, product and club information, and company history.

This chapter can be used in several ways. Retail store buyers can use the listings to contact a company or distributor about purchasing the products for their stores. If the company has a retail catalog or offers direct sales to collectors through a club or outlet location, the listing will give that information as well. Many manufacturers have a special collector's club that offers up-to-date product information and other advantages.

Most manufacturers sell through retail stores only. It is best not to contact a manufacturer about purchasing their products unless the listing specifically states that retail sales are available. The best way to locate a specific company's products is to look in the brand name index for stores carrying them. Some companies may provide a list of stores in your area if you call or write.

Due to the publication time line, it was impossible to get up-to-date product information. We have tried to be as current as possible, but have not mentioned specific new items because they would quickly be out-of-date. For information about new releases, it is best to consult the teddy bear magazines or join the company's collectors club if one exists.

Experienced artists who are interested in selling their designs to manufacturers may use the contact information in this listing for that purpose. See the sidebar by Debbie Kesling in the opening to the artist's chapter for advice on how to go about marketing your designs, and to learn about the advantages and disadvantages to doing so.

Finally, collectors interested in a specific companies may enjoy browsing through the company histories provided. From the oldest to the youngest, these manufacturers all have interesting histories and unique products. Regardless of how you use these listings, we hope they will be helpful. Note: When contacting a foreign manufacturer, it is best to deal with a U.S. or Canadian distributor whenever possible. Most listings include contact information for distributors. If you must make an international phone call, it is best to check the number with your operator first. Foreign city codes change frequently, and different long distance phone companies may have different international dialing methods. ❧

A Salute to the World's Most Popular Toy

BY KEN YENKE

*A*s the teddy bear nears his hundredth birthday, he becomes more and more accepted around the world as a highly treasured work of art. Today, prized teddies are consistently commanding sale prices ranging from one hundred dollars to more than five hundred dollars per inch! As always, the teddy bear is attracting avid collectors. Today, however, a new breed of investor has helped drive prices for the very olde and rare to amounts previously unheard of. Imagine, in the early years of the teddy bear (1905 to 1914), you could purchase a perfect twelve-inch teddy for the tidy sum of twenty-five cents. The best available would run about a dollar or so. The average wage at this time was ten to fifteen dollars a week. And, although the average wage today is significantly higher, we are all surprised at the market prices that antique teddies consistently reach and exceed.

The Early Teddy Bears

The early 1900s were the beginning of a new era, coined the Century of the Child. The world's most prominent leaders boasted large families and began to focus on family-related values and concerns. Germany's Crown Prince Wilhelm ordered many early Steiff items for his four sons, and his family was photographed with an early teddy bear. King Edward (Ted) VII of England was often refered to as "Teddy" in early writings, and his country was one of the largest importers of the early teddy bears and other plush toys.

Of course, President Theodore (Teddy) Roosevelt is credited with providing the most substantial boost to the worldwide popularity of the teddy bear. Not only did he try to spend at least one hour each evening playing with his children, but he also gave the teddy his name. While negotiating a boundary dispute between Louisiana and Mississippi in 1906, President Roosevelt traveled to Smedes, Mississippi. A hunting expedition was planned as a diversion from the business at hand. After a week and a half of no bears, the expedition's organizers captured a small black bear and leashed it to a nearby tree. They summoned President Roosevelt with the hope of providing him with at least one trophy

Ken Yenke began researching the development of the teddy bear about ten years ago. Since then, his collection of olde teddies has grown considerably, and he has become a well-known expert. He enjoys evaluating, identifying and appraising teddy bears and frequently writes articles and gives lectures about teddy bears. A dozen bears from his collection were used in The American Greeting Card Company's 1995 nostalgic collectible calendar. He is a preferred Good Bears of the World appraiser. He lives in Strongsville, Ohio.

for his trip. Roosevelt met the cub, eye to eye, and turned quickly to his cohorts. "I draw the line at shooting anything so small," he said. "My son wouldn't speak to me again if I were to harm that little bear!" The next day, "Drawing the Line at Mississippi," an illustration of the event by Clifford Berryman, appeared in the *Washington Post*. From that day forward, Teddy's bear would grace the multitude of political cartoons as a constant companion of President Theodore (Teddy) Roosevelt. Eventually, "Teddy's bear" became the teddy bear.

It is not surprising that the eye-to-eye, endearing glance of the teddy bear came from real life bears. Before the advent of the plush toy, many highly skilled artists captured an unparalleled character in their paintings and sketches. Bears evoke admiration and respect, not just for their strength, but for several humanlike characteristics. That is why folklore from every culture is rich with tales about bears. Bears walk with a plantigrade step and stand erect just like humans. Bear cubs and children are more ardently protected than nearly any other animals in nature. Admiration and respect translate to "warmth" in the cuddly version of the bear. Nearly without explanation, children will randomly select a teddy bear over any number of other friendly creatures when given the opportunity. I have observed this over and over in my travels, and various controlled tests have produced the same result.

So it makes perfect sense that firms like Steiff, Gebrueder Bing, Schuco, Dean's, Farnell, Ideal, Columbia, Aetna and Gund pioneered an industry based on furry works of three-dimensional art. Artists like Richard Steiff (for Steiff) and Weidlich (for Gebrueder Bing), were two of the pioneering artists at the beginning of this century. Their realistic portrayals were translated to patterns. Add the discovery of mohair as the ultimate covering, put in joints, and voila—a perfect toy!

Many German toymakers were celebrating their hundredth year of toymaking in 1905. These firms welcomed a new sensation. Cottage industries flourished, with families providing most of the original work force. Many of these families worked for more than one manufacturer. Copying patterns, and the movement of knowledgeable employees from one competitor to another, were common practices. Despite these practices, then, as today, there were dramatic differences in quality and craftsmanship.

In general, only the best firms carried their early techniques into the post-World War I era. A renewed worldwide demand for the teddy bear was met with a flourish of manufacturing activity. Every major city in the United States had at least one teddy bear factory. Many of the original makers returned with vigor, including Merrythought, Chad Valley and Chiltern in England. Knickerbocker, Character, Gund and Ideal were four major United States manufacturers at this time. Germany continued to create the teddies that conformed to the highest standards possible, and quickly regained its title as the toy capitol of the world.

A New Interest in Olde Teddies

A dramatic increase in the interest in teddy bears has developed over the past several years—especially in olde teddy bears. But there is a danger in collecting olde bears. Without a basic knowledge of the history of teddy bear manufacturing, one may as well be gambling. But anyone can learn to identify and evaluate these old bears. Trophies abound for collectors who are armed with a trained eye and a keen sense.

Allow me to share one of the many stories I've collected over the years to demonstrate this point. One afternoon, I received a call from a friend at about 3 in the afternoon. She told me she had noticed a two-day estate sale advertised in the local newspaper. An olde long-nosed teddy was being offered. The sale had begun at 7 in the morning, and I knew any "good" olde, long-nosed teddy would have been swooped up by 7:01! Still, with the "excitement of possibility" that every collector knows, I wrote down the address and headed for the sale site. I arrived at a nearly empty house, except for the gracious couple overseeing the sale. I later learned that both had extensive experience in the antique business. When I asked to see the teddy, they pointed to a large mantel in the vast living room area. I looked up, and staring back at me was a circa 1905 teddy bear. I would document this a month later with original photos!

"What is the price?" I asked the couple.

"Five hundred dollars," the man replied.

"I'll take him," (definitely a "he") I said immediately.

The gentleman was astounded that I bought the teddy bear without hesitation. He told me that at least a half dozen antique dealers had pondered buying the teddy, but that all had elected to leave bids of $200-$300 for the next day, instead of paying the $500. "We would have purchased the bear ourselves if it was a Steiff," he told me. "But we knew it wasn't a Steiff because there was no button in the ear."

I explained my decision to purchase the bear using an analogy. "If a Mercedes or Cadillac were parked in

---

LEARN TO LISTEN LIKE A TEDDY BEAR,

WITH EARS OPEN AND MOUTH CLOSED TIGHT.

LEARN TO FORGIVE LIKE A TEDDY BEAR,

WITH HEART OPEN, NOT CARING WHO'S RIGHT.

LEARN TO LOVE LIKE A TEDDY BEAR,

WITH ARMS OPEN AND IMPERFECT SIGHT.

— *Anonymous, contributed by Chris Cassner, artist, Arendtsville, PA*

your driveway, even if the nameplate or hood ornament had been removed, would you be reasonably certain that it was a valuable automobile?" I asked the man.

"Why, certainly," the man replied. "I would recognize a Cadillac or a Mercedes by all its other special features."

"Well, my Mercedes is sitting on the mantel," I said.

The teddy measured twenty-four inches (sixty centimeters). His one-inch long silvery-gray mohair was accented with original felt pads and black cord stitched claws. He had large shoe button eyes and a center-seamed head. Later, a photograph taken at the christening of the original owner confirmed the bear's identity. There, sitting on a park bench near the infant and her mother, was a 1905 (dated) Steiff teddy. No hood ornament, and no nameplate!

At the gentleman's request, I gave a talk to his antique dealer's club at one of their meetings about two months after the estate sale. The topic? How to tell the difference between a $500 and a $5,000 teddy!

Recognizing a Valuable Teddy

I knew the teddy was valuable because I have been collecting and appraising teddy bears for years. But even a beginner, armed with a basic understanding of the history of a toy manufacturer, can identify the manufacturer and the approximate date of a bear—even a bear with no permanent mark. Take Gebrueder Bing, for instance. The German manufacturer was proclaimed to be the largest toymaker in the world around 1907 to 1910. During this period, the company had more than five thousand employees, which represented a tremendous growth from the meager tinware plant they had established in the 1860s. By the late 1800s, the Bing brothers had established themselves as one of the most innovative quality toy firms in the world, specializing in wind-up or clockwork toys.

By 1905 to 1906, Steiff had set the standard for the teddy bear. Bing wanted to share in the market, so the company set out to expand its line of toys beyond mechanical animals—which today are some of the most valued—and enter the teddy bear market. By 1907,

This 1919 Bing teddy bear wears the metal BW tag on its right arm.

teddy mania was making the demand for our furry friend nearly insatiable. With plentiful resources, Bing was able to enter the competition and produce treasured examples until it ceased operation around 1930.

To the best of my current knowledge, Bing produced two basic styles of teddy bears. The first, a small-eared, tip-toe style, is quite easily identified. The original foot design was done to show the teddy was standing on tippy-toes, as if acting as a sentry. The foot pads, of felt, form a point at the heel of the foot. These bears have shoe button eyes, and I have observed these both marked and unmarked. After World War I, this style appears with a metal BW (Bing Werkes) tin button attached to the outer wrist. The grayish felt paw pads are quite unique, and the cinnamon mohair resembles the covering of Bing's early tumbling bears and other mechanical toys. The post-World War I version commonly would have orangish painted glass eyes, sometimes clear as the paint came off. Look for the tip-toe foot!

The nose is a classic trademark for Bing. I believe this rather pronounced snout is distinguished—somewhat exaggerated, but always unique. Many photos exist of this Bing profile, and the sewing pattern should be observed closely. Early Schuco and Steiff bears have artistic nose patterns similar to Bing's. Horizontal noses (usually on the small teddys that were less than fifteen inches tall) and vertical stitch noses (on the bears more than fifteen inches tall) are easily recognizable, especially if you take the time to study the design pattern.

Style number two for Bing would be the classic teddy, which very closely resembles the early Steiffs. The teddy's body is very full, and the large ears are set widely apart and exquisitely done. The long arms and legs have a ratio of measurement similar to the earliest Steiffs. The nose dominates the end of an artistically sloped snout. The outer stitches surround the nose and provide a true signature. The earliest glass eyes (from 1907 special order) are painted brown with black pupils. These eyes offer a very realistic look to the proud teddy bear sporting them.

This prized 1907 teddy bear has the pronounced snout that identifies him as a Bing bear.

Austin still has the rare GBN-Bavaria stamp tin arrow clamped to his ear.

The voices for both the large and small versions of these Bing teddy bears are tilt-type growlers rather than squeeze type. In all of the Bings I have examined, the growlers produce a short, low decible tone, unique from that of other manufactured teddies.

Gebruder Bing marks are easily identified. Originally, Bing bears wore a tin arrow clamped to the right ear. "GBN" (for Gebruder Bing Nurmberg) was painted on the arrow, along with "Bavaria." Steiff took Bing to court, claiming the ear was their territory, and the outcome of the case forced Bing to remove the ear arrow and affix a metal GBN button under the arm. From approximately 1909 until World War I, this button was an established mark. Bing did continue to use the arrow in the ear for mechanical bears and non-teddy animals. After World War I, the round GBN button gave way to Bing Werkes' "BW," which was painted on a round tin disc, either blue or red in color. This tin "BW" was clamped to the wrist of the teddy. This was the final method of marking, which ceased when Bing went into receivership in the early 1930s.

Throughout the world, Bing's products are still among the most highly valued and sought. By reading the special traits as described, studying photographs, and visiting with actual examples through shows and clubs, we can all learn to spot the "Bing." When all else fails, I have a special, new way to determine if a teddy is indeed a Bing. But it will require the talent of a friend or relative—unless you are a seamstress!

My wife, Brenda, is very adept at sewing, and I don't know how we would have progressed to performing minor surgeries for old needy teddies without her skill. The ability to diagnose and historically correct weak or damaged areas is a most important asset. Here is one discovery, made by my wife, which resulted from her sewing ability.

We were most fortunate to receive a 1907, twenty-inch Gebrueder Bing teddy bear. We named him Austin, because he was found in Austinburg. This teddy had a metal arrow in the right ear, brown hand-painted glass eyes, and was covered with 70 years of grey-black soot from storage. After days of meticulous cleaning, a cinnamon-gold mint teddy emerged. Brenda examined the closing stitches on the front of the teddy. The stitching

> TRY TO APPROACH THE MAKING OF EACH NEW BEAR WITH A FRESH EYE, SO THAT
>
> EACH ONE WILL HAVE A UNIQUE QUALITY ALL ITS OWN.
>
> — *Bettina F. Groh, artist, Blue Springs, MO*

consisted of a simple back and forth zig-zag stitch, except at each end, where a unique little box stitch was neatly executed. As far as we know, this style of stitching is unique to Bing bears. If our next Bing is unmarked, he will be identifiable by the stitching alone—thanks to Brenda's careful eye.

Many other well-made teddies from the early 1900s have unmistakable traits. It would have been impossible to cover them all in this article alone, but there are several books available about the history of individual manufacturers and the traits that can be used in identifying the origin of these olde teddies. And of course, your local teddy bear store has several modern manufactured bears in stock. If you don't already have a favorite, check chapter one the stores near you.

We should salute every one of the early teddy manufacturers, including their designers. These artisans provided the spawning grounds from which today's prolific craftspeople arose. And today's designers and manufacturers are busy creating the antiques for upcoming generations!

Manufacturers

AKIRA TRADING CO.
8277 NW 66th St.
Miami, FL 33166

BEARLY PEOPLE
P.O. Box 16267
7250 Radford Ave.
North Hollywood, CA 91615
Phone: 818-982-8082
1-800-227-BEAR
Fax: 818-503-9721
Products: Bearly People creates a collection of jointed, posable plush teddy bears dressed in lavish costumes. Most wear ruffles and elaborate dresses. The company also makes a line of bears wearing antique style clothing. More than 35 new designs are introduced each year, including both open and limited editions.
Company history: Bearly People was established more than 12 years ago by Cheryl DeRose, who began making her own bears and selling them to a few retail stores. Cheryl still designs all the bears herself.

BEARS & BEDTIME MFG. (1994) INC.
4803-52 Ave.
Stony Plain, Alberta T7Z-1C4, Canada
Phone: 403-963-6300 or
1-800-461-BEAR
Fax: 403-963-2134
Sales information: Wholesale and retail sales available. Phone and fax orders accepted. An outlet location is available at the address above.
Products: Bears & Bedtime manufactures limited edition teddy bears. A brochure of their teddies is available upon request. They also carry Cherished Teddies, teddy books, Teddy Bear & Friends, Teddy Bear Review and various gift items such as earrings, mugs and cards.
Club information: Bears & Bedtime's Collectors Club offers collector discounts and up-to-date information about new items. Membership is included with the purchase of a bear.

Call the phone number above or write to the above mailing address for more information. Mark the envelope "Bears & Bedtime Mfg. Collector's Club."
Company history: Bears & Bedtime Mfg. opened as a franchise store in 1993. In February 1994, the company became the only Bears & Bedtime store in Canada. Today, Bears & Bedtime Mfg. is still following the strict standards of the original Bears & Bedtime Teddy Bears. Many original bear designs are still in production, and new and different bears are being developed.

BEAVER VALLEY
18133 NE 68th, Suite D-120
Redmond, WA 98052
Phone: 206-558-0824
Fax: 206-558-0714
Sales information: Wholesale sales only. Orders can be made by phone or fax. Free catalog available. There is an outlet location at the address above.
Products: Beaver Valley bears are realistic bears with accurate claws, noses and open mouths with teeth. They come in limited editions of 100 or less in various sizes, styles and colors. Many are dressed. The company makes other animals as well.
Company history: Beaver Valley was founded in 1983 by Kaylee Nilan. The company has grown to include a dozen craftspeople who work under Kaylee's supervision. She still designs and helps make each bear.

THE BOYDS COLLECTION
P.O. Box 4385
Gettysburg, PA 17325
Phone: 717-359-7312
Products: The Boyds Collection includes affordable, plush bears in many styles, including J.B. Bear & Associates, pellet-filled animals designed by Gae Sharp; The Archive Collection, bears and other animals in the antique style;

T.J.'s Best Dressed, bears and other animals with their own wardrobes; Bears in the Attic, chenille fabric bears for children; and Artist Bears. The company also sells furniture, clothing and accessories for bears. The Bearstone Collection figurines are based on the Boyds plush bears.
Company history: The Boyds Collection began when Gary and Tina Lowenthal decided to wholesale some of the antique reproductions they sold in their antique shop in Boyds, Maryland. In 1987, the company began making plush animals almost exclusively. Since then, the company has grown from a 2-person operation to a company employing more than 40 people.

CANTERBURY BEARS
The Old Coach House, Court Hill, Littlebourn
Canterbury, Kent, U.K.
Phone: 011-44-1227-728238
Fax: 011-44-1227-728238
Distributors:
U.S.A.:
Gund, Runyons Lane, P.O. Box H, Edison, NJ 08818
Phone: 908-248-1500
Sales information: Wholesale sales only through Gund.
Products: Canterbury Bears come in a variety of classic designs and colors. Several limited editions are available, as well as open editions. Canterbury Classic Range bears come in eight different colors and wear bows. Tartan Bears come dressed in more than 600 different tartans made to the customer's specifications.
Club information: Canterbury Bears Collectors Club provides collectors with reservations on limited editions and up-to-date information about new products. For more information, write to Mrs. Donna Saqui, P.O. Box 47, Valpariso, IN 46384, or call 219-465-4084. See the listing in chapter 5.
Company history: Canterbury Bears

were established in 1979 when Mr. Blackburn was asked to design a bear for a woman's 80th birthday. Fifteen years later, the family business has grown considerably, and Canterbury bears are sold all over the world.

COMMONWEALTH TOY & NOVELTY CO., INC.

45 W. 25th St., 5th Floor
New York, NY 10010
Phone: 212-242-4070
Fax: 212-645-4279
Products: Commonwealth Toy & Novelty Co. manufactures several different teddy bear designs per year, including their famous Bialosky Bear. The company manufactures several other toys as well.
Company history: Commonwealth Toy & Noveltly Co. was founded in 1934. Today, the company has a network of 30 factories coordinated in 6 countries.

COOPERSTOWN BEARS LTD.

1275 Busch Pkwy.
Buffalo Grove, IL 60089

DAKIN, INC.

20969 Ventura Blvd., Suite 25
Woodland Hills, CA 91364
Phone: 415-692-1555
1-800-227-6598
Distributors:
Canada:
Hope Gift Distributors, 331 Amber St.
Markham, Ontario L3R 3J7
Products: Dakin's plush line includes plush versions of Enesco's Cherished Teddies; Cuddle Bear, the "all occasion" bear, Gingham and Carmel, bears with two colors of fur that are one of Dakin's best-selling designs; Basic Bears; little bears; oversized bears and more. Bear hand puppets and baby bear items, such as musical mobiles and pull musicals, are also available.
Company history: Dakin was founded in 1955. Today, the company manufactures and distributes more than 900 plush and licensed characters to nearly 30,000 gift and specialty retailers.

DEAN'S RAG BOOK COMPANY LTD.

Pontnewynydd Industrial Estate, Pontypool
Gwent NP4 6YY, U.K.
Phone: 011-44-1495-764881
Fax: 011-44-1495-764883
Distributors:
U.S.A.:
Hobby House Press Inc. 900 Frederick St. Cumberland, MD 21502.
Phone: 1-800-554-1447.
Fax: 301-759-4940.
Sales information: Wholesale only.
Products: Dean's makes several limited edition and open edition mohair bears. Most are traditional in style and wear ribbons. Some are replicas of early Dean's bears. Some special items include Dean's musical bears and Wildlife bear cubs, which are realistic looking polar, grizzly and Panda bears. A wide variety of colors, styles and sizes are available, as well as a selection of other toys. Dean's also sells bear collectibles, including aprons, tote bags, pencil cases, purses, and greeting cards.
Club information: Dean's Collectors Club offers collectors discounts and up-to-date information through a newsletter. The $50 membership price includes a mohair bear. Write to Hobby House Press for more information.
Company history: Dean's was established in 1903 and began making teddy bears in 1915. Many of the Dean's bears are similar to the old bears, and some are made from the old patterns.

DEBRA DOLLS INTERNATIONAL

601 Tradewind Dr., Suite 4
Ancaster, Ontario L9G 4V5, Canada
Phone: 905-304-0192
Fax: 905-648-7103
Products: Debra Dolls International is the Canadian agent and distributor for Merrythought Limited, Gabrielle Designs Limited and Oz International Inc.

DEPARTMENT 56

One Village Place
6436 City West Pkwy.
Eden Prairie, MN 55344
Phone: 1-800-FIVESIX

Products: Dept. 56 produces the Upstairs Downstairs Bears, bear figurines designed by Carol Lawson, a well-known English illustrator and author. The resin bears are handpainted and stand on mahogany bases with porcelain bottom stamps.

DIMENSIONS

641 McKnight St.
Reading, PA 19601-2499
Phone: 610-372-8491
1-800-523-8452
Fax: 610-372-0426
Sales information: Wholesale sales only. Fax and phone orders accepted. Catalogs are free.
Products: Dimensions makes assorted needlecraft kits, iron-on transfer and no-sew appliqué kits in bear designs, including many Lucy Rigg designs.

ENESCO CORP.

1 Elk Grove Plaza
Elk Grove Villa, IL 60007

THE FRANKLIN MINT

U.S. Route 1
Franklin Center, PA 19091
Phone: 1-800-CALL-TFM
1-800-225-5836
Fax: 610-459-6040
Sales information: Retail and wholesale sales available. Phone and fax orders accepted.
Products: The Franklin Mint produces several figurines that are replicas of the figurines in The Teddy Bear Museum's collection in England. The figurines are porcelain, bronze patina, pewter or cast iron. Many are decorated and painted by hand. Other teddy bear items are sometimes available.

GABRIELLE DESIGNS

Great North Road, Adwick-Le-Street
Doncaster DN6 7ES, U.K.
Phone: 011-44-1302-721282
Fax: 011-44-1302-330216
Distributors:
U.S.A.:
Tide-Rider, Inc., P.O. Box 429, Oakdale, CA 95361
Phone: 209-848-4420
Fax: 209-848-4423
Sales information: Wholesale sales only

through Tide-Rider. Tide-Rider accepts fax and phone orders. The company has a factory shop at the address in England.

Products: Gabrielle Designs manufactures the original British Paddington bear. A limited edition bear is available, as well as open edition bears that come dressed in duffel coats, hats and wellingtons. The company also manufactures Aunt Lucy (Paddington's famous aunt) and Winnie-the-Pooh and Friends.

Company history: Shirley Clarkson, the managing director of Gabrielle Designs Limited, designed the original Paddington Bear product more than 25 years ago. Micheal Bond granted Gabrielle Designs the Classic Paddington Bear and limited editions for worldwide distribution. Other character products have since been produced, including Aunt Lucy and Winnie-the-Pooh and friends.

GEBRUEDER BING, INC.

Zwerggasse 1-3, 96047 Bamberg, Germany
Phone: 011-49-951-22978
Fax: 011-49-951-22978
Distributors:
U.S.A.:
European Artist Dolls, 11632 Busy St., Richmond, VA 23236
Phone: 804-379-8595
Fax: 804-379-2780
Sales information: Wholesale and retail sales are available.

Products: Gebrueder Bing classic teddy bears come in limited and open editions and several different styles, colors and sizes. They are all reproductions of old Bing bears.

Club information: Bing 1500 Teddy Bear Club is a free club offering members reservations for limited editions. Members will be kept up-to-date on new editions and will have four weeks after the announcement to purchase their reserved bear. They can choose to refuse specific bears without losing their membership.

Company history: Gebrueder Bing was founded in Nuremberg, Germany in 1863. The company grew to be one of the largest toy companies in the world until 1932, when it closed due to fi-

nancial troubles. The company was revived by Eric Kluge, owner of the Bamberger Puppenwerkstaette 1882, a doll clinic in Bamberg, Germany. Eric met an elderly woman who was related to the former Gebrueder Bing owner during a business trip in Florida. She had original Bing bear patterns traced on an old Nuremberg newspaper, and Eric was able to secure the license to sell reproductions of the bear.

GRISLY SPIELWAREN

D-6719 Kirchheimbolanden, Beethovenstr. 1
P.O. Box 1127, Germany
Phone: 011-49-635-23596
Fax: 011-49-635-267133
Distributors:
Charles R. Moose, importer/distributor, 500 W. 33rd St. Baltimore, MD 21211-2745
Phone: 410-889-5061
Sales information: Wholesale sales are available through the distributor, Charles R. Moose. He will provide direct service to individuals if there is no retail store providing Grisly products in their area. Phone orders are available.

Products: Grisly-Spielwaren manufactures a variety of 100% handmade mohair teddy bears in several sizes and colors. A few limited edition items are produced, but most are open editions. The current line includes about 15 bears and pandas. Some come in choices of 11 colors. They range in size from 4¾"-more than 27". Many are classic in style and wear ribbons. The company's bright red and green mohair teddy bears are quite popular. Hand puppets and a variety of other animals are also available.

Company history: Grisly is a cottage industry founded in 1954 by Karl Theodor Unfricht in Kirchheimbolanden, Germany.

GUND

Runyons Lane, P.O. Box H
Edison, NJ 08818
Phone: 908-248-1500
Sales information: Wholesale only. Retail stores may call 1-800-448-GUND for customer service.

Products: Gund introduces new teddy bears each year. All Gund animals are made of quality materials and are carefully inspected to ensure quality and safety. Gund manufactures several children's toys, as well as the Signature Collection, fine handmade limited edition American-style bears, now in their fifth year. Gund also recently began manufacturing Winnie-the-Pooh products. Gund's Littlest Bears are very popular.

Company history: Gund was founded in 1898 in Norwalk, CT by German emigrant Adolph Gund. It was one of the first companies to produce teddy bears. In 1925, Gund was purchased by Adolph Gund's personal assistant, Jacob Swedlin, who pioneered licensing agreements to produce Walt Disney, King Features and Hanna Barbera cartoon characters. Gund's Collector's Classics were introduced in the 1970s. In 1994, Gund began manufacturing Winnie-the-Pooh products, as well as Bambi and Friends, Frosty the Snowman and Boynton characters. The Signature Collection was introduced in 1990.

HERMANN TEDDY ORIGINAL

P.O. Box 12 07, D-96112 Hirachaid, Germany
Phone: 011-49-954-39161
Fax: 011-49-954-39163
Products: Hermann Teddy Originals include traditional Nostalgic Teddy Bears; 9-jointed Elisabeth; Teddy Replica, a replica of a 1930s original; Hans; Johann, Hans's larger friend; 6" Panda Teddy; Musical Bear that plays Teddy Bears Picnic; Rathskeller Bears, a display piece; Mothers With Baby; Teddy Babies, 6" teddies in yellow, cinnamon or dark brown; Christmas Teddy with Tree; and Jack, an artist bear by Jenny Krantz.

Club information: A Hermann-Teddy Original Club is available, offering a newsletter with company and new product information and more.

Company history: The original Hermann company began more than 80 years ago, when Bernhard Hermann started making teddy bears in Sonneerg. In

1948, Bernhard Hermann and his three sons relocated the business and the factory to the German Democratic Republic in Hirschaid near Bamberg. Since that time, the company has continued to grow, and thousands of Hermann teddies are sold all over the world. Today, Bernhard Hermann's granddaughters own the company, which now employs about 100 people who still make collectible bears in the traditional way. All bears are hand-stuffed and have handstitched noses. They are made of mohair and other high-grade woven materials.

JAKAS SOFT TOYS

85 Lewis Rd., Wantirna
Vic. 3152
Australia
Phone: 011-61-398-873547
Fax: 011-61-398-837553
Sales information: Wholesale and retail sales available.
Products: Jakas Soft Toys teddy bears come in a variety of colors and sizes, including Koalas. Most are plush, but many designs can be made with woollen coats. Some are jointed.
Company history: Jakas Soft Toys was founded in 1956.

KRITTER KAPS

P.O. Box 2480
Oceanside, CA 92051-2480
Phone: 1-800-432-4531
Fax: 619-931-0691
Sales information: Wholesale and retail sales available. Phone and fax orders accepted.
Products: Kritter Kaps makes teddy bear hub caps in 14" and 15" sizes.
Company history: Kritter Kaps was founded about 2 years ago.

MANGO TEDDY BEAR COMPANY

3310 Brookside Dr.
Anchorage, AL 99517
Phone: 907-243-2979
1-800-352-3277
Fax: 406-442-4914
Sales information: Wholesale and retail sales available. Fax and phone orders accepted.
Products: Mango Teddy Bear Company manufactures Peek-A-Boo Bears, bears with magnetic paws that can be

posed in a variety of ways. They come in several colors and styles, including dressed and undressed and Pandas. The company also produces bears that double as backpacks and children's books by Julia Cox.
Company history: The Mango Teddy Bear Company was founded 6 years ago.

MARY MEYER

P.O. Box 275
Townshend, VT 05353
Phone: 1-800-451-4387
Fax: 802-365-4233
Sales information: Mary Meyer has a small retail catalog available, but prefers to sell wholesale and provide collectors with the names of stores in their areas that sell Mary Meyer products. Phone and fax orders are available. A company store, The Toy Store, is located at Putnam Park, Brattleboro, VT 05301. Phone: 802-257-5846.
Products: Mary Meyer manufactures several popular designs, including Green Mountain Bears designed by artist Carol Carini. Bears come in several colors, styles and sizes. Other popular styles include Chocolate Chip, a white bear with brown spots, and Big Bart Bears, polar and black bears that come in 15", 24", 35" and 48" sizes. A wide assortment of additional bears and other animals are also available. Special catalogs for Valentine's Day, Easter and Christmas are published each year.
Company history: Mary Meyer has been in business since 1933. The company is now run by a third generation of the Meyer family. Mary celebrated her 90th birthday in 1994. Several Mary Meyer bears have been nominated for TOBY awards.

MERRYTHOUGHT LIMITED

Ironbridge, Telford
Shropshire TF8 7NJ, England
Phone: 011-44-1952-43316
Fax: 011-44-1952-43254
Distributors:
USA:
Tide-Rider, Inc., P.O. Box 429
Oakdale, CA 95361
Phone: 209-848-4420

Fax: 209-848-4423
Canada: Debra Dolls International Inc., 601 Tradewind Dr., Suite 4, Ancaster, Ontario L9G 4V5
Sales information: Wholesale sales only are available through Tide-Rider, Inc. Orders can be made via phone or fax.
Products: Merrythought bears include mohair classic bears in sizes ranging from 10"-40" in various colors with various ribbons. The Heritage Collection is a collection of dressed character bears. Merrythought also manufactures such special items as bear muffs, bears made especially for small children, and nightwear cases. Finally, the company has an annual international collectors' catalog, with several high quality limited editions bears. Other plush animals are available as well.
Company history: Merrythought was established in 1930 when two mohair manufacturers, W.G. Holmes and G. H. Laxton, joined C.J. Rendle of Chad Valley and A.C. Janisch of J.K. Farnell to manufacture soft toys. Florence Atwood was the company's designer until her death in 1949, and many of her designs are still being produced. The company has been making toys since 1930 except for a brief period when the British Admiralty took over the Coalbrookdale factory buildings during World War II. Today's designer is Jacqueline Revitt, and the managing director of the company is Oliver Holmes, the original founder's grandson.

THE MICHAUD COLLECTION

Tide-Rider, Inc.
Oakdale, CA 95361
Phone: 209-848-4420
Fax: 209-848-4423
Sales information: Wholesale sales only. Phone and fax orders are accepted.
Products: The Michaud Collection includes limited and open edition reproductions of Terry and Doris Michaud's collection. They are mohair bears designed by the Michauds and handmade in Great Britain under their direction. Each bear comes with the story of how it became part of the Michaud's personal collection.
Company history: The Michauds began their famous teddy bear collection in

1972 when they purchased "The Professor." Their Carrousel Museum collection is housed in Chesaning, Michigan.

MIGHTY STAR, INC.

Special Effects Division
925 Amboy Ave.
Perth Amboy, NJ 08861
Phone: 908-826-5200
Fax: 908-826-7370

Products: The Special Effects division of Mighty Star manufactures several different styles of bears, from the forlorn Little Bear Lost in overalls to realistic looking Bear Country bears. The bears and other animals come in a variety of sizes, colors and styles.

Company history: The Special Effects Division of Mighty Star was formalized in 1983. Today, there are more than 200 plush products produced. Despite the company's growth, all design, manufacturing and distribution capabilities are under one roof, to guarantee the quality of their products.

MUFFIN ENTERPRISES, INC.

429 S. 18th St.
Camp Hill, PA 17011
Phone: 717-761-7707
1-800-338-9041
Fax: 717-761-7883

Sales information: Wholesale and retail sales are available. Orders can be made via phone or fax.

Products: Muffin Enterprises, Inc. manufactures Sir Koff-A-Lot, a post-op teddy bear splint with a seamless back used by adults following surgery, and Kiddie Kub Bear, a post-op teddy for children.

Company history: Muffin Enterprises, Inc. is 11 years old. The company was established by two cardiovascular surgeons whose patients didn't want to do respiratory therapy following surgery. They were teddy bear collectors, so they designed a post-op pillow splint in the form of a firm teddy bear called Sir Koff-A-Lot. Since then, Sir Koff-A-Lot has been used by more than 300,000 adults recovering from surgery, and his counterpart, Kiddie Kub, has been used by more than 5,000 children.

NORTH AMERICAN BEAR COMPANY, INC.

401 N. Wabash, Suite 500
Chicago, IL 60611
Phone: 312-329-0020
Fax: 312-329-1417

Products: The North American Bear Company manufactures quality collectibles such as the famous Muffy VanderBear of the VanderBear family, and The V.I.B.s, modeled after historical and famous people. The company also makes many clothes and accessories for Muffy and her family. A full range of other stuffed toys is available, as well as accessories, greeting cards, paper products and a full line of infant plush.

Club information: The Muffy Vander-Bear Club offers collectors up-to-date information about Muffy and her collections. Membership includes stationery, stickers, a pendant, a color history booklet of all collections to date, Muffy Fanfare, and Muffy FunFacts, a newsletter with important information for collectors. Members also receive the North American Bear Newsletter, NAB News, and have the chance to purchase exclusive member-only pieces. Membership is $25 in the USA and $30 outside the USA. For more information, write the Muffy VanderBear Club at the above address.

Company history: The North American Bear Company began when Barbara Isenberg and fashion designer friend, Odl Bauer, designed a bear out of an old sweatshirt. That bear evolved into Albert the Running Bear, a classic bear in a colorful running suit. In 1978, Barbara teamed up with her brother, Paul Levy, to form the North American Bear Co. A year later, the VIB line was introduced. In 1983, the company introduced the VanderBear Family, and in 1984, Muffy Vander-Bear. More bears and animals have followed. Today, Barbara heads the New York studio where all products are created by an in-house team of designers and artists. Paul handles finance, sales and the warehouses in Chicago.

OZ INTERNATIONAL

1601A Dover Hwy.
P.O. Box 637
Sandpoint, ID 83864
Phone: 208-263-7756
Fax: 208-263-7751

Sales information: Wholesale and retail sales are available. Phone and fax orders are accepted. Catalogs are free.

Products: Oz International manufactures mohair and plush bears dressed as the characters in Remi Kramer's books. All have detailed costumes. Open editions and a line of special limited edition bears are available.

Company history: Oz International was founded more than 10 years ago. Remi Kramer wrote *The Legend of LoneStar Bear* in 1988. In 1989, the first versions of LoneStar Bear and his buddy, Barney the Raccoon were released. Since then, there have been two more books about LoneStar Bear and a variety of bears based on the characters in the books. The books, stereo tapes of the books and rubber stamps based on the books are also available.

RUSS BERRIE AND COMPANY, INC.

111 Bauer Dr.
Oakland, NJ 07436
Phone: 201-337-9000
1-800-343-RUSS

Sales information: Wholesale sales only.

Products: Russ Berrie bears are made of fine plush materials in old-fashioned styles. They come in a variety of colors and sizes from 550%"-21". Most wear ribbons.

Company history: Russell Berrie's first job was selling teddy bears in 1956. In 1963, he started Russ Berrie and Company, and has been designing and selling new bears ever since.

SIGIKID H. SCHARRER & KOCH GMBH

21-11 24th Ave.
Astoria, NY 11102
Phone: 718-274-8249
718-274-8834
Fax: 718-274-8249

Sales information: Wholesale sales only. Phone and fax orders accepted. Catalogs are free in USA and $10 overseas.

Products: SIGIKID produces several

styles of bears, from very realistic bears to bears dressed in elaborate costumes. There are both limited and open editions. Several other animals are also available. All textile gift and plush bears are machine washable and guaranteed.

Company history: Previously called H. Scharrer & Koch GMBH, the company that became SIGIKID was founded in 1856 to make glass beads, marbles and wooden toys. In 1968, the company was inherited by Mr. and Mrs. Josef Gottstein and the name SIGIKID was born. Products diversified to include textile gifts for infants, plush animals, dolls, artist dolls and marionettes. In 1993, SIGIKID introduced a sales team that made the company's products available in the USA for the first time.

STEIFF USA, L.P.

200 5th Ave., Suite 1205
New York, NY 10010
Phone: 212-675-2727
Fax: 212-675-5128
Sales information: Wholesale only.
Products: Best known for its bears, the Steiff company also produces a wide range of other animals. Using only the finest and most luxurious fabrics, including mohair, Steiff animals are still cut by hand from bolts of cloth. Many pieces are still stuffed with traditional wood shavings. Steiff bears include classic and realistic styles in a variety of colors and sizes. There are limited editions for collectors and open editions and general toys for children. All Steiff animals wear the famous "Button-in-Ear." Steiff also produces a variety of boutique items including teddy bags, jewelry, watches, china sets and postcards. A book about the company and its history is available.
Club information: Steiff Club offers collectors up-to-date information about the company and its history through its quarterly publication, a sterling silver membership pin and annual renewal gifts, and the opportunity to purchase limited edition Club Exclusives. Membership is $40 per club year, which runs from April 1 through March 31 each year. For more information, write to Steiff Club, 225 5th Ave., Suite 1033, New York, NY 10010, or call 212-779-CLUB.

Company history: Steiff's founder, Margarete Steiff, overcame a disability that confined her to a wheelchair as well as the limitations on women of her time when she became the owner of a successful dressmaking shop in the Swabian town of Giengen on the Brenz in 1880. She began by making small pincushion animals, and went on to experiment with new designs. In 1903, her nephew, Richard Steiff, registered a pattern for a jointed bear. In 1904, to distinguish the company from competitors, the Steiff family began stamping their animals with a distinctive "Button-in-Ear" trademark. Since then, the company has continued to manufacture lifelike and classic designs for bears and other animals.

TIDE-RIDER INC.

614 Hi-Tech Pkwy.
P.O. Box 429
Oakdale, CA 95361
Phone: 209-848-4420
Fax: 209-848-4423
Sales information: Sales to retail stores only. Collectors are welcome to call for information on where to purchase Tide-Rider collectibles in their area, or with any questions they may have concerning the products the company represents.
Products: Tide-Rider is the U.S. distributor for Merrythought, Ltd., The Michaud Collection and Gabrielle De-signs' Original British Paddington.

Company history: Tide-Rider was established in 1950 and has been a family business since its inception.

TRUDI GIOCATTOLI SPA

Via Angelo Angeli, 120, 33017 Tarcento (Udine), Italy
Phone: 011-39-432-791444
Fax: 011-39-432-791664
Products: Trudi manufactures a historical collection of teddy bears. Each design is limited to 200 pieces. Two new designs are added per year. The bears wear historically correct costumes of different historical periods. The bears are entirely handmade under the supervision of Mrs. Trudi Muller Patriarca.
Company history: Trudi has been manufacturing bears for more than 40 years.

THE VERMONT TEDDY BEAR CO., INC

2031 Shelburne Rd.,
P.O. Box 965
Shelburne, VT 05482
Phone: 802-985-3001
1-800-829-BEAR
Fax: 802-985-1304
Sales information: Wholesale and retail sales available. Phone and fax orders are accepted. Fax orders should be on regular order forms. A retail catalog is available. Both retail and wholesale catalogs are free.
Products: The Vermont Teddy Bear Company bears are all handmade in Vermont. They are completely child safe and come in a variety of dressed and undressed styles in many colors and sizes. Special order bears and many outfits and accessories are also available.
Company history: The Vermont Teddy Bear Company has been making bears for more than 15 years.

5
Organizations

How to Use This Chapter

There are several advantages to joining a teddy bear organization. Local and regional organizations foster friendships among collectors and artists and provide members with valuable information and networking opportunities. Many organizations also provide services to the community, such as donating teddy bears to needy people. Others sponsor shows, speakers and other special programs. National and international organizations also offer collectors and artists valuable information and networking possibilities.

This chapter includes several local, regional, national and international organizations. If you are interested in joining an organization in your area, check the geographic index first, and then use the listing to contact the organization. You are bound to make lifelong friends who share your interests. If you are interested in joining a larger organization, such as Teddy Bear Artists of America or Good Bears of the World, you will find contact information for these organizations as well.

Once again, we have tried to be as up-to-date as possible, but a specific organization's meeting places and times are subject to change. It is best to contact someone in the club before attending the meeting. Officers are also bound to change from year to year. Begin by contacting the person in the listing. If she is no longer the club's contact person, she may be able to refer you to someone else. Again, keep in mind that you are likely to be contacting the person listed at home, so be respectful of time zone differences.

Several manufacturers also have clubs for collectors of their bears. These organizations often offer newsletters and reservations on limited editions. Some of these are listed here. If you do not find a manufacturers' club listed here, check the manufacturers' listings.

We hope these listings will help you discover an organization that fits your needs. If there are no local collectors' or artists' organizations, why not start your own? Use these listings to get ideas of the types of activities other organizations are sponsoring. We hope the listings in this chapter will lead to many life-long friendships!

Terrie Stong, Good Bears of the World

BY MEREDITH WOLF

Terrie Stong, Executive Chair of Good Bears of the World, talks about the life-changing power of teddy bears.

*H*ave you offered a good bear hug today?" Every day, Terrie Stong strives to answer this question—the motto of Good Bears of the World—in the affirmative. Terrie has devoted herself to the organization since 1983. She served as chairbear of the Toledo, Ohio den until 1990. She is now the executive chair of the international nonprofit organization that seeks to provide teddy bears for children and elderly people who need solace, comfort and love.

When Terrie's daughter, Anna, was hospitalized with asthma as a child, one of Terrie's friends made a bear for her. Not only did Wellington comfort Anna, but he also became the volunteer recipient of practice shots from diabetic children who were learning how to administer them.

"I read an article in *Prevention* magazine about Good Bears of the World and found out that other bears were doing the same job that Wellington was doing," Terrie says. When she later met GBW founder Jim Ownby, she agreed to hold the first Toledo, Ohio den meeting in her living room. She said that she would serve as chair only until a permanent chairbear was found. She ended up holding that post for seven years.

Good Bears of the World has survived since 1969 thanks to the dedication of people like Terrie. Jim Ownby ran the organization from his radio station, KNDI, in Honolulu, Hawaii until his death in 1986. Since 1969, GBW has expanded to thirty-eight dens across the U.S. and two abroad, in the Netherlands and New Zealand. Members distribute bears around the world in orphanages, battered women's shelters and nursing homes. They also provide bears for police and fire departments and send bears to victims of natural disasters such as floods, fires and earthquakes.

Terrie Stong, the executive director of Good Bears of the World, holds three of the organization's official bears.

Meeting Psychological Needs

The value of giving bears to traumatized individuals stretches beyond simply providing them with something cuddly to hold. Teddy bears meet the psychological needs of people experiencing loss, pain or shock. According to Terrie, the Red Cross used to refuse the bears, saying that their main objective was to provide food, clothing and shelter for disaster victims. Now, however, they often request hundreds of bears at a time.

"They realize that the psychological implications of these disasters need to be met as well as the physical needs," Terrie says. "Sometimes, even when the physical problem is solved, the emotional trauma can hold." And it isn't the victims alone who are affected by the work of GBW. Caregivers of Midwest flood victims in 1994 reported that the arrival of the bears helped raise their own spirits as well as those of the bear recipients.

GBW is serious about helping others—so serious that almost all contributions are used to provide bears for those in need. To cut down on cost, the organization has only one paid employee, administrative assistant

Rose Mulligan. "That means she does everything," says Terrie, including processing the memberships and bear orders, answering the phone and mailing out information. Rose is paid for only twenty hours of work per week, but Terrie estimates that she puts in at least sixty.

GBW's Official Bear

The official Good Bear teddy is 11½ inches tall and chocolate brown with a cream ribbon imprinted with GBW's logo. Terrie says that police usually prefer GBW teddies to bears from other sources, since they can be assured of getting high-quality bears that meet government safety standards. Other organizations often purchase the bears to give away for the same reasons.

"A teddy bear becomes a special friend, especially when it is given at a time when a person is devastated and upset," says Terrie. "The Good Bears teddy bear has an almost human face with a sweet, kindly expression, providing comfort to those in pain."

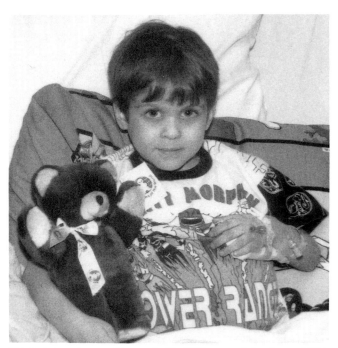

This little boy, the son of bear artist Terri Effan, was glad to have a GBW teddy bear to comfort him when he was in the hospital.

Muffin Enterprises has distributed GBW bears since December 1991. Muffin Enterprises is a company that knew about the healing power of bears long before they began distributing the GBW official bear. The company also manufactures Sir Koff-A-Lot, a bear designed to help patients recovering from surgery. Sir Koff-a-Lot has a seamless back and head that will not irritate an incision, so patients can hug him as hard as they wish to aid in therapeutic coughing and breathing exercises.

Karen Shirley, president of Muffin Enterprises, is yet another individual who went a step beyond her duty as a GBW member. After joining as an individual member, she found a way to produce high-quality bears costing less than those GBW had been using.

Muffin Enterprises also warehouses the bears for free, and charges GBW only after the bears are shipped. This allows GBW full use of its funds and makes it easier to meet demand quickly. Also, shipping costs are much lower from Muffin Enterprise's warehouse in Camp Hill, Pennsylvania, than from the previous warehouse in Hawaii.

"Shipping is still a big overhead cost, but not because it's so expensive," says Terrie. "It's just that we give away so many bears." And she isn't kidding. In 1992, the organization donated 10,321 bears. In 1993, that figure increased by more than 70 percent to 17,600 bears, according to GBW treasurer John Fey.

Terrie gives credit to everyone who helps, emphasizing that the organization's achievements reflect every single member. "No one can do everything, but everyone can do something," she says.

Raising Money

GBW raises money through membership dues and donations. Most members are teddy bear artists and collectors, although Terrie emphasizes that GBW "welcomes everyone with open arms." Many become collectors once they get involved, even if they did not previously collect teddy bears, says Terrie.

GBW also holds auctions to raise money. Teddy bear artists are often willing to donate the bears. "A couple of artists really took up our cause very gallantly," says Terrie. Several show promoters also donate free table space, giving GBW cost-effective exposure.

The Bear Bank

"Unfortunately, the demand for bears continues to grow because there are more disasters, more battered women and more traumatized children every day," says Stong. In order to meet that demand and ensure that there are enough bears at hand, GBW operates a Bear Bank.

"It works just like a regular bank. People can make deposits and withdrawals, except the currency is in bears," explains Terrie. For $7.50, anyone can deposit a bear into the bank, which covers manufacturing, pro-

Police officers often use teddy bears to comfort children in times of trauma.

cessing and shipping costs. Or, they can request a bear from the bank when needed.

GBW Dens

GBW has had nonprofit status for its headquarters, located in Toledo, Ohio, since 1973, but only in 1993 were individual dens granted this status as well. Gaining group exempt status was a major accomplishment since tax deductible donations are more attractive and encourage contributions by large companies and businesses.

Interested people can join as individual members and do the work of GBW on their own, or they can join a den if there is one in their area. Dens operate locally, although many ask headquarters for suggestions about where to give bears, especially when they are just getting established. They are encouraged to give the official Good Bear but sometimes distribute other bears that have been donated to them. Dens donate bears to local individuals, agencies and police departments. They also

join the parent organization in distributing bears when there is a national disaster.

The parent organization usually handles larger and international orders. In 1993, they sent bears to Japan, Germany and Russia. The goals of the national officers are to give away bears, supervise the dens, and publish *Bear Tracks*, GBW's quarterly journal. Recruitment is another unending challenge, and new dens are formed regularly. GBW officers are often on hand at shows to answer questions and recruit.

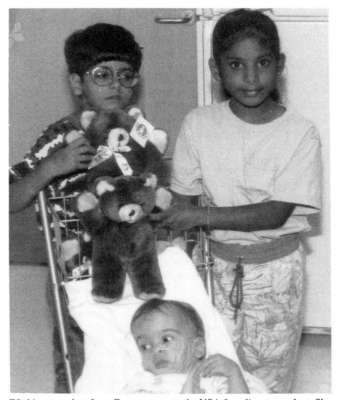

Eftyhia, an orphan from Greece, came to the USA for a liver transplant. She will take home a GBW bear, which has comforted her throughout her ordeal. She is pictured here with two young friends.

"Even if you just give away one bear and make one person feel a little better, you've helped," says Terrie. That's the simple philosophy that has transformed a one-man operation into an international network of people who believe that bears have the power to make the world a better place—with a little help from humans like Terrie, Rose, John and Karen, of course. 🐾

Organizations

BEAR BUDDIES

Susan M. Bartle
P.O. Box 546
North Collins, NY 14111
Phone: 716-337-0273
This is a local organization for artists and collectors of bears and miniature bears.
Established: 1990
Statement of purpose: To provide an opportunity for bear collectors to meet and share information; to provide speakers on bears and bear-related topics; to arrange field trips, communicate with other clubs and organizations, and sponsor shows, sales or other bear collecting activities as agreed upon by the membership.
Members: 38
Membership fee/dues: $12 per year
Meetings are held monthly.
Meeting day/time: 2nd W, 7P.M.
Meeting location: St. Stephens-Bethlehem
United Church of Christ, 750 Wehrle Dr., Amherst, NY
Activities: guest speakers, crafts, field trips, picnics, Christmas parties
Shows: NY

BEAR WITH US TEDDY BEAR COLLECTORS' CLUB

Good Bears of the World Den
Jennifer Anderson
4690 N. Blackstone
Fresno, CA 93726
Phone: 204-222-8031
Office: same as above
Established: 1994
Members: 15
Membership fee/dues: $15
Meetings are held monthly.
Shows: CA

BEARLY OURS TEDDY CLUB

Linda Harris
54 Berkinshaw Cres.
Don Mills, Ontario M3B 2T2
Canada
Phone: 416-445-9417

This is a local organization for artists and collectors.
Established: 1985
Members: 120
Meetings are held monthly.
Meeting day/time: 4th M, 7:30P.M., Sept.-June
Meeting location: Dallington Public School, Dallington Ave., North York, Ontario
Activities: workshops, talks, slide shows about bear-related topics

THE BENEVOLENT BEAR SOCIETY

Terri Kovacs
8442 Ridgewood Ln.
Novelty, OH 44072-9611
Phone: 216-338-8066
This is a local organization for artists and collectors of bears and miniature bears.
Established: 1987
Statement of purpose: To promote the love and education of the arctophile for the teddy bear; to serve as a philanthropic society and distribute teddies to adults, children, nursing homes, hospitals, or where needed; to cooperate, when possible, with other local, national and international organizations with common or related objectives.
Members: 52
Membership fee/dues: $10 per year
Meetings are held monthly. No meetings in August, December or January.
Meeting day/time: 2nd T, 7P.M.
Meeting location: Chagrin Falls Library, 100 E. Orange St., Chagrin Falls, OH
Activities: Sponsors speakers and reps from bear manufacturers; a teddy bear picnic for local children; bear making workshops; spring tea; annual luncheon with Canadian, PA, NY clubs; monthly show and share.

BLUE MT. BEAR TRACKS

Good Bears of the World Den
Gretchen McKillip
45 W. Imperial Dr.
Walla Walla, WA 99362
Phone: 509-525-0395
Catie Walker
309 W. Alder
Walla Walla, WA 99362
Phone: 509-529-8868
Fax: 509-522-0747
Established: 1988
Members: 20+
Membership fee/dues: $15
Meetings are held monthly.
Meeting location: varies
Activities: workshops, luncheons, retreats, talks on bear-related topics.
Shows: OR

CANTERBURY BEAR COLLECTORS SOCIETY

Donna L. Saqui, president
P.O. Box 47
Valparaiso, IN 46384-0047
Phone: 219-465-4084
Office: 159 Moorland Dr., Valparaiso, IN 46383
Fax: 219-465-4084
This is a national organization for collectors of Canterbury Bears.
Established: 1990
Statement of purpose: To better acquaint collectors with Canterbury Bears and their designers, The Blackburns; to provide identification and history of Canterbury Bears; to offer special members-only bears; and to inform collectors when the Blackburns will be visiting from England.
Members: 500+
Membership fee/dues: $10 per year in USA;
$15 per year outside
Shows: FL, VA, OH

CAPERS 'N TEDDIES INTERNATIONAL CLUB

Candy Perry
247 Crum Creek Rd.
Media, PA 19063
Phone: 610-892-7139
Karen Butler
7390 W. David Dr.
Littleton, CO 80123
Phone: 303-933-0562
Fax: 303-978-9164
This is an international organization for collectors, especially collectors of Muffy Vanderbear.
Established: 1990
This organization has branch locations.
Members: 200
Membership fee/dues: $25 per year
Activities: publishes bimonthly newspaper, provides unique products and exclusive offerings to members, hosts teddy bear parties and more.
Shows: UK

COLLECTORS LIFE

Beth Savino
5001 Monroe St.
Toledo, OH 43623
Phone: 419-473-9801
Office: same as above
Fax: 419-473-3947
This is a national/international organization for collectors.
Established: 1984
Members: 1,000
Membership fee/dues: $12-U.S.; $15-outside U.S.
Membership includes quarterly newsletter, membership enamel pin authorized by Steiff, membership card, catalog and price sheet, yearly exclusive limited edition created by Steiff exclusively for The Toy Store.
Shows: OH

GOOD BEARS OF THE WORLD

Terrie Stong, executive director
P.O. Box 13097
Toledo, OH 43613
Phone: 419-531-5365
This is an international organization open to anyone.
Established: 1969
Membership fee: $12-U.S.; $16-outside U.S. Contact dens for den membership fees. Bearo membership one-time $120

Note: Some dens are listed here; many are not. To locate the den nearest you, call or write. See the article opening this chapter for more information.

INLAND EMPIRE TEDDY BEAR CLUB

Marilyn Kurr
P.O. Box 4278
Riverside, CA 92514
Phone: 909-689-1066
Fax: 909-351-8336
This is a local organization for artists and collectors of bears and miniature bears.
Established: 1983
Statement of purpose: To further the knowledge of, compare information about, promote interest in and share and enjoy the hobby of teddy-bear making and collecting, and to develop friendships among people that share the same interests.
Members: 40
Membership fee/dues: $10
Meetings are held monthly.
Meeting day/time: 2nd F, 7:30P.M.
Meeting location: 419 S. 4th St., Redlands, CA 92373
Activities: Sponsors an annual teddy bear show and sale in February of each year, an annual picnic, an annual Christmas party, adopts a needy family each holiday season, bears for neglected, abused and needy children.
Shows: CA

INTERNATIONAL LEAGUE OF TEDDY BEAR COLLECTORS

Pat Todd
P.O. Box 616
Monrovia, CA 91017
Phone: 818-447-3809
Fax: 818-446-2830
This is an international organization for artists and collectors of bears and miniature bears.
Established: 1984
Statement of purpose: A nonprofit organization formed to share an interest in teddy bears and to promote and educate people in teddy bear artistry and collecting.
Membership fee/dues: $10 per year-U.S.; $20 per year-outside U.S.
Meeting location: at annual convention
Activities: Sponsors an annual sale and convention, and publishes an annual

newsletter, Teddy Bear Tabloid, which serves as an information center for members and the clubs they represent.

LUCY & ME COLLECTING NETWORK

Melissa Kelly
P.O. Box 31265
Omaha, NE 68131-0265
Phone: 402-344-0365
Fax: 402-344-0365
This is a national organization for collectors of Lucy Rigg designs.
Established: 1993
Statement of purpose: To bring Lucy & Me collectors, retailers and manufacturers together.
Members: 800+
Membership fee/dues: $27 (collectors); $55 (retailers)

MAINE SOCIETY OF DOLL & BEAR ARTISTS, INC.

Barb Giguere
P.O. Box 124
Scarborough, ME 04070-0124
Phone: 207-883-3771
Office: same as above
Fax: 207-883-0822
This is an international juried organization for bear and doll artists
Established: 1992
Statement of purpose: To educate the public about artist-made dolls and bears, to provide networking and education for artists, to sponsor international doll and teddy bear-making workshops and to promote artist-made dolls and bears as art.
Members: 100
Membership fee/dues: $18 with a one-time $25 jury fee
Meetings are held monthly.
Meeting day/time: Sun, 1P.M. (dates vary)
Activities: Sponsors two shows each year, group participation in trade shows, educational activities, networking, monthly newsletters for members, produces quarterly publication Networking News for Artists and sponsors International Doll & Teddy Bear Making Workshops.
Shows: ME

MOUNTAIN BEAR FAN CLUB

Good Bears of the World den
Jennifer Anderson
4690 N. Blackstone
Fresno, CA 93726
Phone: 204-222-8031
Office: Toni Lagunoff, P.O. Box 307, Oakhurst, CA 93644
Established: 1992
Members: 30
Membership fee/dues: $15
Meetings are held monthly.

THE PETERBOROUGH TEDDIES

P.O. Box 1333
Peterborough, Ontario K9J 7H5
Canada
Phone: 705-743-6415
This is a local organization for anyone interested.
Established: 1985
Statement of purpose: The Peterborough Teddies is a nonprofit volunteer group providing new teddy bears to those in their area needing love, comfort and friendship. New teddy bears or cash donations will help continue their Give A Bear Program.
Members: 12
Membership fee/dues: $10
Meetings are held monthly.
Meeting day/time: M, 7:30P.M.
Meeting location: at members' homes
Activities: fundraising events and presentations

TED-E-BEAR CLUB OF MICHIGAN

Good Bears of the World Den
Grace Coen
5547 Davison Rd.
Lapeer, MI 48446
Phone: 810-653-9421
Meetings are held quarterly.
Members: 50
Membership fee/dues: $20 per year
Meeting day/time: 3rd Sat, January, April, July, October
Meeting location: varies
Shows: KS

TEDDIES TO THE RESCUE

Jeanne Klein
P.O. Box 234
Sutherlin, OR 97479
Phone: 503-459-9517
This is a local organization for anyone interested.

Established: 1992
Statement of purpose: To provide teddy bears for children in traumatic situations in Southwest Oregon; to share our love of teddies with others; to support local artists and businesses associated with bears; to provide ongoing education on bear events, products, techniques, etc. to our members.
Members: 26
Membership fee/dues: $5
Meetings are held ten times a year.
Meeting day/time: 1st T, 6:30P.M.
Meeting location: Shingle Towne Antique Village, Dillard, OR
Activities: Raises money through raffles to buy bears to distribute to battered women's shelters, hospitals, nursing homes and police, fire and EMT departments. Annual Christmas party and summer picnic; programs at each meeting.
Shows: OR

TEDDY BEAR ARTISTS ASSOCIATION

Ron Block/Gene Reising
P.O. Box 905
Woodland Hills, CA 91365
Phone: 818-591-3805 or 818-883-6691
Office: 23961 Craftsman Rd., Suite E, Calabasas, CA 91302
Fax: 818-591-3806
This is a national/international organization for artists and collectors of bears and miniature bears.
Established: 1991
Statement of purpose: A professional association dedicated to the protection, advancement and professionalization of the teddy bear artist through communication and caring. Formed to provide a consistent center of communication to answer and resolve mutual questions and problems about and within the craft and to help promote all activities that cast a positive light on the industry and craft.
Members: 730
Membership fee/dues: $35 per year
Activities: provides information on craftsman protection insurance, liability insurance, term life insurance, Visa and MasterCard plans, and a major medical plan; travel discounts; teddy bear club registry; member survey results, help with collection and laws.

TEDDY BEAR BOOSTERS OF NORTHERN CALIFORNIA

Dan Grunau
3294 Woody Ln.
San Jose, CA 95132
Phone: 408-263-1026
Fax: 408-263-1026
This is a regional organization for artists and collectors of bears and miniature bears.
Established: 1982
Statement of purpose: Providing bears to those in need.
Members: 150
Membership fee/dues: $10 per year
Meetings are held monthly. No meetings in August or December.
Meeting day/time: 2nd F, 7:30P.M.
Meeting location: varies
Activities: Sponsors a 3-day convention once a year, which includes a charity auction.

TEDDY BEAR COLLECTORS ASSOCIATION OF ALBERTA

Shirley M. Clark
P.O. Box 3056
Sherwood Park, Alberta, Canada
Phone: 403-922-3664
This is a regional organization for artists and collectors.
Established: 1992
Statement of purpose: To promote the enjoyment of teddy bears; to provide an opportunity for social as well as educational activities encompassing the theme of teddy bears; to provide community outreach—i.e. information, guest speakers, displays and charitable donations.
Members: 22
Membership fee/dues: $25 per year
Meetings are held monthly.
Meeting day/time: 1st T, 7P.M.
Meeting location: Millwoods Town Centre, Edmonton, Alberta
Activities: Annual Progressive Teddy Bear Project promoting togetherness; donations of bears to charities; TV program for local cable channel on bearmaking; displays in the community to promote bear collecting.
Shows: Alberta, Canada

TEDDY BEAR COLLECTORS CLUB

Marilyn E. Miner
201 W. Collins Ave., #143
Orange, CA 92667
Phone: 714-538-2062
This is a regional organization for artists and collectors.
Established: 1981
Statement of purpose: To further the interest in collecting and the understanding of teddy bears.
Members: 50
Membership fee/dues: $20 per year
Meetings are held monthly.
Meeting day/time: 2nd T
Meeting location: Buena Park Hotel, Buena Park, CA
Activities: well-known speakers, sales and charitable activities.

TEDDY BEAR COLLECTORS OF NORMAN, INC.

Mona Windolph
1919 Elmhurst Dr.
Norman, OK 73071
Phone: 405-329-0767
This is a regional organization for artists and collectors of bears and miniature bears.
Established: 1986
Statement of purpose: An organization for those who love the teddy bear and wish to share that love by learning more about the teddy bear world.
Members: 52
Membership fee/dues: $15 per year
Meetings are held monthly.
Meeting day/time: 1st TH, 6:30P.M.
Meeting location: Ryan's Steak House, 760 N. Interstate Dr., Norman, OK
Activities: Organizes Annual Teddy Bear Affair held in the fall. Auction and banquet associated with the show.

TEDDY BEAR SOCIETY OF ROCHESTER, NY

Barbara Chadwick
311 Mt. Airy Dr.
Rochester, NY 14617
Phone: 716-544-9331
This is a local organization for collectors.

Established: 1983
Statement of purpose: To spread the joy of teddy bears.
Members: 40
Membership fee/dues: $15 per year
Meetings are held monthly.
Meeting day/time: 1st TH, 7:30P.M.
Meeting location: members' homes
Activities: Gives teddy bears to nursing home residents and to the Society for the Prevention of Cruelty to Children. Set up displays of teddy bears in libraries. Has a slide show on the history of the teddy bear to show to community organizations.
Shows: NY

TEDDY BEAR TYMES

Good Bears of the World Den
P.O. Box 21036
St. Catharines, Ontario L2M 7X2, Canada
This is a local organization for artists and collectors
Established: 1987
Members: 60
Membership fee/dues: $20
Meetings are held monthly.
Meeting day/time: 2nd T, 7:30P.M.
Meeting location: St. Catharines Centennial Public Library, St. Catharines, Ontario
Activities: In addition to Good Bears of the World activities, sponsors all Teddy Show & Sale
Shows: Ontario

THEODORE ROOSEVELT ASSOCIATION

Dr. John A. Gable
P.O. Box 719
Oyster Bay, NY 11771
Phone: 516-921-6319
Fax: 516-921-6481
This is a national historical society.
Established: 1919
Statement of purpose: To preserve the memory of Theodore Roosevelt.
Members: 1,500
Membership fee/dues: $30
Meetings are held yearly.
Meeting location: varies
Activities: publishes historical quarterly

TIME FOR TEDDIES

Roberta Rehm
8577 Lantana Dr.
Seminole, FL 34647
Phone: 813-398-7346
This is a local organization for artists and collectors of bears and miniature bears.
Established: 1987
Members: 30-40
Membership fee/dues: $15 per year
Meetings are held monthly.
Meeting day/time: 4th M, 7P.M.
Meeting location: Grandy's, 5 E. Busch Blvd., Tampa, FL
Activities: Sponsors Bearly Spring convention in early March; raffles and show and tell.

TULSA TEDDY BEAR CLUB

Amy Young
Route 1, Box 357
Terlton, OK 74081
Phone: 918-865-3522
This is a local organization for artists and collectors
Established: 1992
Statement of purpose: To come together as a group of people who recognize and appreciate the value of the teddy bear, realizing its ability to give comfort and unconditional love to persons of all ages. The primary objective of this organization shall be to promote good will in the Tulsa area and give as many teddy bears as possible to those in need.
Members: 30
Membership fee/dues: $20 per year
Meetings are held monthly.
Meeting day/time: varies
Meeting location: varies
Activities: Supplies bears and personal care items to the Domestic Violence Intervention Service center, and raises funds for the Tulsa Zoo's new home for polar bears.
Shows: OK

6
Shows

How to Use This Chapter

This chapter is your guide to all the shows, conventions and other events where you can purchase teddy bears and other bear items. The chapter is separated into production companies (companies sponsoring several teddy bear shows a year) and single shows. Production companies are listed first in alphabetical order, and include all companies, individuals and retail stores that sponsor two or more events per year. Single shows are listed after the production companies, beginning with the Amherst Rotary Teddy Bear Rally on page 197. The listings include contact information, time of year, show location and number and types of dealers. Information for dealers, such as the average cost of a booth or table and application and payment information, is also included.

Show names often change from year to year. We have tried our best to list each show under a recognizable name, such as the location or sponsor's name. If you are looking for a show in a specific area of the country and cannot find it under the name you know, check the geographical index at the back of the book.

As always, we have tried to be as up-to-date as possible, but show dates and places are subject to change. Check the teddy bear magazines for current information, or, better yet, write to the show organizer and ask to be included on the mailing list. This is an especially good idea for production companies that sponsor several shows a year in different locations. They are usually happy to include more people on their list and are very good about sending up-to-date information.

Many shows include contests and auctions. Information about contest requirements and charitable organizations associated with the show is also included. Contest requirements are subject to change, but we have tried to include as much information as possible. Contests and auctions that are associated with shows are listed in this chapter only. The additional opportunities chapter includes information on contests and auctions that are not associated with specific shows.

Attending shows is perhaps the best way to meet other teddy bear lovers and purchase unique bears and other items. Shows are also a key opportunity for artists wishing to expand their sales. Best of all, they give artists and collectors alike a good excuse to visit a new state or city!

Winnie's Hometown Festival

BY ROBIN GEE

*H*ere is Edward Bear, coming downstairs now, bump, bump, bump, on the back of his head, behind Christopher Robin. It is, as far as he knows, the only way of coming downstairs, but sometimes he feels that there really is another way, if only he could stop bumping for a moment and think of it. And then he feels that perhaps there isn't. Anyhow, here he is at the bottom, and ready to be introduced to you . . . (—from *House at Pooh Corner* by A.A. Milne)

Fans recognize this scene as the first time they met that plump, honey-loving bear, Winnie-the-Pooh, brought to life in 1926 by British author A.A. Milne. The story goes that Milne often took his young son, Christopher, on outings to the London Zoo, where the boy became entranced by the bears. One of the bears, Winnie, inspired Milne to write a story for his son. In fact, the author wrote several stories which were later collected and published in book form. Two of the most popular of Milne's books were *Winnie-the-Pooh* and *The House on Pooh Corner*, beloved by readers young and old all over the world.

Yet, there's more to this story—Winnie was a Canadian bear, but where she came from and how she got to London was a mystery for many years. It wasn't until 1989 that people learned the real story of Winnie the Pooh and that White River, Ontario, was her home. Since this discovery, White River has paid tribute to its best loved former resident with the annual Winnie's Hometown Festival.

Winnie Goes to London

Festival director and president of the White River District Historical Society, Bernice Makepeace, is often called upon to tell the story of how a White River bear ended up in London and how the town learned of their famous native.

It all started with World War I, Makepeace says. Several regiments of Canadian soldiers were being sent to England to help in the fight. Many of the men wanted to take with them a souvenir of home, something distinctly Canadian to make their separation from friends and family a little more endurable. A few of the regiments chose mascots and what better mascot than a real Cana-

In August 1994, the late Kenneth Saperstone's collection of Winnie-The-Pooh items was unveiled in White River, Ontario. Saperstone, who died in 1994, willed that the collection be kept together in Winnie's hometown. The collection has become a well-loved addition to Winnie's Hometown Festival. Present at the unveiling were (from left to right): Mrs. Thalheimer, Mr. Peter Thalheimer (Member of Parliament), Bernice Makepeace (Winnie's Hometown Festival Co-Chairbear), Daniel Saperstone, Jerry Saperstone, and Reeve Angelo Bazzoni.

dian black bear! An enterprising trapper had the same idea and when he trapped a bear cub in the Ontario woods, he took her to nearby White River, a regular stop for the trains full of soldiers traveling from the western provinces on their way overseas.

One soldier who stopped over at White River was army veterinarian Harry Colebourn. When he saw the bear on the platform of the Canadian Pacific Railroad station, it was love at first sight. Colebourn immediately bought the bear for $20 and named her Winnie after his hometown, Winnipeg, Manitoba. He took Winnie overseas, but left her in the care of the London Zoo when he was called up for active duty in France. Winnie became such a favorite at the zoo that when it came time to return home, Colebourn decided to donate her.

Much later the zoo erected a sign near the bear cages telling visitors the bears were donated by Canadian servicemen during World War I. A mistake in their records, however, made their sign incorrect. The Princess Patricia Regiment of Calgary, Alberta, was credited with donating Winnie. When the Princess Pats held a reunion in the late 1980s, no one remembered a bear, so they took out an ad in the Calgary newspaper asking for information on Winnie.

The Festival Is Born

A friend of Fred Colebourn, Harry's son, saw the ad and contacted him. Fred told the newspaper the story his father had told him many times—Winnie was the mascot of the 34th Fort Garry Horse regiment and belonged to his father, Captain Harry Colebourn, who purchased her in White River. A director from the Ontario Historical society visited White River and the newly formed White River District Historical Society with a question, "What are you going to do about it?" The answer came in the form of the first ever Winnie's Hometown Festival, a three-day celebration of teddy bears, Canadian history and, of course, Winnie-the-Pooh.

About 150 to 200 people attended that first Winnie festival in 1989. Even then it was an exciting event for White River, a small town near the north shore of Lake Superior, about 200 miles north of Sault Saint Marie. Before the festival, the town was known mostly for its lumber industry and sawmills, as well as its close proximity to Canada's gold country. With Pukaskwa National Park nearby, the area remains a favorite of vacationers, but the festival now brings Pooh-lovers and bear enthusiasts from all over Canada and the northern United States.

According to Makepeace, the festival now draws nearly 1,200 people to White River, just about doubling the size of the town itself. The festival is held on a weekend in August each year, from Friday evening until Sunday. In addition to booths featuring bear collections and bears by various artists, the festival includes bear-making workshops, entertainment, a pancake breakfast, a festival dance, food and a parade.

After a little experimentation, Makepeace says the Historical Society decided to hold all the festival events, "under the big top," in the town's community arena. Holding the festival in one central place was "so much better for me, easier for me to keep track of everything that was going on," explains Makepeace, who as president of the Historical Society, is closely involved with operating the festival.

Special Attractions

When she became involved with the Historical Society, Makepeace had no idea what was in store. "I was interested in getting the history of the area, events and people recorded. We had no idea what would develop. We founded the Society just a year before our first festival. All of it came as quite a surprise."

One of the highlights of the festival is the Miss Winnie and Captain contest held on the opening Friday. Adults may enter the name of a girl or a boy, age six to nine, to be selected at random to be either Miss Winnie or the Captain. The children wear costumes and are special guests in the parade. They also take home Winnie-the-Pooh gifts and bear ears as souvenirs.

The festival also holds a contest for teddy bears. "We have 12 different categories, some for adults, some for children," explains Makepeace. "We have all sorts of categories from Best-Dressed Bear to Ugliest Bear to Bear Who Has Traveled the Greatest Distance to Best Made Bear.

"We don't yet have a category for professional artists' bears, but this is what we are hoping to get to. A lot of people have asked about this." One of the people behind the idea to add this category and to promote the work of bear artists at the festival was the late Lee Wansbrough, who was chairbear for Good Bears of the World/Canada. A major supporter of the festival, Wansbrough crafted two different wooden statues of Pooh to be given to winners in each category.

Artists are welcome at the festival and Makepeace hopes to increase their presence each year. In the past between three and seven artists have had booths at the event. Featured artists have included Marcella Pittana, who has a bear in the Teddy Bear Museum in Florida, Debi Hill, from Ontario, who has been steadily building her reputation as an exceptional artist at various bear shows and the B Group, a group of four artists from St. Catharines, Ontario. Another participating bear artist, Grace Foley, happened to live in White River at the time of Winnie's birth. She's become known in and around Ottawa where she uses her bears in therapy for sick and elderly people.

The Town's Bear Collection Grows

Most of the artists who show at the festival donate a bear to the White River District Historical Society's museum, where the group has a growing collection of Winnie-the-Pooh and teddy bear items. The collection grew quickly in 1994, when Winnie collector Kenneth Saperstone of North Dakota left his extensive collection of more than two hundred bears and other items to the Historical Society. His family said it was his ardent wish that the collection be preserved in Winnie's hometown.

"We're not just zeroing in on Winnie-the-Pooh for

our collection," says Makepeace. "We're trying to include the work of teddy bear artists and teddy bears from manufacturers. In 1994 in honor of Smoky the Bear's anniversary, we received a Smoky the Bear from the Department of Natural Resources. We also have in our collection a bear sent to us by the Steiff Company."

Other bears in the collection have ties to children's literature. Each year the Paddington Bear display is a favorite of festival-goers. Makepeace says whenever possible she likes to pair bears with their books as a good way to introduce children to the joys of reading.

The proceeds of the festival go to the Historical Society, its collection and museum. One source of income from the festival is the bear raffle, in which people buy tickets to win one of more than fifty artist-made bears donated for the event.

One of the most unusual bears raffled, says Makepeace, was White River Willy, an old prospector bear. "He had so much character. It turned out my son bought forty dollars worth of tickets and won it for himself. He lets me keep Willy in my collection but makes sure I remember whom he belongs to."

Although Makepeace did not start out as a bear enthusiast, Winnie and the festival have won her over. "I sort of have my own bear collection now and I make a few bears. It does take hold of you and takes over your house!" She says now whenever she walks into a store, her eyes are immediately drawn to bears whether they are china or stuffed. Even her husband says his awareness of bears has grown, and Makepeace can expect to find several bear-related items under her Christmas tree every year. 🐾

Shows

ABC UNLIMITED PRODUCTIONS
Connie Brouillette
1 Thornwood Dr.
Flossmoor, IL 60422
Phone: 708-798-0290
Fax: 708-798-0860
Shows per year: 5
Areas: Mesa, AZ; Schaumburg, IL (one convention, one show); Whippany, NJ; Tampa, FL (convention)
Times of year: January, April, May, September, October
Events generally last for 1-2 days
These events include primarily or only dealers of teddy bears and related items.
Booths for teddy bear artists, retailers, suppliers, restoration services, appraisers, accessories and collectibles dealers and clubs are available.
Application process: Space is available on a first-come, first-serve basis. Apply at least 6 months in advance.
Average cost of booth/table: $175
A deposit is due with the reservation, and the dealer will be billed for the remaining balance.
Advertising: Teddy Bear magazines, local newspapers, mailings.
Conventions include seminars/workshops.
Contests: Any conventioneer may participate. Bears are judged on quality, creativeness and unique design. Contestants may sign up at the show. Collectors, retailers and magazine editors act as judges. The prizes vary. Contest registration is free.
Auctions: Both conventions and one show usually include auctions.
In business for 8 years

ARLAINE ABELLERA
24325 7th Pl. W.
Bothell, WA 98021
Phone: 206-483-5321
Shows per year: several
Areas: Bothell, WA
Times of year: bimonthly
(Classic Doll, Bear & Toy Show & Sale)

twice annually (The Great Northwest Doll, Bear & Toy Extravaganza)
Events generally last for 1-2 days
These events include teddy bears, dolls, miniatures and antiques.
Booths for teddy bear artists, retailers, suppliers, organizations, accessories and collectibles dealers, restoration services and appraisers are available. Apply 1 month in advance.
In business for 8 years

BRIGHT STAR PROMOTIONS
3428 Hillvale Rd.
Louisville, KY 40241-2756
Phone: 502-423-STAR
Areas: throughout USA

CAROL'S DOLL HOUSE
Oak Park Plaza
10761 University Ave. NE
Blaine, MN 55434
Phone: 612-755-7475
Shows per year: 2
Areas: Blaine, MN
Times of year: January and July
Events generally last for 1 day
These events include teddy bears, dolls, miniatures and antiques.
Booths for teddy bear artists, retailers, suppliers, organizations, accessories and collectibles dealers, restoration services and appraisers are available.
Application process: Space is available on a first-come, first-serve basis.
Average cost of booth/table: $35
Payment is due when the reservation is made.
There are door prizes.
Advertising: Teddy Bear magazines, local newspapers, mailings.
Dealers: 75
Average attendance: 600-700
Has been taking place for 15 years

CHINA DOLL SHOWS
Lloyd & Marigold Hogan
5621 Glencrest Lane
Orangevale, CA 95662
Phone: 916-989-9291

Shows per year: 10
Areas: CA
Times of year: January, February, March, May, June, July, August, November
Events generally last for 1 day
These events include teddy bears, dolls, toys, miniatures and antiques.
Booths for teddy bear artists, retailers, suppliers and accessories and collectibles dealers are available.

CODY PRODUCTIONS
Joe Lamothe
P.O. Box 665
Northborough, MA 01532
Phone: 508-393-0016
Hours: M-F, 9:30A.M.-6:30P.M.
Shows per year: 3-4
Areas: Boxborough, MA and throughout USA
Times of year: March, June, September, November
Events generally last for 1 day
These events include primarily or only dealers of teddy bears and related items.
Booths for teddy bear artists, retailers, suppliers, restoration services, appraisers, accessories and collectibles dealers and clubs are available.
Admission fee: $2.50
Includes a ticket for door prize drawing, seminars, workshops, guest signings
Application process: Booths are available on a first-come, first-serve basis. Apply one year in advance.
Average cost of booth/table: $135
A deposit is due with the reservation, and the dealer will be billed for the remaining balance.
Mailing list: 5,000+
Average attendance: 4,000
Dealers: 130-200
Advertising: Teddy Bear Review, Teddy Bear & Friends, local newspapers
Charitable organizations: World Society for the Protection of Animals
Auctions: A special auction of bears handmade by the industry's finest artists will take place in 1996. Proceeds

will be donated to the preservation of the Grizzly Bear.
In business for 7 years

D.L. HARRISON COMPANY
Donna West
279 Capote Ct. W.
Severna Park, MD 21146
Phone: 410-544-4526
Hours: M-F, 10A.M.-5P.M.
Shows per year: 2
Areas: MD
Times of year: spring, fall
Events generally last for 1-3 days
These events include primarily or only dealers of teddy bears and related items.
Booths for teddy bear artists, retailers, suppliers, restoration services, appraisers, accessories and collectibles dealers and clubs are available.
Admission fee: $4.50. Under 12 free.
Includes door prizes every 15 minutes, free parking and exhibits.
Application process: First time exhibitors must send photos.
Apply 6-8 months in advance.
Average cost of booth/table: $115-$150
Full payment is due when the reservation is made.
Mailing list: 1,500
Average attendance: 3,000
Dealers: 200
Advertising: Teddy Bear Review, Teddy Bear & Friends, local newspapers, trade publications
Charitable organizations: Good Bears of the World
Contests: Both shows include contests. Contests include several categories for artist bears and antique bears. There are separate classes for children and adults. All classes have specific qualifications that vary from show to show. There is a $2 registration fee for each class, and contestants should register the morning of the show. A selected group of experts judges the contests. Ribbons and a first prize (varies) are awarded.
Auctions: One show includes an auction. Items are donated. 40% of what is paid for each item is returned to the artist. 10% goes to Good Bears of the World.

FUZZY BEAR PRODUCTIONS
Debbie Ballman
6432 Silverleaf Ave.
Reynoldsburg, OH 43068-1053
Phone: 614-861-3502
John Fey
498 Deer Trail Dr. SE
Thornville, OH 43076-8814
Phone: 614-323-3521
Shows per year: 2
Areas: Columbus, OH
Times of year: Columbus Teddy Bear Fair—last weekend in July
Beary Merry Christmas Show—mid-November
Events generally last for 1-2 days
These events include primarily or only dealers of teddy bears and related items.
Booths for teddy bear artists, antique/vintage bear dealers, retailers, suppliers, restoration services, appraisers, accessories and collectibles dealers and clubs are available.
Admission fee: $5. $2 for children.
Includes chance to win door prizes, meet celebrities
Application process: First-time artists are required to send photos.
Apply 6-8 months in advance. Early applicants' names are included in advertising and mailings.
Average cost of booth/table: $100-$125
Full payment is due when the reservation is made.
Mailing list: 3,400
Dealers: 50-100
Advertising: Teddy bear magazines, local newspapers
Charitable organizations: Good Bears of the World
Contest: The Columbus Teddy Bear Fair in July includes a contest open to all artists, dealers and collectors. There are several categories, including general in several sizes, vintage, show theme, most unusual, and best overall. Registration is on the day of the convention. All convention participants will vote. The cost is $2 per entry, and ribbons are awarded to the winners. All proceeds go to the local den of Good Bears of the World.
Auction: The Columbus Teddy Bear Fair in July includes an auction. Items for auction are donated. All proceeds go to Good Bears of the World.

In business for 2 years

GIGI'S DOLLS & SHERRY'S TEDDY BEARS
6029 N. Northwest Hwy.
Chicago, IL 60631
Phone: 312-594-1540
Fax: 312-594-1710
Shows per year: 2
Areas: Chicago, IL
Times of year: autumn and winter
Location: Chicago South Expo, 171st & Halsted, Chicago, IL
These events generally last for 1 day
They include teddy bears, dolls and miniatures.
Booths for teddy bear artists, retailers, suppliers and accessories and collectibles dealers are available.
Dealers: more than 100
Advertising: Teddy bear magazines, mailings
Has been taking place for 13 years

GROVES QUALITY COLLECTIBLES
Sue Groves
343 S. Jameson Ave.
Lima, OH 45805-3225
Phone: 419-229-7177
Shows per year: 3
Areas: Lima, OH
Location: Groves Quality Collectibles at address above.
Times of year: October
Events: Muffy Party, Ohio Artists Party, Steiff Oktoberfest
Events generally last for 1 day
These events include primarily or only teddy bears and related items.
Booths for teddy bear artists are available.
Application process: Space is available on a first-come, first-serve basis
Apply 6 months in advance
Average cost of booth/table: 35% of gross
Events include seminars/workshops and door prizes.
Advertising: Teddy bear magazines, local newspapers, mailings
Dealers: 30
Average attendance: 1,000
Contest: All three events include contests. Anyone not associated with the show may enter. There are several different categories. Registration is free, and contestants can register the day of the event. Workers judge the entrees.

LINDA'S TEDDY BEAR, DOLL & ANTIQUE TOY SHOW & SALE

Linda Mullins
P.O. Box 2327
Carlsbad, CA 92018
Phone: 619-434-7444
Shows per year: 2
Areas: San Diego, CA
Times of year: January and August
Events generally last for 2 days
These events include teddy bears, dolls, and antique toys.
Booths for teddy bear artists, retailers, suppliers and accessories and collectibles dealers are available.
Admission fee: $5
Average cost of booth/table: $145-$300
Average attendance: 2,000
In business for 13 years

MAINE SOCIETY OF DOLL & BEAR ARTISTS

Barb Giguere
P.O. Box 124
Scarborough, ME 04070
Phone: 207-883-3771
Hours: M-F, 8A.M.-5P.M.
Shows per year: 2
Areas: ME, NH
Times of year: Art Dolls & Bears show in May; Fall Spectacular in October
Events generally last 1 day
These events include teddy bears, dolls and antiques.
Booths for teddy bear artists, retailers, suppliers, accessories and collectibles dealers, restoration services and appraisers available.
Art Dolls & Bears Show in May includes doll and bear artists only.
Admission fee: $2.50
Application process: Space is available on a first-come, first-serve basis.
Apply 5 months in advance.
Average cost of booth/table: $100
Payment is due when the reservation is made.
Average attendance: 2,000
Advertising: teddy bear magazines, doll magazines, TV, radio, newspapers
Contest: Both shows include contests. Artists participating in the shows may enter one doll and/or bear. The public votes for a favorite doll and a favorite bear.
Registration is free and occurs during set up time for the show. A plaque is awarded for 1st place, and ribbons are awarded for 2nd and 3rd.
In business for 12 years

THE MAVEN COMPANY, INC.

Richard N. Robbins
P.O. Box 1538
Waterbury, CT 06721
Phone: 203-758-3880
Hours: 9A.M.-6P.M.
Shows per year: 2
Areas: MA
Times of year: November and April
Events generally last for 2 days
These events include teddy bears, dolls, toys, miniatures and antiques.
Booths for teddy bear artists, retailers, suppliers, restoration services, appraisers and accessories and collectibles dealers are available.
Admission fee: $3.50
Application process: Booths are available on a first-come, first-serve basis.
Apply 6 months-1 year in advance.
Average cost of booth/table: $190
A deposit is due with the reservation, and the dealer will be billed for the remaining balance.
Mailing list: 5,000
Advertising: local newspapers, radio, TV
In business for 18 years

PAT MOORE PRODUCTIONS

Pat Moore
7022 S.E. Holgate
Portland, OR 97206
Phone: 503-775-3324
Hours: 8A.M.-5P.M.
Shows per year: 5
Areas: OR, WA, CO, CA
Times of year: February, May, August, September
Events generally last for 2-3 days
These events include only dealers of teddy bears and related items.
Booths for teddy bear artists, retailers, suppliers, restoration services, appraisers, accessories and collectibles dealers and clubs are available.
Admission fee: $4. Convention fee varies. Convention fee includes meals, programs, souvenirs, workshops, special guest speakers, entertainment
Application process: Show is juried.
Apply 6 months in advance.
Average cost of booth/table: $65-$80

Payment arrangements vary depending on the show.
Mailing list: 10,000
Average Attendance: 1,000-2,000
Dealers: 85-90
Advertising: Teddy bear magazines, local newspapers, flyers at shops and other shows
Charitable organizations: GBW has free table
Contest: Three shows include contests. Contests are based on theme, and categories are dressed/undressed by size, artist vs. hobbyist. Bears are judged on artistic ability and imagination. The registration fee is included in the convention fee. Those in attendance act as judges, and ribbons are awarded to the winners.
In business for 4 years

PRINGLE PRODUCTIONS

John K. Pringle, president
P.O. Box 757
Bristol, CT 06011-0757
Phone: 203-585-9940
Fax: 203-583-3541
Shows per year: 4
Areas: Newport, RI; Danbury, CT
Times of year: February, April, August, and November
Events generally last for 1 day
These events include primarily or only dealers of teddy bears and related items.
Booths for teddy bear artists, retailers, suppliers, restoration services, appraisers, accessories and collectibles dealers and clubs are available. Tables for clubs are free.
Admission fee: $4
Includes door prize drawings every hour, bearmaking demonstrations, lectures, free parking
Application process: First-time artists are juried. Dealers must describe items sold, etc.
Apply 9 months in advance.
Average cost of booth/table: $145-$175
A deposit is due with the reservation, and the dealer will be billed for the remaining balance.
Mailing list: 3,000
Average attendance: 1,500-2,000
Dealers: 50-110
Advertising: Teddy bear magazines, local newspapers, radio, local tourism

bureaus, antique and collectible publications, other shows

Charitable organizations: Good Bears of the World, World Society for the Protection of Animals

Contest: One show includes a contest. Showgoers can dress up their bears to compete in categories such as best-dressed, most athletic, etc. There is no registration fee, and contestants should register no later than a week before the show. Local celebrities and public officials judge the contest. Ribbons are awarded to the winners.

Auctions: Two or three of the shows include auctions. Items for auction are donated. All proceeds go to Good Bears of the World.

In business for 12 years

QUALITY DOLL & TEDDY BEAR SHOWS

Richard & Charles Schiessl
P.O. Box 2061
Portland, OR 97208
Phone: 503-284-4062
Hours: 9 A.M.-5 P.M.
Shows per year: 7
Areas: Portland, OR; Puyallup, WA; Spokane, WA
Times of year: February, August, November (Portland, OR); March, June, October (Puyallup, WA); May (Spokane, WA)
Events generally last for 2 days
These events include teddy bears, dolls
Booths for teddy bear artists, retailers, suppliers, restoration services, appraisers, accessories and collectibles dealers and clubs are available.
Admission fee: $3.75
Application process: Booths are available on a first-come, first-serve basis. There is an ongoing waiting list for most shows.
Average cost of booth/table: $90-$160
A deposit is due when the reservation is made, with full payment due one month before the show. Beginning 30 days before the show, if space is still available, full payment is due with registration.
Dealers: 100-200
Average attendance: 1,600-4,000
Advertising: teddy bear magazines, local newspapers, TV, doll magazines
In business for 15 years

OLGA RODRIGUEZ

10539 NW 35 Ave.
Miami, FL 33147
Phone: 305-696-1334
Areas: Miami, FL
Times of year: February (Doll and Bear Expo), July (Doll and Bear Fair)
Events generally last for 1 day
These events include teddy bears and dolls.
Booths for teddy bear artists, retailers, accessories and collectibles dealers and restoration services are available.
Application process: Booths are available on a first-come, first-serve basis. Apply at least 6 months in advance.
Average cost of booth/table: $75
A deposit is due when the reservation is made, with full payment due two weeks before the show.
There are door prizes.
Advertising: Teddy bear magazines, local newspapers, mailings, other shows, doll publications, shops and other dealers
Dealers: 50
Average attendance: 450
In business for 2 years

SIROCCO PRODUCTIONS, INC.

Tidewater Virginia's Oldest and Best Doll and Bear Show
Gail Monteforte
5660 E. Va. Beach Blvd., #104
Norfolk, VA 23502
Phone: 804-461-8987
Fax: 804-461-4669
Shows per year: 2
Areas: Newport News, VA
Location: Greek Hellenic Community Center, Traverse Rd., Exit 258B off I-64
Times of year: First weekend in May, first weekend in October
These events include teddy bears and dolls
Booths for teddy bear artists, retailers, suppliers, organizations, accessories and collectibles dealers, restoration services and appraisers are available.
Application process: Previous dealers have priority. New dealers accepted if space is available on a first-come, first-serve basis. Ongoing waiting list.
Average cost of booth/table: $150
A deposit is due when the reservation is

made, with full payment due 30 days before the show begins.
Advertising: Teddy Bear magazines, mailings, newspapers, collector magazines, TV spot ads
In business since 1982

THE TOY STORE

Beth Savino
5001 Monroe St., #336
Toledo, OH 43623
Phone: 1-800-862-8697
Shows per year: 2
Times of year: July (Festival of Steiff) and October (The Toy Store's Annual International Doll & Bear Show & Sale)
Events generally last for 3 days
Festival of Steiff includes Steiff dealers only. Annual International Doll & Bear Show & Sale includes doll and bear artists.
Application process: For Festival of Steiff, previous dealers have priority. Additional dealers accepted on first-come, first-serve basis. International Doll & Bear Show & Sale is invitation only.
Apply 6 months in advance for Festival of Steiff.
Average cost of booth/table: $125 for Festival of Steiff; free for International Doll & Bear Show
Dealers: Festival of Steiff: 30; Doll & Bear Show: 80-90
Average attendance: 50,000 for Doll & Bear Show; 125 for Festival of Steiff
Contests: Festival of Steiff: Any participant can apply. Participants are judged on 4 different categories. Terms available after registering.
Judges are Steiff experts. Ribbons are awarded to the winners.
Auctions: Festival of Steiff: Items are submitted, and individual gets the money paid for the item minus a percentage. International Doll & Bear Show & Sale: Items for auction are donated. All proceeds go to Good Bears of the World.

AMHERST ROTARY TEDDY BEAR RALLY

Carlton Brose
36 Triangle St.
Amherst, MA 01002
Phone: 413-256-8425
Jud Ferguson

5 Blackberry Lane
Amherst, MA 01002
Phone: 413-256-1088
Sponsors: Amherst Rotary Club
This outdoor event occurs annually and lasts for 1 day
Time of year: first Saturday in August
Location: Town Common, Amherst, MA
This event includes teddy bears and related items only.
Booths for teddy bear artists, retailers, suppliers, organizations, accessories and collectibles dealers and restoration services are available.
Number of Dealers: 175
Application process: Space is available on a first-come, first-serve basis.
Apply 6 months in advance.
Average cost of booth/table: $70
Payment is due when the reservation is made.
Charitable organizations: local charities
Advertising: Teddy bear magazines, local newspapers, mailings, TV, radio
Average attendance: 20,000
Has been taking place for 13 years

ANNUAL ARTIST SHOW & SALE
Harriet Valdez
1900 Route 70, Suite 210
Lakewood, NJ 08701
Phone: 908-477-2400
Sponsors: Teddy Bears To Go
This indoor event occurs annually and lasts for 1 day
Time of year: March
Location: Teddy Bears To Go at above address
This event includes teddy bears and related items only.
Booths for teddy bear artists are available.
Number of dealers: 4
Application process: personal selection.
Average cost of booth/table: free
Advertising: Teddy bear magazines, local newspapers, mailings
Average attendance: 100
Has been taking place for 4 years

THE BEAR FAIR
Sandy Morrow
Suite 200, Unit 3
317-37 Ave. NE
Calgary, Alberta T2E 6P6, Canada
Phone: 403-230-3554
Sponsors: Trade Show Managers, Inc.

This event occurs annually and lasts for 3 days
Time of year: Fall
Location: Marlborough Inn, 316-33 St. NE, Calgary, Alberta
This event includes teddy bears and related items only.
Booths for teddy bear artists, retailers, suppliers, organizations, accessories and collectibles dealers and restoration services are available.
Number of dealers: 50-60
Application process: Space is available on a first-come, first-serve basis.
Apply 6 months in advance.
Average cost of booth/table: $265 (includes convention package)
A deposit is due when the reservation is made, and the dealer will be billed for the remaining balance.
Convention includes seminars/workshops, a banquet and door prizes.
Charitable organizations: Alberta Children's Hospital Foundation, Hospice Calgary Society
Advertising: Teddy bear magazines, local newspapers, mailings
Average attendance: 1,200
Contest: Any working artist or hobbyist may enter. There are several categories that change annually. All entries must be the artist's original designs, and each artist may submit one entry per category. Decision of the judges is final. Register through the mail by the designated deadline date. Established artists, teachers and restoration experts judge the contest. Prizes include handblown glass paperweights, ribbons and certificates. The grand prize is a large, handblown glass bear sculpture.
Auction: Items for auction are donated, and proceeds go to the Alberta Children's Hospital.
Has been taking place for 3 years

BEARLY SPRING
Edie Rase
4601 Grayview Ct., C201
Tampa, FL 33609-1932
Phone: 813-286-7032
Roberta Rehm
Lantana
Semiole, FL
Sponsors: Time for Teddies Teddy Bear Club

This event occurs in conjunction with Gasparilla parade and art show in Tampa.
It is an indoor, annual event that lasts for 2 days
Time of year: first week in March
Location: Colony Resort, I-275 and 34 Blvd., Tampa, FL
This event includes teddy bears and related items only.
Booths for teddy bear artists, suppliers and accessories and collectibles dealers are available.
Number of dealers: 6-8
Application process: Space is available on a first-come, first-serve basis.
Apply 9 months in advance.
Average cost of booth/table: $145 for convention
A deposit is due when the reservation is made, and the dealer will be billed for the remaining balance.
Show includes seminars/workshops.
Charitable organizations: The Spring
Advertising: Teddy bear magazines, local newspapers, TV, radio
Average attendance: 600
Auction: Items for auction are donated. 75% of the proceeds go to The Spring, a shelter for abused and battered women and children.
Has been taking place for 2 years

BELLEVILLE DOLL, TOY & TEDDY BEAR FAIR
Kay Weber
300 Ross Lane
Belleville, IL 62220
Phone: 618-233-0940
This event occurs in conjunction with Dollhouse & Miniature Show.
This event occurs annually and lasts for 2 days
Time of year: the weekend after the 4th of July
Location: Belle-Clair Expo Building, Route 13 & Route 159, Belleville, IL
This event includes teddy bears, dolls, miniatures, toys and antiques.
Booths for teddy bear artists, retailers, suppliers and accessories and collectibles dealers are available.
Number of dealers: 120
Application process: Space is available on a first-come, first-serve basis.
Apply 6 months in advance.
Average cost of booth/table: $50-$150

Payment is due when the reservation is made.

There are door prizes.

Advertising: Teddy bear magazines, local newspapers, mailings, radio

Average attendance: 2,000

CHRISTMAS DELIGHT

Jane C. Messenger

6892 Route 291

Marcy, NY 13403

Phone: 315-865-5463

Sponsors: The Doll Hospital

This indoor event occurs annually and lasts for 1 day

Time of year: October

Location: First United Methodist Church, 105 Genesee St., New Hartford, NY

This event includes teddy bears, dolls and miniatures.

Booths for teddy bear artists and retailers are available.

Number of dealers: 40

Application process: Space is available on a first-come, first-serve basis.

Apply 6 months in advance.

Average cost of booth/table: $70

Payment is due when the reservation is made.

There are door prizes.

Advertising: Teddy bear magazines, local newspapers, mailings, doll magazines, radio, TV bulletins, posters

Average attendance: 700-800

Has been taking place for 6 years

THE COEUR D'ALENE TEDDY BEAR INVITATIONAL

Mary Nelson

210 Sherman, #161

Coeur d'Alene, ID 83814

Phone: 208-664-2327

Sponsors: Bear Hugs

This indoor event occurs annually and lasts for 2 days

Time of year: 1st weekend in October

Location: The Coeur d'Alene Resort, 2nd and Front Street, Coeur d'Alene, ID

This event includes teddy bears and related items only.

Booths for teddy bear artists are available.

Number of dealers: 5

Application process: The artists are cho-

sen by Ted Menten in conjunction with Bear Hugs.

Average cost of booth/table: free

Show includes seminars/workshops.

Advertising: Teddy bear magazines, local newspapers, mailings

Average attendance: 500

Has been taking place for 3 years

CROSSROADS OF THE WEST DOLL, BEAR, TOY FESTIVAL

Elta Lee Johnson

146 S. Sandrun Rd.

Salt Lake City, UT 84103

Phone: 801-355-3655

Sponsors: Elta Lee Johnson

This event occurs twice a year and lasts for 1 day

Time of year: April and October

Location: Olympus Hotel, 161 West 600 South, Salt Lake City, UT

This event includes teddy bears, dolls and toys.

Booths for teddy bear artists, retailers, suppliers, accessories and collectibles dealers and restoration services are available.

Number of dealers: 60

Application process: Dealers participating in the October show will have priority for the following spring show.

Apply 1 year in advance.

Average cost of booth/table: $40

A deposit is due when the reservation is made, with full payment due on the day the show begins.

Show includes seminars/workshops and door prizes.

Advertising: Teddy bear magazines, local newspapers, mailings, doll clubs, doll magazines

Average attendance: 800-1,000

Contest: The spring show includes a teddy bear exhibit, with a rosette given for the people's favorite bear. A larger competition is also a possibility. The registration fee is $3, and registration occurs through the mail or the day before the show begins. Ribbons are awarded to the winners.

Has been taking place for 3 years

D.A.R.E. BEAR SHOW & AUCTION

Det. Diana L. Herman

6000 Wales Rd.

Northwood, OH 43619

Phone: 419-691-5053

This event occurs annually and lasts for 1 day

This event includes teddy bears and related items only.

Booths for teddy bear artists and organizations are available.

Application process: Space is available on a first-come, first-serve basis.

Apply 8-9 months in advance.

Average cost of booth/table: $85

A deposit is due when the reservation is made, and the dealer will be billed for the remaining balance.

Charitable organizations: local D.A.R.E. program

Advertising: Teddy bear magazines, local newspapers, mailings

Auction: All items for auction are donated. Proceeds go to the local D.A.R.E. program.

Has been taking place for 2 years

DOLL SHOW & SALE

Vi Sands

7960 Jordan Rd.

Cleves, OH 45002

Phone: 513-941-7386

Sponsors: Triple Crown Doll Club

This indoor event occurs annually and lasts for 1 day

Time of year: late September

Location: Marriott Hotel, 11320 Chester Rd., Cincinnati, OH

This event includes teddy bears, dolls, miniatures and antique dolls.

Booths for teddy bear artists, retailers, suppliers, organizations, accessories and collectibles dealers, restoration services and appraisers are available.

Number of dealers: 58

Application process: Space is available on a first-come, first-serve basis.

Apply 5 months in advance.

Average cost of booth/table: $30

Payment is due when the reservation is made.

There are door prizes.

Charitable organizations: several

Advertising: Teddy bear magazines, local newspapers, mailings, doll magazines, TV, dolls and bear stores

Average attendance: 600

Has been taking place for 4 years

DOLL & TEDDY BEAR EXPO
John Bleho
170 Fifth Ave.
New York, NY 10010
Phone: 212-989-8700
Sponsors: Collector Communications Corp. (*Dolls* magazine and *Teddy Bear Review*)
This indoor event occurs annually and lasts for 2 days
Time of year: last weekend in August
This event includes teddy bears and dolls.
Booths for teddy bear artists, suppliers, organizations, restoration services and manufacturers are available.
Number of dealers: 150-200
Application process: Charter participants have priority. Others on first-come, first-serve basis.
Apply 6-9 months in advance.
Average cost of booth/table: $550-$1,495
Twenty-five percent deposit is due with registration, with full payment due by April 1.
Event includes seminars/workshops.
Advertising: Teddy bear magazines, local newspapers, mailings, doll magazines, local and national radio and TV
Average attendance: 6,500
Contest: Dolls Awards of Excellence and Golden Teddy Awards are presented at the banquet at this show.
Has been taking place for 2 years

DOLL & TEDDY BEAR SHOW & SALE
Sponsors: Doll Lover's Doll Club
This indoor event occurs annually and lasts for 1 day
Time of year: mid-October
Location: Greenville, NC
This event includes teddy bears and dolls.
Booths for teddy bear artists, retailers, suppliers, accessories and collectibles dealers and restoration services are available.
Number of dealers: 20
Application process: Space is available on a first-come, first-serve basis.
Average cost of booth/table: $35
A deposit is due when the reservation is made, with full payment due on the day the show begins.
Advertising: Teddy bear magazines, local newspapers, mailings, local TV
Average attendance: 300
Has been taking place for 12 years

ANNUAL DOLLS, TOYS, TEDDY BEARS, & MINIATURE SALE
Sharon Geisen
5827 Balsam Rd. NW
Bemidji, MN 56601
Phone: 218-751-8277
Sponsors: Northwoods Doll Club
This event occurs annually and lasts for 1 day
Time of year: 2nd Sunday in August
Location: Northern Inn, Highway 2 West, Bemidji, MN
This event includes teddy bears, dolls, miniatures, toys, antiques, furniture, clothes and books.
Booths for teddy bear artists, retailers, suppliers, organizations, accessories and collectibles dealers, restoration services and appraisers are available.
Number of dealers: 20
Application process: Space is available on a first-come, first-serve basis.
Apply 1 month in advance.
Average cost of booth/table: $45
Payment is due when the reservation is made.
There are door prizes.
Charitable organizations: public library
Advertising: Teddy bear magazines, local newspapers, mailings, public TV, radio, doll and craft magazines
Average attendance: 300-350
Has been taking place for 8 years

DOLLY'S DOLLS DOLL & BEAR SHOW & SALE
Dolly McGregor
3373 Apple Ave.
Muskegon, MI 49446
Phone: 616-773-7550
Sponsors: Dolly's Dolls
This event occurs in conjunction with Muskegon's Summer Celebration.
This event occurs annually and lasts for 1 day
Time of year: July
Location: Walker Arena Annex, 4th St. at Western Ave., Muskegon, MI
This event includes teddy bears, dolls, and antique dolls.
Booths for teddy bear artists, retailers and accessories and collectibles dealers are available.
Number of dealers: 50
Application process: Space is available on a first-come, first-serve basis.
Apply 4 months in advance.

Average cost of booth/table: $35
Payment is due when the reservation is made.
There are door prizes.
Advertising: Teddy bear magazines, local newspapers, mailings, flyers at other shows
Average attendance: 800-1,000
Has been taking place for 3 years

FOUR CORNERS DOLL, TEDDY BEAR & TOY SHOW & SALE
Lucille Hadley
725 E. 4th St.
Cortez, CO 81321
Phone: 303-565-7828
Joyce Tanner
141 Hwy. 666
Cahone, CO 81320
Phone: 303-565-4713
Sponsors: Four Corners Doll Club
This indoor event occurs annually and lasts for 1 day
Time of year: July
Location: Cortez Conference Center, 2121 East Main, Cortez, CO
This event includes teddy bears, dolls, miniatures and toys.
Booths for teddy bear artists, retailers and suppliers are available.
Number of dealers: 27
Application process: Space is available on a first-come, first-serve basis.
Apply 3 months in advance.
Average cost of booth/table: $10
Payment is due when the reservation is made.
There are door prizes.
Advertising: Teddy bear magazines, local newspapers, mailings, radio, local TV
Average attendance: 300
Has been taking place for 9 years

HELLO DOLLIES ANNUAL DOLL & BEAR SHOW
Jan Rodriguez
P.O. Box 2597
Longmont, CO 80501
Phone: 303-772-3605
Sponsors: Hello Dollies Doll Club
This indoor event occurs annually and lasts for 1 day
Time of year: 3rd Saturday in June
Location: Boulder County Fairgrounds, Hover & Nelson Rds., Longmont, CO
This event includes teddy bears and dolls.

Booths for teddy bear artists, retailers, suppliers, organizations, accessories and collectibles dealers, restoration services and appraisers are available.

Number of dealers: 85

Application process: Space is available on a first-come, first-serve basis.

Apply 4 months in advance.

Average cost of booth/table: $67.50

Payment is due when the reservation is made.

There are door prizes.

Charitable organizations: 10% of profit goes to various charities, depending on year

Advertising: Teddy bear magazines, local newspapers, mailings, doll magazines, flyers at other shows and shops

Average attendance: 2,500

Contest: Anyone can enter. Contestants should sign up the day before the show. Judges change yearly. The fee is $2-$5, depending on the size of entry. Ribbons are awarded to the winners.

Has been taking place for 12 years

HONEY SEEKERS TEDDY BEAR SHOW

Sherri Turner
16778 Pennsylvania St.
Northglenn, CO 80233
Phone: 303-452-2953
Sharon Freehling
12449 Josephine
Thornton, CO 80234
Phone: 303-451-7687
This event occurs annually and lasts for 1 day

Time of year: spring

Location: Regency Hotel, 3900 Elarti St., Denver, CO

This event includes teddy bears and related items only.

Booths for teddy bear artists, retailers, suppliers and accessories and collectibles dealers are available.

Number of dealers: 45

Application process: Space is available on a first-come, first-serve basis.

Apply 5 months in advance.

Average cost of booth/table: $65

Payment is due when the reservation is made.

There are door prizes.

Charitable organizations: Children's Hospital

Advertising: Teddy bear magazines, local newspapers, mailings

Average attendance: 500

Has been taking place for 2 years

HOTEL COLORADO ANNUAL TEDDY BEAR WEEKEND

Valerie Keith
526 Pine St.
Glenwood Springs, CO 81601
Phone: 1-800-544-3998
This event occurs annually and lasts for 3 days

Time of year: August

Location: Hotel Colorado, 526 Pine St., Glenwood Springs, CO

This event includes teddy bears and related items only.

Booths for teddy bear artists, retailers, suppliers, organizations, accessories and collectibles dealers, restoration services and appraisers are available.

Number of dealers: 30-40

Application process: Space is available on a first-come, first-serve basis.

Apply 3-6 months in advance.

Average cost of booth/table: $40

Payment is due when the reservation is made.

Show includes seminars/workshops and door prizes.

Charitable organizations: Children's Hospital

Advertising: Teddy bear magazines, local newspapers, mailings

Average attendance: 400-600

Contest: Anyone who makes bears can enter. Bears should coincide with the theme of the festival. They are judged on design, originality, material, creativity and appropriateness for theme. There is no registration fee. World renowned teddy bear collectors act as judges. Cash prizes (1st- $300; 2nd- $150; 3rd- $50) are awarded to the winners.

Auction: Items for auction are donated. All proceeds go to the Children's Hospital in Denver.

Has been taking place for 3 years

INLAND EMPIRE TEDDY BEAR CLUB SHOW & SALE

Marilyn C. Kurr
P.O. Box 4278
Riverside, CA 92514
Phone: 909-689-1066

Sponsors: Inland Empire Teddy Bear Club

This indoor event occurs annually and lasts for 1 day

Time of year: The Saturday in February following President's Day holiday

Location: Trinity Episcopal Church, 419 S. 4th St., Riverside, CA

This event includes teddy bears and related items only.

Booths for teddy bear artists, retailers, suppliers, organizations, accessories and collectibles dealers, restoration services and appraisers are available.

Number of dealers: 33-38

Application process: Dealers from the previous year have priority. All others are on a waiting list.

Apply 5-6 months in advance.

Average cost of booth/table: $20-$40

Payment is due when the reservation is made.

Charitable organizations: Admission fees and raffle ticket sales go to local hospitals, law enforcement agencies, fire departments, safe houses for abused women & children and convalescent homes

Advertising: Teddy bear magazines, local newspapers, mailings, special event publications, radio, flyers at other shows, clubs

Average attendance: 300

Contest: Any dealer or show attendee may enter. Entry must be related to the show theme. There is no registration fee, and registration takes place the day the show opens. A selected committee judges the contest, and 1st, 2nd and 3rd place ribbons are awarded.

Has been taking place for 13 years

INTERNATIONAL LEAGUE OF TEDDY BEARS CLUB

(name of show changes each year)
Monica Campbell
27 Palermo
Long Beach, CA 90803
Phone: 310-434-8077
Sue Coe
148 Fowler Dr.
Monrovan, CA 91016
Phone: 818-358-2029
This event occurs annually and lasts for 3 days

Time of year: July

Location: Double Tree Hotel, 100 the City Dr., Orange, CA

This event includes teddy bears and related items only.

Booths for teddy bear artists, retailers, accessories and collectibles dealers and restoration services are available.

Number of dealers: 65

Application process: This is a juried show.

Apply 1 year in advance.

Average cost of booth/table: $100

Payment is due when the reservation is made.

Show includes seminars/workshops and door prizes.

Charitable organizations: varies

Advertising: Teddy bear magazines, local newspapers, mailings

Average attendance: 600

Contest: Convention attendees may enter. Entry forms are mailed to attendees prior to the convention. The registration fee is included in the convention fee. Ribbons are awarded to the winners.

Has been taking place for 11 years

ANNUAL INTERNATIONAL TEDDY BEAR CONVENTION

Charles F. Woods
431 Broad, P.O. Box 328
Nevada City, CA 95959
Phone: 916-265-5804
David S. Osborn
American Victorian Museum
203 S. Pine
Nevada City, CA 95959
Phone: 916-265-5804
Sponsors: The American Victorian Museum

This event occurs annually and lasts for 3 days

Time of year: April

Location: Miner's Foundry, BearCastle, and AVMat Powell House, Nevada City, CA

This event includes teddy bears and related items primarily. Also includes dolls, miniatures, toys and antiques.

Booths for teddy bear artists, retailers, and accessories and collectibles dealers are available.

Number of dealers: 65-75

Application process: A committee approves new exhibitors. Returning exhibitors have priority.

Apply 10 months in advance.

Average cost of booth/table: $200

Payment is due when the reservation is made. Other arrangements are possible.

Show includes seminars/workshops and door prizes.

Charitable organizations: American Victorian Museum's nonprofit educational foundation

Advertising: Teddy bear magazines, local newspapers, mailings, TV, radio

Average attendance: 3,500

Contest: Anyone attending can enter. A variety of categories are included in the contest. Registration is free, and contestants can register at the door. An impartial group judges the contest, and banners and badges are awarded.

Has been taking place for 11 years

JENKS TEDDY BEAR CONVENTION

Monica Murray
P.O. Box 728
Jenks, OK 74037
Phone: 918-299-5416
Sponsors: Classic Traditions

This indoor event occurs annually and lasts for 2 days

Time of year: November

Location: First Christian Church, 308 E. Main, Jenks, OK

This event includes teddy bears and related items only.

Booths for teddy bear artists, retailers, suppliers, organizations, accessories and collectibles dealers, restoration services and appraisers are available.

Number of dealers: 73

Application process: Space is available on a first-come, first-serve basis.

Apply 1 year in advance.

Average cost of booth/table: $75

Payment is due when the reservation is made.

Show includes seminars/workshops and door prizes.

Charitable organizations: Good Bears of the World

Advertising: Teddy bear magazines, local newspapers, mailings, TV, clubs

Average attendance: 2,500

Auction: Items for auction are donated, and all proceeds go to Good Bears of the World.

Has been taking place for 3 years

KENNEBEARPORT TEDDY BEAR SHOW

Karen Marie Arel
P.O. Box 740
Kennebunk, ME 04043
Phone: 207-967-0858 or 1-800-982-4421
Sponsors: Kennebunk Kennebunkport Chamber of Commerce

This indoor event occurs annually and lasts for 1 day

Time of year: 2nd Saturday in August

Location: Kennebunk High School, Fletcher St., Kennebunk, ME

This event includes teddy bears and related items only.

Booths for teddy bear artists, retailers, suppliers, organizations, accessories and collectibles dealers, restoration services and appraisers are available.

Number of dealers: 40+

Application process: Space is available on a first-come, first-serve basis.

Apply 6 months in advance.

Average cost of booth/table: $95-$125

Payment is due when the reservation is made.

Show includes seminars/workshops and door prizes.

Advertising: Teddy bear magazines, local newspapers, mailings

Average attendance: 1,000

Has been taking place for 3 years

PEDDLER'S VILLAGE TEDDY BEAR'S PICNIC

Susan Hawthorne
P.O. Box 218
Lahaska, PA 18931
Phone: 215-794-4000
Sponsors: Peddler's Village

This outdoor event occurs annually and lasts for one weekend

Time of year: July

Location: Peddler's Village, Routes 202 & 263, Lahaska, PA

This event includes teddy bears and related items only.

Booths for teddy bear artists, restoration services and appraisers are available.

Number of dealers: 40

Application process: This is a juried show. A crafts committee reviews applications and at least three photographs of work. All work must be handmade by the seller.

Apply in March.

Average cost of booth/table: $40

Payment is due when the reservation is made.

Advertising: local newspapers, mailings

Average attendance: 4,500

Contest: Open to professionals and amateurs. There are several categories. Registration fee is $1-$10. Contestants should register at show. Shopkeepers in Peddler's Village are the judges. Prizes include gift certificates and cash awards.

Has been taking place for 17 years

PLAIN AND FANCY DOLL, BEAR & TOY SHOW

Louise Whittemore
4931 Day Hollow Rd.
Endicott, NY 13760

Phone: 607-785-8939

Sponsors: Broome County Doll Club

This indoor event occurs annually and lasts for 1 day

Time of year: June

Location: Chenango Forks Middle School, 1 Gordon Dr., Binghampton, NY

This event includes teddy bears, dolls, miniatures and toys.

Booths for teddy bear artists, retailers, suppliers, accessories and collectibles dealers and restoration services are available.

Number of dealers: 50-60

Application process: Space is available on a first-come, first-serve basis.

Apply 1-6 months in advance.

Average cost of booth/table: $15

Payment is due when the reservation is made.

There are door prizes.

Charitable organizations: Bears for Broome County emergency squads

Advertising: local newspapers, TV, doll magazines

Average attendance: 400

Has been taking place for 16 years

SEATTLE DOLLHOUSE MINIATURE SHOWS

Pat Williams
1376 SW Station Circle
Port Orchard, WA 98366

Phone: 206-876-6644

Sponsors: Hobby World Exhibits

This event occurs twice annually and lasts for 2 days

Time of year: March and September

Location: Seattle Center Flag Pavillion (near the space needle)

Number of dealers: 100

Apply in August.

Average cost of booth/table: $110

Payment is due when the reservation is made.

Advertising: Teddy bear magazines, local newspapers, mailings, miniature, doll and woodworking publications, calendars, local radio and TV

Average attendance: 1,800-3,500

Has been taking place for 19 years

STORYLAND DOLL & BEAR SHOW & SALE

Judy Vidinich and Adeline Depeder
12240 Rexford
Alsip, IL 60658

Phone: 708-388-7628

Sponsors: Storyland Doll Club

This indoor event occurs annually and lasts for 1 day

Time of year: August

Location: Operating Engineers Hall, 6200 Joliet Rd., Countryside, IL

This event includes teddy bears, dolls, miniatures and toys.

Booths for teddy bear artists, retailers, suppliers, accessories and collectibles dealers, restoration services and appraisers are available.

Number of dealers: 70

Application process: Space is available on a first-come, first-serve basis.

Apply 4 months in advance.

Average cost of booth/table: $55

Payment is due when the reservation is made.

Charitable organizations: Shady Oaks Cerebral Palsy Camp

Advertising: Teddy bear magazines, local newspapers, mailings, shops

Average attendance: 450-500

Has been taking place for 17 years

THE STRONG MUSEUM ANNUAL TEDDY BEAR FESTIVAL, SHOW & SALE

Kathy Castle
The Strong Museum
1 Manhattan Square
Rochester, NY 14607

Phone: 716-263-2700

Donna West, D.L. Harrison Co.
279 Capote Ct. West
Severna Park, MD 21146

Phone: 410-544-4526

Sponsors: The Strong Museum, Steiff USA

This event occurs annually and lasts for 3 days

Time of year: first weekend in June

Location: The Strong Museum at above address.

This event includes teddy bears and related items only.

Booths for teddy bear artists, antique teddy bear dealers, suppliers, organizations, accessories and collectibles dealers and appraisers are available.

Number of dealers: 65-80

Application process: Application and photographs of bears required.

Apply 6 months in advance.

Average cost of booth/table: $75

Payment is due when the reservation is made.

Event includes seminars/workshops, a preview breakfast, a banquet dinner, 2-day sale and children's activities. All this is available for the $4.50 regular entry fee to the museum.

Charitable organizations: All profits go to The Strong Museum

Advertising: Teddy bear magazines, local newspapers, mailings, antique publications

Average attendance: 1,500-2,000

Contest: Anyone can apply. Categories are announced in mailings. May enter only one bear per category. Criteria include quality of costume/decoration, condition of bear and general appeal. There is a $2 registration fee per bear. Contestants sign up the day of the contest. Bear dealers and artists act as judges. Prizes include ribbons and T-shirts.

Has been taking place for 4 years

ANNUAL TEDDY BEAR AFFAIR

Mona Windolph
1919 Elmhurst Dr.
Norman, OK 73071

Phone: 405-329-0767

Sponsors: Teddy Bear Collectors of Norman

This indoor event occurs annually and lasts for 1 day

Time of year: September

This event includes teddy bears and related items only.

Booths for teddy bear artists, retailers, suppliers, organizations, accessories

and collectibles dealers, restoration services and appraisers are available.
Number of dealers: 50
Application process: Space is available on a first-come, first-serve basis. Apply 6 months in advance.
Average cost of booth/table: $40
Payment is due when the reservation is made.
Show includes seminars/workshops and door prizes.
Charitable organizations: Norman Women's Resource Center, Norman Regional Hospital Oncology Unit, Health for Friends, Salvation Army, OKC Peds. Hemophilia Unit, Moore Police Dept., Kingfisher Hosp., Binger Police Dept., OKC Zoo
Advertising: Teddy bear magazines, local newspapers, mailings, radio, TV
Average attendance: 300-350
Contest: All exhibitors and club members who are teddy bear artists may enter. The bear entered must have been made by the contestant. There are three size categories and a best of show award. Contestants should send their contest registration along with their registration for the show. 1st, 2nd and 3rd place satin ribbons are awarded in each category, and a purple ribbon is awarded for best of show.
Auction: All items for auction are donated. All proceeds go to purchase bears for the charities listed above, and to sponsor a Grizzly bear at the OKC Zoo.
Has been taking place for 9 years

TEDDY BEAR BOOSTERS OF NORTHERN CALIFORNIA ANNUAL CONVENTION

Dan Grunau
3294 Woody Ln.
San Jose, CA 95132
Phone: 408-263-1026
Karen Sawin
130 Fig Tree Lane #2A
Martinez, CA 94553
Phone: 510-379-8198
Sponsors: Teddy Bear Boosters of Northern California
This event occurs annually and lasts for 3 days
Time of year: 3rd week in July
Location: Red Lion Hotel, Gateway Blvd., San Jose, CA

This event includes teddy bears and related items only.
Booths for teddy bear artists, retailers, suppliers, organizations, accessories and collectibles dealers and restoration services are available.
Application process: Space is available on a first-come, first-serve basis to full paid conventioneers. Apply 2 months-1 year in advance.
Average cost of booth/table: $60 and convention fee
A deposit is due when the reservation is made, with full payment due three months in advance of the show.
Convention includes seminars/workshops, door prizes and a banquet.
Charitable organizations: local charities
Advertising: Teddy bear magazines, local newspapers, mailings
Average attendance: 800-1,000
Contest: The contest is open to conventioneers only. There are several categories, as well as competitions for small, medium and large bears and a best of show award. Each contestant may enter up to three categories. There is no registration fee, and contestants must register on the first day of the convention. The public judges the contest, and ribbons are awarded for 1st, 2nd and 3rd in each category.
Auction: Items for auction are donated. All proceeds go to local charities or toward the purchase of teddy bears that are distributed to the community.
Has been taking place for 14 years

TEDDY BEAR CHRISTMAS

Laura Turner
1940 Old Taneytown Rd.
Westminster, MD 21158
Phone: 410-875-2850
Sponsors: Small Wonders Antiques
This event occurs annually and lasts for 3 days
Time of year: 2 weeks before Thanksgiving
Location: Small Wonders Antiques at above address
This event includes teddy bears and related items only.
Booths for teddy bear artists and accessories and collectibles dealers are available.
Application process: Space is available on consignment by invitation.

Advertising: local newspapers, mailings, flyers
Average attendance: 500
Has been taking place for 15 years

TEDDY BEAR FAIR

Gordon J. Marrin or Jeanna Ross
Palisades Interstate Park Commission
Bear Mountain State Park
Administration Building
Bear Mountain, NY 10911
Phone: 914-786-2701
Sponsors: Palisades Interstate Park Commission, ARA Leisure Services, Westchester Teddy Bear Club
This outdoor event occurs annually and lasts for 2 days
Time of year: 1st weekend in June
Location: Bear Mountain State Park, Route 9 West, Bear Mountain, NY
This event includes teddy bears and related items only.
Booths for teddy bear artists, retailers, suppliers, organizations, accessories and collectibles dealers, restoration services and appraisers are available.
Number of dealers: 20
Application process: Space is available on a first-come, first-serve basis. Apply 3-4 months in advance.
Average cost of booth/table: $50
Payment is due when the reservation is made.
Advertising: Teddy bear magazines, local newspapers, mailings
Average attendance: 3,000
Contest: Dealers and patrons may apply. There is no registration fee. Contestants should register on the day of the event. The Westchester Teddy Bear Club judges the event. Various small prizes are awarded.
Has been taking place for 6 years

TEDDY BEAR JUBILEE

Dolls, Bears & Funny Hares
Daniel Epley and Joel Hoy
6015 Johnson Dr.
Mission, KS 66202
Phone: 913-677-3055
Sponsors: Dolls, Bears & Funny Hares
This event occurs in conjunction with GBW annual membership meeting.
This event occurs annually and lasts for 3 days
Time of year: June
Location: Double Tree Hotel, 10100

College Blvd., Overland Park, KS

This event includes teddy bears and related items only.

Booths for teddy bear artists, retailers, suppliers, organizations, accessories and collectibles dealers, restoration services and appraisers are available.

Number of dealers: 95

Application process: The Teddy Bear Jubilee showroom is juried. Artists must send photos of their work along with an application.

Apply 1 year in advance.

Average cost of booth/table: varies

Payment is due when the reservation is made.

The convention includes seminars/workshops and two banquets.

Advertising: Teddy bear magazines, local newspapers, mailings, TV, national magazines

Average attendance: 2,000

Contest: Anyone registered as a participant in the Jubilee can register. The contest is limited to three entries per person. Entries may not take more than 24 square inches of table space. Other information is included in the Jubilee registration information. The cost is $3 per entry. Teddy Bear Jubilee participants judge the contest. 1st, 2nd, and 3rd place ribbons are awarded in each category. There is also a Bill Boyd award and a Best of Show award.

Auction: Items for auction are donated. All proceeds go to Good Bears of the World.

Has been taking place for 5 years

TEDDY BEAR LOVERS

Sharon Freehling

12449 Josephine St.

Thornton, CO 80241

Phone: 303-451-7687

This indoor event occurs annually and lasts for 1 day

Time of year: October or November

Location: Regency Hotel, 3900 Elati, Denver, CO

This indoor event includes teddy bears and related items only.

Booths for teddy bear artists, suppliers, accessories and collectibles dealers and restoration services are available.

Number of dealers: 50

Application process: Space is available

on a first-come, first-serve basis.

Apply 4 months in advance.

Average cost of booth/table: $55-$65

Payment is due when the reservation is made.

There is a door prize.

Charitable organizations: varies

Advertising: Teddy bear magazines, local newspapers, mailings, TV announcements

Average attendance: 500+

Has been taking place for 4 years

TEDDY BEAR SHOW & SALE

Pam Ruiter

Phone: 616-458-4329

Sponsors: Trinity United Methodist Women

This event occurs annually and lasts for 1 day

Time of year: 2nd Saturday of October

Location: Trinity United Methodist Church, 1100 Lake Dr. SE, Grand Rapids, MI

This event includes teddy bears and related items only.

Booths for teddy bear artists, retailers, suppliers and accessories and collectibles dealers are available.

Number of dealers: 15

Application process: Space is available on a first-come, first-serve basis.

Apply 6 months in advance.

Average cost of booth/table: $35

A deposit is due when the reservation is made, and the dealer will be billed for the remaining balance.

There are door prizes and activities for children.

Charitable organizations: Trinity United Methodist Women's Mission Fund

Advertising: Teddy bear magazines, local newspapers, mailings, yard signs, posters

Average attendance: 300-600

Has been taking place for 5 years

ANNUAL TEDDY BEARFEST

John Moore

P.O. Box 232, Route 896

Strasburg, PA 17579

Phone: 717-687-6954

Tracy Palmer

same address/phone

Sponsors: Moore Bears Shoppe

This indoor event occurs annually and lasts for 1 day

Time of year: first Saturday in September

Location: Moore Bears Shoppe at above address

This event includes teddy bears and related items only.

Booths for teddy bear artists, suppliers, organizations, accessories and collectibles dealers and appraisers are available.

Number of dealers: 20-24 artists

Application process: Space is available on a first-come, first-serve basis.

Apply 6 months in advance.

Average cost of booth/table: $75

Payment is due when the reservation is made.

There are door prizes.

Charitable organizations: Leukemia Society, S. June Smith Center, American Heart Association

Advertising: Teddy bear magazines, local newspapers, mailings

Average attendance: 1,000-2,000

Contest: The contest is open to anyone who makes bears as a hobby or profession. Only one entry per contest is permitted. Contestants must be present to win. Admission is $1 per bear. There are 8-9 categories plus a best of show contest. Categories vary. Registration begins at 10 A.M. on the day of the event. Bear artists judge the contest, and a bear is awarded to each winner.

Auction: Items for auction are donated. Proceeds go to the charities listed above.

Has been taking place for 8 years

TEDDY TRIBUNE EVENT AND ALL TEDDY BEAR SALE

Barbara Wolters

254 W. Sidney

St. Paul, MN 55107

Phone: 612-291-7571

Sponsors: Teddy Tribune Warehouse

This event occurs annually and lasts for five days

Time of year: July

Location: Convention: Holiday Inn Express, 1010 Bandana Blvd. West, St. Paul, MN; Sale: Bandana Square, 1021 Bandana Blvd., St. Paul, MN

This event includes teddy bears and related items only.

Booths for teddy bear artists, retailers, suppliers, organizations, accessories

and collectibles dealers, restoration services and appraisers are available.
Number of dealers: 40-50
Application process: Space is available on a first-come, first-serve basis. Apply 3 months in advance.
Average cost of booth/table: $50
Payment is due when the reservation is made.
There are door prizes.
Advertising: Teddy bear magazines, local newspapers, mailings, advertising at Bandana Square
Contest: Anyone may enter. Bears must be original in design. They may be any size and type, dressed or undressed. Related bear items may be entered in the "creative bear" category. Contestants are judged on quality of workmanship and originality. Registration is $4 per entry, and contestants should register one month before the contest. Local collectors and teddy authorities act as judges. Ribbons and certificates are awarded to the winners.
Auction: Items for auction are donated. Proceeds go to help cover convention costs.
Has been taking place for 15 years

TIDEWATER TEDDY BEAR & DOLL SHOW
Nancy Walker
1888 Brookwood Rd.
Norfolk, VA 23518
Phone: 804-588-6165
Edna Smith
1018 Colonial Ave.
Norfolk, VA 23507
Phone: 804-622-0982
Sponsors: ABC Toys & Toysmiths
This event occurs annually and lasts for 1 day
Location: Lake Wright Resort & Convention Center, 6280 Northampton Blvd., Norfolk, VA
This event includes teddy bears, dolls and doll supplies and accessories.
Booths for teddy bear artists, retailers, suppliers, organizations, accessories and collectibles dealers and restoration services are available.

Number of dealers: 35
Application process: Space is available on a first-come, first-serve basis. Apply 6 months in advance
Average cost of booth/table: $125
Show includes seminars/workshops and door prizes.
Charitable organizations: Candii House (Children With Aids)
Advertising: Teddy bear magazines, local newspapers, mailings, TV, doll magazines, local events calendar
Average attendance: 400-500
Has been taking place for 4 years

TWO SAILS PRODUCTIONS DOLL, BEAR & ANTIQUE TOY SHOW & SALE
Suzanne Morris
15 West View Dr.
Hoquiam, WA 98550
Phone: 206-533-4555
Donna Roberts
706 Washington Ct.
Hoquiam, WA 98550
Phone: 206-533-7650
Sponsors: Suzanne Morris and Donna Roberts
This event occurs annually and lasts for 1 day
Time of year: Second or third Saturday in September
Location: Ocean Shores Convention Center, 120 West Chancealamer, Ocean Shores, WA
This event includes teddy bears, dolls, miniatures, toys and antiques.
Booths for teddy bear artists, retailers, suppliers, organizations, accessories and collectibles dealers and restoration services are available.
Number of dealers: 49+
Application process: Space is available on a first-come, first-serve basis. Apply 150% months in advance.
Average cost of booth/table: $50
Payment is due when the reservation is made.
There are door prizes.
Advertising: Teddy bear magazines, doll magazines, local newspapers, mailings, radio, Accent magazine, Country Pleasures, handbills at shows.

Average attendance: 500
Has been taking place for 2 years

WINNIE'S HOMETOWN FESTIVAL
Bernice Makepeace
P.O. Box 31
White River, Ontario P0M 3G0, Canada
Phone: 807-822-2783
Shirley Sholdice
Winnipeg St.
White River, Ontario P0M 3G0, Canada
Sponsors: White River District Historical Society, Ministry of Culture, Tourism and Recreation
This event occurs annually and lasts for 3 days
Time of year: August (usually third weekend)
Location: Community Arena, White River, Ontario
This event includes teddy bears and related items only.
Booths for teddy bear artists, retailers, suppliers, organizations, accessories and collectibles dealers, restoration services and appraisers are available.
Application process: Space is available on a first-come, first-serve basis. Apply 3-6 months in advance.
A deposit is due when the reservation is made, with full payment due on the day the show begins.
Show includes seminars/workshops and door prizes.
Charitable organizations: local museum and historical society
Advertising: Teddy bear magazines, local newspapers, mailings, other shows, posters
Average attendance: 1,000+
Contest: Anyone can enter the contest. There are various categories each year, and previous winning bears cannot be entered. Visiting bear artists judge the contest. A special trophy designed by the late Lee Wansbrough, chairbear of Good Bears of the World-Canada is awarded to the winners.
Auction: Items for auction are donated. All proceeds go to the White River Museum.
See the article opening this chapter.

7

Museums

How to Use This Chapter

*T*eddy bears are an important part of many nations' histories, so it is no surprise that museums throughout the world have teddy bear collections. Several museums listed are exclusively for teddy bears or have large teddy bear collections. Others house several different items, including some teddy bears. All make enjoyable additions to a vacation. This chapter is wonderful for collectors or artists who are planning a trip—whether to Florida, New York, California or Europe.

The listings include contact information, basic information about the museum's collections, and days and hours that the museum is open to the public. It is best to call to verify the hours if you are planning a long trip, as they are subject to change. Special events sponsored by the museum are also listed. It might be fun to plan a trip around one of these events.

Planning is the key to making the most of a trip to a museum. Guided tours are the best way to see a museum. Guides are trained to answer your questions and give thorough explanations about the bears. Many of the museums listed offer tours at certain times during the day. Some museums require reservations for such tours.

These museums house everything from artist bears to antique bears, miniature bears to modern bears. To learn more about a museum before visiting, you may want to request information through the mail. This is a great way to make a trip both fun and educational for the whole family! Note: When contacting a museum outside the U.S. and Canada, it is best to check the number with your operator before making an international phone call. Foreign city codes change frequently, and different long distance phone companies may have different international dialing methods. ❦

George Black, on The Teddy Bear Museum

BY ARGIE MANOLIS

George Black, director of The Teddy Bear Museum of Naples, Florida, describes a place for arctophiles of all ages.

*W*hat do you buy a woman who has everything?

That's what Frances Pew Hayes's five-year-old grandson wanted to know when he drew her name for the family gift exchange one Christmas about nine years ago. She thought for a moment and told the young boy that she wanted paper clips and rubber bands—items he could surely afford.

But as George Black, Frances's son, tells it, that little boy was a child wiser than his years. "He said, 'Na, I can't do that, because if somebody asks me what I gave my grandmother for Christmas and I say rubber bands and paper clips, he'll think I'm a cheapskate!' "

Frances thought for a moment, and finally she said, "Well, it's the year of the bear in China. Why don't you give me a teddy bear?"

That Christmas, she opened her first teddy bear, an M&Ms bear from Hershey, Pennsylvania. That bear led to a collection of thousands of bears that eventually became The Teddy Bear Museum of Naples, Florida.

"With older people, you can never figure out what to give them, because they already have everything. Or else they get so set in their ways that if you don't give them a shirt exactly like the one they're wearing, they won't like it," George explains. "So, when everybody heard my mother wanted a teddy bear, they thought, 'I can do that.' "

So the collection multiplied, and Frances, having always been a collector of everything and anything, began buying bears for herself as well.

"She doesn't like this part when I tell it," George says, "but basically, she was living in a retirement community, and she would do a lot of holiday decorating using her bears. This decorating brought attention to her collection, and many people began to ask to see it. She had to clean her place every time she had someone

This parade scene is just one of the many displays at the museum.

over to see her collection. So, she finally struck upon the idea that 'If I can build a museum, I won't have to clean. Somebody else will do it.' "

And that was the beginning of the first and only known museum in the world that was built from the ground up to house and promote the collection and appreciation of teddy bears.

"There are other museums that have a lot of bears. I believe that most of the other museums took existing buildings and put up a few displays," says George, who has been the museum's director since it was founded in 1990. "But we basically took some bears and put a whole building up around them."

The Collection

The museum now houses about three thousand bears, including a Steiff bear dated from 1903 or 1904, and several bears worth tens of thousands of dollars. Also on display are all types of "bearafurnalia," such as paintings, posters, Native American bear artifacts and figurines.

"About the only bear-related items you won't find here are taxidermied bears or 'real bear' stuff," George says. "You won't find a bear's head, for instance, or a bear rug. I won't include them because many bears are endangered or heavily poached."

The museum acquires bears any way it can. Some are purchased, but many of them have been donated. For instance, there was the elderly man who had owned

This is Klondike, a big bear by the Manhatten Toy Company, one of the many bears awaiting your visit to the museum.

his Steiff bear all his life—since 1907—and wanted to give him a permanent home.

"He couldn't bear the thought that if something happened to him and his wife, the bear would be thrown out," George recalls. When a bear is donated, George asks for a picture of the owner to display with the bear.

Artist Bears

The museum includes artist bears as well as manufactured bears. George regularly purchases them at shows, conventions and auctions. In addition, he often writes to artists asking for donations.

"We've been quite successful at acquiring artist bears, because we also tell artists that if they are in the museum, to some degree, we will represent them," George says. Because the museum keeps careful records of all artists, visiting collectors can use the museum's resources to contact an artist if they see a bear they like.

In addition, visitors can purchase bears and bear items in the gift shop, which provides much of the revenue for the museum's upkeep. The rest comes from donations, the minimal admission fee, and fees for mu-

seum-sponsored classes, speeches and teddy bear repairs.

George says there are no requirements for acceptance in the museum. Any artist can donate a bear. "I guess we're sort of like the United States," he says. "We never turn down a bear seeking asylum. But they do have to go through some sort of immigration policy. The way I explain it is this: I would certainly love to have Michelangelo's first drawing, but to get that, I probably wouldn't have known how popular he was going to be. So if you decided to be a teddy bear artist, and you offered me your first bear, I wouldn't turn it down."

However, not all the bears donated will be displayed. George says he expects newer artists to participate in shows and establish a following before he will put their bears on display.

Joanne Mitchell's limited edition artist bear, Rusty, is one of the many artist bears on display.

The Library and Archives

In addition to the more than three thousand bears and bear items, the museum houses a teddy bear manufacturers' and artists' archives. These archives include information on about fifteen hundred bear artists, as well as every major manufacturer. Because several of the bears in the museum have not been identified, George understands first hand the importance of the archives.

"There are many unknowns among the antiques. For instance, take Ideal," George says. "Ideal doesn't exist today. I don't have their old catalogs at this point. I would love to have them, so I could look through them and tell someone with an Ideal bear exactly when it was manufactured and how much it cost at the time. What I'm trying to do through the archives is to put an end to future unknowns."

George says that the artists' archives are as important as the manufacturers' archives.

"Ten years from now, I presume that a bunch of these artists, either by choice or by chance, aren't going to be around," George says. "And yet, their bears may very well be."

He predicts that there will be some confusion in the future over who made which artist bear. Because of the huge number of bear artists, there are bound to be artists with similar company names who have never heard of each other. He hopes that the archives will help alleviate confusion.

The museum also houses a library of hundreds of books about bears and bear collecting, including antique books about teddy bears and golliwogs that visitors can ask to see.

Educational Opportunities

Perhaps most importantly, the museum provides educational opportunities for people of all ages and interests. Aspiring artists can sign up for the bearmaking classes that the museum regularly sponsors. Collectors can listen to speakers on a variety of topics—funny and serious.

Education includes the history of the teddy bear, which is quite mysterious, George says. Americans claim the name came from Teddy Roosevelt, and there are several stories about Roosevelt's love—or dislike—of the bear. Germans claim that they were the first to make a teddy bear, but no one really knows for sure. George says the museum tries to collect these stories as part of the education objective.

The museum also seeks to educate the public about real bears. "Education includes everything. For instance, if you study the natives of almost any land, with the exception of the Aborigines in Australia, every other tribe from Alaska to the Seminoles have as the symbol of one of their major clans a bear," George says.

The museum also provides talks to schoolchildren. Teddy bears can be used to educate children as young as five years old. George says that when he is asked to speak in a school library, he asks the children to look around and notice the different subject headings on the shelves, including natural history, animals, religion, geography, mythology and environment.

"I explain to the kids that by talking about either real bears or teddy bears, I could hit virtually every subject in that multimedia room," George says.

A Universal Appeal

And that is part of the reason for the universal appeal that teddy bears have. "I say the museum is for children of all ages," George says. "Virtually everybody has some connection to teddy bears. You get the young ones in here, and they can play in a playhouse or look at the mechanical displays we have. The older people once had a teddy bear, so they're looking back at their childhoods. They also see the bears as an art form. It is one of the few places that grandmothers can bring their children and grandchildren, and everyone will enjoy it."

Even men enjoy the museum, once they get inside. George says that men will often start out by looking at some of the more "acceptable" art forms in the museum, such as the paintings and statues. Eventually, they, too, will get hooked.

A Never-Ending Interest

Over the years, the museum's collection has nearly outgrown the building. There is a possibility of expansion, or even moving, George says. But whatever the future holds, one thing is for certain: The museum will always be bears only, as long as there is an interest in teddy bears. And, George predicts, there always will be.

"It's like asking, do you think there will ever be a lack of interest in painting? Well, as long as there are painters, no. The style may change, but there will always be paintings in one form or another," George says.

"And the same goes for bears. When the teddy bear industry began, they were probably all mohair. Since then, we've seen a variety of fabrics, traditional looks, dressed looks, wooden faces, porcelain faces, felt faces, jointed and non-jointed, and now they're coming out with air brushing. But it's just like painting. There are cubists and serialists and landscapists, and I think you need that to appeal to the masses."

George says that teddy bears should be taken seriously as works of art. They are a form of soft sculpture. "Instead of a hammer and chisel, bear artists use fabric, needle and thread," he says.

But the appeal goes much deeper than the art form. "In the beginning, bears were touted as the boys' an-

swer to dolls," George says. "And to some degree girls picked it up, because back then all the dolls were porcelain. If you threw them down, they broke. Teddy bears were a lot more forgiving that way. They would absorb a lot more tears, and stay awake at night and protect you from all those things you knew were hiding under the bed or in the closet. And they do the same things for children today."

Museums

THE BEAR CASTLE

431 Broad St.
P.O. Box 328
Nevada City, CA 95959
Phone: 916-265-5804
Contact: Charles F. Woods, secretary David S. Osborn, president
Hours: vary
Closed: holidays
Please make reservations 4-5 days in advance.
Tours: by request
Admission: $2
Discounts: children
The collection includes antique bears, bears manufactured between WWI and WWII, bears manufactured between 1945 and 1970, modern manufactured bears, artist bears, Teddy Roosevelt antiques, teddy bear collectibles, miniature teddy bear houses and the miniature Bearsonian Cultural Center.
Special programs: Annual International Teddy Bear Convention in April.
History: The 1863 Victorian building was slated to be torn down for a parking lot. It was saved and reconstructed as a Victorian Gothic Folly since 1981 using old pieces and parts of other buildings.

THE BEAR MUSEUM

38 Dragon St.
Petersfield, Hants GU314JJ, UK
Phone: 011-44-1730-265108
Contact: Judy Sparrow, owner/curator
John Sparrow, owner/curator
Hours: M-Sat, 10A.M.-5P.M.
Closed: Sundays
No reservations required.
Admission: free
The collection includes antique bears, bears manufactured between WWI and WWII, bears manufactured between 1945 and 1970, modern manufactured bears, artist bears, teddy bear collectibles, carved wooden bears from the black forest, mechanical bears, books and postcards. There is a Teddy Bears' Picnic in the Cellar.
Special programs: The museum includes a shop where many bears and bear-related items are sold.
History: The museum was founded by Judy Sparrow in 1984. Judy is one of the world's foremost restorers, although she has given up restoration due to the increase in museum visitors. She is an artist, collector and author of Teddy Bears, which has been sold in great volume throughout the world. About half the contents of The Ultimate Teddy Bear Book by Pauline Cockrill were photographed in the museum.

DEUTSCHES PUPPEN-UND BARENMUSEUM LORELEY

Sonnengasse 8, D-56329 St. Goar, Germany
Phone: 011-49-6741-7270
Fax: 011-49-6741-1770
Contact: Eleonore Goedert, owner
Hours: 10A.M.-6P.M. daily
Closed: January 15-March 15
Tours: call first
Discounts children, students, groups
The collection includes antique bears, bears manufactured between WWI and WWII, bears manufactured between 1945 and 1970, modern manufactured bears, Teddy Roosevelt antiques and teddy bear collectibles.

KATHE KRUSE POPPEN MUSEUM

Binnenhaven 25
1781 Bk Den Helder, The Netherlands
Phone: 011-31-2230-16704
Fax: 011-31-2230-16704
Contact: Tiny Riemersma, director
Hours: TH-Sat, 2P.M.-5P.M. & appointment
Please make reservations for groups on closed days (Sun-W), 1 week in advance.
Admission: $5
Discounts: children, groups
The collection includes bears manufactured between WWI and WWII, bears manufactured between 1945 and 1970 and modern manufactured bears.
Special programs: Every three months there is a seminar about a subject relating to the museum.
History: Tiny Riemersma, a local of Den Helder, is a collector of Kathe Kruse dolls. The museum is the first one to display four generations of Kathe Kruse dolls, from 1911 to today

LONDON TOY & MODEL MUSEUM

21-23 Craven Hill
London W2 3EN, UK
Phone: 011-44-171-262-9450
Fax: 011-44-171-703-1993
Contact: H. Macgillivray, curator
Closed: holidays
The collection includes antique bears, bears manufactured between WWI and WWII, bears manufactured between 1945 and 1970, Paddington and Peter Bull Collections.

DREAMWEAVER

I SEE HIM FIRST IN MY DAYDREAMS
AND WIND HIS IMAGE
THROUGH MY MIND
AND ONTO PAPER
THEN INTO A SCULPTURE
OF FUR, STUFFING, THREAD
THAT EMERGES
A SOFT AND CUDDLY
FRIEND,
WOVEN OF WHIMSY,
WHO WILL JOURNEY
FROM MY DAYDREAM
THROUGH MY HANDS
AND INTO YOUR HEART.

I AM THE TEDDY BEAR ARTIST.

– *Gloria Adams*

THE MICHAUD COLLECTION MUSEUM

505 W. Broad St.
Chesaning, MI 48616
Phone: 517-845-7881
Fax: 517-845-6650
The Michaud Collection Museum includes all the original bears from the Michaud's collection, one of the most famous collections in the U.S.

MUSEUM OF CHILDHOOD

42 High St.
Edinburgh, Scotland, UK
Phone: 011-44-131-529-4142
Fax: 011-44-131-558-3103
Contact: Ian Gardner, asst. keeper
John Heyes, keeper
Hours: M-Sat, 10A.M.-6P.M. Oct.-May, 10A.M.-5P.M.
Closed: holidays
Please make reservations for groups only, as early as possible.
Tours: audio tour available
Admission: free
The collection includes antique bears, bears manufactured between WWI and WWII, bears manufactured between 1945 and 1970, modern manufactured bears and teddy bear collectibles.
Special programs: The museum has five public galleries packed full of childhood memories. Temporary exhibitions are staged throughout the year. Contact the museum for details.

POLLOCK'S TOY MUSEUM

1 Scala St.
London W1P 1LT, UK
Phone: 011-44-171-636-3452
Contact: Mrs. V. Sheppard, curator
Hours: M-Sat, 10A.M.-5:30P.M.
Closed: Sundays, most holidays
Please make reservations for groups only, one month in advance.
Admission: 2 pounds

Discounts: children, free on Saturdays
The collection includes antique bears; bears manufactured between WWI and WWII; board games; optical, mechanical and constructional toys; English tin toys; puppets; wax and composition dolls; lead miniatures; dolls' houses; folk toys from the Alps, Russia, Poland and the Balkans; dolls of china, wood, fabric and celluloid; a 1900 young girls' nursery; English dolls; folk toys from Europe, India, Africa, China and Japan; and toy theaters.
History: Benjamin Pollock was well known for his Juvenile Dramas. He devoted his life to toy theaters. By the time Mr. Pollock died in 1937, he had become quite famous among publishers, writers, artists and actors who flocked to his shop. When the shop was destroyed during World War II, his old customers rallied to save the Juvenile Drama from extinction. The museum opened in 1956 in a single attic room where Pollock's toy theaters were sold. By 1969, the collection had outgrown its original space and was moved to the current location.

RIBCHESTER MUSEUM OF CHILDHOOD

Church St.
Ribchester, Lancashire PR3 3YE, UK
Phone: 011-44-012-548-7852
Fax: 011-44-012-548-2397
Contact: Ankie Wild, co-director David Wild, co-director
Hours: T-Sun, 10:30A.M.-5P.M.
Closed: M
Tours: on request
Admission: 2 pounds
Discounts: senior citizens, children
The collection includes antique bears, bears manufactured between WWI and WWII, bears manufactured between 1945 and 1970, modern manufactured bears, artist bears and teddy bear collectibles.
History: The museum originated from

the collection of childhood memorabilia formed by Ankie Wild in Sweden. It is now one of the largest exhibitions of its type in the UK.

THE STRONG MUSEUM

1 Manhattan Sq.
Rochester, NY 14607
Phone: 716-263-2700
Fax: 716-263-2493
Contact: Ellen Manyon, curator
Kathy Castle, director of merchandising
Hours: M-Sat, 10A.M.-5P.M. Sun, 1-5
Closed: most holidays
Admission: $4.50
Discounts: senior citizens, children, student, groups
The museum collections number some 500,000 items that reflect the national consumer culture of the 19th and 20th centuries. Included are furnishings, household objects, table wares, textiles, art, ephemera, dolls, games and toys (including a small group of antique bears and bears manufactured between WWI and WWII)
Special programs: The Strong Museum's annual teddy bear festival, show and sale is held the first week of June.
History: Margaret Woodbury Strong, who died in 1969, left her collections to form a museum. In 1982 a 156,000 square foot building opened in downtown Rochester, New York to house her collection. The museum is dedicated to the exploration of everyday life in the United States from 1820 to today

THE TEDDY BEAR MUSEUM LTD.

19 Greenhill St
Stratford Upon Avon CV37 6LF, UK
Phone: 011-44-1789-293160
Contact: Sylvia Coote, manager
Hours: 7 days, 9:30A.M.-6P.M.
Closed: Christmas Day, Boxing Day
Please make reservations for parties of 20 or more.
Admission: 1.95 pounds
Discounts: children, groups
The collection includes antique bears, bears manufactured between WWI and WWII, bears manufactured between 1945 and 1970, modern manufactured bears, artist bears, teddy bear collectibles and bears with famous owners.

History: The museum was founded in 1988 by Michele and Gyles Brandreth.

TEDDY BEAR MUSEUM OF NAPLES

2511 Pine Ridge Rd.
Naples, FL 33942
Phone: 813-598-2711
Fax: 813-598-9239
Contact: George B. Black, director
Hours: W-Sat, 10 A.M.-5 P.M. Sun, 1 P.M.-5 P.M.
Closed: Christmas, New Years Day, Thanksgiving, July 4
Tours: 10:30 A.M., 2:30 P.M.
Admission: $5 adults
Discounts: senior citizens, children, groups
The collection includes antique bears, bears manufactured between WWI and WWII, bears manufactured between 1945 and 1970, modern manufactured bears, artist bears and teddy bear collectibles.
Special programs bearmaking classes, artist and manufacturers' archives, video shows, school teddy awareness talks.
History: See the article opening this chapter.

TEDDY MELROSE: SCOTLAND'S TEDDY BEAR MUSEUM

The Wynd
Melrose, Scotland, UK
Phone: 011-44-1896-822464
Contact: Felix Sear, owner Sue Niccol, bear maker
Hours: 7 days, 10 A.M.-5 P.M.
Closed: Christmas
Tours: 10:30 A.M., 2:30 P.M.
Admission: 1.50 pounds
The collection includes antique bears, bears manufactured between WWI and WWII, bears manufactured between 1945 and 1970, modern manufactured bears, artist bears and teddy bear collectibles.
Special programs: A one-hour talk by Felix Sear on the history of teddies, from the first bearmaker, Agnes Farnell, to today's artist makers. The talk includes a light lunch and bearmaking presentation by Sue Niccol, who founded Romsey Bears 22 years ago.

THEODORE ROOSEVELT INAUGURAL NATIONAL HISTORIC SITE

641 Delaware Ave.
Buffalo, NY 14202
Phone: 716-884-0095
Fax: 716-884-0330
Contact: Janice Tomaka, special events coordinator
Hours: M-F, 9 A.M.-5 P.M. Sat, Sun, noon-5 P.M.
Closed: Saturdays in Jan., Feb., and Mar.; holidays
Tours: Anytime. Groups by appointment only.
Admission: $2
Discounts: senior citizens, children
The collection includes antique bears, bears manufactured between WWI and WWII, bears manufactured between 1945 and 1970, modern manufactured bears, artist bears and Teddy Roosevelt antiques.
Special programs: A wide range of educational programs relating to Teddy Roosevelt and life at the turn of the century. Different programs are geared toward pre-K through high school, college students and adults. A gift shop with a wide variety of teddy bears is also available.
History: The museum is located in the former home of Ansley and Mary Grace Wilcox, friends of President Theodore Roosevelt. Roosevelt was sworn in as the 26th president of the United States in the Wilcox home, where he arrived after hearing the news of President William McKinley's death.

TOY AND MINIATURE MUSEUM OF KANSAS CITY

5235 Oak St.
Kansas City, MO 64112
Phone: 816-333-9328

THERE IS NOTHING MORE REWARDING THAN FINDING AN OLD BEAR, ONE WHO'S BEEN THROUGH MORE DIFFICULT TIMES THAN MOST OF US COULD EVER IMAGINE. OLD BEARS ARE FIGHTERS. THEY TUG ON THE HEARTSTRINGS OF BOTH YOUNG AND OLD.
— *Steve & Sybille Howard, owners, Teddy Bar Circa 1900, Oakville, Ontario, Canada*

Fax: 816-333-2055
Contact: Mary Wheeler, collection manager
Hours: W-Sat, 10 A.M.-4 P.M. Sun, 1 P.M.-4 P.M.
Closed: holidays, the first 2 weeks after Labor Day
Please make reservations for groups of ten or more and guided tours two weeks in advance.
Tours: advance reservations
Admission: $3
Discounts: senior citizens, children, students, groups, AAA
The collection includes bears manufactured between 1945 and 1970, modern manufactured bears, artist bears, teddy bear collectibles and $\frac{1}{12}''$ scale miniature bears.

TOY MUSEUM IN WETTSTEINHAUS

Baselstrasse 34
4125 Riehen
Switzerland
Phone: 011-41-61-641-2829
Fax: 011-41-61-641-1124
Contact: Lawrence Landolt
Hours: W, 2 P.M.-7 P.M.; TH-Sat, 2 P.M.-5 P.M.; Sun, 10 A.M.-12 P.M., 2 P.M.-5 P.M.
Closed: M, T, Sun noon-2 P.M.
Tours: on advance request
Discounts: senior citizens, children, student, groups.
The collection includes antique bears, bears manufactured between WWI and WWII, bears manufactured between 1945 and 1970, modern manufactured bears, teddy bear collectibles, historical games and toys, miniature worlds, dolls and dollhouses.
Special programs: Play hours and afternoon actions with and for children.
History: The Wettsteinhaus is a Basel manor that originally belonged to the monastery of Wettingen. The mayor of Basel, Johann Rudolf Wettstein, acquired the manor in the middle of the 17th century. The community of Riehen bought the estate in 1958. Since its renovation (1968-1971), it has housed the Toy Museum and the Village and Viniculture Museum. The Toy Museum was set up in 1972, founded by the community of Riehen and the Swiss Folklore Museum of Basel.

No matter how many bears are in your collection, make room, because when you least expect it, another will grab your heart.
— *Patricia Brink, owner, Pat's Kountry Kitchen and Kollectibles, Old Saybrook, CT*

THE WAREHAM BEARS
Wilton House
Wilton, Salisbury SP2 0BJ, UK
Phone: 011-44-1722-743115
Contact: Alun Williams, tourism and marketing manager
Hours: 11 A.M.-6 P.M.
Closed: End of Oct.-Easter
Admission: 5.75 pounds
Discounts: senior citizens, children, students, groups
The collection includes miniature teddy bears.
Special programs: Teddy Bears Picnic in the summer.

History: The Wareham bears were made by Mary Hildesley to amuse family and friends, particularly her own children and grandchildren. In 1975, John Honeychurch of Market Lavington was commissioned to build the bears' house and later the stable block. A series of 12 stories were written based on the bears, and the books are illustrated by John Doubleday. After moving to Wareham, Mary and Paul Hildesley converted the basement of their home to a small museum and opened it to the public. In 1993, Paul and Mary decided to retire, and the bears found a new home at The Wilton house, a museum dedicated to the memory of the Earls of Pembroke. The museum includes two hundred original paintings and 21 acres of landscaped parkland.

WENHAM MUSEUM
132 Main St.
Wenham, MA 01984
Phone: 508-468-2377
Contact: Lorna Lieberman, curator of dolls
Hours: M-F, 11 A.M.-4 P.M. Sat, 1 P.M.-4 P.M. Sun, 2 P.M.-5 P.M.
Closed: holidays
Please make reservations for groups only, several days in advance.
Tours: on request
Admission: $3
Discounts: senior citizens, children, groups, AAA
The collection includes antique bears, bears manufactured between WWI and WWII, Teddy Roosevelt antiques, almost 5,000 dolls (2500 B.C. to the present), dollhouses, miniature rooms and antique toys.
Special programs: Colonial Household programs for grades 3 and 4 in local schools, including Colonial cooking for grade 3 and spinning and weaving for grade 4.

8

Additional
Opportunities

How to Use This Chapter

*T*his chapter has everything you need that wasn't included in the previous chapters. Whether you are a beginning or an experienced artist or collector, you are bound to find something you need in these pages. Artists at all levels will find instructional videos and workshops to help them with their craft, contests to enter, tours to take, and photographers for their furry friends. Collectors will find appraisal and restoration services, tours and insurance for their collections. There are publications and books that will be of great interest to collectors and artists alike, as well as other opportunities and products.

The listings include contact and price information (when available) and specific information about the product or opportunity available. There are a few things to keep in mind for all these opportunities. When calling or faxing, as always, keep time zone differences in mind. Like the artist's listings, many of these listings are home businesses, and it is important to be courteous.

When looking at the books listed here, keep in mind that most publishers will not allow you to purchase a book directly from them. It is best to ask your local bookstore to order the book if it is not in stock. Most large bookstores, and some smaller bookstores, now handle special orders. The information provided should be all they need.

Many of these opportunities and products can be ordered through the mail. It is common courtesy to pay for shipping both ways in these cases, particularly if the businessperson is offering the service for free or at an exceptionally low rate, as is often the case with appraisals. When conducting business through the mail, always contact the person or business listed before shipping anything. Never send a bear or other item unannounced to an appraiser or a restoration business.

The contests and auctions listed here are those that are not associated with a specific show. See the show listings for more contests and auctions available. There are several, and you do not always have to be a show participant to attend the auction or enter the contest.

Whether you are an artist, a collector, or both, you may need some of these additional products and services when you least expect it, so keep this book handy! 🐾

Teddy Love Can Take You Anywhere

BY NEYSA PHILLIPPI

*W*ho would have guessed when I was a child, growing up on a small farm in Homer City, Pennsylvania, that I would end up making teddy bears for a living, and planning tours to Europe for other artists and collectors? As a child, I never even had a teddy bear! Who needed stuffed animals when you had plenty of the real thing? My furry friends came in all sizes and shapes, from horses, cows and pigs to everyday "Heinz 57" variety dogs and cats. All my pets had personality and were real characters. Charley, my second pony, was fond of doing anything to embarrass me, while my dog Fatso never left my side, even on schooldays. Quasimodo, a chicken who could only walk in circles, also contributed to my active imagination, which ran wild! I am convinced that these experiences with "real" animals later gave me the insight to create special personalities for each of my bears.

I had always been interested in art, and in 1975 I attended the Art Institute of Pittsburgh and received a degree in Photography/Multi-Media. Upon graduation I became a freelance agricultural/nature photographer. That was when I developed a love for traveling. The Artists for Artists tours I organize prove that I still can't get enough.

Neysa Phillippi has been making bears fulltime since 1985. In 1994, she began Artists for Artists European Tours. Her bears have appeared in *Teddy Bear Review, Teddy Bear & Friends* and other newspapers, magazines and books. They are sold in the USA, Canada, the Netherlands, Belgium and Germany. She has been a celebrity guest at the Toy Store Annual International Tribute to Teddies for three years, and was also featured on a local TV station. She lives in Indiana, Pennsylvania.

Discovering the Teddy Bear

In 1978 I let my friends talk me into applying for a full time "real" job—something a little more dependable than what I was doing. I accepted a job as a graphic arts technician in the advertising department at Gimbels in Pittsburgh, where I worked for six years. My best friend, Adrienne Sempr, was very interested in dolls, and she knew of a wonderful toy store across the street from Gimbels. Every payday Adrienne and I would cash our checks and cross the street to spend the next hour looking at dolls. One day a teddy bear spoke to me.

Soon I was buying bears regularly. When I attended the toy store's annual doll and bear festival and purchased my first Steiff, I was hooked. I took him home, and my husband Gerry asked, "How much did that cost?" I just mumbled. I couldn't afford many Steiff

bears, and my first purchases lost their appeal. They were cute, but had no real character or personality. That was important to me. I outgrew them as a child outgrows her toys.

The Beginning of a Business

I began making bears shortly after that. My mother gave me a bolt of furry coat lining. I bought a bear pattern, made a bear, took it to work and came home with orders for ten. The last two years I worked for Gimbels I made bears from purchased patterns. One day I decided I could do better and created my first original bear. We all have our beginnings. Some of them aren't pretty. I didn't like cute. Character and personality were more important, and who said they had to have short arms and legs and look like manufactured bears? Mine never did.

A lot of me goes into my creations. "Normal" doesn't describe my bears, or me, if you look back at all I've done. I have delivered pizzas and worked as a welder, a weaver and a graphic artist. I photographed cows and now I'm a teddy bear artist. All have taught me discipline, productivity, creativity and a sense of satisfaction that I can do anything I put my mind to. These are attributes that all teddy bear artists must acquire. I believe they led me to a successful bear-making business, as well as the success of the Artists to Artists tours that followed.

In 1984 I quit my job. By May of 1985, I was attending craft shows and selling my bears full time. I have always liked being my own boss. By then I was almost thirty-two and on my way, but being married also helped with my decision to quit a job with a weekly paycheck. Gerry supported my initial decision. Today, I am supporting myself and my business without his help. It is a good feeling.

The First Trip to Europe

By 1992, my business was doing well and I was ready for something new. I was asked to participate in a thirteen-day tour of Holland and Germany. We would participate in four shows while there. I had always wanted to go to Europe, but the timing was never right. This sounded like a good opportunity to expand my business. While in Europe, I sold forty of the forty-five bears that I took with me! But there were some problems with the tour: The price was high, the organizer was gruff, and we saw little of the countries we visited.

On that trip I met Nick Kesteloot, the driver for the coach company that the tour organizer used. Little did I know that the coach company was owned by Nick's inlaws! Nick, his wife Kathy, and I became instant friends, and before we knew it, we were planning the first Artists for Artists tour. Gerrit Cars of Zwevegem, Belgium (A5379) is a travel agency and coach company that has been a successful family business for the past fifty years. Nick had experience conducting tours throughout Europe and England. This proved to be a great asset.

We wanted to bring American teddy bear artists and collectors to Europe. I wanted a reasonably priced tour with plenty of sights, good food and fun. After all, as the U.S. organizer, I had to be able to afford to go to Europe every year. For me to do this, the price had to be good. Nick could function as driver, tour guide and translator for all of us and provide a big savings. I knew he and his wife were honest people who wanted to give their customers the most for their money and the best of everything. Family is important to them, and they wanted their customers to feel like part of their family. Nick is also very personable, and I knew that this would be a big help for our public relations.

European Advantages

We spoke often about the opportunities Europe offered. I learned that there were many advantages to selling in Europe. For one thing, the market for artist bears was relatively new. Art in Europe is well respected, and for

This bear seems to be enjoying a leisurely boat trip in Brugge, Belgium.

the first time, Europeans were becoming interested in bears other than the manufactured ones. Today Europe is where we were in the mid-1980s as far as collecting goes, but the market is definitely expanding. Many new shops are opening. I realized that if we offered European collectors good designs from the very beginning, we would be selling in Europe for years to come. European collectors were looking to America and the rest of the world for something new. Our teddy bear magazines were reaching them, and they were familiar with many artists' names if not their bears. Getting in on the ground floor seemed important.

Another advantage for American artists touring Europe is that the collectors only have one opportunity to buy directly. They know that if they don't buy, they will miss their opportunity until the next year. This is different than the situation at U.S. shows, where collectors have less incentive to buy right away because they know they can always find the artist again if they later decide they want a bear.

The participants in the May 1994 Artists for Artists tour enjoy a moment of relaxation in Castle Burg ELZ Germany.

Finally, competition in Europe is primarily from antique bears, dolls and toys. The European teddy bear artists are on the rise and are producing beautiful bears. Many are truly original. Still, the competition in Europe does not even begin to compare with home competition, where shows often include more than two hundred tables of artists' bears.

Artists for Artists Is Born

Here at home, in all aspects of business, I've always felt that money and connections are everything. Since I had neither of these, Europe seemed the only place to go. Expensive advertising helps the artist become well known in the U.S. Not having money to advertise often keeps many of us from making it big. My idea for the tour was to give the "little person" the chance to become known worldwide, not just in his or her home area or nearby shows. I wanted us, the bear artists, to make money—not the travel agency or the tour guide. Finding a name for the tour was easy. I was an artist trying to make it easy for other artists and myself to go to Europe and sell. "Artists for Artists" came from my wanting the artists and the artists alone to benefit from the trip. "Artists for Artists" said it all!

In October 1993, artist Sharon Agin, of Sharon's Bears, and I went to Europe and spent nineteen very prosperous days selling in Holland, Belgium and Germany. Nick provided us with transportation, and we worked to set up the tour for May 1994. Nick and I spoke with every promoter, shop owner and artist we could. We asked their opinion of our idea and were pleased with their response. It wasn't hard to convince them it was a wonderful opportunity for them as well.

We decided that Nick and Kathy would be the organizers in Europe. They would stay in touch with promoters and work to set everything up to our mutual satisfaction. I would be the American organizer and contact. It would be my job to find the artists and collectors and keep them informed of our progress. We also chose the month of May for the tour. Because May is off-season for tourists, air fare and hotel rooms are cheaper. The tourist season doesn't reach full swing until June, so Nick would be available to us. May is also a slow show month at home, so planning the tour for that month made the most sense.

In October of 1994, Jackie Morris, of Blacklick Bears, and I worked with Nick to set up the May 1995 tour, while selling at shows and to shops to keep our businesses going. Many European promoters are now approaching us about their shows. Our plans for May 1995 include visiting many sights in Holland, Belgium, France and Germany. We are working with promoters to participate in five shows throughout these countries. We will see and enjoy everything we can possibly fit into our schedule. In future years we hope to go to England and Switzerland as well.

In 1996, we're also hoping to bring a tour of European artists and collectors to the United States. We hope to bring them in the month of September and give them as much opportunity to sell and collect as possible.

Tips for Selling in Europe

Entering the European market is like stepping into a whole new world of opportunity. But believe it or not, selling in Europe is much the same as it is here in the states. Until the European collectors speak, you won't even realize you're not at home. They love their bears just the same. The collectors in Europe also like to get to know you before they buy, just as American collectors do. Europeans, especially Germans, appreciate fine art and are willing to pay for it. But that doesn't mean you can charge anything you want for your bear. Keep your prices consistent with the U.S.; Europeans read U.S. magazines.

Ninety percent of the time you must tell Europeans, "You can pick the bear up if you want to." This surprises some collectors, who, out of respect, will not touch your bears. You must hand them the bears to hold. I like this form of respect, but I also feel that allowing the collector to hold the bear helps sell it.

There is only one major difference between selling in Europe and in America—money. We can't accept checks, and if we accept Visa or MasterCard, our merchant numbers are not valid outside the U.S. This means you can accept payment with credit cards but you have no number to call to verify the sale until you return home. In my opinion this is a big risk. Once home, if the charge doesn't clear, you have no way to collect. My advice is to accept cash only, and all money up front, whether it's from collectors or shops. Don't deviate from this just to make a sale. I know from personal experience—money first!

When you begin selling to stores in Europe, remember that travel in Europe is less common than it is in the U.S. At home we think nothing of driving six hours to a show or any other event. In Europe, traveling two hours is considered too long to drive. This means you can sell to more shops because you won't have to worry as much about selling to shops that are close together. Don't sell to shops that are next door to each other, but remember gasoline costs three times as much in Europe as in the United States. For example, the Dutch don't generally travel to their neighbor Germany to attend a show, even if it is only a three-hour drive. It's too far, and costs too much.

Obviously, you should always treat Europeans with the same openness and honesty with which you treat American collectors. Language can be a real barrier, depending on how well they speak and understand the English language. Be very clear; speak slowly, and make sure all is understood. You don't need a representative in Europe. Dealing directly with the shops is preferable. If they don't speak English, they will usually know someone who can translate. All Europeans now begin learning English in school when they are ten years old. Germans speak English because of the American military bases. Chances are that wherever you go in Europe, the person standing next to you will speak English or at least have a general understanding of the language. During the tours, we count on Nick to translate, because he speaks five languages fluently. Here in the states, if you are conducting business with someone of a foreign country and are having trouble, contact the nearest school or college language department.

Handling Orders From Europe

A definite must in dealing day to day with Europe is a fax machine. Those of us who have them wonder what life was like without them. In dealing with European buyers, accepting mail, phone or fax orders is most common. Prepayment is vital, but don't accept payment until your order is ready to ship. This above all else is the most important factor in dealing with Europeans!

Using your local post office is great for small bears and small orders. Air mail is especially useful. If using your local post office, however, you must add shipping to your price. Let your customer know that shipping is added. I personally ship through a large company (Burlington Air Express) that deals daily with the rest of the world. The heavier the box, the more reasonable the shipping price. Delivery time is four or five days, and shipping, tax and duty is collected in Europe from the customer. Make sure your customers understand that they are paying all these fees, and that the price you quote them is only for the bear itself.

Despite the extra work it may take to adjust to selling internationally, you, the artist, are the one who benefits most in the long run. The Artists for Artists tours will hopefully continue for years to come, giving artists the opportunity to travel with Nick, Kathy and I down that long and not so lonesome highway of the teddy bear world.

BEAR MAKERS, MAKE ONLY WHAT YOU LOVE—SOMEONE ELSE WILL LOVE IT, TOO!
— *Carol Adrian, artist, Beaver Falls, PA*

For the collector, the tours offer a chance to collect both manufactured and artist bears from Europe. Some of these bears are not available in the United States. An educated collector will find many bargains.

Love in Any Language

My hope for the future is a better understanding of our two worlds. We must earn respect from our European friends. We must accept them for what they believe. Americans adapt to their changing environment. Europeans, under the surface, cling to their beliefs and find it harder to accept change.

But teddy bears are love in any language. We are opening the eyes of European collectors to a new form of bear. We are making friends a world away who will enrich our lives forever. We artists want our furry friends to help us bridge the way.

Come along and join us! 🐾

> KEEP ALL YOUR TAGS ON ALL YOUR COLLECTIBLES TO GAIN THE MOST VALUE IN YEARS TO COME.
> — *Karen Nelson, owner, Chubby's Cubby, Occoquan, VA*

Appraisals

BEARS & BAUBLES
Denise Parsons
1603 Solano Ave.
Berkeley, CA 94706
Phone: 510-524-4794
Accepts: personal check, money order,
   Visa, MasterCard, Discover, Ameri-
   can Express
Mail order: Package contents well. Send
   UPS insured. Denise must see the
   item in order to appraise it. Her spe-
   cialty is Steiff.
She has been with Bears & Baubles for
   2 years

THE COUNTRY BEAR
Jay Hadly, owner
Route 73, P.O. Box 17
Skippack, PA 19474
Phone: 610-584-4055
Jay has been in the bear business for more
   than 13 years

OLD-TIMERS ANTIQUES
Elizabeth Neitz, owner
3717-B South Dixie Hwy.
West Palm Beach, FL 33405
Phone: 407-832-5141
Fax: 407-832-5141
Elizabeth has a thorough knowledge of
   the Steiff line, both old and new.

P J BEARS
Pat Johnson
2121 Contra Costa Ave.
Santa Rosa, CA 95405
Phone: 707-578-8809
Accepts: personal check, money order
Mail order: Wrap in cloth, put in plastic
   bag, attach name, address and phone
   number. Pack in box, send UPS.
Pat offers appraisals for $10. If she also
   restores the customer's bear, the appraisal is free. She specializes in Steiff
   bears.

THE TEDDY BEAR GARDEN
Ruth E. Fraser
366 Eglinton Ave.
Toronto, Ontario M5N 1A2, Canada
Phone: 416-322-3277
Fax: 416-322-5527
Mail order available at customer's convenience. Ruth must see the item in order to appraise it. There is no charge
   for appraisals. An evaluation and
   identification certificate is issued.

KEN YENKE
P.O. Box 361633
Strongsville, OH 44136
Phone: 216-238-5363
Ken Yenke is an experienced appraisal,
   evaluation and identification expert.
   He also buys and sells old teddy bears.
   See the article opening chapter four
   by Ken.

Auctions

These listings include only auctions that are not associated with any shows or conventions. For auctions that are associated with shows or conventions, see the show/convention listings.

CHRISTIE'S

Christie's Publications Dept.
21-24 44th Ave.
Long Island City, NY 11101
Phone: 1-800-395-6300
Fax: 1-800-395-5600
Auctions are held in 15 major cities around the world. Write to the above address for information about a subscription to the Dolls, Toys, Teddy Bears and Juvenilia catalog, which will give you information on auction lots that include teddy bears. A yearly subscription to this catalog costs $70.

TEDDY BEAR AUCTION

Arlene Demirjian
Children's Safety Project,
Greenwich House
New York, NY 10014
Sponsors: Greenwich House Inc.
This event occurs annually in the spring or fall
Items for auction are donated. All proceeds go to the Children's Safety Project, Greenwich House.
Has been taking place for 3 years

RECIPE FOR A LOVE-FILLED TEDDY BEAR

1 POUND MOHAIR

4 WOOL PAW PADS

8 CUPS STUFFING

5 MOVABLE JOINTS

2 GLAZED GLASS EYES

1 ENORMOUS HEART

SEW TOGETHER WITH TENDER CARE. JOINT HEAD, ARMS AND LEGS FOR MOVEMENT. STUFF WITH LOVING HANDS. PLACE EYES FOR THE GIFT OF SIGHT. SEW ON NOSE AND MOUTH FOR SMELLING AND TASTING HONEY. LAST OF ALL, GIVE TEDDY A HUGE HUG TO ACTIVATE THE ENORMOUS HEART. NOW TEDDY WILL CONTINUE HIS WORK—GIVING LOVE—'CAUSE THAT'S A TEDDY BEARS JOB!

— *Susan L. Paul, owner, Beary Best Friends, East Stroudsburg, PA*

Books/Publishing Companies

THE BEAR AFFAIR
by Cynthia Powell
Avalon Books
Thomas Bouregy & Company, Inc.
The Bear Affair is a love story with bear characters.

BEARS REPEATING
by Terry and Doris Michaud
Price: $14.95
Nostalgic stories about teddy bears in the Michaud's collection.

BETTY LAMPEN KNITTING BOOKS
Betty Lampen
2930 Jackson St.
San Francisco, CA 94115-1007
Betty's books include patterns for teddy bear sweaters.

COLLECTOR'S GUIDE TO MINIATURE TEDDY BEARS
by Cynthia Powell
Collector Books
A Division of Schroeder Publishing Co., Inc., Paducah, KY
This book documents the history of miniature bears from 1903 to the present. It includes color photographs, descriptions and prices for miniature bears. The book includes old, new, manufactured and artist miniature bears as well as collecting tips and historical information.

CONTEMPORARY TEDDY BEAR PRICE GUIDE—ARTIST & MANUFACTURERS
by Terry and Doris Michaud
Price: $16.95
This book includes selected artists with current values on their bears and a scientific approach to pricing. Also includes Steiff, Hermann and other contemporary manufactured bears.

HOBBY HOUSE PRESS
1 Corporate Dr.
Grantsville, MD 21536
This company publishes a wide variety of books about bears and bear collecting.

HOW TO MAKE & SELL QUALITY TEDDY BEARS
by Terry and Doris Michaud
Price: $12.95
A step-by-step guide to designing, creating and producing top-quality teddy bears.

JUST BEARS
by Sue Quinn
Salamander Books Ltd.
London, UK
This book includes instructions on how to make a variety of bear items, including gift wrap, greeting cards, cushions, sweaters and more.

THE LITTLE BOOK OF BEAR CARE
THE LITTLE BOOK OF CELEBRITY BEARS
THE LITTLE BOOK OF TRADITIONAL BEARS
all by Pauline Cockrill
(sold individually and as a set)
Dorling Kindersley, Inc., New York, NY

MAKE YOUR OWN CLASSIC BEARS
by Julia Jones
Crescent Books
Distributed by Outlet Book Co.
Avenel, NJ
This book includes 14 bear patterns with instructions.

MAKE YOUR OWN TEDDY BEAR
Running Press Book Publishers
Price: $9.95
This book includes a fully illustrated, step-by-step instruction book and the materials needed to make a 5½" teddy bear.

MAKING TEDDY BEARS
by Joyce Luckin
BT Batsford Ltd.
London, UK
This book includes patterns and step-by-step instructions.

OFFICIAL PRICE GUIDE TO ANTIQUE & MODERN TEDDY BEARS
by Carol-Lynn Rossel Waugh & Kim Brewer
House Collectibles
New York, NY
Price: $10.95
Published in 1990, this book gives beginning and advanced collectors the information and background they need to purchase bears.

RUNAWAY BEAR
by Chester Freeman and John E. McGuire
Pelican Publishing Co.
Price: $14.95
A children's story about a teddy bear that runs away, his adventures and his return.

TEDDY BEAR
Courage Books
Running Press Book Publishers
Price: $12.98
This book traces the history of the teddy bear from the story of Margarete Steiff to recent years. It also includes a study of how bears are made and profiles of famous bears.

THE TEDDY BEAR ENCYCLOPEDIA
by Pauline Cockrill
Dorling Kindersley, Inc.
New York, NY
Price: $34.95
The Teddy Bear Encyclopedia is a com-

prehensive book on collecting and identifying teddy bears.

THE TEDDY BEAR KIT
by Alicia Merrett
St. Martin's Press
New York, NY
Price: $19.95
The book includes instructions, patterns and materials for three bears.

> BEARS ARE AN INVESTMENT YOU CAN LIVE WITH!
> — *Shalmir Pinney, owner, Comfrey Corner, Inc., Heath, OH*

THE TEDDY BEAR LOVER'S COMPANION
by Ted Menten
Courage Books
Running Press
Price: $9.98
A book about collectible teddy bears that covers bear fashions and crafts, documentation of collectible bears, and caring for antique bears.

TEDDY BEARS: A GUIDE TO THEIR HISTORY, COLLECTING, AND CARE
by Sue Pearson and Dottie Ayers
Macmillan Books
New York, NY

Price: $19.95

TEDDY TALES BEARS REPEATING, TOO!
by Terry and Doris Michaud
Price: $19.95
A book about the love between people and teddy bears.

THE ULTIMATE TEDDY BEAR BOOK
by Pauline Cockrill
Dorling Kindersley, Inc.
New York, NY
A comprehensive book on collectible teddy bears.

Computer Services

TEDDY BEAR INVENTORY
Rob Blerstein
RR 2, Box 994
Milton, PA 17847
Phone: 717-437-3123
Price: $30
Accepts: personal check, money order
Mail order: 1-2 weeks

Teddy Bear Inventory is a database for teddy bear collectors that can be used to enter their teddy bear data information. The database can be used on IBM PCs or compatible systems with at least one disk drive. Two drives are recommended. The program comes with a booklet with step-by-step instructions on how to enter, change, print, copy, delete, sort and search for important teddy bear data. Shipping and handling are free.

> IF YOU SEE A BEAR THAT REALLY GRABS YOUR HEART, DON'T HESITATE. BEARS ARE CRAFTY CREATURES AND YOU OFTEN DON'T GET A SECOND SHOT AT THEM. I'VE WASTED A LOT OF TIME AND MONEY TRYING TO TRACK DOWN BEARS THAT GOT AWAY!
> — *Edie Barlishen, aritst, St. Albert, Alberta*

Contests

These listings do not include contests associated with a show or convention. See the show/convention listings for additional contests.

GOLDEN TEDDY AWARDS
Teddy Bear Review
Collector Communications Corp.
170 Fifth Ave.
New York, NY 10010
Phone: 212-989-9700
212-645-8976
Price: $10 per entry for hobbyists. $25 per entry for artists and manufacturers.

The Golden Teddy Awards are among the most prestigious awards that teddy bear artists, hobbyists and manufacturers can win. To enter, send a clear, color photograph of the bear or a 4″ × 5″ or larger transparency, a completed entry form and the entry fee. See Teddy Bear Review for the due date. Each bear must have a separate entry form. Photographs of the nominated bears appear in the July/ August issue of Teddy Bear Review. Readers select their favorites from among the nominees, and winners are featured in the November/December issue. Hobbyist, artist and manufacturer bears are eligible for the contest, and categories are by size and dressed/undressed under these headings.

TOBY AWARDS
Teddy Bear & Friends
David L. Miller, editor
Cowles Magazines
Kable News Company
Kable Square
Mount Morris, IL 61054
Phone: 1-800-435-9610
The Toby award is one of the most prestigious awards in the teddy bear industry. The contest includes 10 categories, 5 for artists and 5 for manufacturers.

> DON'T EVER LIMIT YOURSELF TO A PARTICULAR TYPE OF BEAR BECAUSE YOU MIGHT MISS THE MOST SPECIAL ONE TO ADD TO YOUR COLLECTION.
> — *Roberta A. Rehm, artist, Seminole, FL*

Insurance

**AMERICAN COLLECTORS
INSURANCE, INC.**
Collectibles Underwriter
P.O. Box 8343
385 N. Kings Hwy.
Cherry Hill, NJ 08002
Phone: 609-779-7212
   1-800-360-2277
Fax: 609-779-7289
Accepts: personal check, money order
Mail order: 7-10 days to review application

American Collectibles insurance specializes in insuring antique and contemporary collectibles. They provide collections with all-risk, agreed value coverage at an extremely affordable rate. Many different types of collections, including teddy bears, may qualify for their program. A completed application and photo of any item exceeding $1,000 in value is necessary.

A BEAR IS AN EMOTIONAL INVESTMENT, AND IF YOU KEEP THAT IN MIND YOU WILL NEVER HAVE TO THIN THE
"JUNK" OUT OF YOUR COLLECTION. IT IS FAR BETTER TO HAVE A SMALL COLLECTION THAT YOU LOVE THAN
HUNDREDS OF BEARS THAT YOU NO LONGER CARE ABOUT.

— Monty & Joe Sours, artists, Golden City, MO

Lectures

CHESTER FREEMAN
398 S. Main St.
Geneva, NY 14456-2614
Phone: 315-781-1251
Fax: 315-781-0643
Chester gives lectures on the therapeutic value of the teddy bear, and also speaks about his children's book, Runaway Bear.

LOVE'S LABOURS
Kara L. Anderson
428 Highland Terrace
Pitman, NJ 08071-1522
Phone: 609-589-5818
Accepts: personal check, money order
Kara provides lectures and slide shows on two topics: 1. Miniature teddy bears—how to display them, slide show featuring different artists' creations, info on similarities/differences between miniature teddy bears and dollhouse miniature worlds and 2. "More Time For Teddies"— how to organize your "stuff" to be free to do what is most important to you.

MONICA MURRAY
P.O. Box 728
Jenks, OK 74037
Phone: 918-299-5416
Monica gives lectures on bears and related subjects.

KEN YENKE
P.O. Box 361633
Strongsville, OH 44136
Phone: 216-238-5363
Ken Yenke is an appraisal, evaluation and identification expert. He gives lectures on a variety of teddy bear topics. See the article opening chapter four written by Ken.

Periodicals

BEAR TRACKS

Box 13097
Toledo, OH 43613
Phone: 419-531-5365
Fax: 419-531-5365
Bear Tracks is the journal of Good Bears
of the World. It is published quarterly
and includes artist profiles, updates on
den activities, a calendar of events and
other items.
Advertising: Both display ads and classified ads are included.

THE SPARKLER

Valerie Rogers, editor
Bright Star Promotions
3428 Hillvale Rd.
Louisville, KY 40241-2756
Phone: 502-423-STAR
A publication for the advancement and
growth of the miniatures and teddy
bear artists industry, published by
Bright Star Promotions. Includes features, letters and up-to-date show information.

TEDDY BEAR & FRIENDS

David L. Miller, editor
Joan Bohnert and Lisa Faus, advertising
reps
Cowles Magazines
Kable News Co., Kable Square
Mount Morris, IL 61054
Phone: 1-800-435-9610
Fax: 717-540-6728
Price: $17.95 (subscription). $3.95 per
issue.
Teddy Bear & Friends has been serving
teddy bear collectors and artists for
more than 11 years. The magazine includes national and international show
information, features on bear collectors and artists, general information
about collecting and bear artistry, and
bear patterns. It is published six times
a year and has a paid circulation of
42,000.
Submissions: Teddy Bear & Friends accepts unsolicited manuscripts, but

prefers contact from the writer prior
to submission. Pay varies depending
on content.
Advertising: Contact the magazine for
more information.

TEDDY BEAR REVIEW

Stephen L. Cronk, editor
Lorelei Aubrey and Bernice Silbaugh,
ad reps
Collector Communication Corp.
170 Fifth Ave., 12th Floor
New York, NY 10010
Phone: 212-989-8700
1-800-347-6969
Fax: 212-645-8976
Price: $16.95 subscription. $3.95 per issue.
Teddy Bear Review has been serving the
teddy bear community for more than
9 years. It has a circulation of nearly
60,000. The magazine is published six
times a year and includes profiles of
artists and manufacturers, information
about bearmaking, the business, and
restoration and repair, as well as patterns for bears and costumes and coverage of innovative bearmaking techniques. Other features include updates
on auction results for antique bears, a
show calendar, recipes, book reviews,
paper teddy bears, identification of
rare and unusual teddies, new teddy-
related products and annual contest,
the Golden Teddy Bear Awards. The
Bear Gallery includes new artist creations chosen by the editorial staff,
and The Bear Shoppe includes new
designs offered by studios and manufacturers. Submissions for these columns should be made to the address
above and include quality photographs and appropriate information as
designated in the columns.
Advertising: Contact the magazine for
more information.

TEDDY BEAR TIMES

Julie Martini
Heritage Press
3150 State Line Rd.
North Bend, OH 45052
Phone: 513-353-4052
Fax: 513-353-3933
U.K. Address: Ashdown Publishing
Limited, Avalon Court, Star Road,
Partridge Green, West Sussex, RH3 8RY.
Price: U.S.A.: $6 per issue, $32 subscrip-
tion. Canada: $45 subscription.
Teddy Bear Times is published in England
and distributed in the USA through
Heritage Press. It includes articles on
all aspects of the teddy bear world.
Submissions: Contact the magazine for
details.
Advertising: Contact the magazine for
details.

VICTORIAN HARVESTER/
TEDDIES' OWN JOURNAL

Linda Singleton
438 Draycott St.
Coquitlam, British Columbia V3K 5K2,
Canada
Phone: 604-937-5119
Fax: 604-937-5119
Price: Canada: $4 per issue, $20 subscription. U.S.A.: $21 subscription.
The Victorian Harvester/Teddies' Own
Journal, Canada's only teddy bear
magazine, has been serving the teddy
bear world since 1992. Features include teddy bear artist profiles, bear
artist's corner, teddy bear club listings,
classified ads, calendar of events on
local, national and international shows
and bearmaking tips and patterns.
The magazine is published 6 times a year
and has a circulation of 500.
Submissions: The magazine accepts
typewritten, unsolicited articles with
or without photographs. Pay is 3 cents
per word and $1 per photograph. Pay
will increase as the magazine grows.
Advertising: Contact the magazine for
more information.

Photographers

A THOUSAND WORDS PHOTOGRAPHY

Stacey Stucky

123 Pasto Rico

Rancho Santa Margarita, CA 92688

Phone: 714-589-9886

Price: $45-$85 per photo shoot, depending on subjects to be photographed. Large orders are quoted.

Accepts: money order, Visa

Stacey takes photographs for personal use, contests, appraisers, ads and brochures or catalogs. Her photos have been published in Teddy Bear and Friends and Teddy Bear Review magazines, as well as the book A Tribute to Teddy Bear Artists by Linda Mullins. She specializes in capturing tiny teddy creations on film.

PAW PRINTS

Kristina Shankel

851 South Frost

Saginaw, MI 48603-6029

Phone: 517-793-5256

Accepts: personal check, money order
Kristina photographs bears for personal use, insurance records and appraisers. She can also make postcards, prints, photo button pins, calendars and other gift items from the photographs.

JEFF RUHNKE

4434 S. St. Louis Ave.

Chicago, IL 60632

Phone: 312-254-1086

Price: prices vary depending on what the customer wants. A deposit of $20 is usually required.

Accepts: personal check, money order

Mail order: 2 weeks

Jeff photographs bears for personal use, appraisers, insurance providers and ads. He can also make photo buttons, mirrors, magnets, key chains and ID cards for teddy bears. His photographs have been published in Teddy Bear & Friends, Teddy Bear Review, newspapers and store flyers. He will work with any customer to meet their special needs. As a Bearo and a board member of Good Bears of the World, he offers a discount to fellow members.

CAROL-LYNN ROSSEL WAUGH

5 Morrill St.

Winthrop, ME 04364-1220

Phone: 207-377-6769

Fax: 207-377-6769

Price: Sitting fee is $100, plus the cost of photographs, which are $25 and up.

Accepts: personal check, money order

Mail order: Bears are shipped to the photographer, and the client pays postage both ways. 1 month for delivery.

Carol-Lynn Rossel Waugh provides photographs for personal use, contests, appraisers, insurance providers, ads, and publicity. Her photographs have been published in Teddy Bear Review, Teddy Bear & Friends, Dolls, Doll Reader, Doll Making, National Doll World, Maine Antique Digest, and many other books and magazines. She has won national awards for her photographs of dolls and bears. As a freelance writer and well-respected speaker, Carol-Lynn often uses photographs taken for other purposes in her articles and presentations, giving her clients added exposure.

Restoration Services

A SWEET REMEMBRANCE
Paula Walton
172 Aspetuck Ridge Rd.
New Milford, CT 06776-5611
Phone: 203-355-5709
Accepts: personal check, money order,
 layaway
Mail order: Must be well-packed and insured. Allow 2-6 weeks.
Paula has been restoring bears since
 1986. She will replace or restore ears,
 eyes, growlers, joints, noses, paws,
 stitching and stuffing as needed. She
 will dye and distress new fur if necessary to match old fur. Fur cannot be
 woven into an existing backing. She
 tries to duplicate all methods and materials used when the bear was originally made. She also cleans bears using museum quality textile restoration
 washing paste. She gently dries and
 fluffs fur. She recommends an inde-
 pendent professional appraisal on an
 antique bear before having work done
 to be aware of how restoration will af-
 fect the bear's value.

BEARS & BAUBLES
Denise Parsons
1603 Solano Ave.
Berkeley, CA 94706
Phone: 510-524-4794
Accepts: personal check, money order,
 Visa, MasterCard, Discover, American Express
Mail order: Package contents well. Send
 UPS insured.
Denise restores antique and modern
 stuffed toys to prolong their life and
 increase their value. She replaces or
 restores eyes, ears, fur, growlers,
 joints, noses, paws, stitching and
 stuffing. She also cleans and replaces
 weaving and old fur. She also surface
 washes bears by hand. She never
 makes a repair that cannot be "unre-
 paired," as this can damage value. Every repair is approached in a manner
 so as not to show the bear has been
 repaired.

BEARWORKS HEALTH SPA
Debra Metler
4274 Claire
West Bloomfield, MI 48323
Phone: 810-855-1874
The Bearworks Health Spa is a clinic and
 resort for distressed bears.

THE COUNTRY BEAR
Jay Hadly, owner
Route 73, P.O. Box 17
Skippack, PA 19474
Phone: 610-584-4055
Jay has been in the bear business for more
 than 13 years

MAR-KE MOHAIR
Martha L. Anderson
611 Morelock Dr.
Richmond, VA 23236-3355
Phone: 804-276-3900
Accepts: personal check, money order
Mail order: Bears should be shipped insured. Name, address, phone number
 and work desired should be enclosed.
Martha offers restoration services on a
 first-come, first-serve basis. She replaces or restores ears, eyes, growlers,
 joints, noses, paws, stitching, stuffing
 and squeakers. She does not remove
 anything original to a toy except for
 damaged eyes, and she discusses with
 her customers the extent of the restoration they desire. She also cleans
 bears using a solution she has developed that cleans but does not damage
 delicate mohair.

LEOTA ORDIWAY
4104 Tretorn Ave.
Bakersfield, CA 93313
Phone: 805-835-8508
Leota restores old, hurt teddy bears. She
 gets a feeling of accomplishment in
 knowing she has prolonged a teddy
 bear's life.

JAMI SANTOS BEAR CARE & REPAIR
Jami Santos
26305 Loch Glen
Lake Forest, CA 92630
Phone: 714-586-2086
 714-847-6266 (work)
Accepts: personal check, money order
Mail order: Customer must pay UPS
 charge.
Jami has been restoring bears for more
 than 10 years. Ears, eyes, growlers,
 joints, noses, paws, stitching and
 stuffing can be restored or replaced.
 Jami cleans the bears using a bear bath
 or Woolite. They are air dried only.
 Jami does not clean wool paw pads
 because they do not clean well. She
 will replace mohair or wool on pads
 if required, or cover them with net-
 ting. All items are replaced with the
 closest possible materials. Jami provides service at shows in Orange
 County, CA. and at the store DNJ
 Bears & Dolls, 18563 Main St., Huntington Beach, CA 92648.

THE TEDDY BEAR GARDEN
Ruth E. Fraser
366 Eglinton Ave. W.
Toronto, Ontario M5N 1A2, Canada
Phone: 416-322-3277
Fax: 416-322-5527
Accepts: personal check, Visa, Master-
 Card, American Express
Mail order: may take many weeks
Ruth restores or replaces eyes, ears,
 growlers, joints, noses, paws, stitching and stuffing. She restores as much
 of an antique or aging bear as the customer desires, trying to return it as
 much as possible to its original condition. She also cleans bears using a
 small amount of mild liquid rug
 cleaner mixed with cold water. She
 shakes the liquid in a tight container,
 and suds are applied with a nylon
 brush. The bears are dried overnight,
 then brushed gently with a wired
 brush. She repeats the process if

needed. Nothing is ever done to a bear that cannot be reversed.

TEDDY TRAUMA CENTER OF P J BEARS

Pat Johnson
2121 Contra Costa Ave.
Santa Rosa, CA 95405
Phone: 707-578-8809
Accepts: personal check, money order
Mail order: Wrap in cloth, put in plastic bag, attach name, address and phone number. Ship UPS. Always insure.

Pat has been restoring bears for more than 13 years. She can restore or replace eyes, ears, fur, growlers, joints, noses, paws, stitching and stuffing. She can dye fur to match color and distress fabric when necessary for missing body parts, and can also re-weave damaged parts. She makes an effort to leave original body parts intact, replacing only to preserve the bear (to keep the stuffing from spilling out). Research is made as to proper eyes and their placement. She also cleans bears, and her methods vary depending on the condition and material of the bear. Old and brittle bears, animal skin or fur, synthetic fabrics and mohair are all treated differently. Owners are advised of the estimated value of the bear, and then Pat discusses how to bring the bear to an optimum value and preserve the original parts and appearance. Her unique service is called the Teddy Trauma Center. Steiff USA, Steiff Club, FAO Schwartz, Dakin, Pauline Cockrill, ABC Productions, Basic Brown Bear, Bears In The Wood and many other shops and companies refer to the Teddy Trauma Center.

WINEY BEAR CLINIC

Sally Winey
900 Market St.
Lemoyne, PA 17070
Phone: 717-774-7447
Fax: 717-737-0231
The Winey Bear Clinic is the official repair company for Steiff USA.

Tours

ARTISTS FOR ARTISTS EUROPEAN TOURS
Neysa A. Phillippi
45 Gorman Ave.
Indiana, PA 15701
Phone: 412-349-1225
Fax: 412-349-3903
Accepts: personal check, money order, Visa, MasterCard
The tours go to The Netherlands, Belgium and Germany. More countries may be added in upcoming years. They last 17-18 days in May. Exact dates change from year to year. Teddy bear and doll artists have the chance to sell their creations at least 5-6 shows. Collectors have the opportunity to buy European bears and dolls. Tours include 11-13 days of sightseeing. See the article opening this chapter for more information.

BRITISH BEARINGS
Ruth or Lloyd Fraser
156 Shaughnessy Blvd.
Willowdale, Ontario M2J 1J8, Canada
Phone: 416-493-2944
Fax: 416-322-5527
British Bearings is a 12-day tour to Great Britain that occurs in August. The tour includes visits to teddy bear shops, museums, factories, festivals, as well as historical sites such as castles, churches, ancient monuments, etc.

KEYSTONE TRADERS, LTD.
Annual Teddy Tour to Great Britain
505 W. Broad St.
Chesaning, MI 48616
Phone: 517-845-7881
Fax: 517-845-6650
Accepts: personal check, Visa, Master-Card, Discover, American Express
The Annual Teddy Tour to Great Britain is a 12-day tour that occurs the last week of June to the first week of July. The tours are in their eighth year, and include visits to leading factories, shops and markets.

TEDDY BEAR REVIEW TOURS
Stephen Cronk
170 Fifth Ave.
New York, NY 10010
Phone: 212-989-8700
Fax: 212-645-8976
These tours to Germany and Austria last 10 days and 14 days. They take place in July and September. The tours take the collector behind the scenes to visit bear and doll artists and factories that are not available to the general public.

Videos

CASEY'S BEAR FACTORY
Rita Casey
110 Village Landing
Fairport, NY 14450
Phone: 715-223-6280
715-425-3566
Accepts: personal check, money order,
Visa, MasterCard, Discover
Mail order: 1 week
Rita Casey's bear-making video offers in-
struction on how to make and design
bears and clothing for bears. It is for
beginning, intermediate and advanced
bear artists.

HEIRLOOM BEARS VIDEO
Dennis Pace
1881 Old Lincoln Hwy.
Coalville, UT 84017
Phone: 801-336-2780
Price: $10
Accepts: personal check, Visa, Master-
Card
Mail order: 2 weeks
The video teaches how to make bears.
Kathy Pace is the instructor. The
video is aimed at beginning and inter-
mediate artists.

TEDDY TRIBUNE WAREHOUSE
Barbara Wolters
254 W. Sidney
St. Paul, MN 55107
Phone: 612-291-7571
video mail order catalog
Teddy Tribune Warehouse offers artists
and collectors the opportunity to sell
their bears on a consignment basis.
The seller sets the price, and Teddy
Tribune Warehouse takes a percentage
of that price: 30% for items valued at
$399 or less, 20% for items valued at
$400-$799, and 15% for items valued
at $800 or more. Bears are sold on a
video mail order catalog. Artist and
collectible bears are offered to buyers
on videos. There is no cost to participate, and the company takes the percentage only if the item is sold. The
video catalogs are $6 each.

TRIPLE "L" PRODUCTIONS
1715 Dean Rd.
Suite C
Temperance, MI 48182
Phone: 313-847-8888
Fax: 313-847-0416
video

Price: $49.95 + $4 for shipping and handling
Accepts: personal check, money order,
Visa, MasterCard
Mail order: orders purchased with
money orders and credit cards are
shipped immediately. Orders purchased with checks have a 1-week
waiting period.
Triple "L" Productions offers "The Secrets of Miniature Bear Artistry with
Debbie Kesling." The 90-minute
video goes from fabric selection and
tools you will need, to tying the first
knots, to stuffing, jointing and applying the finishing touches. The video
comes with a kit to make a 2″ bear.
The tape includes a "showcase" of
work by other artists. It is available in
NTSC and PAL format and will soon
be available in Japanese.
See the article opening the miniature index and the sidebars in the introduction for collectors and chapter three,
all by Debbie.

Workshops

A SWEET REMEMBRANCE
Paula Walton
172 Aspetuck Ridge Rd.
New Milford, CT 06776-5611
Phone: 203-355-5709
Price: beginning classes: $100. Advanced classes: $140
Accepts: personal check, money order
Workshops are taught by Paula Walton and cover how to make a bear. They take place at least twice a year at the above address. Participants should apply a month in advance. Materials are included in the cost.

CELIA D. BAHAM
1562 San Joaquin Ave.
San Jose, CA 95118
Phone: 408-266-8129
Fax: 409-978-2888
Celia travels all over the country teaching bearmaking.

BEARLY AVAILABLE
Jean Myers, owner
31 Centra Square New Rd. (Route 9)
Linwood, NJ 08221
Phone: 609-926-2272
Bearmaking workshops held at the shop.

BLACKWOODS DESIGN BEAR MAKING CLASS
Terry John Woods
Dale West
RR 1, Box 840
Eastham Rd.
Shrewsbury, VT 05738
Phone: 802-492-3715
Price: Classes start at $130
Accepts: personal check, money order, Visa, MasterCard
Terry John Woods's bear-making classes take place 4 times yearly at the above address. The classes teach how to make bears and how to make them look antique. They are aimed at beginning, intermediate and advanced artists. Materials are included in the cost.

CASEY'S BEAR FACTORY
Rita Casey
110 Village Landing
Fairport, NY 14450
Phone: 716-223-6280
716-425-3566
Price: $40.00
Accepts: personal check, money order, Visa, MasterCard, Discover
The workshops are offered weekly at the address above. Rita is also willing to travel to other states to teach. Materials are not included in the cost of the workshop. Rita teaches beginning, intermediate and advanced bear artists how to design and make regular sized and miniature bears, and how to design and make clothes for bears.

CHARMANT TEDDY BEARS
Donna McPherson and Armand Thibodeau
RR #1
Napanee, Ontario K7R 3K6, Canada
Phone: 613-354-6393
Fax: 613-354-6393
Accepts: check, money order, Visa, MasterCard
Bearmaking workshops available.

THE COUNTRY BEAR
Jay Hadly, owner
Route 73, P.O. Box 17
Skippack, PA 19474
Phone: 610-584-4055
Jay teaches bearmaking classes.

MARTHA DERAIMO
635 Hickory, Suite 142
West Bend, WI 53095
Phone: 414-338-6954
Martha teaches bearmaking classes and conducts seminars on using accessories and costuming.

DIANE GARD'S TWO-DAY MASTER BEARMAKING CLASS
Diane Gard
1005 W. Oak St.
Fort Collins, CO 80521

Phone: 303-484-8191
Fax: 303-484-0090
Cost: $265-$275
Cost includes all materials except mohair.
Accepts: check, money order, Visa, MasterCard, American Express
Diane teaches bearmaking to artists and aspiring artists at all levels. Her class is offered 4-5 times a year. Interested people should apply 2-3 months in advance. See the article opening Chapter 3 by Diane.

NOLA HART
90 Berkinshaw Cres.
Don Mills, Ontario, Canada
Phone: 416-444-4038
Fax: 416-322-5527
Nola has been teaching bearmaking and bear design classes for 4 years. She enjoys showing people how to unleash the hidden bear inside them.

H.E.A.R.T.T. PRODUCTIONS
(Having Enthusiasm About Really Tiny Teddies)
Gretchen McKillip
Catie Walker
45 W. Imperial Dr.
Walla Walla, WA 99362
Phone: 509-525-0395
509-529-8868
Fax: 509-522-0747
Price: prices vary
Accepts: personal check, money order
H.E.A.R.T.T. Productions offers miniature bearmaking classes and mini conventions centered around how to make miniature bears and accessories including pins, necklaces, etc. Catie Walker and Gretchen McKillip are the instructors, with others joining them at the mini-conventions. The classes and mini conventions are for beginning and intermediate artists. Conventions vary, but there is a quarterly workshop that can be taken through the mail.

ANITA KELSEY
12345 Lake City Way NE #198
Seattle, WA 98125
Phone: 206-365-8753
Anita teaches bearmaking classes 3 times
    per year

LOVE'S LABOURS
Kara L. Anderson
428 Highland Terrace
Pitman, NJ 08071-1522
Phone: 609-589-5818
Price: varies depending on project.
Usually between $30-$100
Accepts: personal check, money order
Kara conducts workshops on how to
    make miniature bears and other bear-
    related items such as pins. Her work-
    shops can be adjusted for all levels of
    expertise, from beginners to advanced
    artists. Her workshops are usually
    held at conventions. Materials are
    usually included in the cost.

TERRY & DORIS MICHAUD
505 W. Broad St.
Chesaning, MI 48616
Phone: 517-845-7881
Fax: 517-845-6650
Price: $75 or less
Accepts: personal check, Visa, Master-
    Card, Discover, American Express
Well-known collectors and artists Terry
    & Doris Michaud offer workshops on
    how to make bears for beginning, in-
    termediate and advanced artists. They
    are offered twice a year (spring and
    fall) at the address above. The Mi-
    chauds also teach workshops through-
    out the country. Times and places
    vary. Materials are included in the
    cost.

BONNIE H. MOOSE
500 W. 33rd St.
Baltimore, MD 21211-2745
Phone: 410-889-5061
Price: $40-$130
Accepts: personal check, money order

Bonnie conducts workshops on how to
    make bears and miniature bears and a
    variety of jointing methods and de-
    signs. The workshops are for begin-
    ning and intermediate artists. She con-
    ducts her workshops at the address of
    the person sponsoring them, and has
    conducted workshops in three states.
    The workshops are available upon re-
    quest, and materials are included in
    the cost of the workshop. Most are
    2-day workshops. Miniature work-
    shops are 1 day.

MONICA MURRAY
P.O. Box 728
Jenks, OK 74037
Phone: 918-299-5416
Price: $65-$125
Accepts: personal check, money order,
    Visa, MasterCard
Monica Murray teaches several bearmak-
    ing classes a year on how to make reg-
    ular sized and miniature bears. Her
    classes are aimed at beginning, inter-
    mediate and advanced bear artists.
    She teaches at different locations each
    year. Materials are included in the
    cost, and participants can enroll by
    mail.

KAREN I. PRINGLE
11 Rodger St.
St. Catharines, Ontario L2N 3J5, Canada
Phone: 905-937-1411
Karen teaches biweekly classes on every-
    thing from making miniature bears to
    making full-size mohair bears, to an-
    tiquing, to designing original patterns.

STEVE SCHUTT
201 First Ave. NW
Clarion, IA 50525
Phone: 515-532-2591
Steve has taught bearmaking classes
    throughout Europe and in California
    and Florida.

FREDERICK M. SLAYTER
3020 N. Federal Hwy.
Ft. Lauderdale, FL 33306
Phone: 305-563-5353
Frederick teaches classes in bearmaking
    from beginning to advanced.

THE TEDDY BEAR GARDEN
Ruth or Lloyd Fraser
366 Eglinton Ave. E.
Toronto, Ontario M2J 1J8, Canada
Phone: 416-493-2944
Fax: 416-322-5527
Price: $35-$120
The classes are taught by various Cana-
    dian artists. Bearmaking, miniature
    bearmaking, design, finishing and
    dressing are all covered. The class is
    open to beginners as well as interme-
    diate and advanced artists. Classes
    take place 2-3 times a month in fall,
    winter and spring. Applicants should
    register one month in advance. Ma-
    terials are included in the cost.

TEDDY TRIBUNE WAREHOUSE CLASSES
Barbara Wolters
254 W. Sidney
St. Paul, MN 55107
Phone: 612-291-7571
Price: free
The Teddy Tribune Warehouse offers
    classes on how to make craft items
    that are bear-related, including orna-
    ments, decorations, bear wear, etc.
    The classes are taught by Barbara
    Wolters or a guest instructor. Partici-
    pants should apply one week in ad-
    vance. There is an average of 1 work-
    shop per month at the above address.
    Interested people should call and ask
    to be put on the mailing list.

SALLY WINEY
900 Market St.
Lemoyne, PA 17070
Phone: 717-774-7447
Fax: 717-737-0231
Sally Winey has been teaching bear-mak-
    ing classes for more than 10 years

General Index

Indexed here are all retail stores, suppliers, artist's names (by last name), artist's company names, show names, production company names, organization names, museum names, and names of listings in the additional opportunities chapter. This index will help you quickly find the page number for your favorite business, show, etc., and will also help if you remember an artist's company name but not his or her last name.

Geographical Index

This index will help collectors and artists locate resources in their home states and countries. States are listed alphabetically, with foreign countries following. All resources are listed along with the page numbers on which they appear.

Brand Name Bear Index

This index is designed to help you quickly find the stores that sell your favorite brand of bear. Included are all the brands mentioned in the book as well as the retail businesses at which they can be purchased. Page numbers are listed for each retail store.

NOUNOURS/AUX NATIONS/AJENA

OLD WORLD CHRISTMAS BY HERMANN

ORZEK

OSHKOSH

PADDINGTON

Accessories, Collectibles and Figurines Index

This index will help you locate whatever bearafurnalia you need to add to your collection, whether it be a new dress for your bear, a specific brand name figurine, or a Winnie-the-Pooh collectible. All items are listed alphabetically under one of these three major categories, and include page numbers of stores that sell the item.

FIGURINES

Lucy Rigg, Self-Taught Figurine Artist

BY ARGIE MANOLIS

*L*ucy Rigg has done it all: Sculptor, artist, greeting card designer, children's author, mother, wife. Most teddy bear collectors, however, know her as the designer of the bear figurines, now manufactured by Enesco, that have found their way into more than seven-thousand collectors' homes around the world.

That's pretty amazing for a little girl who got her start when she sculpted some small pixies for a project for Bluebirds in second or third grade.

"Everybody loved them and wanted to buy them, from the time I was a little girl," says Lucy. "That was the first time I sculpted anything. The second time, I was twenty-six."

When Lucy was pregnant with her daughter Noelle in 1969, she had a lot of free time on her hands. She decided to sculpt a mobile for the baby's nursery. That project gave her the idea to sculpt little people out of baker's clay—a mixture of flour, salt and water. The clay was rather crude, Lucy admits, but she was able to paint each figurine with great detail.

"At first, I made them for Christmas presents," she says. "But I don't do anything in a small way. When I get into something, I'm into it."

The Beginning of a Business

When Lucy decided to stay at home with her stepson and daughter, she began making and selling figurines to raise some extra income for the family. Her stepson named those first figurines "Rigglets." Soon she began making angels and bears in addition to the little people.

"I was all over the place—art fairs, university fairs, flea markets. As far as categories, I sold to all kinds of people, not just the more elite people," says Lucy. "Wherever I went, people liked the teddy bears. It was a universal thing." Both her daughter and her son liked her bears as well, so she realized they appealed to all ages and both sexes.

In 1977, when her daughter was in fourth grade, Lucy decided she was ready for something new. She and a friend started a greeting card company called Lucy & Me.

"My friend would say, 'Someday Lucy and me are

Lucy Rigg is wearing one of her many famous hats in this photograph with daughter and long-time partner, Noelle.

going to do something together,' " Lucy says. "And that's where we got the name Lucy & Me."

The team began making their greeting cards at home. Lucy took a printing class and learned to print in black line, sometimes with one or two colors added. The cards looked like silk screen, Lucy says. As their business expanded, they moved into the lunchroom of a company owned by her partner's father. Although the business eventually ended, it played an important role in the expansion of Lucy's figurine business.

"We started out really slowly because of the limitations with money," Lucy says. "To make money for the cards, I sold my Rigglets, and my friend sold paintings." At that time, Lucy was making more than one hundred Rigglets a day, and selling them for $1 or $1.25.

"That would be a lot more now, to put it mildly. But it still didn't amount to very much money," Lucy says. "I perfected my method, and I was making three or four at a time. I'd make three heads, three noses, three bodies. Eventually I was making different sizes, too."

Enesco's Discovery

A friend of the president of Enesco discovered her at a street fair at the University of Washington in 1978. At that point, she had been sculpting Rigglets for nearly ten years. The man introduced himself and asked if he could buy some of her figurines to take to his friend at Enesco. Lucy gratefully gave him some.

"He was actually the second person that asked to bring them to a bigger company," Lucy says. "The first time, I liked my life the way it was and I didn't want to get any bigger."

But when Enesco wanted to reproduce some of her greeting card drawings on collector plates, Lucy decided it was a good opportunity.

"I was so excited that my artwork was on a plate that I bought cases of them," Lucy says. "Unfortunately, no one else did. No one knows what happened to all those plates."

Enesco then tried to mass-produce some of her figurines. "It's funny, because they didn't go for the bears at all," she says. "They liked the little people."

But the little people didn't sell well, either, and Lucy was convinced that Enesco could do better. When her husband got a half-price plane ticket from work, Lucy decided to take her daughter to Enesco and talk to the company face to face about her products. After looking at other figurines the company was producing, she had a better idea of the changes she wanted to make in her own.

"They were very kind," Lucy recalls. "They were willing to work with me. Enesco is a very sincere company. They knew that what they were doing wasn't what I expected. You don't have to get tough with a company like that. I was very blessed to be associated with Enesco."

The Bears Take Off

Finally, Enesco began producing Lucy's bear figurines, and the rest is history.

"At first, the bears stood like paper dolls or little statues, because the ones I had made with baker's clay stood up like that," Lucy says. "You couldn't create a lot of animation using baker's clay, because the oven's heat would cause it to fall over. So all the first ones were either sitting or standing very straight, with their legs together, because Enesco tried to reproduce my original designs."

Today, the company produces ceramic bears using drawings and ideas that Lucy creates. She usually sends about one hundred drawings, and the company chooses from among them. They work in themes, and are constantly coming up with new ideas.

The ideas always have a personal touch, Lucy says.

For instance, a line of limited edition figurines—bears wearing elegant hats with real feathers—are called Chapeau Noelle. They were named for Lucy's love of hats (Chapeau is the French word for hats), and after her daughter and long-time partner, Noelle.

"I wear all kinds of hats—derby hats, hats with a brim, baseball hats, berets," says Lucy. "Enesco wanted me to come out with a line of bears wearing hats. My original idea was to do a garden bear with a hat with a flowerpot on top of it, a summer bear wearing a baseball cap—things like that." But Enesco wanted a more elegant look, and Lucy was willing to compromise.

Family First

The name "Noelle" is appropriate for the Chapeau Noelle figurines not only because Lucy was pregnant with Noelle when she rediscovered her sculpting ability, but also because her daughter has been instrumental in the success of her business. Noelle has worked with Lucy nearly all her life, and has helped with both the artistic and the business side of Lucy's work.

Lucy's close relationship with her daughter reflects the philosophy she has tried to live by throughout her life. "I always tried to keep my priorities in line, to put my family first," she says.

Noelle recently moved on to plan her wedding and begin a new life, but Lucy says the support she has received from her family over the years has been very important. Today, Lucy's mother helps her by sending out orders and answering the phone.

A Self-Taught Artist

With so much family support, it's no wonder that Lucy has persevered and become successful. But perhaps the most amazing part of her story is the fact that she never received any formal art training. Her training consisted of a couple of introductory art classes at a community college. In one of them, her teacher recognized her talent and was very encouraging, but she never imagined she would become an artist by profession.

"I went to school for five years and never got a degree," Lucy says. "I guess I never really wanted to take that chemistry course."

Much later, when Lucy's business was flourishing, her grandmother asked her if she regretted the fact that she had never graduated. She offered to pay for Lucy to go back to school. Lucy applied at an art school in Seattle.

"They were really honest with me," Lucy says. "They said they didn't want me because it wouldn't do me any good. They told me that most people go all the way through school, and what they're looking for is their own style. I already had my own style, they said, so there was nothing they could help me with."

Lucy believes that her success lies in her careful attention to detail. The favorite item she has ever sculpted is a tiny toy sack with little toys when she was just getting started. She painstakingly sculpted each toy to look as realistic as possible.

"I made the toys out of white bread and Jergen's lotion," says Lucy. "Now people use professional materials, but I didn't know about those things back then."

Living With Success

Lucy is very humble about her own work. "It's really very primitive," she says. "I guess I just did it by imitating. I mean, you can tell I haven't had any training."

But the more than 650 people in the Lucy & Me Collecting Network, an organization for collectors of Lucy's figurines, certainly don't see her art as primitive. Members pay $27 to receive a bimonthly newsletter updating them on Lucy's creations. They also have the opportunity to purchase exclusive Lucy collectibles and to enter contests for prizes donated by various manufacturers of Lucy's products. In addition to the 650 in the network, there are more than seven-thousand bear enthusiasts around the world who have extensive Lucy & Me collections.

Today, more than thirty different manufacturers produce her products. She says the manufacturers she has chosen do not compromise the quality of her products. In the long run, mass-manufacturing her work was the best choice for her.

"I felt that the business part of it took more time than I really had. Being a business person and publishing and printing and managing an office and doing shows, I was always behind," Lucy admits. "It was more than I could handle."

This gives Lucy more time to spend in her studio. She says she is there about forty hours a week. Lucy loves her work, but admits that if she could do anything in the world, she would choose shopping and decorating. But it is her hard work and determination that has made her so successful, and she is aware of that.

"I never learned how to play tennis, or how to relax at a concert," Lucy says. "I'm not disappointed, but those are the things I had to give up. But it's not too late."

Lucy is modest about her success. She says she doesn't feel that she is all that well known. Few people recognize her out of context.

"I don't think too much about the money. It's amazing," Lucy says. "I don't think any artist does. But unfortunately, that is the way people usually measure your success."

She says the best payoff for the success she's acquired is the confidence it has given her. She has learned that no matter what her latest project, the important part is to do it to the best of her ability.

"I think the key is determination," Lucy says. "Things didn't always go the way I wanted them to go. But you just have to remember that there's always something else when things don't work out."

Miniature Index

This index includes all the resources that miniature collectors and artists can use. Because of the tremendous growth of the miniature teddy bear industry, we felt that this was an important addition to our book. Included are retail stores that sell miniature bears and accessories for miniature bears, artists who make miniature bears, suppliers that sell miniature bear supplies, manufacturers of miniature bears, and other resources of interest to miniature bear artists and collectors. All are listed under subject headings with page numbers.

SUPPLIERS

Eyes

Fur

Joints

Miscellaneous

Patterns

The Wonderful World of Tiny Teddies

BY DEBBIE KESLING

The current teddy bear phenomenon is not limited to bears that fill your arms. Some of the most incredible teddies to be found are no bigger than your thumb! Miniature bears are enjoying a resurgence in popularity. For many people, full-size teddy bears take up too much room. For others, the wee teds are a special kind of magic, seemingly created by fairies. One cannot help but marvel at the expressions captured on these little faces, the attention to detail in their trimming, and the incredible personalities they exude. In these pages, we will introduce you to the individuals who create these tiny wonders, as well as the suppliers who can get you started making your own!

Defining the Miniature Bear

First of all, what is a miniature teddy bear? To some, a miniature bear is simply a bear that is smaller than your average teddy. To purists, a miniature must conform to standard dollhouse scale, which is 1 inch to 1 foot. That would mean that a 24-inch full-size bear would be represented in miniature by a 2-inch bear, an 18-inch full-size bear would be represented by a 1.5 inch bear, and so on. *Teddy Bear Review* magazine considers miniature bears to be 3 inches or less for their annual Golden Teddy Awards. That is the criteria we have adopted for this section of *The Teddy Bear Sourcebook*.

The History of Miniature Bear Artistry

Miniature teddy bears evolved soon after the appearance of the first full-size teddy bear, around 1903. These first tiny teds didn't always conform to our current criteria for miniatures. Several manufacturers, such as Steiff, Schuco, Alpha-Farnell and others, have produced small bears over the years. Schuco was particularly known for the surprises they incorporated into their designs, such as compacts, flasks and yes/no bears.

The "teddy bear artist" was born when Beverly Port created her unique Time Machine Teddies. Beverly's daughter, Kimberlee Port, created the first miniature bears. Kim made her first tiny teddy in 1974. In those early years of the artist bear, a few individuals stood alone as the creators of miniature bears. Elaine Fujita-

Debbie Kesling has been involved in the teddy bear world since the early 1980s as a collector and artist. Her teddy bears, both full-size and miniature, have been featured in many books and periodicals. She received a Golden Teddy Award in 1991, and was the cover artist for the Spring 1990 issue of *Teddy Bear Review* magazine. In 1994, she released her how-to video, *Secrets of Miniature Bear Artistry*. Debbie lives in Lambertville, Michigan with her husband, John, two dogs and a flock of parrots.

Gamble, Dickie Harrison, Sara Phillips, Kim Port, Laurie Sasaki, and April Whitcomb-Gustafson were true trailblazers in the field of miniature bear artistry. The little gems they created were few and far between, however, leaving collectors hungry for more. The number of artists working in miniature has grown dramatically in recent years. An "open audition" of miniature teddies held in 1994 for a feature article in *Teddy Bear & Friends* magazine drew more than two hundred entries! While some of these artists come from the full-size bear market, others have always concentrated on miniatures.

My Old Ted, created in 1994 by Debbie, is a traditionally jointed bear with custom-made German glass eyes and Ultrasuede pads. He is made with vintage upholstery fabric and is stuffed with cotton batting. He wears a silk ribbon collar with goldtone beads. A one-of-a-kind bear from the collection of M. Smith, he illustrates how a classic look can be achieved in miniature by using a four-piece body pattern.

Finding Supplies

One of the most difficult aspects of making miniature bears is finding appropriate supplies. Although some miniature artists use mohair as their medium, most use upholstery fabric. Not just any upholstery fabric will do. There is a particular type of backing that works best when making bears on such a small scale. The finish and length of nap (fur) is important as well. The most commonly available fabrics are shiny or sparkly, with a very short nap. Longer napped fabrics with no sheen are usually preferred for traditional minis, though these fabrics can be incredibly difficult to find. The time taken to track down fabrics, while certainly not wasted, does take away from time spent actually making bears. That time, when added to the cost of phone calls and correspondence, can increase the actual cost of the fabric tenfold. Thanks to suppliers such as Tracy Main, today's miniature bear artists have a much wider variety of fabrics at their disposal than ever before. And using this sourcebook, it's easier than ever for miniature artists to find the supplies they need!

It used to be that most miniature bears were string-jointed, but more and more artists are devising clever ways to joint their bears in a "big bear" way. String joints can be very stable, when done properly, and some well-established artists use them exclusively. The trend, however, appears to lean more toward a scaled-down version of traditional disk joints.

As with humans, a teddy's eyes are the windows to his soul. Small glass eyes on wires (such as are used on full-size bears) are available, though they vary greatly in size and shape. This makes finding a perfectly matched pair quite an undertaking. Another option is to use beads. Many artists use seed beads and onyx beads. Some artists make their own eyes, usually by painting jewelry head pins with automotive enamel, then baking them. These eyes give a great look, but they can be prone to chipping. Some artists achieve the desired effect with expertly executed French knots. Whatever the eyes are made of, when you look at the bear, he should look right back at you, preferably straight into your heart!

This 2⅞″ clow purse by Debbie Kesling is an example of a specialty piece.

Building Your Collection

When figuring the work that goes into a particular miniature bear, begin by looking at the number of pieces used in the bear's construction. Some bears may have forty pattern pieces or more, while others have as few as fourteen. However, complexity does not necessarily indicate a superior bear. There are some bear makers who have perfected the two-piece head, which utilizes no head gusset. Others never put paw or foot pads on their bears. Most artists use two-piece bodies, though some like the design control you can achieve with a four-piece body. Incorporating clothing (non-removable clothing that is incorporated into the bear's design) is a nice way for an artist to dress a bear without the bulkiness of applied clothing (clothing added to a bear after its completion). These dressed bears, whether the clothing is incorporated or applied, take an extra degree of time and care to create.

Another point to consider is the sewing method used. A few artists are able to sew tiny bears on sewing machines before they are cut out, but the majority are hand-sewn. Some stitch their bears on the outside with good results. The majority of today's mini artists sew their bears as big bears are sewn: right sides together, then turned. Even with these traditionally sewn bears, the paw pads may be "applied," or stitched on after the bear is otherwise completed. Though their methods may vary, the best artisans will end up with a teddy bear that appears to be seamless with no stitches visible.

Specialty pieces are being created by many artists. This would include items such as compact or perfume bottle bears, tiny teddy purses, yes/no bears, and even tiny mechanical acrobat bears. Miniature scenes, complete to the finest detail, are also available. Some artists create jewelry from their designs. Little stuffed bear-head earrings, pins and necklaces are a wonderful way to take a wee bit of your collection with you wherever you go. Keep in mind that these special bears take extra time and effort to create, so don't be surprised if the price is appreciably higher than a traditional bear by the same artisan.

Once you have begun your collection, you will need to find a way to display these little treasures. Full-size bears typically inhabit chairs, shelves and baby buggies. With miniatures, you have many more options available. You could move a little bear family into a dollhouse. Curio cabinets offer another solution, as you can fit literally hundreds of tiny teddies inside! Some collectors create shadow box scenes that can be wall mounted. You can even decorate a tabletop Christmas tree with miniature bears! At bear shows, you may see collectors wearing hats that are virtually covered in little bears. Because these little bears fit in almost anywhere, you are limited only by your imagination.

The Business of Miniature Bears

Whether the artist makes regular sized bears, miniature bears, or both, the same business etiquette applies. Make sure you read the artist's listing before contacting him or her. For more information about the business of bear artistry, see the sidebar on this topic in the introduction to the artist's section.

Because miniatures are labor intensive, it is common for an artist to base his or her prices on time spent on each bear. An artist would need to charge approximately $20 per hour for their bears to earn $13 per hour after taxes and expenses. This is, of course, assuming they will be able to work forty hours per week, and that they will be able to sell all the bears they create. If it takes this artist eight hours to make a bear, that bear would need to retail for about $160. Of course, as with regular sized bears, a collector should keep in mind that a higher price is not always an indication of a better bear.

Mass-Manufactured Miniature Bears

As the market for miniature bears increases, more manufacturers are adding tiny bears to their lines. If you are a miniature bear artist who is thinking about approaching a manufacturer about mass-manufacturing your designs, be sure to read the sidebar in the artist's chapter on this topic. If you collect miniature bears, you should know that a few manufacturers specialize in recreating the designs of select artists. In these cases, the bears are clearly marked as being designed by a particular artist, but manufactured by, for example, the Akira Trading Company. The prices of these teddies may be significantly lower than an original piece from the artist might be. With the very limited production of some artists, this provides an opportunity for collectors to obtain pieces designed by individuals whose work might otherwise be virtually unobtainable.

ATTEND SHOWS AND ASK THE ARTISTS ANY QUESTIONS YOU MIGHT HAVE. YOU WILL RECEIVE PLENTY OF FREE INFORMATION AND POSSIBLY EVEN SOME USEFUL TIPS!
— *Leann M. Snyder, artist, Upper Sandusky, OH*

A Special Excitement

If you are interested in making miniature bears, there are several artists who offer patterns, kits, books and videotapes to aid you. These items are available through some of the suppliers listed in this book, or from the artists themselves. There are also clubs where makers and collectors of miniature bears may share ideas and techniques.

There is a special excitement that comes from being able to hold an entire collection in the palms of your hands. With so many wonderful miniature teddy bear

> JOIN A TEDDY BEAR CLUB IF YOU CAN. THEY'RE GREAT FOR SWAPPING IDEAS AND TECHNIQUES AND PURCHASING LARGE QUANTITIES. THEY CAN BE VERY HELPFUL, SINCE BEARS DON'T GIVE OUT ADVICE—JUST HUGS.
> — *Pauline M. Conrad, artist, Allentown, PA*

artists working today, there is certain to be a new temptation around every corner. Perhaps you will decide to add some miniature bears to your collection, or, better yet, to try your hand at creating these little gems. Well, what are you waiting for? We can't wait to see them!

Did We Miss You?

We attempted to make *The Teddy Bear Sourcebook* as all-inclusive as possible. We apologize to those who did not receive a questionnaire. If you would like to be included in our next edition, please type or neatly print your name and address below, and circle the surveys you would like to receive. Please be patient—there will be about two years between editions!

Name: _____

Address: _____

_____

Phone: _____

I would like to receive the following questionnaires for inclusion in *The Teddy Bear Sourcebook*:
(please circle your choices)
1. Retail stores/businesses
2. Suppliers (sellers of supplies, including furs and patterns)
3. Artists (must make and sell your own designs on a regular basis to be included in the book)
4. Manufacturers
5. Shows or show promoters
6. Clubs or organizations
7. Museums
8. Additional opportunities (anything not included above—please specify below)

_____

_____

_____

Comments

We want to know what you think about *The Teddy Bear Sourcebook*! Please type or neatly print your comments in the space provided below, so we can make the next edition even better!

_____

_____

_____

_____

_____

_____

_____

_____

_____

_____

_____

_____

_____

_____

_____

_____

Please send comments and requests for questionnaire to: Betterway Books, *The Teddy Bear Sourcebook*, Attn: Argie Manolis, 1507 Dana Ave., Cincinnati, OH 45207.

More Great Books
for Collectors and Crafters!

The Crafts Supply Sourcebook—Turn here to find the materials you need—from specialty tools and the hardest-to-find accessories, to clays, doll parts, patterns, quilting machines and hundreds of other items! Listings organized by area of interest make it quick and easy! *#70253/$16.99/288 pages/25 b&w illus./paperback*

The Complete Book of Silk Painting—Create fabulous fabric art—everything from clothing to pillows to wall hangings. You'll learn every aspect of silk painting in this step-by-step guide, including setting up a workspace, necessary materials and fabrics, and specific silk painting techniques. *#30362/$26.99/128 pages/color throughout*

Fabric Sculpture: The Step-By-Step Guide & Showcase—Discover how to transform fabrics into 3-dimensional images. Seven professional fabric sculptors demonstrate projects that illustrate their unique approaches and methods for creating images from fabric. The techniques—covered in easy, step-by-step illustration and instruction—include quilting, thread work, appliqué and soft sculpture. *#30687/$29.99/160 pages/300+ color illus.*

Decorative Wreaths & Garlands—Discover stylish, yet simple to make wreaths and garlands. These twenty original designs use fabrics and fresh and dried flowers to add color and personality to any room, and charm to special occasions. Clear instructions are accompanied by step-by-step photographs to ensure that you create a perfect display every time. *#30696/$19.99/96 pages/175 color illus./paperback*

The Complete Flower Arranging Book—An attractive, up-to-date guide to creating more than 100 beautiful arrangements with fresh and dried flowers, illustrated with step-by-step demonstrations. *#30405/$24.95/192 pages/300+ color illus.*

The Complete Flower Craft Book—Discover techniques for drying fresh flowers and seedheads, creating arrangements to suit all seasons and occasions, making silk flowers, potpourri, bath oil and more! This guide is packed with photographs, tips, and step-by-step instructions to give you a bouquet of ideas and inspiration! *#30589/$24.95/144 pages/275 color illus.*

Jewelry & Accessories: Beautiful Designs to Make and Wear—Discover how to make unique jewelry out of papier mâché, wood, leather, cloth and metals. You'll learn how to create: a hand-painted wooden brooch, a silk-painted hair slide, a paper and copper necklace and much more! Fully-illustrated with step-by-step instructions. *#30680/$16.99/128 pages/150 color illus./paperback*

The Art of Painting Animals on Rocks—Discover how a dash of paint can turn humble stones into charming "pet rocks." This hands-on easy-to-follow book offers a menagerie of fun—and potentially profitable—stone animal projects. 11 examples, complete with material list, photos of the finished piece, and patterns will help you create a forest of fawns, rabbits, foxes and other adorable critters. *#30606/$21.99/144 pages/250 color illus./paperback*

Decorative Boxes to Create, Give and Keep—Craft beautiful boxes using techniques including embroidery, stencilling, lacquering, gilding, shellwork, decoupage and many others. Step-by-step instructions and photographs detail every project. *#30638/$15.95/128 pages/color throughout/paperback*

Elegant Ribboncraft—Over 40 ideas for exquisite ribbon-craft—hand-tied bows, floral garlands, ribbon embroidery and more. Various techniques are employed— including folding, pleating, plaiting, weaving, embroidery, patchwork, quilting, applique and decoupage. All projects are complete with step-by-step instructions and photographs. *#30697/$16.99/128 pages/130+ color illus./paperback*

Paint Craft—Discover great ideas for enhancing your home, wardrobe and personal items. You'll see how to master the basics of mixing and planning colors, how to print with screen and linoleum to create your own stationery, how to enhance old glassware and pottery pieces with unique patterns and motifs, and much more! *#30678/$16.99/144 pages/200 color illus./paperback*

Nature Craft—Dozens of step-by-step nature craft projects to create, including dried flower garlands, baskets, corn dollies, potpourri and more. Bring the outdoors inside with these wonderful projects crafted with readily available natural materials. *#30531/$14.95/144 pages/200 color illus./paperback*

Paper Craft—Dozens of step-by-step paper craft projects to make, including greeting cards, boxes and desk sets, jewelry and pleated paper blinds. If you have ever worked with or wanted to work with paper you'll enjoy these attractive, fun-to-make projects. *#30530/$16.95/144 pages/200 color illus./paperback*

Everything You Ever Wanted to Know About Fabric Painting—Discover how to create beautiful fabrics! You'll learn how to set up work space, choose materials, plus the ins and outs of tie-dye, screen printing, woodgraining, marbling, cyanotype and more! *#30625/$19.99/128 pages/color throughout/paperback*

Holiday Fun with Dian Thomas—Discover how to turn mere holiday observances into opportunities to exercise imagination and turn the festivity all the way up. You'll find suggestions for a memorable New Year's celebration, silly April Fool's Day pranks, recipes and ideas for a Labor Day family get-together, creative Christmas giving and much more! *#70300/$19.99/144 pages/150 color illus./paperback*

Master Strokes—Master the techniques of decorative painting with this comprehensive guide! Learn to use decorative paint finishes on everything from small objects and furniture to walls and floors, including dozens of step-by-step demonstrations and numerous techniques. *#30347/$29.99/160 pages/400 color illus.*

Master Works: How to Use Paint Finishes to Transform Your Surroundings—Discover how to use creative paint finishes to enhance and excite the "total look" of your home. This step-by-step guide contains dozens of exciting ideas on fresco, marbling, paneling and other simple paint techniques for bringing new life to any space. Plus, you'll also find innovative uses for fabrics, screens and blinds. *#30626/$29.95/176 pages/150 color illus.*

Creative Paint Finishes for the Home—A complete, full-color step-by-step guide to decorating floors, walls and furniture—including how to use the tools, master the techniques and develop ideas. *#30426/$27.99/144 pages/212 color illus.*

Stencil Source Book—Transform a room from plain to remarkable. This guide combines inspiration with practical information—and more than 180 original designs you can turn into stencils. *#30595/$22.95/144 pages/150 color illus.*

Painting Murals—Learn through eight step-by-step projects how to choose a subject for a mural, select colors that will create the desired effects, and transfer the design to the final surface. *#30081/$29.99/168 pages/125 color illus.*

The Christmas Lover's Handbook—Everything you need to plan and create a fabulous Christmas season. You'll find specific ideas for getting yourself and those around you in the holiday spirit. Plus, you'll find festive ideas for planning everything, from selecting or making cards to gift wrapping with imagination. *#70221/$14.95/256 pages/170 b&w illus./paperback*